LIMNOLOGY

LIMNOLOGY

SECOND EDITION

Alexander J. Horne

Department of Civil and Environmental Engineering
University of California, Berkeley

Charles R. Goldman

Division of Environmental Studies
University of California, Davis

McGraw-Hill, Inc.

New York   St. Louis   San Francisco   Auckland   Bogotá
Caracas   Lisbon   London   Madrid   Mexico City   Milan
Montreal   New Delhi   San Juan   Singapore   Sydney   Tokyo   Toronto

This book was set in Times Roman by Ruttle, Shaw & Wetherill, Inc.
The editors were Kathi M. Prancan and John M. Morriss;
the production supervisor was Kathryn Porzio.
The cover was designed by Carla Bauer;
Cover photograph was taken by Alexander J. Horne.
Project supervision was done by Ruttle, Shaw & Wetherill, Inc.

LIMNOLOGY

15 16 17 18 19 20   QWFQWF   0 5 4 3

ISBN 0-07-023673-9

Library of Congress Cataloging-in-Publication Data

Horne, Alexander J.
    Limnology / Alexander J. Horne, Charles R. Goldman. — 2nd ed.
       p.   cm.
    In the previous ed. Charles R. Goldman's name appeared first on
t.p.
    Includes bibliographical references.
    ISBN 0-07-023673-9
    1. Limnology.   I. Goldman, Charles Remington, (date).
II. Title.
QH96.H6   1994
574.5′2632—dc20   93-38109

ABOUT THE AUTHORS

ALEXANDER J. HORNE became fascinated with lakes and ponds in his early childhood and remembers being allowed out late at night so he could look at "pond bugs" with a flashlight. Initial training in chemistry and zoology culminated with studies of the, then new, subject of biochemistry at the University of Bristol in England, where he became interested in the process of biological nitrogen fixation. Graduate work in limnology and oceanography began at the University of London in the mid-1960s and culminated at the University of Dundee, Scotland, following research on nitrogen and carbon fixation in the English Lake District, African Rift Lakes, Antarctic lakes and wetlands, and the Antarctic Ocean. He came to California to study eutrophication in the large Californian lake, Clear Lake, which now belies its name, and has taught pure and applied limnology and oceanography at the University of California at Berkeley since 1971. He has studied lakes and oceans in many areas of the world. Although still concerned with nitrogen fixation by blue-green algae and the associated processes of eutrophication, he has spent considerable time on the management of lakes, wetlands, rivers, estuaries, and tropical oceans, especially with regard to the ecological effects of pollution. A former director of the North American Lake Management Society and President of the California chapter, his current interests include nitrogen fixation in saline desert lakes, nitrogen and heavy metal removal in wetlands, and kinetics of polyaromatic hydrocarbon distribution in estuarine sediments. His hobbies include mountain hiking and leading an intermittent rock and roll-blues band called "Any Waters."

CHARLES R. GOLDMAN's early interest in limnology came via his fishing expeditions to midwestern streams with his father. Early training in geology and zoology at the University of Illinois lead to graduate work in limnology and fisheries at the University of Michigan in the mid-1950s. His Ph.D. research on primary productivity in oligotrophic lakes of the Alaskan Peninsula required development of the newly discovered carbon-14 radioisotope method for both field use and as a laboratory assay for the effects of various nutrients including trace metals. These methods were put to further use in California at Castle Lake and Lake Tahoe when he took up a faculty position at the University of California at Davis in 1958. His studies on productivity and cultural eutrophication in these lakes continues to the present day. This unique long-term data set has produced major advances in limnological understanding ranging from the effect of deep water column mixing on year-to-year variations in lake productivity, the unexpected results of additions of nonnative zooplankton on Lake Tahoe, to the dominant influence on lakes of "El Nino" weather patterns. At Tahoe he has been successful in translating scientific research into information convincing to politicians who must fund restoration of this large lake. He has carried out research in Antarctica, where a glacier bears his name, and Africa, as well as in several other countries. A Fellow of the California Academy of Sciences, former President of the American Society of Limnology and Oceanography, and current Executive Vice President of the International Society of Limnology, Professor Goldman has received numerous awards, including a Guggenheim fellowship, the Canadian Vollenweider Lectureship, a Chevron Conservation Award, and the Earle A. Chiles Award from the High Desert Museum. He has published over 375 papers, edited three books, and produced four ecological documentary films. He was founding director of the Institute of Ecology and has served as major professor to 80 graduate students at the University of California. A current interest is research at Lake Baikal in Siberia, where he has conducted six expeditions. His hobbies include fishing, skiing, cooking, and travel, which he combines with observation of lakes.

To Our Mentors:
W. T. Edmondson
G. E. Fogg
G. E. Hutchinson
G. Lauff
J. W. G. Lund
and W. D. P. Stewart
To the Students
Past, Present, and Future

CONTENTS

PREFACE

The primary goal of this book is to present a balanced, comprehensive, and contemporary view of limnology, the study of inland waters. It is designed for undergraduates, graduate students, and those who deal professionally with lakes, streams, rivers, estuaries, and wetlands. Textbooks at this level can be organized in two ways: (1) in the traditional manner presenting the physics, chemistry, and biology of lakes first, then moving into ecosystem examples or (2) by launching directly into ecosystems or complex examples, incorporating the needed physics, chemistry, and biology on the way. We have again chosen the former, traditional route. Our combined 60 years of teaching limnology suggest that this is the most efficient way for students to learn and understand the basics of the subject.

To add interest we have used many realworld situations as an integral part of the text. Many of the examples are drawn from the lakes and reservoirs we have personally studied in North, South, and Central America, Africa, New Guinea, New Zealand, Japan, Europe, Antarctica, and the Arctic. Lakes in these regions differ markedly from one another in size, basin shape, climate, and biota yet illustrate a unity of principles important to the science of limnology.

Some major limnological principles are, however, best illustrated in other kinds of aquatic environments. In our own pure and applied work we have benefited from the work of others not only on lakes but also on streams, rivers, wetlands, estuaries, and even the world's oceans. Nevertheless, because lakes have been studied so extensively and have so much unity of physical, chemical, biological, and evolutionary structure, the field of limnology has largely developed through the study of lakes. Although we give examples from rivers, estuaries, and wetlands where appropriate, it is often impossible to generalize for all aquatic ecosystems. The fact remains that most limnologists work on lakes or reservoirs, and frequently the comprehensive examples best suited for a text of this type are lake-derived.

At the beginning of each chapter we provide an overview to provide the student with a general idea of the extent of the chapter and begin to familiarize the student with the key terms. Limnology is essentially a practical discipline, and a short methods section reminds the reader that a chapter's content is based on and restricted by the measurements available. However, these short sections are no substitute for the analytical handbooks, which are referenced. Technical terms are italicized when they first appear in the text. Excessive references tend to interrupt the flow of the text, so we have limited them to key papers, review articles, or books. Figures and tables contain additional references to specific items. A short reading list of key papers and reviews is provided at the end of each chapter to direct more extensive reading if desired.

This edition is updated to reflect the changes that have occurred over a decade. Two completely new chapters on wetlands and large rivers follow the emerging trend for limnologists to broaden their horizons beyond lakes and streams. The chapters on light and phosphorus were completely rewritten to incorporate a wider spectrum of information. The chapters on phytoplankton, zooplankton, fish, and food chains have been extensively revised in response to requests from colleagues and students for more biological emphasis. Almost all other chapters either have been rewritten or have new sections added to include exciting new developments. For example, we added a section on the Wedderburn number in Chapter 4, on denitrification in Chapter 8, on periphyton and on phytoplankton energetics and chemical defenses in Chapter 12. In addition, we cover the top-down, bottom-up food web concept and chemomorphosis in Chapter 13 and habitat preference in larval and adult fish in Chapter 14. The microbial loop and nutrient regeneration in the mixed layer are added in Chapter 15 and the river continuum hypotheses is included in Chapter 16. As we revised the text we integrated common features and ideas that link separate topics such as water movement, nutrients, and plankton. As always we welcome any suggestions and comments from our readers for incorporation in future editions.

McGraw-Hill and the authors would like to thank the following reviewers for their many helpful comments and suggestions: David C. Beckett, University of Southern Mississippi; Michael Brett, University of California, Davis; David C. Brubaker, Seattle University; Thomas W. Collins, Moorhead State University; Marcie Commins, Lafayette, California; Cliff Dahm, University of New Mexico; Arthur C. Hulse, Indiana University of Pennsylvania; H. B. Noel Hynes, (retired) University of Waterloo, Ontario; Daniel A. Livingstone, Duke University; and Dennis Todd, University of Oregon.

Alexander J. Horne

Charles R. Goldman

LIMNOLOGY

CHAPTER 1

Limnology: Past, Present, and Future

OVERVIEW

Limnology is the study of fresh or saline waters contained within continental boundaries. Limnology and the closely related science of oceanography together cover all aquatic ecosystems. Although many limnologists are freshwater ecologists, physical, chemical, and engineering limnologists all participate in this branch of science. Limnology covers lakes, ponds, reservoirs, streams, rivers, wetlands, and estuaries, while oceanography covers the open sea. Limnology only evolved into a distinct science during the last two centuries, when improvements in microscopes, the invention of the silk plankton net, and improvements to the thermometer combined to show that lakes are microcosms of life with a distinctive structure.

Today limnology plays a major role in water use and distribution as well as in wildlife habitat protection. Limnologists work on lake and reservoir management, water pollution control, stream and river protection, artificial wetlands construction, and fish and wildlife enhancement. The field is unique in that theory and practice often go hand-in-hand, both inside and outside academia. The pressing needs of applied limnol- ogy continually stimulate new experimental and theoretical developments in the basic science. An important goal of education in limnology is to increase the number of people who, although not full-time limnologists, can understand and apply its general concepts to a broad range of related disciplines.

In this chapter we describe the early limnologists and the great laboratories; limnology today; and the future of limnology.

INTRODUCTION

In addition to lakes, ponds, streams, rivers, marshes, swamps, bogs, and estuaries, limnology embraces a host of microhabitats often overlooked by the casual observer. These include springs, caves, old watering troughs, tree holes, and even the unique environments formed in abandoned cans or in the water- and enzyme-filled cavities of insectivorous pitcher plants. Limnology applies to running, or *lotic,* as well as standing, or *lentic,* waters, as defined by the International Association of Theoretical and Applied Limnology (SIL) in 1922. In this text limnology includes standing and running water, both salt and fresh, as long as the body of water is not oceanic. Brackish waters in estuaries also constitute important areas of limnological investigation.

The open ocean is in the realm of oceanography, which shares basic principles with limnology. The coastal ocean and shoreline and small enclosed seas, such as the Black Sea, are best served by a knowledge of both limnology and oceanography. Ground water, an important source of drinking water and irrigation supply, is the province of hydrologists but limnologists also play a role. Ground water is a known source of nitrates, which can lead to eutrophication in lakes and streams, and therefore affects lakes as large as Lake Tahoe or as small as the forest lakes of northern Wisconsin. Studies of microbiology, pollution, and benthic invertebrates in groundwater often employ limnologists who can transfer their skills to this expanding field.

The Early Limnologists

Originally the word *limnology,* derived from the Greek word *limnos* (''pool, lake, or swamp''),

was used to mean the study of lakes. It first appeared in *Le Léman: monographie limnologique,* the work of F. A. Forel, who studied Lake Geneva, Switzerland, also known by its French name, Lac Léman. The first two volumes, published in 1892 and 1895, consist of the geology, physics, and chemistry of the lake (Fig. 1-1), while the third volume, published in 1904, deals with the lake's biology. Earlier, in 1869, Forel published a paper on the bottom fauna of Lake Geneva, ''Introduction à l'étude de la faune profonde du Lac Léman.'' In 1901 he published the first textbook on limnology, *Handbuch der Seenkunde: allgemeine Limnologie.* Forel, then a professor at the University of Lausanne, is justifiably considered the father of limnology.

Biological limnology studies were initiated by Leeuwenhoek in 1674, with the first microscopic description of the filamentous green algae *Spirogyra* from Berkelse-Lake, a shallow lake in the Netherlands. Although Leeuwenhoek considered himself a microbiologist, his report contains the first account of the seasonal cycles of algae in lakes, hints about food chain dynamics, and

FIGURE 1-1 Diagram of thermal stratification patterns through the year for an idealized temperate lake as presented in Forel (1892). The double line at 39.2°F (4°C) is the maximum density of water. P_1, P_2 are depths, and m_1, m_2, n_1, n_2 are the isotherms showing the depth at which temperatures m_1, m_2, n_1, n_2 . . . are found at any period during the year. (For a more modern approach, see Fig. 4-2.)

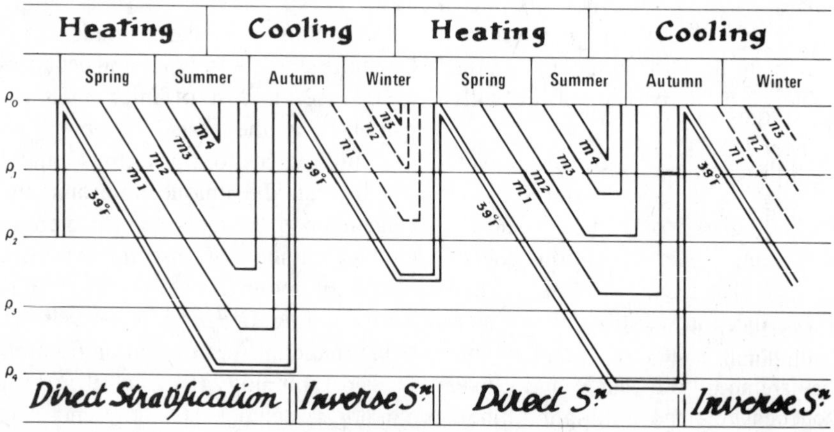

the influence of winds on algal ecology. He wrote:

> About two Leagues from this Town (Delf) there lyes an Inland-Sea, called Berkelse-Lake, whose bottom in many places is very moorish. This water is in Winter very clear, but about the beginning or in the midst of Summer it grows whitish, and there are then small green clouds permeating it, which the Country-men, dwelling near it, say is caused from the Dews when failing, and call it *Honeydew.* This water is abounding in Fish, which is very good and savoury. Passing lately over this Sea at a time, when it blew a fresh gale of wind, and observing the water as above described, I took up some of it in a Glass-vessel which having view'd the next day, I found moving in it several Earthy particles, and some green streaks, spirally ranged . . . . and the compass of each of these streaks was about the thickness of a man's hair on his head. (quoted in Fogg, 1969)

Leeuwenhoek was sampling a lake with a peat bottom. It was probably an old Iron Age peat digging area, and he thus found a strong similarity between the lake sediments and peat bogs, which are still called moors in England and the northern Netherlands.

Physical limnology began in 1730 in Switzerland, when the engineer F. de Duillier measured a periodic surface wave, or *seiche.* Fifty years later, Saussure discovered thermal stratification after devising a method to make temperature observations in deep water. The first description of how light, heat, water temperature, and wind mix to form the structure so important in lake ecosystems (Chap. 2) was given by Sir John Leslie, who interpreted studies in Scottish lakes made by the civil engineer James Jardin from 1812 to 1814. Leslie could almost have composed the introduction to Chaps. 3 to 5 in this text when he wrote:

> But the rays which fall on seas or lakes are not immediately arrested on their course; they penetrate always with diminishing energy till, at a certain depth, they are no longer visible. This depth depends without doubt on the clearness of the medium, though probably not one-tenth part of the incident light can advance five fathoms [10 m] in most translucid water. The surface of the ocean is not, therefore, like that of the land, heated by direct action of the sun during the day, since his rays are not intercepted at their entrance, but suffered partially to descend into the mass, and to waste their calorific power on a liquid stratum of ten or twelve feet in thickness. . . . But the surface of deep collections of water is kept always warmer than the ordinary standard of the place, by the operation of another cause, arising from the peculiar constitution of fluids. Although these are capable, like solids, of conducting heat slowly through their mass, yet they transfer it principally in a copious flow by their internal mobility. The heated portion of the fluid being dilated, must continue to float on the surface; while the portions which are cooled, becoming consequently denser, will sink downwards by their superior gravity. Hence the bed of a very deep pool is always excessively cold, since the atmospheric influences are modified in their effects by the laws of statics. (quoted in Murray and Pullar, 1910)

The discovery of animal plankton was another important milestone in aquatic biology. Although it is not certain who first described plankton, Johannes Muller conducted some of the earliest studies around 1845. A short time later another Muller, Peter Erasmus, observed microscopic crustacea for the first time, in Swiss lakes. These events launched the classification of freshwater and marine microorganisms. The word *plankton,* which means "wandering," was first used by Hensen in 1887 to describe the suspended microscopic material at the mercy of the winds, currents, and tide. The meaning of the word was later expanded by the German biologist Ernst Haechel to include larger pelagic organisms. For a time only those organisms retained by a fine silk net were known, since those whose dimensions were less than 0.067 mm passed between the threads of the cloth and were not observed. Later these important smaller organisms were discovered and given the name *nannoplankton.*

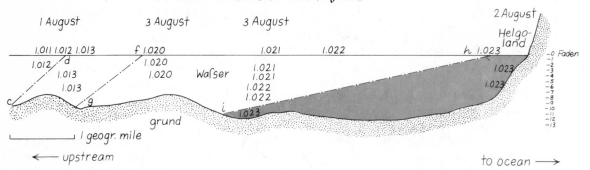

FIGURE 1-2 The estuarine salt wedge as discovered by J. R. Lorenz at the mouth of the River Elbe, Germany, in 1862. The island of Helgoland lies in the open North Sea (far right) and the dense sea water of specific gravity 1.023 to 1.025 forms a sharp submerged wedge under the outflowing fresh and lighter river water (see line *hi* and shaded area). The salt wedge becomes less pronounced upstream (lines *fg* and *cd*). Lorenz made these measurements in a drifting boat over 3 days in August using a homemade sampling device that frequently became jammed with sand or damaged by the swift estuarine current of about 180 cm s^{-1}. He commented, "I spent many a bitter day in such exhausting exercises." Depth is shown in Faden (fathom, or about 2 m) on the right of the figure. Much simplified from the original, Lorenz, (1863).

The scientific study of the flowing waters of estuaries began in the 1860s, with the discovery by J. R. Lorenz of the salt wedge in the River Elbe in Germany (Fig. 1-2). At the same time, pollution research began in the River Thames in England. Meyer and Mobius (1865; 1872) recognized the problems of survival in the variable salinity of brackish waters and initiated a biological approach.

Limnology in the United States began in the middle of the nineteenth century, when Louis Agassiz (1850) published *Lake Superior: Its Physical Character, Vegetation, and Animals,* which was primarily concerned with the fishes of Lake Superior. The first limnologist to describe lakes as ecosystems was Stephen A. Forbes, who in 1887 presented "The Lake as a Microcosm" to the Peoria, Illinois, Historical Society. The ecosystem concept has been particularly important in the development of limnology. The term *ecosystem* was first used by the terrestrial English botanist A. G. Tansley but was put into popular usage in 1942 by G. E. Hutchinson and R. L. Lindeman in the latter's "The Trophic-Dynamic Aspect of Ecology."

At the turn of the century American limnology was dominated by four investigators: E. A. Birge and C. Juday, studying Wisconsin lakes; C. A. Kofoid, working on the Illinois River; and James G. Needham, working on New York lakes. Professor Birge is especially noteworthy for contributing a greater biological dimension to the field of limnology through his study of the plankton of Lake Mendota. He is also noted for studies of physical limnology, which included light penetration, gases, currents, and the thermal characteristics of lakes. Birge's administrative duties at the university left the execution of much of his limnological research and teaching to his close associate, Chauncy Juday. Their first joint paper was published in 1908, the last about 30 years later. Birge is the subject of a biography by G. C. Sellery (1956) that includes a review of his limnological contributions by C. H. Mortimer, a pioneer of physical and chemical studies in lakes. Juday's contributions are documented in a short monograph by Beckel (1987). The limnological laboratory established by A. D. Hasler on the shores of Lake Mendota continues the work of Birge and Juday.

Paul S. Welch wrote the first American textbook, *Limnology,* in 1935. Franz Ruttner's *Fundamentals of Limnology,* which first appeared in German in 1940, in his own modest view "will in no way replace the introductions to limnology (Thienemann, Brehm, Lenz, and Welch) but complement them in certain respects." Many found the 1964 translation by D. G. Frey and F. E. J. Fry a useful introductory text well into the 1970s. At Yale University G. Evenly Hutchinson produced the first volume of his comprehensive *Treatise on Limnology* (1957), which became a standard reference work throughout the world. This was eventually followed by three more volumes (1967; 1975; and 1993), the later published posthumously.

In 1966 Bernard Dussart produced *Limnologie: L'étude des eaux Continentales,* a text emphasizing biology and evolution. An individualistic treatment of the subject, *Physiological Limnology,* by H. L. Golterman, appeared in 1975, the same year Robert. G. Wetzel published the first edition of his text, *Limnology.* Two texts on streams appeared in the 1970s: Hynes's *The Ecology of Running Waters* (1972) and Whitton's edited text *River Ecology* (1975). Other introductory texts, such as these by Cole (1975), Reid and Wood (1976), and Moss (1980), cover the ecology of inland waters. A collection of essays on some aspects of physical and chemical limnology is given in the text edited by Lerman (1978), and Volume 31 (1974) of the *Journal of the Fisheries Research Board of Canada* is a review of Canadian limnology. Junk publishes monographs about individual lakes and rivers, including many lakes outside the United States. The Ecological Studies series of Springer-Verlag

has at least 83 volumes to date, several of which concern rivers, estuaries, and watersheds. Individual lakes or lake systems are the subject of many publications, including those of the Internal Limnology Society (SIL). Several reviews consider estuarine limnology from various viewpoints (Lauff, 1967; Perkins, 1974; Chapman, 1977; Day et al., 1989).

At the same time limnology was beginning in the United States, the science was well developed in Europe. F. Simony studied thermal stratification in Austrian lakes about 1850, and Anton Fritsch in lakes in the Bohemian forests around 1888. It is now recognized that temperature change with depth is one of the most important characteristics of lake structure, since it sets the stage for the spring phytoplankton bloom. Simony made his investigations by lowering a crude wood-insulated thermometer, allowing it to equilibrate, retrieving it rapidly, reading it before the temperature rose at the surface. (Some of the authors' students, before they had any limnological training, devised almost identical methods when they were sent by a government agency to report on mountain lakes. They suspended a large soft drink bottle overnight in deep water. Pulling it up quickly they were able to determine the lake bottom water temperature quite accurately!)

The secchi disk, a white plastic or metal disc used to determine the transparency of water, is among the oldest of limnological devices and was invented by the Italian astronomer and Jesuit priest Pietro Angelo Secchi (Tyler, 1968; Peskova, 1990). He was asked to assist the commander of the papal ship *S.S. I'Immacolata Concezione* in measuring the transparency of coastal waters in the Mediterranean Sea. In April 1865, he experimented with a 43-cm-diameter disk of white clay and a 60-cm-diameter disk of white-painted sailcloth stretched over an iron ring. The disks were lowered until they became invisible, a depth that was to become known as the secchi depth. Over the next few weeks he tested brown and yellow discs, sometimes shading them from the sun with umbrellas and hats, and also determining the secchi depth in calm and stormy weather. Secchi was aware of the reasons for some of the variations in secchi depth that are now used in mathematical modeling of phosphorus and secchi depth:

> We do not wish to pass over a circumstance which is pointed out to us that in these months (April and May) the sea is more transparent than in summer, perhaps owing to the lesser amount of animalcules and other organisms which grow there in the summer season (quoted in Peskova, 1990).

Secchi concluded that the critical factors in the estimation of secchi depth were the diameter of the disk, its spectral reflectance, the presence of waves, reflections of sun and sky on the water surface, shadows on the submerged light path, and the amount of plankton in the water. The secchi disk is still one of the most valuable instruments in the limnologist's tool kit, because it is inexpensive and almost indestructible.

Studies on temperature and water movement became popular in Europe in the early 1900s, particularly in Switzerland and Scotland (Figs. 1-1, 1-3). These studies, especially those concerning Forel's theory of surface seiches, soon established the worldwide similarity of a variety of lake phenomena. In contrast, early Russian limnologists emphasized aquatic bacteriology, and S. N. Vinogradskiy, S. I. Kutznetsov, G. G. Vinberg, and V. I. Romanenko helped originate microbial limnology. Rhode in Sweden, Ohle and Elster in Germany, Jagg and Vollenweider in Switzerland, and several others expanded limnology into a broader science.

The Journals

In the nineteenth century the need arose to establish journals to assemble the increasing volume of information. Despite the existence today of many limnological journals, a thorough search of the limnological literature includes publications in a variety of other fields. This underscores the fact that limnology is a truly interdisciplinary science. On January 1, 1936, the Limnological Society of America was founded; in 1948, it was reorganized as the American Society of Limnology and Oceanography, to integrate limnology, oceanography, and marine biology. The interrelationship of interest and activity was expressed

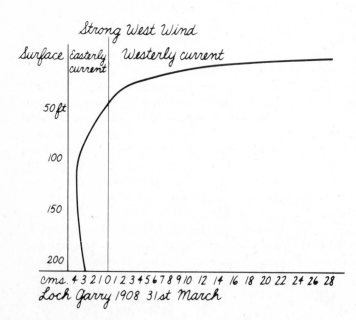

FIGURE 1-3   Measurements of the water currents in Loch Garry, Scotland, in 1908. This original figure shows rapid surface water movement downwind and slow return flows below the thermocline at about 50 ft (17 m). Water speed is given on the horizontal axis in cm s⁻¹, and water depth, in feet, on the vertical axis. Unfortunately, most copies of this work were lost in a fire in London before they could be distributed. From Murray and Pullar (1910).

by the president of the new society in the first issue of its official publication, the journal *Limnology and Oceanography:*

> The American Society of Limnology and Oceanography was established in response to a need felt by its members for a common outlet for the publication of scientific papers on all aspects—physical, chemical, geological, and biological—of phenomena exhibited by natural bodies of water.

Limnology and Oceanography, which had about 2500 subscribers in 1993 and is available in virtually every major university library, was followed by other new journals that catered to more specialized topics. Journals with international coverage that emphasize fresh and brackish waters are listed at the end of this chapter.

The Great Laboratories

The year 1948 also marked the formation of the Freshwater Biological Association in Britain. Several decades of work distinguish this laboratory on the shores of Lake Windermere, which maintains a continuous record of physical, chemical, and biological information on 17 lakes in the English Lake District. The works of LeCren, Lund, Macan, and Talling on the Lake District are often referred to in this text. In Italy, the Istituto Italiano di ldrobiologia, first under the direction of Vittorio Tonolli and later Livia Tonolli, furthered the science through intensive study of northern Italian lakes. The institute also became a Mecca for visiting scientists, who enjoy the intellectual climate and excellent library. Similar world-renowned institutes, such as those at Plön, Germany; Uppsala and Lund, Sweden; Copenhagen, Denmark; Lake Constance, Germany; Lake Baikal, Siberia, were established about this time, and many more have since joined them.

LIMNOLOGY TODAY

Modern limnologists are concerned with the advancement of their science, but also with its application to the preservation and enhancement of aquatic ecosystems. Lakes and rivers accumulate pollutants and are easily damaged. Very few new lakes, rivers, or wetlands are being created by natural means. In fact, some small lakes created by glacial action are slowly vanishing, and many wetlands have already been lost to agriculture and urban development.

However, large new lakes are formed behind dams and many small lakes are created as the focal point of housing developments. Wetlands are created or restored in land swaps or as mitigation for destroyed sites, and streams are sometimes formed or augmented with treated wastewater discharges. An increasing number of limnologists are involved in optimizing these new aquatic environments for both utility and beauty.

Since the 1970s a heightened awareness of the deterioration of the aquatic environment and the need for action has attracted engineers as well as a new generation of limnologists. It is essential that aquatic resources are managed more sensibly on both local and global scales. This problem is so pressing that it has greatly influenced contemporary research in limnology. For example, the eutrophication of lakes has degraded water quality for both humans and fish. In the 1960s the problem was considered to be entirely due to excessive loading of phosphate from agriculture, sewage, and detergent. A major effort was made to reduce phosphate loading and thereby decrease algae growth. It is now recognized that phosphorus is not the only nutrient that can limit algal growth, especially away from the temperate zone lakes familiar to most limnologists. Colimitation by both nitrogen and phosphorus, with different species of algae being limited by different nutrients, is probably the rule rather than the exception. Thirty years later, theorists predict that much of the effect of eutrophication can be removed by modifying the top of the food chain, the large fish. This top-down rather than bottom-up approach may or may not be widely successful, but the example demonstrates how the science continually mixes theory and practice.

Today, limnologists are engaged in lake and reservoir modeling, a topic considered in the future in the first edition of this text. The overoptimistic supermodels of the past have been replaced by less all-encompassing models that better serve the limnologist. For example, the current WQRRS (water quality for river or reservoir systems) model can predict with reasonable accuracy the one-dimensional changes in temperature and dissolved oxygen under different conditions. The model must be calibrated with actual data from the lake or reservoir, and some of the assumptions are not very realistic, but it works well enough for most purposes. The Great Lakes total phosphorous model, devised by Chapra and Sonzogni in the late 1970s, has also delivered good results recently. An example of the data predicted by this "simple" multicompartment model in 1977-1979 compared with

data collected in the 1980s is shown in Fig. 1-4. Reckow and Chapra (1983), in their excellent two-volume book *Lake Modeling,* discuss the use of models. They also give an example of how the precision of a computer model can vary over time in response to uncertainty in the data input (Fig. 1-5).

Limnologists today are called upon to provide data for environmental planning studies, such as Environmental Impact Reports. Such studies are gaining use in many parts of the world, because funding decisions are often based in part on consideration of environmental problems. The World Bank, for example, recently doubled its environmental staff. When a large reservoir was proposed in the the Skippack watershed near Evansburg, Pennsylvania, 1969–1970, environmental analyses, including alternative strategies, were undertaken. Due to the projected undesirable limnological consequences, the project was abandoned in favor of several smaller reservoirs

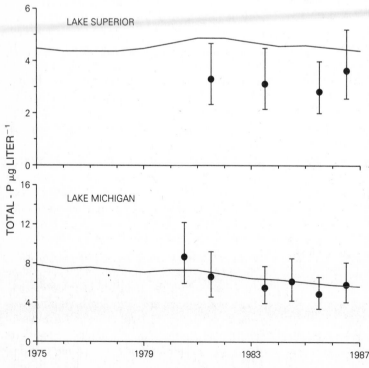

FIGURE 1-4 The total phosphorus concentrations predicted by a "simple" multicompartment lake model (continuous line) in two large lakes as compared with data (dots, shown as annual averages) collected after the predictions were made. Note how the model overestimated future phosphorus levels in Lake Superior but was more accurate for Lake Michigan (lower panel) as well as the other Great Lakes (not shown). The error was probably due to poor estimations of the phosphorus-removal mechanisms in this largest of lakes. Error bars for the actual data are about 30 percent of the mean. No error is shown for this computer model output, but see Fig. 1-5. Original model by Chapra (1977) and Chapra and Sonzogni (1979). Modified from Lesht et al. 1991.

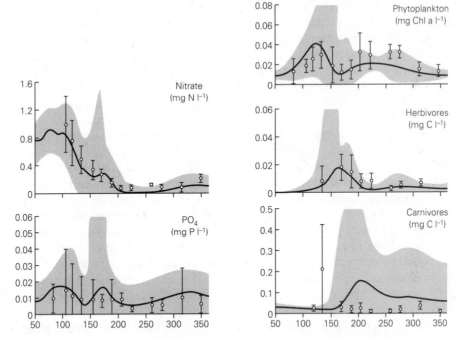

FIGURE 1-5 Dynamic eutrophication simulation model for Saginaw Bay in Lake Huron, which shows the variability in both computer output and field data. Several trophic levels are shown. Note that for most parameters, the May–June "spring" bloom (150–180 days) is very poorly predicted by the model since there is very high variability. In summer and fall there is less variability in the prediction. The limnologist interprets the high variability in spring as a higher risk of being incorrect in predictions. Note also that the highest trophic level, the zooplankton (carnivores), is very difficult to predict with any certainty when using this kind of "bottom-up" model. This is a result of the many links in the food chain between nutrients, algae, herbivores, and carnivores. Modified from Scavia et al. (1981).

(McHarg and Clarke, 1973). In Papua, New Guinea, a proposed huge hydroelectric scheme involved as many as 10 dams on the Purari River. After environmental analysis and review by the United Nations Development Program, the project was abandoned by its sponsor (Goldman and Hoffman, 1977). A reassessment of overall costs often allows for the development of less costly and less environmentally damaging alterative programs and mitigating measures.

THE FUTURE

The future of limnology is closely tied to the general advancement of science and technology.

Six areas that offer good prospects are analysis of long-term data, replicated studies in large enclosures, better-integrated laboratory and field studies, whole-lake food web manipulation, comparative limnology of lakes and rivers, and wetlands management.

Long-Term Data Sets

A very powerful method of analysis is to use long-term physical, chemical, or biological data sets. Data are now available on more than 60 years in the marine sciences and over 40 years in limnology (e.g., Figs. 12-5, 13-10, 13-11, 14-11, 14-14, 16-12, 20-10, 22-6). The false results that can occur using only short-term data have been demonstrated for the water transparency in Lake Tahoe (Goldman, 1988) and for fish data in the Apalachicola River Estuary (Livingstone, 1984). The U.S. National Science Foundation has funded 10 long-term studies of individual lakes, which should provide better insight into the interactions between climate, watersheds, and long-term succession of aquatic organisms.

Long-term data need not be sophisticated. For example, over the last decade, coral reefs in the Pacific and Caribbean Sea seem to be losing their algae symbionts, bleaching and dying. This may be associated with global warming and may be due to a 2 to 3°C increase in water temperature. There are hundreds of university and other marine stations situated near coral reefs, and daily or weekly temperature data could easily have been collected over the last few decades using simple automatic recording devices or even taken by hand. It is a tragedy that not one laboratory maintained a long-term temperature record that can be correlated with coral bleaching (Brown and Ogden, 1993).

Integration of Laboratory and Field Research

Limnology provides a unique opportunity to combine observations with laboratory and field experimentation. The methods can be divided into three types: field measurement, pure culture studies, and mesocosm and microcosm experiments. The results of field measurements, although inherently highly variable, are usually directly applicable. Pure culture studies using a single species of algae, invertebrate, or fish have the advantage of low variability but the disadvantage of limited applicability to real systems. The benefits and drawbacks of using scaled analog models of the aquatic ecosystem, called *enclosures, microcosms* or *mesocosms* (Fig. 1-6), lie between the other two. The advantages are that (1) micro- and mesocosms ecosystems can be easily adjusted to enable prediction of future effects; and (2) the experimental design can be changed to give the degree of precision required

by the investigator. Manipulation, while decreasing variability, has the inherent danger of departing from reality. For example, in a planktonic or riverine mesocosm, zooplankton or benthic invertebrates can be excluded to establish more precisely the relationships between algae and nutrients without the complicating effects of grazing. In the example of coral bleaching mentioned above, despite field studies that showed that polyp deaths were probably due to increases of 1 to 2°C occurring over months to years, all experiments to date have used temperatures of 6°C over 16 to 72 hours (Brown and Ogden, 1993). This poor integration of laboratory and field studies can now easily be remedied.

Studies in large enclosures, such as those of the English Lake District (Fig. 1-7) or the giant CEPEX bag experiments in the Pacific Ocean near Vancouver, Canada, give some idea of what might be done in the future. These experiments lacked the replication needed to determine between-bag variation and thus a level of statistical reliability for future predictions. The multiple ponds at Cornell, New York (Hall et al., 1970), or the multiple-model estuary system at the University of California's Berkeley Field Stations at Richmond are examples of well-replicated analog systems (Fig. 1-6a).

Whole-Lake Manipulation

The manipulation of whole lakes remains an excellent vehicle for future limnological research efforts. The entire food web can be explored, and the long-term changes measured are not confounded by "enclosure effects" inherent in even the largest bottles or bags. Typical enclosure effects are those due to the larger amount of wall surface relative to lakes and the inability to support less abundant migratory species or large predatory fish. In most whole-lake manipulations, nearby lakes or the lake's past history are used to establish baseline conditions. Since all lakes are individuals, adjacent "control" lakes are not always adequate, and several years of data, at all trophic levels, must ideally be col-

(a)   (b)

FIGURE 1-6   Experimental mesocosms (analogs) of aquatic ecosystems. (*a*) A medium-sized estuarine mesocosm. Electric pumps provide tidal motion and allow use of any desired hydraulic residence time. Replication is possible in these systems, but the cost of construction and maintenance is high. The figure shows part of 20 tanks of 4 m^3 used for flow-through tests in the San Francisco Bay Estuary. Precise amounts of waste can be added continually via Plexiglas header tanks (center right), and plants or animals can be held under precise experimental conditions for months or even years. This facility is part of the University of California, Berkeley, Environmental Engineering and Health Laboratory's lake and wetlands mesocosm system. (*b*) An in situ lake mesocosm experiment showing 5 of 12 separate 0.7-m^3 containers made of 4-mil polyethylene (2.5 m deep $\times$ 0.7 m wide, tied at the bottom). Replication of controls and experimental treatments can easily be made. Polybag mesocosms are inexpensive and variations of this system are commonly used in many lakes throughout the world. Although oxygen or temperature are identical to those in the surrounding lake, heavier phytoplankton tend to settle out. They can be resuspended using a secchi disk on a pole, as illustrated by one of us in the 1970s. In this case each mesocosm was suspended on springs to enable experiments in the center of large Clear Lake, California ($A = 17,000$ ha), where wave action is often great. Mesocosms designed and built by C. J. W. Carmiggelt and J. C. Roth.

FIGURE 1-7 Large-scale mesocosms. Three 46-m-diameter, 12-m-deep enclosures in Blelham Tarn in the English Lake District. These experiments are too large to replicate easily but can simulate lake conditions for a whole season and were run continually for 11 years. The enclosures are made of butyl rubber and are dug about 1 m into the mud. The central tube has a spring bloom of the blue-green algae *Oscillatoria agardhii,* which appears white in this picture. The effect is due to a complex several-month interaction between fungal parasitism, zooplankton grazing, and fertilization with phosphate and silicate in the previous fall. Photograph by J. W. G. Lund, F.R.S..

lected prior to manipulation. One of the first examples of whole-lake manipulation was Castle Lake, California, where the effects of molybdenum addition were studied (Goldman, 1964) (Fig. 10-12). The studies in some of the 1000 lakes in the Experimental Lakes Area (ELA) in Canada have made extensive use of whole-lake manipulations to study the effects of nutrient additions and, more recently, acid rain (Schindler et al., 1985). The Hubbard Brook experimental watershed, where whole sections of the watershed can be cleared of vegetation provides a flowing water equivalent of whole lake experiments (Likens et al., 1977). Such studies on lakes and streams could be extended elsewhere, but the difficulties in undertaking them and in interpreting the results should not be underestimated (Fee, 1980; Schindler, 1980). Unforeseen events, such as the forest fires that have complicated some ELA studies as well as those at Lake Tahoe (Goldman et al., 1990), must be incorporated into future designs.

Comparative Limnology

The study of lakes within a lake district or between similar lakes in different regions is likely to produce valuable limnological insights (Chap. 21). The greatest challenge is the comparative limnology of large lakes, rivers, and estuaries. The Laurentian Great Lakes, the African Rift lakes, and the Amazon, Nile, and Rhine rivers pose formidable logistic and financial problems.

Helicopters, float planes, satellites, and other remote data-analyzing devices are being more
widely used for large ecosystems.

Wetlands Management

Much current research is devoted to wetlands,
which are in some ways the most difficult of the
habitats limnologists study due to their spatial
heterogeneity (Plate 5). Nevertheless, the loss of
wetlands, which are valuable as wildlife reserves
and clean some polluted waters, makes future
study of wetlands desirable. Methods are needed
to design replicated mesocosms in wetlands that
allow for the natural spatial heterogeneity at all
levels as well as an ecosystem maturity that is
measured in years, rather than days or weeks as
for many planktonic systems. Long-term studies
are needed to determine whether nutrient removal will reach equilibrium, if heavy metal accumulation will result in poisoning, as occurred
with selenium in the Kesterson Marsh in Central
California, and how are polluted fresh and saline
wetlands to be restored.

Finally, limnologists should continue to seek
close working relationships with marine scientists. Both groups benefit from this interaction,
and there is no logical reason to feel restricted
to either ecosystem.

The next chapter considers in detail the
"structure" of lakes, streams, wetlands, and estuaries. The physical, chemical, and biological
elements of aquatic systems produce distinct
temporary or permanent compartments akin to
the rooms in a house. This structure changes with
time and depth, and the study of these variations
provides the basis of limnology. Additional understanding can be gained by comparison of different bodies of water.

FURTHER READING

Limnological Journals

Limnology and Oceanography
Journal of Plankton Research
Journal of Plankton Ecology
Journal of Freshwater Ecology
Journal of Freshwater Biology
Canadian Journal of Fisheries and Aquatic Science
Australian Journal of Freshwater and Marine Science
*New Zealand Journal of Freshwater and Marine Sci-
ence*
Hydrobiologia
Archiv für Hydrobiologie
Swiss Journal of Hydrobiology (abbr. *Schweiz. Z. Hy-
drol.*)
*Proceedings of the International Association of The-
oretical and Applied Limnology* (abbr. *Ver. Int. Ver.
Limnol.*)
Journal of Great Lakes Research
Memorie dell'Istituto Italiano di Idrobiologia
Hydrobiological Journal (USSR)
Journal of Lake and Reservoir Management

Journals That Publish Some Limnological Articles

Ecology
Journal of Ecology
Oikos
Water Research
Water Resources Research
Ecological Monographs
Journal of Phycology (US)
British Journal of Phycology
Phykos
Bioscience
Estuaries
Proceedings of the Royal Society (UK) Series B.
British Antarctic Survey Journal
Polar Research

Other Readings

Beckel, A. L. 1987. "Breaking New Waters." *Trans.
Acad. Wis. Soc. Arts Lett.* Special Issue. 122 pp.
Bloech, J. (ed). 1989. "Mesocosm Studies." *Hydro-
biologia,* **221.**
Elster, H. J., 1974. "History of Limnology." *Mitt.
Int. Ver. Theor. Angew. Limnol.,* **20:**7-30.
Giesy, J. P. 1980. "Microcosms in Ecological Re-
search." Technical Information Center, U.S. De-
partment of Energy, Springfield, VA. (DOE Sym-
posium Series 52). Conf.-781 101. 1110 pp.
Rodhe, W. 1979. "The Life of Lakes." *Arch. Hydro-
biol. Beth.,* **3:**5-9.

CHAPTER 2

The Structure of Aquatic Ecosystems

OVERVIEW

Lakes, streams, estuaries, and wetlands have distinct structures determined by basin morphometry and physical, chemical, and biological interactions. These elements provide a simple way to describe many important lake features. Morphometry refers to the shape of the underwater basin. The physical structure is determined by the distribution of light, heat, waves, and currents and varies by day and season. The chemical structure results from the uneven distribution of chemicals such as nutrients and dissolved oxygen. Superimposed on these abiotic components is the distribution of living organisms. The characteristics of the watershed and airshed are also important determinants in lake structure, mostly due to their role in nutrient cycles.

In this chapter we describe lake structure based on these parameters and then consider ponds, streams and rivers, and estuaries.

LAKES

Morphometry

A lake's morphometry is a function of underwater contour lines, the shape of the lake, and its geologic origin. The lake's morphometry is basic to its structure; for example, deep, steepsided lakes are quite different in almost all respects from shallow ones. Once the lake basin is formed, physical, chemical, and biological factors interact to produce discernible structure within the water. This structure persists despite the continual movement of the water that is characteristic of all aquatic ecosystems. The relatively still waters of lakes have led to their designation as *lentic* environments, in contrast to flowing, or *lotic* systems, such as streams.

The lake basin, as opposed to the drainage basin, is the portion that holds the water. The topography of the surrounding area may provide clues to the lake basin's morphometry, but details such as depth and contour of the bottom must be measured by sounding with a weighted line or an echo sounder. Often, a detailed morphometric map is available, but in a surprising number of cases this information is absent, inadequate, or outdated due to sedimentation.

Measures of lake morphometry provide a useful means of description, which we use frequently throughout this book. Lake surface area (A) is measured with a planimeter from a good map or aerial photograph that includes elevation of the water surface relative to mean sea level. In most temperate lakes, the area is quite constant except during severe droughts. In tropical or dry climates, however, the area may change dramatically with the season and in wet and dry years. Reservoirs are often drawn down in summer, producing large changes in both area and volume. Volume (V) can be calculated using underwater contour lines, by summing the volume of the various layers of water contained between all depth contours. Volume is most conveniently expressed in cubic meters or cubic kilometers, although the term acre-foot (1 acre, 1 foot deep) is still commonly used in engineering and agriculture in the United States. Mean depth ($\bar{z}$) is obtained by dividing the volume V of the lake by its surface area A. Other frequently used morphometric terms are maximum depth (z_{max}) and length (L) of the shoreline.

One of the most useful ways to present data is to use a *hypsographic curve,* a plot of depth along the vertical axis and either volume or area along the horizontal axis (Fig. 2-1). These plots indicate the lake volume or area at any desired depth. They are vital for controlling reservoirs, since the best way to release or store a known volume of water is to lower or raise to the water level, which is easily measured.

Shoreline development (D_L) reflects the degree of shoreline irregularity and is expressed as the ratio of the length L to the circumference of a circle of area equal to that of the lake surface. The more irregular the shoreline, the greater D_L. Some of these measurements for selected lakes are given in Table 2-1 and for two well-known lake districts in Tables 21-1 and 21-3.

The time required to refill an empty lake with its natural inflow is termed the *hydraulic residence time.* It is calculated by dividing the volume by the inflow or outflow rate. This is an important parameter in lake pollution studies and for nutrient dynamics calculations. It is mainly determined by the interplay between lake inflow and basin morphology, in that a large, deep lake with a moderate water inflow will have a long hydraulic residence time but a small, shallow lake with the same inflow volume will have only a short residence time.

FIGURE 2-1 (*a*) The relationship between absolute surface area and depth in the steep-sided Lake Tahoe, as indicated by cumulative hypsographic curves derived from measurement by planimetry. (*b*) Relative hypsographic curves for three of the glacially excavated Laurentian Great Lakes and the pan-shaped Lake Milaren, Scandinavia. Modified from Hakanson (1981).

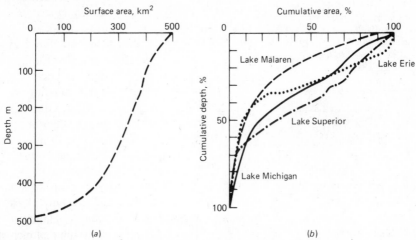

TABLE 2-1

PHYSICAL DIMENSIONS AND HYDRAULIC RESIDENCE TIMES (WHERE AVAILABLE) FOR SELECTED LAKES AND RESERVOIRS THROUGHOUT THE WORLD

	V, km³	A, km²	$\bar{z}$, m	$z_{,max}$, m	Retention time, years
Americas					
Tahoe, California	156	499	313	501	~700
Castle, California	0.0023	0.201	11.4	35	3–5
Clear, California	1.4	176	~8	14	~3
Superior, North America	12,000	83,300	144	307	184
Pyramid, Nevada	~25	~500	~50	~100	Sink
Okeechobee, Florida	~6	1,880	~3	~4.5	
Crater, Oregon	20	55	364	608	
Winnipeg, Canada	311	24,530	13	19	
Managua, Nicaragua	~8	~1,000	5	19	Sink
Titicaca, Andes	866	8,100	107	281	70
Europe					
Esrom, Denmark	0.21	17.3	12.3	22	8.5
Windermere, England	0.35	14.8	24	67	0.75
Balaton, Hungary	~1.8	596	~3	~4	
Constance, Germany	49.3	540	91	252	
Tjeukemeer, Netherlands	~0.03	~20	~1.5	~3	
Africa					
Victoria, East Africa	2,700	68,800	40	79	
George, Uganda	0.63	250	2.4	3	0.34
Tanganyika, East Africa	18,940	34,000	557	1,470	Sink
Chad, Chad	20–40	16,000	1.5–4	12	Sink
Kariba (reservoir), Africa	130	4,300	30	93	~3
Kainji (reservoir), Africa	15.6	1,280	12.3	50	0.25
Asia					
Biwa, Japan	28	685	41	104	5.4
Baikal, Siberia	23,000	31,500	730	1,741	
Caspian Sea, former U.S.S.R.	79,319	436,400	182	946	Sink
Kinneret, Israel	4,301	168	26	43	7.32
Antarctica					
Vanda, Dry Valley	0.15	5.2	29	66	Sink
Lake 2, Signy Island	0.00009	0.04	2	6	

The *retention time* of a nutrient may be somewhat different from the hydraulic residence time, since sedimentation and recycling take place within the lake. For example, in winter, soluble nutrients such as nitrate or phosphate have a residence time similar to that of a water molecule. In spring, their passage through the lake is delayed because some are removed by algae growth. Some nitrogen and phosphorus may be released by decomposition later in the year and flow out of the lake but some algae containing nutrients may remain in the sediments forever. Other compounds arrive in the lake in particulate form, sink and form permanent sediments. The residence time of most chemicals and particulates thus depends on both the substance itself and its interactions with biotic and abiotic factors.

Table 2-1 gives hydraulic retention times for selected lakes and reservoirs. Table 21-3 shows similar data for the Laurentian Great Lakes. Lake Tahoe, with a retention time of about 700 years, is almost a permanent sink for nutrients. In contrast, Marion Lake, in Canada, has a hydraulic retention time of only a few days, and most nutrients pass out almost as fast as they enter. It is difficult to generalize for the "typical" lake, but residence times of 1 to 10 years are common for both natural lakes and reservoirs.

Surface water has two major regions, with exact analogies in the marine environment. The *littoral zone* extends from the shore just above the influence of waves and spray to a depth where the well-mixed warm surface waters still reach the lake bed in summer (Fig. 2-2). Organisms that live in this zone must be able to tolerate strong wave action and most are firmly attached to rocks or plants. The shallow littoral zone often contains abundant populations of animals and plants, although too much light, wave action, and rocky or mobile sand substrate can prevent plant attachment (Plate 2). Beyond the littoral zone lies the open water, the *pelagic* or *limnetic zone,* which is characterized by an absence of contact with either the lake bottom or shore. Organisms that inhabit the pelagic zone must be adapted for swimming or flotation; otherwise, they would sink to the bottom.

Light and Temperature

Lake physics, especially the interaction of light, temperature, and wind mixing, establishes the second major element of lake structure.

Light Zonation Zones based on the amount of sunlight at a particular depth establish a major element of lake structure. The sunlit upper waters constitute the *photic* or *euphotic zone* extending from the lake surface down to where light dims to about 1 percent of that at the surface (Fig. 2-2). During the day the photic zone is a region of net oxygen production by plants. During the

FIGURE 2-2 The influence of the distribution of light and temperature on the physical structure of a lake (see also Fig. 2-3). The situation shown is typical of a small temperate lake in summer. The zones are not exact, and in turbid lakes or near dawn and dusk in any lake the photic zone may extend only partway down the mixed layer. In winter the mixed layer usually extends to the lake bed. Strong wave action along the shore as well as favorable light establish the limits of the littoral zone. The term *thermocline* has sometimes been restricted to the zone with a change of at least 1°C m^{-1} of depth. This unnecessarily restrictive definition has limited value, particularly in the tropics, and is not adhered to in this text.

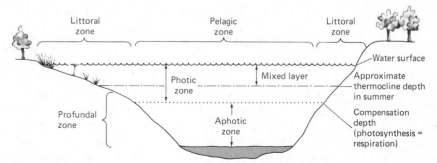

night photosynthesis ceases but respiration by animals and plants continues and oxygen may decline. All of the littoral zone and the upper parts of the pelagic zone are contained within the photic zone.

The *aphotic zone* extends from below the photic zone to the bottom of the lake. In this zone light levels are too low for photosynthesis. Respiration, however, proceeds at all depths, so the aphotic zone always comsumes oxygen. This region is also called the *profundal zone,* since it is usually deep. The lower boundary of the photic zone varies daily and seasonally with changing solar intensity and water transparency. For example, the photic zone is reduced if transparency is decreased by algae blooms or suspended sediment. In the most transparent lakes, such as Lake Tahoe, a small amount of light penetrates to great depths and a few specialized primitive plants grow at depths greater than 150 m where light is only a fraction of 1 percent. This deepest area of plant growth is the *sublittoral zone,* a transition between littoral and profundal zones. Shallow lakes with transparent water, such as pools in the high mountains or deep in forests, may have no sublittoral, profundal, or aphotic zones. Thick growths of mosses or algae may cover the entire lake bed and the entire water column is sufficiently illuminated to permit photosynthesis.

In contrast to shallow transparent lakes, shallow lakes with low transparency often have an aphotic zone where no plant growth can occur. Turbidity from algae and suspended sediments shades out the growth of attached plants within a few meters of shore, despite the shallow depth.

Temperature Zonation   The water mass itself has a characteristic vertical temperature structure that is independent of the shape of the basin. In summer swimmers find that slightly colder water is only a short distance below the surface, and anglers can cool their bottled drinks to refrigerator temperature on a hot summer day by suspending them 20 to 30 m below the surface. In winter this structure is absent.

During *thermal stratification,* three vertical zones are found in temperate lakes. The upper warmer water is called the *epilimnion;* the middle portion, where the rate of temperature change with depth is greatest (the *thermocline*), is called the *metalimnion;* and the deepest portion is the *hypolimnion* (Fig. 2-3). All or part of the epilimnion may be well stirred, and the *mixed layer* is simply the water that is well mixed by the wind (Fig. 2-2). The mixed layer may be very deep or quite shallow, depending on the season and the interaction between wind and sun on any given day. In summer, all or part of the epilimnion constitutes the mixed layer. In autumn and spring the entire water column is mixed top to bottom and ice cover prevents wind mixing in winter. Shallow lakes may not exhibit thermal stratification at all, with the entire lake mixed more or less continually.

The structure of the water column as determined by temperature is a reflection of the differences in water density. The warmer, less dense water layer floats at the surface; the colder, denser water sinks to the bottom; and there is a zone of rapidly changing density in between (Fig. 2-3). Although storms may stir the warm waters of the epilimnion into furious motion, little energy is transmitted through the thermocline to the cool, quiescent hypolimnion. Stable thermal stratification is very important in determining the distribution of dissolved chemicals, gases, and the biota.

In the autumn less solar radiation reaches the water and greater heat losses occur at night. Convection and wind mixing begin to weaken the thermocline. The epilimnion increases in depth as it decreases in temperature. Eventually, the difference in temperature and density between the overlying water and that beneath is so slight that a strong wind overcomes the remaining resistance to mixing and the lake undergoes the *fall overturn.* The stratified structure is lost and the lake becomes homothermous; that is, it has a uniform temperature from surface to bottom. In cold climates mixing and further cooling continue until the surface of the lake freezes. Freez-

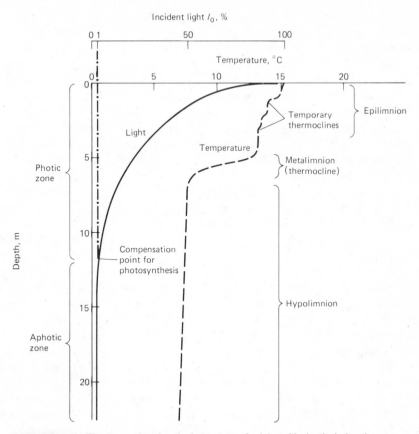

FIGURE 2-3 The thermal and optical structure of a lake with depth during the period of summer thermal stratification.

ing occurs only when surface waters reach 0°C on a windless, cold winter night. Some slightly warmer water remains below the ice.

During the *spring overturn,* the ice melts and wind mixes the cold water until the water temperature increases sufficiently to reestablish thermal stratification. Other patterns of circulation are established in tropical regions and at high latitudes or altitudes (Chap. 4). It will suffice at this point to note that there is a greater density change per degree of temperature change in warm water than in cold. For example, it takes about 30 times as much energy to mix equal volumes of 24 and 25°C water completely as it takes to mix the same volumes of water at 4 and 5°C! Herein lies the explanation for thermal

stratification and the remarkable stability of the epilimnion. A useful classification of lakes has been developed on the basis of how often and how completely their waters mix (Chaps. 4, 5).

Chemical Factors

The distribution of chemicals, especially nutrients, provides the third major element of lake structure. After the onset of thermal stratification, nutrients often become depleted in the epilimnion or photic zone while at the same time remaining constant or even accumulating in the hypolimnion or aphotic zone (Figs. 7-9, 8-3, 10-9). By analogy with temperature, the depth at which rapid change in a substance occurs is called the *chemocline.* In a few lakes the chemocline is a permanent feature (Chap. 4), but usually chemical stratification is determined by thermal stratification. Very deep lakes, such as Lake Superior, Lake Tahoe, or Lake Tanganyika, in Africa, may have chemical stratification that is independent of temperature and depends on microbial processes. There is rarely any stable vertical stratification of chemical constituents in the well-mixed littoral zone. Horizontal nutrient zonation may occur, however, with the highest concentration near the shore or in shallows. The littoral zone and the bed of a shallow lake provide a good habitat for bottom-dwelling organisms, whose foraging, burrowing, and excretion aid in recycling nutrients from the bottom. If the shoreline has numerous bays and points (i.e., D_L is large), there will be more contact of open water with the shore and bottom. This causes nutrients such as phosphorus, nitrogen, iron, and trace elements to dissolve into the lake waters, increasing their concentration in those shoreline regions.

The vertical component of lake chemical structure is seasonal and depends on the presence of layers of density-stabilized water. The horizontal component may occur year-round and results from the influence of the lake's edge and bottom.

Biological Zonation

The fourth major element of lake structure is biological. Most organisms may be classified on the basis of their most common habitat. Except for fish and floating or emergent plants, lake organisms are invisible to the casual observer but use of a microscope reveals a myriad of tiny organisms living in the open water. *Plankton,* (derived from the Greek term for "wanderer") are the floating or weakly swimming organisms at the mercy of waves and currents. The animals of this group are called *zooplankton* and the algae are termed *phytoplankton.* Planktonic bacteria, fungi, and viruses are also present but are usually associated with suspended particles. The stronger swimming animals, such as fish, that inhabit the pelagic zone and are masters of their position in the water column are called *nekton.* There is also a special community of organisms, the *neuston,* that inhabit the surface of the water. One part of the neuston is the *pleuston,* which comprises large floating assemblages blown about by the wind. In African lakes the large aquatic macrophyte *Pistia* (water cabbage) can be an abundant component of the pleuston and may completely cover small bays and coves.

Among the biota of the littoral zone the *attached algae* are important where rocks or higher plants provide a firm substrate. Higher plants, the *aquatic macrophytes,* are likely to dominate the sandy or muddy littoral zones of lakes if wave action does not uproot them. The whole community of microscopic attached organisms composed of algae, bacteria, fungi, protozoa, and small metazoa is called *aufwuchs.* This term, which has no English equivalent, is derived from German and means "living on." Aufwuchs communities are responsive to environmental change and serve as excellent biological indicators of lake fertility.

The organisms associated with the lake bottom are called *benthic organisms,* referred to collectively as *benthos.* These include all forms found in or on submerged substrates, regardless of whether they are in the littoral, sublittoral, or profundal zone. Those that live and move about on the lake bottom, such as crayfish and dragonfly larvae, are called *epibenthic organisms,* and those that burrow beneath the mud surface, such as aquatic worms and some insect larvae, are known as *infauna.* The *epifloral* habitat of submerged vegetation also provides a home for many types of algae and small invertebrates.

Watershed and Airshed

The lake's watershed and airshed constitute the fifth element in lake structure. The size, slope, geological composition, and climate of the lake's drainage basin influence the identity and quantity of minerals suspended or dissolved in the lake or deposited in its sediments. Farmers know that the granite basins of the Precambrian shield of Canada, Scandinavia, and Scotland are infertile and the same factors apply to lakes. In contrast, lakes farther south, in areas of glacial drift and sedimentary rock, are able to produce large algal and fish crops (Figs. 21-1, 21-2). The size of drainage area in relation to the surface area is also important; higher fertility in lakes is often associated with large drainage areas (Table 20-1).

Climate also influences sediment and nutrient transport. In temperate climates rain falls for much of the year and is rarely torrential. Such rain patterns produce a continuous vegetative cover in both forests and grasslands, one result of which is little natural soil erosion. By contrast, regions with semiarid climates have a few, often severe, rainstorms. Here ground cover is not continuous, soil erosion is frequently extensive, and sediments move more easily from watershed to lake. Nutrients such as phosphorus or iron, which are generally transported as salts adsorbed to soil particles, also move more easily in semiarid climates. By contrast, nitrogen, silica, or sulfur are usually present in soluble chemical forms easily transported by either clear or muddy water. The main source of nitrogen in all watersheds is rainfall, and the main source of phosphorus is soil erosion. Rivers and lakes in semiarid climates tend to have excess phosphate and to be nitrogen-limited, while those in temperate climates have excess nitrate and tend to be phosphorus-limited. Other limitations imposed by trace elements or silica are controlled more by the geology of the basin than by the climate.

Acid rain affects lakes primarily via the watershed. Sulfuric and nitric acid deposited in rainfall and on dry particles may pass directly to the lake or be buffered by alkaline soils that contain carbonates. The acidity may even have an indirect toxic effect on lake biota by liberating aluminum ions from the watershed soils and passing them to the lake.

Climate, too, influences the damage caused by acid rain. Because snow melt has a lower pH than water that has percolated through the soil's buffering system, lakes in cold regions are more likely to receive a discharge of very-low-pH water than those in regions where snow does not accumulate.

Freshwater lakes without an outflow eventually become salt lakes through evaporation and may dry up completely as the climate becomes drier. The great Bonneville Salt Flat, now used as a track for developing land-speed records, was once an enormous freshwater lake. There is almost as much water contained in saline lakes, including the inland "seas," as in freshwater lakes (Table 3-1, Chap. 21). Many of these lakes are situated far from the ocean, usually in the rain shadow of high mountain ranges. For example, salt lakes are found north of the Himyalas, in eastern Australia, in Central Canada, in Nevada and Utah, and in the western deserts of North America.

In addition to natural sources of chemicals from sediment or erosion and leaching of the watershed, there are agricultural, forest, and urban sources. These sources not only alter the morphometry of most larger lake basins by filling, they also modify the chemical environment. Urban and agricultural erosion can be so severe that some small ponds and reservoirs require dredging every 10 years. The main effect of humans on the watershed is pollution from erosion, careless disposal of toxic chemicals, and nutrients present in sewage.

PONDS VERSUS LAKES

Where a pond ends and a lake begins has been the subject of considerable definition and redefinition. P. S. Welch (1935) concluded that to be considered a lake, a body of water must have a barren wave-swept shore. Forel (1892) considered ponds to be lakes of slight depth. This definition seems inappropriate for lake waters such as Lake Chad in Africa or Lake Winnipeg in

Canada, which are large but very shallow. The presence of higher aquatic plants is considered important in Welch's definition of ponds. He would classify as lakes all the shallow coastal waters of the Antarctic, regardless of their shallow depth and small size. We conclude that a precise definition is not essential but that one can use the type of lake mixing to aid in definition. In lakes wind plays the dominant role in mixing, but in ponds, gentler convective mixing predominates. By definition ponds are shallow but often thermally stratified waters, with abundant growths of rooted and floating aquatic macrophytes. Employing this definition, Lakes Chad and Winnipeg are lakes and the familiar tree-shaded ponds are not. The abundant shallow-water bodies of the tundra that are subject to extensive wind mixing are probably more similar to the littoral zone of lakes than to ponds.

STREAMS AND RIVERS

The physical structure of flowing waters is more easily seen than that of lakes. When viewing the lotic or running-water environment from a stream bank, one is struck by the variety of habitats that occur over a short distance. Undercut banks, small sandbars, overhanging trees, old snags, and large rocks forming miniature islands all sit in a turbulent flow of water. Closer examination reveals a definite structure largely determined by water velocity and underlying geology. Water splashes over shallow gravel-covered *riffles* that shimmer in the sunlight and alternate with deep quiet *pools*. In the shady conditions, falling leaves provide the main organic carbon source for invertebrates. As with lakes and ponds, the distinction between streams and rivers is vague, but rivers are larger, faster-moving, and often warmer. We use the terms *river* and *stream* interchangeably in this text. Chapter 16 deals with smaller rivers and streams and some special features of food-chain dynamics, cold-water streams. Large rivers are covered in

Chap. 17, and river pollution is discussed in Chaps. 15, 21, and 22.

The dominant feature that structures the lotic environment is the swift unidirectional water flow. The *discharge* (volume per time) and *current* (distance per time) interact with the substrate to determine whether the streambed will be stony or composed of mud and detritus. Most streams possess a series of distinct physical structures that have a regular vertical and horizontal periodicity. Horizontal *meanders* occur in the flatter portions of the watercourse, no matter if the stream is large or small, mountain or lowland. Meanders are due to the water seeking the least energetic path and produce deeper, swifter flows near the eroding, outer edge of the meander circle and shallow areas of deposition on the opposite bank (Fig. 2-4). In the broad valleys of major rivers, extensive meanders create *oxbow lakes* in abandoned channels and *scroll lakes* through deposition at existing bends (Fig. 2-4).

Along the stream the periodicity of riffles and pools referred to above has long fascinated limnologists. One effect of periodicity in streams may be a regular periodic chemical recycling, which Elwood et al. (1981) have called *nutrient spiraling*. This spiraling may produce the same general kind of periodicity as the power spectrum effect produces for waves in lakes and oceans (Fig. 5-7). Streams have a great biotic variability, even over short distances, some of which may be due to this effect.

Thermal or chemical density stratification is usually unimportant in the turbulent lotic environment, and plankton normally play no role in the biotic structure. However, in very large rivers the mixed layers may not reach the bottom. There the stream resembles an elongated lake, and definite thermal and chemical stratification as well as a true plankton community are evident.

The physical structure of streams provides an abundance of specialized biological niches. For example, there is a fast current on the upstream face of a rock and an eddy formed behind. Beneath the rock lies a well-protected dark hiding

(a)

(b)

FIGURE 2-4   (*a*) Meanders, which occur in flat areas in almost every river and stream as shown on the Salado River in Argentina. Oxbow lakes (see text) are formed when the meander becomes cut and blocked off at the ends. (*b*) Meanders may form a series of multiple oxbows or scroll lakes as deposition moves the river channel to a new bed.

place for small animals, while the upper surface provides a well-lighted site for attached algal growth. Much of the biological structure of streams is dependent on the spatial patterns of *drift* and *detritus,* which reflect the dominant effect of currents. Drift consists of living benthic invertebrates and algae that have released or lost their attachment to the substrate. Swept downstream by the current, they may find another favorable site or source of food. Fish and invertebrates that feed on drift are distributed to make optimum use of this food supply. Detritus, also important in lake sediments and estuarine environments, consists of dead organic fragments coated with bacteria and fungi, small protozoans, and rotifers (Chap. 16).

ESTUARIES

An estuary is the place where the river meets the sea. Estuarine structure is modified by the morphometry of the estuary, the tide, and the amount of inflowing fresh water. Estuaries are discussed in more detail in Chap. 19. The density difference provided by the salt and fresh water results in a *salt wedge,* which provides a structure to the water mass not unlike that caused by thermal stratification in lakes. However, the salinity effect dominates over thermal stratification, which is usually unimportant in most estuaries. The salt wedge, because of its high salinity, is heavier

than the overlying fresh water and therefore extends upstream beneath it (Fig. 2-5). The wedge advances upstream at high tide and retreats at low tide. In most regions freshwater inflow varies considerably during the year, and this modifies the degree of separation between the fresh and salt water as well as the upstream extension of the salt wedge.

At the interface between the saline and freshwater masses, small particles and some dissolved organic material ''salt out'' or flocculate into larger, heavier detrital aggregates. The saline bottom water collects particles settling into it which may be returned upstream with each high tide. The area covered by the salt wedge as it moves up and down the estuary is often an area of high productivity for both plankton and benthos.

There are more distinct physical elements to estuarine structure than are found in lakes and rivers. In addition to pelagic and littoral zones, estuaries frequently have extensive mud flats and tidal marshes exposed at each low tide. The tide mixes soluble nutrients and food particles between these structural elements. This interaction produces profuse growth of plants and small animals; estuaries are important nursery areas for fish, shellfish, and birds. The influence of the tide varies greatly according to its height and the estuary's morphometry. The daily tidal variation is over 10 m in some funnel-shaped estuaries,

FIGURE 2-5 A typical estuary, showing the salt wedge. Outflowing fresh water overlies the denser sea water to create the wedge. This is also the site of ''salting out,'' or flocculating of small silt particles (Chap. 19).

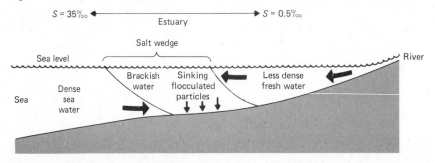

such as the Severn estuary in Britain or the Bay of Fundy in Newfoundland, Canada. In contrast, in the Mediterranean Sea or San Francisco Bay tides are only 1 to 2 m in height and are less than 1 m in the great Chesapeake Bay.

WETLANDS

Wetlands have few of the structural elements of lakes, rivers, or estuaries. Marshes, swamps, and bogs are all characterized by shallow fresh water, and may even be dry for part of the year. Thus thermal or density stratification and water currents are usually unimportant. The most important structural elements in wetlands are vegetation. In fact, the main types of wetlands (marshes, swamps, and bogs) are defined by the dominant vegetation (emergent macrophytes, trees, and *Sphagnum* moss, respectively). Another feature of wetlands is their extreme spatial heterogeneity. Here a small reed-fringed pool lies near a large patch consisting entirely of cattails filled with breeding redwing blackbirds. Next to that a soggy zone mostly filled with submerged waterweeds is interrupted by small stands of reeds or cattails and pockmarked by more small open water pools. Since water motion does not dominate the wetlands habitat as it does in lakes and rivers, this heterogeneity can persist for months or even years.

Their heterogeneity makes wetlands more difficult for limnologists to study, since samples must be taken at more sites to characterize the ecosystem fully. In the example of a marsh given above, separate samples from the cattail patch, the small and large open water pools, the reed fringes, the different species of submerged weed, and the mixed small cattail and reed islands would be required. Each of these must be examined for its physical characteristics, such as temperature and dissolved oxygen, as well as for chemistry and the number of animals and plants present. There may be abundant oxygen in the water of the pool or macrophyte beds, but anoxia will prevail in the sediments. The larvae of insects such as chironimid midges and dragonflies will be abundant in the submerged weeds but rare in the adjacent reed beds and open water, even if these are only a few centimeters distant.

The degree of structure imparted by the various physical, chemical, and biological components discussed in this chapter provides a common conceptual thread that ties together lakes, streams, estuaries, and wetlands. In the following chapters on the characteristics of water and the distribution of light, heat, and water motion, it should be increasingly evident that aquatic ecosystems, despite their great diversity of type, have a remarkable continuity of structure that makes them ideal subjects for intensive ecological study.

FURTHER READINGS

Hakanson, L. 1981. *A Manual of Lake Morphometry.* Springer-Verlag, New York. 78 pp.

Hutchinson, G. E. 1957. *A Treatise on Limnology,* vol. 1, chap. 2. Wiley, New York.

Rawson, D. S. 1955. "Morphometry as a Dominant Factor in the Productivity of Large Lakes." *Verb. Int. Ver. Limnol.,* **12:**164–175.

CHAPTER 3

Water and Light

OVERVIEW

Most of the structural elements of aquatic eco-systems are a result of the unusual properties of water and its interactions with light. The molecular structure of water allows weak *hydrogen bonding* between the hydrogen and oxygen atoms of adjacent water molecules, producing a matrix known as a *liquid crystal*. This interlinking of molecules is responsible for many unique properties, such as a high boiling point. Hydrogen bonding is also the reason the maximum density of water is at 4°C, rather than at the freezing point, as is common with most liquids. Once lake water reaches 4°C, further cooling at the surface produces lighter water and eventually ice, leaving warmer, denser water below. The ice formed insulates the liquid water and prevents deeper lakes from freezing solid. Few organisms can survive in solid ice. In streams and sometimes in lakes with rocky bottoms, *anchor ice* may form on the bottom.

At the other extreme, the high specific heat of water allows it to absorb large amounts of heat with only a small temperature increase. This enables aquatic organisms to survive even the in-tense solar radiation at the equator, which results in only a small increase in lake temperature. Surface heating is also reduced by evaporation and convection. In warmer water density changes rapidly with shifts in temperature, but in cool water the density changes with shifts in temperature are smaller. Density changes with depth are responsible for the remarkable resistance to wind mixing of stratified lakes. The water's viscosity plays an important role in determining the shape of fish and insect larvae in streams.

The intensity, color, direction, and distribution of light in lakes are major components in the structure of lake ecosystems. Light provides the energy for primary production, signals for migration in plankton and fish, and gives a characteristic hue to many lakes. But before sunlight reaches the lake it is modified in both intensity and color as it passes through the atmosphere. Ozone absorbs ultraviolet radiation, while carbon dioxide absorbs radiation in the far infrared. Clouds and dust particles further change the spectral composition and intensity of light. More important for limnologists, reflection, refraction, scattering, and selective absorption of certain wavelengths occur in water. Light absorption is measured by the absorption coefficient ϵ_λ, which is fairly specific for each lake and wavelength of light. Transparent lakes have a low ϵ_λ, while eutrophic and muddy waters have a high ϵ_λ. In the visible range blue-green light penetrates farthest and red and violet wavelengths are most rapidly absorbed. Blue light is also strongly backscattered by water molecules, which produces the characteristic blue color of transparent mountain lakes. However, ultraviolet light can cause strong surface inhibition of photosynthesis at the lake surface. Through the water column, water molecules and suspended particles reflect a variety of colors back to the observer. This *apparent color* is further modified by the *true color* imparted by dissolved substances.

In this chapter we discuss global distribution of water; properties of water; importance of light; light as energy; measurement of light; light in the atmosphere; light under water and photosynthetically active radiation; lake color and absorption coefficients; reflection; and remote sensing.

WATER

Global Distribution

Water covers seven-tenths of the earth's surface, 98 percent of which (over 10^9 km^3) is found in the oceans (Table 3-1). Relatively little fresh water is present in rivers or in the atmosphere, and fresh water in lakes is relatively scarce (Fig. 3-1). Lake Baikal in Siberia, the oldest and deepest lake in the world, contains about 20 percent of all unfrozen fresh water. The five Great Lakes of North America contain an almost equal volume. The relative rarity of fresh water is of interest as well as concern to the modern limnologist, who must protect both the quantity and quality of lake water during increasing use by an

TABLE 3-1

DISTRIBUTION OF FRESH AND SALINE, LIQUID AND FROZEN WATER IN THE WORLD

Most surface fresh water is trapped in the Antarctic ice cap, and ground water is the other major freshwater reserve. Lakes contain relatively small amounts, and the volume of saline lake water ($<$ 3 ppt salinity) roughly equals that of freshwater lakes. The largest uncertainty is in the estimation of groundwater volume.

Site	Volume (km^3)
Oceans	1,322,000,000
Polar ice caps and all glaciers	29,200,000
Exchangeable ground water	24,000,000
Freshwater lakes	125,000
Saline lakes and inland seas	104,000
Soil and subsoil water	65,000
Atmospheric vapor	14,000
Rivers and Streams	1,200
Annual inputs	
Surface runoff to ocean	37,000
Ground water to sea	1,600
Precipitation	
Rainfall on ocean	412,000
Rainfall on land and lakes	108,000

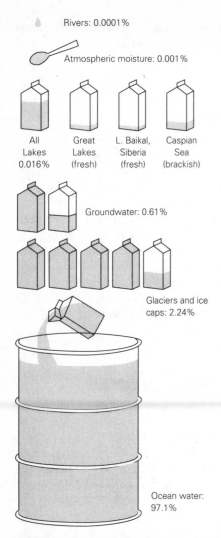

Rivers: 0.0001%

Atmospheric moisture: 0.001%

| All Lakes 0.016% | Great Lakes (fresh) | L. Baikal, Siberia (fresh) | Caspian Sea (brackish) |

Groundwater: 0.61%

Glaciers and ice caps: 2.24%

Ocean water: 97.1%

FIGURE 3-1 Distribution of water on earth. The majority of all water is salty and in the oceans, while most fresh water is locked up in the great polar ice caps. Some ice caps and glaciers are over 1000 m thick. Fresh water in lakes is quite rare, and about 40 percent of it is contained in two large lake areas: Lake Baikal in Siberia and the North American Laurentian Great Lakes (Superior, Michigan, Huron, Erie, and Ontario). About half of lake water is brackish (variable salinity) and cannot be drunk by most animals. The Caspian Sea in Russia contains about half of all saline lake waters. Rivers and streams (Chaps. 16, 17) contain a miniscule proportion of the world's fresh water yet are major sites for waste disposal and fishing activity. Modified from American Chemical Society (1985).

expanding population. Most of the world's nutrients and toxic wastes flow through the small volume of fresh water in rivers and lakes. Unfortunately, they tend to accumulate pollutants, and water quality is degraded.

Less well known are the inland saline lakes that contain almost as much water as the freshwater lakes. They range from slightly to highly saline, some being saltier than the ocean. Most were formed in the interior of large continents from evaporation of fresh water (Chap. 21). Examples in the United States are the Great Salt Lake in Utah and the very saline Mono Lake in California. Salt lakes, called *athalassohaline* (Greek for "not a sea"), have a chemistry dominated by the salts derived from evaporation of calcium, magnesium, and sulfate. A few salt lakes including the largest, are relics of the sea and have sodium and chloride as the main ions. All continents, including Antarctica, contain salt lakes.

Most of the earth's estimated 1 million-plus lakes are quite small and contain fresh water. The world's largest lake, by area and volume, is the vast and saline Caspian Sea, which lies on the border of the former USSR and Iran. The freshwater lakes Superior in the United States and Victoria in East Africa follow but cover much less area than the Caspian Sea (Table 3-2). Classification by depth would give a very different ranking. The relatively small Crater Lake, with an area of only 54 km^2, ranks eighth in the world in terms of depth. Large lakes are somewhat different from other water bodies and are discussed in more detail in Chap. 21.

Fluctuations over Time

Lakes and rivers are sensitive to changes in climate, and estuaries are particularly influenced by changes in sea level. Lakes vary in depth over time, but because of the essentially panlike shape of most lake basins, these changes are most obvious as changes in lake area. For example, the surface area of Lake Chad, on the southern

TABLE 3-2

THE WORLD'S TEN LARGEST LAKES, LISTED BY AREA

Most large lakes are either fresh or formerly marine. Very deep large lakes, such as Tanganyika, may have nonmarine salts in the bottom water, but these do not normally mix with the surface freshwaters.

Lake	Area (km^2)	Volume (km^3)	Salinity
Caspian, former USSR/Iran	374,000	78,200	Mostly marine
Superior, US/Canada	82,100	12,230	Fresh
Victoria, East Africa	68,460	2,700	Fresh
Aral, Southwest former USSR	64,100	1,020	Mostly marine
Huron, US/Canada	59,500	3,537	Fresh
Michigan, US	57,750	4,920	Fresh
Tanganyika, SE Africa	32,900	18,900	Mostly fresh
Baikal, East former USSR	31,500	22,995	Fresh
Great Bear, NW Canada	31,326	3,381	Fresh
Great Slave, NW Canada	28,568	2,088	Fresh

Modified from Herdendorf (1990).

fringes of the Sahara Desert, has fluctuated dramatically during the twentieth century. Its area has ranged from 24,000 km^2 in 1917 to as little as 9000 km^2 in 1973 km^2 (Fig. 3-2). These fluctuations were of natural origin, as a dry period occurred in the sub-Saharan region of Africa during this period.

In contrast, humans are the main agent of change in the huge Sea of Aral in Russia. Water levels in this inland saline lake, once the fourth largest lake in the world, have dropped by 13 m since reaching their peak in 1960. The lake has shrunk to 60 percent of its original area and lost two thirds of its volume over the last 30 years (Fig. 3-2). This decrease is attributed to diversions of inflowing river water for crop irrigation in the arid lower drainage basin. Together with contamination of the lake by salt and pesticides in the agricultural drainwater, the situation is viewed as a major ecological disaster. The situation is even worse in the western United States where Walker Lake, Nevada has lost about 70 percent of its volume over the last 100 years due to increased upstream irrigation.

Increases in water level cause problems as well. The relatively small rise of about 50 cm in the surface of the Great Lakes in 1986 caused great damage to shoreline structures and coastal bluffs. A similar rise in the Great Salt Lake, Utah followed heavy rains in 1983 and flooded roads and buildings for several years.

Ground water, a subject at the boundaries of limnology, is intimately connected with lakes and streams, which can be thought of as depressions in a larger and mostly subsurface water table. Ground water studies are still bedeviled by measurement problems, since each sampling requires drilling a well rather than just lowering a collection bottle. Although the volume of ground water is much larger than that of surface water, the exact value depends on how deep the ground is thought to extend. In many areas this underground resource is being rapidly depleted. The huge Agolalla aquifer, which stretches from Wisconsin to Texas and was formed 10 million years ago, is pumped extensively for crop irrigation. Current estimates are that it will be virtually dry within the next century.

Properties of Water

Compared with other compounds of similar shape and molecular weight, water exhibits

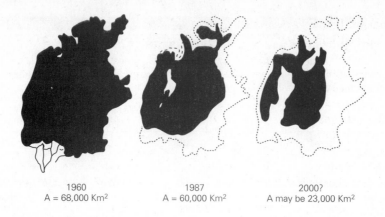

1960
A = 68,000 Km²

1987
A = 60,000 Km²

2000?
A may be 23,000 Km²

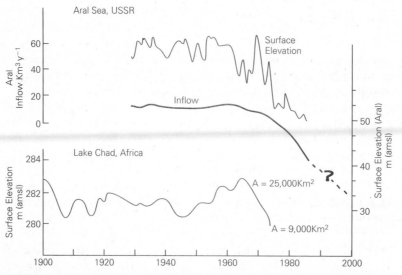

FIGURE 3-2 Drastic changes in lake size due to natural climatic changes (Lake Chad, West Africa) and diversion of inflows for agriculture (Aral Sea in the southwestern former U.S.S.R.). Because most large lakes have an extensive shallow littoral zone, small changes in elevation result in big changes in water surface. In Lake Chad, with a very flat bathymetry, a 3-m change in lake level reduced the lake area by 60 percent. A drop of 10 m was required for a similar change in the Aral Sea. Note the continual variation in water level in Chad over time and the recent decline in Aral. The upper figures show the changes in the shape of the Aral Sea. If the prediction for the year 2000 is correct this lake will have dropped from being the fourth largest in the world to the thirteenth! Modified from Lemoalle (1975; for Lake Chad) and Micklin (1988; for the Aral Sea).

anomalous behavior. If water (H_2O) behaved at normal environmental temperatures as do H_2S, NH_3, or HF, it would be present only as a vapor. It is one of the two inorganic liquids (together with mercury) that can exist at the earth's surface under ambient pressure and temperature.

Many of water's unique properties result from its molecular structure. Oxygen is highly electronegative and in water shares its outer shell valence electrons with its two associated hydrogen atoms. The covalent chemical bonding has electrons skewed in the direction of the strongly negative oxygen atom. This results in a slight negative charge on the oxygen atom and a slight positive charge on the hydrogen atoms. The charge asymmetry in water molecules allows the oxygen molecule to form a weak hydrogen bond with the oppositely charged hydrogen bond of an adjacent molecule (Fig. 3-3). The hydrogen bond is strongly directional, and the covalent chemical bond —O—H of one molecule must point almost directly at the oxygen nucleus of another molecule to form a bond with the hydrogen atom (Fig. 3-3). In a true fluid individual molecules move freely. This is not true for water which consists of a continuous network of randomly connected hydrogen bonds that form a liquid crystal. The liquid crystal structure of water in a lake provides an uninterrupted network of hydrogen bonds running in all directions throughout its entire volume. Thus, in theory, water molecules in Chicago's waterfront on Lake Michigan are connected with those in remote bays in northern Lake Superior hundreds of miles away.

Covalent bonds are too strong to be significantly deformed by hydrogen bonding. As water changes from ice to liquid and then to vapor, hydrogen bonds strain or break. The crystalline matrix of liquid water is not static but undergoes continual topological reformation. As the covalent molecular bonds twist and turn, the hydrogen bonds continually switch their attachment sites in the liquid crystal matrix. This complex bonding holds the water molecules together as a liquid to a much higher temperature than H_2S, HF, or NH_3, all of which are vapors at room temperature.

Water expands when it freezes, so that the ice formed requires more volume than liquid water. The expanding frozen surface of a lake may groan and crack as it expands. It can exert enor-

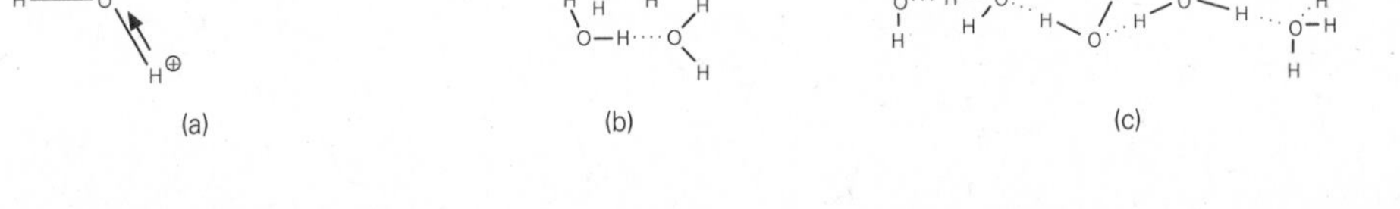

FIGURE 3-3 (*a*) Hydrogen bonding (dotted lines) in water. The small electronegative oxygen atom attracts part of the valence electron cloud, leaving a positively charged hydrogen atom. A hydrogen bond forms between the positive hydrogen atom of one molecule and the negative oxygen of another. The bond is weak and contains only about 1/16 the energy of a normal covalent bond but is more flexible. (*b, c*) Likely polyhedra formed by water molecules at about 10°C. Bond angles at the oxygen atom are close to tetrahedral. There is a continual reformation with new water molecule groups as hydrogen bonds are broken and reformed. Modified from Stillinger (1980).

(a)　　　　(b)　　　　(c)

mous pressure around the lake's margin, resulting in a ridge of soil called an *ice ramp*. As the ice melts the water molecules can move more freely and assume different hydrogen bond angles than those formed in the more rigid ice crystal, allowing the molecules to pack together. Therefore, water density increases between 0 and 4°C. The counteracting process of vibrational motion caused by heating predominates over packing above 4°C, and the water becomes less dense.

One important consideration of heating or cooling water is that its heat capacity, or *specific heat*, is higher than that of all elements except liquid lithium, hydrogen, and helium. Specific heat is the ratio of a substance's thermal capacity to that of water at 15°C. The specific heat of water is defined as unity, since it takes 1 cal to heat 1 g of water by 1°C. Water also has a high latent heat of fusion, that is, heat required to melt ice.

Lakes affect the surrounding land, with the extent of the effects dependent on the size of the lake. Because water stores a lot of heat per unit volume, large volumes of water can alter climate. The Great Lakes, for example, protect nearby orchards from spring frosts. The region north of the Arctic Circle in Swedish Lapland has a much milder climate than the tundra at similar latitudes in Alaska. Here the tropical Gulf Stream current warms the coast of western Britain and Scandinavia.

The difference in density of hot and cold water is responsible for the great resistance to mixing of water masses. The rate of change of water density is not constant with changes in temperature: the density decreases more rapidly at higher temperatures (Fig. 3-4). Water density is influenced by factors other than temperature. Dissolved salts increase density and give stability to meromictic lakes. Salinity-induced density effects dominate over temperature-induced ef-

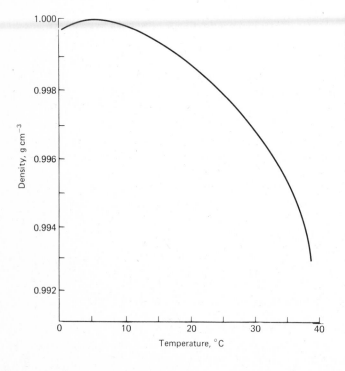

FIGURE 3-4   Changes in the density of pure fresh water with temperature. Note that the maximum density of water is 3.94°C and the almost exponential decrease in density at higher temperatures (see also Fig. 4-4).

fects in estuaries and oceans. The density of pure water at 4°C is 1.000 mg cm^{-3} and that of normal seawater at 35 ppt (parts per thousand) salinity is 1.028. This decreases seawater's temperature of maximum density to -3.5°C. A solution's freezing point is lowered as salinity increases. On Mono Lake, with salinity of 70 ppt, ice will not form until the temperature reaches -2.5°C.

Other properties of water important in limnology include viscosity and surface tension. *Viscosity,* a measure of a liquid's resistance to flow, produces *viscous drag* to organisms moving through it and serves to slow the rate of sinking of plankton. Viscosity is much higher at lower water temperatures (Table 3-3).

Surface tension, like viscosity, results from cohesive hydrogen bonding in the liquid crystal lattice. Certain animals and plants maintain their position in the water by using surface tension and water striders (Gerridae) skate on the water surface. Dissolved salts, in addition to increasing water density and viscosity, also increase surface tension. In contrast, organic surfactants—foaming or wetting agents produced by aquatic plants and animals—reduce surface tension. Lines of foam that accompany some water motions, such as Langmuir spirals, are often caused by natural surfactants (Fig. 5-14). Natural foam is often mistaken for foam caused by detergent pollution.

TABLE 3-3

INCREASE IN VISCOSITY OF WATER WITH TEMPERATURE

Temperature, °C	Viscosity, cP
0	1.79
5	1.52
10	1.31
15	1.14
20	1.00
25	0.89
30	0.80
35	0.72
40	0.65

LIGHT

Solar radiation provides the heat that drives the world's wind patterns. Wind energy passed to surface water provides mixing in both lakes and oceans. Much of the structure of aquatic ecosystems described in Chap. 2 is directly related to solar radiation, which heats and lights the water. Heat produced by the transformation of light energy interacts with wind mixing to produce thermal stratification characteristic of deeper lakes in summer. In addition, light establishes the zonation that restricts plant photosynthesis to the upper, illuminated or photic zone. Finally, the movement and migration of many aquatic creatures is guided by light intensity or direction.

The photosynthetic base of the aquatic food chain in lakes, estuaries, and streams is represented by large and small attached or free-floating plants. These owe their existence to solar radiation; where it is low, as under a dense leafy canopy of riparian vegetation, plants are scarce. The distribution of most animals is also strongly influenced by light. Moonlight and starlight (1/30,000 to 1/50,000 that of the sun) aid nocturnal migration of zooplankton and fish but are an insignificant source of energy. Unlike humans, aquatic animals are able to detect light that has been polarized into a unidirectional plane. Polarized light serves as underwater guideposts for the distribution of aquatic animals. One important example is the migration of salmon from the ocean back to their spawning areas. Although they use chemical clues or smell in their local streams, these are of no use in the ocean. Instead the sunlight, polarized by water, provides a compass for these long journeys, which may cover thousands of kilometers (Hasler, 1966).

The behavior of both higher and lower organisms is strongly influenced by the strength of the underwater light field. This is exemplified by the diurnal migration of animal plankton in response to the daily changes in sunlight (Fig. 13-5). The fish predators of these migrating zooplankton follow their prey and often show a similar light-regulated pattern (Fig. 14-3). Epibenthic animals, those that live on but not in the sediments, avoid light and predators by hiding under stones during the day to emerge and feed at night. In streams a drift of small invertebrates, usually insect larvae, moves to new habitats only at night, again to avoid sight-feeding predators. Night dives with underwater lights reveal fish that inhabit deep waters by day moving into the shallows to feed by the dim light of dawn or dusk and crayfish and other benthic predators emerging from under rocks or vegetation to forage after sundown.

Measurement

Estimates of total solar radiation are made at the lake's surface using continuously recording *pyroheliometers*. This simple instrument records changes in light by mechanical tension produced by differential expansion of an absorbing black surface and a reflecting silver surface. Other types of pyroheliometers convert light energy to electricity by using photovoltaic solar cells. Light energy is measured in microeinsteins or watts, but references to langleys (gram-calories cm^{-2}) are found in the older literature.

Underwater light is usually measured with waterproofed photocells and compared with readings taken simultaneously with a deck cell at the surface. The deck cell compensates for passing clouds during the underwater measurements and is not needed on cloudless days. Spectral discrimination is accomplished by adding selective colored filters over the photocell to enable measurement of different wavebands of light. The limnologist can then compute the percentage of various wavelengths of light penetrating to any particular depth. Some modern instruments are full-fledged spectroradiometers equipped with submersible quartz-fiber optical probes, which cover the whole visible and near infrared spectrum from 400 to 800 nm.

A simple, inexpensive, and robust device to measure the transparency of lake water is the *Secchi disk*, discussed in Chapter 1. The white disk is lowered into the lake until it disappears from sight. This distance is the *secchi depth*. The secchi depth of eutrophic and muddy lakes, estuaries, and big rivers ranges from almost 0 to 2 m, but in oligotrophic lakes or blue-water oceans can be as great as 40 m. In many lakes the secchi depth is approximately one-third the depth of the photic zone. Such simple, inexpensive measurements as the temperature-depth profile and the secchi depth can tell the experienced limnologist a great deal. The clarity of any lake varies with season due to algal blooms or suspended sediment and these changes are well demonstrated by the secchi depth. The annual variation in secchi depth for a well-studied midwestern lake, Lake Madison in Wisconsin, is shown in Fig. 3-5a. The average values range from 1 to 8 m, depending on the season. The deepest individual values are 9.5 to 13.2 m, but there is no evidence of long-term decreases due to eutrophication in this lake since the maximum depths recorded in 1916 have been equaled or exceeded in the 1960s and 1970s (Stewart, 1976). In contrast, the secchi depth in the very clear waters of ultraoligotrophic Lake Tahoe is very high—up to 30 m (Fig. 3-5b). The gradual eutrophication in this beautiful lake over the last 30 years is evidenced by pronounced decline in secchi measurements (Fig. 22-7).

Light as Energy

Light reaching the earth can be thought of as a continuous flow of electromagnetic waves or, alternatively, as photons (quanta), which are discrete packages of energy. Wavelength is a useful measure of light color, and quanta describe light energy. An important characteristic of a light beam is its *intensity*, which is the number of *quanta* or *photons* passing through a given unit area. Another important feature of a beam of light is its wavelength (λ, *lambda*), or color, which is a qualitative measure of light energy. Light from the sun is a mixture of many different

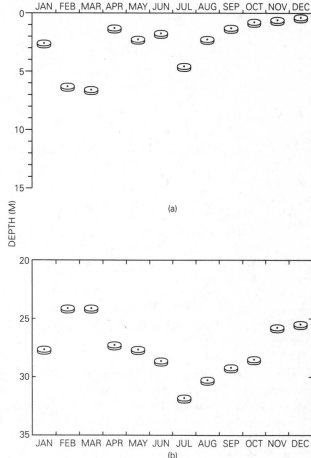

(a)

(b)

FIGURE 3-5 Seasonal variation in secchi depth in 1981 for two contrasting lakes: (*a*) the moderately eutrophic Lake Mendota in Wisconsin and (*b*) the very transparent and ultraoligotrophic Lake Tahoe in California-Nevada. Note the lowest values (least transparent water) in spring and July in Lake Mendota corresponding to the two phytoplankton blooms of temperate lakes (Chap. 12). In Lake Tahoe, which is much deeper, algal blooms are later (Chap. 4; Table 4-2) and only a summer bloom is noticeable. The lower winter transparency is due to sediments. Once out on the lake or on a pier, a secchi disk reading takes only a minute to carry out and can provide invaluable data on water quality. Modified from Brock (1985) and Goldman (unpublished).

wavelengths, which are considerably modified as they pass through the earth's atmosphere.

Light in the Atmosphere

As it leaves the sun light has a very wide and uneven spectral distribution ranging from very short ultraviolet to very long infrared wavelengths. Even the overall intensity of solar radiation is uneven, and sunspot cycles with periodicity of 11 and 22 years are superimposed on other aperiodic changes. The penetration of light through the earth's atmosphere and through water results in the selective absorption and scattering of light, particularly at the ends of the spectrum. The spectral composition and percentage of light of various wavelengths arriving at the lake surface is crucial, since scattering, absorption, reflection, and suitability for photosynthesis of photons depends on the wavelengths actually reaching the pigments. Figure 3-6 illustrates the spectral distribution of light outside the atmosphere and at ground level and the portion of the visible spectrum visible to the human eye.

The spectrum and intensity of direct sunlight reaching the lake surface depends on various transient phenomena in the atmosphere, such as

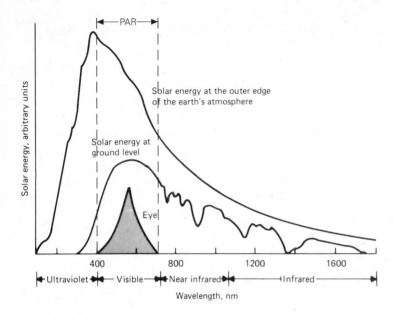

FIGURE 3-6 Solar energy as it reaches the earth's atmosphere and at lake (ground) level. The shaded area shows the sensitivity of the human eye (400 to 700 nm), which is also the range of photosynthetically active radiation (PAR). Thermal radiation (now shown) is at about 5000 to 14,000 nm. Much energy that could be used for photosynthesis is absorbed by the atmosphere, which also reduces harmful ultraviolet light.

clouds, dust, and fog, which determine which wavelengths will be absorbed or scattered. In Fig. 3-6 the essentially smooth solar spectrum becomes jagged after passage through the atmosphere. The dips are due to selective absorption by gases and particles of water, carbon dioxide, and ozone. The increase in CO_2, which absorbs infrared light, is projected to cause some global warming over the next century. If this occurs, changes in temperature, sea level, and rainfall distribution will change the shape of many lakes and estuaries. The highly reactive ozone gas (O_3) absorbs ultraviolet light. Ozone in the upper atmosphere may be decreasing due to reaction with atmospheric pollutants such as fluorocarbons. So far, long-term measurements do not show any increases in ultraviolet light at the earth's surface, but total ultraviolet light reaching the atmosphere may also be influenced by trends in solar radiation itself. Any substantial increase in ultraviolet light could increase skin cancer in humans and also add to photoinhibition of photosynthesis in surface phytoplankton (Warrest et al., 1981). The changes will be similar to those experienced when moving from the lowlands to the mountains. Increased ultraviolet light due to the ozone depletion in the Antarctic is a topic of much interest that requires careful experimentation (Roberts, 1989; Trodahl and Buckley, 1989). The way in which phytoplankton can adapt to such increases in light intensity and wavelength by sinking deeper in the water column is illustrated for the rapid change from spring ice cover to summer sunshine in a lake in the European Alps (Fig. 21-10). In contrast, the failure of phytoplankton to accomplish this in shallow lakes in the Antarctic is shown in Fig. 21-9.

The angle of incidence of sunlight to the lake's surface determines the distance light must travel through the atmosphere before it reaches the lake. Because the sun's angle varies with different latitudes, seasons, and time of day, the distance and thus the amount and quality of light penetrating the atmosphere also varies. This variation in color and intensity is one reason to use in situ (in lake) incubations for estimates of primary production (Chap. 15). The distance traveled by sunlight through the atmosphere is also less at high altitudes than at sea level.

The solar radiation incident on the lake surface is both *direct* sunlight and *indirect*, or *diffuse*, light, which is scattered and reflected off mountains, clouds, and atmospheric particles. The ratio of indirect to direct light depends on the amount of atmosphere to be traversed, the amount of scattering constituents, and the local topography. Indirect radiation accounts for about 20 percent of the total but is extremely variable. The land and vegetation surrounding lakes also influences the kind and amount of light reaching the lake surface. For example, mountains, give shade early and late in the day. Cloud cover or haze reduces light intensity and filters out some wavelengths. Besides the direct shading effect of clouds at low sun angles, scattered clouds above the lake or snow-covered slopes nearby may reflect light onto the lake and actually increase the overall intensity of solar radiation at the water surface.

In summary, light arriving from the sun has a characteristic wavelength, intensity, and direction. Light enters the earth's atmosphere and is selectively absorbed, scattered, and bent or refracted before it reaches the surface of the lake. Once in the lake it is further modified by the denser liquid medium.

Light under Water: Photosynthetically Active Radiation

Light penetrating water is also refracted, scattered, transmitted, or absorbed. As light moves between media of different optical densities, as from air to water, it is bent by refraction. This is why submerged objects appear slightly out of line to above-water observers. Birds such as kingfishers must correct for this displacement when diving for fish. The refractive index is higher for shorter wavelengths and lower for longer wavelengths. Thus blue light is bent the most and red light the least. White sunlight is refracted by raindrops in the sky, which act as tiny prisms to produce rainbows. Light is scattered as well as absorbed or refracted by particles and some molecules. A shaft of light coming through a window is actually invisible but can easily be seen in a dusty room as the light is scattered by the dust particles. A similar process occurs in muddy water. An unpolluted sky or a transparent lake appear blue because oxygen molecules in the air or pure water scatters blue light more than other colors. Transmitted light passes through the water column. As the light penetrates and is absorbed, it is converted to heat. The discontinuous vertical distribution observed for temperature (Fig. 2-3) would be observed for light if it were not for the unique physical properties of water, specifically the density differences and resistance to mixing mentioned previously.

Light intensity decreases exponentially with depth (Fig. 2-3). This loss of light is expressed mathematically by the extinction coefficient ϵ_λ, (*epsilon-lambda*), of the solution, the fraction of light absorbed per meter of water. The higher the value of ϵ_λ, the lower the transmission of light or the less transparent the water. For parallel beams of monochromatic (single-wavelength) light, the intensity I at water depth z when the sun is directly overhead is given by the formula:

$$I_z = I_0 e^{-\epsilon_\lambda z}$$

where I_0 = intensity penetrating the surface
$\quad\quad z$ = path length
$\quad\quad \epsilon_\lambda$ = extinction coefficient for the wavelength in question

The percentile transmission is 100 times the fraction of light of a given type transmitted through 1 m. For distilled water and daylight, transmission is approximately 50 percent. The extinction coefficient can also be expressed as

$$\epsilon_\lambda = \epsilon_w + \epsilon_d + \epsilon_p$$

where ϵ_w = extinction due to water molecules
$\quad\quad \epsilon_d$ = extinction due to dissolved materials
$\quad\quad \epsilon_p$ = extinction due to particulate matter

For pure water, $\epsilon_d = \epsilon_p = 0$, and extinction $\epsilon_\lambda = \epsilon_w$.

Under natural conditions, light falls as a complete spectrum but each wavelength follows the above equation. Only about half of the underwater spectrum of transmitted light can be used by algae for photosynthesis. This fraction is known as photosynthetically active radiation (PAR), and it covers 400 to 700 nm (Fig. 3-6).

Unlike their terrestrial equivalents, which absorb almost all sunlight falling on the ground, aquatic plants live in an optically dense medium and must compete with several other light-absorbing sources. Phytoplankton and submerged macrophytes must grow in a foglike milieu of suspended particles. The fraction of PAR absorbed by phytoplankton can vary greatly, from 2 to 60 percent of the total. Figure 3-7a shows the percentage of light absorbed by algae relative to all other components, going down the water column in a large oligotrophic lake in Europe. The way the water modifies the underwater light climate can be seen clearly if the seasonal changes in the detailed spectrum of surface incident PAR (I_0) is compared with that at the approximate depth of maximum photosynthesis (Fig. 3-7 b, c). The light is much reduced in intensity, almost tenfold. There is relatively less PAR in autumn and winter, but smaller amounts of light are adequate for photosynthesis in winter-adapted phytoplankton.

In general, more light means more photosynthesis, but in almost all lakes on sunny days, the intense midday radiation inhibits photosynthesis. The effect is most evident in clear air and in mountain or polar regions. Mild photoinhibition is caused by surplus electrons generated by the initial capture of light filling all of the electron "holes" in the chlorophyll molecules which acts as living semiconductors. Similar electron saturation occurs when a camera's light meter is exposed to a very bright light. After some time in less intense light these "holes" become unblocked and the passage of electrons from pigment to other cellular processes can resume. More permanent damage can occur due to ultraviolet light, analogous to the way human skin is sunburned. The most damaging wavelengths, called UVB (290 to 320 nm), can destroy the DNA in chloroplasts (Bauer et al., 1982) and decrease fecundity in zooplankton (Karanas et al., 1981). In the most extreme cases, entire surface algal blooms can be destroyed by too much sunlight and the milky cell contents of blue-green algal summer blooms can be seen from miles away.

Lake Color, Absorption and Extinction Coefficients

As light penetrates lake water there is selective absorption, which is most pronounced at both ends of the spectrum (Fig. 3-8). Absorption differs slightly between cloudy and clear water because the scattering effect of turbidity permits greater penetration of long-wavelength red light than is encountered in clear water (Figs. 3-8a, 3-9). In all cases, the ultraviolet and infrared ends of the spectrum are absorbed first and therefore penetrate least. Deeper in the water there is a progressive narrowing of the spectrum, so that in a deep, transparent lake like Lake Tahoe, only blue-green light remains at 100 m (Fig. 3-8b). If we divide the spectrum into the categories ultraviolet (UV), blue (B), green (G), red (R), and infrared (IR), we discover that for pure water the order of increasing extinction, or decreasing light transmission, is B, G, UV, R, IR. In lakes that contain dissolved substances, ϵ_d will be highest for short wavelengths (UV). The resulting order of transmission is then G, B or R, UV, and IR. If there is a great deal of colored particulate matter, such as phytoplankton (when ϵ_p becomes more important), the above order of absorption may alter since water may assume the color of the particles. For example, the presence of a surface bloom of blue-green algae may produce a green or turquoise-colored lake even if the water remains quite clear. In some alkaline African lakes bacteria can produce a burgundy color. Perhaps the most extreme example is shown in muddy lakes and estuaries, where red light may penetrate furthest, although no light will pene-

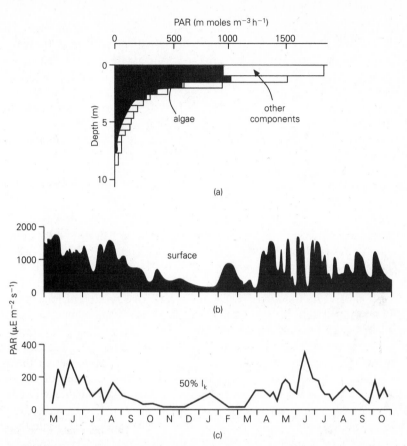

FIGURE 3-7 (*a*) Absorption of photosynthetically active radiation (PAR) by phytoplankton (black bars) and other light-absorbing components (clear bars). Values shown at several depths for Lake Constance, a large mesoeutrophic water body near the Alps in July. Unlike some lakes (Table 3-4), most of the summer sunlight here is taken up by algae, except near the surface. In November (not shown) only a small amount of light was absorbed by algae, which are at their annual minimum. (*b*) Seasonal changes in the mean solar radiation falling on the lake surface. Note the different effect of clouds in producing peaks and troughs of summer radiation in the two years. (*c*) Underwater light field at the approximate depth of half-maximum light saturation of photosynthesis (I_k). Note the relatively dim light intensity needed by algae for good growth (40-210 μE m^{-2}s^{-1}) relative to the very bright, inhibitory intensity (> 300 μE m^{-2} s^{-1}) recorded at the surface on clear days. Redrawn from Tilzer (1983; 1984).

trate far compared with transparent lakes or the open ocean. The absorption of light in a real lake is even more complex than the simple equations indicate. For example, absorption is partitioned among four of the light-absorbing components at 3 m deep in a small mesotrophic Californian lake (Table 3-4). Algae account for only 19 percent of the light absorbed in this small subalpine lake; nonchlorophyll particles and detritus from the surrounding land and sediment disturbance

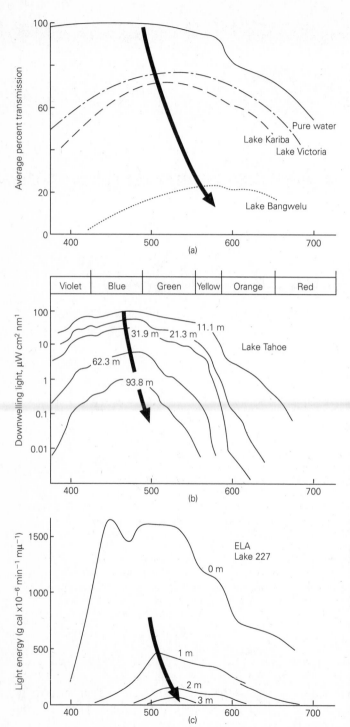

FIGURE 3-8 The color of light transmitted by different lakes and changes in color with depth in two contrasting ones. (*a*) The average transmission of various colors (wavelengths) in pure water and in the relatively transparent African lakes Kariba and Victoria and the shallow, less transparent Lake Bangwelu, which has more suspended particles and humic acids from its papyrus swamp drainage. Note that the maximum transmission shifts (arrow) from the short wavelengths (blue in pure water) through green in normal lakes to long wavelengths (orange-red) in the muddy, productive lake Bangwelu. The spectrum for Lake Victoria is similar to that of many European and North American lakes. Modified from Balon and Coche (1974). (*b*) A partial shift toward longer wavelengths also occurs with increase in depth (arrow), even in very transparent lakes such as Lake Tahoe. Here the shift is only from blue to green. Modified from Smith, Tyler, and Goldman (1973). (*c*) A similar shift (arrow) occurred when Lake 227 in the Experimental Lakes Area (ELA) was converted from oligotrophic to eutrophic as part of an experiment on nutrient additions. Only 19 percent of I_0 remained at 1 m and 1.3 percent at 3 m. Modified from Schindler (1971).

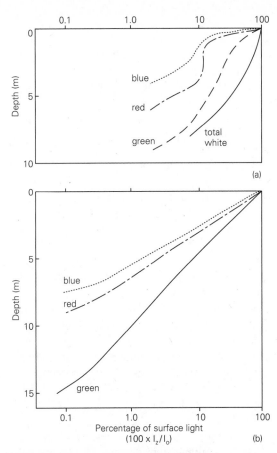

FIGURE 3-9 Absorbance of different colors of light on a log scale by (*a*) a highly productive, shallow reservoir with dense populations of phytoplankton and (*b*) a relatively oligotrophic lake. Algae are colored because they contain the green pigment chlorophyll *a*, which absorbs blue and red light and reflects or transmits green light. Note that in the productive lake (*a*), blue and then red are most quickly absorbed and green light penetrates most. In the more transparent unproductive lake, the same pattern is observed but each color penetrates deeper. In theory and assuming uniform phytoplankton distribution, the lines should be straight, but these are real-lake data sets collected by a student class.

TABLE 3-4

LIGHT EXTINCTION PER METER OF WATER THICKNESS DUE TO FOUR COMPONENTS OF LIGHT-ABSORBING MATERIAL IN MESOTROPHIC SUBALPINE CASTLE LAKE, CALIFORNIA

Measurements were made at depth of 3 m.

Component	Percent absorbed
Chlorophyll *a*	10
Dissolved substances	1
Nonchlorophyll particles	73
Water	16

Modified from Priscu (1983).

Algae can alter their pigment concentration to utilize the light available at the depths at which they live. This applies more to attached forms growing in dim light and phytoplankton in stable layers near the thermocline, where light is often low. Phytoplankton in the turbulent mixed upper water are usually stirred from high to low light too rapidly for adaptation to occur. Shade-adapted algae are distinguished by unusually high pigment-to-cell volume ratios. Adaptation can also occur in very high light levels. Some algae living in clear shallow water, where solar radiation is intense, manufacture extra pigments to protect them from cellular damage. Benthic blue-green algae, which form thick feltlike layers on the bottom of shallow Antarctic lakes (Plate 1*b*), have a layer of orange carotene-rich cells above the green photosynthetically active ones. The absence of this protection in phytoplankton is presumably the reason for their scarcity in such lakes (Fogg and Horne, 1970; Goldman, Mason, and Wood, 1963). Chromatic adaptation, the production of pigments that absorb the most abundant (blue-green) light deep in lakes and oceans, is now considered unimportant compared with changes in the main light-absorbing pigments (Dring, 1981).

The blue color of oligotrophic lakes is one of the features that distinguishes them from lakes of different trophic states. Much of the blue color is due to scattering by water molecules. The

account for the bulk of the absorption (73 percent). Even though humic acids are quite common in these small mountain lakes, the contribution of dissolved substances to the underwater light climate is negligible (Table 3-4).

shortest wavelengths are scattered the most, with the effect proportional to $(1/\lambda)^4$; blue light is thus the dominant color scattered back to the surface in transparent lakes. Scattering of blue light by water molecules back to the observer's eyes gives ultraoligotrophic lakes a deep cobalt blue color (Plates 1a, 2b) and a clear sky its blue color. The effect is heightened by wearing polarized sunglasses or looking down on the lake from a high cliff and diminished by clouds or observing the water from the lake's edge. In less transparent lakes, dissolved and particulate matter normally obscure backscattering of blue light. Absorption of the scattered light is due to suspended particles, including living phytoplankton, as well as colored but dissolved substances. A common example is the tan-colored water of bog lakes and streams that contain humic acids (Plates 4b, 5a).

The color of lakes to the human eye is one of their most appealing features. Who has not been cheered by the blue of a lake glimpsed down a mountain valley or between the trees in a woodland? Likewise, some people may be disappointed if the lake is a muddy brown or green. Lake color is composed of reflected light from two sources, *true* and *apparent color*. True color is the color of the water and its contents as would be measured in a spectrophotometer. Apparent color is the color as seen by the observer on the lake shore. The apparent color depends on the interaction between the wavelengths that are scattered back to the eye and the absorption of these wavelengths in the water between the depth of the scattering and the surface. Changes in daily and seasonal spectral distribution of incident radiation, cloud cover, reflection of vegetation, and hills around the lake modify the apparent color of the water. Also influencing what the eye perceives is *bottom color* in shallow lakes or at the edges of deeper ones. We can make the following generalizations. If there is little or no dissolved or suspended matter, a deep lake will appear blue (Plate 2b). However, under storm clouds even these ultraclear waters will take on some of the grey, leaden hue of the clouds. If there is a moderate amount of dissolved matter and some phytoplankton then the lake will probably appear green. Polarizing sunglasses or a polarizing filter on a camera "brings out" the true over the apparent color. A green color is also produced by the presence of fine suspended particles. The prettiest examples of this phenomenon are found in the middle of a series of glacial lakes. The upper lake is grey or whitish, due to a dense suspension of fine rock particles, called *glacial flour* (Plate 3). The middle lakes of the chain appear chalky green and only the finer particles remain suspended. The lower lakes, where all particles have settled out, are blue. Under some circumstances, phytoplankton use up so much dissolved carbon dioxide in the lake water that a fine precipitate of calcium carbonate is produced. This causes *lake whitening*, and the cloudy water can be seen clearly even in lakes as large as Lake Michigan (Fig. 3-10).

If there are large quantities of dissolved material, especially organics, the lake appears yellow or brown (Plate 4b). Some very acid lakes are deep green due to the presence of dissolved colored metallic ions made soluble in large amounts by the acidity. Even if few dissolved colored compounds are present, lakes often contain quite large amounts of colored particulate matter, which can dominate the apparent color. The dense phytoplankton blooms of eutrophic lakes can impart a dull green cast, and "red tides" of dinoflagellates impart a rusty brown tint. Blue-green algae can make lakes appear dark green, milky, or brown, depending on species and health. Where lakes are rich in dissolved organic matter and low in dissolved oxygen, photosynthetic bacteria turn the water to a blood color. Shallow pools on esturarine mud flats provide habitat for sulfur-oxidizing bacteria, which produce sulfur particles and give a milky whitish yellow color to the water. Because these bacteria use hydrogen sulfide as a substrate, the color is often accompanied by the characteristic smell of rotten eggs.

(a)

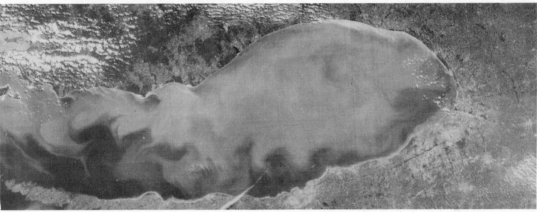

(b)

FIGURE 3-10 Reflection of light by suspended particles as seen from satellite photographs of Lake Michigan. In this lake whitening event increased photosynthesis combined with a shortage of carbon dioxide caused precipitation of a fine suspension of calcium carbonate. The upper photograph shows the normal lake, the lower one the lake whitening, which covers most of the south and east of the lake (right and top in this picture). From Strong and Edie (1978).

Reflection (Albedo)

Although some light striking the lake surface is absorbed, some is reflected and never penetrates the water. This reflection is often apparent to the observer early and late in the day, when the water assumes a metallic sheen as low angled light is reflected at a similarly low angle to the observer on the shore. The fraction of light reflected is called the *albedo*. Light coming from overhead has a lower angle of incidence and thus a lower reflection than slanted light. Reflection from a mirror-calm lake is therefore at a minimum at noon and maximum at sunrise and sunset, as well as for much of the day in the seasons of low sun angle. Since real water surfaces are frequently roughened by waves, there will be a continuous variation in reflection even at noon, because the waves themselves present a variety of surfaces to the incoming light ranging from horizontal to perpendicular. In most lakes there is more wind in the afternoon than in the morning, which causes an asymmetrical underwater distribution of photosynthetic energy. For example, in Lake Tahoe, the onset of waves can change the secchi depth from 30 m at 11 a.m. to 18 m at 1 p.m. while the solar radiation remains more or less constant.

Ice is quite transparent, but snow cover greatly increases albedo so that up to 90 percent of sunlight will be reflected. In contrast, backscattering by water molecules will reflect only about 5 percent of incident light. In Antarctic Lake Vanda, 14 to 20 percent of the incoming sunlight penetrates the 4-m-thick layer of permanent ice that covers this unusual lake.

Remote Sensing

In summer blue-green algae and submerged macrophytes often form dense layers just beneath the surface. These photosynthetic organisms absorb light strongly in the red and blue regions but reflect near infrared (NIR) and green light. Other algae reflect much less NIR but similar amounts of green light (Fig. 3-11). Since NIR is invisible to the human eye, lakes with dense blue-green algae blooms or thick macrophyte stands appear green. Diatoms and green algae rarely form dense near-surface layers, and their green reflection is greatly modified by absorption due to dissolved and nonliving materials in the water column. Despite its invisibility to humans and the absorption of NIR by water, the strong reflection by some plants is of some value to

FIGURE 3-11 Reflection of light by aquatic plants. Note the two peaks of reflectance. The small peak in the green-yellow-orange (525 to 625 nm) is due to green chlorophyll *a* and yellow-orange accessory pigments, such as carotene, common to most aquatic photosynthetic organisms. High near-infrared (NIR) reflectance is shown by the large colonial blue-green alga (*Aphanizomenon flos-aquae*) and the floating higher plant duckweed (*Lemna*). Gas vacuoles of the blue-green algae and the air spaces inside the duckweed provide many air-water interfaces that preferentially reflect NIR. The diatom (*Cymbella*) has no air spaces. Modified from Anderson and Horne (1975).

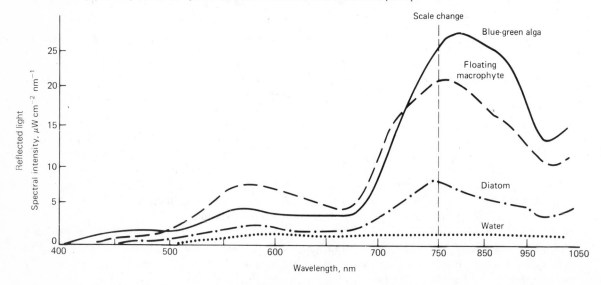

limnologists. False-color infrared film accurately records NIR reflection. Photographs made using this method show the complex patterns formed by surface blooms of blue-green algae or dust and debris, such as floating dead grass, leaves, and submerged macrophytes (Figs. 3-11, 5-3). Muddy water and some pollutants also produce distinct reflection patterns on lakes, but at shorter wavelengths. Pictures made from satellites or airplanes reveal the instantaneous distribution of highly variable phenomenon, especially on large lakes where conventional limnology covers too small an area.

Color IR photographs are routinely used to map wetland vegetation, since the large stands of single species create blocks of different re-

FIGURE 3-12 Horizontal variation in water clarity in a very large reservoir, Lake Mead in Arizona, in June 1988. These images were reconstructed from NASA's Landsat satellite, which orbits about 580 km from earth. Large arrows indicate the Colorado River, small arrows temporary washes and small rivers. The inflowing Colorado River (right) is muddy (cross-hatched; 0.5 to 1.5 m secchi depth), as is the Overton Arm (top), which receives input from the Muddy River. Once the sediment settles out most of the lake is clear (unshaded; 4 to 5 m secchi depth) since it is oligotrophic. Patches of very transparent water (dotted; 6 to 7.5 m secchi depth) occur in some areas. Eutrophication from the discharge of treated sewage is evident in Las Vegas Bay (lower left), where algal growth decreases transparency to 2 m. The effect of the artificial fertilization is reflected in the lower secchi depths in the upper Overton Arm. The area of lake shown is 642 km^2 (247 mi^2) and the resolution of the pixels in the picture is about 60 m. Drawn from a picture by D. Eckhardt, U.S. Bureau of Reclamation.

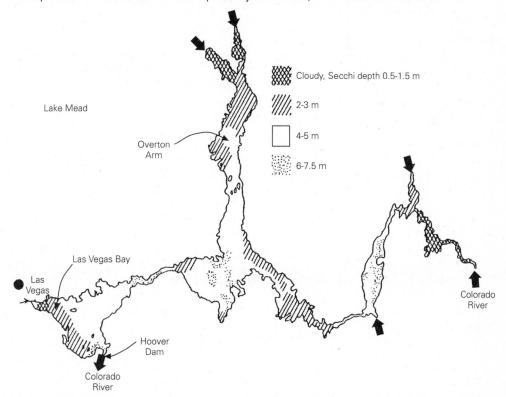

flectance patterns. Recently, video images of wetlands have been input directly to computers to produce high-resolution maps. If calibrated by some ground truth, the digitized data can be programmed to provide a direct readout of the areas of types of vegetation. Not only algae but also temperature and turbidity can be mapped by remote sensing. The technique is especially useful for very large lakes and reservoirs. An example is Lake Mead on the Colorado River. This reservoir is the largest in the United States and has recently been the site of a fertilization experiment to increase fish yields (Vaux, 1990). The spatial pattern of water transparency (secchi depth) in June as determined from Landsat satellite images is shown in Fig. 3-12.

This chapter has stressed the important aspects of the quality and quantity of light in the aquatic ecosystem. Light that is not reflected or backscattered is absorbed and converted to heat by the water or the organisms, particles, and pigments it contains. This heat produces the important thermal structure of lakes that is described in Chap. 4.

FURTHER READING

Bauer, H., M. M. Caldwell, M. Tevini, and R. C. Worrest. 1982. Biological Effects of UV-B Radiation. Proc. Workshop Munich Min. Res. Tech. (Munich) and US EPA (Covallis, Oregon) BPT-Bericht 5/82. 231 pp.

Hutchinson, G. E. 1957. *A Treatise on Limnology*, vol. 1, chap. 6. Wiley, New York.

James, H. R., and E. A. Birge. 1938. ''A Laboratory Study of the Absorption of Light by Lake Waters.'' *Trans. Wis. Aca. Sci. Lett.,* **31**:1–154.

Jerlov, N. G. 1968. *Optical Oceanography*. Elsevier, London. 194 pp.

Mortimer, C. H. 1988. ''Discoveries and Testable Hypotheses arising from Coastal Zone Color Scanner Imagery of Southern Lake Michigan.'' *Limnol. Oceanogr.*, **33**:203–226.

Smith, R. C. 1968. ''The Optical Characterization of Natural Waters by means of an 'Extinction Coefficient.' ''*Limnol. Oceanogr.*, **13**:423–429.

Talling, J. F. 1971. ''The Underwater Light Climate as a Controlling Factor in the Production Ecology of Freshwater Phytoplankton.'' *Mitt. Int. Ver. Theor. Angew. Limnol.*, **19**:214–243.

Tyler, J. ''The Secchi Disc.'' *Limnol. Oceanogr.* **13**:1–6.

Tyler, J. E., and R. W. Priesendorfer. 1962. ''Transmission of Energy within the Sea.'' pp. 397–451. In M. N. Hill (ed.). *The Sea*.

Vollenweider, R. A. 1961. ''Photometric Studies in Inland Waters. I. Relations Existing in the Spectral Extinction of Light in Water.'' *Mem. Ist. Ital. Idrobiol.*, **13**:87–113.

Wyatt, P. J., and C. Jackson, 1989. ''Discrimination of Phytoplankton via Light-Scattering Properties. *Limnol. Oceanogr.*, **34**:96–112.

CHAPTER 4

Heat

OVERVIEW

Heat in aquatic ecosystems performs two functions: it establishes thermal stratification in water bodies and it regulates the rates of chemical reactions and biological processes.

Thermal stratification, resulting from heating by the sun, is the most important physical event in the lake's annual cycle and dominates most aspects of lake structure. Heating decreases the density of the upper water, which, in combination with the wind, results in a three-layered system. If the lake is deep enough, summer stratification produces an upper warm, lighter layer—the *epilimnion;* a cool denser layer—the *hypolimnion;* and a transitional zone between them—the *metalimnion.* The regions of greatest change in temperature are called *thermoclines.* In many temperate lakes the seasonal thermocline spans a difference of 10 or even 15°C. Tropical lakes, due to the unique temperature-density relationship of water, have stable stratification with a thermocline spanning only 1 to 3°C.

The parent or seasonal thermocline is not fixed in depth. It gradually descends during the summer until the lake turns over in the autumn. The seasonal thermocline occurs in the meta-limnion, but temporary thermoclines are common in the epilimnion. Temporary thermoclines are mixed on a daily basis down to intermediate depths by afternoon winds or nocturnal convection. Two or three thermoclines may form this way, depending on recent mixing events, but eventually all are mixed down to the seasonal thermocline by the next strong wind. During the summer the volume of the epilimnion increases at the expense of the hypolimnion. Finally, de-stratification occurs in the autumn as heat losses from conduction and evaporation exceed the supply of solar heat. Once destratified, lakes that mix from top to bottom are termed *holomictic;* very deep or chemically stratified ones that mix only partially are called *meromictic. Dimictic* lakes mix twice, once in the autumn and once in the spring, they are covered with ice in winter and may show *inverse stratification. Monomictic* lakes do not freeze; they have one long mixing period all through the winter. *Polymictic* lakes are shallow; they mix every few days or even daily all year round. *Amictic* lakes have year-round ice cover and never mix.

A lake's *maximum heat content* is the heat entering between the lowest winter and highest summer temperatures. It is mainly a function of mean depth and is useful in predicting the onset of thermal stratification. In deep lakes with a large maximum heat content, the water takes a long time to heat or cool. Thus deep lakes stratify, destratify, freeze, and thaw more slowly than shallower lakes in the same vicinity. Maximum heat content is greater in hot climates, but evaporative cooling may almost equal solar input. If it were not for evaporative cooling, many lakes would become too hot for most organisms to survive. In streams, rivers, and estuaries where thermal stratification rarely occurs, the daily or spatial changes in temperature are most important in regulating metabolism.

In this chapter we discuss the importance of heat in aquatic ecosystems, measurement of heat in lakes, thermal stratification and lake classification, thermocline formation in spring, seasonal and daily heating and cooling in the epilimnion, the end of stratification at the fall overturn, heat cycles and heat budgets, and waste heat discharges.

THE IMPORTANCE OF HEAT IN LAKES

Heat in lakes, rivers, and oceans plays two distinct roles, one in lake structure and the other in chemical and biological reactions. The heat transmitted with light is responsible for establishing various kinds of thermal stratification in water bodies. Heat also regulates the rates of chemical reactions and biological processes.

An increase in heat during the summer turns the metabolic wheels at a faster rate. The rate of recycling of organic and mineral components in lakes increases with temperature, because in general chemical reactions and biological activities such as respiration double if the temperature rises 10°C. Thus zooplankton or fish in winter use much less energy but grow more slowly than in summer. This temperature-metabolic relationship is called the Q_{10} index. As just indicated, $Q_{10} = 2$ for most organisms, but in some cold environments Q_{10} may be higher. For some Antarctic wetland algae, the Q_{10} for N_2-fixation may

be as high as 6 at temperatures between 0 and 5°C. This gives an obvious advantage during the few sunny days of the coastal Antarctic summer (Plate 6a). As the water temperature rises, the increased metabolic rates of lake and river organisms place additional demand on the supplies of dissolved oxygen. We will discuss this oxygen depletion in greater detail in Chap. 7. As temperatures reach their maximum in summer, the filtration and excretion rates of zooplankton also increase. All this activity increases the mass of fecal pellets available for bacteria to regenerate and recycle. The inorganic nutrients released by bacteria and zooplankton support the small summer phytoplankton crop, since earlier plant growth has depleted the nutrients built up over the winter. Even the cold-blooded or *poikilothermal* fish become more active and both adults and young juveniles feed more voraciously in the warmer seasons. In fact, as we show in Chap. 14, young fish often survive better in warm years because they can grow more quickly to a size at which predation is less severe.

Phytoplankton also respire more at higher temperatures and, since they do not increase photosynthesis to the same extent, are less efficient in warmer water. In the 25 to 35°C water of tropical Lake George, Uganda, gross primary production, measured as oxygen produced, is very high at 15.6 g O_2 m^{-2} in the 12 hours of daylight. However, respiration over the same 12 hours is so high that it consumes 9.1 g O_2 m^{-2}, leaving a net usable production of only 6.5 g O_2 m^{-2} (Ganf and Horne, 1975). If the estimated (lower) rate of nocturnal respiration is taken into account, only the tiny amount of 0.1 g O_2 mg C m^{-2} is available for new algal growth. In contrast, in the frigid waters of the Antarctic Ocean respiration rates are low; since net growth is not hindered by large respiratory losses, the huge blooms of phytoplankton at the edges of the continental ice shelf appear quickly.

Heat is gained in lakes by the absorption of solar radiation. Most radiation entering water is converted to heat quickly, but the lake temperature increases slowly because water has an enormous capacity for heat storage. Major heat losses occur by evaporation and conduction to the air and, to a lesser extent, the sediments. The slow but continuously changing heat content of temperate lakes, rivers, and estuaries is an important part of the structure of aquatic systems described in Chap. 2. In tropical regions the annual change in heat content closely reflects the seasonal pattern of temperature and, as expected, varies much less during the year than in temperate regions. Lakes and streams at high latitudes and elevations, although subject to more intense radiation in summer, tend to be cooler because of lower ambient air temperatures. Winter ice in these areas may persist well into summer, and the open water season may be very brief. In one cool summer at Signy Island in the Weddel Sea, Antarctica, the small, shallow Heyward Lake became ice-free for only 1 day (Plate 1*b*).

Although the effects of heat and temperature in streams and estuaries are similar to those in lakes, streams and estuaries do not show significant thermal stratification. Shading by riparian vegetation is very important in streams but less so rivers and larger lakes. Solar heating of exposed mud flats is unique to estuaries since tidal action is involved. Very shallow water flowing across sun-warmed rocks is a characteristic of many shallow streams and rivers. For these reasons features of heat and temperature peculiar to rivers and estuaries are discussed in Chaps. 16 to 19.

MEASUREMENTS

An ordinary mercury-in-glass thermometer or electric thermister is adequate for most limnological purposes. *Thermistors* measure the change in resistance with temperature of a metal probe in a tiny gas bubble under a thin glass cover. Achieving accuracy greater than $\pm 0.01°C$ using thermistors with a remote readout requires more effort and cost. Modern devices transmit data about temperature as well as other variables (pH,

conductivity, dissolved oxygen, depth) directly to a computer file. Temperatures can be measured every few millimeters of depth for detailed investigation of water movement and heat fluxes.

Another device, used extensively in the 1940s and still common in oceanographic work, is the *bathythermograph,* a rocket-shaped instrument that is lowered rapidly to the lake bed on a hydrograph wire. On the way down to the lake bed, the bathythermograph records both temperature and depth by producing a continuous trace that is etched on a piece of smoked or gold-plated glass. Bathythermographs can be recoverable or expendable. The expendable type, frequently used at sea, transmits temperature and depth information back to the ship as it free-falls to the bottom.

A method of temperature measurement now coming into wider use is *remote sensing,* which detects heat radiation (5,000 to 14,000 nm) emitted by water. The signals are recorded by sensors in low-flying aircraft or satellites and are computer-processed to produce a visual image. In addition, some ''water truth,'' the equivalent of ground truth, is needed if the temperatures are to be accurate ($<1°C$). Although expensive, the advantages of synoptic coverage of large areas often makes remote sensing worthwhile.

Incoming radiation, which is used for the calculation of heat cycles, can be measured directly or calculated using data from existing metrological stations in the vicinity. Thermopiles and pyroheliometers record solar radiation in gram-calories per centimeter per minute, which can be integrated over any time period. More detailed work requires calculation of net radiation, which is incoming radiation minus back radiation reflected from the surface.

THERMAL STRATIFICATION AND LAKE CLASSIFICATION

Sunlight heats water near the surface and forms a layer of less dense warm water overlying a denser cool zone. Since the absorption of light

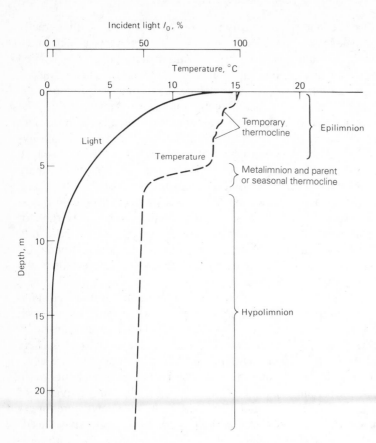

FIGURE 4-1   Idealized summer distribution of light and heat in a stratified lake. Note the irregular distribution of heat and sharp thermoclines and the smooth exponential curve for light distribution. An example from a lake is given in Fig. 5-19, which shows complex temporary thermoclines.

in lakes is nearly exponential with depth, one might expect a similar distribution of heat. However, because of stirring by convection and the wind, a layer of water is formed that has a more defined boundary than the illuminated zone (Fig. 4-1). The lake is then stratified and divided into three separate layers: the *epilimnion*—the warmer, less dense upper layer; the *hypolimnion*—a cooler less dense lower layer; and a layer of intermediate density—the *metalimnion*—which lies between them. The exact boundaries of these three layers are not always easy to detect, and the layers are dynamic, with some fluctuation in the size of each layer occurring over the season. The other important zone in the lake is the *thermocline,* which is the region where temperature changes rapidly with depth.

Historically the thermocline has been defined as the region where temperature changes are greater than 1°C per meter of depth. Although suitable for many temperate lakes, this definition breaks down in tropical and other warm waters, where very stable stratification can occur with only 1 to 3°C difference from surface to bottom. In addition, small, temporary density-stratified layers occur within the epilimnion on most calm, warm days, and these thermoclines also show only a small difference in temperature with depth. These phenomena came to light long after the initial definition was coined. In this text we use a more general definition of thermoclines: we consider them to be the regions of greatest inflection in the temperature depth curve.

The deepest thermocline, the *parent* or *sea-*

sonal thermocline, always lies within the metalimnion. *Temporary* or *daily thermoclines* are shallower and may lie in the metalimnion or in the epilimnion. In common usage the terms (*parent*) *thermocline* and *metalimnion* are often used interchangeably, since they are in a similar general region of the lake. Students should be careful to distinguish between the two terms where a separation is warranted. In lakes the epilimnion may range from the surface to as little as 2 m to more than 20 m. The metalimnion is often several meters thick, and the hypolimnion is thick only in deep lakes.

Lakes at midlatitudes form a thermocline in spring, if they are deep enough, and lose it in the autumn. Many form thick ice cover in winter. In tropical climates the rainy season is often the time of mixing equivalent to the winter in temperate lakes. All lakes mix to some extent almost all the time, but a useful method of classifying them is based on how completely they mix in the vertical plane during the season of lowest temperature and greatest turbulence. Lakes that have winter ice cover are called *dimictic* since they mix twice a year—in autumn before ice cover and in spring after ice out. Full mixing occurs only in the short periods between ice breakup and the onset of thermal stratification in spring and between the breakdown of thermal stratification and formation of ice cover in winter (Fig. 4-2*c*). The ice cover prevents wind energy from mixing the cold water lying beneath the ice and conserves heat much as a swimming pool cover does in the winter months. Most temperate lakes are dimictic. Typical dimictic lakes are Lake Mendota, Wisconsin, and Castle Lake, California. *Monomictic* lakes are never completely ice-covered and winter is a single continuous wind-stirred event (Fig. 4-2 *a, b*). Typical monomictic lakes are the Great Lakes except for Lake Erie, Lake Tahoe, and Lake Windermere, England.

If a lake is shallow and exposed to the wind, thermal stratification may last for a week or two, be destroyed by a storm, reestablish for a few days, be disrupted again, and so on. This rather common type of lake is called *polymictic,* because it mixes many times per year. Examples are Clear Lake, California, and Lake George, Uganda (Fig. 4-2*a*).

Two other classifications are based on the degree of lake mixing and its seasonal variation. If during the annual mixing cycle a lake mixes from top to bottom, it is said to be *holomictic* (*holo* meaning ''whole'' and *mixis* meaning ''mixing''). If, on the other hand, it is so deep that there is insufficient energy to overcome stratification and stir it top to bottom, it is called *meromictic.*

Some of the world's deepest lakes in tropical climates, such as Lake Tanganyika, an African Rift Valley lake, are meromictic, as are some isolated deep ocean basins. Lake Tanganyika has a permanent thermocline at about 400 m and seasonal thermoclines between 20 and 100 m. Lakes with significant accumulations of dense, salty water near the bottom also may not mix. Such lakes are chemically meromictic and have a warm bottom water layer or *monimolimnion,* where the additional upward buoyancy of the deep, warm water is counterbalanced by the increased density from dissolved salts. Runoff from deicing salts in roadways has created some new chemically meromictic lakes in the colder parts of the United States. Occasionally, meromictic lakes are mixed by severe storms. This mixing is dramatic, because hydrogen sulfide accumulated in the anoxic bottom water reaches the surface, oxygen is depleted, and massive fish kills result. The nutrients released in meromictic overturns usually produce a series of algae blooms until equilibrium is reestablished. A similar meromixis and fish kill can occur in the vicinity of stagnant coastal lagoons when storms flush the anoxic lagoon waters into nearby shallow seas.

One dramatic problem resulting from the overturn of meromictic lakes occurred in the 1980s in tropical Lake Nyos, in the Cameroons. Lake Nyos is a small lake formed in a volcanic

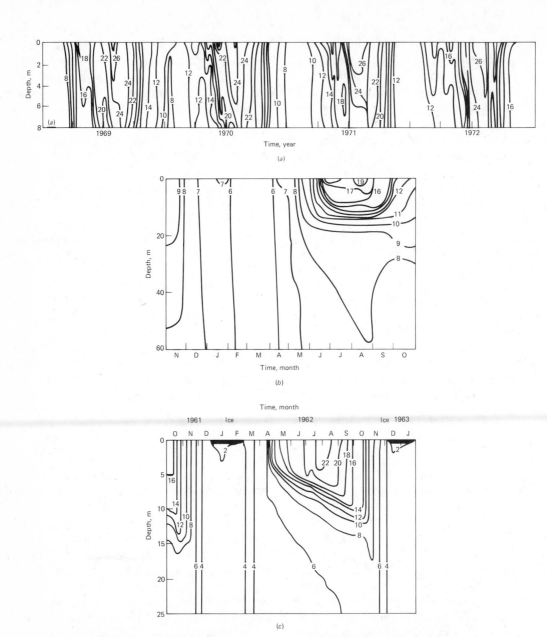

Figure 4-2 The seasonal variations in temperature with depth for three contrasting lake types. (*a*) Warm, shallow polymictic Clear Lake in California. Redrawn from Horne, (1975). (*b*) Deep monomictic Lake Windermere, England. Redrawn from Jenkin, (1942). (*c*) Dimictic Mountain Lake, Virginia. Redrawn from Roth and Neff, (1964). The values are shown in isotherms at 2°C intervals for (*a*) and (*c*) and 1°C intervals for (*b*). Note the regularity of the seasonal stratification (horizontal lines close together) and winter mixed regime (vertical lines far apart). Winter temperatures are uniform from top to bottom in monomictic lakes, but in dimictic lakes ice cover prevents wind action and slight inverse stratification often occurs.

explosion crater; it is steep-sided and stratifies easily. Dozens of local villagers were found dead near the lake, and the cause of death was presumed to be suffocation by carbon dioxide released in huge quantities from the monimolimnion. The exact cause of the overturn and the toxicity are part of a limnological puzzle for which all the answers are not yet known. No measurements of carbon dioxide were made prior to the event in this remote and little-studied area. A team of geologists rushed to the area presumed the carbon dioxide had built up over time from volcanic vents, but these vents have never been found and little carbon dioxide has accumulated in the deep water since the event. An alternative source of carbon dioxide would be bacterial respiration in the lake sediments. It is also possible that hydrogen sulfide, a very toxic gas common in the lower waters of productive stratified lakes (Chap. 10), was the toxic agent. Hydrogen sulfide is a common cause of fish deaths in some fish hatcheries fed by hypolimnion releases from reservoirs. Differences in

the mode of toxic action of the two gases on the lungs could distinguish which caused these deaths, but reliable postmortem examinations were not performed.

Most of the world's lakes are dimictic, monomictic, or polymictic, but there are a few curious examples with different mixing patterns. Lakes that are always covered with ice and never mix are called *amictic*. Lakes Vanda and Boney in the Antarctic (Figs. 4-3, 21-12) are examples of permanently ice-covered large lakes, but many smaller lakes at high altitudes or latitudes are also amictic. Other lakes found in less extreme climates may thaw only once every few years. Such lakes are called *oligomictic*.

THERMOCLINE FORMATION IN SPRING

The formation of the thermocline in spring, with consequent restriction of nutrient circulation, is the single most important physical event for lake biota. The wax and wane of the spring bloom of

Figure 4-3 An amictic lake, Lake Vanda, Antarctica. This large lake ($A = 5.2$ km^2, $-z = 29$ m) is permanently covered with a thick layer of ice. The lake lies in a dry valley, but adjacent hills were covered by snow in summer when this picture was taken. Although the wind cannot mix this lake because of its ice cover, sufficient light passes through the ice in summer to heat the water and produce convective mixing. The combination of convective mixing and light supports an algae-based food chain.

diatoms is an obvious biological change directly associated with thermocline formation (Chap. 12).

An approach to thermocline formation useful to biologists and chemists considers energy as a unifying concept. Boyce (1974) uses a mechanical energy budget for the water column and relates this to a critical wind speed and rate of surface heating or cooling (see Eq. (2 and 3)). First, the sun heats the water surface. The wind stirs this warmer, lighter water down to a depth where the turbulence is eventually dissipated. This depth becomes the top of the thermocline. Most heat is absorbed in the first few meters and to extend farther down water must be physically stirred by wind or convection-induced turbulence. The downmixing water is warmer and positively buoyant and resists mixing in proportion to the density difference between the warm and cold water. The density of water changes rapidly with temperature (Fig. 4-4), so a large effect can be expected with a few days of sunshine and calm weather.

Why, then, when sunshine and calm weather occur in winter, does not a thermocline appear, at least temporarily, when the winds resume? The answer lies in the relative strengths of the turbulent wind mixing and the warmer water's buoyant resistance to mixing. These forces can be compared by using the *Richardson number, R_i*, which is expressed by the equation:

$$R_i = \frac{g \, d\rho/dz}{\rho \, (dU/dz)^2} = \frac{\text{buoyancy}}{\text{mixing}} \qquad (1)$$

where R_i = the Richardson number, a dimensionless quantity
g = acceleration of gravity
ρ = density of the fluid
U = horizontal water current
$g \dfrac{d\rho}{dz}$ = a measure of the water's buoyancy
z = depth
$\rho \left(\dfrac{dU}{dz}\right)^2$ = a measure of the stirring due to shearing of water currents

Richardson's number defines the ratio of work done by stirring to overcome the stabilizing buoyancy forces relative to the available kinetic energy. Where R_i becomes critical, there is adequate kinetic energy available as wind stirring to produce a shearing stress sufficient to overcome the buoyancy forces. This R_i (critical) is close to $1/4$. When R_i is less than $1/4$, stirring increases and stratification is destroyed. Above this value buoyancy dominates and thermal stratification is preserved. In winter R_i is low because there is too much kinetic energy available compared to the small buoyancy effects caused by heating the cold water with weak winter sunshine. Under this circumstance mixing prevails.

Students studying small lakes are often surprised at the rapidity with which the thermocline forms in spring. This can occur in a matter of only a few days. Such speed would not be expected from a uniform diffusion process based on steadily increasing solar radiation. A good explanation employs a nonuniform event such as a storm. Above a critical wind speed ($U_{a,\,\text{crit}}$) the rate of change of potential energy (dP/dt) supplies sufficient surface turbulence to entrain deeper water layers. To do this the resistance of any density gradients must be overcome. At thermocline onset the sun warms the lake surface and wind blows across it (Boyce, 1974). Then

$$\frac{dP}{dt} = 0 \doteq \gamma_w U_{a,\,\text{crit}}^3 + \gamma_h g \frac{\alpha_{vs}}{C_P} q_s D \qquad (2)$$

where γ_w = a constant dependent on environmental conditions encompassing wind drag and vertical wind mixing efficiency
γ_h = a constant also dependent on environmental conditions that represents the fraction of heat energy used in mixing of the water column
α_{vs} = volume coefficient of thermal expansion of the surface water
C_p = specific heat of water
q_s = net heat flux across the water surface

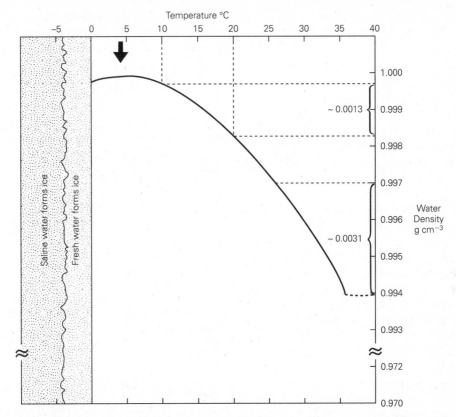

Figure 4-4 Changes in fresh water density with temperature. Ice is much less dense than water (-0.9100 g cm^{-1}) and thus floats. Note that the maximum density (arrow) of 1.000 g cm^{-1} occurs at $+4°$C. Because the actual temperature, not only the temperature difference, is important in thermocline stability, a few degrees difference creates stable thermoclines in tropical lakes but not in temperate waters. The reason is that there is a greater decrease in density per degree rise in temperature at higher temperatures than at lower temperatures (see above). In fact, much of the curve is parabolic. For example, from 10 to 20°C density changes by about 0.0013 g cm^{-1}. In contrast a similar 10°C rise starting at 25°C, reduces water density almost 3 times as much (approx. 0.0031 g cm^{-1}). The wind is not as important in this geographical difference since its speed, and thus wind stirring of the water, is similar the world over. The important factor is that warm water is more resistant to wind mixing than cold water.

$D =$ depth over which heat is distributed, that is, depth to which uniform vertical mixing proceeds for $U_{a,\ crit}$

Equation (2) says that a lake's potential energy may change in two ways: The first term ($\gamma_w U_{a,\ crit}^3$) is wind stirring, which redistributes layers of different densities; the second term

($\gamma_h g \dfrac{\alpha_{vs}}{C_p} q_s D$) shows that heat loss or gain can change the density distribution.

When the wind blows at speeds faster than $U_{a,\ crit}$, as in a mild storm, dP/dt is positive, and active turbulent entrainment proceeds down from the surface.

Rearranging Eq. (2),

$$U_{a,\,\mathrm{crit}} = \left(\frac{\gamma_h g \alpha_{vs}}{C_p \gamma_w}\right)^{1/3} (-q_s D)^{1/3} \qquad (3)$$
$$= \beta(|q_s|D)^{1/3}$$

This has been related to values in a lake by Boyce (1974), where in summer $\gamma_h = 1$, $g = 980$ cm s^{-2}, $\alpha_{vs} = 10^{-4}$°C^{-1}, $C_p = 1$ cal g^{-1}°C^{-1}, $\gamma_w = 1.9 \times 10^{-9}$, and thus $\beta = 372$ (cgs units). For $D = 10$ m and heating rate q_s of 400 cal cm^{-2} day^{-1} (4.6×10^3 cal cm^{-2} s^{-1}),

$$U_{a,\,\mathrm{crit}} = 618 \text{ cm s}^{-1}$$

A wind velocity of 6 m s^{-1} (10 mph) is a typical spring storm wind speed. The extra inputs of turbulent energy increase entrainment, overcoming the previous slight temperature gradients, and establish permanent stratification with 1 or 2 days. Unlike many other lake mixing processes, once the spring thermocline has formed it is thermodynamically stable and can be destroyed only by cooling the epilimnion. Hurricane-strength winds will sharpen the boundaries of the three water layers but will not cause the lake to destratify.

The Thermal Bar

In the special case of very large cold lakes, such as the Great Lakes, the thermocline does not form all over the lake at the same time. In spring the waters of the Great Lakes are divided in two sections, offshore unstratified water at less than 4°C and a warmer weakly stratified mass near shore. The 4°C water between the two is the densest (Fig. 4-4) and sinks. The zone of dense sinking water is called the *thermal bar* (Fig. 4-5): it gradually moves offshore until the entire lake stratifies. The near-shore water becomes warmer than the main water mass because it is relatively shallow and so heat is contained in a small volume. In smaller lakes near-shore water would quickly be wind mixed horizontally into the offshore water. The thermal bar enhances early algal growth by effectively trapping heat. Nutrients and toxicants from spring meltwater are also trapped within the thermal bar.

HEATING AND COOLING IN THE EPILIMNION AND MIXED LAYERS

The discussion that follows is applicable to the epilimnion and mixed layers as well as to polymictic and unstratified lakes and even rivers, since their single mixed layer is similar to an epilimnion in stratified lakes. It is important to forecast changes in the epilimnetic temperatures of lakes to enable prediction of, to name a few examples, the onset of ice, the effect of thermal discharges on lakes, the effect of dry cloudless summers on reservoir levels, the rate of egg development in zooplankton and stream invertebrates, and the success of some fish year classes. Unfortunately, because of variability of the weather, this is often difficult. A basic problem is that lakes do not heat up in direct proportion to applied light and heat inputs. Evaporative cooling and back radiation also occur, and the balance between these losses and solar heating determines the resulting lake temperature. The fraction of incoming radiation absorbed by the epilimnion is calculated from pyroheliometer measurements, lake extinction coefficients, and the lake's altitude and latitude. Evaporation depends largely on relative humidity, lake surface temperature, and wind speed. Further, the strength of the wind may vary considerably over the lake surface. Some recent advances in equipment facilitate many of the measurements required to study lake mixing in more detail.

Daily Mixing Cycles in the Epilimnion: Customizing for Individual Lakes Using the Wedderburn Number

Many important planktonic processes depend on the continual mixing of the epilimnion. For example, if the epilimnion is not stirred almost every day, heavy species such as diatoms will sink into the dark hypolimnion. Small, immature zooplankton and fish larvae, which are weak swimmers, are swirled about and dispersed by turbulent mixing in the epilimnion. However, calm periods are also important. The success or failure of some fish year classes can depend on

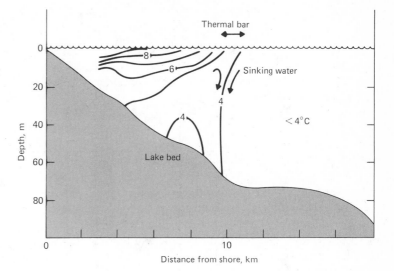

Figure 4-5 The thermal bar in Lake Ontario resulting from the differential effect of solar heating in the open lake and at the margin of the lake. The warmer water is confined to shallows by a sinking mass of dense 4°C water derived from lighter, cooler water offshore that must be less than 4°C for a thermal bar to form. Redrawn from Boyce, (1974).

the occurrence of a few days of calm weather in spring or summer. When mixing in the epilimnion is low, zooplankton are dispersed slowly by turbulence and reach high densities. These dense zooplankton patches are essential for the survival of some newly hatched pelagic fish larvae. Unlike larger fish, which survive poor conditions by using stored fat, larvae must find a good food source within a few days of hatching or starve to death (Peterman and Bradford, 1987).

How can these short-term mixing events be described? The stability of the seasonal thermocline can be predicted using the Richardson number (R_i). However, this number is a general expression for the stability of all water and covers oceans as well as lakes. The hydrodynamic characteristics of a particular lake are related to such unique features as the depth of mixing and the fetch. A more customized approach for individual lakes is to modify R_i to become the *Wedderburn number, W* (Thompson and Imberger, 1980). This dimensionless number is defined below:

$$W = \frac{g'h^2}{u_*^2 L} = \frac{\text{depth-based buoyancy}}{\text{length-based wind mixing}} \quad (4)$$

where g' = reduced gravitational acceleration due to the density jump across the base of the thermocline
h = depth of the mixed water layer
u_* = characteristic shear velocity (based on wind speed, Fisher et al., 1979)
L = fetch (basin length in direction of the wind)

The Wedderburn number explains short-term mixing patterns in the epilimnion. Low values ($W = 0.01$ to 1.0) indicate unstable conditions and high values ($W = 1$ to 15) show high stability in the mixed layer. Examples of the use of the Wedderburn number for a temperate lake in Australia are shown in Figs. 4-6 and 4-7. When W is high, large amounts of energy (sunlight, wind, evaporation) must be supplied to change the existing surface water mixing patterns. As described earlier, the epilimnion is defined as the area above the thermocline, but it may not always be completely mixed. The *mixed layer* is defined as the water recently mixed by wind or convection currents. On stormy days the mixed layer encompasses the entire epilimnion, while on calm days it may be only a thin surface layer. The uppermost mixed layer has a temporary ther-

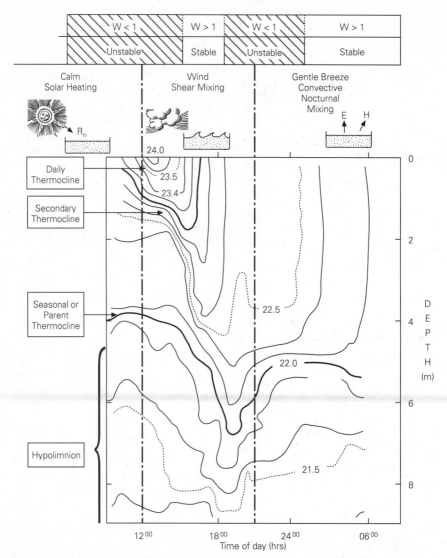

Figure 4-6 The daily cycle of temporary thermoclines in a temperate lake. The isotherms are shown every 0.2°C (thin lines), 0.5°C (dotted lines), and 1.0°C (heavy lines). On the first calm morning the sun heats a thin surface layer of water to give a temporary thermocline at about 0.5 m (upper horizontal isotherms) over a secondary one formed previously at 1.5 m. The Wedderburn number, W, is low, indicating low stability in the mixed layer. Strong afternoon winds mix the hot water down to the seasonal thermocline (vertical isotherms), destroying both temporary thermoclines. The mixed layer is then moderately stable ($W > 1$), but as the wind dies in the evening the water is too warm to be stable ($W < 1$). Following a misty night, the now cooler mixed layer is very stable ($W \gg 1$) in contrast to the previous morning. This figure should be read in conjunction with Fig. 4-7. Modified from Imberger (1985).

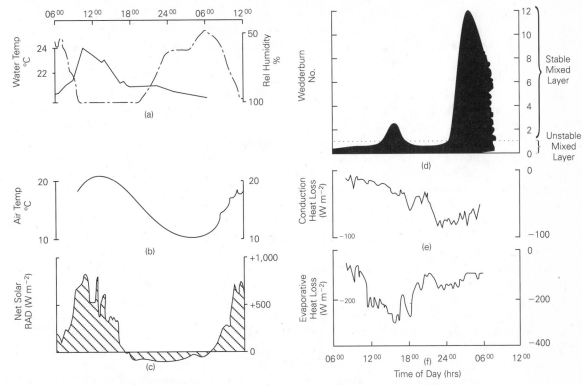

Figure 4-7 The diel cycle of the mixed layer. Variations in most of the important parameters of the heat balance of a lake during a daily cycle (Fig. 4-6). The stability of the mixed layer is indicated by the Wedderburn number ($W > 1$ = stable, $W < 1$ = unstable). Note how the solar heating, air and water temperatures, conduction to the air, and evaporative heat fluxes interact and modify the effects of the wind (Fig. 4-6) to alter the stability of the mixed layer. Modified from Imberger (1985).

mocline below it. There may be one or more deeper secondary thermoclines formed by winds of varying strength over the last few days. The epilimnion thus consists of several slabs of water separated by temporary thermoclines that lie above the seasonal or parent thermocline (Fig. 4-6).

The mixed layer receives energy more directly from wind and solar radiation than do the deeper layers. When $W < 1$, depth-based buoyancy is low but mixing energy is abundant and the mixed depth (h) is small. This condition is unstable and the mixed layer deepens rapidly, since the shear velocity u_* is high [Eq. (4), Fig.

4-6]. As the thermocline deepens and h increases, the stability of the new mixed layer increases. W remains high when the winds drop, since the deeper mixed layer persists until a new shallow thermocline is established. Thus deep mixed layers and calm windless periods are characterized by $W > 1$.

The Wedderburn number is particularly useful in comparing the high mixing stability of tropical lakes with those in temperate climates. In turn, this partially explains why blue-green algae and dinoflagellates are so common in warm and tropical lakes. Evaporative cooling is much more important in the heat budget of tropical lakes than in temperate lakes. Even on calm nights, overnight evaporation and cooling of the surface water in the tropics produces strong convective mixing. Convection reduces depth-based buoyancy (a small numerator in Eq. (4)), even with a deeper mixed layer, since g' falls as the mixed layer cools and the density difference across the thermocline is reduced. The surface layer of any lake will heat up by about only 5°C in one day, although the initial water temperatures in tropical and temperate zones will be very different. An increase of a few degrees centigrade in a tropical lake (33 to 35°C) will decrease water density about 3 times more than if the water was initially only 10 to 15°C (Fig. 4-4). Thus the density jump across the thermocline (g') will be high in the tropical lake and the mixed layer can be much thinner for the same high W value than in a temperate lake. Because high W indicates great stability, the thin hot mixed layer in the tropical lake will resist mixing by the afternoon winds. Under these conditions, heavy diatoms will sink out and buoyant blue-green algae or swimming dinoflagellates will tend to dominate the phytoplankton of smaller tropical lakes and temperate lakes in late summer.

The Summer Season: Heat Balance, Upwelling and Hypolimnetic Entrainment

An important feature of lake heating is the average summer temperature of the epilimnion and hypolimnion. The epilimnion heat balance is complicated since heat losses at night and back radiation or evaporative cooling vary with day-to-day weather patterns. The situation in the hypolimnion is much simpler since heat flows are buffered by the lake bed and the blanket of the epilimnion. The main factor influencing the hypolimnetic temperature is the onset of stratification. If the lake stratifies early in the season, when the water is cold, the hypolimnion will be cooler than when stratification occurs later. The first permanent thermocline is usually established by a storm, and storms do not occur at the same time each year.

Once stratification is established, *direct heating* is the only important heat source for the hypolimnion in most lakes. Direct heating occurs when the lake is sufficiently transparent to allow light to penetrate below the thermocline. As described earlier, long-wave radiation, including thermal radiation, is absorbed in the first few centimeters of lake water. The thermocline depth and that of the photic zone are roughly equal in many lakes, but in transparent lakes this is not so. Visible light penetrates deeper and is converted to heat in the hypolimnion. In transparent lakes with dark rocky or muddy bottoms the lake bed is directly heated and releases heat to the overlying water. In Castle Lake, most of the heating of the upper hypolimnion is due to direct conversion of visible radiation into heat (Bachmann and Goldman, 1965).

Upwelling of cold nutrient-rich water in the ocean along the western shores of the major continents produces rich fisheries. Upwelling also occurs in lakes when high winds drive the warm, less dense epilimnion to the lee shore and expose the underlying thermocline to the wind. Cold hypolimnetic water may then upwell to the surface, where the wind mixes it into the epilimnion. Upwelling is most noticeable in larger lakes like Baikal, Michigan, and Lake Tahoe but occurs less dramatically in smaller lakes.

One might expect indirect heating of the hypolimnion by conduction from the warmer adjacent epilimnion. Heating would thus be regulated by the thermal conductivity of the metalimnion in the same way as a window controls heat flow from a warm room to the outside air. Since the metalimnion is a dynamic mobile layer, this uniform heat flow does not, in fact, occur as expected. What actually happens is that the thermocline in lakes gradually descends from spring to autumn and the epilimnion becomes deeper at the expense of the hypolimnion (Fig. 4-2c). This process is not uniform, and the thermocline may fall and rise over some weeks (Fig. 4-8). The upper part of the hypolimnion is incorporated into the epilimnion throughout the

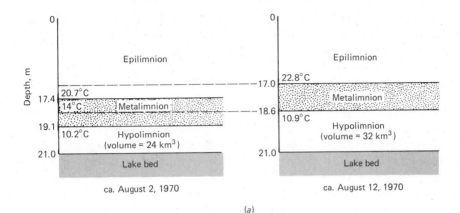

ca. August 2, 1970 ca. August 12, 1970

(a)

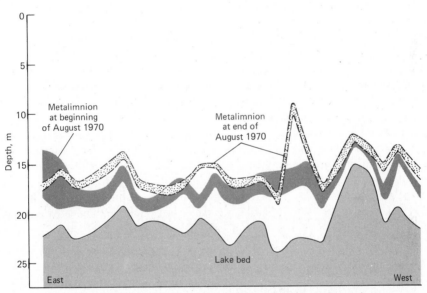

Distance along lake (stations start near the east and proceed to west)

(b)

Figure 4-8 Hypolimnetic entrainment in Lake Erie in summer. Short bursts of high wind after periods of calm caused the changes shown. Heat, water, and nutrients were transferred indirectly between hypolimnion and epilimnion via the metalimnion. The effect on the otherwise isolated hypolimnion was more obvious than in the epilimnion, where heat losses and gains can occur continually due to solar heating and evaporative cooling. The effect was also exaggerated because Lake Erie has an unusually thin hypolimnion for such a large lake. (a) In 10 days, 10^{15} kcal of heat and 8 km³ of water were transferred down into the hypolimnion. During relatively calm conditions (early August) the metalimnion was thicker (1.7 m) than after some windy days (1.58 m). The metalimnion incorporated water from both the hypolimnion and the epilimnion in calm weather but was reduced in size by winds that moved water to the epilimnion. (b) Hypolimnetic entrainment varied spatially over a longer time period. Note that the metalimnion and hypolimnion varied considerably from the average values shown in (a). Large gravity waves (Chap. 5) on the metalimnion caused the up-and-down motion so obvious in (b). Modified from Burns and Ross (1972).

summer by storm-induced turbulence near the top of the thermocline, by upwelling, or by hypolimnetic entrainment (Fig. 4-8).

The very existence of a thermocline is testimony to its strong resistance to vertical mixing. Diffusion (Table 5-8) across the metalimnion is very low, but some transfer of nutrients has been observed. This transfer can occur if the hypolimnetic water moves, carrying nutrients with it (Fig. 4-8). Vertical migrations of fish, zooplankton, and flagellate algae also account for the transfer, as they may feed in one place and excrete in another. In many cases physical transfer of water can account for nutrient transport. Movement of hypolimnetic water across the thermocline occurs in several lakes, including Lake Perris, California, a popular recreational reservoir east of Los Angeles. This reservoir has an anoxic hypolimnion in late summer. When nutrients in the epilimnion of this lake are monitored on a diel cycle, there is a sudden rise in epilimnetic iron and hydrogen sulfide during the period of maximum wind in midafternoon (Table 4-1). This upward movement of iron and hydrogen sulfide indicates entrainment of hypolimnetic water into the epilimnion.

In some large lakes edge leakage is sufficiently small relative to the epilimnetic volume to allow measurement of the transfer of heat and nutrients across the thermocline. This process, called *hypolimnetic entrainment,* involves an initial transfer of water from hypolimnion and epilimnion to the metalimnion during calm weather (Bums and Ross, 1972; Blanton, 1973). During a storm the metalimnion decreases in thickness, transferring water back to the epilimnion and sometimes to the hypolimnion (Fig. 4-8). Relatively small changes in wind speed affect the thermocline depth (Boyce, 1974). During calm weather the thermocline depth decreases and the metalimnion volume increases at the expense of both the epilimnion and the hypolimnion. Thus hypolimnetic water is incorporated into the metalimnion. When strong winds resume, the epilimnion reincorporates some of the metalimnion and, indirectly, some of the hypolimnion water. Figure 4-8 indicates changes in volumes of these three layers of Lake Erie. The volume of water transferred occurs over several days and is quite small compared to that of the entire epilimnion. The effect on the temperature of the epilimnion is thus minimal. The most significant effect of hypolimnetic entrainment is the transport of relatively large amounts of growth-limiting elements upward.

TABLE 4-1

DIEL VARIATIONS IN CONCENTRATIONS OF TOTAL DISSOLVED IRON (μg liter^{-1}) IN PERRIS RESERVOIR, CALIFORNIA, ON AUGUST 17, 1976, DUE TO TRANSFER OF IRON FROM THE ANOXIC HYPOLIMNION THROUGH OR AROUND THE THERMOCLINE

Note that in the lower epilimnion at 10 m iron a noticeable smell of H_2S increaed following afternoon winds.

Depth, m	Hour		
	0900	1200	1500
0	7.5	6.0	9.0
10	7.5	17.3	20.3
16	47.1	53.4	49.9

From Elder and Horne (1977).

THE END OF STRATIFICATION: THE FALL OVERTURN AND WINTER

The prime reason for the loss of thermal stratification in autumn is the reduction in heat input from solar radiation, which occurs while evaporative cooling continues at high summer rates. Most lakes experience a gradual lowering of the thermocline in late summer (Fig. 4-2c). The eventual total mixing or *overturn* is of such great importance in stratified lakes because only then can nutrients and gases such as oxygen be uniformly distributed. In summer the lighter epilimnion overlies the denser hypolimnion to produce a low overall center of gravity. The large turbulent energy input due to storms raises the center of gravity of the lake water to the winter position. From Eqs. (3) and (4), a decrease in heat inflow q_s amplifies the effect of wind speed U_a^3 on the thermocline depth D. The net effect is a series of declining thermoclines. This incorporation from below of hypolimnetic water into the epilimnion provides nutrients for the autumn algal bloom (Fig. 12-3).

Evaporation at the lake surface in autumn cools the water, increasing its density. However, the cooling is not uniform across the water surface. One can see this by observing the patches of smooth and ruffled water on a lake as the wind swirls across. For this reason temporary patches of downwelling several meters across appear and vanish on the lake surface in autumn. These cool sinking patches are analogous to the air thermals so effectively utilized by soaring birds and gliders. They help to maintain the underwater microclimate and high species diversity often found in the autumn plankton.

The Winter Lake: Inverse Stratification and Ice Cover

In cold climates ice forms within a month or two of destratification and may persist for several months. Ice cover isolates the lake water from the mixing forces of the wind. Ice forms at 0°C at the very surface of the lake, but the rest of the lake water is somewhat warmer, between 0 and 4°C (Chap. 2). This is because water's maximum density is at about 4°C and thus ice and the coldest water float near the surface. Under these conditions an *inverse thermal stratification* can occur (Fig. 4-2). Inverse stratification can only occur between 0 and 4°C and persists only where ice isolates the lake from the wind. In lakes where the ice cover is not permanent, inverse stratification tends to be lost during open water periods.

HEAT CYCLES AND HEAT BUDGETS

The effects of the mechanisms already described can be summarized in the concept of the *heat cycle* (Fig. 4-9). In contrast to upwelling and entrainment, heat cycles are relatively easily measured. They give a total accounting of the gain and loss of heat by the system during a specified time period, expressed as calories transferred per square centimeter of lake surface. The length of the water column considered is the average depth of the lake. The heat income and losses from a lake surface vary greatly with time of day, latitude, altitude, and exposure to the sun as well as shading from surrounding mountains. In general, there is greater variation in heat input and output at higher elevations and latitudes than there is for the more uniform climate of the equator (Fig. 4-10 *a, b*).

The components of a lake's heat cycle are summarized in the following equation:

$$S = R_n - E - H - Q \qquad (5)$$

where S = storage rate of heat in lake
R_n = net radiation
E = evaporation
H = sensible heat transfer, which is roughly equal to conduction
Q = advective heat inputs and outputs due to water currents or inflow and outflow of streams

In detail, S is the rate of heat entering a lake (cal cm^{-2} min^{-1}) and is due to the following processes:

R_n (net radiation) is the direct and indirect solar radiation absorbed at the lake surface (Chap. 3) plus the long-wave radiation given off by the air minus long-wave radiation back-radiated from the water surface. Net radiation depends on air temperature, air vapor pressure, and cloud cover.

E (evaporation) is the amount of heat lost by evaporation and depends on the wind, surface temperature, and air vapor pressure.

H (sensible heat transfer) is the amount of heat lost by conduction from the water to air and depends on the difference between the air and

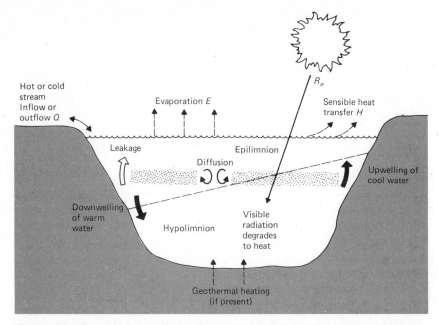

Figure 4-9 The major heat and water flows across the edges of the metalimnion during summer. Bold lines are advective flows of water (currents); thin lines are diffusive transfer. Upwelling is most obvious in large lakes when the thermocline tilts significantly, as often occurs at the upwind end of a large lake during storms. Leakage probably occurs continually as an irregular flow around the edge of the thermocline where it meets the lake bed. Heat diffusion is always present but very difficult to measure directly. In transparent lakes some sunlight will penetrate below the thermocline and directly heat the hypolimnion or sediments.

the water surface temperature as well as the wind velocity.

Q (advective heat inputs and outputs) is the heat loss due to an outflow of warm surface water being replaced by an inflow of cold stream water (may be reversed in special circumstances, e.g., hot springs).

We neglect here geothermal heating, loss by conduction to the basin sediments, or the solar heating of sediments.

Thus the storage rate S depends on solar radiation, cloud cover, surface and air temperatures, humidity, and wind speed as well as the net amount of heat entering the lake. The changes in this complex set of variables are shown for an actual lake over a day or so in Fig

4-7. As already noted, lakes at high altitudes or low latitudes receive more heat from the sun than those near sea level or nearer the north and south poles (Fig. 4-10). A deep lake with a large water volume may contain more heat than a shallow lake at the same location merely because it has more water (Table 4-2). Local effects, such as exposure to sunlight, protection from the wind, and warm submerged springs, are most important in smaller lakes. Large lakes such as the Great Lakes actually modify the surrounding area by virtue of their great heat content. The microclimate created may be locally important in preventing early frosts.

The *maximum heat content,* once called the *annual heat budget,* of a lake is the total heat per unit surface area that enters the lake between the

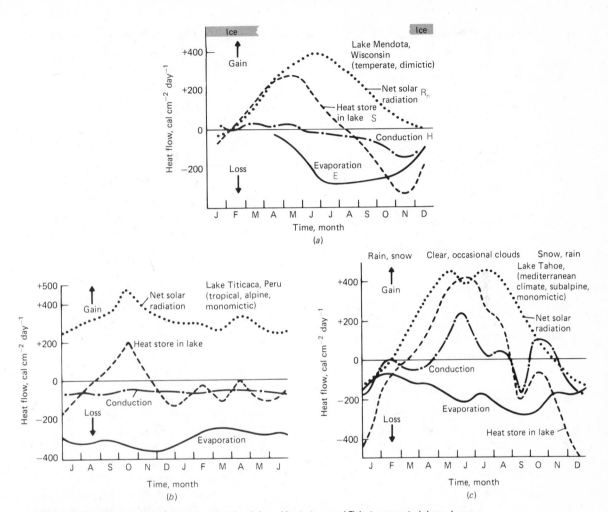

Figure 4-10 Heat cycles in three contrasting lakes. Heat storage (*S*) in temperate lakes shows a single large and regular annual cycle, while tropical lakes have smaller and irregular heat storage cycles. Evaporation (*E*) in temperate lakes is relatively low compared with that in tropical lakes. (*a*) In the typical temperate, dimictic Lake Mendota, Wisconsin, spring and summer radiation (*R*ₙ) heat the lake and heat losses are minimal. After midsummer the now warm epilimnion loses substantial amounts of heat via evaporation. This loss continues at much the same rate through autumn, when sensible heat loss (*H*), akin to conduction, amplifies total heat losses. Redrawn from Ragotzkie (1978). (*b*) In large, high-altitude, monomictic tropical Lake Titicaca, both net radiation and evaporation are more uniform and show little seasonal change. Redrawn from Kittel and Richerson (1978). (*c*) In subalpine monomictic Lake Tahoe, summers are relatively cloudless and the net radiation input peaks markedly. Redrawn from Myrup et al. (1979).

TABLE 4-2

PHYSICAL CHARACTERISTICS, MAXIMUM HEAT CONTENTS, STRATIFICATION PERIOD, AND LENGTH OF ISOTHERMAL MIXING FOR THREE ADJACENT WISCONSIN DIMICTIC LAKES AND THREE MONOMICTIC LAKES IN BRITAIN

Note that the deeper the lake, the greater the heat stored and the longer the period of isothermal mixing.

Lake	$\bar{z}$, m	Mean max. temp., °C	Heat contents, cal cm^{-2}	Area, km^2	Volume, m$^3 \times 10^6$	Isothermal mixing, days	
						Fall	Spring
Mendota	12.4	20.0	24,100	38.7	480	50 or 66	73
Monona	7.7	23.3	17,600	14.0	108	66	63
Waubesa	4.6	25.2	11,400	8.3	38	Polymictic in summer	
Windermere: North Basin	27	~20	17,500	8.2	221	All winter (Nov-May)	
South Basin	19.4	~20	15,700	6.1	118	All winter (Oct-May)	
Loch Ness	133	~20	37,200	56.4	7500	All winter (Jan-June)	

Modified from Stewart (1973), Moritimer and Worthington (1942), and Mill (1895).

time of lowest and highest temperatures. It is not a true budget since it only contains heat gains and the term *maximum heat content* is a more appropriate term. The maximum heat content reflects the total heat input from the coldest winter day to the warmest summer day without considering daily fluctuations in between. Not all the heat is in the water, as some is absorbed by the sediments. The maximum heat content of a lake is the product of the weighted averages of mean lake temperatures and lake depth. Mean temperature is measured by summing the product of temperature and volume fractions for a series of layers of the lake. The mean temperature is the content of heat per unit volume (cal cm^{-3}), assuming density and specific heat are equal to unity. Total heat is heat per unit area (cal cm^{-2}) above 0°C (Birge, 1915; Stewart, 1973).

The maximum heat contents of dimictic Lake Mendota and adjacent lakes near the center of the continental United States may be considered rather typical of inland temperate lakes near sea level (Table 4-2). Those of the monomictic lakes of the English Lake District and Loch Ness, Scotland, are typical of coastal waters (Table 4-2). Table 4-2 shows that mean depth is the dominating factor in maximum heat content (Gorham, 1964). Shallow lakes stratify, destratify, freeze, and thaw more rapidly than adjacent deep lakes.

The effect of increasing the maximum heat content is to delay the freezing of dimictic lakes. Inflowing sediment and nutrients as well as thermal power plant discharges may also affect heat cycles. Pollution may change freezing and thawing dates or the onset of thermal stratification, which will affect the lake's chemistry and biota.

The onset of freezing and the time of thermal stratification are important. They produce major physical and, later, chemical changes to which almost all lake biota must respond. The most obvious effect of stratification is to isolate the photosynthetic zone from the aphotic zone and thus stop the mixing of algae into dark waters. Variations in the times of maximum blooms of the diatom *Asterionella* in various lakes of the English Lake District are due to the mean depth of the lakes and associated maximum heat contents since the shallower lakes stratify before the deep ones. Stratification eventually results in nutrient depletion in the epilimnion, since nutrients in the hypolimnion are not mixed into the upper waters as long as stratification persists.

Stratification also affects the oxygen cycle in lakes. In the fall dimictic lakes have only a short period of holomixis in which to satisfy any summer oxygen debt that has accumulated in the hypolimnion. In some mountain and high-latitude lakes autumn overturn is followed so rapidly by ice formation that there is insufficient time to transfer all the needed oxygen from the air to the water and sediments. This condition is most obvious in eutrophic lakes. Similarly, limited holomixis may occur in the spring, when a warm period melts the last of the ice cover and produces thermal stratification within a week in small sheltered lakes.

Winter kills, in which large numbers of fish can die, occur where under-ice oxygen is depleted. Since most fish do not overwinter in lakes without oxygen, the variable period of autumnal mixing prior to ice formation is a deciding factor in the winter kill. The problem is aggravated by snow cover, which prevents light from providing photosynthetically generated oxygen during winter.

Cold air temperatures, evaporative cooling, and wind mixing will produce a water column temperature below 4°C prior to ice formation. Often the entire water column will be about 1°C when ice forms. After freezing, the lake water gains some heat from the sediments, which cool more slowly than the water itself. Any heat losses occur via the latent heat required to thicken the ice layer, which increases through midwinter. When lake ice melts there is a slight dip in the spring temperature rise caused by the latent heat required to melt the ice. This is not surprising; in Lake Mendota, for example, the heat required to freeze and melt the ice cover is about a quarter of the heat content of the lake (Stewart, 1973).

In a few lakes other sources of heating are important for the lake heat cycle. In amictic Lake Vanda, Antarctica, geothermal heating of the lake sediment and overlying water occurs in the salt-stabilized monimolimnion at 25°C, which exists beneath a layer of 8°C water. Geothermal heating can also occur in lakes in areas of volcanic activity, where heat transfer may be direct or may result from hot springs entering the lake. The dramatic thermal vents in Yellowstone National Park in Wyoming also heat the lakes and streams around them, some to the boiling point. Lake Managua in Nicaragua has hot springs entering it that could be tapped for geothermal steam and used for electric power generation (Fig. 4-11).

WASTE HEAT DISCHARGES

The effects of changes in heat content due to thermal discharges are of major concern to limnologists and environmental engineers. The example of Lake Monona, Wisconsin, illustrates this. A power station there uses lake water for cooling that could, theoretically, increase the temperature of the entire lake by 10°C each year (0.03°C per day). This represents 50 percent of the total heat content of the lake. Despite the heating, the lake temperature remains unaltered, because 0.03°C is a very small change compared with the daily 2 to 3°C change due to solar heating and evaporative cooling and conduction. These daily heat fluxes mask the effects of thermal pollution. Similarly, the natural heat-buffering capacity of any lake prevents large or rapid changes in temperature on unusually sunny or cloudy days. The absolute amounts of daily heating and cooling in the mixed layer are large compared with the amount retained or lost in the epilimnion. Slow, small changes in temperature

Figure 4-11 Volcanic heating of Lake Managua, Nicaragua. The bare areas contain hot springs with water at near-boiling temperatures, which runs into the lake. The heat from the slopes of Momatombo Volcano (to the right) extends below the water's edge. Geothermal heating is, however, insignificant in most of the world's lakes.

have little effect on living communities because they adapt to the temperature changes.

The hot water from the power station is discharged to the surface waters. If it were discharged to the hypolimnion in summer, drastic changes in the lake heat cycle would occur, because the epilimnion would insulate the hypolimnion, preventing heat loss to the atmosphere. A probable result would be destratification. Only by hypolimnial heating can waste heat discharges produce large shifts in lake heat content and cause biotic changes.

One noticeable effect of thermal pollution in Lake Monona is the accelerated ice breakup in spring. Over a period of 115 years, the average difference in ice breakup in lakes Mendota and Monona was only 1 day; for the 15 years since construction of the power station Lake Monona has opened 19 days before Lake Mendota. The reason is that the heat from the water discharged by the power station cannot be dissipated to the atmosphere in winter because the snow-covered ice acts as an insulating blanket.

Of course, in very small lakes waste heat can produce larger effects. Some factors that affect heat content are not easily changed. These include mean depth as well as all of the other variables in Eq. (4).

Stratification of heat and light imposes on lakes a fundamental physical structure within which animals and plants must live. Waves and currents weave an organized pattern on the stratified water column, modifying the distribution of plankton within and among the layers. This motion is described in Chapter 5. A study of water motion is perhaps less intuitive than the topics discussed thus far, in that it requires a more mathematical approach, but it reveals an important aspect of lake structure.

FURTHER READINGS

Birge, E. A. 1915. ''The Heat Budgets of American and European Lakes.'' *Trans. Wis. Acad. Sci.,* **18**:166–213.

Boyce, F. M. 1974. ''Some Aspects of Great Lakes

Physics of Importance to Biological and Chemical Processes.'' *J. Fish. Res. Board Can.,* **31:**689–730.

Denison, P. J., and F. C. Elder. 1970. ''Thermal Inputs to the Great Lakes 1968–2000.'' *Proc. 13th Conf. Great Lakes Res.,* pp. 811–828.

Gorham, E. 1964. ''Morphometric Control of Annual Heat Budgets in Temperate Lakes.'' *Limnol. Oceanogr.,* **9:**525–529.

Hutchinson, G. E. 1957. *A Treatise on Limnology,* vol. 1, chap. 7. Wiley, New York.

Imberger, J. 1985. ''The Diurnal Mixed Layer.'' *Limnol. Oceanogr.,* **20:**737–770.

Lewis, W. M. 1973. ''The Thermal Regime of Lake Lanao (Philippines) and Its Theoretical Implications for Tropical Lakes.'' *Limnol. Oceanogr.,* **18:**200–217.

Likens, G. E., and N. M. Johnson. 1969. ''Measurement and Analysis of the Annual Heat Budget for the Sediments in Two Wisconsin Lakes.'' *Limnol. Oceanogr.,* **14:**115–135.

Stewart, K. M. 1972. ''Isotherms under Ice.'' *Verh. Int. Ver. Limnol.,* **18:**303–311.

Talling, J. F. 1969. ''The Incidence of Vertical Mixing, and Some Biological and Chemical Consequences, in Tropical African Lakes.'' *Verh. Int. Ver. Limnol.,* **17:**998–1012.

CHAPTER 5

Water Movement

OVERVIEW

The motion of water has profound consequences for the chemistry and biology of lakes. Wind is the primary force moving lake water at all depths, although the mixing due to evaporative cooling discussed in Chap. 4 is important. The combination of heat and wind produces a lake structure consisting of many short-lived layers or patches that are more turbulent and chemically and biologically distinct from the surrounding water. The kinetic energy of the wind is transferred to the water to produce an irregular *turbulent* cascade of kinetic and potential energy from that contained in large lake-sized eddies to the smaller, more rapid ones. The distribution of energy over various wavelengths, called an *energy spectrum,* can be used as a unifying concept for understanding the complexity of features that characterize movement in an enclosed body of water.

There are two kinds of water motion, *periodic* or *rhythmic waves* and *nonperiodic* or *arrhythmic currents.* Waves consist of the rise and fall of water particles, involving some oscillation but no net flow. Currents consist of net unidirectional flows of water. Currents and waves nor-

mally occur together. Part of the wind's kinetic energy goes into the continuous formation of surface waves, which lose their form and dissipate their energy as they break on the downwind shore. Currents build up much more slowly than waves but eventually contain most of the lake's kinetic energy. In addition, the wind induces *internal waves* in the thermocline and the hypolimnion.

Water currents at the lake surface are called *surface drift.* In large lakes and estuaries surface currents eventually flow at approixmately 45° to the direction of the prevailing wind. This flow results from the effect of the earth's rotation. Water currents below the surface move at progressively greater angles to the wind the greater the distance from the surface. Finally the deepest currents flow in the opposite direction to the wind. This spiral-staircase-like flow of currents is called an *Ekman spiral.*

Lakes are mixed most vigorously by storm winds, which produce surface and internal waves as well as strong horizontal currents. Although surface waves are obvious, internal waves occur at the thermocline. The short-wavelength, low-amplitude surface gravity wind waves are familiar. Less familiar are the very long surface waves, which may resonate and reflect back and forth from shore to shore. These are termed *surface seiches.* The natural resonant frequencies of the basin also select among the large-amplitude *internal gravity waves* for certain wavelengths. These are the *internal seiches,* which occur at the thermocline. Short-wavelength internal gravity waves may become unstable and break in midlake, causing considerable local turbulent mixing and even transfer of hypolimnion water into the epilimnion. Formation of these *turbulent billows* is most pronounced near the base of the thermocline.

Vertical mixing and horizontal flow are caused by the surface wind. The currents of the Ekman spiral may be thought of as slabs of water moving at different speeds and directions. The contact between these layers imparts a vertical displacement or shear stress to the water in each layer, producing vertical mixing between them. *Surface wind-shear* effects are mostly confined to the epilimnion. *Breaking waves* contribute to vertical mixing, and *Langmuir spirals* provide a more organized vertical mixing energy with a wavelength about equal to the depth of the thermocline. At certain times of year evaporative cooling at the lake surface is the major vertical mixing force. Nocturnal sinking of cooler waters to the bottom of the epilimnion stirs the mixed layer by *convective mixing.* This process is more efficient than wind mixing and is sometimes the main source of mixing in stratified lakes in temperate and tropical climates. The epilimnion usually mixes daily unless prevented by thermal barriers, which occur during sunny, windless periods. Turbulent energy is finally lost as heat. Movement in deep water below the thermocline is slow, and substances near the lake bed are only gradually circulated throughout the hypolimnion. In large lakes the main energy for deep water mixing may come from large-amplitude, long-period internal gravity waves at the thermocline. The resulting turbulence at the lake bed moves dissolved substances up from the sediment-water interface. In large exposed lakes *upwelling* and *downwelling* produced at the lake edges by storms are a major mixing force.

Inflowing rivers are usually more important sources of biostimulants and toxicants than of kinetic energy. River plumes extending into lakes spread more horizontally than vertically and sink if their density is greater than that of the lake. However, mixing of discrete plumes into a lake is quite small, and there is a tendency for such inflows to cling to one shoreline. Water movement in estuaries, rivers, and streams has many features in common with lakes, but important differences are discussed in Chaps. 16 and 19 on flowing waters and estuaries.

In this chapter we consider the importance of water motion and its measurement, laminar and turbulent flow, the kinetic energy spectrum, advective and diffusive transport of energy, motion in the epilimnion, at the thermocline, and in the hypolimnion, and the effect of rivers.

INTRODUCTION: IMPORTANCE OF WATER MOVEMENT

The continual motion of the aquatic environment provides its unique character among ecosystems (Fig. 5-1). In lakes water movement transports phytoplankton from a high-light, low-nutrient, low-predator environment near the surface to the dark nutrient-laden deeper waters, which contain numerous predators. The one-way rapid water currents dominate the ecology of plants and animals in rivers, streams, and estuaries (Chaps. 16, 19). On land large physical changes in the environment tend to take place over a period greater than the life span of most terrestrial organisms, which promotes specific adaptations. Aquatic organisms must adapt to a wide range of conditions, and even then are truly at the mercy of their ever-changing environment.

Water movements are critical to the distribution of all forms of energy, momentum, nutrients, dissolved gases, algae, some zooplankton, and sedimentary material. The distribution of solar

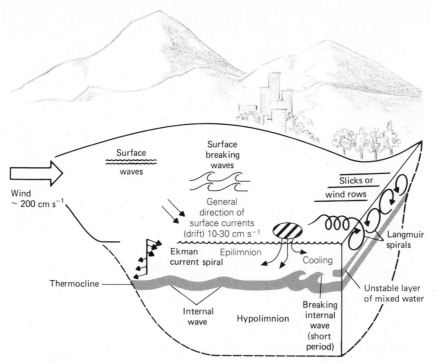

FIGURE 5-1 Forces (wind, gravity, evaporation, and the earth's rotation) and the resultant water currents and waves. Wind moves the water, gravity makes horizontal flow easier than vertical, evaporation cools surface water which then sinks, and the earth's rotation moves surface flows to the right (northern hemisphere) and to the left (southern hemisphere).

and wind energy produces some form of thermal stratification in all lakes and stable summer stratification in most (Chap. 4). The lack of water mixing between the warm epilimnion and cooler hypolimnion is a major factor determining lake productivity. Similarly, the rapid top-to-bottom stirring in shallow lakes during the summer is extremely important in recycling the nutrients, which often support high levels of productivity.

MEASUREMENT

Lake currents range from almost 0 to more than 30 cm s^{-1}. The measurement of rapid water currents is relatively straightforward for horizontal flows, but weak and vertical currents are very difficult to estimate accurately. The three principal devices used are current meters, drifters, and dyes. The basic instrument for measuring

strong water flow usually consists of a propeller that is turned by the water current. A common choice is the Savonius rotor. Some instruments swivel horizontally and vertically and thus always face into the current (Fig. 5-2). A number of current meters are available but most are too insensitive or fragile for routine use. For example, for rapidly changing currents a meter with speedy response, such as the delicate hot-film probe, may be necessary.

Alternatives to current meters are *drifters* and *drogues,* which present a large surface area to the current. Except at the water surface, a marker such as a small flag must be attached so that movements can be followed. The drag of the surface marker should be slight compared to that of the main device. Usually several drogues are placed at different depths. Motion can be plotted over time using photography or observations

FIGURE 5-2 A profiling current meter. The current velocities are measured by a freely suspended vane (white can-shaped object). The direction of the current flows are measured by first finding the position of the vane (which has an electrode) relative to the two other pairs of electrodes (sticklike objects) that are also freely suspended. The vane electrode picks up signals at different frequencies from the two pairs of electrodes, indicating its orientation and hence the direction of the water current. Results from this apparatus are shown in Figs. 5-22 and 5-23. Photograph courtesy of S. A. Thorpe, Institute of Oceanographic Sciences, England.

from a ship's crow's nest or the nearest hillside. This method is normally used over a few hours on calm days.

Fluorescent dyes have been used in studies of horizontal and vertical water motion. This method requires many measurements of a moving and expanding dye patch but is not recommended for measuring strong currents.

The inexpensive but effective method of using an orange attached to a fine fishing line was demonstrated by I. R. Smith in Lake George, Africa. The neutrally buoyant orange is carred by the surface currents. Keeping the line taut and placing knots at 50-m intervals gives an accurate short-term current measurement. A similar technique on the ocean prompted the seamen of old to call the velocity term a *knot.*

Remote sensing from aircraft or satellites measures surface-water masses over periods of days provided a sufficiently obvious feature is available, for example, a sediment plume or temperature difference. The method can be extended to shallow-surface films by using the high reflectance of blue-green algae in the near-infrared (NIR) wave bands. Repeated photography of distinct features shows movement relative to a fixed point, normally the shoreline (Fig. 5-3). The effects of a typical daily wind pattern as it affects near-surface organisms are given in Fig. 5-4.

LAMINAR AND TURBULENT FLOW

We experience laminar and turbulent flows every day. *Laminar flow* is the smooth slipping of water particles past each other or an obstruction and has little drag on moving objects. Dolphins, most fish, and submarines possess body designs that maximize laminar flow past them, causing minimal energy expenditure. In contrast, *turbulent flow* is the random, chaotic tumbling of the

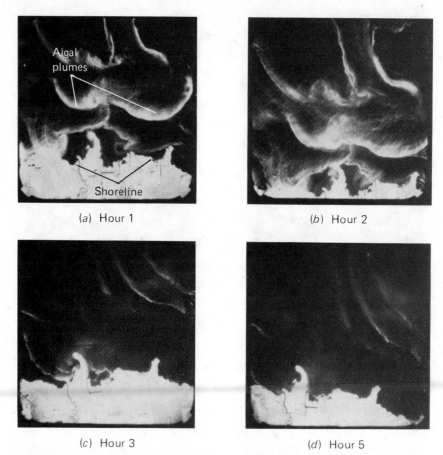

(a) Hour 1

(b) Hour 2

(c) Hour 3

(d) Hour 5

FIGURE 5-3 Changes in surface patterns over a 5-h period in Clear Lake, California, beginning at 7 a.m. The large turbulent eddy is outlined by the high reflectance of blue-green algae in the near-infrared (Fig. 3-7). Note how the eddy vanished in a few hours, probably due to the setting up of a temporary thermocline. The areas shown are 5 km across. There was no inflow to the lake at this time, and there was also no wind. Thus motion was mostly generated by convection currents due to evaporation. From Wrigley and Horne (1975).

water particles around each other or any object passing through the water. These tumbling motions are described as *eddies*. Most lake, river, or estuarine flow motions are turbulent. A burning cigarette provides a good example of the two types of motion: the initial smoke plume is laminar while the more distant plumes show turbulent flow. A drop of dye in a beaker of water or the pouring of milk into a cup of coffee produces three-dimensional turbulence.

The onset of turbulence in a lake can be predicted from the *Reynolds number, R_e*, the ratio of inertial forces ($\sim U^2/d$) to viscous forces ($\sim vU/d^2$).

Thus

$$R_e = \frac{Ud}{v} = \frac{\text{stirring energy}}{\text{viscosity of water}} \qquad (1)$$

where U = water-current velocity

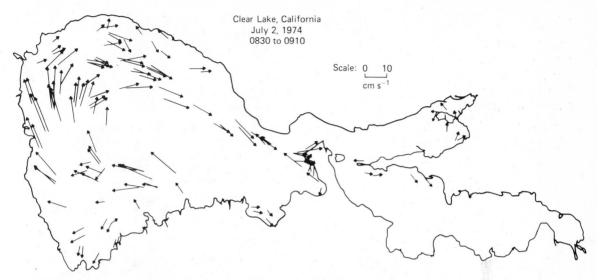

FIGURE 5-4   Vector diagram of wind-driven resuspended sediment movements on July 2, 1974, as recorded by remote sensing. The length of the lines is proportional to the water velocity. Most sustained currents are in the range of 2 to 15 cm s^{-1}. From Wrigley and Horne (1975).

d = depth or thickness of water layer concerned

v = kinematic viscosity of water, a property of the water molecules (Table 3-3)

A large R_e value implies high water velocities, a thick water layer, low viscosity, or a combination of these three factors. A value can be assigned to R_e to distinguish turbulent from laminar flows. When the Reynolds number is less than a critical value ($R_e \sim 500$), the flow will be laminar, and at $R_e \sim 2000$ the flow will be turbulent (Fig. 5-5). It is now accepted that most lake motion is turbulent and that if laminar flows are present they are in transition to a turbulent state. For a typical lake, values might be $U = 10$ cm s^{-1}, $d = 10$ m (depth of lake or thermocline), $v = 0.01$ cm^2 s^{-1}. Thus from Eq. (1), $R_e = 10^6$, much larger than 2000, and the flow is turbulent. In a stratified fluid, such as a lake, the balance between the buoyancy of a water mass and the mixing power of the wind must also be considered. The ratio of these two forces, the *Richardson number,* and its adaptation to any given lake

using the *Wedderburn number,* was considered in Chap. 4. Detailed analysis of turbulent flows has been described as "one of the last unsolved problems of classical physics." However, some progress can be made by considering the typical scales or dimensions of various lake motions, which are usually measurable as waves. For example, the common surface waves, surface gravity waves, have approximately the following dimensions:

Length L:
  Horizontal, 10 m
  Vertical, 1 m
Time T, 1 s
Velocity V, 10 m s^{-1}

Another common lake surface phenomenon, Langmuir spirals (Figs. 5-13, 5-14), has very different dimensions: L (horizontal) = m to km, L (vertical) = 10 m, $T = 10^3$ s, $V = 1$ cm s^{-1}. Using these scales, a kind of taxonomic order can be given to these apparently chaotic motions (Table 5-1).

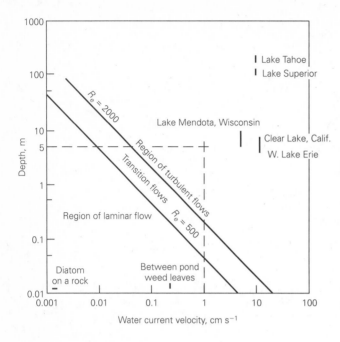

FIGURE 5-5 Idealized diagram to illustrate the conditions for turbulence in lakes. Lake surface currents are rarely slow enough to allow laminar flow. Lake water motion is almost always turbulent. Laminar flow can occur in aquatic ecosystems in very calm, very small sites, for example, between the leaf blades of a submerged aquatic plant such as *Potomogeton,* the common pondweed. Here *d* in equation 1 is < 1 cm and, as these plants are characteristic of slow-moving waters, $U = 1$ cm s^{-1}. Thus $R_e = 50$ and flow is laminar. Pennate diatoms gliding over rocks and logs are almost always in the laminar layer. Modified from Smith (1975).

THE KINETIC ENERGY SPECTRUM

Energy of motion is designated kinetic energy (KE) and manifests itself in two main phenomenona: periodic wavelike motion and aperiodic currents. Each type of wave and current has captured a characteristic proportion of the applied wind energy. Waves are characterized by distinctive lengths, heights, periods, and frequencies (Fig. 5-6). *Length* is measured between two adjacent crests or troughs. *Height* is the vertical distance between the crest and trough, and the *amplitude* is half this distance. *Period* is the time required for the passage of two crests or two troughs past a fixed point. The inverse of the period is called the *frequency.* The major types of motion occurring in lakes are shown in Table 5-1 and Fig. 5-1.

After KE is transferred from wind to the water surface, the energy is distributed vertically through the water column. Energy is not imparted to the whole lake but is transferred unevenly depending on the lake's morphometry and latitude and on the irregular nature of the wind. As mentioned previously, free wind-driven surface waves have wavelengths up to about 10 m and regular periodicity of approximately 1 s. Wavelength and period are mainly determined by the *fetch,* or distance of open water over which the wind blows. *Surface waves* retain little of the wind's energy and merely oscillate water particles in a small ellipse (Fig. 5-6, Table 5-1). In contrast, wind-driven horizontal lake *currents* are basinwide, and the eddies or gyres produced may be 10^5 m in diameter in large lakes. They have an irregular "periodicity" of about 10^5 seconds. These large-scale currents contain the major part of the applied wind energy and cause much of the vigorous horizontal and vertical mixing in lakes (Table 5-1, Figs. 5-1, 5-7).

Measurement of lake waves shows that motions are restricted to certain time and space scales. We call KE(λ_1, λ_2) the kinetic energy in lake water motion between two wavelengths λ_1 and λ_2. For small intervals,

$$\text{KE}(\lambda_1, \lambda_2) = \bar{E}_{(\lambda)} (\lambda_1 - \lambda_2) \qquad (2)$$

TABLE 5-1

SIZE, FREQUENCY, VELOCITY, AND IMPORTANCE OF WAVES, CURRENTS, AND OTHER LAKE WATER MOTIONS

Type of motion	Length scale		Time Scale	Velocity scale	Importance to kinetic energy spectrum	Importance for plankton (P_t) or nutrient recycling (R)
	Horizontal	Vertical				
Horizontal Surface systems						
Wind-driven surface gravity waves	1–10 m	1 m	1 s	10 m s^{-1}	Small	P_t, R: small
Standing surface gravity waves (surface seiches)	1 km–100 km	10 cm	2–10 h	2 cm s^{-1}	Small	P_t, R: small
Surface wind drift and whole-lake gyres	1 km up	1–25 m	Days	1–30 cm s^{-1}	Large	P_t, R: large
Deep-water systems						
Short freely propagating internal waves	100 m	2–10 m	2–10 min	2 cm s^{-1}	Major mixing energy at the thermocline	R: summer moderate
Long freely propagating internal waves steered by lake shape (including internal seiches)	to 10 km	2–20 m	1 day	50 cm s^{-1}	Major source of motion in hypolimnion of large lakes	P_t, R: moderate
Vertical (in epilimnion) Random flows						
Vertical diffusion of momentum	1 cm–100 cm	1 cm–10 m	1 min	1 cm s^{-1}	A major vertical force	P_t, R: important
Breaking waves	1 m	1 m	Mins	50–500 cm s^{-1}	Moderate to small	P_t: moderate
Organized flows, Langmuir spirals	50 m–100 m	2–20 m	5 min	0–8 cm s^{-1}	Moderate to small	P_t: important
Hypolimnial	1 km up	Up to 200 m	long	0.5 cm s^{-1}	Small	P_t: important in clear lakes R: small

Modified from Boyce (1974).

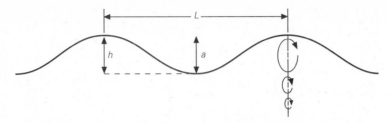

FIGURE 5-6 The motion of water parcels and the various linear definitions of a rhythmic wave. The water parcels oscillate elliptically but show no net lateral motion. The motion of the water parcels is not exactly to scale. The amount of movement decreases exponentially with depth. L = wavelength, h = wave height, a = wave amplitude ($= \frac{1}{2}h$).

or, more generally,

$$\mathrm{KE}(\lambda_1, \lambda_2) = \int_{\lambda_1}^{\lambda_2} E_{(\lambda)}\, d\lambda$$

where $\bar{E}_{(\lambda)}$ is the average value of $E_{(\lambda)}$ over the interval (λ_1, λ_2). $E_{(\lambda)}$ is called the KE spectral density. It is also called the *energy* or *power spectrum.* More precisely, it is the KE per unit mass per unit wavelength interval.

The energy spectrum shows that KE cascades from large lake-sized eddies driven by storms down to smaller eddies and is eventually lost as heat. It is often convenient to plot the log of the KE density on the vertical axis and the log of the wavelength on the horizontal. Such a plot produces peaks of energy connected by smooth curves. The energy spectrum is shown for an idealized large lake in Fig. 5-7, where the sizes of the various types of motion are shown. For a smaller lake the spectrum would be similar in shape but with different absolute values. Familiar lake phenomena such as waves and currents show up as peaks in the density of KE and are well-defined in both time and space. The smooth curve connecting the energy peaks indicates its redistribution into turbulent, chaotic eddies as energy cascades down the spectrum.

An important feature of lake structure is the space-time scale of turbulent eddies. The size and energy of these motions can be seen in Fig. 5-7 and Table 5-1. The lake can be thought of as containing a series of patches of water, each with slightly different physical and chemical constituents (Fig. 5-23a). Whether plankton inside a patch will be broken into new patches depends on the size of the patch, the size and strength of nearby turbulent eddies, and the organisms' swimming ability. As can be seen from Fig. 5-7, the most energetic water turbulence is in long wavelengths, greater than 100 or 1000 m. This motion also has a period of many hours. Thus organisms in a patch 50 m across will only be moved (i.e., *advected*) along with the patch by the most energetic eddies. Eddies of a smaller size and more rapid period will penetrate and increase the separation or *diffusion* of individuals within the patch. Mobile plankton such as *Daphnia* or buoyant blue-green algae can move several meters in an hour. They can thus counteract the smaller eddies and either maintain or disperse from the patch. Other nonmotile plankton, like many of the algae, depend entirely on small-scale low-energy turbulence to diffuse them out of their nutrient-depleted patch into richer waters.

Limnologists using the concept of energy density, or power spectrum, usually know the scales or wavelengths of motion of common lake phenomena. Reference to the energy spectrum will show approximately how energetic the water motion is at that wavelength. For example, consider the difference between two types of lake water movement, *mean flow* and *turbulent flow.*

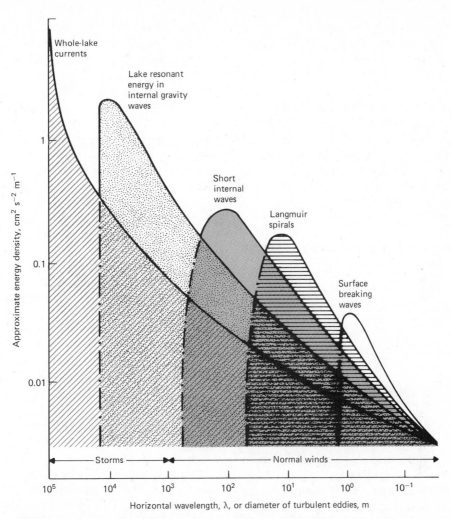

FIGURE 5-7 Wind-energy distribution in a hypothetical large lake. Surface wind waves (λ = 10 m) have little energy and do not show on this figure. An energy or power spectrum can be measured in lakes by using current meters. $E_{(\lambda)}$ = KE spectral-density function, where $E_{(\lambda)}\,d\lambda$ is proportional to the KE in the wavelength range $\lambda = -d\lambda/z$ to $+d\lambda/z$.

Mean flow has a specified direction and *advects* substances around the lake, while turbulence is random in direction and causes *diffusion* and spreading of a patch. The relative amounts of energy in the advective and diffusive motions can be found in the appropriate segments of the energy spectrum (Fig. 5-7).

Kinetic energy in lakes is finally dissipated as heat in small eddies of about 10^{-2} m. Lakes do

not heat up despite the enormous input of wind energy. Similarly, white-water streams on steep mountain slopes do not heat up as the water loses potential energy in its descent. The reason water in motion does not heat significantly is its high heat capacity (Chap. 3). The calorie, the energy needed to heat 1 cm³ water by 1°C, is very large in comparison to the energy generated by environmental scales of motion. For example, water must fall 418 m to gain a KE equivalent of 1 cal. In the heyday of Victorian physical sciences Lord Kelvin, known for the absolute temperature scale and Kelvin waves on the thermocline, met Mr. Joule, who had defined an energy unit bearing his name. Joule was in the Swiss Alps carrying an enormous thermometer in search of a high waterfall to measure the amount of heating produced. Unfortunately, Joule was unsuccessful in measuring a temperature difference, largely due to the ability of water to absorb heat with little temperature increase.

ADVECTIVE AND DIFFUSIVE TRANSPORT OF ENERGY

Mean horizontal movement or advection as of, for example, a dissolved substance in water, can be described by

$$\frac{\delta s}{\delta t}\,(\text{advective}) = \frac{\delta(us)}{\delta x} - \frac{\delta(vs)}{\delta y} - \frac{\delta(ws)}{\delta z} \quad (3)$$

where s = concentration of substance
$u,\ v,\ w$ = current velocities in the three dimensions x, y, z (width, breadth, depth of water layer), respectively

Here we visualize motion as a simple directional movement of water particles.

Diffusion is random, chaotic motion. The flux of a substance due to diffusive transport is proportional to the spatial gradient of concentrations between the substance and the surrounding water. The proportionality constant is an *eddy diffusion constant, K*. The rate of change of a substance due to diffusive transport of a substance S in water is described as

$$\frac{\delta S}{\delta t}\,(\text{diffusive}) = \frac{\delta}{\delta x}\!\left(K_x\frac{\delta S}{\delta x}\right) \quad (4)$$

$$+ \frac{\delta}{\delta y}\!\left(K_y\frac{\delta S}{\delta y}\right) + \frac{\delta}{\delta z}\!\left(K_z\frac{\delta S}{\delta z}\right)$$

where K_x, K_y, and K_z are the eddy diffusion coefficients in the three directions x, y, and z de-

scribed above. Note the formal similarity between *us, vs, ws,* and $K_x\,\delta S/\delta x$, $K_y\delta S/\delta y$, $K_z\,\delta S/\delta z$. The values of the various diffusion coefficients are given in Fig. 5-8.

Note that by including the pressure gradient and Coriolis force due to the rotation of the earth, the "substance" can become momentum in Eq. (4). The equations that result are called *equations of motion.* More advanced discussions of water movement begin with these equations, and the reader is referred to Pond and Pickard (1978) for an example. Other discussions with a biological or chemical orientation are the reviews by Boyce (1974), Mortimer (1974), Csanady (1975), and Smith (1975).

Horizontal eddy diffusion is several orders of magnitude faster than that in the vertical plane (Fig. 5-8), since no buoyancy forces have to be overcome. Although less easily seen in water than in the atmosphere, advection usually involves wavelengths greater than 1000 m, while diffusion or small-scale turbulence occurs at wavelengths less than 10 m (Figs. 5-7, 5-9). The

FIGURE 5-8   Various diffusion coefficients in lakes. Modified from Murphy (1972).

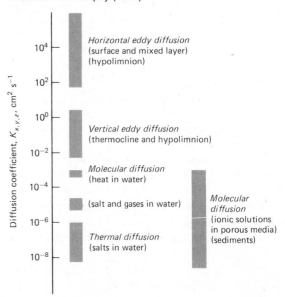

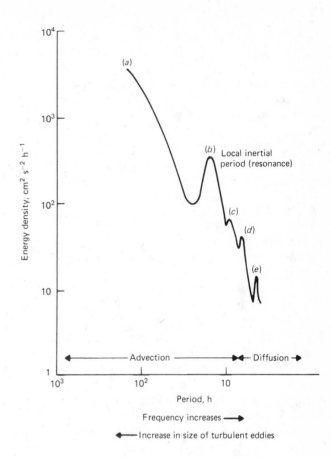

FIGURE 5-9 Input of the KE of wind into the waters of Lake Ontario. Note advective energy peaks for (a) whole-lake motion, (b) lake resonance, and (c), (d), and (e) other unidentified peaks, which may be Langmuir spirals or gravity waves. The values were measured 6 km offshore, $z = 8$ m; total variance of the measurements $= 107$ cm^{2}s^{-2}. Modified from Boyce (1974).

average velocity of the turbulent flows in all directions is zero due to their random eddying characters. However, the energy involved in random motion does not vanish and can be described as the sum of the mean square values (or the variance) for each dimension averaged over a given time period. Thus for energy of turbulent flow,

Turbulent KE per unit mass:

$$E' = \frac{1}{2}[\overline{(u')^2} + \overline{(v')^2} + \overline{(w')^2}] \qquad (5)$$

where u', v', and w' are fluctuating water-velocity components and are averaged over a suitable time scale (denoted by an overbar). For energy of the mean flow,

Mean KE per unit mass:

$$E = \frac{1}{2}(\overline{u}^2 + \overline{v}^2 + \overline{w}^2) \qquad (6)$$

where u, v, and w are as in Eq. (3). Total energy in the water motion is the sum of E and E', which are separated only for convenience. Generally, for the surface of the lake in windy conditions, E (associated with advection) is greater than E' (associated with diffusion), but at depth or on calm days the opposite may be true.

Kinetic energy in the water may be estimated directly from long-term measurements of horizontal lake currents. This is how Fig. 5-8 was derived for Lake Ontario. Storms commonly produce large horizontal water currents (Fig. 5-22), but such events occur infrequently. If whole-lake horizontal current speeds are high, overall lake energy content is high. This is shown graphically by values at the upper left-hand section of Figs. 5-7 and 5-9. By contrast, rapid, common surface waves represent a low-energy component for the lake.

Another peak of energy density is often found at the wavelength of breaking waves. Effects due to surface waves are indicated in Fig. 5-7 and in detail in Fig. 5-16. The breaking of both surface and internal waves imparts turbulence to lake waters. It is an important way in which vigorous mixing can occur between layers of water with different density that form below the surface in stratified lakes.

Waves break when the slope of the leading edge becomes too steep. The increased slope occurs because the velocity of water at the base of the slope is held back by friction more than the upper part. Photographic and schematic representations of turbulent billows produced by such mixing is shown for an internal wave in Fig. 5-10a and b. Such mixing is called *Kelvin-Helmholtz mixing* or *Kelvin-Helmholtz instability* and is most important at the lake surface or in the layers of slightly different density within the thermocline (Fig. 5-23).

MOTION IN THE EPILIMNION

The main sources of water currents are the wind, which is the major force; pressure gradients, caused by nonequilibrium distribution of water masses; buoyant forces, caused by heating and cooling from evaporation, which can lead to vertical motion (Chap. 4); and (4) inflowing and outflowing rivers. These are modified by the *Coriolis effect,* especially in large lakes, and by bottom and side friction, which is most important in small lakes. Wind is usually the major energy-supplying agent but may not always be the most significant from the view of lake biology or chemistry, since convection currents are also important (Chap. 4). Friction develops when wind blows over the surface of a lake, resulting in a

shear stress at the wind-water interface. The air movement sets up a corresponding motion in the upper water layer, which will reduce the stress; that is, a current develops in the same direction as the wind at a reduced velocity.

Surface Drift

Under most conditions the wind, if allowed to reach a steady state, would impart a fairly constant fraction of its speed (roughly 3 percent) to the surface layers of the water over which it moves. This is largely attributable to the differences in density between the two fluids, air and water. When the stress of the air on the water (τ_{air}) is equal and opposite to the stress of the water on the air (τ_{H_2O}), we can use the fact that the stress on a fluid should be proportional to fluid density $\rho \times$ (velocity u_*)^2 to find

$$\tau_{air} = \rho_{air}\, u_{*air}^2 = \rho_{H_2O}\, u_{*H_2O}^2 = \tau_{H_2O} \quad (7)$$

so that

$$\frac{u_{H_2O}}{u_{*air}} = \left(\frac{\rho_{air}}{\rho_{H_2O}}\right)^{1/2} \approx \left(\frac{10^{-3}}{1}\right)^{1/2} \approx 0.03$$

over real lakes. That is, water speeds equal about 3 percent of wind speeds at equilibrium. Under most lake conditions this value is only an approximation. Lake water speeds generally range up to 30 cm s^{-1} and are much slower than the water velocity of a typical stream.

The earth's rotation is important for lake currents. In large lakes the water does not move in exactly the same direction as the wind: it moves at an angle to the wind due to the rotation of the earth. The apparent force produced is called the *Coriolis force,* and the surface drift to the right in the northern hemisphere and to the left in the southern hemisphere is referred to as *Ekman drift.* The deflection of the surface current is less pronounced in shallow lakes but may be as great as 45° to the direction of the wind in deep lakes and in the ocean.

Water blown to one end of a lake must return eventually, and this occurs either at the lake surface or, more usually, by return flows deeper

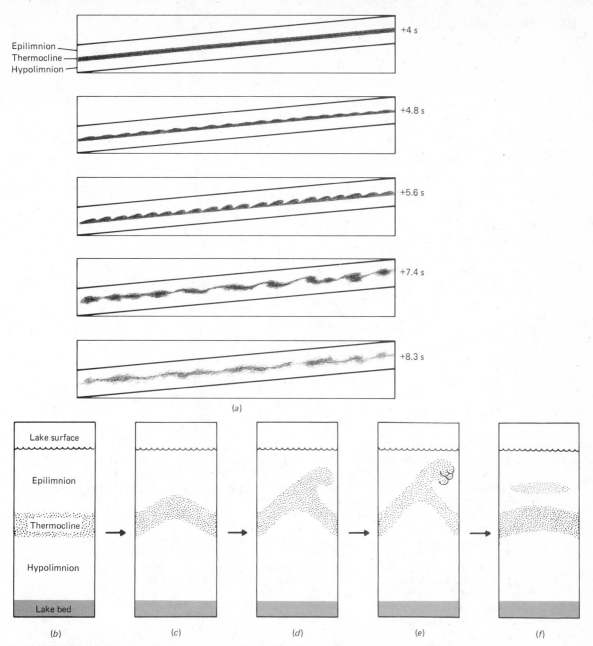

FIGURE 5-10 Kelvin-Helmholtz mixing (or instability). (*a*) Onset of Kelvin-Helmholtz shear instability in a three-layer experiment with densities 1.000 (epilimnion), 1.092 (thermocline), and 1.172 g cm^{-3} (hypolimnion). The central dyed layer had an initial thickness of 1.3 cm. Initially horizontal the tube was tilted 5.6°. The first diagram, taken 4 s after tilting, shows the smooth three-layered system. Kelvin-Helmholtz instability occurred soon after. The values to the right show the elapsed time after tilting occurred. Billows formed by mixing represent conditions similar to those found in lakes where internal waves occur. Redrawn from Thorpe (1971). (*b*)–(*f*) Representation of changes shown in (*a*). (*b*) Condition prior to wave initiation. (*c*) An internal wave forms, (*d*) becomes unstable, (*e*) breaks and incorporates different water layers at the crest, and (*f*) produces a layer of water of intermediate density. See also Fig. 5-23.

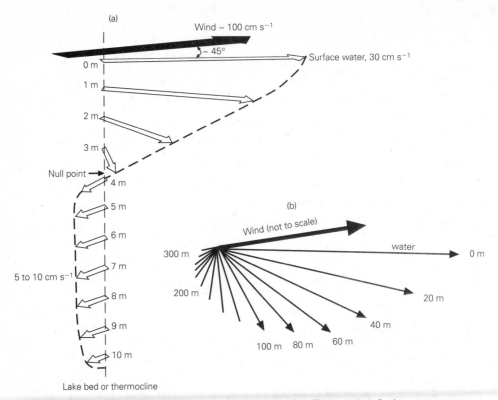

FIGURE 5-11 (*a*) Idealized and (*b*) measured diagrams of an Ekman spiral. Surface water moves most quickly at the surface and, in theory, at about 45° to the wind direction due to the Coriolis force imparted by the earth's rotation. Motion is to the right (northern hemisphere) and to the left (southern hemisphere). In this figure the water is considered to be layers of equal thickness moving in various directions. Note how the flows spiral down to give a complete reversal of the direction in deeper water. To conserve mass, the volume of water moving downwind should approximately equal that returning. At the null point no net flow occurs. (*a*) The expected scale of movement for a typical lake. Modified from Gross (1977). (*b*) Changes in current velocity and direction with depth measured using a profiling current meter in the Pacific Ocean, where depths are larger in most lakes. Redrawn and modified from Stacey et al. (1986). Currents are shown relative to the surface velocity. Note that in the real example the water moves at a much smaller angle to the wind than theory predicts. This smaller angle also probably occurs in lakes as well as oceans. For an Ekman spiral shown in context of other water flows see Fig. 5-22.

down in the water column. Most studies have been carred out in rectangular lakes; in these, return flows are often just above the thermocline under stratified conditions (Fig. 5-22) or near the bottom when the lake is unstratified. The maximum current at the surface decreases with depth to a point of zero net flow. Below this depth there is a fairly uniform return flow, which is much slower than the near-surface flow. In ad-

dition, due to the Coriolis force, movement down the water column is twisted into a coiled spiral known as an *Ekman spiral* (Fig. 5-11). Large deviations from a perfect spiral may form during high or changeable winds or where basin bathymetry is irregular. The Ekman spiral is a classical but useful simplification found in large deep lakes and the ocean, particularly when steady, strong winds blow in one direction (Fig. 5-22).

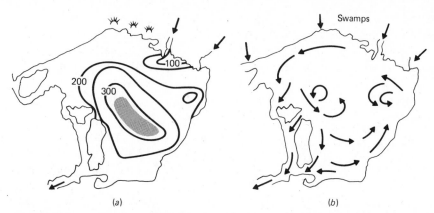

FIGURE 5-12 Surface-drift patterns in shallow tropical Lake George, Uganda, Africa. (*a*) Chlorophyll *a* at the surface in milligrams per cubic meter. Isopleths at intervals of 50 μg liter^{-1}. Redrawn from Burgis (1971). (*b*) Water currents derived from changes in chlorophyll. Redrawn from Ganf (1974).

Surface drift can be a nuisance in eutrophic or polluted lakes because concentrations of algae, bottles, cans, or dead fish are rapidly moved by wind. Movements of floating algae are shown in productive Clear Lake, California (Fig. 5-3*a* to *d*), and in eutrophic, tropical Lake George, Uganda (Fig. 5-12).

Another type of whole-lake surface drift occurs in most lakes in the northern hemisphere— a slow mean flow in a counterclockwise direction (Emery and Csanady, 1973). This circular motion with a relatively stagnant center is familiar to oceanographers and is called a *gyre*. The importance of gyres is that lake organisms can be transported without energy expenditure. For example, it may be advantageous for plankton to pass near a nutrient-laden inflow. In rectangular lakes, especially in those with a flat bottom, the wind produces topographic gyres. Usually two gyres form, a cyclonic one to the right of the wind and an anticyclonic one to the left (Csanady, 1975).

Surface Waves

Wind-driven surface gravity waves are the normal waves observed on the lake surface. Although less impressive on lakes than on the ocean, there is little difference between the two except that in lakes they are smaller. Their properties are described in Table 5-1 and Fig. 5-7, and they contain little of the lake's total KE.

Standing surface gravity waves or *surface seiches* are the regular, resonating waves that pass from one edge to the other and back. Surface seiches were among the first physical events noted by early European limnologists. In other parts of the world their existence did not go unnoticed. In beautiful Lake Wakitipu in New Zealand the slow seiche rhythm gave rise to a Maori legend that a sleeping giant lay breathing on the lake bed. The word *seiche* may be derived from the French word *seche,* which means "dry," and was originally used because one shore of the lake becomes exposed and dry while the other becomes flooded.

Seiches are commonly generated when winds blow fairly constantly from one direction, driving the surface water downwind. The wind piles up water on the lee shore, holding it there until the wind drops, at which time the driving force is released and the accumulated water mass flows back under the influence of gravity. This produces a standing wave that rocks back and forth with gradually decreasing motion. A series of waves is produced, which are called standing surface gravity waves, surface seiches, or simply seiches. It is a common property of mechanical systems that inputs of energy at any of a wide range of frequencies will excite the resonant or harmonic frequencies more than others. Thus the sloshing back and forth of the water produces a standing wave at the resonant frequencies of the lake in the same way that a plucked guitar string produces one main note irrespective of the plucking frequency. In lakes, surface seiches have a period given by

$$T = \frac{1}{n} \frac{2L}{\sqrt{gZ}} \qquad (8)$$

where T = resonance period

  Z = lake depth where the lake is a rectangular basin

  n = number of nodes of the standing wave

  L = basin length

Surface seiches are apparent on lakeshores as regular but small (≤ 10 cm) up-and-down motions of the lake surface. They are of little importance for lake biology or chemistry, as their energy is low. They dissipate their energy by frictional shear at the air-water interface and at the lake edges.

FIGURE 5-13 As viewed downwind, wind-produced Langmuir spirals show surface water mixed down between two adjacent left- and right-handed spirals.

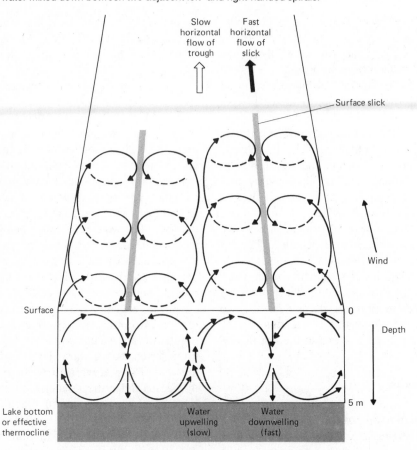

FIGURE 5-14 Langmuir spirals in Clear Lake, California, as seen from an aircraft 2000 m above the lake. Wind is blowing from the west (left to right). Boundaries of Langmuir spirals are indicated by white streaks parallel to the wind. Wave fronts are obvious as ripples at right angles to the wind. Wind speed was approximately 6 m s^{-1}. The Langmuir spirals are about 2 to 3 m across per cell in this photograph. The picture shows an area approximately 2 km across.

Langmuir Spirals

Langmuir spirals are often as obvious as breaking waves. On a windy day it may be possible to see lines of foam, called *windrows,* oriented in the same direction as the wind and at right angles to the waves (Figs. 5-13, 5-14). These lines mark the boundaries of pairs of *Langmuir spirals,* a series of adjacent vertical clockwise and counterclockwise rotating cells of water. They produce alternate areas of upwelling and downwelling, and foam accumulates above the downwelling zone. Windrows, also called *slicks,* contain algae and zooplankton as well as oily substances or natural foaming agents from the death and decay of plankton or shoreline vegetation (Fig. 5-14). Langmuir-type circulation is due to an interaction between surface waves and wind-driven drift currents. A detailed explanation of this circulation can be found in Craik and Leibovich (1976). Langmuir spirals produce downwelling flows of between 2 and 8 cm s^{-1} (Fig. 5-15). This is considerably faster than the swimming of most zooplankton or algae. Langmuir spirals may rapidly mix plankton, heat, or dissolved gases throughout the epilimnion. Upwelling is much less concentrated than downwelling, and currents may be slower. In many cases the spirals have a diameter approximately equal to the depth of the thermocline or to the total depth of shallow lakes.

An important feature of these rapid vertical movements is their effect on algal photosynthesis and zooplankton. Zooplankters such as *Daphnia* may concentrate in the slicks (Chap. 13), presumably offsetting the disadvantages of being eaten there against the advantages of concentrations of food in the form of algae and bacteria. The inhibition of algal photosynthesis by exposure to surface-light intensities is well known, and rapid mixing in Langmuir spirals may in-

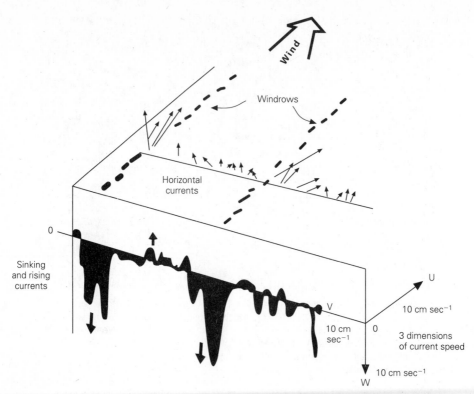

FIGURE 5-15 Water currents in three dimensions showing some Langmuir circulation. Note the large downwelling currents, over 10 cm s⁻¹ (shaded areas), relative to the slower upwelling velocities. The sinking flow will overpower even strongly swimming zooplankton and even highly buoyant phytoplankton. Horizontal "jets" of up to 20 cm s⁻¹ occurred in the surface layers (small arrows). These data were obtained from an oceanic floating platform where the slicks were about 20 m apart. The data are from a depth of 23 m to avoid interferences by surface waves and mixing. Lake examples generally have less distance between the slicks and effects will be shown at lesser depths, but currents should be similar. Redrawn and modified from Weller et al. (1965).

crease light inhibition and reduce primary production. Thus the system of bottles suspended at fixed depth normally used to estimate photosynthesis (Chap. 7) may not reproduce the natural-light regime.

Random

A combination of the diffusion of momentum from the surface with additional energy provided by breaking waves accounts for random mixing of the lake's epilimnion. Wind blowing over lakes causes fluctuating turbulent movement in the vertical as well as horizontal direction. Because surface water is almost always warmer and thus more buoyant than deeper water, more energy is needed to mix vertically than horizontally. Since turbulence is essentially a random three-dimensional motion, its effect is to mix or diffuse adjacent water masses. Such mixing is important in the exchange of nutrients and heat between top and bottom water.

The vertical transfer of the wind's energy is similar to that described for a substance in Eq. (4) but is further modified by pressure gradients and the Coriolis force. This gives a slightly larger diffusion coefficient for momentum than for dif-

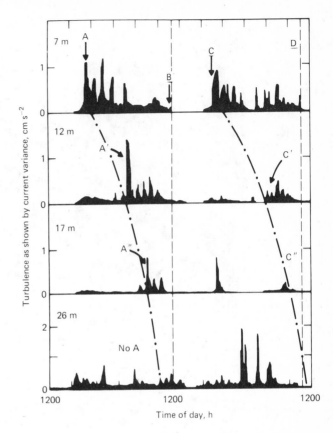

FIGURE 5-16 Mixing in the epilimnion of Lake Tahoe. The afternoon wind mixes the lake down to the top of the thermocline (20 m). Turbulence starts with the afternoon wind near the surface (*A, C*) and drops down to the top of the thermocline (dotted lines *A', A'', C', C''*). By midmorning, solar heating restratifies the epilimnion and extinguishes turbulence (*B, D,* dashed line) until the onset of the next afternoon wind. Redrawn from Dillon and Powell (1979).

fusion of a substance. A 5- to 20-m-thick layer of epilimnion in a temperate lake is well mixed vertically each day by the shear stress imparted by moderate winds (Fig. 5-16).

Breaking Waves

Extra energy is available for both vertical and horizontal transport via breaking waves or whitecaps when organized wave motion is degraded into turbulence. The energy concentrated in breaking waves can be measured directly as part of the whole-lake energy-frequency spectrum (Fig. 5-7). Measurements of this spectrum in a lake with and without breaking waves demonstrate the formation and decay of energy at a particular wavelength due to breaking waves (Fig. 5-17).

The thermocline is stably stratified and thus resists mixing from the cascade of random, chaotic turbulence. Most motion at the thermocline appears as organized waves.

MOTION IN THE THERMOCLINE

The fairly gentle turbulence introduced by internal waves at the thermocline (Fig. 5-10) helps prevent the stagnation that would otherwise prevail due to the slowness of molecular diffusion (Fig. 5-8). This may be insufficient if detritus or zooplankton cause metalimnetic oxygen depletion. Gentle mixing may be one reason for the abundant growth of algae and bacteria around the thermocline. The danger of being swept into unfavorable zones is minimal, but stirring provides fresh supplies of nutrients from the

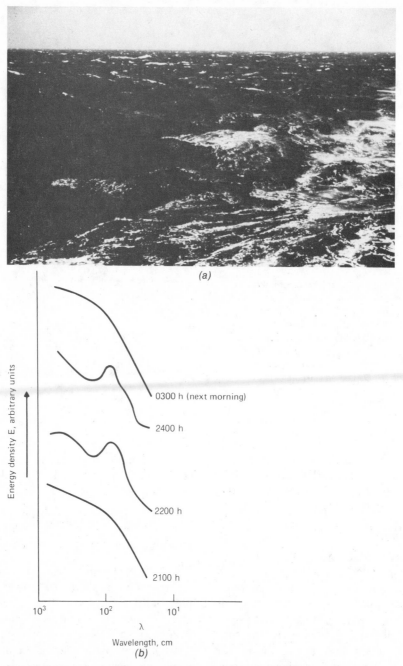

FIGURE 5-17 (*a*) Large whitecapped waves in the South Atlantic Ocean. (*b*) Transfer of energy due to whitecapping (breaking waves) into energy of vertical mixing. This occurred after a windy afternoon was followed by a calm evening on Lake Ontario. Note the rise of a turbulent energy peak with a wavelength of about 100 cm, which is similar to the size of a breaking wave crest. Modified from Lemmin et al. (1974).

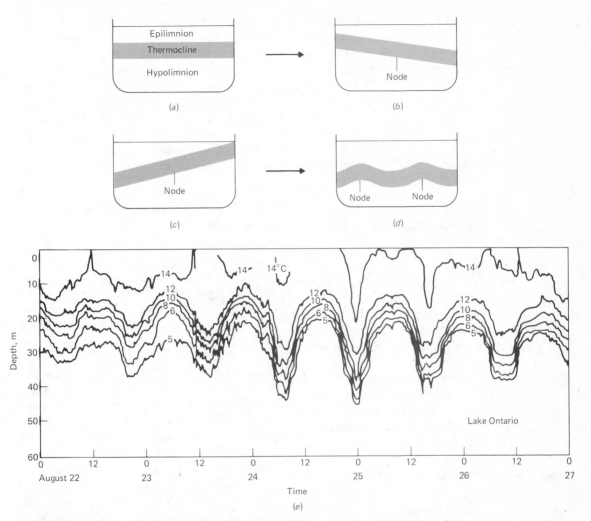

FIGURE 5-18 Internal gravity waves or seiches. (*a*) to (*d*) Representation of the initiation of internal gravity waves. The single central node is usually replaced by several nodes. (*a*) Calm three-layered structure. (*b*) After strong winds the epilimnion becomes displaced downwind, depressing the thermocline. (*c*) After the wind stops, the epilimnion tilts back due to gravity. (*d*) After a few hours or days of oscillation, internal gravity waves are set up on the thermocline. These waves may persist for several days. (*e*) Internal gravity waves on Lake Ontario, Canada (Station 6, off Oshawa, northwest of lake), as recorded by thermocline movement. Redrawn from Boyce (1974).

hypolimnion. Internal waves are usually detected by the periodic rise and fall of the thermocline (Fig. 5-18*e*). Some types of waves, such as the Kelvin and Poincaré waves discussed later in this chapter, are important only in large lakes, while others, such as short freely propagating internal gravity waves, occur in almost all stratified lakes.

Internal Gravity Waves

Internal gravity waves (internal seiches), which can be formed only under stratified conditions, are not apparent from the lake surface. They are usually much larger than surface waves and may be as much as 10 m high. In a rectangular basin the period of an internal seiche is given by

$$T = \cfrac{2L}{\sqrt{g\left(\cfrac{\rho_h - \rho_e}{\rho_h}\right) \bigg/ (z_h^{-1} + z_e^{-1})}} \qquad (9)$$

where ρ_h, ρ_e = densities of hypolimnion and epilimnion, ≈ 1 g cm^{-3}, respectively

z_e, z_h = respective thicknesses of epilimnion and hypolimnion

L = basin length

Figure 5-18 *a* to *d* shows the growth of internal gravity waves on the thermocline. Figure 5-18*e* also shows the dramatic changes in the horizontal position of the thermocline after the passage of Hurricane Agnes over Lake Ontario in 1972.

Small lakes are little affected by internal waves. The height of all waves increases with fetch, so waves on small lakes have a small amplitude and wavelength. Kettle lakes, for example (Chap. 20), have extremely stable stratification, and motile or buoyant algae dominate the phytoplankton (Chap. 12).

Short-Period Internal Gravity Waves

These freely propagating waves within the thermocline may cause the intricate patterning indicated by taking very accurate depth-temperature profiles. An example from Lake Tahoe is shown in Fig. 5-19. These could be due to the breaking of the waves from a Kelvin-Helmholtz instability. These short-period waves have a maximum frequency $N/2\pi$, where N, called the *Brunt-Vaisala frequency* is:

$$N^2 = -\frac{g}{\rho}\frac{d\rho}{dz} \qquad (10)$$

where ρ = water density

z = depth

g = acceleration of gravity

For Lake Tahoe these waves would pass an observer on the thermocline every 100 s during late-summer stratification.

Planktonic organisms in the grip of turbulence from the breaking of these short-period internal waves are vertically mixed toward or away from light over periods of several hours. Such turbulence may assist metalimnion populations of the blue-green algae *Oscillatoria rubescens,* which grew so abundantly in Lake Zurich during periods of enrichment.

Long-Period Internal Waves: Kelvin and Poincaré Waves

These two long propagating internal waves are probably the only types that produce significant currents in the hypolimnia of large lakes. They are internal gravity waves, which differ from previously discussed internal seiches because they are modified by basin morphometry and latitude. They normally reach large size on the thermoclines of stratified lakes. The rotational influence of the earth, the Coriolis force, is vital for their maintenance, so they occur only in large lakes. Kelvin waves are low-frequency waves whose frequency depends on the size of the lake basin and its resonant frequency. Kelvin waves are important only in lakes with a minimum fetch in any direction of about 5 km. Poincaré waves have a frequency close to the inertial frequency (or period), which depends on the latitude of the lake. The *inertial period* is the period of a wave acted on only by Coriolis force. It is about 17 h for the North American Great Lakes (45°N) and is much longer for an equatorial lake such as Lake Tanganyika (6°S) (Fig. 5-20). Poincaré waves occur only in the very largest lakes.

Kelvin waves have a pronounced effect in nearshore waters less than 5 km from the lake edge. When an internal seiche forms in a large lake, the Coriolis force induces a counterclockwise rotation (northern hemisphere) on the single plane whose node is at the center of the lake (Fig. 5-21). Kelvin waves may displace the thermocline several meters near the lake edges and

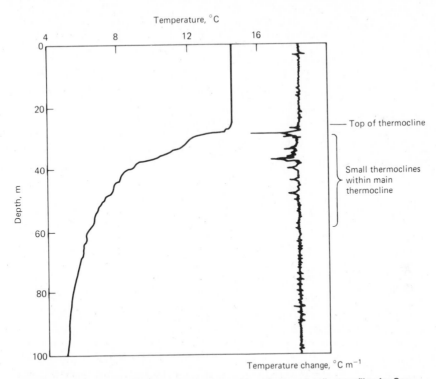

FIGURE 5-19   Temperature microstructure and temperature-gradient profiles for September 29, 1973, Lake Tahoe, midlake. Note the fine detail of thermal microstructure and several small thermoclines. Some of these may be only temporary and will be modified by the next storm. Redrawn from Dillon, Powell, and Myrup (1975).

will pass around the lake at its inertial period. The motion imparted may be important in causing "leaks" around the edges of the thermocline, which allow nutrients from the hypolimnion to reach the epilimnion and increase algal growth. Kelvin waves may be important in shoreline areas where fisheries are concentrated since this region of the lake is the major source of sediment-nutrient recycling during stratification.

Poincaré waves influence the hypolimnion in the open waters away from the shores of large lakes. They are very large waves, and their effects on water currents may extend 50 m or more below the thermocline. Poincaré waves can be visualized by imagining the thermocline to be divided into huge squares of alternating black and white colors. Initially, all the black squares will be depressed toward their centers like a pit while the white ones will be elevated like a hill. After a period near the inertial frequency, the positions will be reversed with black hills and alternating white pits. This will continue producing alternating water mounds and depressions. In addition, horizontal water currents will be caused by Poincaré waves.

MOTION IN THE HYPOLIMNION

Sources of organized motion in this layer are generally absent and most mixing is diffusive and weak. Some motion is due to Poincaré and Kelvin waves. These waves have large vertical

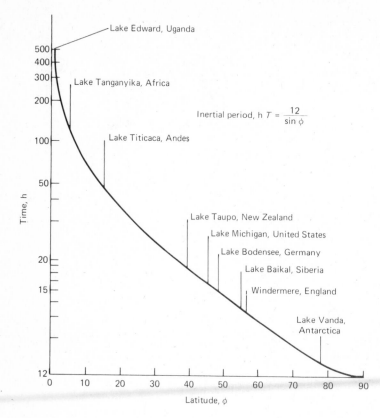

$$\text{Inertial period, h } T = \frac{12}{\sin \phi}$$

FIGURE 5-20 Inertial period as a function of latitude. This is the period of a wave acted upon only by the Coriolis force of the earth's rotation. Courtesy of C. P. Duncan and G. Schladow.

displacements (Table 5-1 and Fig. 5-18e) and produce a back-and-forth movement of water over the sediment. This motion sets up turbulence, especially in lakes with irregular beds, and mixes substances dissolved in interstitial water into the open water (Powell and Jassby, 1974). Wave turbulence is negligible at a depth equal to half the wavelength. Thus even a high wave must have a long wavelength to affect deep water. Since such waves are generally stable and do not break, there is no source of vigorous mixing in the hypolimnion.

The amount of nutrient release depends on the composition of the lake bed, which may range from soft muds to hard stony areas. Some lakes have oozes that are protected from mixing by a rigid crust formed by insect activities.

In eutrophic lakes where the bottom sedi-

ments become anoxic, large quantities of nutrients diffuse out of the interstitial mud water. This outflow is much less in the oxygenated muds of very oligotrophic lakes but is still significant, since important algal growth occurs in the hypolimnion of very clear lakes (Goldman et al., 1973; Fee, 1976). It is important to know how this layer of nutrient-rich water overlying the sediments is circulated throughout the hypolimnion. First, it should be noted that such mixing does not always occur. In small, well-stratified lakes, such as Castle Lake, California, mixing over the sediment surface is slight and progressive depletion of near-bottom nitrate occurs, probably by denitrification in the mud. This chemical stratification indicates that mixing is weak at best. Because of the relatively weak currents, bottom hardness, biotic activity, and tem-

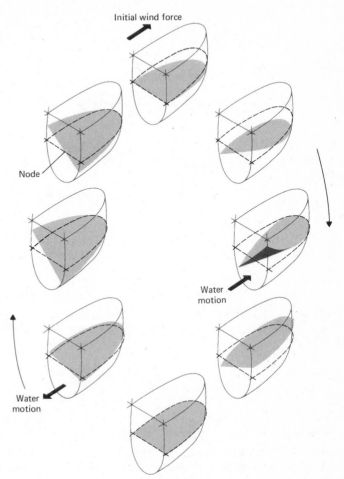

Initial wind force

Node

Water
motion

Water
motion

FIGURE 5-21 One cycle of a Kelvin wave (an internal gravity wave) on the thermocline of half of large northern-hemisphere lake. The wave has a counterclockwise rotation (due to the Coriolis force) about a stationary center-lake node. Note the large wave near the lake edge, which characterizes a Kelvin wave. Also note the reversal of net water flow in the hypolimnion during the cycle. This flow reversal also applies to any internal gravity wave in large lakes. Modified from Mortimer (1974).

perature remain the most important factors in establishing the absolute quantity of nutrients in the hypolimnion.

AN OVERALL VIEW

A good example of overall current patterns for a short period during a storm is that for Loch Ness. Fig. 5-22 shows strong surface flows and slower deeper flows in the reverse direction. An alternative view of these data is estimation of changes in turbulence. Turbulence is essentially random and cannot be measured directly. If current or temperature measurements are known accu-

rately, the proportion of the water that is unstably stratified relative to the surrounding water can be calculated. After mixing, some parts of the epilimnion have a greater or lesser density than the water around them, since they originated from warmer or cooler layers. This produces unstable stratified water since heavier water overlies lighter warm water. Eventually, turbulent diffusion will eliminate these density differences. Until that time, the proportion of unstably stratified water, χ, called an *intermittency index,* measures the amount of turbulence in the water. When greatly above zero, χ indicates downmixing of surface water, internal waves, and possible

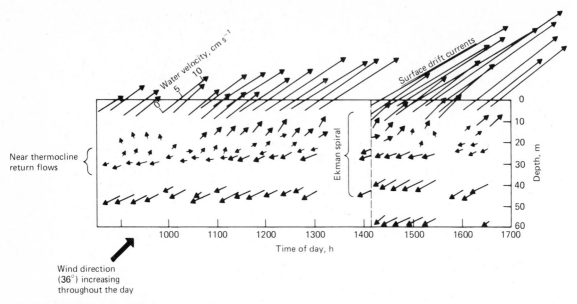

FIGURE 5-22 Currents measured as a storm moves across Loch Ness, Scotland. The long axis of the lake is downwind (at 36°). Note the very rapid rise in surface flows as the day progresses and as winds increase. Slower return flow is indicated at depth. Ekman spirals are also shown. Modified from Thorpe (1977).

Kelvin-Helmholtz mixing (Fig. 5-10a to f). In Fig. 5-23 the intermittency index χ is plotted for Loch Ness in September. The resultant layered structure of turbulence is similar to that found in Lake Tahoe (Fig. 5-19). Most turbulence (χ > 30 percent) is found near the surface. Layers of lesser turbulence are interleaved between 10 and 30 m; below this there is little turbulence. As would be expected, turbulence is low in deep water.

EFFECT OF RIVERS

Most rivers flowing into large lakes have only a local effect on water movement. Some smaller lakes, such as Marion Lake in British Columbia, are essentially riverine. Lakes of this sort have very short retention times of only a few days. Since rivers transport most of the annual supply of nutrients, pollutants, and toxicants, the dispersion of river inflow in lakes is particularly

important. Plumes of inflowing muddy water are easily seen (Fig. 5-24). The horizontal spread of a plume can be approximated where the horizontal eddy diffusivity coefficient is K_y [see also Eq. (4)]

$$K_y = \text{const. } U \frac{\delta w}{\delta x} = \text{const. } w^{4/3} \quad (11)$$

where w = width of a plume at distance x from the source (river mouth)
U = horizontal water-current speed.

The vertical spread of the plumes is usually negligible compared with horizontal spread (refer to Csanady, 1969, for further details).

Near the river mouth, in the initial phases of plume spreading,

$$w = \text{const. } \mathbf{x}^{3/2} \quad (12)$$

That is, there is an initial rapid and nonlinear horizontal spread of the plume that is due to

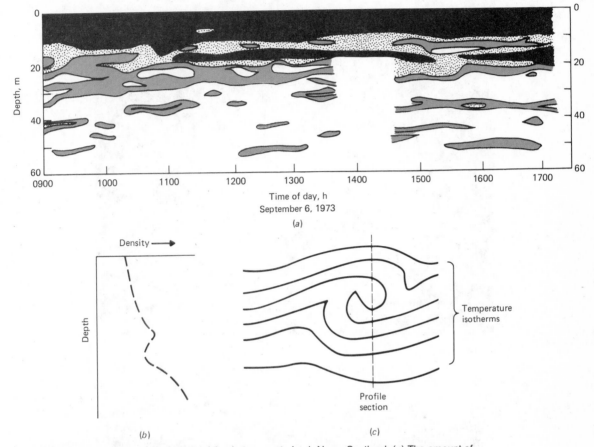

FIGURE 5-23 Estimated turbulent mixing in temperate Loch Ness, Scotland. (*a*) The amount of turbulence over one day as measured by the function χ, which increases as instability and mixing increase. χ represents the frequency of the occurrence of density inversions, that is, regions of gravitational instability in which the density increases upward. Such inversions are caused by the Kelvin-Helmholtz mixing shown in Fig. 5-10 and in parts (*b*) and (*c*) below (see text for further details). Solid black = high turbulence ($\chi > 30$ percent), dotted = lower turbulence ($\chi = 15$ to 30 percent), grey = low turbulence ($\chi < 15$ percent). Clear areas of no density inversions have little turbulence. (*b*) the density measured by an instrument as it profiles the billow. The instrument normally measures temperature, which is converted to density before plotting (*b*). (*c*) The buildup of a Kelvin-Helmholtz billow. Redrawn and modified from Thorpe (1977).

incorporation of larger and larger eddies up to 50 m in diameter. Soon after this, plume dissipation slows. A few kilometers farther out the plume meanders and often follows the shoreline, especially in calm weather.

Turbidity or Density Plumes

Runoff in the snowmelt season is often cold and denser than lake water. When it arrives at the lake the inflow will sink to the bottom or to an intermediate depth where its density equals that of the surrounding water. This discrete underwater plume is called a *density current*. In more arid climates and often when land disturbance has caused erosion, the inflowing river water can be laden with sediment and also much denser than the lake, even if both water masses have the same temperature. In this case the underwater

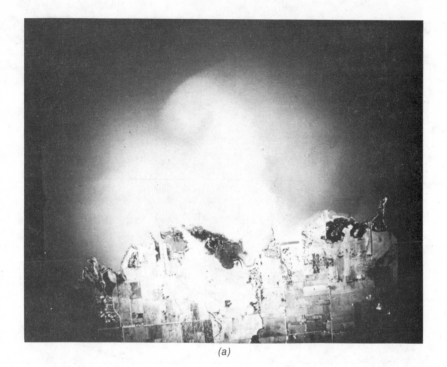

(a)

(b)

FIGURE 5-24 (a) Black-and-white rendering of a color infrared photograph of the muddy plume of the inflowing river at flood stage at Clear Lake, California. Note the large eddy forming at the end of the sediment plume. The view shown is about 5 km across. Photograph courtesy of R. C. Wrigley. NASA, Ames. (b) Normal spectral range photograph of the muddy plume of the Flathead River as it enters Flathead Lake, Montana, during a high flow period. Photographed by T. J. Stuart.

plume is called a *turbidity current*. Density and turbidity currents behave similarly. Their importance to lakes is that they can impart a lot of kinetic energy to the sediments. In larger lakes and estuaries and especially on the ocean coast, deep trenches have been dug in the benthic sediments by the passage of turbidity currents. These may travel for more than a kilometer before eventually slowing down and gradually dispersing. Although the effects are rarely seen by shoreline observers, they are much larger agents of disturbance in the deepwater sediments than any other mechanism, such as the large internal Poincaré waves.

Because of their visual impact, sediment plumes are likely to arouse public concern and are particularly good subjects for monitoring by remote sensing (Fig. 5-24, see also Lathrop et al., 1990). Plumes provide direct evidence of the dispersion into lakes of nutrients, particularly nitrogen and phosphorus from the watershed. Chaps. 6 to 10 deal with nutrients and their transformations in aquatic ecosystems.

FURTHER READING

Boyce, F. M. 1974. "Some Aspects of Great Lakes Physics of Importance to Biological and Chemical Processes." *J. Fish. Res. Board Can.,* **31:**689–730.

Burns, N. W., and C. Ross. 1972. "Project Hypo: An Intensive Study of the Lake Erie Central Basin Hypolimnion and Related Surface Water Phenomena." Canadian Centre for Inland Waters, Paper 6. 182 pp.

Carmack, E. C., R. W. Wiegand, R. J. Daley, C. B. J. Gray, S. Jasper, and C. H. Pharo. 1986. "Mechanisms Influencing the Circulation and Distribution of Water Mass in a Medium-Residence-Time Lake. *Limnol. Oceanogr.,* **31:**249–265.

Csanady, G. T. 1969. "Dispersal of Effluents in the Great Lakes." *Water Res.,* **3:**835–972.

Imberger, J., and J. C. Patterson. 1990. "Physical Limnology." *Adv. Appl. Mech.,* **27:**303–471.

Lathrop, R. G., J. R. Vande Castle, and T. M. Lillesand. 1990. "Monitoring River Plume Transport and Mesoscale Circulation in Green Bay, Wisconsin, through Satellite Remote Sensing." *J. Great Lakes Res.,* **16:**471–484.

Mortimer, C. H. 1974. "Lake Hydrodynamics." *Mitt. Int. Ver. Theor. Angew. Limnol.,* **20:**124–197.

Patalas, K. 1984. "Mid-Summer Mixing Depths in Lakes of Different Latitudes." *Vert. Int. Ver. Limnol.,* **22:**97–102.

Smith, I. R. 1975. "Turbulence in Lakes and Rivers." *Freshwater Biol. Assoc. U.K.* **29.** 79 pp.

Thorpe, S. A. 1977. "Turbulence and Mixing in a Scottish Loch." *Philos. Trans. R. Soc. London,* **286:**125–181.

CHAPTER 6

Introduction to the Chemistry of Natural Waters

OVERVIEW

The chemical composition of natural waters is regulated by the age-old processes of rainfall, erosion and solution, evaporation, and sedimentation. Daily, seasonal, and long-term cycles of the major elements are also influenced by the biological components of the watershed, stream, and lake waters. Microbial activity in soils is still another factor in modifying the chemical composition of runoff. In this chapter we introduce the broad spectrum of chemicals present in natural waters in relation to each other and to the watershed, from which most of them originate. Because of its importance, we also discuss the impact of human activities on global water chemistry. Acid rain is used as an example of the linkages between atmospheric chemistry, watershed soil buffering, and the leaching of soil metals with the deaths of fish and invertebrates in lakes and streams.

In this chapter we discuss methods of chemical study, organic and inorganic compounds in water, the influence of climate and watershed, the atmospheric contribution, chemical pollution, logging and erosion, and acid rain.

METHODS

Detailed methods of determining the concentration of important chemicals should be sought in such references as the latest edition of *Standard Methods for the Examination of Water and Wastewater* (American Public Health Association, 1992) and *Limnological Analyses* (Wetzel and Likens, 1991). Most biologically important chemicals can be detected in the waters of lakes and streams, although sometimes advanced analytical methods may be needed. Chemical methods change, and the current literature should be examined when low concentrations are investigated.

ORGANIC AND INORGANIC COMPOUNDS IN WATER

Lake and stream waters are never chemically pure H_2O and, since water is the "universal solvent," they contain an array of inorganic and organic molecules that are present as dissolved solids and gases. Chemicals in lakes, streams, estuaries, and wetlands may exist as simple molecules but are often complex combinations of organic and inorganic compounds. Water constantly picks up impurities of all kinds from the air as well as from the land, and some of these provide the growth factors needed to support the aquatic food chain. Organisms already present in the water excrete ammonia, phosphate, carbon dioxide, and a large percentage of everything they have eaten. Even distilled water usually carries enough trace quantities of nutrients to grow bacteria and algae. The *Legionella* bacteria that has caused numerous human fatalities lives in damp spots in the air conditioning systems of large buildings. The disease was a mystery for some time and the bacterium was not easily isolated. *Legionella* is an obligate oligotroph and cannot compete with other bacteria in the rich organic soup usually used by bacteriologists, thus the almost distilled water produced by condensation was its preferred habitat.

If one places an open container of sterile, highly purified water outdoors, life will quickly colonize it. First the water will come into equilibrium with the dissolved gases carbon dioxide, oxygen, and nitrogen. Some nutrients will dissolve from the walls of the container and some enter as aerosols or from atmospheric dust. Spores or resting stages of bacteria, algae, fungi, protozoans, and some small higher animals drift in on the wind and colonize the water, and evaporation concentrates the dilute nutrients until growth is possible.

Inorganic nutrients provide the chemical constituents on which the entire food chain is based. The multitude of inorganic salts and dissolved gases in natural waters can be conveniently divided into three groups: (1) major and minor nutrients (Chaps. 7 to 10); (2) those whose effect is largely ionic (Chaps. 10, 19); and (3) toxicants (Chap. 10). The nutrients that are important in lakes are those which are often in short supply and which limit growth of plants and animals. Common nutrients needed in large quantities for cell development include CO_2, O_2, NH_4, NO_3, PO_4, SiO_2, SO_4, and Fe. Important minor nutrients that may occasionally be in short supply

include manganese, cobalt, molybdenum, copper, and zinc. Sodium, potassium, and chloride ions are often abundant in lakes, but their effect is largely ionic and occurs at the surface of delicate membranes through which ions are exchanged.

Some common inorganic substances, such as copper and zinc, can act either as toxicants or as growth stimulators. Although copper is an essential trace element for algae, high levels of copper sulfate (called bluestone) have been used for many years to poison algae in reservoirs, recreational pools, and lakes. These metals are normally present at low levels or in a nontoxic form, but they may become toxic under unusual, acid conditions, such as in some volcanic springs or in the leachate from coal and metal mining operations. Some organisms can adapt to toxic metals if given sufficient time for physiological adaptation. We have observed streams below 20-year-old copper and zinc mines that were totally devoid of life, but have found organisms below mines abandoned in Roman times.

Small quantities of *organic compounds* are common in natural waters, especially in estuaries and eutrophic lakes. The organics can be divided into seven classes by their source or function in aquatic ecosystems: (1) refractory compounds; (2) those providing food for microbes; (3) chelating compounds; (4) extracellular enzymes; (5) those used by animals for communication; (6) those used for chemical defense, which is akin to chemical warfare; and (7) odiferous substances, which are notable because they cause problems in water supplies for humans.

1. *Refractory compounds* are those that are decomposed very slowly, if at all, thus they tend to accumulate even in oligotrophic lakes. The most common refractory compounds are the family of brownish *humic acids* leached out of the soil mantle. It is these compounds that give the characteristic yellow-brown color to bogs and dystrophic lakes and even large rivers such as the Rio Negro in the Amazon (Plate 4*b*, Fig. 17-1). On very rainy days the water supply at some remote limnological laboratories set in wooded areas becomes the color of weak tea, which is nonetheless consumed by the scientists as part of the limnological experience. Although aesthetically unappealing, humic acids are not toxic. In many areas ground water is not used for drinking due to the presence of humic acids; they are so chemically stable that it is very costly to remove them in water treatment plants.

2. Bacteria, fungi, some protozoans, and a few dinoflagellates are dependent for their growth on a supply of soluble and readily decomposable organic compounds. These substances are provided by many processes in lakes, including feeding and bacterial and fungal decomposition, and are also added from the inflows. Most lower animals and plants leak organic compounds through their cell membranes since they do not possess the waterproof skin of higher organisms. Acetate, glucose, and glycolate are common organic compounds consumed by lake bacteria that keep the level of such desirable organic foods low. All of these, particularly glycolate, are lost from phytoplankton that are stressed by high light or salinity.

3. One very important group of organic compounds acts as *chelating agents,* which change the ionic state of metals that might otherwise be toxic. They may even make available for assimilation some metals that are normally chemically inert. Some chelating agents are produced by algae and some animals in response to a need for the dissolved metal or as protection from its toxic effects. Humic acids and citrate are common natural chelating agents produced by decomposition of leaves in lakes and streams. The word *chelator* is derived from the word *chela,* or claw, of crustaceans such as crabs. The metal is held by a weak chemical bond between parts of the organic molecule in the same way a food particle is held between the two pincers of a crab. Chelation complexes play an important role in blood pigments and in the structure of the chlorophyll molecule (Fig. 10-4).

4. Most enzymes are retained in the plant cell, but extracellular enzymes play a role in lake waters in summer. The *alkaline phosphatases* are a group of enzymes that act on nonmetallic nutrients. These enzymes are excreted by algae when dissolved phosphate is scarce and function by splitting off phosphate originally bound to an organic molecule. Half the total phosphorus that zooplankton excrete may be organic phosphorus, but this fraction would be unavailable for plant growth if it were not for the existence of alkaline phosphatases. A *siderochrome* is a similar organic compound excreted by blue-green algae to make organically bound iron available.

5. Animals communicate chemically in water as they do on land (Hasler, 1966). Very dilute quantities of organic compounds play a vital role in the return of salmonid fish from the ocean to the freshwater streams where they were originally spawned. Other aquatic animals key their reproductive behavior to dissolved organic excretions. The common zooplankter *Daphnia* modifies its shape to become less easily attacked in response to chemicals released, presumably unwittingly, by one of its invertebrate predators (Chap. 13).

6. Animals and plants have probably engaged in a form of chemical warfare for hundreds of millions of years. Some plant leaves, for example, are toxic to deer or caterpillars, which thus feed elsewhere. Toxic compounds such as alkaloids require energy and scarce nutrients for their synthesis and are not always present. In fact, recent research suggests that some plants may actually produce toxic substances only when they are browsed upon by animals. Algae, like higher plants, excrete organic compounds that inhibit the growth of their competitors. This chemical warfare is often called *allelochemistry,* and the substances responsible are collectively called *antimetabolites.* Although important in terrestrial plant ecology and known to occur in dense cultures of algae, allelochemical effects are unlikely to be common in aquatic ecosystems due to the enormous dilution of any excreted material.

Other toxic compounds released by phytoplankton and attached algae seem to have less direct advantage to them. Some organic compounds produced by freshwater blue-green algae or red tides of marine and brackish-water dinoflagellates are among the most toxic substances known, but they do not kill the organisms that feed on them. For example, paralytic shellfish poisoning of humans is due to neurotoxins called saxitoxins concentrated in shellfish that have fed on a toxic dinoflagellate. Blue-green algae synthesize a saxitoxin and a hepatotoxin that can destroy the liver in mammals, including humans, although proven cases are rare. The reason for the toxin production in blue-green algae is not clear. Every year dozens of cows and hogs die when they drink water containing toxic blue-green algae, but millions of others that drink water containing similar algae are unharmed. This is one of the more fascinating applied limnology problems and requires the full armory of chemical tests such as high-pressure liquid chromatography and immunoassays.

7. Geosmin and MIB (2-methyl-isoborneol) are two of many organic compounds secreted by some algae and fungi that impart a musty odor to water. As with the toxins discussed above, there is no apparent reason for the production of these compounds. They are a nuisance in water supply systems that depend on eutrophic reservoirs as their source. Odor removal requires expensive chemical treatment, such as oxidation or filtration through activated carbon at the treatment plant.

THE INFLUENCE OF THE CLIMATE AND WATERSHED

To understand the chemical composition of the waters of a particular drainage system, we must consider the nature of the vegetation, the weathering of the parent rock, and climatic factors. The dissolution of rock is dependent on the solvent properties of water, the length of time the water has contact with the substrata, and temperature fluctuations.

The parent rock, climate, topography, and vegetation cover determine the chemistry of

water draining the lake's watershed. The gradual weathering and decay of the parent rock releases material directly to the runoff water. A general rule is that the *soft waters* of mountain lakes and streams in resistant, old rocks, such as granite, metamorphosed grits, or volcanic "tuffs," resemble rainwater in their chemical composition. Sedimentary rocks dissolve more easily to produce lakes and streams with *hard water* (Chap. 10), which is unlike rainwater. Climate strongly influences the rate of weathering and dissolution of minerals. Extreme heat and cold speed the weathering process by cracking rocks and altering soil conditions. Temperate climates with year-round rainfall usually produce well-vegetated soils that are resistant to erosion. Lakes and streams in these areas often have ample nitrogen but may be deficient in phosphorus or silica. In climates where a few heavy storms provide most of the water and erode the sparsely vegetated soils, nitrogen is often in short supply (Chaps. 8, 9).

Basin topography controls the stability of the site and regulates erosion. The chemical composition of streams fed by the snow and rain falling in a volcanic caldera is little altered by short passage down the small volcanic rim to the lake (Plate 2b). In contrast, inflows to a lake with a large drainage basin collect more dissolved nutrients. The ratio of lake surface area to drainage basin area is a major factor influencing the lake's trophic state (Table 20-1).

The nature of the vegetation in the watershed modifies the quality of soil water. A good example concerns the nitrogen cycle. Most nitrogen in the watershed comes from nitrate or ammonia in rainfall, but a few watershed bacteria can convert atmospheric nitrogen gas into a biologically available form (Chap. 8). In leguminous plants, nodules form on the roots and provide a site where these bacteria are provided with sugars by the plant in symbiotic exchange for the release of fixed nitrogen. Some nonlegumes, such as alder bushes and buckbrush, have similar root nodules for N_2-fixation. After these symbiotic N_2-fixing plants decay, the soil becomes enriched in nitrogen. Farmers take advantage of this process when they alternate crops of N_2-fixing legumes such as peas or beans with nitrogen-demanding crops such as corn. For limnologists this soil enrichment becomes important in drainage basins where nitrogen may limit phytoplankton growth in the lake.

For example, most tree leaves are deficient in nitrogen and phosphorus, which are conserved over the winter by being withdrawn into the trunk prior to leaf fall. Alder trees contain more nitrogen in their leaves due to the extra supply from N_2-fixation, and more of this nitrogen remains in the leaves when they fall. After decomposition, the nitrogen from the alder leaves passes on to increase the soluble nitrogen content of near-surface ground water. Castle Lake, California, is a small mountain lake that receives most of its water directly from snow melt, small springs, and groundwater seepage. Although these account for most of the lake's annual nitrogen, approximately one-third of its nitrogen is derived from leachate of the humus layer that develops beneath the trees under the N_2-fixing mountain alder, *Alnus tenuifolia.* The distribution of nitrogen between lake, spring water, trees, and soil is shown for Castle Lake in Fig. 6-1.

THE ATMOSPHERIC CONTRIBUTION

The airshed, the aerial counterpart to the watershed, is an important source of chemicals for the aquatic ecosystem. Even rainwater, which has been distilled from the surface of the ocean, brings with it measurable quantities of sodium and halogens (chlorine, bromine, iodine, and fluorine). The farther one gets from the seacoast, the smaller the proportion of sodium and halogens relative to such continental contaminates as sulfate. Iodine is essential for the functioning of the thyroid gland, and deficiencies of this element in food produce a swelling of the neck called *goiter,* once known as *Derbyshire neck* in that English county which has no seacoast. The central United States was once referred to as the *goiter belt,* and iodized salt has become the normal table salt in these areas. Goiter is not a forgotten disease: it was still pronounced in some mountain villages in Spain as recently as 1984.

Anyone who has attempted to prepare ammonia-free blanks in the laboratory appreciates water's great affinity for picking up ammonia from the atmosphere. Aerosols containing ammonia and some other chemicals are frequently produced by animals and can travel great distances (Chap. 8). There is an interesting study of a pig farm near, but not draining into, a pond that was carefully sloped so the drainage from the pigs would not pollute it. Despite this precaution, the pond was fertilized by aerial transport of ammonia from pig excreta to the pond.

Fires, dust storms, and volcanic activity are major contributors to the atmospheric load. Dust contains adsorbed nitrogen and phosphorus as well as trace metals. Airborne dust may be a major source of trace metals in some areas but is apparently insignificant in others.

SOIL EROSION AND SEDIMENTS

Erosion and runoff from timber harvesting, agriculture, road construction, and housing development all supply sediment to receiving waters. Particles of eroded sediment cause turbidity in streams and lakes. This is usually undesirable, as sediments may kill fish or impair their respiration by clogging the gills, smother fish spawning gravel, and bury submerged plants (Fig. 6-2).

Another concern is that sediments in lakes and streams act as sites for ion exchange between aquatic and solid phases (Eq. 2 in Chap. 9). If nutrients, trace elements, or biocides are in high concentration in the water, the sediments may remove them by adsorption; if their concentration is low, they tend to be released from the sediment into the water. Thus a dynamic equilibrium or buffering system exists between the nutrients adsorbed to sediment particles and the surrounding water, and an increase in the amount of sediments may upset this equilibrium. This is

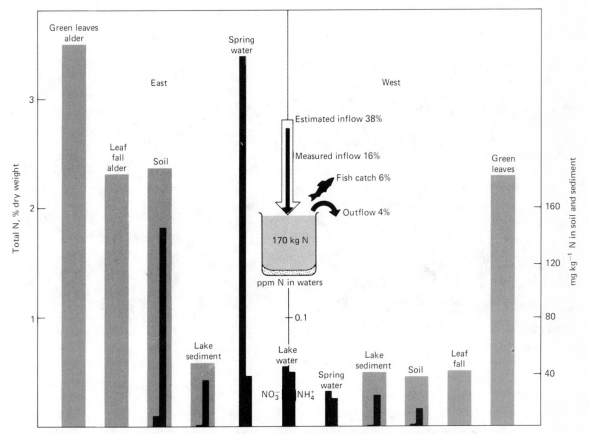

FIGURE 6-1 The contribution of nitrogen by alder trees (*Alnus tenuifolia*) to the nitrogen budget of Castle Lake, California, is evident from a comparison of the nitrogen distribution on the east and west sides of the lake. Alders are common on the east side and the west side is mostly covered with conifers. Grey bars represent the total organic nitrogen as percent dry weight of the alder and other deciduous plant leaves, the soil, and lake sediment. Solid bars are NO_3—N and NH_4—N levels in the soil and sediment in accordance with the scale on the right side of the figure. Lake water and spring water values (μg liter^{-1}) are indicated by the more exaggerated scale in the center of the figure. The average nitrogen content of the 19-ha (40 acre) lake with inflow, outflow, and fish removal as percentages of this average value is also given. Data from Goldman (1961). Figure redrawn from Frey (1963).

well documented for phosphate (Chap. 9). Bacteria, utilizing sediment and detritus for attachment, benefit from concentration of dissolved organic matter at the particle-water interface (Fig. 6-3).

Timber harvesting removes the natural vegetation cover for several years, until young trees spring up again. In addition, forests are frequently cut on steep slopes using heavy equipment, and many require road construction. The importance of the forest cover is twofold: it protects the soil from physical erosion; and root uptake recycles nutrients released by decomposition on the forest floor. With the vegetation removed, the loss of sediments and soluble plant nutrients from the land is greatly accelerated.

FIGURE 6-2 Extensive sediment deposits in a stream valley resulting from a mud flow in the hills of this tropical watershed. The erosion was caused by poor land management. The original stream is now buried by 10 m of soil.

Likens et al. (1970) have demonstrated that a forest will release large quantities of soil nutrients to the drainage system if recycling is interrupted by killing the vegetation.

Forest fires not only remove vegetation as effectively as lumberjacks, they also produce ash rich in minerals, which is easily blown or washed away. The combination of erosion of unprotected soil and production of ash decreases fertility on the land and increases fertility to too great a level in receiving waters. Controlled forest burns are a management strategy designed to reduce the fuel level of the forest floor to prevent the catastrophic effects of wildfires (Richter et al., 1982).

After point sources of pollution such as sewage outfalls, the diffuse pollution of sediments and soluble nutrients from poor land use tends to dominate the degradation of lakes and streams. Urbanization has created an ever-increasing diffuse source of sediments and other nutrients to the aquatic environment. Roads increase runoff and promote erosion along their margins. Fertilizers used for lawns and golf courses contribute to eutrophication. Studies are needed to determine what land development strategies are least harmful and how best to regulate the use of heavy earth-moving equipment to reduce vegetation loss and soil disturbance. This is particularly important in mountain habitats and at high latitudes, where regrowth is extremely slow as a result of cold winter and dry summer conditions.

HUMAN EFFECTS ON GLOBAL WATER CHEMISTRY: ACID RAIN

Plants, animals, and humans have always affected water chemistry. About 3 billion years ago blue-green algae became common. They were the first organisms to release oxygen from photosynthesis, and the resulting oxygen ''pollu-

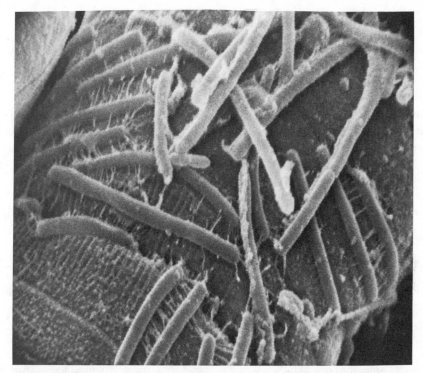

FIGURE 6-3 Detritus, magnified 4000 times. In this case dead stream algae have become covered with long rods of bacteria, whose pinlike appendages hold them to the algae in the fast-flowing waters. The bacteria also bind many small algae together to form larger clumps of detritus, which become food for animal suspension feeders. SEM photograph by H. W. Paerl.

tion'' changed forever global chemistry in the land, air, and water. Human effects on the landscape due to cutting, grazing, and burning of forests date back more than 10,000 years, but it is only over in the last century that humans have had a global influence. Examples include the increase in carbon dioxide due to burning of fossil fuels, the fluorocarbon-promoted ''ozone hole'' in the southern stratosphere, and the worldwide presence of the volatile pesticide DDT in animal fats.

On a lesser, but still very large, scale, mining has contaminated large rivers with copper, zinc, and other heavy metals. The use of the antiknock agent tetraethyl lead in gasoline has had a similar result, although low-lead gasoline is now common. Fish in some parts of the Great Lakes and the Hudson River are contaminated by careless disposal of the insulating oil polychlorinated biphenyl (PCB). Acid rain is an example of the large-scale effects of human activities.

Acid rain, a phenomenon that has generated much publicity since the 1970s, is rain with a pH of less than 5.0 (5.5 according to some authorities). Acid rain may seem to be a simple problem: sulfur oxides released from power stations dissolve in pure rainwater to form sulfuric acid, which then falls on lakes and streams, making them acidic; this acidity kills fish. However, the effects on any lake or stream may vary from no effect to almost total destruction of the biota.

Toxic effects may be due as much to dissolved metals and the geology of the watershed as to the acidity of the rain.

Acid rain was first reported in the mid-1880s (Smith, 1852; Barret and Brodin, 1955; Gorham, 1955) and exists in most industrialized areas of the world, for example the German Ruhr, Pittsburgh, Pennsylvania, and Gary, Indiana. One of the authors was raised in the industrial northern England town of Doncaster in the 1950s and remembers when acidic particles from the local steel mills and domestic coal fires would burn holes in laundry drying in the yard. Fifty years of acid rain and soot also had a dramatic effect on churches and public buildings. To reduce the risk of fire, these building were often built of local limestone, which has a pale creamy yellow color. After 100 years of the industrial revolution, all of the buildings were black and encrusted with hard grime, and the delicate carvings of the churches were reduced to featureless blobs.

In a famous example, the normal light colored individuals of one species of pale brown moth began to become less common than dark individuals that were thus camouflaged from predators when they alighted on black, soot-covered vegetation. In the 1950s tall smokestacks, some over 300 m high, were constructed to disperse the acid pollution over a much larger area, and alkaline particles were removed by electrostatic precipitation. This had the effect of leaving acid gases such as sulfur dioxide, while removing some of the balancing alkalinity. More widespread acid pollution resulted, which crossed national boundaries and created modern acid rain pollution.

Acidity in Natural and Polluted Rain

Uncontaminated rain water is naturally acidic. At equilibrium with the air, water contains atmospheric gases, including carbon dioxide. Carbonic acid forms when the carbon dioxide dissolves. With a pH of about 5.6 (on a log scale where 7 is neutral; see Chap. 7 for details), this weak acid is 25 times more acid than distilled water. Some natural rain can be more acid than 5.6 due to the addition of sulfates from volcanic eruptions and nitrogen oxides formed during lightening storms. Rain having a pH of less than 5.0 is usually due to human activities. The relative acidity or alkalinity of various waters is shown in Fig. 6-4. In many areas acid rain has a pH of less than 4.5 (Fig. 6-5).

Acid rain occurs after gases formed by burning fuels that contain sulfur and nitrogen are released into the air. Since coal and oil are the compressed and modified remains of ancient forests and animals, it is not surprising that they contain many elements in addition to carbon. The most important of these are sulfur and nitrogen, which may contain various numbers of oxygen atoms and are commonly referred to as NO_x and SO_x. Sulfur dioxide (SO_2) is the most stable SO_x emitted during combustion. When released to the atmosphere, it reacts with photochemically produced ozone to produce sulfur trioxide. In turn, this dissolves in water droplets to produce sulfuric acid. The photochemical process is an essential component in most, if not all, acid rain formation. The basic equations are shown below.

$$SO_2 + O_3 \rightleftharpoons SO_3 + O_2 \text{ (all in the gas phase)}$$
$$\rightleftharpoons SO_3 \text{ (gas)} + H_2O \rightleftharpoons H_2SO_4$$

Similarly, the most thermodynamically stable NO_x at high temperatures emitted from smokestacks is nitrous oxide (NO). Like sulfur dioxide, as it cools it first reacts with ozone in the air to produce nitrogen dioxide (NO_2), which dissolves in the rain water to give nitric acid and more nitrous oxide:

$$3NO_2 \text{ (gas)} + H_2O \rightleftharpoons 2HNO_3 + NO$$

In most areas acid rain is primarily due to sulfur oxides emitted from conventional oil- or coal-fired power stations and other industrial energy plants. Nuclear, solar, and hydropower electricity generating plants do not emit NO_x or SO_x, but geothermal power plants may release sulfur

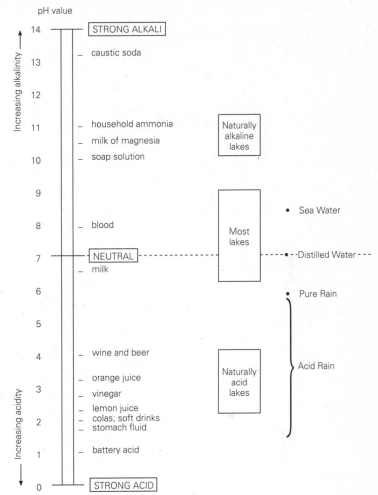

pH value

FIGURE 6-4 Acidity of natural lakes and acid rain as compared with common substances. The pH scale is logarithmic; a difference of 1 pH unit indicates a change of 10 in the number of hydrogen ions, which are the agents of acidity. Unpolluted lakes can range from very alkaline (pH 11) to very acid (pH 2), but most lie between 6.5 and 9. The pH of most acid rain is about 4.5 or 12 times more acid than pure rainwater (pH 5.6). The very high acidity of soft drinks and colas would be harmful if they were not neutralized by the body. Most wines and soft drinks will easily dissolve varnishes, and the sting of soap in one's eye is due to its high alkalinity. Modified from Park (1987).

gases such as hydrogen sulfide. These can be oxidized in the atmosphere to produce SO_x. Tall smoke stacks spread SO_x far and wide, as can be seen from the extent of acid precipitation in North America shown in Fig. 6-5. Quite clearly the acidity is downwind of major industrial areas such as the midwestern United States and Ontario, Canada. The situation is similar downwind of industrial areas in Europe. In parts of North America the rainfall in summer has a pH as low as 3.5, about 125 times more acid than normal rainfall. Rainfall with pH values of 4 to 4.5 are

common in parts of Canada, Scandinavia, and eastern Britain.

In most areas of the world the acid rain is dominated by sulfates. In contrast, in parts of the western United States, the acid gases in the atmosphere are often dominated by NO_x released from automobile exhaust. This typically occurs during photochemical smog events on calm sunny days, so the acid rain is better termed *acid fog* or *acid dew*. It is actually produced at night or in the early morning when condensation occurs. The pH levels are usually similar to those

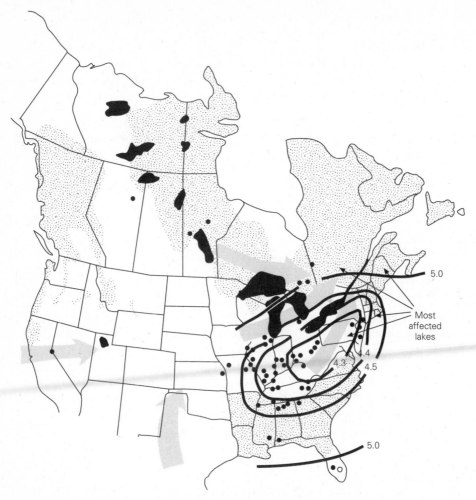

FIGURE 6-5 Interaction of meteorology, watershed soil chemistry, and location of sulfur-producing power plants on the location of acid rain and the production of acid lakes. Isopleths show the average annual pH in rainwater for the eastern United States and Canada. Most acid rain occurs in the northeast of the continent. Serious problems begin when the pH drops below 4.5. Large dots represent areas having over 100,000 tons of SO_2 emissions annually; arrows, the prevailing winds; and dotted areas, granitic areas where the soils have little buffering capacity to neutralize the acidity in the rain. Note that the most acid rain does not always produce the most acid lakes. A combination of low pH rain and a poorly buffered watershed produces an acid lake. Modified from the Canadian Embassy (1989) and Cogbill (1976).

for sulfur-dominated acid rain but may fall as low as 2 in smog droplets. Less NO_x is produced in the rainy season, and most rainfall in the mountains downwind of Los Angeles, for example, has a pH between 5 and 5.4. Finally, not all acid rain is due to inorganic acids. In urban areas acid dew may derive as much as one-fifth of its acidity from organic acids, primarily formic and acetic acids (Pierson et al. 1988).

Dry fallout occurs in all areas but is obviously

more important in summer or in dry climates, when deposition of nitrates and sulfates in particles and aerosols is a major contributor to the overall acidity. Although termed dry, there are often small amounts of moisture adsorbed on the surface of airborne particles and acids can form in this water layer.

Effect of the Watershed on Stream Acidity

The combination of low pH in rainwater and low buffering capacity in soils eventually results in acid lakes. Normal lakes have a pH of 6.5 to 9, well above the natural acidity of rainwater (pH 5.6). Most lakes affected by acid rain have a pH between 4.5 and 6.0 and most are less acid than the rainwater that falls in their watersheds, with a pH of 4.5 to 5.0. The discrepancy is due to the buffering of the hydrogen ions in acid rain by the soil. Rain falls to the ground and percolates through the shallow ground water to the streams and lakes. As it does so it encounters the soil buffering system, which is primarily calcium carbonate or limestone. This process is discussed in detail in Chap. 7. In brief, acids in rainwater can be neutralized by the calcium salts present in normal or alkaline soils. Thus lakes and streams tend to have a near-neutral pH despite the natural acidity of rain.

Some watersheds are low in calcium and other buffering salts in the rocks and soils. These are on granite rocks, such as the precambrian shield of eastern Canada and New England (Fig. 6-5) and similar regions in Scotland and Scandinavia. Lakes in these regions tend to have a lower pH than lakes in other areas, and the best-documented cases of long-term declines in fish populations are also from these regions.

Free hydrogen ions, the actual acid part of acid rain, are very active. They will replace calcium in limestone, as discussed above, but they will also replace many other cations bound in various ways by soil. As hydrogen ions pass through the soil they cause the release of free ions of copper, zinc, aluminum, and some other heavy metals. At elevated concentrations these

ions can be directly toxic to fish, invertebrates, and algae. The actual toxicity depends on the amount of other salts in the water as well as the amount and kind of organic compounds. These interact with the metals to change their chemical availability by chelation, as was discussed earlier in this chapter.

Acid Rain Effects on Biota

Most lakes and streams frequently experience changes in pH between 6.5 and 7.5 with no ill effects on the animals and plants. When the pH falls below 6 over the long term, there is a noticeable reduction in the abundance of many species, including snails, amphibians, crustacean zooplankton, and fish such as salmon and some trout species. Many other species, such as the brook trout, eel, some insects, and rotifers, may be unaffected by relatively small pH declines. Amphibians such as frogs and toads are very sensitive to acidity in the egg and tadpole stages, and even modest declines in pH may reduce their numbers. Other amphibians, such as newts, are less affected by acidity and may even increase in abundance as competition from other amphibians declines.

However, a long-term pH level of 5 will kill most organisms. Experimental studies in which sulfuric acid was added to lakes have shown that organisms gradually die off as the pH is lowered. Reproduction is impaired and although, for example, adult fish may linger on for many years, the eggs or young will die. Not all life perishes, and a few species of attached green algae may actually flourish. Acid-loving *Sphagnum* moss, for example, may become more common in the shallow littoral zones. In this way the overall lake primary production may remain constant for some time even though the species diversity falls and production at higher trophic levels is drastically reduced.

The complexity of the acid rain story becomes obvious when one tries to model the toxicity of the rain. The model compares experimental results of whole-lake acid additions with actual

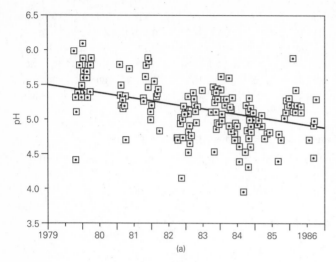

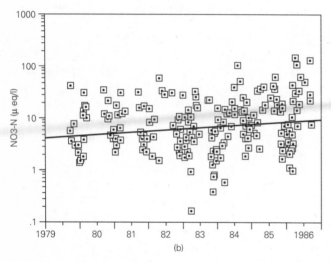

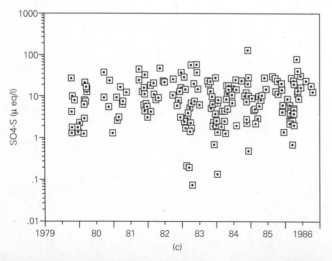

FIGURE 6-6 Acid rain as a source of nutrients. Trends in (*a*) rainfall acidity (pH), (*b*) nitrate, and (*c*) sulfate in rainwater and dry fallout in the Lake Tahoe basin. In the western United States the increase in acidity that forms acid rain is mostly due to nitric acid produced from the NO_x gases in automobile exhausts. (*a*) A small decrease in pH between 1979 and 1986. (*b*) A small but statistically significant ($P <$ 0.01) increase in nitrate. (*c*) An insignificant change in sulfate over the same period. These data were collected in a small granitic watershed that flows to the lake. Phytoplankton growth was limited by nitrogen in 1979 but the increase in acid rain nitrate shifted the limitation more to phosphorus by 1986. Modified from Byron et al. (1991).

data from lakes and streams in granitic watersheds. Even though these little-buffered systems are more easily acidified, it is apparent that some lakes and streams are much more affected than would be predicted from the model based on measured acidity. In other words, the fish and invertebrates in most lakes have not vanished due to the increased acidity alone. Other factors, primarily metals and irregular events such as storms, play a pivotal role in the indirect manifestation of the toxic effect of acid rains in fresh water.

When present in sufficient quantities, aluminum becomes toxic to fish when the pH drops below 6.2. The toxic effect is thus due to the release of soil-bound aluminum ions combined with increased lake acidity. In some only slightly acid waters Al^{3+} is the primary cause of fish deaths. In clean mountain water and at a pH below 6, the aluminum ion precipitates on the gills of fish and interferes with the transfer of calcium and sodium between the blood and the water. The fish produce mucus on their gills to ward off the toxicant, which unfortunately also prevents efficient transfer of oxygen. The net result is that the fish suffer respiratory stress and may eventually die because they have lost the ability to control the ionic balance in their blood.

Increases in aluminum may also reduce the productivity of the lake. At near-neutral lake pH values aluminum is thermodynamically more stable as aluminum phosphate than as the free ion Al^{3+}. In fact, aluminum salts such as alum are often added to lakes to decrease the phosphates added from detergents or agricultural runoff. Even if the lake can buffer the acidity of the inflowing acidic stream, the extra aluminum load may precipitate soluble phosphate, which sinks to the lake bed and is no longer available for algal growth. Phytoplankton decline and in turn the zooplankton, which serve as fish food, also decrease. Most acid lakes are more oligotrophic than in their original state.

The opposite effect is also possible, since nitrate in acid rain can increase eutrophication in unproductive lakes. For example, Lake Tahoe is a very unproductive lake where algae growth in summer was originally limited by the amount of nitrate in the epilimnion. Over the last 10 years the amount of acid deposition, both rain and dry fallout, has risen slightly (Fig. 6-6). The increase can be attributed to more automobile use in the local lake basin and in the San Francisco and Sacramento metropolitan regions, which lie downwind. The small but statistically significant trend of increasing nitrate in the lake parallels a steady increase in algal growth. Lake Tahoe has so few nutrients of any kind that even the relatively small amount of nitrate added each year by fallout has caused the phytoplankton to become increasingly phosphorus-limited. Over the years the total amount of nitrate in the lake has increased by several hundred tons. Similar increases in nitrate in rainfall have occurred in other regions, but with lesser effects on eutrophication due to the larger amounts of nitrate already present in most lake waters. For example, Lake Michigan is oligotrophic and downwind of several major urban regions (Fig. 6-5). However, its epilimnion contains over 100 μg liter^{-1} NO_3–N during the summer, compared with only about 1 to 4 μg liter^{-1} NO_3–N in Lake Tahoe. In addition, as was described earlier, in most situations sulfate contributes much more to acid rain than does nitrate.

Chemistry provides the third element in the structure of aquatic ecosystems. In the next four chapters we discuss in greater detail the limnological chemistry of lakes. Where it is different from lakes, stream chemistry is covered in Chap. 16.

FURTHER READING

DeMort, W. R. 1986. "The Role of Taste in Food Selection by Freshwater Zooplankton." *Oecologia* **69**:334–340.

Droop, M. 1957. "Auxotrophy and Organic Compounds in Nutrition of Marine Phytoplankton." *J. Gen. Microbiol.*, **16**:286–293.

Charles, D. F. (ed.). 1991. *Acid Deposition and Aquatic Ecosystems: Regional Case Studies.* Springer-Verlag, New York. 747 pp.

Fogg, G. E. 1971. "Extracellular Products of Algae in Freshwater." *Arch. Hydrobiol. Beih.,* **5:**1–25.

Folt, C., and C. R. Goldman. 1981. "Allelopathy between Zooplankton: A Mechanism for Interference Competition." *Science,* **213:**1133–1135.

Gold, K. 1964. "Aspects of Marine Dinoflagellate Nutrition Measured by ^{14}C Assimilation." *J. Protozool.,* **11:**85–89.

Goldman, C. R. 1961. "The Contribution of Alder Trees *(Alnus Tenuifolia)* to the Primary Productivity of Castle Lake, California." *Ecology,* **42:**282–288.

Golterman, H. L., and R. S. Clymo (eds.). 1967. *Chemical Environment in the Aquatic Habitat.* Noord-Hollandsche Uitgevers-Mij., Amsterdam. 322 pp.

Haines, T. A. 1981. "Acidic Precipitation and Its Consequences for Aquatic Ecosystems: A Review." *Trans. Am. Fish. Soc.* **110:**669–707.

Isom, B. G., S. D. Dennis, and J. M. Bates (eds.). 1986. *Impact of Acid Rain and Deposition on Aquatic Biological Systems.* Publication 04-928000-16. ASTM, Philadelphia. 114 pp.

Kaushik, N. K., and H. B. N. Hynes. 1971. "The Fate of Dead Leaves That Fall into Streams." *Arch. Hydrobiol.,* **68:**465–515.

Mann, K. H. 1988. "Production and Use of Detritus in Various Freshwater, Estuarine, and Coastal Marine Ecosystems." *Limnol. Oceanogr.* **22:**910–930.

Park, C. C. 1987. *Acid Rain: Rhetoric and Reality.* Methuen, 272 pp.

Paerl, H. 1973. "Detritus in Lake Tahoe: Structural Modification by Attached Microflora." *Science* **180:**496–498.

Provasoli, L. 1963. "Organic Regulation of Phytoplankton Fertility." pp. 165–219. In M. N. Hill (ed.). *The Sea.*

Saunders, G. W. 1971. "Carbon Flow in the Aquatic System." pp. 31–45. In J. Cairns (ed.). *Structure and Function of Freshwater Microbial Communities.* Research Division Monograph 3. Virginia Polytechnic Institute, Blacksburg.

Tjossem, S. F. 1990. "Effects of Fish Chemical Clues on Vertical Migration of *Chaoborus.*" *Limnol. Oceanogr.,* **35:**1456–1468.

CHAPTER 7

Oxygen and Carbon Dioxide

OVERVIEW

Oxygen and carbon dioxide can be considered together in lakes since they are so closely inter-related in photosynthesis and respiration. Oxygen participates in many important chemical and biological reactions, and dissolved oxygen is a variable frequently measured by limnologists. It is continually consumed in respiration by both plants and animals but is produced by plant photosynthesis only when sufficient light and nutrients are available. Cold, well-oxygenated water contains less than 5 percent of the oxygen contained in a similar volume of air, and this amount rapidly decreases as water temperature increases. Water contains so little oxygen due to the combination of a relatively low partial pressure of oxygen in the atmosphere (0.21 atm) and its low solubility. The lack of oxygen in water relative to air means that oxygen is easily depleted by respiration and decomposition unless continually replenished by the air. The short- and long-term variations in dissolved oxygen of lakes and rivers are a good measure of their trophic states. For example, oligotrophic waters show little variation from saturation, while eutrophic

ones may range from virtual anoxia in the hypolimnion to supersaturation in the epilimnion. When oxygen is depleted to a low level it causes a change in the reduction-oxidation state (*redox potential*) and solubility of many metals and some nutrients. Organic matter from natural sources or domestic and industrial wastes may result in serious depletion of dissolved oxygen. When this occurs most aquatic organisms perish or are replaced by a few specialized organisms tolerant of low oxygen levels.

Carbon dioxide concentrations in water frequently show an inverse relationship to oxygen. Carbon dioxide is a product of respiration by both plants and animals and also provides the major carbon source for photosynthesis. Although only a minor component of air, CO_2 is quite abundant in water because its solubility is more than 30 times that of oxygen. Carbon dioxide dissolves in water to produce carbonic acid (H_2CO_3), which dissociates into various fractions (CO_2, HCO_3^-, CO_3^{2-}) depending on the hydrogen-ion concentration (pH). At typical pH levels of 6 to 8, bicarbonate is the most abundant carbon fraction and the rate-limiting step from bicarbonate to CO_2 is dehydration of the carbonic acid intermediate. This reaction may limit photosynthetic rates for a short time during calm days in some productive waters where free CO_2 levels are low relative to plant demand. When the demand for CO_2 for photosynthesis is high, precipitation of calcium carbonate occurs, especially in hard-water lakes. This results in two common lake phenomena: benches of limestone or marl are deposited around the edges of *marl lakes* and colloidal suspensions of calcium carbonate produce a *lake whitening,* which decreases water clarity.

The single most important environmental factor regulating the concentration of oxygen and carbon dioxide is temperature, but the levels also depend on photosynthesis of plants, respiration of all organisms, aeration of the water, presence of other gases, and any chemical oxidations that may occur. Further, oxygen and carbon dioxide can enter or leave an aquatic ecosystem chemically combined with other elements as well as dissolved in water or as gas.

In this chapter we consider O_2 and CO_2 dissolved gases: measurement; sources; pH and the carbonate-bicarbonate-CO_2 equilibrium; temperature, salinity, and biotic effects; seasonal and diel variations and the hypolimnetic oxygen deficit; CO_2 as a limiting nutrient; O_2 and CO_2 in streams; and the redox potential.

MEASUREMENT

The distribution of oxygen and carbon dioxide in natural waters provides a convenient measure of organic production and decomposition and forms the basis of most methods of measuring primary productivity (Chap. 15). The first extensive measurements of dissolved oxygen were probably in the estuary of the River Thames, England, in 1882 (Fig. 22-14). S. A. Forel studied oxygen in Lake Geneva, Switzerland, in 1885, and modern studies of oxygen distribution began with Birge and Juday in 1911. The Winkler titration method for measuring oxygen concentration, devised in the 1860s, is a simple oxidation-reduction reaction routinely performed by aquatic biologists. Oxygen-sensitive electrodes, which are regularly calibrated with the Winkler method, have facilitated continuous measurement and have broadened our knowledge of the distribution of oxygen in all aquatic ecosystems. Redox potential or reduction-oxidation status of the water is also easily measured with a probe. The main problem with most oxygen probes is that the delicate membrane over the electrode must be replaced frequently. Computer models based on the annual cycles of dissolved oxygen and temperature are often used for pollution control. Such models are particularly useful for predicting the quality of hypolimnion releases below large dams.

Carbon dioxide is less frequently measured but is needed to estimate organic production and decomposition. Total inorganic carbon (CO_2 + HCO_3^- + CO_3^{2-}) is easily measured by titration or gas analyzers. A common technique involves sealing a small water sample in a glass ampule. This is later opened and the CO_2 released by acidification and flushing with inert carrier gas. Acidification converts all of the inorganic carbon to carbon dioxide, which is measured by its adsorption spectrum in an infrared gas analyzer. If the original pH and temperature of the lake are known, free carbon dioxide can be determined from the total inorganic carbon present using standard tables of dissociation constants.

OXYGEN AND CARBON DIOXIDE IN LAKES

Figure 7-1 illustrates the distribution of oxygen, free carbon dioxide, and temperature with depth during summer stagnation in a eutrophic lake. Dissolved oxygen is high in the epilimnion and low in the hypolimnion. The oxygen decline in the hypolimnion is indirectly due to the productivity of the epilimnion, since the more organisms of all types in the epilimnion the more dead and decomposing material will sink through the hypolimnion to the lake bottom and use up oxygen. The depth distribution of free CO_2 is the

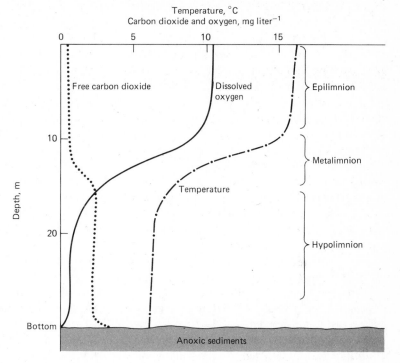

FIGURE 7-1 Changes in dissolved oxygen, carbon dioxide, and temperature with depth for midsummer in a typical eutrophic lake. None of the dissolved gases are in perfect equilibrium with the concentrations in air, since biological processes and temperature effects in the water and sediments are more rapid than the fluxes through the air-water interface or across the thermocline. Note that the plots of free CO_2 and dissolved O_2 are virtual mirror images.

mirror image of that of oxygen (Fig. 7-1), because the photosynthetic reaction that produces oxygen in the epilimnion is reversed to favor respiration in the hypolimnion. Thus carbon dioxide increases due to decomposition of organic matter.

SOURCES OF OXYGEN AND CARBON DIOXIDE

One main source of oxygen and carbon dioxide for all aquatic ecosystems is the atmosphere. Additional CO_2 is produced from organic carbon by respiration, especially in the sediments. Additional O_2 is released from the photolysis of water in the epilimnion during photosynthesis.

Diffusion from the Atmosphere: Solubility of Gases

Both oxygen and carbon dioxide are important constituents of air. Air contains about 21 percent oxygen by volume, or 300 mg oxygen per liter

of air, but water at 0°C at sea level contains only 14.6 mg liter^{-1} O_2. Carbon dioxide in the atmosphere is about 0.033 percent by volume, and water at 0°C at sea level contains 1.10 mg liter^{-1} CO_2. While both gases diffuse slowly into static liquids, solution is accelerated by turbulent mixing, as occurs in a lake epilimnion or in streams.

The laws of Henry and Dalton govern the solution of gases. Henry's law, on the mixture of gases, states that the concentration of a solution of a gas which has reached equilibrium is proportional to the partial pressure at which the gas is supplied. Dalton's law also applies to a mixture of gases in solution and states that the pressure of each component of gas is proportional to its concentration in the mixture, the total pressure of all gases being equal to the sum of the components. Nitrogen (79 percent of air) has a partial pressure of 0.79 atm, oxygen (21 percent) a partial pressure of 0.21 atm, and carbon dioxide (0.033 percent) a partial pressure of 0.00033 atm. The gases dissolved in well-aerated water will come into equilibrium with the atmospheric mixture of gases. Their different solubilities, however, determine how much of a given gas water can hold. A combination of partial pressure and solubility determine exactly how much of each gas is dissolved. Oxygen is about 2 times as soluble as nitrogen, but its partial pressure is one-quarter that of nitrogen (Table 7-1). Thus the ratio of both gases dissolved in water is roughly 1:1.4 (O_2:N_2). Carbon dioxide is about 35 times more soluble than oxygen and has a partial pressure about 1/700 that of oxygen. Unlike nitrogen and oxygen, carbon dioxide is more abundant in water than in the air. Changes in barometric pressure alter the concentrations of dissolved gases, since all are more soluble at higher pressures. Lakes at high elevations contain less dissolved gas per unit volume than lakes of equal temperatures at sea level.

Wind plays an important role in the distribution of dissolved gases by providing the energy to stir the water column. As they splash over rocks, streams are naturally aerated and are usually saturated with oxygen. As a result, streams provide an effective system of self-purification from organic matter pollution, which has long been exploited by streamside civilizations. Waves breaking on shore also expose a large surface area for diffusion and, like the water in the rapids of a stream, are saturated with dissolved gases.

Artificial oxygenation by bubbling air or pure oxygen into polluted waters is a technique used for lake and river restoration (Chap. 22). The method is in particular demand for maintaining a salmonid or other cold-water fishery in otherwise anoxic hypolimnia. Large reservoir operations, such as those of the Tennessee Valley Authority, inject pure oxygen into the hypolimnion and also to the outflows from their reservoirs. Without augmentation, the river below the dam will not contain sufficient oxygen to meet water standards.

Carbon dioxide in the atmosphere has more than doubled over the last 100 years due to the burning of fossil fuels. Although this increase may cause global warming, it has had no apparent effect on photosynthesis in lakes and oceans. However, since algae respond to an increase in CO_2 by increasing their growth rates, eventually some of the more productive lakes and oceans may come to contain more phytoplankton.

Photosynthesis and Respiration

Photosynthesis produces oxygen and consumes carbon dioxide, while respiration consumes oxygen and produces carbon dioxide. It is thus convenient to consider photosynthesis and respiration together:

$$nCO_2 + H_2O \rightleftharpoons (CH_2O)_n + O_2 \qquad (1)$$

where n is usually 3, 6, or 12 (e.g., pyruvate, glucose, or sucrose). Relative concentrations of carbon dioxide and oxygen depend on whether the process is going from left to right or from right to left. In productive waters photosynthesis and respiration are dominant in establishing the levels of oxygen and carbon dioxide, but in oligotrophic waters these processes have only a slight influence.

Photosynthetic activity of algae and higher plants is, along with the atmosphere, one of the major sources of oxygen in the aquatic environment. For plants, oxygen is essentially an unwanted byproduct of photosynthesis and originates from the water molecule, not from carbon dioxide. Photosynthetic oxygen is released dur-

TABLE 7-1

SOLUBILITIES OF THE MAIN ATMOSPHERIC GASES IN WATER AT 1 ATM AND 0° AT SEA LEVEL

The combination of solubility and partial pressure gives water in equilibrium with air a total dissolved gas content of about 1.1 mg liter^{-1} (CO_2), 14.6 mg liter^{-1} (O_2), and 20 mg liter^{-1} (N_2).

Gas	Solubility, cm^3 per 100 ml water	Percent in air
Carbon dioxide	171	0.003
Oxygen	4.9	21
Nitrogen	2.33	79

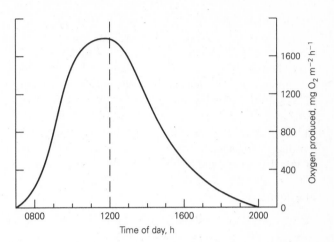

FIGURE 7-2 Photosynthesis is an important source of dissolved oxygen in many lakes. The other main source is diffusion from the air. In an extreme case—very eutrophic Lake George, Uganda—photosynthetic rates are so high that supersaturation of O_2 to as much as 250 percent can occur. Modified from Ganf and Horne (1975). In oligotrophic lakes, in contrast, photosynthesis is a very small source of dissolved oxygen. Photosynthesis is a true new source of oxygen, since it is derived from the splitting of the water molecule in photosystem II .

ing daylight, in an amount proportional to the productivity of the water (Fig. 7-2). High rates of production in the epilimnion during the day greatly increase oxygen levels. Carbon dioxide levels decrease as oxygen output rises but are supplemented to some extent by the reserve of bicarbonate and carbonate (HCO_3^- and CO_3^{2-}). The penetration of light influences the distribution of both oxygen and carbon dioxide in the aquatic system since photosynthesis can occur only in the photic zone (Fig. 2-2).

Respiration occurs at all depths, both day and night, and, together with the atmosphere, is the other main source of CO_2 for the lake. The amount of respiration is roughly proportional to biomass and is particularly high in organically rich sediments where bacteria are abundant. Most of the organic matter in large lakes originates from phytoplankton that grow in the lake. In small mountain or woodland lakes and in most lowland streams, dead leaves and branches are an important source of organic matter. When it decays the structural carbon from cellulose is converted to carbon dioxide.

At high rates of photosynthesis, oxygen production may exceed the diffusion of oxygen out of the system, and *oxygen supersaturation* may result. Very productive lakes, such as Lake George, Uganda, or Clear Lake, California, may reach 150 to 250 percent O_2 saturation. In other

situations, bubbles of oxygen are easily seen on the algae-covered rocks or on the leaves of submerged plants. In a common classroom exercise, bubbles forming on sunlit aquatic plants may be captured by placing an inverted funnel over them and leading the gas produced to an inverted test tube. A glowing splint or taper, when placed inside the tube, will burst into flames, demonstrating the presence of elevated concentrations of oxygen inside the tube. If filamentous green algae are present in lakes, oxygen bubbles may float them to the surface, forming scumlike mats that blow up on shore, to the annoyance of lakeside dwellers.

pH and the Carbonate-Bicarbonate-Carbon Dioxide Equilibrium

As discussed in the previous chapter the acidity or alkalinity of lakes is measured in units called pH, an exponential scale of 1 to 14 (Fig. 6-4). The term *pH* is derived from the French *puissance d'hydrogène* ("strength of the hydrogen"), because the hydrogen ion H^+ controls acidity. pH is defined as the negative log of the hydrogen-ion concentration. An *acid* solution is one with pH of 0 to 7 and *alkaline* from 7 to 14. Most lakes have a pH of 6 to 9; naturally acid lakes have a pH of 5 to 6; and leachate from mine tailings can be as low as pH 2. Some very eutrophic lakes and some soda lakes have pH values as high as 10 to 11.5 (Fig. 6-4). The hydrogen-ion concentration also controls the chemical state of many lake nutrients, including carbon dioxide. Changes in pH influence other important plant nutrients such as phosphate, ammonia, iron, and trace metals (Chaps. 8 to 10).

Carbon dioxide gas dissolves in water to form soluble carbon dioxide. This reacts with water to produce undissociated carbonic acid (H_2CO_3), which dissociates and equilibrates as bicarbonate (HCO_3^-) and carbonate (CO_3^{2-}) according to the equation:

$$\underset{\text{Gas}}{CO_2} \rightleftharpoons \underset{\substack{\text{Dissolved} \\ \text{gas}}}{CO_2} \overset{H_2O}{\rightleftharpoons} \underset{\substack{\text{Undissociated} \\ \text{carbonic acid}}}{H_2CO_3} \rightleftharpoons \underset{\text{Bicarbonate}}{HCO_3^-} + H^+$$

$$\rightleftharpoons \underset{\text{Carbonate}}{CO_3^{2-}} + 2H^+ \tag{2}$$

This series of reversible chemical changes is the most important of the several reactions that control pH in natural waters. As CO_2 is used up in photosynthesis or dissolves in from the air, the pH should change, since carbonic acid is either removed or added [Eq. (2)]. However, the pH shift is reduced or buffered by the huge reservoirs of carbonate and bicarbonate present (Fig. 7-3). The inorganic carbon equilibrium is the major pH *buffering system* for lakes and streams, which generally remain at a pH between 6 and 9. Reactions involving silica, discussed in Chap.

10, play a subsidiary role in the overall buffering of lake and stream waters.

The relative abundance of each ionic or molecular state at various pH levels is shown in Figs. 7-3 and 7-4. The precise levels of each component phase will vary with both the temperature and the ionic strength of the lake water. The free CO_2 necessary to maintain HCO_3^- in solution is called *equilibrium CO₂*. Most plants can utilize only CO_2 for photosynthesis. Since CO_2 can be supplied by diffusion from the air, from HCO_3^-, or from CO_3^{2-} [Eq. (2)], there is a potentially inexhaustible supply of carbon for plant growth. Some plants may also use HCO_3^- after converting it to CO_2 by using the enzyme *carbonic anhydrase*. However, for all practical purposes, the amount of equilibrium CO_2 available will depend on the rate at which the various reactions in Eq. (2) reach equilibrium.

The relative rates of reaction and amounts of the various inorganic carbon fractions in typical lake water are shown in Fig. 7-4. The rate-limiting step is obviously the hydration-dehydration of carbon dioxide to carbonic acid. Carbon dioxide is used during photosynthesis from a relatively small reservoir of dissolved CO_2. Away from the lake surface, where atmospheric CO_2 is available, HCO_3^- and CO_3^{2-} represent the main reserve of CO_2.

Since the H_2CO_3, HCO_3^-, CO_3^{2-} inter-

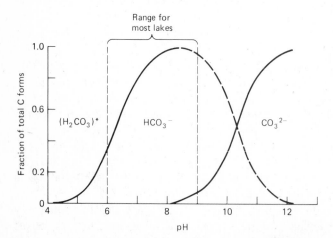

FIGURE 7-3 Changes in the three forms of inorganic carbon in a lake with changes in pH: $(H_2CO_3)^* = H_2CO_3 + CO_2$. Note that at the usual pH range in lakes, bicarbonate (HCO_3^-) is most abundant. Carbon dioxide is most abundant at low pH, while CO_3^{2-} dominates in high pH conditions. About 35 percent of the total inorganic carbon is present as bicarbonate at pH 6, but this fraction rises to 95 percent at pH 8. Algae and higher plants mostly use only CO_2, so little usable CO_2, (derived from $H_2CO_3^*$), is present in eutrophic lake surface waters.

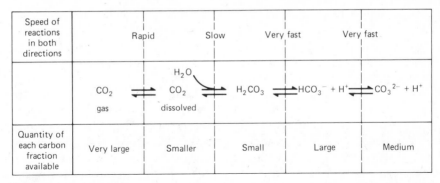

Speed of reactions in both directions	Rapid	Slow	Very fast	Very fast
	CO_2 gas $\rightleftharpoons$ CO_2 dissolved $\xrightarrow{H_2O}$ H_2CO_3 $\rightleftharpoons$ $HCO_3^- + H^+$ $\rightleftharpoons$ $CO_3^{2-} + H^+$			
Quantity of each carbon fraction available	Very large	Smaller	Small	Large	Medium

FIGURE 7-4 Reaction rates and amounts of carbon fractions in a typical lake at about pH 7 and 15°C. The slowest rate, the hydration-dehydration of CO_2, will potentially limit photosynthesis. Note the small amount of dissolved CO_2 available for photosynthesis relative to the large HCO_3^- and atmospheric CO_2 pools.

changes are very fast, Eq. (2) can be simplified to:

$$CO_2 \underset{\text{rapid}}{\overset{\text{rapid}}{\rightleftharpoons}} CO_2 + H_2O \underset{\text{slow}}{\overset{\text{slow}}{\rightleftharpoons}} \begin{pmatrix} H_2CO_3 \\ HCO_3^- \\ CO_3^{2-} \end{pmatrix} \quad (3)$$

$$\text{Gas} \qquad \text{Dissolved}$$

or away from the lake surface,

$$\underset{\text{Dissolved}}{CO_2} + H_2O \underset{\text{slow}}{\overset{\text{slow}}{\rightleftharpoons}} \begin{pmatrix} H_2CO_3 \\ HCO_3^- \\ CO_3^{2-} \end{pmatrix} \quad (4)$$

In the simplified form [Eq. (4)], the rate-limiting step for photosynthetic carbon uptake is more clearly the dehydration of carbonic acid. This does not usually limit the overall photosynthetic carbon yield, since wind mixing normally replaces CO_2 as it is used up. During short periods of intensive photosynthesis, however, this source may be insufficient to meet the maximum demands of the plants for CO_2 (Talling, 1976).

In some lakes precipitation of solid calcium carbonate occurs during periods of high photosynthesis. Such lakes are called *marl lakes,* and layers of whitish precipitate are formed around the lake edges below the surface. As deposits build up they form a characteristic marl bench in the euphotic zone. Where higher aquatic plants are present, marl may precipitate on them

and slowly encapsulate the leaves and stems in calcium carbonate. Obviously, the process can occur only in hard-water areas where there is a good supply of calcium. In these lakes the precipitation removes much of the available CO_2 reservoir in a form that is not returned to the lake waters.

The reaction of carbonic acid (H_2CO_3) in rainwater as it flows through the soil is:

$$H_2CO_3 + CaCO_3 \rightarrow Ca^{2+} + 2HCO_3^- \quad (5)$$

Thus inflowing streams contain both calcium ions and bicarbonate. The calcium ions enter the lake from the inflowing rivers and react with the most abundant inorganic carbon ion, bicarbonate, as follows:

$$Ca^{2+} + 2 HCO_3^- \rightleftharpoons Ca(HCO_3)_2 \rightarrow$$
$$\text{Soluble} \qquad \text{Soluble} \qquad\qquad (6)$$
$$\underset{\text{Insoluble}}{CaCO_3 \downarrow} + H_2O + CO_2 \underset{\text{by plants)}}{\text{(taken up}}$$

The reaction in Eq. (6) that produces $CaCO_3$ is essentially irreversible in lakes, since the weak carbonic acid (H_2CO_3) which could redissolve the $CaCO_3$ is soon lost to CO_2 uptake by plants. The photosynthetic uptake of equilibrium CO_2 continually pulls the reaction toward $CaCO_3$ until photosynthesis is stopped by darkness, lack of CO_2, or other limiting nutrients. The $CaCO_3$ precipitated may form solid masses, such as lime-stone, or remain as a colloidal suspension. Either of these forms can coprecipitate other chemicals or become coated with a layer of organic compounds. This coating can be of great importance to the allochthonous carbon budget of marl lakes (Wetzel and Otsuki, 1974). The fine suspension of $CaCO_3$ particles can rapidly reduce the light penetration in some lakes. This widespread phenomenon is called *lake whitening*. The chemistry causing the precipitation is not fully understood (Kelts and Hsu, 1978) but whiting occurs even in large lakes such as Pyramid Lake, Nevada, or Lake Michigan, where it can reduce the secchi depth from 9 to 3 m in a short time. A fine example is shown for Lake Michigan in Fig. 3-10.

TEMPERATURE, SALINITY, AND BIOTIC EFFECTS ON DISSOLVED OXYGEN

The concentration of oxygen in solution is inversely proportional to temperature. Boiling will produce an oxygen-free solution of water. At any given pressure, cold waters contain a higher oxygen concentration when saturated than warm waters. Of course, photosynthesis and respiration may alter this relationship in either direction. In unpolluted lakes and streams, the greatest loss of oxygen from the system occurs during the summer warming period. Temperature increase during spring and summer alone can account for a loss of 50 percent of the dissolved oxygen content of the coldest water. Figure 7-5 illustrates this important relationship between temperature and dissolved oxygen concentration.

It is often desirable to know whether lake or stream water is fully saturated with oxygen at a particular temperature. Oversaturation can indicate high levels of photosynthesis while undersaturation indicates organic pollution or natural respiration, as occurs after leaves fall into streams in autumn. The relationship between the measured dissolved oxygen, its percentage saturation, the water temperature, and altitude are traditionally interpreted using a nomograph of the type shown in Fig. 7-6. Increasing salinity has only a minor effect on dissolved oxygen con-

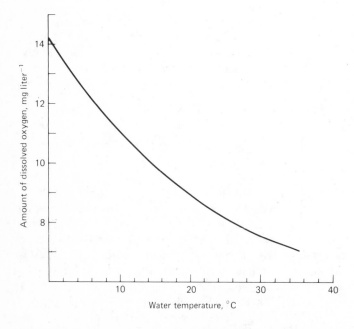

FIGURE 7-5 Relationship between dissolved oxygen and water temperature. Values are shown for a well-mixed system of pure water at sea level and at 760-mm Hg pressure. There is less dissolved oxygen at higher altitudes and in very saline water. The percent saturation is often used to illustrate oxygen deficits (Figs. 22-13, 22-14).

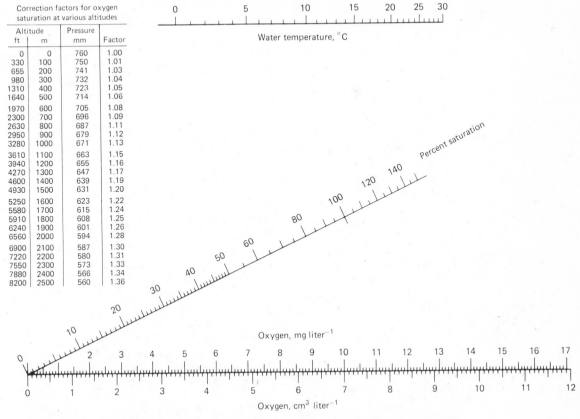

Correction factors for oxygen saturation at various altitudes			
Altitude ft	m	Pressure mm	Factor
0	0	760	1.00
330	100	750	1.01
655	200	741	1.03
980	300	732	1.04
1310	400	723	1.05
1640	500	714	1.06
1970	600	705	1.08
2300	700	696	1.09
2630	800	687	1.11
2950	900	679	1.12
3280	1000	671	1.13
3610	1100	663	1.15
3940	1200	655	1.16
4270	1300	647	1.17
4600	1400	639	1.19
4930	1500	631	1.20
5250	1600	623	1.22
5580	1700	615	1.24
5910	1800	608	1.25
6240	1900	601	1.26
6560	2000	594	1.28
6900	2100	587	1.30
7220	2200	580	1.31
7550	2300	573	1.33
7880	2400	566	1.34
8200	2500	560	1.36

FIGURE 7-6 Nomograph for calculating the percent dissolved oxygen at various temperatures, pressures, and altitudes. To obtain, for example, the amount of oxygen at saturation at 6°C, place a straight edge to cover both 6°C and 100 percent. The line extends down to 12.5 mg liter^{-1} for a freshwater lake at sea level. If the measured oxygen level was only 5 mg liter^{-1}, then the straight line between 5 mg liter^{-1} and 6°C intersects the percent saturation line at about 50. This indicates that the water was only 40 percent saturated with oxygen and that some pollution or high rate of respiration might be suspected. If the lake was at 1500 m (about 5000 ft), where air pressure is lower, the water would be fully saturated at a lower oxygen concentration. Altitude correction factors are shown in a table in the upper left; for 1500 m the correction is about 1.2. Thus a measured value of 10 mg liter^{-1} (as shown for Standley Lake in Fig. 7-8) is multiplied by 1.2 to give 12 mg liter^{-1}. This shows that 10 mg liter^{-1} at 5000 ft represents full saturation, not a situation where pollution has reduced the surface oxygen level. Drawn from data of Truesdale, Downing, and Lowden (1955). A more precise nomograph is in Mortimer (1981).

centration, namely that salts dissolved in water reduce the intermolecular space available for oxygen. Unless salinities are very high, such as in some Texas salt ponds (Simpson and Gunther, 1956), the Great Salt Lake, Utah, and Mono Lake, California, salinity influences on dissolved oxygen content are very small indeed.

Nomenclature of Oxygen-Depth Curves

Four general types of oxygen distribution in thermally stratified lakes are recognized. In waters of low productivity, oxygen distribution will largely be a function of temperature, resulting in fairly uniform *orthograde* distributions (Fig. 7-

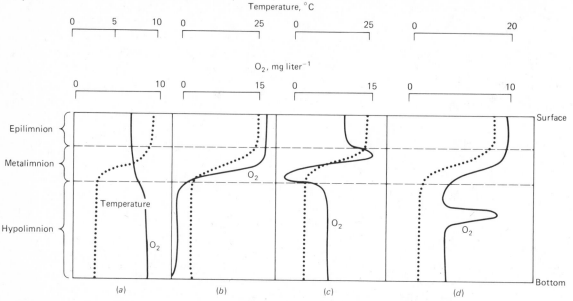

FIGURE 7-7 Types of oxygen distribution with depth. (a) Orthograde curve typical of an unproductive lake. (b) Clinograde curve from a productive lake. (c) Positive and negative heterograde curves. Here photosynthesis from a layer of algae just above the thermocline raises oxygen in the upper part of the metalimnion. Respiration occurring during bacterial decomposition and zooplankton grazing lowers oxygen levels just below the thermocline (metalimnion minimum). (d) Anomalous curves due to the inflow of dense, cool, oxygen-rich stream inflows, which form a discrete layer. In this example, the oxygen-rich stream inflow, is in midhypolimnion.

7a). This curve is characterized by no appreciable decrease or increase in oxygen concentration with depth. A *clinograde* curve is characterized by relatively higher oxygen content near the surface, where photosynthesis releases oxygen (Fig. 7-7b). It will occur if productivity is high, since oxygen depletion occurs both in the hypolimnion in summer and during winter stagnation under ice. A *heterograde* oxygen curve (Fig. 7-7c) exhibits an irregular slope from the lake surface to the depths. Concentration of animals may produce a *negative heterograde distribution* if respiration (oxygen consumption) dominates at some middepth, or a *positive heterograde distribution,* if photosynthetic organisms (oxygen producers) are concentrated in the same fashion. Other anomalous oxygen distributions may result from the settling of cooled high-oxygen surface waters or by layering at intermediate depths

of inflow waters (Fig. 7-7d) that have a different oxygen concentration than the lake.

Arctic and tropical lakes present different problems in terms of their oxygen distribution. The high temperatures of tropical lakes may preclude deep mixing if they are protected from wind and not at high elevation. These lakes may have permanent hypolimnetic oxygen deficits together with high concentrations of methane or hydrogen sulfide. Some very deep tropical lakes, such as Lake Tanganyika in Africa, may never mix or mix only on very rare occasions during unusual tropical storms. They are characterized by permanent clinograde oxygen curves frequently reaching zero below the density discontinuity. In the Arctic and Antarctic, lakes often pass from an ice cover to a continuously mixed condition and never warm sufficiently to stratify. Some lakes are permanently ice-covered, as in the case of the lakes Vanda and Bonney in the Antarctic. If they were more productive, these lakes would show severe oxygen depletion near the bottom. However, because of the clear ice, low productivity, and very low respiration, they do not have severe oxygen depletion despite the fact that they are permanently frozen over.

SEASONAL AND DIEL CHANGES IN OXYGEN AND CARBON DIOXIDE

Measurements of the distribution of oxygen and carbon dioxide in lake waters provide the limnologist with a great deal of information about the nature of the lake, including its trophic status. The concentration of oxygen in an aquatic environment is a function of biological processes such as photosynthesis or respiration and physical processes such as water movement or temperature. The concentrations of these two gases change over short and long time intervals. We discuss the annual change, as illustrated by the summer condition, and a *diel* (24-hour) cycle.

Seasonal Variations in Oxygen and Carbon Dioxide

As noted in Chap. 2, there is a distinct chemical structure in lakes and one aspect of this is the

FIGURE 7-8 Seasonal changes in dissolved oxygen in a mesotrophic lake. The lines are isopleths of dissolved oxygen at 1 mg liter^{-1} intervals, with heavy lines at 5 and 10 mg liter^{-1}. The dark area indicates levels of functional anoxia ($<$ 1 mg liter^{-1}). The horizontal lines close together at about 20 m from the lake bed indicate the thermocline. This lake, Standley Lake, is actually a reservoir and is situated at about 1500 m (5000 ft) in the foothills of the Rocky Mountains, near Denver, Colorado. Because it is so high the air pressure is less and oxygen saturation at about 6°C is only 10 mg liter^{-1}. If magically moved to sea level this lake would absorb 2 mg liter^{-1} more oxygen (Fig. 7-5). This figure uses a moving surface to indicate that the reservoir level changes over time. Thus depth is given from the bottom, not the surface, as is usual for most lakes. From Horne (unpublished).

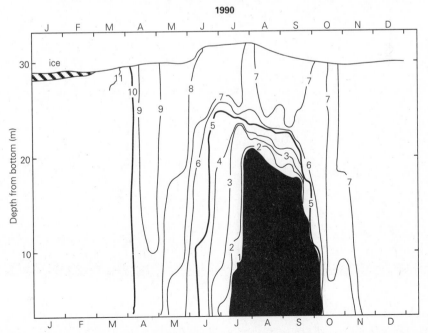

seasonal changes in oxygen that occur in moderately productive lakes (Fig. 7-8). This figure is made from many daily depth oxygen profiles of the type shown in Fig. 7-1. During the winter or spring mixing period, oxygen and carbon dioxide levels reach equilibrium with the atmosphere. As thermal stratification occurs, oxygen decreases until most of the hypolimnion water is anoxic. *Summer kills* are a result of the depletion of ox-

ygen in both stratified and unstratified lakes. Large numbers of dead fish may litter beaches when this occurs. In warm, unstratified lakes oxygen-depleted water may form overnight during windless periods. In deep oligotrophic lakes, such as Lake Superior or Lake Baikal in Siberia, changes in dissolved oxygen are negligible.

The seasonal changes in total inorganic carbon and free CO_2 in a productive Danish lake

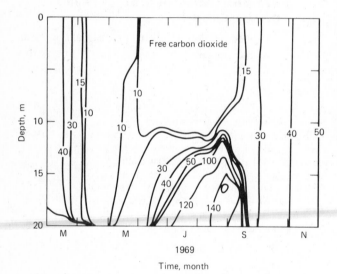

(a)

FIGURE 7-9 Seasonal changes in (a) free CO_2 and (b) total inorganic carbon in productive Lake Estrom, Denmark. Free CO_2 levels are reduced in surface water in summer by photosynthetic uptake. Carbon dioxide is abundant near the sediments due to the respiration of benthic organisms. Total inorganic carbon, which can buffer photosynthetic uptake of free CO_2, shows much less variation. Units are in mmol liter^{-1}. Redrawn from Jonasson et al. (1974).

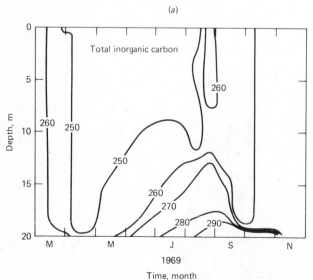

(b)

are shown in Fig. 7-9. As expected, the pattern is the inverse of that shown by dissolved oxygen in Fig. 7-8. Free or equilibrium CO_2 falls from over 40 mmol liter^{-1} during the holomictic period prior to thermal stratification to less than 10 mmol liter^{-1} in the epilimnion in summer (Fig. 7-9a). Due to intense respiration in the sediments of this eutrophic lake, hypolimnion levels of CO_2 rise to over 140 mmol liter^{-1} in summer. In contrast, the total inorganic carbon values change little over the season (Fig. 7-9b). This is because the changes in free CO_2 are buffered by decreases in HCO_3^- and CO_3^{2-}, as explained earlier.

In autumn, as the waters cool and the resistance to mixing decreases, a storm will mix the waters from top to bottom. Oxygen and carbon dioxide levels will once again begin to approach equilibrium with the atmosphere. However, the sediments of a eutrophic lake may take several weeks of holomixis before their oxygen debt is fully repaid and CO_2 releases return to normal. This may not occur if the lake freezes over quickly and ice prevents mixing with the atmosphere. If snow covers the ice, and during winter darkness at polar latitudes, the lake waters are without light for much of the winter. Then photosynthesis ceases or is limited to a small twilight zone immediately beneath the ice. Under such conditions, *winter kills* of fish and other animals may occur. As radiation increases in early spring,

photosynthetic oxygen production under the ice may produce the highest dissolved oxygen values of the year, even in oligotrophic lakes (Fig. 7-10). In lakes protected from winds (Fig. 20-5), as in some volcanic cones or in cirque basins such as Castle Lake, a calm spring period with high solar radiation may establish summer stratification without allowing spring overturn. This carries any winter oxygen deficit into the summer stagnation period.

Diel Variations in Oxygen and Carbon Dioxide

Diel means day plus night, or over 24 hours. *Nocturnal* is nighttime, in contrast to *diurnal,* which is the lighted period of the day. Over a diel cycle a eutrophic lake often passes from below-oxygen saturation in the early morning to supersaturation in late afternoon. Carbon dioxide typically has an inverse relationship to oxygen. Because of biological modification of the oxygen and carbon dioxide regime, the more productive the environment, the greater the fluctuation in concentration of these two gases during the day.

Figure 7-11a shows the diel cycle of oxygen in a very productive tropical African lake with surface values of over 250 percent saturation during the daylight hours. The integrated values for the entire water column were shown in Fig. 7-1. So much photosynthetic oxygen is produced that even night respiration reduces the value to

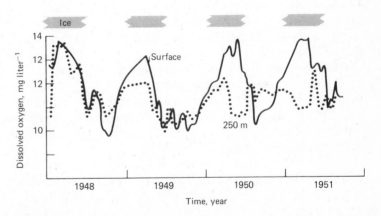

FIGURE 7-10 Seasonal changes in dissolved oxygen in oligotrophic Lake Baikal, Siberia (solid line = surface; dotted line = 250 m; shading indicates ice cover). Note that there is little difference between the two depths except under ice cover in spring during the main phytoplankton bloom. Redrawn from Kozhov (1963).

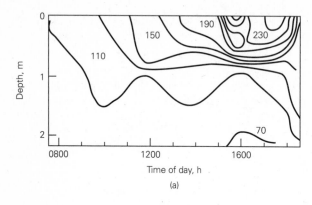

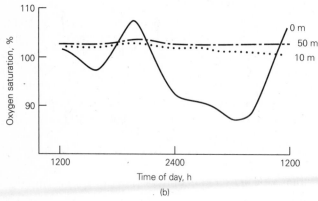

FIGURE 7-11 Diel (24-hour) changes in dissolved oxygen in lakes. (*a*) In a very productive lake, Lake George, Uganda, isopleths of oxygen saturation are at 20 percent intervals. Numbers are percent oxygen saturation. These changes are mostly due to algal photosynthesis and respiration. From Ganf and Horne (1975). (*b*) In Lake Baikal, an unproductive system. These changes are mostly due to temperature fluctuating faster than O_2 can equilibrate with the atmosphere. Redrawn from Kozhov (1963). Both are shown at periods of maximum algal photosynthesis. Note the very small diel changes (± 10 percent) in the oligotrophic lake (secchi depth 10 to 25 m) and very large changes from below saturation (70 percent) to supersaturation (250 percent) for the eutrophic lake (secchi depth 0.5 m).

only about 110 percent. During other seasons and in the deeper water more oxygen consumption occurs. Even some unproductive lakes show small changes (Fig. 7-11*b*), but these are mostly due to diel temperature cycles. It takes time for the warming and cooling water to release oxygen, so the changes from 90 to 110 percent in saturation often occur in the surface waters. In the depths, where no temperature changes occur, no change from 100 percent saturation is seen (Fig. 7-11*b*).

Photosynthesis in eutrophic waters generally follows the changes in available sunlight, with a midday peak (Fig. 7-2). This fact can be used to model photosynthesis using only light intensity and chlorophyll concentration (Chap. 15). The most dramatic example is a sewage oxidation lagoon where a high concentration of nutrients supports such high algal growth that oxygen lev-

els may reach supersaturation during the day and drop to zero during the night. The magnitude of variations in oxygen concentration in some lakes is also influenced by macrophytes. Large variations in oxygen concentration may occur near shore where these higher aquatic plants are abundant.

Sediments often contain decaying organic material and a coating of photosynthetic organisms if there is sufficient light. The respiratory activity of benthic invertebrates in the sediments creates a continuous exchange of carbon dioxide and oxygen with the overlying water. At night the combination of respiration by plants, bacterial decomposition, and invertebrate respiration can deplete oxygen from the overlying water and exchange carbon dioxide and dissolved nutrients in the process. This benthic contribution to the oxygen deficit is particularly important in shallow, thermally stratified lakes with a small hy- polimnetic volume. An example is Lake Erie, in which the epilimnion is about 17 to 20 m thick, but in some places the underlying hypolimnion is only 2 to 3 m thick (Fig. 4-8).

The Hypolimnetic Oxygen Deficit

In the hypolimnion of mesotrophic or eutrophic lakes dissolved oxygen is reduced from satura- tion by the oxygen demand of decaying phyto- plankton. The amount of the decrease is an ox- ygen debt that must be satisfied during the fall or winter overturn. Low oxygen in the hypolim- nion affects the survival of fish and benthic an- imals, increases the recycling of nutrients, and may produce compounds such as hydrogen sul- fide, which cause problems if the water is used as a drinking water supply. Thus a more precise estimate of the amount of the oxygen debt, es- pecially if it is increasing over the years, is im- portant.

The *oxygen deficit* in a lake is the amount of oxygen needed to reach saturation minus the amount of oxygen present. For example, at a temperature of 11.5°C, the amount of oxygen to reach saturation (10.6 mg liter^{-1}) minus the amount of oxygen actually present (9.0 mg li- ter^{-1}) is equal to the deficit (1.6 mg liter^{-1}).

The *relative areal hypolimnetic oxygen deficit* (RAHOD) is the difference between the oxygen content of the hypolimnion and that empirically determined at the end of spring mixing before thermal stratification. It is defined as the mean oxygen deficit below 1 cm^2 of hypolimnion sur- face. The volume of the hypolimnion is assessed by summing a series of layers of water each with its own oxygen content. An example for a 10-m- deep lake is shown in Table 7-2. The respiration that results in a loss of oxygen in the hypolim- nion is directly related to the amount of phyto- plankton that grew in the epilimnion. Thus the RAHOD can also be used to estimate the lake's productivity.

It is not easy to estimate several of the param- eters used to measure RAHOD, especially the

TABLE 7-2

RELATIVE AERIAL HYPOLIMNETIC OXYGEN DEFICIT (RAHOD)

In a small lake prior to the onset of thermal stratification in spring, the water was at 12°C and fully saturated with dissolved oxygen (DO = 11.8 mg liter^{-1}). The volume of the lake was 6000 m^3, so the mass of oxygen in the whole lake was 64.8 kg. The surface area of hypolimnion was 2500 m^2 (2,500,000 cm^2). The RAHOD was as- sessed after 100 days by summing the volume and DO content of the hypolimnion as shown. Note that this is a low value for RAHOD, and this lake is oligotrophic (< 0.017 mg DO cm^{-2} day^{-1}) rather than eutrophic (> 0.033 mg DO cm^{-2} day^{-1}).

Strata	Volume, m^3	Mean DO, mg liter^{-1}	Total DO in strata, kg
6–8 m	4000	7.1	28.4
8–10 m	2000	7.0	14.0
Total	6000	—	42.4

Relative aerial hypolimnetic oxygen deficit is (64.8 kg DO − 42.4 kg DO/2,500,000 = 0.896 mg cm^{-2} = 0.00896 mg cm^{-2} day^{-1}

surface area of the hypolimnion. The exact po- sition of the upper boundary of the hypolimnion on the temperature-depth curve is somewhat ar- bitrary, but with practice it is possible to obtain good results. In the example of Lake Erie, men- tioned above, there is still dispute over how much of the small hypolimnion is actually hy- polimnion rather than metalimnion. This affects the history of the eutrophication of the lake when measured by loss of benthic oxygen (Charlton, 1987).

CARBON DIOXIDE AS A LIMITING NUTRIENT

Despite the reservoir of carbonate in water, ex- perimental additions of carbon dioxide or car- bonate to phytoplankton from eutrophic lakes usually result in an increase in photosynthesis if two conditions are met: (1) the increase in pho- tosynthesis must be measured in a sealed bottle that restricts atmospheric input; and (2) the additions must be made when natural CO_2 levels are low relative to the algal demand. Carbon, often as CO_2 gas, is frequently used to stimulate photosynthesis in algal cultures or sewage oxidation ponds. Some scientists have even speculated that the increase in the world's CO_2 levels will eventually be counterbalanced by an increase in algal growth and CO_2 uptake.

The role of CO_2 as a limiting nutrient in algal production is disputed. Much of the controversy was engendered by the rapid cultural eutrophication of some lakes caused by pollution. Some limnologists blamed phosphorus from detergents; others believed nitrogen from sewage and agriculture was more important. The detergent industry, which manufactures phosphate-containing products, took the position that nitrogen or phosphorus pollution was irrelevant to the eutrophication of lakes and that CO_2 limitation was the main factor controlling phytoplankton growth. These arguments all have some elements of truth. An important question is: "When does the natural influx of CO_2 from the atmosphere balance the demand for CO_2 at peak photosynthesis?" The general conclusion from several studies in the unbuffered Canadian lakes, where CO_2 was low, the English Lake District, and the deep oceans is that carbon dioxide availability may restrict daily production in some waters. The result is that the crop may be slightly delayed in reaching its seasonal maximum, which

is then controlled by other factors such as the supply of nitrogen, phosphorus, or silica. Therefore, over the course of any one day, CO_2 availability may limit the rate of primary production. In contrast, overall seasonal production or annual yield is limited by other nutrients or by the turbidity or turbulence of the water.

Several aspects of algal ecology, such as the rising and sinking of blue-green algal colonies and competition between species based on relative growth rates (Chap. 12), are related to carbon dioxide metabolism. Of particular interest is the use of photosynthetically produced carbohydrate "ballast" and the squashing of small gas vesicles with the osmotic pressure that results when small photosynthetically produced sugars are released inside the cell (Chap. 12).

OXYGEN AND CARBON DIOXIDE IN STREAMS

When unpolluted streams contain a large population of algae and benthic invertebrates, they frequently show considerable diel variation in oxygen in the warmer months (Fig. 7-12). This may be used to estimate primary production. Most rivers and streams in inhabited areas receive organic pollution, and oxygen levels may fluctuate more drastically. Modern sewage treatment plants greatly reduce the biological oxygen demand of their effluent, but where no treatment

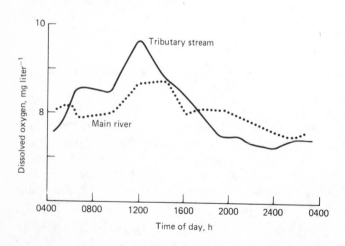

FIGURE 7-12 Diel changes in dissolved oxygen in rivers and streams. Note that both show changes over 24 hours, but the river shows the smaller variation due to its larger volume. The changes are not related to temperature but to respiration by the extensive benthic invertebrate population, which exceeds river reaeration at night. During the day reaeration and diatom photosynthesis increase oxygen levels. Data from the Truckee River, California, and a small tributary, Martis Creek, in August 1979. Data from F. R. McLaren.

or only primary treatment is provided a permanent oxygen depletion, called an *oxygen sag,* occurs below the outfalls. This downstream region has a characteristic flora and fauna. Diffuse sources of organic materials can dramatically reduce oxygen levels in streams. For example, in the Chicago area a great deal of material, including dead leaves, dog excreta, and other debris, washes into the main waste diversion canal with each summer storm. The oxygen demand of these nonpoint source pollutants is so great that it alone reduces the stream oxygen to zero even without the addition of any sewage effluent. Unpolluted streams also become clogged with dead leaves in fall, and during low flow this produces oxygen depletion.

Rivers have much less ability to reoxygenate their waters since the water is deep. Many rivers have had all rapids, waterfalls, and shallows removed or flooded by dams to facilitate navigation. This has the unfortunate effect of removing almost all natural rapid reaeration. In the River Thames in England, pure oxygen is added following the influx of oxygen-demanding storm debris to enhance the now-reduced natural aeration processes. Supersaturation of oxygen and nitrogen to values of 105 to 140 percent saturation occurs beneath the spillways of high dams like those on the Columbia River in the United States. This supersaturation causes the grotesque *gas bubble disease,* which kills salmon during migration.

When mixing is vigorous, CO_2 is usually at saturation levels in streams. Some plants, particularly aquatic mosses and the common stream blue-green alga *Nostoc,* require such a high level of CO_2 that they can grow well only in very turbulent water. Consequently, such plants are usually found only in rapids or small waterfalls.

THE REDOX POTENTIAL

The *redox potential* or *reduction-oxidation potential* E_h, is the electrical voltage that exists after connecting two electrodes, one made of hydrogen and the other made of the material under consideration. It is called a potential because the materials are not actually connected in nature. The change in the oxidation state of many metal ions and some nutrient compounds is defined by their redox potential. For example, at neutral pH and 25°C, oxygenated lake water has a redox potential of about +500 mV. Under these conditions most common metals and nutrients are thermodynamically stable in their most oxidized forms. Iron will be present as Fe^{3+} (ferric iron), not Fe^{2+} (ferrous iron). Similarly, nitrate rather than nitrite or ammonia will be present, and sulfate will be more stable than sulfide. As the name indicates, oxygen is closely involved with redox potential; as oxygen falls, the redox potential drops. When the oxygen is used up, a series of substances undergo chemical reductions, each at a specific redox potential. For example, between an E_h of +450 and +300 mV, ammonia becomes favored over nitrate, and between +300 and +200 mV, Fe^{2+} is favored over Fe^{3+}. When E_h falls to almost zero, hydrogen sulfide is favored over sulfate and sulfur. All of these reactions will tend to reverse if oxygen is reintroduced and E_h rises again to the +500-mV level of fully oxygenated water.

Although the effect of the redox potential extends throughout the water, the effect is strongest in a thin layer, the *oxidized* or *reduced microzone,* at the sediment-water interface (Chap. 10). All of the above-mentioned redox changes will occur slowly in sterile water, but in lakes and streams living organisms greatly increase the rates over the purely chemical reactions. Most oxidation-reduction reactions are carried out by bacteria that gain energy from converting the substance to the thermodynamically favored state as oxygen and redox potentials change. In situ estimation of redox potentials in natural waters has been possible for many years (Mortimer, 1942) and is now routinely measured using a submarine probe in the same way as for oxygen.

Changes in the redox potential are most important in eutrophic conditions and special environments such as highly reducing acid bogs.

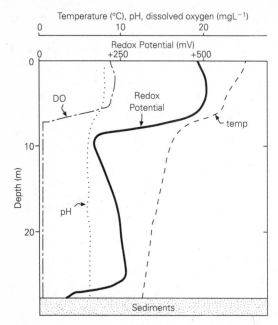

FIGURE 7-13 Depth profile of the redox potential and associated variables in a eutrophic lake. Fully oxygenated epilimnion water (about 8.4 mg liter^{-1} at 25°C) has a redox value of about 500 mV. The redox potential measured by a probe has been corrected for pH, which is slightly alkaline in this lake (pH = 8) due to moderate algal photosynthesis. The rapid decline in redox and oxygen occurs in the metalimnion. In the hypolimnion, dissolved oxygen decreases to 0.2 mg liter^{-1}, temperature falls to 16°C, and pH falls to about 6. The very low redox (< 100 mV) near the sediments was characterized by the production of hydrogen sulfide. A. J. Horne (unpublished data).

In most lakes the redox potential remains at about +500 mV because dissolved oxygen never falls far from 100 percent saturation. In eutrophic lakes the low oxygen concentrations near the mud-water interface usually lower the redox potential to below +200 mV (Fig. 7-13). As mentioned above, this converts oxidized ferric iron (Fe^{3+}) to ferrous iron (Fe^{2+}), a process that changes the insoluble ferric phosphate molecule to ferrous phosphate, which is soluble. Thus phosphate ions may assist in accelerating eutrophication during the descent of the thermocline in the summer. Similarly, ammonia is

favored over nitrate at redox of less than 350 mV, and at very low redox (< 100 mV) and anoxic conditions hydrogen sulfide is favored over sulfate.

In the limnological cycles of oxygen and carbon dioxide the gaseous form plays a major role. In Chap. 8 we discuss nitrogen, whose gaseous phase is less important, despite the abundance of nitrogen gas in the atmosphere and in the water. The chemical inertness of nitrogen relative to the oxygen, and carbon dioxide molecules causes this difference. As we see in Chap. 8, the N≡N bond can be cleaved only by a few specialized organisms and only by using large amounts of metabolic energy.

FURTHER READING

Birge, E. A., and C. Juday. 1911. "The Inland Lakes of Wisconsin: The Dissolved Gases and Their Biological Significance." *Bull. Wis. Geol. Nat. Hist. Surv.,* **22.** 259 pp.

Charlton, M. N. 1987. "Lake Erie Oxygen Revisited." *J. Great Lakes Res.,* **13:**697–708.

Ohle, W. 1952. "Die hypolimnische Kohlendioxyd-Akkumulation als produktionsbiologischer Indikator." *Arch. Hydrobiol.,* **46:**153-285.

Pamatmat, M. M., and K. Banse. 1969. "Oxygen Measurements by the Seabed. II. *In Situ* Measurements to a Depth of 180 m." *Limnol. Oceanogr.,* **14:**250–259.

Rosa, F., and N. M. Burns. 1987. "Lake Erie Central Basin Oxygen Depletion Changes." *J. Great Lakes Res.,* **13:**684–696.

Shapiro, J. 1960. "The Cause of a Metalimnetic Minimum of Dissolved Oxygen." *Limnol. Oceanogr.,* **5:**216–227.

Sugawara, K. 1939. "Chemical Studies in Lake Metabolism." *Bull. Chem. Soc. Japan,* **14:**375–451.

Talling, J. 1976. "The Depletion of Carbon Dioxide from Lake Windermere by Phytoplankton." *J. Ecol.,* **64:**79–121.

Walker, W. W. 1979. "Use of Hypolimnetic Oxygen Depletion Rates as a Trophic State Indicator for Lakes." *Water Resour. Res.,* **15:**1463–1470.

Wetzel, R. G. 1960. "Marl Encrustation of Hydrophytes in Several Michigan Lakes." *Oikos,* **11:**223–236.

CHAPTER 8

Nitrogen

OVERVIEW

Most of the nitrogen in aquatic ecosystems is present as the gas N_2. Nitrate (NO_3^-), ammonia (NH_4^+), nitrite (NO_2^-), urea ($CO[NH_2]_2$), and dissolved organic compounds are less abundant but usually of more biological interest. Nitrogen cycles between all these compounds in gaseous, soluble, and particulate forms in both oxic and anoxic conditions. The concentration of most nitrogen compounds in lakes and streams tends to follow regular seasonal patterns. Biological uptake lowers concentrations in the photic zone in spring and summer. During the fall and winter, releases from sediments, tributary inflows, precipitation, and replenishment from the hypolimnion increase the nitrate and sometimes the ammonia concentrations. The availability of various nitrogen compounds influences the variety, abundance, and nutritional value of aquatic animals and plants. Nitrogen is the fourth most common cellular element; living matter contains about 5 percent nitrogen by dry weight. However, nitrate and ammonia are not always present in adequate amounts in natural waters and may limit plant growth. Nitrogen limitation is common in the ocean and in lakes in warm climates and where phosphorus and silicon are naturally present in relatively large quantities or where pollution has increased phosphorus relative to nitrogen.

Nitrate is normally the most common form of combined inorganic nitrogen in lakes and streams. The concentration and rate of supply of nitrate is intimately connected with land use practices on the watershed. For example, acid rain contains nitric as well as sulfuric acid, and the nitric component is higher where there are more automobiles. Nitrate ions move easily through soils and are quickly lost from the land. This contrasts with phosphate or ammonium ions, which are retained by the soil. Natural changes in the vegetation of the drainage basin caused by fires, floods, or artificial clearing increase the nitrate levels in streams. Nitrogen derived from waste discharges from agricultural fertilizers and waste discharges from cities greatly increase nitrate in streams and lakes. If streams are diverted through wetlands, it is possible to remove nitrate by denitrification.

Ammonia is the preferred form of N for plant growth, since the reductive metabolism of nitrate to the amino group—NH_2, requires additional energy as well as the presence of the enzyme *nitrate reductase.* Ammonia may become harmful to animals and plants, especially at elevated pH levels when toxic ammonium hydroxide forms. Ammonia excretion by animals recycles nitrogen back to plants. Its high turnover rate both intrigues limnologists and explains the ability of phytoplankton and stream algae to grow when other nitrogen supplies have been exhausted.

Nitrogen gas is almost inert and is utilized for growth only by some blue-green algae and bacteria capable of *nitrogen fixation.* In some lakes this is an important source of plant nitrogen. *Denitrification,* the bacterial reduction of nitrate to nitrite and then to N_2 gas, occurs at low oxygen levels in sediments and the hypolimnion. Denitrification is important in the nitrogen budget of lakes, wetlands, streams, and, especially estuaries, and is often closely coupled with *nitrification,* the conversion of ammonia to nitrate. All waters contain both dissolved and particulate organic nitrogen, which are generally not available to higher organisms until modified by bacteria and fungi. The organic products range from readily available urea and proteins to complex humic acids, which are biologically inert. However, some of these large inert molecules do play a significant role in the chelation of dissolved metals. The deposition of particulate organic matter onto the sediments provides a major nitrogen sink.

INTRODUCTION

After carbon, hydrogen, and oxygen, the most abundant element in living cells is nitrogen. All proteins contain nitrogen and, since enzymes are made from proteins, it is essential for almost all biochemical reactions. The quantity of nitrogen accumulated by each animal or plant varies from 1 to 10 percent of dry weight and to some extent reflects the availability of nitrogen in the adjacent environment (Gerloff and Skoog, 1954; Fitzgerald, 1969). However, most of the earth's nitrogen is present in the chemically inert gaseous N_2 form, which is not used directly by most organisms because it requires considerable energy to split the N≡N triple bond. Growth that is limited by nitrogen is sometimes supplemented by N_2 fixation. This gives only minimal evolutionary advantage, because limitations due to phosphorus, iron, and other nutrients soon develop. The aquatic nitrogen cycle has two interesting undirectional components, N_2 fixation and denitrification. Both can occur only when oxygen is virtually absent. Denitrification of nitrate to N_2 gas in lake and estuarine sediments may cause considerable loss of nitrogen from the system. In most oligotrophic lakes and oceans, the recycling of nitrogen from plants and animals back to ammonia or nitrate is the main source of nitrogen in summer. This remineralization is often tightly coupled with bacteria playing an important role.

In this chapter we discuss nitrogen measurement, the nitrogen cycle, forms of nitrogen in lakes and their seasonal cycles, and nitrogen transformations.

MEASUREMENT

The concentrations of nitrate, nitrite, ammonia, and organic nitrogen are estimated using traditional chemical analyses (Solorzano, 1969; Strickland and Parsons, 1972; Jenkins, 1975; APHA, 1989). At moderate to high levels (> 1 mg liter^{-1}) inorganic nitrogen compounds can be measured with specific ion electrodes. Organic nitrogen can be estimated using the acid Kejeldahl digestion procedure or with an automatic analyzer (which simultaneously analyzes carbon and hydrogen). Many plants can take up nitrate or ammonia at levels so low they are at the limits of detection of most analytical methods. Concentrations of nitrate, nitrite, or ammonia should always be expressed as elemental nitrogen. Thus nitrate is expressed as NO_3—N in micrograms or milligrams per liter or in microgram atoms (i.e., 14 g of N per mole of NO_3), and never as NO_3 (that is, 62 g per mole of NO_3). In the older literature and in some current engineering and public health reports, the reader is not certain how the nitrogen is reported. Dissolved N_2 gas can be measured by complicated extraction methods (Benson and Parker, 1961), using mass spectrometry or gas chromatography for final assay. A less accurate method uses volumetric analysis (Sugawara, 1939). The major problem in lakes and rivers is collecting and keeping water at its original temperature and pressure until gases are analyzed.

Nitrogen fixation can be measured in lakes by using the heavy nonradioactive isotope of nitrogen, $^{15}N_2$, which is incorporated into blue-green algae or bacteria (Neess et al., 1962; Fogg and Horne, 1967). This procedure requires several chemical transformations and the use of an isotope mass spectrometer or optical device for detection of the ^{15}N atoms among the more numerous ^{14}N atoms. Most limnologists now use the acetylene-reduction method to measure N_2 fixation. The technique depends on the ability of an enzyme to reduce acetylene, which has a molecular shape (H—C≡C—H) similar to that of N≡N. Acetylene is reduced to ethylene and measured on a gas chromatograph (Stewart, Fitzgerald, and Burris, 1967; Horne and Goldman, 1972). Three molecules of ethylene are produced for every N_2 molecule that would have been fixed. *Denitrification* in aquatic systems can be measured by mass balance when denitrification is the only unknown component. An alternative is to use the stable isotope ^{15}N (Nishio et al., 1983) or the radioactive isotope ^{13}N (Gersberg et al., 1976). Bacterial denitrification occurs in anoxic sediments where nitrate is present (Keeney et al., 1971). When $^{15}NO_3$ or $^{13}NO_3$ is added to lake muds, the labeled gas that evolves is a measure of the amount of denitrification. Unfortunately, there are problems with all of these methods due to sediment disturbance, the very short half-life of ^{13}N, the large amounts of ^{15}N needed, and the difficulty of balancing the gains and losses of nitrogen in whole-lake systems.

Today most quantitative estimates of denitrification are made using the acetylene blockage technique of Sorensen (1978). Acetylene is added in excess and the N_2O intermediate (Fig. 8-1) released is measured using gas chromatography. A problem with this method concerns the diffusion of the gases in and out of the mud. Collection of N_2 gas as it naturally bubbles out of the lake muds is usually unreliable because any gas leaving the mud comes into equilibrium with the other gases dissolved in the water. Thus bubbles of methane (CH_4), a common gas produced by anoxic lake muds, acquire N_2 gas from the water as the bubbles rise. The origin of gases collected in containers on the lake bed is therefore uncertain. In some shallow lakes, however, denitrification is so vigorous that direct gas collection can be used. Recently, sediment cores have been sealed into N_2-free chambers and the N_2 and N_2O released measured directly. With all environmental measurements, care should be taken to obtain representative samples to describe horizontal, vertical, daily, seasonal, and year-to-year variations adequately.

THE NITROGEN CYCLE

In aquatic ecosystems the major forms of nitrogen available to bacteria, fungi, and plants are nitrate and ammonia, just as they are for terrestrial systems. Since nitrogen is often in short supply for plant growth on land, it is not surprising that it may be a growth-limiting factor in water. In some aquatic ecosystems nitrogen is the nutrient element that most limits plant growth. This tends to occur most frequently in lakes at the eutrophic or oligotrophic ends of the trophic spectrum.

Before considering the spatial and temporal variations of nitrogen in various aquatic ecosystems, it is important to understand the interactions between each form. This is best accomplished by examining the nitrogen cycle illustrated in Fig. 8-1 and typical lake situations in Figs. 8-2 to 8-4. The cycle applies to all eco-

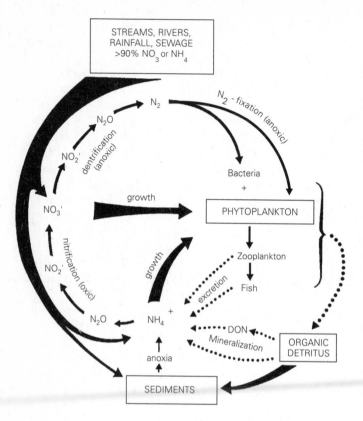

FIGURE 8-1 The nitrogen cycle in freshwater aquatic ecosystems. Thick black lines indicate the main pathways in terms of mass transfer; dotted lines, those involving recycling and mineralization in the water column. Most biologically available nitrogen is present as nitrate, which passes from rain to rivers and lakes, where much of it is taken up by algae, used for growth, and then deposited in the sediments. Nitrogen in algae eaten by zooplankton (lakes) and insect larvae (lake benthos and streams) is excreted as ammonia, which is recycled back to algae in the summer. Note the two anoxic sections of the cycle (N_2 fixation and denitrification), which involve blue-green algae and bacteria, in contrast to the rest of the cycle that occurs under oxygenated conditions. Most N_2 fixation occurs in the plankton, whereas most denitrification occurs in the sediments, especially in estuaries and wetlands. Most organic nitrogen in aquatic ecosystems is present as plant or animal nitrogen and organic detritus (particulate or DON = dissolved organic nitrogen).

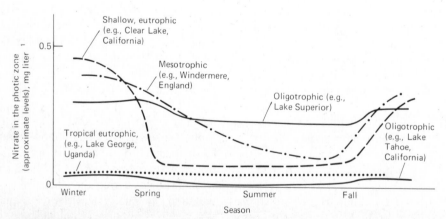

FIGURE 8-2 Idealized representation of seasonal changes in nitrate available for plant growth. Figure shows the situation for temperate-zone eutrophic, mesotrophic, and oligotrophic lakes and a tropical eutrophic lake. Actual data are shown for some lakes in Figs. 8-4 and 8-6 and Table 8-1.

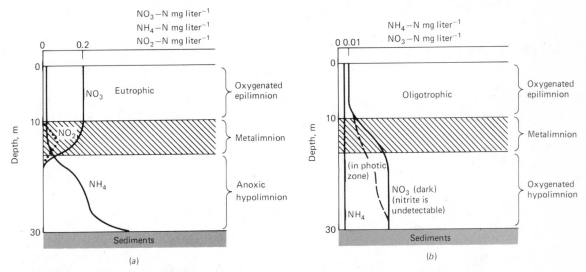

FIGURE 8-3 Idealized distribution of nitrite, nitrate, and ammonia with depth for two stratified lakes (oligotrophic and eutrophic) in midsummer. Note that the oligotrophic example shown here has low nitrate levels (e.g., Lake Tahoe) but could have high nitrate levels (e.g., Lake Superior) since lack of other nutrients may cause the low productivity.

systems, but the presence of oxygen may be most important in aquatic systems. As previously discussed (Chap. 7), an oxygen shortage is more likely in water than in air. The nitrogen cycle involves all of the oxidation states of the nitrogen atom, from $+5$ (NO_3) to -3 (NH_4) and is thus more complex than that of many other elements. In aquatic systems N_2 fixation and denitrification are the ultimate sources and sinks of combined nitrogen available to algae. Both transformations involve enzyme systems requiring anoxic conditions, although specialized cells (heterocysts) or anoxic microzones may permit the processes to occur in the presence of oxygen.

FORMS OF NITROGEN IN LAKES AND THEIR SEASONAL CYCLES

Nitrate and Nitrite

Nitrate is the most highly oxidized form of nitrogen and usually the most abundant form of combined inorganic nitrogen in lakes and streams (Table 8-1). Nitrite, the partially reduced form of nitrate, is usually present in very small quantities.

Plant cells use reduced nitrogen, which is often transferred intercellularly as the amino group $-NH_2$. The transfer involves enzymes, the best known of which are *nitrate reductase* and *nitrite reductase*. Nitrate reductase catalyzes the reaction $NO_3 \rightarrow NO_2$, has a molecular weight of about 250,000, and contains molybdenum at its reactive center. The nitrite is then converted to nitrogen gas. The nitrite reductase enzyme, which catalyzes the reaction $NO_2 \rightarrow N_2$, is a relatively small enzyme (m.w. = 63,000). This enzyme contains iron at its reactive center and requires copper as a cofactor.

Nitrate is metabolized by algae only after transformation by nitrate reductase. The induction period for this enzyme is quite long, several hours to a few days, and thus increased nitrate uptake is slow relative to uptake of ammonia. This becomes important when nutrients are sup-

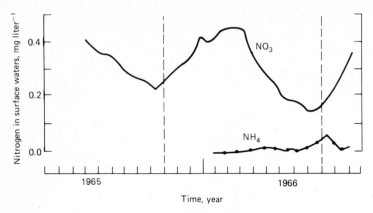

South Basin: Windermere, England
(monomictic, mesotrophic)

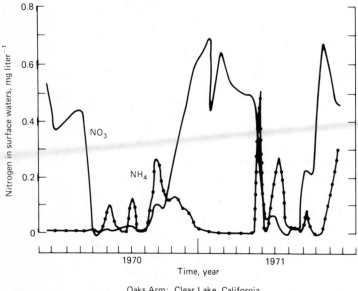

Oaks Arm: Clear Lake, California
(polymictic, eutrophic)

FIGURE 8-4 Seasonal variation in ammonia and nitrate in the photic zone of various lakes (see also Table 8-1). Vertical dashed line represents the autumn overturn for the stratified lake. Clear Lake is nitrogen-limited and Windermere is phosphorus- or silicon-limited. Nitrate fluctuates at relatively high levels in Windermere, which is typical of many temperate lakes in Europe and North America. In contrast, in summer nitrate is reduced to insignificant levels in Clear Lake, typical of warm-climate eutrophic lakes. Note that ammonia from the deeper water caused an increase in photic zone ammonia at overturn but that the increase was much larger in the more productive Clear Lake. Windermere data courtesy of the U.K. Freshwater Biological Association; Clear Lake data from California Department of Water Resources and Horne (1975).

plied in pulses such as occur after rains or from excretion by individual animals. Nitrate reductase is low in algal populations growing where nitrate levels are low but is present even if the plants are utilizing ammonia. The presence of high levels of ammonia causes direct feedback inhibition and repression of nitrate reductase synthesis. Fortunately for the plants, the levels of ammonia in most aquatic systems are too low to cause this repression.

Competition for nitrate often proceeds by the type of enzyme kinetics described in Chap. 15. The rate of nitrate uptake V and the affinity of the enzyme for its substrate (K_s) vary with species and cell size as well as the nitrate preconditioning the plants have experienced (Table 8-2). For example, some algal species can use low levels of nitrate if grown in a low-nitrate environment but lose this ability in high-nitrate situations. These biochemical adaptations may be

TABLE 8-1

CONCENTRATION OF INORGANIC NITROGEN (μg liter^{-1}) IN THE SURFACE WATERS OF VARIOUS LAKES AND RIVERS

Note the very wide range of total inorganic nitrogen (NO_3 + NH_4) available for plant growth. Values less than 100 μg liter^{-1} may limit growth, while levels above 400 would not. Both eutrophic and oligotrophic lakes may have very low or very high levels of total inorganic nitrogen.

Lake or river	Relative trophic state and mixing type	NO_3—N* Summer	NO_3—N* Winter	NH_4—N* Summer	NH_4—N* Winter	References[†]
Tahoe, Calif.	Oligotrophic, monomictic	4	μ–25	<2		1
Castle, Calif.	Mesotrophic, dimictic	<5	10–50	<5	10–50	2
Clear, Calif.	Eutrophic polymictic	μ–100	400–600	μ–300	μ–20	3
Superior	Oligotrophic monomictic	≈230	≈280	<10		4
Windermere	Mesotrophic monomictic	100–200	300–400	≈10		5
Esthwaite Water	Eutrophic monomictic	μ–100	400–500	≈30		6
George, Uganda	Eutrophic polymictic	μ		<10		7
Baikal, U.S.S.R.	Oligotrophic dimictic	0–20	45–80	μ		8
Titicaca, Andes	Mesotrophic monomictic	40–100	100–200	μ		9
Cayuga, N.Y.	Eutrophic monomictic	50–800	≈800	100–300	≈80	10
Uganda Rivers (annual mean)		530		24		11
Truckee River at km 3		—	20	—	<10	12
Hubbard Brook		—	440	2500	40	13

* μ = undetectable, generally < 10 μg liter^{-1}.
[†] References: (1, 2) Goldman, various sources; (3) Horne and Goldman, 1972; (4) Dobson et al., 1974; (5, 6) Heron, 1961; Horne and Fogg, 1970; (7) Viner, 1969; (8) Kozhov, 1963; (9) Richerson et al., 1977; (10) Oglesby, 1978; (11) Viner and Smith; (12) McLaren, 1977; (13) Likens et al., 1977.

short-lived and reversible. Table 8-2 shows some values for nitrate uptake in phytoplankton. In general, the smaller species have a competitive advantage in oligotrophic nitrogen-limited systems. In addition, some algae simply have more enzymes than others. For example, the green algae *Chlorella* may have 3 times more nitrate reductase per unit biomass than the blue-green algae *Microcystis* (Pomiluyko and Ochkivskaya, 1970).

Nitrate is usually not toxic in the quantities found in lakes and rivers—up to 10 mg liter^{-1} NO_3—N, the human drinking water standard. Even at higher levels the health hazard of nitrate itself is apparently small. These limits are placed on nitrate to ensure that water containing high

TABLE 8-2

ENZYME UPTAKE OR GROWTH KINETICS OF NITRATE AND AMMONIA FOR SOME NATURAL POPULATIONS OF PLANKTON AND ATTACHED DIATOMS AND SOME CULTURES OF A FLAGELLATE, A DINOFLAGELLATE, SOME DIATOMS, AND BLUE-GREEN ALGAE FROM WATERS OF DIFFERING FERTILITIES

Note that the half-saturation constant K_s generally increases with cell size and with increases in the average ambient nutrient levels (Table 8-1). Thus small algae in oligotrophic waters usually have low K_s values. The change in K_s in response to the environment is even shown by different races (oceans, estuaries) of the same species *Cyclotella nana*.

Dominant algal type/or habitat	Cell size, μm	K_s, μliter^{-1}		Max. growth rate, doublings day^{-1}	References*
		NO$_3$	NH$_4$		
Oligotrophic					
General marine	—	3	5	—	1
Chaetoceros gracilis	5	3	6	3.2	2,3
Cyclotella nana (from ocean)	5	7	5.6	—	3,4
Coccolithus huxleyi	5	4	1.4	1.7	3
Mesotrophic					
General marine	—	14	18	—	1
Asterinella japonica	10	14	15	2.0	2,3
Cyclotella nana (from estuary)	5	21	—	—	4
Skeletonema costatum	8	6	28	2.4	3
Melosira in aufwuchs	10–20 × 1000	—	70	—	5
Eutrophic					
Gonyaulax polyedra	45	130	80	0.5	4
Pseudoanabaena caterata	—	—	170	—	6
Anabaena sp.	100	70	—	—	7
Oscillatoria aghardhii	—	420	180	0.4	8
Castle Lake (mesotrophic)					
3 m, 50% blue-greens, 50% dinoflagellates	—	9–14	2–7	—	9
20 m, 75% dinoflagellates	—	10–16	3–14	—	9
25 m, 75% dinoflagellates		35–80	6–9		
Periphyton		200–500	200–1000		

* References: (1) MacIsaac and Dugdale, 1969; (2) Eppley and Thomas, 1969; (3) Carpenter and Guillard, 1971; (4) Eppley et al., 1969; (5) Horne and Kaufman, 1974; (6) Healy, 1977; (7) Mitchell, personal communication; (8) Zevenboom and Mur, 1981; Zevenboom et al., 1980; Zevenboom, 1978; (9) Priscu, 1982; Axler et al., 1982; Reuter, 1982.

levels of nitrate are not fed to babies under about 6 months of age, who have relatively low gastric activity that allows bacteria to reduce nitrate to nitrite. Nitrite can form methemoglobin, which reduces the oxygen-carrying capacity of the blood. This oxygen starvation in the tissues can produce a fatal condition known as *blue baby*. In most humans methemoglobin is broken down quickly, but very young babies lack the necessary enzyme (Magee, 1977). Both nitrate and nitrite have been used to preserve meat and fish for many years. Altought there is a risk of nitrite poisoning or infant methemoglobinemia, these risks are balanced against the protection from the deadly bacterial toxin from *Clostridium botulinum* (Raveis, 1976).

Nitrite is generally present only in trace quantities in water exposed to oxygen, where it is transformed to nitrate. Occasionally well waters in areas of manure accumulation are seriously polluted with nitrites. Polluted streams can contain up to 10 mg liter^{-1} NO_2—N, generally below sewage treatment plants that discharge ammonia. A small area near the thermocline of lakes may contain relatively large quantities of nitrite (Fig. 8-3a).

Major sources of nitrates in streams and lakes are runoff from agriculture and sewage discharges from cities. Ground water can become seriously contaminated with agricultural nitrate, especially from intensive livestock farming such as cattle feed lots. Nitrate can be removed from sewage, but the process is expensive. Recently the process of denitrification, or conversion of nitrate to nitrogen gas, discussed later in this chapter, has been used to remove nitrate from streams and treated sewage. Wetlands are used to treat the wastewaters because the anoxic conditions always present in waterlogged marsh soils encourage denitrification. However, the process is not yet reliable and cost-effective in all situations.

Seasonal Cycles of Nitrate

Nitrate is the most common form of nitrogen and is the form most used by phytoplankton in their major growth event, the spring bloom (Fig. 8-1). The major changes occurring between autumn and winter and between winter and spring fall into three categories (Fig. 8-2):

1. Oligotrophic phosphorus- or silicon-limited lakes in which nitrate levels remain almost constant, such as Lake Superior
2. Oligotrophic or eutropic nitrogen-limited lakes where nitrate levels fall to almost zero, such as Lake Tahoe or Lake George, Uganda
3. Mesotrophic lakes in which nitrate levels fall but may not become limiting, such as Lake Windermere and Lake Mendota

The cycle is shown in diagramatic form in Figs. 8-2 and 8-3 and real data are given in Fig. 8-4. In winter, nitrate inflow exceeds uptake by algae and more nitrate is mixed up from the hypolimnion. In summer, nitrate uptake by plants exceeds inflow, and input from the hypolimnion is physically limited by the thermocline. In the anoxic hypolimnia of eutrophic lakes, demand for electron acceptors often completely removes nitrate (Fig. 8-3a), which is either denitrified or converted to ammonia. A similar condition exists in eutrophic lakes under winter ice. In contrast, nitrate in the hypolimnia of deep oligotrophic lakes persists unchanged or may even increase near the lake bed as organic nitrogen is converted to nitrate and diffuses from the sediments (Figs. 8-3b, 8-8). In oligotrophic lakes the photic zone often extends below the thermocline and algal growth occurs in the hypolimnion. Algal depletion of nitrate then extends into the hypolimnion (Fig. 8-3b).

The major source of nitrogen for lakes is the nitrate in rainfall and dry precipitation on their watersheds. In large lakes, such as the Laurentian Great Lakes, rain on the lake is also important. Both wet and dry precipitation contain relatively large amounts of nitrates, up to 500 µg liter^{-1}. Much nitrate passes directly from the rain in the watershed to the lake via streams or falls directly on the lake. Even when it soaks into the ground, nitrate moves freely through soils to the lake along with subsurface waters. In this it contrasts with ammonia, phosphate, and most metal ions, which tend to be adsorbed by clay particles or organic matter. For example, if water rich in both nitrate and phosphate passes through soil, the outflowing water becomes depleted in phosphate but the nitrate remains little changed.

Acid rain contains dilute nitric acid derived from combustion of fossil fuels and thus can supply considerable amounts of nitrogen as well as acidity. Lakes, especially those on alluvial soils, can have considerable nitrate input from ground water. For example, many of the lakes of the lake district of northern Wisconsin are almost completely supplied with ground water. Below the root zone the ground water is usually a more concentrated solution of nitrate than stream water, since there is little opportunity for its removal by plants. Instream uptake by plant growth, together with any input from geological weathering, sewage, or other wastes, further modifies the stream water's nitrogen content.

Ammonia and the Ammonium Ion

Ammonia, present in aquatic systems mainly as the dissociated ion NH_4^+ (ammonium), is much more reactive than nitrate due to its higher chemical energy. Its positive charge enables it to form bonds with negatively charged clays, which are common in many inflowing streams. Although it is not strictly correct, most people use *ammonia* to describe ammonium (NH_4^+) as well as ammonia (NH_3). Ammonia differs from nitrate in both toxicity and mobility. Ammonia has a high toxicity and ammonium ions are retained by most soils.

The ammonium ion is rapidly taken up by phytoplankton and other aquatic plants (Toetz, 1971). The uptake of the ammonium ion, like that of nitrate, often follows classic enzyme kinetics (Chap. 15). Some available values of kinetic constants representative of major algal groups are given in Table 8-2. Despite its rapid uptake by algae ammonia persists in small quantities because it is also the major excretory prod-

uct of aquatic animals (Fig. 8-1). This *recycled* nitrogen is often distinguished from *new* nitrogen, which is that present in spring or derived from the inflows (see Chap. 15 for further details on general nutrient recycling). The actual amount of ammonia present at any time depends on the balance between animal excretory rates, plant uptake, and bacterial oxidation. Ammonia in the epilimnion may vary considerably with daily vertical migrations of zooplankton and fish through the thermocline. For example, fish are known to excrete sufficient ammonia to stimulate phytoplankton metabolism. The variations in ammonia with depth for typical oligotrophic and eutrophic lakes are shown in Fig. 8-3.

The toxicity of ammonia to aquatic animals and plants is of great practical importance. The gas ammonia (NH_3) dissolves readily in water and forms ammonium hydroxide (NH_4OH), which dissociates to give ammonium (NH_4^+) and hydroxyl ions (OH^-) as shown below:

$$NH_3 + H_2O \rightleftharpoons NH_4OH \rightleftharpoons NH_4^+ + OH^- \quad (1)$$

The reaction equilibrium lies far to the right at neutral pH 7 and 25°C, where only 0.55 percent of total ammonia is present as NH_4OH, almost none as NH_3, and the rest as NH_4^+. Changes with pH and temperature are shown in detail in Table 8-3. Under acid conditions the percentage of NH_4OH decreases; in alkaline conditions it increases. Undissociated NH_4OH is toxic, but the ion NH_4^+ is almost harmless. Ammonium hydroxide toxicity to aquatic organisms varies not only with pH but with temperature, dissolved oxygen levels, the hardness or salt content of the water, and animal species and age. For example, even under normal physiochemical conditions (pH = 6 to 7, temperature = 5 to 10°C), young rainbow trout fry are rapidly killed by the toxicity of ammonium hydroxide if the total ammonium concentration exceeds 0.3 mg liter^{-1} NH_4—N. In contrast, minnows and other non-salmonid fish are generally more tolerant, surviving to 10 times the quantity toxic to trout.

TABLE 8-3

RELATIONSHIP OF pH AND TEMPERATURE TO THE PERCENTAGE OF UN-IONIZED AMMONIA [NH_4OH + NH_3 (dissolved)] IN FRESHWATER

Note the very large increase in this toxic fraction as pH and temperature rise to levels often found in productive lakes and streams.

pH	Temperature, °C				
	5	10	15	20	25
6.5	0.04	0.06	0.09	0.13	0.18
7.0	0.12	0.19	0.27	0.40	0.55
7.5	0.39	0.59	0.85	1.24	1.73
8.0	1.22	1.83	2.65	3.83	5.28
8.5	3.77	5.55	7.98	11.2	15.0
9.0	11.0	15.7	21.4	28.5	35.8

Trussell, 1972.

Aquatic invertebrate zooplankton such as *Daphnia* apparently tolerate levels as high as 8 mg liter^{-1} NH_4—N.

Ammonia in most lakes and streams is generally well below 0.1 mg liter^{-1} (Table 8-1, Fig. 8-4), and detrimental effects of naturally occurring ammonia are uncommon. Most toxic effects of ammonia on animals are due to pollution, generally sewage outfalls that contain 10 to 30 mg liter^{-1} NH_4—N before dilution by the receiving water. In lakes and rivers, at least a few days are required before this ammonia is removed by plant growth or transformed to nitrate. Plant photosynthesis due to the increased nutrient supply removes carbon dioxide and increases the pH of the water, which greatly increases the toxicity of ammonia (Table 8-3). During the night, when oxygen levels are low or when the oxygen demand of wastes exceeds photosynthetic production of oxygen, the susceptibility of animals to ammonia poisoning is increased.

The ammonium ion NH_4^+ is not toxic to most plants except at very high concentrations or elevated pH values. However, values of as little as 0.5 mg liter^{-1} are known to inhibit photosynthesis slightly in a species of blue-green algae and some estuarine diatoms at pH 7.5 to 9 (Horne and Kaufman, 1974). For most waters, values in the hundreds of milligrams per liter are needed for toxic effects since some algae can live in ponds where concentrations exceed 500 mg liter^{-1} NH_4—N.

Seasonal Cycles of Ammonia

In general, two types of patterns are followed, depending on the trophic state of the lake (Figs. 8-4, 8-5). In oligotrophic and mesotrophic lakes, ammonia in the epilimnion varies around a low value of about 5 μg liter^{-1} throughout spring and summer and any excess is taken up by phytoplankton. Ammonia often increases during the autumn overturn and decreases in winter in monomictic lakes. If the lake is ice-covered, moderate levels of ammonia may persist until spring. For eutrophic lakes, summer values of ammonia in the epilimnion may fluctuate considerably over periods of a few days. At autumn overturn, ammonia levels rise considerably but then fall. In winter, ammonia may increase to very high levels ($>$ 1 mg liter^{-1}), particularly under ice.

The major source of ammonia is from inflowing rivers, precipitation, atmospheric dust, or indirectly from N_2 fixation. Most of the ammonia in rain is probably derived from aerosols originating in ocean, animal, or bacteria excretions rather than in volatilization of ammonia gas from the lake surface. Direct volatilization does not seem to occur even in warm lake water at high pH values, but losses of ammonia do occur from stockyards or cattle feedlots. The excreted urea is converted to ammonia by soil bacteria. Hutchinson and Viets (1969) have demonstrated that ammonia from such feedlots can be detected in large quantities several kilometers downwind. Some soils and natural concentrations of animals such as seal wallows produce ammonia-rich aerosols. Flooded streams and rivers also often contain relatively large quantities of ammonia because there is insufficient time or there are no sites for plant uptake or microbial transformation of ammonia to nitrate.

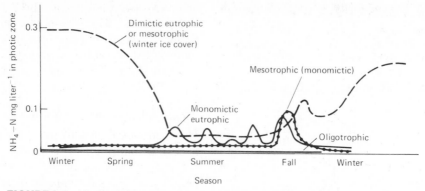

FIGURE 8-5 Idealized diagram of seasonal changes in photic-zone ammonia for various lake types. Actual data are given in Fig. 8-4 and Table 8-1. Random summer increases in ammonia occur in eutrophic lakes due to decay of algal blooms or irregular inputs from the hypolimnion. Most productive lakes show an increase in surface ammonia at the fall overturn. In nitrogen-limited lakes, ammonia recycled from excretions of zooplankton and fish may be the only source of nitrogen for phytoplankton growth in summer.

Dissolved Organic Nitrogen

All natural waters contain some dissolved organic nitrogen (DON), which is more abundant in eutrophic than oligotrophic systems (Manny, 1971). Dissolved organic nitrogen ranges from simple nutrients like urea to large complex molecules whose roles are little known. Urea is a common animal excretory product that serves as an excellent nitrogen source for phytoplanktonic growth (McCarthy, 1972; Carpenter et al., 1972). Urea is rapidly broken down to ammonia by bacteria or by the extracellular enzyme *urease,* which is present in most waters. Simple DON compounds, such as amino sugars, are excreted by some plants (Jones and Stewart, 1969; Walsby, 1974) and can be utilized as both energy and nitrogen sources. The uptake of organic compounds for energy, termed *heterotrophy,* is discussed in Chap. 11. However, most algae and other aquatic plants are not heterotrophic, and thus DON plays a minor role in the energetics of lakes.

The other major role of DON is as a chemical modifier that alters the ionic state of many metals. The ability of nitrogen (as $-N=$) to form complexes with metal ions is enhanced by DON when some nitrogen is present in the amine group $-NH_2$. The presence of large quantities of DON is apparently a prerequisite for the growth of many algae, particularly N_2-fixing blue-greens (Pearsall, 1932; Horne and Fogg, 1970; Fogg and Thake, 1987). This may be due to the toxic and stimulatory roles played by several metals whose state of chelation depends on organic compounds such as DON (Chap. 10).

Gaseous Nitrogen

N_2 gas is the most abundant form of nitrogen because it is little used and because the lake surface waters are in continual contact with the inexhaustible reservoir of the atmosphere (79 percent nitrogen). Nitrogen is present in volumes comparable with those of oxygen despite its lower solubility because N_2 has a greater partial pressure in the atmosphere. N_2 levels generally show no seasonal or depth variations except those resulting from temperature changes. Nitrogen is a conservative gas, and its variations are biologically insignificant. An exception is the supersaturation with nitrogen gas occurring below some large dams, where N_2 bubbles form in fish blood, resulting in high mortality. This is similar to "the bends" in humans, which occurs after breathing compressed air during diving and returning too rapidly to surface pressures.

NITROGEN TRANSFORMATIONS

Biological Nitrogen Fixation

Biological nitrogen fixation occurs in only a few genera of bacteria and blue-green algae (cyanobacteria) and is defined as the transformation of nitrogen gas to ammonia by an enzyme. Nitrogen (N_2) fixation in lakes is carried out mostly by blue-green algae—in contrast to dry land, where symbiotic bacteria-plant systems containing legumes such as alfalfa and peas dominate. In wetlands, nonlegumes, such as alder trees and *Ceanothus* bushes, as well as blue-green algae are important. N_2 fixation is important in lakes because it can be a major source of new, usable nitrogen (see nutrient recycling in Chap. 15). This is most obvious when supplies of phosphorus and iron as well as warm weather are favorable. Under these conditions, N_2 fixation can accelerate lake eutrophication even when other nitrogen sources are very low. A few genera of photosynthetic blue-green algae—*Aphanizomenon, Anabaena, Gleotrichia,* and *Nodularia*—dominate N_2 fixation in lakes. *Nostoc* is common in streams (Horne, 1977), and *Nodularia* and *Aphanizomenon* are characteristic estuarine forms (Huber, 1986). Under the anoxic conditions found in the hypolimnion of some lakes, photosynthetic N_2-fixing bacteria are important.

The enzyme responsible for N_2 fixation, called *nitrogenase,* has two components. One has a molecular weight of 300,000 and contains iron and molybdenum in a ratio of 20:1; the other component has a molecular weight of 35,000 and contains only iron. Nitrogenase is irreversibly denatured by oxygen. It may seem paradoxical that nitrogenase cannot function in the presence of oxygen, since in blue-green algae it requires the energy generated by photosynthesis, which produces oxygen. Further, N_2 fixation occurs in well-oxygenated waters, where oxygen can easily diffuse into the algal cells. This dilemma is resolved in special thick-walled cells called *heterocysts,* which consume oxygen through very high rates of respiration (Figs. 11-1c, 12-1d). The thick wall restricts the inflow of oxygen as well as nitrogen. Nitrogenase is fully saturated even at only 0.2 atm N_2. So N_2 fixation is not affected by the reduced gas permeability. Heterocysts also lack photosystem II, the part of the photosynthetic apparatus that produces oxygen. The result is anoxia inside the heterocyst that allows the nitrogenase to function despite the oxygen in the surrounding cells and medium. Heterocyst formation is induced by intracellular nitrogen shortages that occur when the C:N ratio exceeds 8:1.

Nitrogen compounds in lake water affect nitrogenase. Activity is repressed by the presence of ammonia while nitrate represses further enzyme synthesis. Because nitrogenase contains considerable quantities of iron and molybdenum, N_2 fixation places an additional demand on these two metals, which must be extracted from the water. These and other micronutrients, called *transition metals,* are also needed for the increased ferridoxin and cytochromes involved in the electron transport pathway of respiration, which is high in the heterocyst. The relative scarcity of iron and molybdenum may be responsible for the general low levels of N_2 fixation in estuaries and oceans (Howarth et al., 1988) as well as in some lakes (Wurtsbaugh and Horne, 1983). Micronutrient availability can influence both algal species composition and productivity (Chap. 10). For example, an iron limitation might cause a switch away from N_2-fixing *Aphanizomenon* to a flagellated green alga.

Where other nitrogen supplies are low or exhausted, summer or autumn blooms of N_2-fixing blue-green algae are common in most eutrophic lakes throughout the world. The significance of N_2 fixation in lakes of various types is shown in Table 8-4. In very eutrophic lakes it may be the major nitrogen source, but N_2 fixation plays a

TABLE 8-4

PERCENT CONTRIBUTIONS OF NITROGEN FIXATION AND DENITRIFICATION TO THE ANNUAL NITROGEN BUDGETS OF LAKES, RIVERS, AND ESTUARIES

The largest contribution to the annual nitrogen budget and the highest rates of N_2 fixation (not shown) are found in the plankton of eutrophic lakes. N_2 fixation is most important where other sources of nitrogen, such as nitrate from rainfall and runoff, are low. These conditions are found in dry climates, such as California, and reach extreme levels in desert lakes such as Pyramid Lake, Nevada. Denitrification in fresh waters is most important in sediments where nitrate can become mixed into anoxic sites. These are most often found in estuaries and wetlands. Most denitrification values are estimated by difference; those marked with an asterisk were measured directly

Water Body	N_2 fixation	Denitrification	Reference
Eutrophic lakes			
Mendota, Wisconsin	5–10	36	1
Clear, California	30–60	5	2
ELA 227, Canada[†]	22	1.4*	3
Okeechobee, Florida	0?	9–23*	4
George, Uganda	33	<5?	5
Erken, Sweden[‡]	80	?	6
Valencia, Venezuela	23	?	7
Windermere, England	0.2–0.5	?	8
Mesotrophic lakes			
Pyramid, Nevada	0–81	?	9
Rivers			
Delaware	0–5?	20*	10
Potomac	?	35*	10
Estuaries			
Delaware	< 1?	46*	10
Baltic Sea	0–20?	40–55*	11
Tejo, Portugal	< 1?	45*	12

References: (1) Torrey and Lee, 1976; Seitzinger, 1988; (2) Horne and Goldman, 1972; (3) Flett et al., 1980; (4) Messer and Brezonik, 1983; (5) Horne and Viner, 1971; (6) Granhall and Lundgren, 1971; (7) Levine and Lewis, 1987; (8) Horne and Fogg, 1970; (9) Horne and Galat, 1985; Rhodes and Reutter, personal communication; (10) Seitzinger, 1988; (11) Shaffer and Ronner, 1984; Larson et al., 1985; (12) Ronner, 1985.
[†] Originally oligotrophic, this lake was experimentally fertilized.
[‡] Values for Lake Erken have been recalculated.

minor role in the nitrogen budget of oligotrophic lakes. In Lake Mendota, Wisconsin, typical of many eutrophic lakes in wetter climates where nitrate is more abundant, N_2 fixation makes up only 5 to 10 percent of the annual supply. In contrast, in Clear Lake, California, N_2 fixation regularly provides about half the lake's annual nitrogen supply. In Pyramid Lake, Nevada, over 80 percent of the annual nitrogen supply comes from N_2 fixation in some years (Table 8-4). In Clear Lake, N_2 fixation enables the spring bloom of *Aphanizomenon* (Fig. 8-6) to persist until mid-

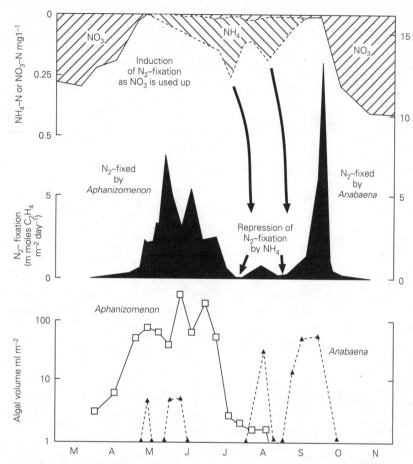

FIGURE 8-6   Seasonal variation in N_2 fixation and associated factors in the Upper Basin of Clear Lake, California. In this polymictic eutrophic lake, the spring bloom of *Aphanizomenon flos-aquae* (bottom panel) initially grew using nitrate (upper left panel) but when this was depleted *Aphanizomenon* was responsible for a long-lasting period of N_2 fixation (middle panel). In summer ammonia released from the anoxic sediments (arrows) repressed N_2 fixation. In autumn sediment ammonia releases declined and a brief but intense spell of N_2 fixation was initiated by a bloom of *Anabaena solitaria* and *Anabaena* sp. The rise in nitrate in autumn terminated the N_2 fixation. Modified from Horne and Goldman (1972).

summer (Horne and Goldman, 1972; Horne, 1979b). Without N_2 fixation the bloom would collapse in late spring after the winter accumulation of nitrate is depleted. In summer, the release of ammonia from the anoxic sediments is sufficient to repress N_2 fixation (Fig. 8-6). In autumn a characteristically ephemeral bloom of N_2-fixing *Anabaena* dominates the plankton due to its ability to grow in the highly nitrogen-depleted water (Fig. 8-6). The ability to change from the use of NH_4 to NO_3 and then to N_2 as each nitrogen source is depleted was demon-

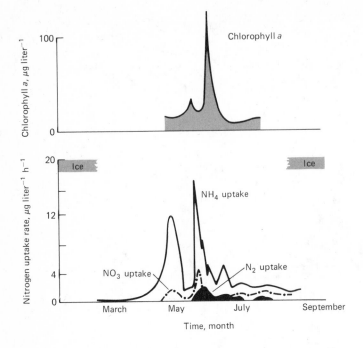

FIGURE 8-7 Sequential use of ammonia, nitrate, and nitrogen gas (N_2) by a bloom of N_2-fixing algae in a shallow eutrophic Alaskan lake. As one nitrogen source becomes depleted (not shown; see Fig. 8-4 for typical seasonal changes), the next source available with least energy expenditure is used. The uptake rates were determined using ^{15}N tracers for each compound. Redrawn from Billaud (1968).

strated in an elegant experiment on an *Anabaena* bloom in Smith Lake, Alaska, using ^{15}N labeling (Billaud, 1968; Fig. 8-7). In mesotrophic Windermere, nitrate and ammonia become depleted in late summer when the N_2-fixing alga *Anabaena* reaches its maximum. Although amounting to < 1 percent of the lake's annual nitrogen budget, N_2 fixation supplies between 10 and 70 percent of the nitrogen used by these alga, depending on the year (Horne and Fogg, 1970).

Various N_2-fixing organisms live in close proximity to aquatic higher plants. Most common are the symbiotic blue-green algae and bacteria in the root zone or rhizosphere of *Lemna,* the duckweed, and *Anabaena* associated with *Azolla,* the water fern (Chap. 11). N_2-fixing organisms secrete some of the fixed nitrogen (Jones and Stewart, 1969; Walsby, 1974), which is then used by the associated plants. A common example is in traditional rice culture in Asia, where for centuries N_2 fixation associated with *Azolla* has passed nitrogen to rice. N_2 fixation also occurs in flowing waters where planktonic algae are absent. *Nostoc* is common in streams, springs, and polar wetlands throughout the world up to altitudes of 2000 m (Plate 6a). Often the dominant genus in shallow streams, *Nostoc* can fix considerable quantities of N_2 (Horne and Carmiggelt, 1975).

Denitrification and Nitrification

The production of N_2 gas from nitrate counterbalances N_2 fixation in the global cycle. In most aquatic systems denitrification rates are usually greater than nitrogen fixation rates (Table 8-4). The balance is made up by nitrogen input from streams and rainfall. Another part of the nitrogen cycle (Fig. 8-1) is nitrification—the conversion of ammonia or organic nitrogen to nitrate. Nitrification and denitrification are discussed together because the processes are often tightly coupled in aquatic ecosystems (Seitzinger, 1988).

Denitrification is carried out by many common facultatively anoxic bacteria and seems to occur whenever conditions are suitable. The microbes reduce nitrate instead of dissolved O_2 during respiration at low oxygen levels in lake muds or anoxic hypolimnia. Biochemically, reduction is the gain of electrons (negative charge); in denitrification the nitrogen in nitrate is reduced from the fully oxidized $+5$ state to the $+0$ state in N_2. The N_2 produced is actually an unwanted byproduct of the metabolism. Ammonia is not directly transformed to N_2: nitrate must be formed first. Denitrification is an energy-demanding process that requires the presence of organic carbon, but nitrification, the oxidation of ammonia, produces energy for the bacteria. The nitrification-denitrification interaction in sediments can be likened to a factory assembly line where ammonia from organic matter is oxidized to nitrate, which is passed along to be converted to N_2. However, the two processes cannot occur in exactly the same place, since denitrification occurs under anoxic conditions but nitrification requires O_2. Denitrifying bacteria do not have specialized structures like the heterocyst of blue-green algae where anoxic conditions can be maintained in a highly oxygenated environment, so spatial separation of the two reactions is needed. Generally, nitrification occurs in the upper 5 cm of mud where nitrate concentrations in the interstitial water are higher than those in the overlying water. Nitrate diffuses either up to the water or down to the anoxic zone, where it is denitrified (Fig. 8-8). The resulting N_2 gas then diffuses slowly upward to the mud surface, into the lake water, and is eventually vented to the atmosphere. Sediment denitrification may continue at variable rates for much of the year,

FIGURE 8-8 Nitrification and denitrification in lake or estuarine sediments. Detritus such as dead algae and fish contain organic nitrogen, which undergoes decomposition with ammonia released as a bacterial waste product. This ammonia is rapidly oxidized to nitrate (nitrified) by other bacteria in the oxic upper mud since this is an energy-producing reaction. The nitrate can then diffuse either up to the water or down to the anoxic region, where it is denitrified, releasing N_2 gas, which diffuses up to the water. Complete anoxia is not needed for denitrification, one reason it is a very common process.

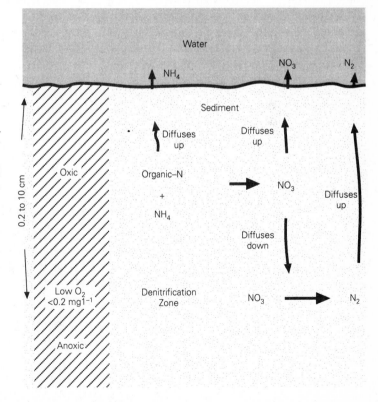

whereas denitrification in lake water occurs for only short periods until the nitrate is depleted (Brezonik and Lee, 1968). In most cases ammonification, the conversion of nitrate to ammonia, accounts for all observed losses of nitrate in anoxic lake hypolimnia. Although denitrification occurs at slower rates in the hypolimnion than in the sediments, the overall importance of the conversion to the lake depends on the relative volumes of the sediment and hypolimnion.

Denitrification in the sediments could be fueled by nitrate from the overlying water, but most studies indicate that the sediments release more nitrate and ammonia than diffuses into them (Fig. 8-8; Seitzinger, 1988). However, some lakes with oxygenated hypolimnia show a decline in nitrate in the deepest water, near anoxic sediments. This could be due to nitrate diffusing into the sediments or other processes, such as conversion to ammonia, may be involved. In shallow productive estuaries with large exposed intertidal areas, nitrates are denitrified as they pass from river to sea. Nitrate is often abundant in rivers, and estuarine sediments are usually anoxic. As the water surface passes over the exposed intertidal zone, wave mixing stirs the nitrate into the sediments. Mixing is less at high and low tides and the sediments settle and become anoxic. Bacterial denitrification then uses up the nitrate. Twice-a-day tidal mixing is much faster than slow molecular diffusion (Table 5-8), thus denitrification is more efficient at removing nitrate from the water than in nontidal regions. Estuarine denitrification is one possible reason why the ocean is limited by nitrogen and not phosphorus, as in many lakes. It is estimated that as much as 40 to 55 percent of all nitrogen flowing into estuaries is lost by denitrification (Table 8-4).

In the watershed, away from the lake, nitrate-rich ground waters permeate anoxic soil pockets rich in organic matter to create ideal denitrification sites. When nitrate-rich ground water upwells through anoxic lake or marsh sediments, it may be largely denitrified before it reaches open water. In Lake Mendota sediment denitrification of ground water produces considerable quantities of nitrogen gas (Brezonik and Lee, 1968; Table 8-4). In wetlands, higher plants play an important role in denitrification. The internal gas circulation system assists oxygen to penetrate the waterlogged anoxic soil near the roots (Chap. 17). Because of this oxygen supply, nitrification occurs near the root hairs. As oxygen becomes depleted away from the roots, the nitrification zone becomes surrounded by a zone of denitrification analogous to the coupled layers in lake and estuarine sediments. For example, about one-third of $^{15}NH_4$ added to wetland sediments was denitrified in laboratory experiments using the macrophytes pickerelweed and soft rush (Reddy et al., 1989). As mentioned earlier, this transformation is one of the ways in which wetlands can be used to treat domestic wastewater.

Nitrogen and phosphorus are nutrients required in moderate quantities in aquatic and terrestrial ecosystems, but both may become limiting for plant growth in lakes and streams. The water chemistry of nitrogen is complicated by its positive and negatively charged forms (NH_4^+, NO_3^-, and NO_2^-) as well as its gaseous phase. In contrast, phosphorus in aquatic systems has no gaseous form and only one type of ion (PO_4^{3-}), but, as will be seen in the next Chapter, the limnological chemistry of phosphorus is complicated by its adsorption onto solid particles.

REVIEWS AND FURTHER READING

Brezonik, P. L. 1973. *Nitrogen Sources and Cycling in Natural Waters.* Ecological Research Series. EPA-660/3-73-002. 167 pp.

Brock, T. D. 1985. pp. 66–71. In *A Eutrophic Lake, Lake Mendota, Wisconsin.* Springer-Verlag, New York.

Corner, E. D. S., and A. G. Davis. 1971. ''Plankton as a Factor in the Nitrogen and Phosphorus Cycles in the Sea.'' *Adv. Mar. Biol.,* **9**:101–204.

Ganf, G. G., and P. Blazka. 1974. ''Oxygen Uptake, Ammonia and Phosphate Excretion by Zooplankton of a Shallow Equatorial Lake (Lake George, Uganda). *Limnol. Oceanogr.,* **19:**313–325.

Howarth, R. W., R. Marino, J. Lane, and J. J. Cole. 1988. "Nitrogen Fixation in Freshwater, Estuarine, and Marine Ecosystems. 1. Rates and Importance. 2. Biogeochemical Controls." *Limnol. Oceanogr.,* **33:**669–687, 688–701.

Horne, A. J. 1978. "Nitrogen Fixation in Entrophic Lakes." pp. 1–30. In R. Mitchell (ed.). *Water Pollution Microbiology,* vol. 2. Wiley, New York.

Horne, A. J., and M. L. Commins. 1987. "Macronutrient Controls on Nitrogen Fixation in Planktonic Cyanobacterial Populations." *N.Z. J. Marine Freshwat. Res.,* **21:**413–423.

Keeney, D. R. 1972. "The Fate of Nitrogen in Aquatic Ecosystems." *Univ. Wis. Water Resour. Cent. Lit. Rev.* **3.** 59 pp.

National Academy of Sciences. 1975. *Nitrates: An Environmental Assessment.* Environmental Studies Board, National Research Council, Washington. 750 pp.

Paerl, H. W., K. L. Webb, J. Baker, and W. J. Wiebe. 1981. "Nitrogen Fixation in Waters." pp. 193–240. In W. J. Broughton (ed.). *Nitrogen Fixation,* vol. 1. Clarendon, Oxford.

Seitzinger, S. P. 1988. "Denitrification in Freshwater and Coastal Marine Ecosystems: Ecological and Geochemical Significance." *Limnol. Oceanogr.,* **33:**702–724.

CHAPTER 9

Phosphorus

OVERVIEW

Phosphorus is a common growth-limiting factor for phytoplankton in lakes because it is often present in low concentrations. Most phosphorus is held in a biologically unavailable form by particles in lake water. In addition, plant roots and the soils of the watershed retain phosphorus much more than nitrogen. The quantities of phosphorus needed by living plants and animals (0.3 percent of body weight) are much smaller than those for carbon, silicon, or nitrogen. A common N:P ratio is 10:1, with higher ratios indicating a deficiency of phosphorus. The phosphorus cycle in lakes involves organic and inorganic phosphorus in both soluble and particulate forms as well as transfers between the different fractions. These transfers occur more quickly than with nitrogen or silicon. Of all the phosphorus compounds present in lakes, phytoplankton can use only soluble phosphate (PO_4) for growth. By late spring, phosphate, which accumulates over the winter, is usually reduced to levels (< 2 μg/liter) well below the K_m for phytoplankton growth. For the rest of the year the remaining phosphorus compounds, and phos-

phorus taken up by algae, are continually *recycled* back to phytoplankton via excretion from fish, zooplankton, and bacterial activity. When algal growth is phosphorus-limited, the rate of photosynthesis is determined by the amount of biologically available phosphate. In contrast, the phytoplankton standing crop is proportional to total phosphorus (TP = soluble + particulate), most of which is assumed to be recyclable. During the summer and fall recycling is likely to be the major source of phosphorus for phytoplankton, even for dense algae blooms in eutrophic lakes. In oligotrophic lakes the role of recycling is less certain. Even with recycling almost all TP sinks out from the epilimnion by the end of the summer. In shallow lakes or in the littoral zone, direct replenishment of PO_4 from the sediments is important. This is the process of *internal loading*. In deeper lakes winter or spring mixing is most important in returning phosphorus to the epilimnion.

Algae have developed special mechanisms to reduce the severity of phosphorus limitation. When supplies are low, phytoplankton can excrete extracellular enzymes called *alkaline phosphatases,* which can cleave the chemical bond between PO_4 and organic molecules. In times of high PO_4, such as early spring, algae can store excess phosphorus in polyphosphate granules. This *luxury consumption* allows the cell to divide several times when external PO_4 supplies are depleted.

In streams and rivers where mineral particles are abundant, a *phosphate buffer system* occurs whereby PO_4 is adsorbed or desorbed from particles depending on external PO_4 concentrations and salinity. Phosphate reacts with inorganic suspended particles in a two-step process. Adsorption occurs initially at a fast rate and is easily reversible. The second stage is slow, less easily reversed, and involves solid-state diffusion of PO_4 into the interior of the particle. Some reversal of the processes occurs in oligotrophic waters or saline estuaries, giving a more constant ''buffered'' PO_4 equilibrium concentration.

In the watershed, PO_4 is readily immobilized in the soil and even that from fertilizers soon becomes unavailable for plant growth. Thus PO_4, in contrast to NO_3, CO_2, and SiO_2, does not move easily with ground water to recharge surface streams. The inflow of large amounts of TP in lakes and rivers results mainly from erosion of soil particles from steep slopes and disturbed ground during floods and storms. Only a small percentage of the TP in streams is in soluble form. More than 90 percent of all phosphorus eroded from continental rock is carried to the sea or deep lakes in an inert form. Worldwide, phytoplankton in wet climates tend to be growth-limited by phosphorus rather than nitrogen. The opposite is true in dry climates because the main nitrogen sources are rainfall and the main phosphorus sources are in the watershed.

Domestic, agricultural, and some industrial wastes are sources of soluble phosphate and have caused cultural eutrophication in many lakes. Secondarily treated sewage effluent contains 5 to 8 mg/liter^{-1} of PO_4—P, which must be removed almost completely by further treatment or diluted at least a thousand times to reach typical lake PO_4 concentrations. The logic behind

this process is that in phosphorus-limited lakes the amount of algal growth in summer is proportional to the phosphorus loading from the surrounding watershed. In addition, phosphorus-limited lakes show a simple linear relationship between TP and chlorophyll. This relationship has been used in mathematical models to predict the benefits of reducing phosphorus inputs and reversing eutrophication. Use of such models has resulted in at least partial restoration of, for example, Lake Erie.

In this chapter we consider measurement of phosphorus, the phosphorus cycle, uptake of phosphorus; and phosphatase induction, recycling in the water column, phosphorus and nitrogen limitation in lakes, and the relative importance of phosphorus as a limiting nutrient.

INTRODUCTION

Phosphorus is essential for all living organisms; living matter contains about 0.3 percent dry weight phosphorus. It plays an irreplaceable role as a structural link in the genetic materials DNA and RNA. In adenosine triphosphate (ATP) phosphorus is involved as short-term energy ''currency'' in biochemical reactions, and it is a component in the phospholipid membranes of cell walls. Although phosphorus is not needed for growth in such large amounts as carbon, oxygen, hydrogen, or nitrogen, it is perhaps the most common growth-limiting element in fresh water. There are four main reasons for phosphorus limitation in lakes: (1) rock breakdown in the watershed releases little biologically available phosphorus to streams and lakes; (2) the root zone on land intercepts and retains most soluble P compounds; (3) there is no gaseous phase in the phosphorus-cycle and thus rainwater contains little phosphorus; and (4) any soluble PO_4 released into water is rapidly adsorbed onto particles or precipitated with other compounds and is not readily available to algae.

Inorganic phosphorus is widely distributed and makes up about 0.1 percent of continental

TABLE 9-1

CONCENTRATIONS OF INORGANIC PHOSPHORUS (μg liter^{-1}) IN THE SURFACE WATERS OF VARIOUS LAKES AND RIVERS

Note the wide range of PO_4—P available for plant growth from limiting levels ($<$ 2 to abundance, $>$ 10). Also, note that eutrophic and oligotrophic lakes may have similar levels.

Lake or river	Relative trophic state and mixing type	Soluble PO_4—P Summer	Winter	References[*]
Tahoe, Calif.	Oligotrophic monomictic	≈2		1
Castle, Calif.	Mesotrophic dimictic	≈2	—	2
Clear, Calif.	Eutrophic polymictic	≈20	≈10	3
Superior	Oligotrophic monomictic	0.5		4
Windermere	Mesotrophic monomictic	5	30	5
Esthwaite	Eutrophic monomictic	5	≈30	5
George, Uganda	Eutrophic polymictic	<2		6
Baikal, Siberia	Oligotrophic dimictic	≈2	6	7
Titicaca, Andes	Mesotrophic monomictic	≈15	≈15	8
Cayuga, NY	Eutrophic monomictic	>5	≈12	9
Uganda rivers	—	80–230		10
Truckee River at km 3	—	≈10	—	11
Hubbard Brook	—	3	2	12

* References: (1, 2) Goldman, various sources; (3) Horne, 1975; (4) Schelske and Roth, 1973; Dobson et al., 1974; Ragotskie, 1974; Bennett, 1978; (5) Heron, 1961; (6) Ganf and Viner, 1973; (7) Kozhov, 1963; (8) Richerson et al., 1977; (9) Oglesby, 1978; (10) Viner, 1973; Golterman, 1975; (11) McLaren, 1977; (12) Likens et al., 1977.

rocks. In a few sites phosphorus comprises up to 7 percent of the rock and is mined for fertilizer. Some small and beautiful tropical islands have been almost mined away to supply the world's agricultural needs. The large phosphorus mining industry in Florida has produced considerable environmental concern because it involves the excavation of so much rock and disposal of waste tailings in a region with a very high water table.

The average concentrations for phosphorus in some of the world's lakes and rivers are given in Table 9-1. Comparison with similar figures for nitrogen (Table 8-2) shows that the N:P ratio varies widely. Since living matter typically requires an N:P ratio of 7:1 by weight or 16:1 by element, phosphorus depletion is likely in many fresh waters where nitrate levels are high ($>$100 μg liter^{-1}). In general, if the ratio N:P $>$ 10 (by weight), phosphorus is considered to limit phytoplankton growth, and if N:P $<$ 10, nitrogen limits growth. Where PO_4 concentrations are very low or undetectable, this approximation is used for total phosphorus and total nitrogen. Where PO_4 is higher, and thus more precisely measured, the ratio is derived using soluble inorganic fractions (PO_4 and $NO_3 + NH_4$).

MEASUREMENT

Phosphorus is measured spectrophotometrically by the blue color PO_4 produces with acid molybdate solution. Organic phosphorus requires a stronger acid digestion prior to assay. Since only PO_4 can be used directly by algae, this form is of most interest. However, in many lakes PO_4 is often present at concentrations near analytical detection limits so it cannot be measured precisely. There is also some question as to whether the molybdate test is a true measure of biologically available PO_4. This uncertainty arises because the acid molybdate solution hydrolyzes some lightly bound small particulate PO_4. This fraction passes thorough the 0.45 μm filter conventionally used to separate ''soluble'' from ''dissolved'' substances in aquatic chemistry. In practice, the molybdate method may overestimate or underestimate soluble PO_4 (Tarapchak and Rubitschun, 1981). The rapid recycling of phosphorus between most fractions means that PO_4 may not be the most appropriate measure for the phosphorus available for phytoplankton growth. To overcome these problems normally several forms of phosphorus are measured in lakes and rivers. For unfiltered water, two forms are analyzed: *total reactive phosphate* (TRP), the PO_4 that reacts with molybdate, and *total phosphorus* (TP). Total phosphorus is all phosphorus fractions present, including any released from soluble and particulate phosphorus compounds after perchloric acid digestion. For filtered water, the direct measure of PO_4 is *total soluble phosphate* (TSP; also called *total dissolved phosphate,* TDP), the dissolved PO_4 that reacts with molybdate, which has the drawback of including some lightly bound organic phosphorus. Total phosphorus measurement has proven useful in understanding the role of phosphorus in eutrophication (Sas, 1989; Wilson and Walker, 1989). Both TRP and TSP correlate well with biologically available phosphorus as measured by the growth of algae (Bradford and Peters, 1987). The distribution of some of these fractions in some North American lakes is shown in Table 9-2.

Details of phosphorus analysis, including other phosphorus fractions such as soluble organic phosphorus, are available in the literature (for fresh waters, Golterman et al., 1978; APHA, 1989; for saline waters, Parsons et al., 1984). The radioisotopes $^{32,33}P$ are used to measure the kinetics of recycling as well as phytoplankton uptake at low PO_4 concentrations (Rigler, 1975). Where phosphorus limits growth, the amount of *biologically available phosphorus* (BAP) determines phytoplankton standing crop. Biologically available phosphorus cannot be measured chemically and must be determined by lengthy algal bioassay. Total soluble phosphorus, the PO_4 present in filtered water, correlates well with BAP in eutrophic lakes and rivers. Total reactive phosphate, the PO_4 in unfiltered water, gives a better correlation with BAP in less productive lakes.

THE PHOSPHORUS CYCLE

Phosphorus in lakes occurs in both organic and inorganic forms. In many northern temperate lakes, PO_4 is scarce and organic phosphorus dominates (Tables 9-1, 9-2). At normal lake pH ranges most soluble phosphate is present as orthophosphate in two ionic forms: monophosphate ((HPO_4^{2-}) and dihydrogen ($H_2PO_4^-$) phosphate ions. However, changes between these forms occur rapidly as pH changes. Although linear chains of condensed soluble polyphosphates are common algal storage products, they are scarce in lake waters. Dissolved cyclic metaphosphorus compounds are also uncommon in lakes. Dissolved organic phosphorus (DOP) usually represents the bulk of the total soluble phosphorus.

TABLE 9-2

DISTRIBUTION OF THE MORE COMMONLY MEASURED PHOSPHORUS FRACTIONS IN SOME NORTH AMERICAN LAKES

The very high TSP value in Lake Onondaga in 1969 is due to phosphorus from sewage pollution, which was much reduced by 1975. For many lakes, SRP, TRP, and BAP are quite similar. Where TP is >30 µg/liter, the various phosphate fractions are also higher. Note that TP varies seasonally much less than SRP.

Temperate lakes	TP	BAP	TSP	TRP	SRP	NSP
39 Canadian rivers & lakes	59	28	28	28	19	18–30
19 Canadian lakes, TP <30 µg/liter	17	5	8	5	4	7–9
10 Canadian lakes, TP >30 µg/liter	64	31	32	24	19	24–36
10 Canadian rivers, TP >30 µg/liter	134	68	62	76	46	55–62
Lake Menodota, 1978–9 winter	165	—	—	—	101	—
summer	107	—	—	—	22	—
Cayuga NY, 1968–70 summer	17	—	—	—	1.8	—
Chatauqua, NY 1975	31	—	13	11	7	—
Onondaga, NY, 1969	—	—	2,350	940	—	—
1975	—	—	200	—	150	—
8 Finger lakes, NY summer	13	—	—	—	0.6	—
spring	12.8	—	—	—	5.2	—
Lake Superior, 1971 summer	3.3	—	2.0	—	0.5	—
West Lake Erie, 1971 summer	49	—	17	—	3	—
spring	—	—	27	—	21	—
10 ELA Lakes, Canada summer	—	—	4.6	—	1.3	—

References: Canadian waters, Bradford and Peters, 1987; Mendota, Brock, 1985; Cayuga, Oglesby, 1978; Chatauqua, Mayer et al., 1978; Onondaga, Murphy, 1978; Eight Finger lakes, Shaffner and Oglesby, 1978; Great Lakes, Dobson et al., 1974; Lesht et al., 1991; ELA lakes, Armstrong and Schindler, 1971.
Key: TP = total phosphorus (unfiltered, digested), BAP = biologically available phosphorus (algal assay), TSP = total soluble phosphorus (included digestion, varying % bioavailable), TRP = total reactive phosphorus (unfiltered, undigested), SRP = soluble reactive phosphorus (no digestion − varying % bioavailable), NSP = vigorous treatment with UV radiation or enzyme digestion.

This organic fraction is made up of many different classes of compounds, but there is no general agreement as to which are the most important. The best estimates are that DOP is dominated by various types of nucleic acids, for example, RNA and DNA. A small fraction of TP is usually present in colloidal form, with molecular weights running to the millions. In most aquatic environments, total particulate phosphorus is present in much larger quantities than soluble phosphorus. Particulate phosphorus encompasses bacterial, plant, and animal phosphorus as well as that adsorbed or an integral part of suspended inorganic particles, such as clays and other minerals.

Although they are interrelated, the geochemical, pelagic water, and sediment cycles of phosphorus are sufficiently different that they are treated separately below.

Phosphorus Cycles from the Landscape

The *geochemical cycle of phosphorus* is essentially a one-way transport of weathered rock fragments from the continental crust to the sediments of lakes and oceans (Fig. 9-1). Changes in patterns of erosion and sediment transport thus strongly influence the overall phosphorus-transport processes. Increases in river discharge increase the transport of particles from source to sink (Chap. 16; Figs. 16-5, 16-6). In natural waters only 5 to 10 percent of phosphorus is carried in soluble form; the rest is inert and moves as sediment particles. Sewage and agri-

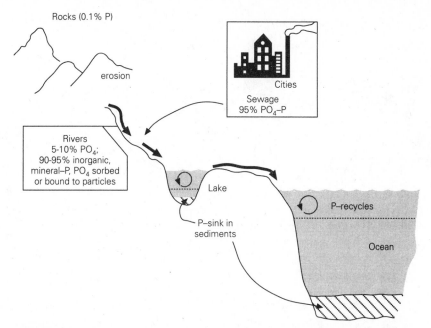

FIGURE 9-1 The geochemical cycle of phosphorus. Almost all (90 to 95 percent) of phosphorus derived from rock breakdown is passed in an inert form to permanent sinks in the sediments of large lakes or the ocean. Phosphate is released by plant decomposition and is quickly taken up by living plant roots and the soil. Soluble, biologically available phosphate is scarce (2 to 10 μg liter^{-1} PO_4—P) in many lakes and rivers, but sewage (5000 to 8000 μg liter^{-1} PO_4—P) and agricultural drainage water (up to 20,000 μg liter^{-1} PO_4—P) are rich sources and contribute to lake eutrophication. In some regions the watershed and thus the streams and lakes are naturally enriched with phosphate. Recycling in the mixed layer of lakes and oceans is a major source of summer phosphate.

cultural runoff disturbs this balance since this pollution contains mostly soluble PO_4 and little particulate phosphorus. Any BAP is rapidly incorporated into algae, which eventually sink to join the inorganic phosphorus in the sediments (Fig. 9-1). Uplifting of the sediments over geological time eventually restarts the cycle.

Because phosphate is both quickly released and adsorbed by particles, an equilibrium arises between phosphate ions and mineral particles in streams and rivers. This is called a *phosphate buffer system* (Froelich, 1988) and is similar to the familiar pH buffer systems used to maintain a desired acidity in a water sample. The buffer system is most applicable in streams and rivers where mineral particles are abundant. Phosphate ions (PO_4^{3-}) are adsorbed or desorbed from particles depending on the external phosphate concentrations and the salinity. Suspended inorganic particles react with PO_4^{3-} in a two-step process. In the first stage adsorption onto the surface layers occurs rapidly—in minutes to hours. This process is easily reversed. The second stage is solid-state diffusion of PO_4 into the interior molecular spaces of the particle. This process is slow, requiring days to months for completion, and is less easily reversed. When the equilibrated particles encounter different external conditions,

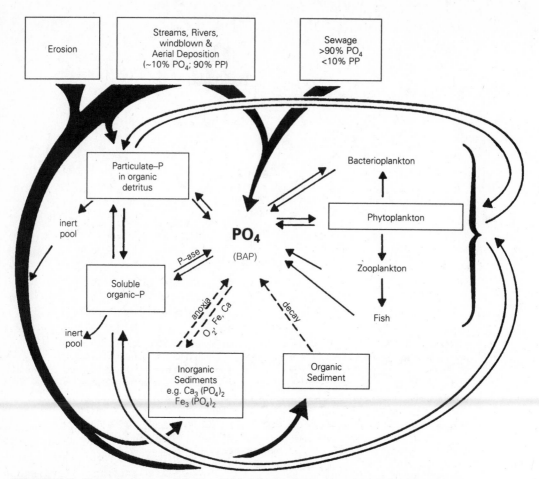

FIGURE 9-2 The phosphorus cycle in lakes. Heavy lines indicate external loading; dashed lines, internal loading; other lines, internal recycling. Although some interconnections are omitted, almost all phosphorus in lake water is present in organic form as living or dead biomass. Sorption and desorption of PO_4 onto organic and inorganic particles surfaces dominates phosphorus chemistry in natural waters, but true compounds, such as the mineral apatite [impure $Ca_3(PO_4)_2$] are also formed. Desorption from particles releases biologically available phosphorus (BAP), which is available as PO_4 for phytoplankton growth. Boxes indicate the largest quantities of phosphorus in lakes; the actual values and relative importance vary with season. Since input of phosphorus in summer is often low and sediments are usually isolated from the photic zone, recycling comprises much of the activity in the pelagic phosphorus cycle. The major inputs of phosphorus to the cycle are from the inflow of streams and discharges of human wastes. Dust may transport phosphorus to some lakes. PP = particulate-phosphorus.

the reversal of the process releases phosphate. For example, when stream waters flow into an oligotrophic lake or the higher salinity waters of an estuary, PO_4 is released, mostly by reversal of surface adsorption. The overall result is a more constant "buffered" equilibrium phosphate concentration.

Even where soluble phosphate is released in the watershed it tends to be retained by most soils, so leachates and ground waters in general are much lower in phosphate than in nitrate. When water polluted with nitrogen and phosphorus from domestic sewage is passed through soil, as in a septic tank leach field, the percolate is much more depleted in phosphate than in nitrate.

Phosphorus Cycle in Pelagic Waters

The major pathways of the phosphorus cycle in lakes and the approximate quantities to be found in the various fractions are shown in Fig. 9-2. At the center of the cycle is soluble BAP. Almost all phosphorus in lake water is present in organic form as living or dead biomass. Since the input of phosphorus from the watershed in summer is often low and deep sediments are isolated from the photic zone, recycling comprises much of the activity in the pelagic phosphorus cycle. Both soluble and organic phosphorus are excreted by zooplankton, fish, and bacterioplankton. Decomposition of dead plants and animals releases DOP and phosphate.

The seasonal phosphorus cycles in several kinds of lakes are shown in Fig. 9-3. The major inputs of phosphorus to the cycle are from the inflow of streams and rivers and, nowadays, discharges of human wastes. Dry deposition and dust contains more phosphorus, at least in some lakes (Cole et al., 1990). In summer, shallow, eutrophic lake sediments may release large amounts of phosphate (Williams and Barker, 1991). This *internal loading* is the reason many shallow lakes remain eutrophic once polluted with sewage, even if the phosphorus supply is terminated (Fig. 22-5). In deep lakes internal loading is restricted, thus they recover more rapidly from phosphorus pollution. Some phosphorus is transferred to the epilimnion by hypolimnetic entrainment, thermocline descent in the autumn, and leaking around the edges of the metalimnion following internal waves (Chaps. 4, 5). However, phosphate released from the sediments or from the hypolimnion may not pass to the photic zone in some small, protected lakes (Lehman and Naumoski, 1986). The main role of ground water in the phosphorus cycle of seepage lakes appears to be the flushing of phosphate from the sediments. Between 10 and 30 percent of the annual phosphorus loading to ground water-fed lakes may come via these routes (Kenoyer and Anderson, 1989; Shaw et al., 1990).

The major loss of phosphorus from open water is sedimentation of the biota or chemically formed precipitates. Most of this phosphorus becomes part of the permanent accumulation of sediments. The annual layers of sediment are often clearly distinguishable and can be used to document changes in phosphorus input to the lake over time (Fig. 20-9). Addition of iron to a pure sodium phosphate solution precipitates ferric phosphate ($FePO_4$), depending on oxygen and pH. Inorganic solid phosphate phases are formed with calcium, aluminum, and iron, while clay particles ''scavenge'' phosphate by sorption. Many of these solid-liquid phase equilibria can reach completion in the time required for the particle to sink.

In the Sediment

Sediments consist of solid particles separated by liquid-filled *interstitial spaces* containing pore water. They are mixed by larger benthic organisms and wave action. The *sediment-water interface* or *microzone* is the barrier to free interchange of phosphorus between sediments and the lake waters. If the interface is anoxic, phosphate ions can pass across at a rate dependent on the concentration gradient between sediment pore waters and the water. If the interface is oxygenated, phosphate ions are scavenged and do not pass freely to the lake water. Anoxic sediments release phosphate as much as 1000 times faster than releases from oxygenated sediments. This is attributable to both classical chemical bonding and physiochemical sorptive mechanisms. The reactions

$$Fe(III)PO_4 \text{ (insoluble)} \rightleftharpoons Fe(II)_3(PO_4)_2 \text{ (soluble)}$$
$$\rightleftharpoons Fe^{2+} \text{ (free)} + PO_4^{3-} \text{ (free)} \qquad (1)$$

may be less important than reactions of the type

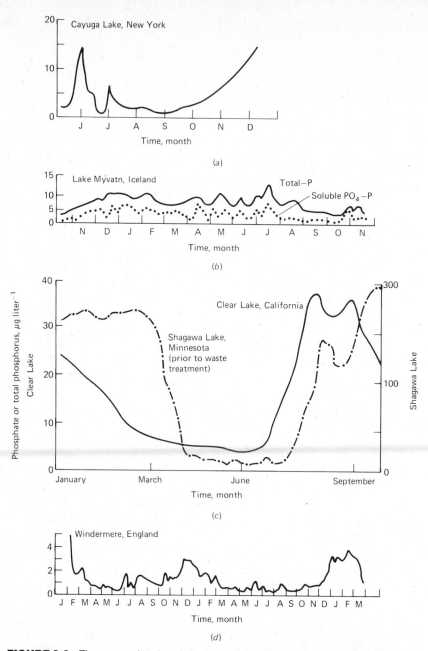

FIGURE 9-3 The seasonal cycles of phosphate in five lakes. Total-P is shown only for Lake Mývatn. In most lakes soluble phosphate concentrations fall from relatively high winter levels at the start of the spring bloom and continue low until early winter. Luxury uptake by phytoplankton (see text) may use up many times the requirement for one cell division (Table 9-1) and may account for the rapid decline in spring levels. Clear Lake, California, has naturally high phosphate levels; Shagawa Lake, Minnesota, was polluted by sewage; the levels in the other lakes are similar to the low levels found in many lakes. *Modified from (a) Oglesby, 1978; (b) Olafsson, 1979; (c) Horne, 1975; Lallatin, 1972; Malueg et al. 1973; (d) Heron, 1961.*

$$Fe^{3+}(OH)_3 + PO_4^{3-} \text{ (sorbed)}$$
$$\rightleftharpoons Fe^{2+}(OH)_2 + PO_4^{3-} \text{ (free)} \quad (2)$$

where the ferric hydroxide or oxyhydroxide may be replaced by numerous other sorption sites such as clays. For this reason, Eq. (2) is not balanced stoichiometrically. The sorption equilibria in Eq. (2) are sensitive to pH, the redox potential E_h, and dissolved oxygen. Unfortunately, the heterogeneous nature (solid-liquid phases) of the reactions prevents easy extrapolation of laboratory results to real-lake sediment systems.

The most important reactions in the sediments are those that change phosphorus from a solid phase into soluble phosphate in the interstitial waters, which may then in turn be released to overlying waters. Sediment samples reflect the relative fertility of the lake and contain 0.06 to 10 mg liter^{-1} of soluble interstitial phosphate. These levels are many times greater than those of the overlying waters (0.002 to 0.05 mg liter^{-1}). The amount of clay in a lake sediment is perhaps the most important factor in determining its phosphorus-holding capacity. Unfortunately from the standpoint of prediction of its effect on phosphates, clay is a rather variable mineral. Clay consists of complex silicates of aluminum and iron together with their oxides. The purest form of clay, china clay or kaolin, has the formula $AlO_3 \cdot 2SiO_2 \cdot 2H_2O$. Clays sorb phosphorus by the specific chemical interaction of PO_4^{3-} with Al^{3+} on the edges of the clay plates (Stumm and Leckie, 1971). Phosphate is also sorbed directly onto hydrous iron or aluminum oxides, particles of calcite (impure calcium carbonate), and apatite (impure $Ca_3[PO_4]_2$). Phosphate may also be occluded within iron oxides and some sediments. This inclusion, or internal absorption, is part of the phosphorus buffering system discussed earlier.

The amount of precipitated phosphate, as distinct from sorbed phosphate, is also controlled by pH and E_h. As the concentration of phosphate and pH vary, different metallic phosphorus compounds are precipitated. When the process is re-versed, the quantity of phosphate released into sediment interstitial waters is regulated by minerals that buffer releases from other minerals. In addition, organic phosphorus released from decaying organic matter further modifies the amount of phosphate present in the pore water. Biological activity also affects pore water phosphate, since sediments are a food source for various *detritivores,* such as insect larvae, worms, and crustaceans. These organisms excrete soluble phosphorus compounds in the pore waters as they burrow and feed in the upper few centimeters of newly deposited sediment.

UPTAKE OF PHOSPHORUS AND INDUCTION OF PHOSPHATASES

Algae have evolved three main methods to overcome phosphorus deficits: (1) luxury consumption; (2) an ability to use phosphate at low levels (low K_m); and (3) alkaline phosphatase production.

Luxury consumption of phosphate occurs in almost all phytoplankton. More phosphate is taken up than is required for growth and the excess is stored in the cell. Microscopic examination of algal cells grown under nonlimiting conditions reveals highly refractive cellular inclusions called *polyphosphate granules.* They form very rapidly, often within hours, when phosphate is added to a phosphorus-deficient culture (Stewart and Alexander, 1971). Polyphosphate granules disappear rapidly when the surrounding medium becomes depleted in phosphorus, but the store in the granules can support up to 20 cell divisions. An obvious advantage to the cell containing polyphosphate granules is their lack of osmotic or toxic effects. This is in contrast with most nitrogenous products, which do not readily condense to a suitable storage form and must be kept as protein or pigments.

Polyphosphate granules are easily released from cells by boiling; algal physiologists have used the amount of phosphate released as a mea-

TABLE 9-3

ENZYME GROWTH AND UPTAKE KINETICS OF PHOSPHATE FOR TWO DIATOMS AND A GREEN ALGA

Note the superiority of *Asterionella* and *Selenastrum* at low levels of lake phosphate. They can take up PO_4—P at lower levels and use it faster.

Species	K_3, µg liter $^{-1}$	Max. growth rate µ, doublings day^{-1}	Uptake rate V_{max}	Luxury uptake coeff. R^*	References[†]
Asterionella formosa	0.6	0.9	13×10^{-9}	82	1
Cyclotella meneghiniana	8	0.8	5×10^{-9}	6.6	2
Selanastrum capricornutum	1.3	1.2	—	57	2

[*] The luxury uptake coefficient R is the ratio of the cell quota of a nutrient when it is limiting to when it is abundant (Droop, 1974). Here *Asterionella* and *Selenastrum* are superior to *Cyclotella*.
[†] References: (1) Tilman and Kilham, 1976; (2) Brown and Button, 1979.

sure of the degree of cellular phosphorus depletion (Fitzgerald and Nelson, 1966). In most lakes the *phosphate growth constant, K_m,* is very low for natural phytoplankton (Table 9-3; Chap. 15). It is generally in the range of 1 to 3 µg liter^{-1} PO_4—P which means the enzyme system in algae is not saturated for much of the time under natural lake conditions (Tables 9-1, 9-2). Particularly in summer, phosphate levels in unpolluted lakes often fall to extremely low levels. In contrast, lakes polluted with sewage or those with high natural phosphorus inputs usually have phosphate levels (Fig. 9-3) that will saturate the uptake system of the phytoplankton. There may be considerable variation in K_m between species, and as available phosphate decreases this could play a role in species succession (Chap. 15; Figs. 15-7, 15-8). Because phosphate is recycled rapidly, the rate of phosphate uptake (V_{max}) is also important. A higher uptake rate can thus compensate, to some degree, for the lack of a mechanism to remove phosphate at very low levels.

The enzyme *alkaline phosphatase* is an esterase that, by hydrolysis, cleaves the bond between phosphate and the organic molecule to which it is attached. The result is free phosphate available for plant growth. The production of alkaline

phosphatases by planktonic algae is a remarkable adaptation to an environment low in phosphate but comparatively rich in larger phosphorylated compounds. These may be either organic or condensed inorganic polyphosphates. The enzyme is attached near the cell surface and is produced in response to phosphorus deficiency. Synthesis of new enzyme is repressed by the addition of phosphate to the medium. Algae deficient in phosphorus may contain up to 25 times more alkaline phosphatase than algae with surplus phosphorus (Fitzgerald and Nelson, 1966; Bone, 1971). It is unfortunate that increases in phosphatases do not always predict phosphorus deficiency in phytoplankton. Phosphatases are reviewed by Jansson et al. (1988).

Even more remarkable than the production of alkaline phosphatase is its release in free dissolved form into the environment. The extracellular enzyme quickly hydrolyzes much of the previously unavailable TP (Berman, 1970; Petterson, 1980). The releases are roughly proportional to algal biomass and lake trophic state (Jones, 1972). Phosphatases are nonspecific: the phosphate released by one species is available to all the others. The competitive advantage of phosphatase release to the individual algal cell appears uncertain; it is possible that the entire population of phytoplankton may benefit. If this were so, the process of natural selection would be operating at a community level, which is not expected in ecology theory. However, due to the very viscous nature of water and the scale of the individual alga, most organic phosphorus encountered by the alga is very close to its cells. Thus they may be able to take advantage of their own phosphatase more than other algae. In addition, the life of the enzyme in fresh waters is quite short—hours to days. The free-solution reactions involving phosphatases are a major reason for the short turnover time of most phosphorus compounds in lakes, estuaries, and seas and the utility of TP as a predictor of algal biomass.

The use of extracellular enzymes by phytoplankton is almost unique to phosphorus metabolism, the only analogous mechanism being that for iron (Chap. 10). Phosphorus and iron are among the few elements most likely to be growth-limiting in natural situations. There are other free-solution reactions that liberate both iron and phosphorus. For example, insoluble inorganic phosphates such as $FePO_4$ and $AlPO_4$ can be solubilized by sediment bacteria. This is accomplished by the production of organic acids rather than phosphatases (Harrison et al., 1972).

PHOSPHORUS RECYCLING IN THE WATER COLUMN

The Role of Zooplankton and Fish

Zooplankton and fish excrete nutrients directly into the water, where they are available for phytoplankton growth. Zooplankton excrete approximately 10 percent of their body phosphorus daily, but there is considerable variation depending on feeding rate, temperature, type of food, time of day, and larval stage (Corner and Davis, 1971). Of the phosphorus excreted, roughly half is phosphate and the remainder is organic. Thus excretion is the main source of readily available phosphate in the epilimnion of lakes where phosphorus limits growth. Although zooplankton

phosphorus excretion varies, it may supply most of the daily demand of phytoplankton in more eutrophic lakes where zooplankton standing crops are large. One explanation for the changes in phytoplankton in lakes is thus related to changes in zooplankton numbers.The effect of a drastically lower zooplankton excretion rate has been discussed for Lake George, Uganda, a nonseasonal equatorial lake. Ganf and Blaika (1974) predict that decreased zooplankton grazing would result in a "bloom and crash" phytoplankton population in place of the present constant algal densities (Fig. 21-5). The theory is that with few grazing zooplankton, the phytoplankton will grow until all phosphorus supplies are exhausted. The bloom will then decay rapidly, and phosphorus will be released in huge quantities by cell lysis and bacterial decay to start the cycle again. With more zooplankton there is always a supply of phosphate from excretion, and phytoplankton growth continues at a high but controlled rate.

The diel vertical migration of zooplankton (Chap. 13) also influences the nutrient cycle. To avoid consumption by predators that rely on sight, most herbivorous zooplankton move into the surface waters at night. During the day they remain in the dark, cool deeper water where digestion and excretion are slowed by the lower temperatures. Thus in shallow lakes the cycling of phosphorus in the euphotic zone is favored by their nightly vertical migrations to the warmer surface zone.

Role of Rooted Macrophytes and Algal Decomposition

Wetland plants can modify the phosphorus cycle in lakes by transporting phosphates from sediments to the open water. Many lakes are fringed with emergent reeds and submerged macrophytes (Fig. 11-6). In small lakes these wetland plants are the dominant primary producers and also constitute the largest biomass. Uptake of phosphate can occur through the leaves of macrophytes when the water is rich in phosphate (McRoy et al., 1972). However, Tables 9-1 and

9-2, show lake waters are usually low in available phosphate. In contrast, the pore waters of the sediments are 9 to 600 times richer in phosphate than the overlying waters. Thus rooted macrophytes normally obtain about 85 percent of their phosphorus by absorption of phosphate directly from the interstitial soil pore water (Carignan and Kalff, 1980). Over the year, this phosphorus is released to the water by the decay of freshwater macrophytes. Macrophyte decay can be rapid; for example, over half of plant phosphorus is lost in 12 days in eutrophic Lake Wingra, Wisconsin (Carpenter, 1980). The quantities of phosphorus transferred are sometimes large enough to be important to lake phosphorus loading. Smith and Adams (1986) showed that the decay of *Myriophyllum spicatum* added about half as much phosphorus to Lake Wingra each year as was contributed by the entire watershed runoff. However, *Myriophyllum* is an invading weed in this lake and the amounts transferred in other lakes may be lower. When a macrophyte stand reaches steady state, such as a mature *Phragmites* reed bed, there will be a steady release of phosphate from decay. In fresh water, phosphorus transfer depends on death and decay of the plant. Little phosphate leaks directly out from the leaves and stems of freshwater macrophytes. In contrast, for living estuarine eelgrass beds, about 30 percent of the phosphorus taken up daily by the roots was almost immediately released as phosphate to the surrounding water (McRoy and Barsdate, 1970).

Like macrophytes, phytoplankton and attached algae release phosphorus when they decay. If algae are placed in darkness to simulate the deeper waters of the lake, they decompose in three stages: (1) within 24 hours both release and uptake of phosphorus occur, depending on the original conditions of the cells; (2) over the next several days there is a stage of little net activity; (3) over a few hundred days active nutrient regeneration takes place, with releases to solution (Foree et al., 1971). Much of the cellular phosphorus is not released. This is called *refractory*

phosphorus and constitutes roughly one-third of the initial particulate phosphorus. It is the refractory phosphorus that constitutes the bulk of the sedimented organic phosphorus.

The Role of Planktonic Bacteria

Bacteria require organic carbon to grow but also need nitrogen and phosphorus. Culture studies indicate that at low phosphate levels, bacterial uptake should predominate over phytoplankton uptake (Berman, 1983; Currie and Kalff, 1984). Studies of natural populations using radioactive tracers show that where phosphorus is low, most added phosphate is found in the small ($< 0.5 \, \mu m$) particle fraction composed of bacteria. At higher concentrations of phosphate, algae can compete more successfully, probably because bacteria become carbon-limited (Currie, 1990). When phosphorous is low it is difficult to imagine how algae obtain phosphate if bacteria are present. One solution is the luxury consumption of phosphate early in the season when it is present in higher quantities. However, bioassay studies show that where phosphorus limits growth, additions of phosphate stimulate algae productivity, so there must be some method by which algae obtain needed phosphorus. The solution may involve patchiness, found in almost all aquatic systems. In nature, scarce nutrients are found in patches where there has been a recent excretion by zooplankton or fish (Lehman and Scavia, 1982); the concentration of all nutrients is higher in these patches. Algal phosphate uptake would be competitive with that of bacteria. In addition, most bacteria are eaten by rotifers and other small zooplankton and their phosphorus soon excreted at a relatively high concentration. Further experiments are needed to determine the competitive role of bacteria under natural conditions.

This discussion has been confined to unproductive, phosphorus-limited waters. Where phosphate is more common, as in estuaries, rivers, and some lakes, the distribution of TP between bacterioplankton and phytoplankton is more even and algae may take up almost all of

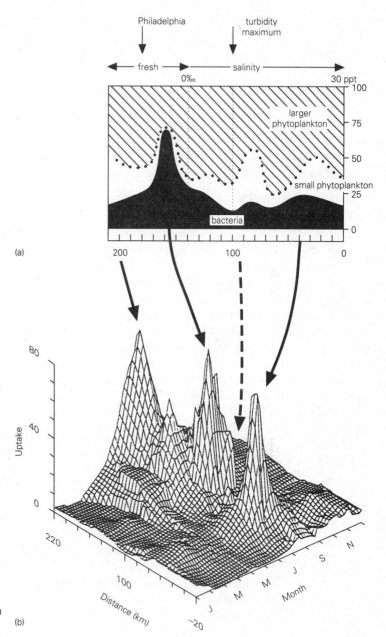

(a)

(b)

FIGURE 9-4 Phosphate uptake and its distribution between phytoplankton and bacterioplankton in the Delaware Estuary, a river-estuary continuum. (*a*) The contribution by bacterioplankton (approx. 0.5 μm diameter), small phytoplankton (1 to 3 μm), and larger phytoplankton (> 3 μm) to PO_4 uptake along the length of the river and estuary. Note that in this system, where concentrations are usually > 60 μg liter^{-1} PO_4—P, the bacteria are generally unimportant in PO_4 removal. This may not be the case in phosphorus-limited lakes (1 to 5 μg liter^{-1}, PO_4—P), where they may remove almost all added phosphate. (*b*) The seasonal and spatial variation of uptake (nm liter^{-1} h^{-1}) as shown by orthogonal three-dimensional projection. The greatest uptake is in summer. Peak uptake is in fresh water near the sewage outfalls of Philadelphia and in saline water to either side of the muddy turbidity maximum. Modified from Lebo (1990).

added phosphate. This situation is shown in Fig. 9-4*b* for a river that becomes an estuary in its lower reaches. Most uptake occurs in spring and summer. Only in the muddy turbidity maximum

is uptake low (Chap 19). The distribution of the uptake between bacterioplankton and phytoplankton is shown in Fig. 9-4*a*. Here bacteria account for less than a quarter of phosphate uptake, except near the sewage discharges, which provide an organic carbon source. In this region, about 75 percent of phosphate uptake is bacterial. In this estuary, as in many productive waters, the large algae (> 3 μm) dominate both the biomass and the phosphate uptake.

PHOSPHORUS AND NITROGEN LIMITATION IN LAKES

The Phosphorus-Chlorophyll Relationship and Phosphorus-Loading Curves

In most lakes there is a direct relationship between the concentration of the growth-limiting nutrient and the maximum crop of phytoplankton. In the temperate zone there are many lakes where the amount of total phosphorus is statistically well-related to the maximum phytoplankton abundance, as expressed by chlorophyll a. Frequently regression coefficients (r^2) as high as 0.9 are recorded, indicating that 90 percent of the variation in algae is explained by variations in TP. In other lakes, especially those in dry climates, the r^2 for TP may be < 0.1, indicating that other factors control algal abundance. The TP-chlorophyll relationship is shown in Fig. 9-5. The same relationship applies for nitrogen and silica in lakes where these elements limit algal growth, although these limitations are less common in temperate lakes. The ability to predict the changes in phytoplankton from changes in TP is nevertheless useful, even though it is an empirical relationship that must be established for each lake or group of lakes. The theory of the TP-chlorophyll relationship assumes that all TP (or a large and constant fraction) is recycled (Fig. 9-2). Thus the easily measured TP fraction present in early spring is a guide to the maximum phytoplankton crop produced in spring and summer. Keep in mind that it is necessary to use TP, since phosphate is difficult to measure accurately at low concentrations (< 2 μg liter^{-1}).

The TP-chlorophyll relationship can be extended to predict the effects of the watershed on

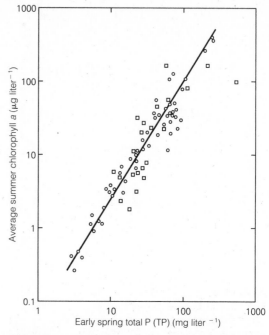

FIGURE 9-5 Relationship between total phosphorus (TP) and chlorophyll a in some temperate lakes. If TP is measured in early spring before algal growth has begun, this relationship can be used to predict the mean summer phytoplankton crop. Note that phosphorus must be the limiting nutrient for this relationship to be appropriate. The regression line and dots represent values from the original Dillon and Rigler paper (1974), and squares represent values from a more recent Canadian lakes study (Prepas and Trew, 1983). Quite large deviations from the relationship are obscured by this log-log plot. Nevertheless, the TP-Chlorophyll a relationship is useful to limnologists.

phytoplankton blooms. Again, if phosphorus is the growth-limiting element, the amount of TP entering the lake each year should be related to the phytoplankton standing crop. This type of relationship is called a *phosphorus loading curve,* a simple example of which is shown in Fig. 9-6. There are several ways to present loading curves but all place the loading values on the y axis and a lake-related parameter such as depth on the x axis. The initial loading curves for both nitrogen and phosphorus were developed by Vollenweider in the 1960s. He used loading in

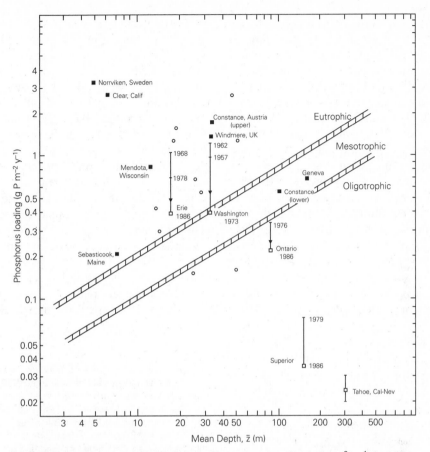

FIGURE 9-6 Loading curves for phosphorus in lakes. Loading (g P m^{-2} y^{-1}) from the watershed is plotted against mean depth, which is frequently related to the residence time of phosphorus in the lake. Lakes can be separated into three groups: above the upper trend line are eutrophic lakes, below the lower line are the oligotrophic lakes, and in between the lines are the mesotrophic ones. If phosphorus is growth-limiting and the TP-chlorophyll *a* relationship (Fig. 9-5) applies, then changes in loading will change chlorophyll and thus the trophic state. Examples are shown where phosphorus was decreased by sewage diversion or treatment. Lakes Washington (Chap. 22), and Erie changed from relatively eutrophic to mesotrophic (vertical lines). Also shown are two shallow nitrogen-limited lakes, Clear Lake, California (phosphorus naturally high), and Norrviken, Sweden (phosphorus-polluted). Their very high phosphorus loading sets them apart from the others. Set apart are the very oligotrophic lakes Tahoe and Superior, in which the low phosphorus input from the relatively small drainage basins is highly diluted by their enormous volumes. Open circles indicate European lakes in the original Vollenweider (1968) plot.

grams (phosphorus or nitrogen entering the lake from rivers, streams, and wastewater effluents) per square meter of lake surface per year against mean depth (Vollenwieder, 1968). Mean depth is a general indicator of hydraulic residence time and also indicates the amount of internal loading expected from the sediments. Shallow lakes have a rapid turnover of inflowing nutrients, so a single year's loading from the watershed is important. Internal loading is facilitated by shallow water since much of the sediment area is exposed to wave mixing. Deep lakes have only a small fraction of their sediments above the thermocline, and thus sequester nutrients more effectively than shallow ones. More sophisticated models include aerial fallout in the loading data as well as hydraulic or particulate residence time.

When many lakes are plotted on a nutrient loading curve they can be fitted into three distinct groups, depending on where they lie relative to the 45° trend line (Fig. 9-6). Those lakes that lie well below this line are deep and have a low nutrient loading; these are oligotrophic lakes. Those that lie well above the line are shallow, have a high nitrogen or phosphorus loading; these are eutrophic lakes. Those that lie on or near the trend line tend to be mesotrophic. If a lake lies out of position relative to its mean depth, trophic status may have changed (see eutrophication, Chap. 20; regional limnology, Chap. 21). In Fig. 9-6 two lakes are shown to have changed from eutrophic to mesotrophic. These changes were partially due to reduction in phosphorus pollution. Some examples of lake restoration by removal of phosphorus or nitrogen from inflows are discussed in detail in Chap. 22. As it has immediate relevance to phosphorus, the example of Lake Erie is discussed below.

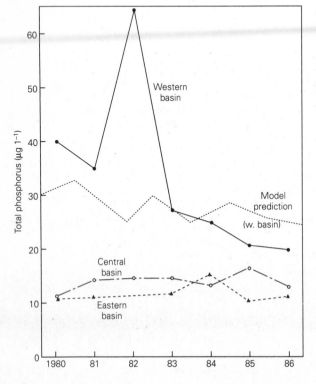

FIGURE 9-7 Changes in annual TP concentration in the surface waters of Lake Erie, 1980–1986. Samples are from only deep water sites and thus exclude near-shore influences. Total phosphorus in the most polluted Western Basin declined by over 40 percent due to phosphorus removal from sewage discharges. The larger, deeper, less polluted Central and Eastern Basins show no trends over this time period. Note that the model prediction, made using 1970s data (see text), underestimates the measured decline and also did not predict the doubling of TP in 1982. Based on data from Lesht et al. (1991).

Lake Erie is a large water body receiving sewage, industrial, and agricultural runoff. Using the TP-chlorophyll and nutrient loading curves discussed above, phosphorus was determined to have been a major cause of eutrophication. There is a considerable excess of nitrate in this lake, so phosphorus is a logical candidate for the growth-limiting nutrient. Early in the 1970s serious attempts to reduce phosphorus loading were made by removing phosphate from secondarily treated domestic sewage effluent and by a partial ban on the sale of detergents containing high levels of phosphates. It takes a long time for large-scale restoration projects to produce results that are clearly distinguishable from natural year-to-year variations in nutrients and algae. Often changes in weather patterns, such as an unusually windy or hot spell, cause divergence from the trends due to the cleanup.The results of the 1970s restoration are only now becoming evident (Fig. 9-7). Despite a temporary upswing, there has been a decline in TP in the western part of Lake Erie since 1980. This shallow, western basin was particularly affected by pollution. In 1980–1981 the annual mean TP ranged from 35 to 37 μg liter^{-1} but by 1985–1986 the annual means had fallen about 40 percent, to 20 to 22 μg liter^{-1}. Declines in TP in the less-polluted Central and Eastern Basins, however, showed no obvious change in TP, remaining at 11 to 17 μg liter^{-1}. Also shown on Fig. 9-7 is the prediction made using a simple model of the lake that considers it as a series of 7 or 11 connected segments (Lesht et al., 1991). Each segment is considered as a well-mixed reactor and the change over time of the phosphorus mass is calculated as a linear function of the loading, upstream and downstream flows, mixing between adjacent sections, and loss to the sediments (Chapra and Sonzogni, 1979). Considering all the complexities, the predictions for Lake Erie are quite good. However, the change in TP from 35 μg liter^{-1} (1981) to 64 μg liter^{-1} (1982) and back to 27 μg liter^{-1} (1983) was not predicted at all, even by recent, more sophisticated models. Although the TP in Lake Erie's Western Basin has fallen by 41 percent, the real test of the cleanup will be a decline in chlorophyll, as would be expected from a close TP-chlorophyll relationship.

THE RELATIVE IMPORTANCE OF PHOSPHORUS AS A LIMITING NUTRIENT

Although phosphorus is generally considered the most common limiting nutrient for algae growth in many lakes, limitation of plant growth by deficiencies in nitrogen, silicon, carbon dioxide, and some metals, such as iron and molybdenum, can occur in a variety of lakes, reservoirs, estuaries, and coastal waters. For example, Fig. 9-6 can be redrawn for the same lakes using nitrogen loading to give a similar grouping of lakes by trophic status. A recent review of laboratory and whole-lake experiments on the limitation of phytoplankton growth by nitrogen and/or phosphorus shows that a more balanced view of which nutrient most limits phytoplankton growth is needed (Elser et al., 1990). The review considered 62 lake studies; in most of them the algae were deficient in *both* nitrogen and phosphorus. When added together they greatly stimulated phytoplankton growth. In contrast, additions of nitrogen or phosphorus alone usually stimulate less algal growth (Fig. 9-8). This was shown for some Canadian whole-lake experiments in the 1970s (Fee, 1979). Only if the stimulation of nitrogen or phosphorus alone equals the stimulation of nitrogen and phosphorus together is it certain that, in an ecologically important sense, only one nutrient was limiting. These results apply to natural populations of algae found in the lake and not the pure culture of *Selenastrum capricornatum* often used for laboratory studies of filtered lake water. Pure culture tests are less realistic but indicate more stimulation by phosphorus than nitrogen (Miller et al., 1974). This result is probably an artifact due to the particular high phosphorus requirements of *Selenastrum*. It was once thought that nitrogen fixation could overcome the lack of nitrate or ammonia in lakes

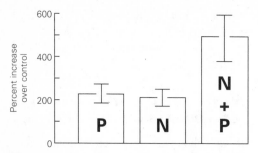

FIGURE 9-8 Responses of indigenous lake phyto-plankton to additions of nutrients. Results are for about 50 different lakes in North America and error bars are 95 percent confidence limits. Note that, although either nitrogen or phosphorus stimulates an average doubling of growth, the two added together produce an average five-fold increase. When this large number of lakes is compared, equal numbers respond to either nitrogen or phosphorus. Most of the world's unproductive lakes have low concentrations of *both* nitrogen and phosphorus. Obvious exceptions to this are the nitrate-rich waters such as the Laurentian Great Lakes, Lake Windermere in England, and some of the Finger Lakes in New York State. On the other extreme are lakes such Pyramid Lake, Nevada, Lake George, Uganda, and Lake Rotonaio, New Zealand, where phosphate is always abundant. Modified from Elser et al. (1990).

if phosphate was added. Now it is clear that the stimulation of nitrogen fixation is a more complex process (Wurtsbaugh, 1988; Horne and Commins, 1989). In contrast to fresh waters, the ocean is generally limited by nitrogen. The reasons for the differences in the importance of phosphorus in lakes and oceans is still uncertain (Howarth et al., 1988a; 1988b).

Regional Influences on Phosphorus and Nitrogen Limitation

The previous section on phosphorus limitation was limited to temperate lakes since this is where there is most concern about lake eutrophication. Not all areas regard moderate eutrophication as a problem. In tropical countries the fish from productive lakes provide scarce protein. In addition, warm-water fisheries are less affected by mild eutrophication, because they do not support salmonid fish. In these areas reduction in the

water quality in reservoirs may be the most important effect of eutrophication. Whatever the reasons, identifying the growth-limiting nutrient(s) is of worldwide concern for limnologists.

One simple difference between regions is the climate and thus the amount of precipitation. Rainfall carries much less phosphorus than nitrogen, and one can formulate regional (climatic) difference as to which nutrient is likely to limit algal growth in lakes. The difference is based on the amount and frequency of rainfall, the vegetation cover, and the transport of phosphorus-rich particles by storm flows. Most nitrogen in a watershed is derived from rainfall, so lakes in wet climates receive relatively more nitrogen than phosphorus. The watersheds of lakes in dry climates tend to be sparsely covered with vegetation and often consist of large areas of seasonal grass cover interspersed with small shrubs. These soils are easily eroded by the infrequent but heavy storms characteristic of semiarid regions. In contrast, the watersheds of lakes in wetter climates are usually well-covered with vegetation, especially trees and plants that grow throughout the summer. These watersheds have lower rates of erosion.

An important reason for this is the effect of vegetation on the first stages of soil erosion. The leaves of trees and grasses greatly reduce the velocity of raindrops before they strike the ground. Some rainwater evaporates before it even reaches the ground and some runs down the tree trunk to the soil. Because the first step in soil erosion is the raindrops hitting and loosening the soil, a reduction in the number and speed of raindrops reduces erosion under vegetation. The overall effect can easily be seen in runoff after storms. Even small streams in dry areas are often brown-colored with suspended silt, whereas streams in wet regions are typically clear. Since erosion is the removal of solids, much of which are clay, the phosphate sorbed to the clay is carried off with the silt. Particles in the silt provide the high phosphorus input typical of dry regions lakes, while nitrogen in rainfall and runoff dominates in wet regions.

The slope of the land, the type of soil, and human land use practices also influence the amount of erosion. Where the soil is geologically unstable or ground cover is absent, erosion occurs (Figs. 5-23, 6-2). Such erosion is common in mountainous areas such as the southwest of North America, Alaska, the Rift Valley of Africa, and the Himalayas. In these areas we would expect nitrogen to be more limiting to algal growth than phosphorus. In contrast, in the older mountain areas of middle and eastern North America and much of northern Europe, particulate inflows would be relatively low and phosphorus limitation would be expected. The flow of phosphorus into rivers is highly correlated with the average slope of the drainage basin (Table 9-4). If the stream channels are long relative to the drainage area, greater phosphorus loading may be expected (Kirchner, 1975).

We have now discussed in detail the *major nutrients,* carbon, oxygen, hydrogen, nitrogen, and phosphorus. Chapter 10 deals with the equally essential *minor and trace elements.* This diverse group has historically received less attention but may provide the key to some of the yet-unexplained fluctuations in plant and animal productivity.

FURTHER READING

Berman, T. 1970. ''Alkaline Phosphatase and Phosphorus Availability in Lake Kinneret.'' *Limnol. Oceanogr.,* **15:**663–674.

Confer, J. L. 1972. ''Interrelations among Plankton, Attached Algae, and the Phosphorus Cycle in Artificial Open Systems.'' *Ecol. Monogr.,* **42:**1–23.

Elser, J. J., E. R. Marzolf, and C. R. Goldman. 1990. ''Phosphorus and Nitrogen Limitation of Phytoplankton in the Freshwaters of North America: A Review and Critique of Experimental Enrichments.'' *Can. J. Fish. Aquat. Sci.,* **47:**1468–1477

Froelich, P. N. 1988. ''Kinetic Control of Dissolved Phosphate in Natural Rivers and Estuaries: A Primer on the Phosphate Buffer Mechanism.'' *Limnol. Oceanogr.,* **33:**649–668.

Ganf, G. G., and P. Blaizka. 1974. ''Oxygen Uptake, Ammonia and Phosphate Excretion by Zooplankton of a Shallow Equatorial Lake (Lake George, Uganda).'' *Limnol. Oceanogr.,* **19:**313–325.

Griffith, E. J., A. Beeton, J. M. Spencer, and D. T. Mitchell (eds.). 1973. *Handbook of Environmental Phosphorous.* Wiley, New York. See especially the chapters by H. L. Golterman, ''Vertical Movement of Phosphorus in Freshwater,'' and F. H. Rigler, ''A Dynamic View of the Phosphorous Cycle in Lakes.''

Jansson, M., H. Olsson, and K. Pettersson. 1988. ''Phosphatases: Origin, Characteristics and Function in Lakes.'' *Hydrobiologia,* **170:**157–175.

Lebo, M. E, 1990. ''Phosphate Uptake along a Coastal Plain Estuary.'' *Limnol. Oceanogr.,* **35:**1279–1289.

Lehman, J. T. and T. Naumoski. 1986. ''Net Community Production and Hypolimnetic Nutrient Regeneration in a Michigan Lake.'' *Limnol. Oceanogr.,* **31:**788–797.

Lesht, B. M., T. D. Fontaine, and D. M. Dolan. 1991. ''Great Lakes Total Phosphorous Model: Post Audit and Regionalized Sensitivity Analysis.'' *J. Great Lakes Res.,* **17:**3–17.

Vollenweider, R. A. 1976. Advances in Defining Critical Loading Levels of Phosphorus in Lake Eutrophication.'' *Mem. Ist. Ital. Idrobiol.,* **33:**53–83.

TABLE 9-4

INCREASE IN TRANSPORT OF NITROGEN AND PHOSPHORUS WITH INCREASE IN THE SLOPE OF ARABLE LAND IN WISCONSIN DRAINAGE BASINS

Note that as slope increases relatively more phosphorus is lost than nitrogen. This is because phosphorus is transported mostly as particulates (Table 16-1) and soil erosion also increases with slope. Nitrogen, in contrast, is usually lost as soluble nitrate.

Slope	N, kg ha^{-1}	% increase	P, kg ha^{-1}	% increase
8°	16	—	0.45	—
20°	34	210	1.6	360

Modified from MacKenthun et al., 1964.

CHAPTER 10

Other Nutrients

OVERVIEW

Silicon, calcium, magnesium, sodium, potassium, sulfur, chlorine, iron, and the minor metals constitute most of the plant and animal nutrients not covered in Chaps. 7 to 9. Diatoms require large quantities of silica for their cell walls and silica can be a limiting element for phytoplankton growth where diatoms are the predominant algae. This element is derived from the weathering of soils, especially those containing the class of minerals called *feldspars*. Silica incorporated into many species of diatoms is insoluble and therefore less easily recycled than most other elements. Diatom shells, called *frustules*, accumulate in sediments, and the changes in different species with time are used by the paleolimnologist to reconstruct the trophic history of lakes.

Calcium is the main skeletal component of many animals and some plants, but it is also the main buffering system in lake waters. Precipitation of $CaCO_3$ during intensive photosynthesis and its solution by rainwater in the watershed control the supply of this element. Magnesium, which has a water chemistry similar to that of calcium, is vital for energy transfer in any cell since it catalyzes the change from ATP to ADP.

Plants also require magnesium to form the active center of their major pigment, chlorophyll *a*.

Sulfur is an essential structural component of proteins and has an important gaseous phase when hydrogen sulfide is released from anoxic decaying sediments. Hydrogen sulfide is usually oxidized to sulfate at the aerated microzone of the sediments of some lakes and estuaries. Chlorine, as the chloride ion, is present in small quantities in fresh water but becomes a dominant ion in estuaries and the sea. Disinfection during municipal and industrial water treatment produces chlorinated compounds, which can be very toxic to animals and plants. Iron is needed in relatively large quantities by plant and animal cells although it is often considered a minor element. The two or three outer-shell electrons of the iron atom dominate the electron-transport pathway of respiration. Iron is essential to hemoglobin in blood and for enzymes involved in nitrogen metabolism. Phosphate in lakes is often lost from the photic zone by precipitation or by sorption onto the outside of complex iron-containing particles. Iron availability may limit growth of algae in lakes and streams, especially when nitrogen fixation is important. Molecules called *siderophores* are produced by some algae when dissolved iron is scarce. These make organically bound iron available for algal growth.

Natural waters are extremely dilute chemical solutions with very small quantities of several essential metals, including manganese, copper, zinc, cobalt, and molybdenum. These elements are required by animals and plants in minute quantities and for this reason are often called *trace elements* or *micronutrients*. Their main role in the cells is at the active center of enzymes or as cofactors in enzyme reactions. Algae in some oligotrophic lakes show growth limitation from shortages of one or more trace metals. Toxicity to plants and animals can result from high concentrations of trace metals. Toxicity is most likely to occur if the metal is in an ionic *unchelated* state. Animals and plants tend to accumulate trace metals far in excess of their immediate needs. Where trace element limitation occurs, the basic cause is a geochemical shortage of the element in the drainage basin.

In this chapter we cover those elements sometimes required in large quantities (silicon, calcium, magnesium, sodium, potassium, sulfur, and chlorine), iron, the trace metals (manganese, zinc, copper, molybdenum, and cobalt), and other trace minerals such as selenium.

ELEMENTS SOMETIMES REQUIRED IN LARGE QUANTITIES

Silica and Silicon

In lakes and seas silica plays an intriguing role since it apparently accounts for the success of diatoms, which dominate most aquatic systems (Fig. 12-4). Most algae and animals have at best only a minor need for silicon, but in the diatoms, silica (SiO_2) forms the rigid algal cell wall or *frustule*, which may account for half the cell's dry weight. Some chrysophycean flagellates and a few other algae also possess silica cell walls. The form of silicon when used as a structural component in algae is hydrated to form amorphous silica ($SiO_2 \cdot nH_2O$), or opal. This rigid

material is highly perforated and surrounded on both sides by a thin cell membrane (Figs. 10-2, 11-1). Freshwater sponges contain needlelike inclusions called *spicules*, which are also almost pure silica and, like diatoms, leave a permanent record of their presence. Lake Baikal has large numbers of sponges, many of which are endemic to this ancient lake, and masses of spicules are to be found on its beaches.

Silica is normally measured as "reactive" silicate, that is, the molecule H_2SiO_4 and its short-chain polymers. Longer polymers of three or four units are not measured, although they are present in natural waters (Parsons et al., 1984). Reactive silica is probably the only form available for diatom growth. The most common test used is spectrophotometric measurement of the blue color produced when a silicomolybdate complex is reduced.

The Silica Cycle The *silica cycle* illustrates the nearly one-way flow of this compound from rocks in the watershed to the lake sediments (Fig. 10-1). Such a pattern is very different from the cycles of nitrogen, phosphorus, iron, and other nutrients where plant and animal cells take up and excrete large amounts in various forms. There are only two major sources of silica in lakes: inflows and from below the photic zone. Animal recycling of silica is generally believed to be unimportant in lake waters, but some release of silica occurs from anoxic sediments. Certain diatoms release up to 15 percent of the silica they take up (Nelson et al., 1976).

The world average concentration for dissolved silica in large rivers is about 13 mg liter^{-1}, while lakes show values from less than 0.5 to 60 mg liter^{-1} (Table 10-1). Silica-containing rocks make up 70 percent of the earth's crust and therefore provide the major minerals in contact with streams and ground water. Rainwater, springs, and the leachate from soils are all high in carbon dioxide, which weathers rocks to release soluble silica (SiO_2). Feldspar is an important class of minerals that contain large amounts

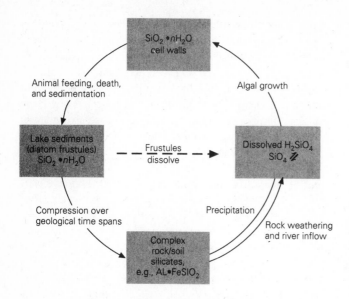

FIGURE 10-1 The silica cycle in lakes, emphasizing the role of diatoms. Although SiO_2 is not digested by any predator, it does not always protect against crushing or digestion of the cell contents by many invertebrates or fish that excrete SiO_2 fragments unchanged chemically. This is in contrast to nitrogen, iron, phosphorus, and most other elements.

of silicon. White or pinkish feldspar crystals are a main component of granite. The reaction can be illustrated as follows, where feldspar is weathered by weak carbonic acid to china clay, or kaolinite:

$$2NaAlSi_3O_8 + 2CO_2 + 3H_2O \rightleftharpoons 4\ SiO_2$$

| Sodium feldspar | Rainwater, streams, springs | Dissolved silica |

$$+\ Al_2Si_2O_5(OH)_4 + 2Na^+ + 2HCO_3^-\quad(1)$$

Kaolinite

This weathering is also an important source of sodium ions, and in the buffer system of natural waters bicarbonate produced in silica release is another important byproduct (Chap. 7; Bricker and Garrels, 1967).

Silica exists in lakes in many forms, but only silicic acid (H_2SiO_4), which is partially dissociated at normal lake pH values, can be used by algae (Lewin, 1962; Darley, 1974). Other forms, such as colloidal silica and clays, play a physicochemical role by providing sorption sites for phosphate and ammonia.

Silica and Diatoms Diatom productivity can be very great. For example, the production of 15 million tons of opaline diatom frustules each year in the inner Amazon estuary removes 25 percent of the river's dissolved silica (Milliman and Boyle, 1975). Since 25 to 60 percent of the dry weight of diatoms is silica, silicon can become a limiting nutrient for diatom growth, primarily because of the absence of significant recycling. There is no mechanism for silica storage when it is abundant, although some diatoms may be able to make a few further divisions by thinning their walls. The interactions between silica and diatom blooms are discussed in more detail for *Melosira* and *Asterionella* in Chap. 12. As for phosphorus, the silica growth constant K_s indicates that the enzyme system often operates below saturation in some lakes (Tables 10-1, 10-2).

Compared to the levels of other pollutants, such as nitrogen or phosphorus, waste discharges of silica are minor. A shortage of silica relative to the other nutrients has major consequences in cultural lake eutrophication (Chap. 20). Lakes may change from aesthetically pleasing diatom waters to less desirable ones dominated by blue-green algae. The high loading of nitrogen and phosphate favors algae that do not require silica. The nearshore waters of Lake Michigan show

TABLE 10-1

CONCENTRATIONS (mg liter⁻¹) OF SOLUBLE MAJOR NUTRIENTS (OTHER THAN NITROGEN AND PHOSPHORUS) IN THE SURFACE WATERS OF VARIOUS LAKES AND RIVERS

The very dilute lakes, such as Tahoe or the Experimental Lakes Area (ELA) lakes in Ontario, contrast with terminal lakes such as Mono, where the conservative elements accumulate. Note how conservative elements increase downstream in rivers, indicating that dilute lakes need small watersheds to remain low in conservative elements.

Lake or river	Conductivity, μmho cm^{-1}	SiO_2	Ca	Mg	Na	K	SO_4—S	Cl	HCO_3	References*
Tahoe	92	—	9.4	2.5	6.1	1.7	2.5	1.9	40	1
Castle, Calif.	30	1.3	1.6	2.6	1.1	0.2	0.2	0.1	20	2
Clear, Calif.	250	14	23	15	10	2.0	9	6	145	3
English Lake District, average	—	—	4.5	1.0	3.9	0.5	6.3	7.1	7.8	4
South Basin, Windemere	—	—	6.2	0.7	3.8	0.6	7.6	6.7	11	4
Erie	6	0.3	38	8.5	7.2	0.6	22	15	118	5
Superior	79	2	12.4	2.8	11	0.6	3.2	1.9	28.1	5
ELA lakes, average	19	≈1	1.6	0.9	0.9	0.4	3.0	1.4	3.8	6
Cayuga, N.Y.	56	—	44	10	51	2.6	36	81	122	7
Mono, Calif.	—	—	—	60	28,000	1400	9000	17,500	18,800	8
George, Uganda	223	20	17.2	7.4	20	4.2	14.6	8.4	99	9
Biwa, Japan	—	≈1	≈10	≈2	≈5	≈2	≈6.8	≈7	—	10
Titicaca, Andes	—	0.07–1.1	66	34	176	14	282	260	—	11
Tanganyika	—	0.3	11	39	63	33	6.3	26	—	12
Baikal, Siberia	—	≈3	15	4.2	6.1		4.9	1.8	≈60	13
World average lakes and rivers	—	12	15	4.1	6.3	2.3	11.2	7.8	58.6	14
North American rivers, average	—	9	21	5	9	1.4	20	8	68	14
European rivers, average	—	7.5	31	5.6	5.4	1.7	24	7	95	14
Nile, Khartoum	—	26	17.4	5.2	30.7	11.8	0.44	8	149	14
Rhine, Netherlands	—	5.7	42	6.1	10.1	6.4	19.5	11.3	113	14
Amazon (Narrow Santarem)	—	11.1	12.5	1.5	1.1	1.4	4.3	2.3	41	14
Truckee at km 10	—	—	8.5	4.3	6.1	1.7	2.9	≈3	—	15
Truckee at km 15	—	16	9.5	4.8	12.4	1.8	3.5	5.9	48	14, 15
Lower Congo River, Kinshasa	105	7.5	10.8	3.9	14.2	—	7.8	6.1	—	16
Hubbard Brook, N.H.	≈25	4.5	1.7	0.38	9.1	0.21	6.3	5.4	<1	17

* References: (1,2) Goldman, various sources; (3) Horne, 1975; Lallatin, 1972; (4) Macan, 1970; (5) Schelske and Roth, 1973; Dobson et al., 1974; Ragotzkie, 1974; Bennett, 1978; (6) Armstrong and Schindler, 1971; (7) Oglesby, 1978; (8) Mason, 1967; Livingstone, 1963; (9) Viner, 1973; Ganf and Viner, 1973; (10) Itasaka and Koyama, 1980; (11) Richerson et al., 1977; (12) Hecky et al., 1978; (13) Livingstone, 1963; Kozhov, 1963; (14) Livingstone, 1963; (15) McLaren, 1977; (16) Visser and Villeneuve, 1975; (17) Likens et al., 1970.

TABLE 10-2

ENZYME UPTAKE KINETICS OF SILICA FOR THREE DIATOM SPECIES AND THREE CLONES OF THE SAME SPECIES FROM DIFFERENT ENVIRONMENTS

Note the similarity in K_s but difference in V_{max} for the clone from the relatively eutrophic estuary compared with those from the oligotrophic Sargasso Sea. The freshwater diatom *Asterionella* has a higher K_s than *Cyclotella* and will thus outcompete it when nutrients are high, for example, in spring (Chap. 12).

Species	K_s, µg liter^{-1}	Max. growth rate $\hat{\mu}$, doublings day^{-1}	Uptake rate V_{max} µg SiO$_2$ cell^{-1}h^{-1}	References[*]
Asterionella formosa	230	1.1	36×10^{-3}	1
Cyclotella meneghiniana	84	1.3	15×10^{-3}	1
Thalassiosira pseudonana	102	—	—	2
T. pseudonana (estuarine clone)	90	3.2	16×10^{-3}	3
T. pseudonana (ocean clone)	90	1.0	60×10^{-3}	3

* References: (1) Tilman and Kilham, 1976; (2) Paasche, 1973; (3) Nelson et al., 1976.

this shift in algal species composition (Schelske and Stoermer, 1972).

After death, bacterial and fungal decay removes the organic material, leaving only the stable diatom frustule. These may be heated to redness or boiled in acid to remove any remaining organic material. Diatom frustules are symmetrical and are laced with minute holes and often crowned with sharp spines (Fig. 10-2). Since diatom frustules remain unchanged over millenia in the sediments, their types and numbers can be used to help the paleolimnologist interpret the trophic status of a lake through time (Chap. 20). In parts of the ocean bed, frustules constitute most of the sediment, and diatomaceous earth is produced from previous deposits (Chap. 11).

Calcium

Calcium is essential for metabolic processes in all living organisms and as a structural or skeletal material in many. An example of its biochemical role is the relaxation of animal muscle after contraction, which depends on depolarization of the cell membranes by an inflow of Ca^{2+} ions in the same manner that nerves require an inflow of

Na^+ ions. Virtually all vertebrates, mollusks, and certain other invertebrates require large quantities of $CaCO_3$ as a major skeletal-strengthening material. In addition, some marine and marsh algae use $CaCO_3$ in the cell wall. Coral reefs represent the ultimate expression of $CaCO_3$ skeletons. Since carbonate is more soluble in cold than warm waters, arctic mollusks have greater difficulty precipitating it and may substitute strontium in their shells. The fragile, paper-thin shells of dead snails in some Alaskan lakes contrasts with the strong, thick shells typical of a midwestern lake. Since the need for calcium in animals is large, growth limitation might be anticipated for some invertebrates. In contrast, the nonskeletal demands by aquatic plants are met by normal lake calcium levels.

An important role of calcium is its effect on pH and the CO_2—HCO_3^- system (Chap. 7). Calcium is present in ionic form and as suspended particulates, mainly $CaCO_3$. Calcium salts are the main cause of hard water, which can be softened by substituting sodium for calcium and magnesium or circumvented by adding detergent phosphates. About half the phosphate in sewage

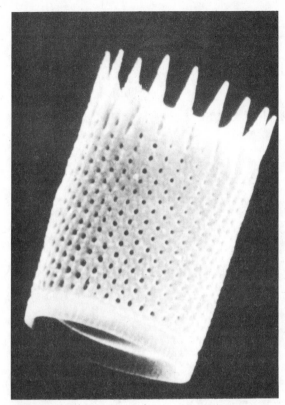

FIGURE 10-2 Scanning electron micrograph of the silica cell wall of half a small diatom, *Melosira crenulata*, from oligotrophic Lake Tahoe, California (magnification ×4000). The cell has been treated with acid to clear the cell membrane (see text). Note the elaborate structure where the spines of the "crown" connect with the adjacent cell (not shown) and the numerous wall pores, which allow nutrients to flow freely into the cell. Photo by H. W. Paerl.

Although this is the main buffering system in natural waters, it is overcome when the bicarbonate or CO_2 is removed by photosynthesis, and $CaCO_3$ is precipitated. This is a common phenomenon in hard-water lakes, especially marl lakes (Chap. 7). In these lakes the water precipitates so much $CaCO_3$ at the height of algal blooms that the sediments show alternate layers of $CaCO_3$ and darker organic material deposited in periods of lower productivity. The precipitation of $CaCO_3$ has dramatic effects on both the organic and inorganic nutrient levels in marl lakes.

Calcium, bicarbonate, pH, and specific conductivity are only approximately correlated in lake waters. Conductivity measures the number of charged ions in the water (e.g., Ca^{2+}, Na^+, SO_4^{2-}). Calcium in most temperate waters is often correlated with most other minor and major ions (Table 10-1). This gives rise to a general lake classification by ionic strength. *Soft-water lakes* can be distinguished from *hard-water* ones by their lower conductivity (Fig. 10-3). Since calcium is one of the most abundant and easily measured ions, it is often used as an indication of lake hardness.

One might expect an analogy between terrestrial and aquatic ecology through the presence of aquatic *calciphobes* (calcium-hating organisms) and *calciphiles* (calcium-loving organisms). There is little evidence that planktonic algae show such traits (Fig. 10-3). The apparent calciphobic distribution of oligotrophic desmids appears to be a chance association having no metabolic cause. Lund (1965) suggests calcium's main effect on phytoplankton is the buffering of lake pH.

Magnesium

Magnesium is often associated with calcium, primarily due to its similar chemistry (Table 10-1). Dolomite, the major rock of the Dolomite Mountains in the European Alps, is a magnesium calcium carbonate. Dolomite is a fairly common

is derived from the detergents used, which contributes to lake eutrophication (Chap. 20).

Rain and soil water contain weak carbonic acid, which is a major carbon source for receiving waters [Eq. (2), Chap. 7]. Basic carbonate rocks, such as limestone in the lake watershed and sediments, neutralize this acid by the reaction.

$$CaCO_3 + H_2CO_3 \rightleftharpoons CaCO_3 + CO_2 + H_2O \rightleftharpoons$$

$$Ca(HCO_3)_2 \rightleftharpoons Ca^{2+} + 2HCO_3^- \qquad (2)$$

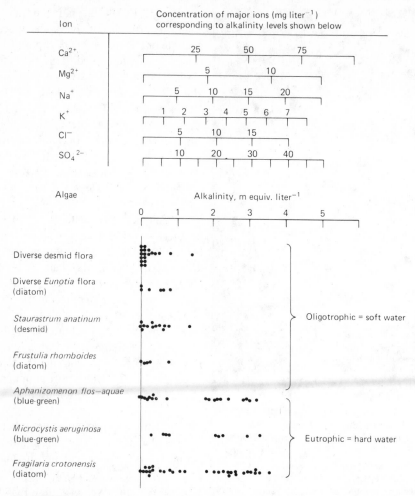

FIGURE 10-3 The distribution of species of algae with respect to alkalinity and major ions in fresh water. Four examples are indicators of oligotrophy; three are typical of eutrophic waters. Desmids are a type of green algae, Chlorophyceae (Table 11-3). Modified from Moss (1972).

rock in many parts of the world, although it is rare in central and southern Africa.

Magnesium is needed by all cells for phosphate transfer involving adenosine triphosphate and diphosphate (ATP and ADP), as shown in the following equation:

$$ATP \underset{Mg^{2+}}{\rightleftharpoons} ADP + P + energy \qquad (3)$$

This step is the major short-term energy-transfering reaction in living cells. The exact role of magnesium is unknown for many other reactions, but the magnesium requirement has been well-established. Magnesium in plants serves as the transition metal at the heart of the reactive center in the chlorophyll molecule (Fig. 10-4). Despite its major role in algal photosynthesis, there are only a few instances of either magne-

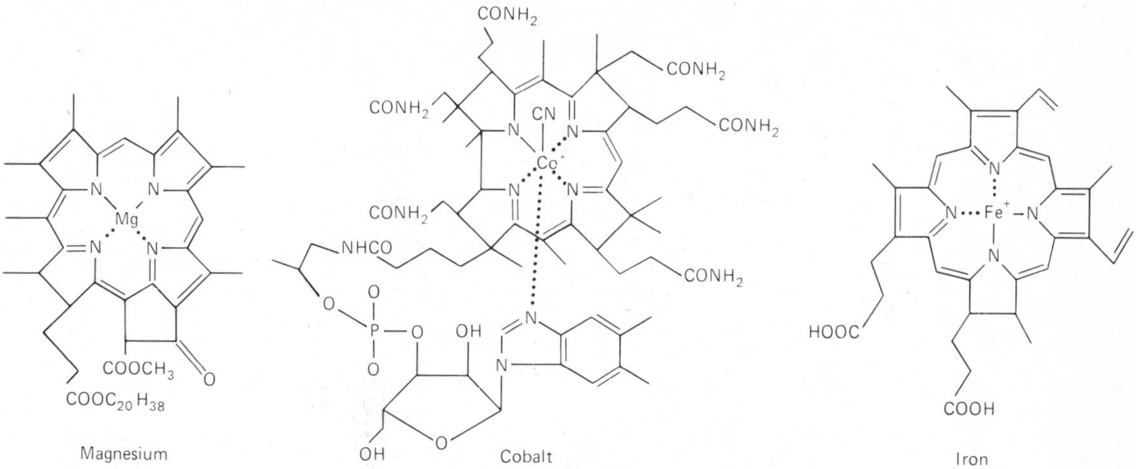

FIGURE 10-4 Examples of how iron and trace metals play a major role in aquatic biota. The changes in the oxidation-reduction state of the metal, for example ferrous (Fe^{2+}) to ferric (Fe^{3+}), involve the addition or subtraction of one electron. The resulting changes in molecular structure or electron transport permit, for example, blood to carry or off-load oxygen or chlorophyll a to capture solar energy in photosynthesis. Note the metal ion in the heart of the molecule, surrounded by a porphyrin ring made of four pyrrole rings in a proline chain of alternating double and single carbon bonds, which hold the resonating electrons. (*a*) Magnesium in the photosynthetic pigment chlorophyll. (*b*) Cobalt in vitamin B12. (*c*) Iron in the blood pigment hemoglobin. Copper in the molluscan blood pigment hemocyanin does not contain a porphyrin ring, and its detailed structure is uncertain.

sium deficiency or toxicity in lakes (Goldman, 1960).

The element is usually present in aquatic systems in large amounts relative to plant needs (Table 10-1). From this we must conclude that magnesium does not play a major role in limiting the growth or distribution of animals or plants in most waters. In Brooks Lake, Alaska, magnesium limitation of algal growth was attributed to the higher-than-normal sodium levels. Plants may show magnesium deficiency when sodium levels are high because sodium competes for binding sites in the cell.

Sodium and Potassium

One of the greatest chemical differences between terrestrial plant growth and that of phytoplankton is the minor role played by potassium in waters. Most water appears to possess adequate supplies of sodium for plant growth (Table 10-1). Agri-

cultural land is fertilized with nitrogen, phosphorus, and potassium, but cultivated lakes such as fish ponds need only nitrogen and phosphorus. Potassium is required for all cells, principally as an enzyme activator, and is present in larger quantities inside the cells of aquatic biota than in the surrounding medium. Since lakes are much less concentrated solutions of potassium, cell membranes must continually pump in potassium and pump out sodium, a process requiring the expenditure of large amounts of energy. In saline lakes (Chap. 21) and estuaries (Chap. 19) too much sodium, along with other ions, restricts the biota to a few species that can tolerate the osmotic stress.

Sulfur and Chlorine

Sulfur is important in protein structure but rarely limits the growth or distribution of the aquatic biota. This is due to the abundance of the ele-

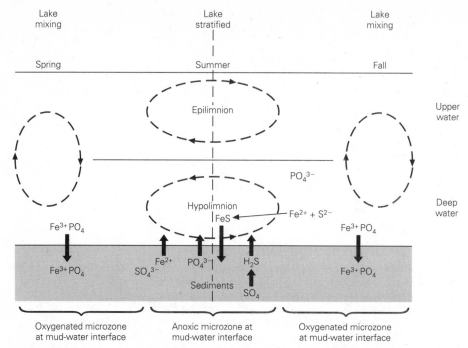

FIGURE 10-5 The iron, sulfur, and phosphorus interaction in eutrophic lakes. During overturn and whole-lake mixing, oxygenated water precipitates ferric (Fe^{3+}) phosphate. During the summer anoxic period, eutrophic lake sediments release ferrous (Fe^{2+}) ions, phosphate ions (PO_4^{3-}), and hydrogen sulfide (H_2S). The dissociated sulfide ion (S^{2-}) from H_2S can precipitate ferrous sulfide, a very insoluble substance, and remove iron and sulfur from the system.

ment, primarily in its most energetically stable form, sulfate (SO_4^{2-}) (Table 10-1). The complex three-dimensional structure of enzymes and other proteins is partially due to bridges between two sulfur atoms, which stabilize the geometry of the enzyme. This is the main use of sulfur in all cells, but the element plays a role in other metabolic processes, such as cell division.

Anoxic sediments rich in organic matter release gaseous hydrogen sulfide (H_2S) to produce the familiar rotten-egg smell of decaying vegetation. In lakes and estuaries this H_2S is oxidized to SO_4^{2-} at the mud-water interface so long as there is an oxygenated microzone. Once this layer is reduced by bacterial respiration and chemical oxygen demand, H_2S is released into the air or overlying water (Fig. 10-5). Hydrogen

sulfide may form a highly insoluble black ferrous sulfide precipitate, effectively removing available iron from solution (Fig. 10-5).

Industrialization has greatly affected aquatic sulfur cycles. In recent times much sulfur in some rivers and lakes has originated from the burning of fossil fuels (Kellogg et al., 1972). The major source in most rivers remains that derived from the breakdown of parent material in the drainage basin. Atmospheric pollution caused by burning fossil fuels is largely in the form of SO_2, which forms sulfuric acid (Fig. 10-6) and is the major contributor to *acid rain*. Tide flats and salt marshes release enormous quantities of sulfur to the atmosphere from bacterial reduction of sulfate to hydrogen sulfides in the mud.

Among the halogens (chlorine, bromine, io-

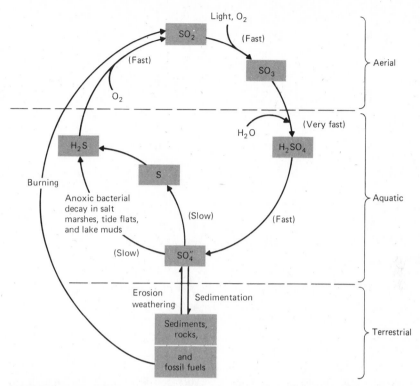

FIGURE 10-6 Sulfur cycle in water, on land, and in the air. Sometimes all the aerial stages may take place in oxygenated mud or water. In the figure, slow means days and fast means hours. Sulfur occasionally produces a white or yellowish precipitate on the surface of exposed mud at lake edges or in salt marshes. Hydrogen sulfide (H_2S), a poisonous gas, is a major nuisance for humans near rotting vegetation and is extremely toxic to fish and other animals. Lower plants, however, may use H_2S if a little light is available. Blue-green algae grow in the upper layers of anoxic hypolimnia or as felts in salt marshes. Greatly modified from Kellogg et al. (1972).

dine, and fluorine), chlorine is the most abundant. The chloride ion is required by photosynthesizing cells for the photolysis of water to release oxygen, for ATP formation, and for certain phosphorylation reactions. In contrast, free chlorine is very toxic, even at low concentrations. Because chloride is easily measured, it is frequently used to identify water masses in pollution studies of chlorinated waste. Toxic chlorinated wastes are discharged to lakes and seas in ever-increasing quantities. Free chlorine is used as a disinfectant for waste discharges primarily to kill harmful bacteria and in power

plants to curb slimes in the heat-exchange pipes. A new use is to kill the larvae of the zebra mussel, which has invaded the Great Lakes from eastern Europe. The adult mussel, although only 1 to 2 cm across, can become so numerous that they block water intake pipes, which must be backwashed with a chlorine solution. Chlorine kills by oxidation of the cell membranes but lasts only a few minutes as free chlorine in most systems. It is then either converted to the harmless chloride ion by sunlight or combined with organic compounds. Of the resulting compounds, chloramines are the most toxic in fresh water and last for several days before conversion to less harmful states. In estuaries, toxic bromamines are produced since seawater contains abundant bromine. Even at great dilution, chlorinated and brominated organics may harm or even kill algae, zooplankton, and the larvae of commercially important fish and shellfish. To prevent toxicity, sewage and power plants should dechlorinate with bisulfite, which nullifies most of the chloramine or bromamine toxicity (Stone, Kaufman, and Horne, 1973).

Iron, the "Trace" Element Needed in Moderate Quantities

Iron is needed by most living organisms in larger quantities than any other element apart from the structural atoms carbon, oxygen, hydrogen, nitrogen, and phosphorus. Clifford Mortimer's classic studies are good examples of the major sediment-water interactions of dissolved iron (Mortimer, 1941–1942; 1971). As noted, iron is an essential constituent of many enzymatic and other cellular processes. Oxidative metabolism in all organisms and photosynthesis in plants involves cytochromes, which contain iron. Iron is needed in the hemoglobin of blood and has a vital role in the nitrogenase enzyme of some lower plants and bacteria. Plants and animals have evolved to take advantage of the oxidation-reduction reaction of iron. The unique feature of iron is the little energy required to change from ferrous (Fe^{2+}) to ferric (Fe^{3+}), and vice versa. It is not surprising that iron is also easily transformed by changes in lake oxygen concentration.

Because iron is so important to all organisms, there is considerable demand for it in the environment. Lakes in semiarid climates may show an iron shortage, and iron limitation in temperate lakes was first described long ago (Rodhe, 1948; Gerloff and Skoog, 1957; Schelske, 1962; Goldman and Mason, 1962). Iron is one of the most common metals in the earth's crust and occurs in small amounts in almost all clays, soils, and granite rocks. Organic and inorganic forms of iron exist in particulate and dissolved phases in most water. For convenience, we consider all iron attached to organic material as "organic" even though the attachment may be sorption rather than chemical bonding. Lakes generally have particulate iron on the order of 1 mg liter^{-1}, most of which is contained in the lake biota. Oligotrophic lakes have less, since they have sparse populations of algae and zooplankton. Soluble iron ranges from 100 to 3000 μg liter^{-1} in most waters (Table 10-3) but may drop below 2 μg liter^{-1} in some lakes, particularly in semiarid regions (Fig. 10-9). Under normal oxidizing conditions (Fig. 10-5) ferric iron (Fe^{3+}) predominates over ferrous iron (Fe^{2+}). Because ferric iron forms insoluble compounds, it rapidly disappears from the lake's mixed layer and is deposited on the sediments as a rust-colored layer called *ocher* ($Fe(OH)_3$).

Measurement   Dissolved iron (inorganic plus organic) is generally measured by using acid and Ferrozine or bathophenanthroline (Parsons et al., 1984). Most natural chelating or sorption reactions that bind soluble organic iron are broken down by the acid reaction. Sodium EDTA, a common metal chelating agent used in laboratory cultures, is so strong that it prevents breakdown to free iron.

Iron Cycles   The loss of ferric iron from oxygenated water occurs as precipitation of ferric hydroxide. Phosphate ions are adsorbed onto this hydroxide. Approximately equal quantities of Fe^{3+} and PO_4^{3-} in the lake epilimnion could result in precipitation of both elements. In many temperate and polar lakes where iron predominates, phosphorus may limit phytoplankton growth. This principle is used to clean up eutrophic lakes where the phosphate can be removed by precipitation with added metals. Iron salts can be used, but it is cheaper to use alum, or aluminum hydroxide. In semiarid zone lakes there is often sufficient phosphate to precipitate most soluble iron, and soluble iron may then limit plant growth. The next stage in the iron

TABLE 10-3

CONCENTRATION OF SOLUBLE MINOR NUTRIENTS (μg liter^{-1}) IN THE SURFACE WATERS OF VARIOUS LAKES AND RIVERS

Although present in relatively low concentrations, most are not limiting or toxic to the biota. Both ionic and chelated metals are present in unknown proportions in the soluble, or filterable, fraction.

Lake or river	Fe	Mn	Cu	Zn	Co	Mo	References*
Tahoe	<10	2.6	Trace	<14	<0.6	0.5	1
Castle, Calif.	<10	<1	<0.5	<2	<1	<0.5	2
Clear, Calif.	5–20	4.6	2–30	<14	<1.4	<0.3	3
Windermere	5	8.5	2.2	3.1	>0.1	>0.1	4
Cayuga, N.Y.	3–80	1–30	0.6	2.7	0.005	—	5
Biwa, Japan	40	5–17	>2.5	5.30	0.03	—	6
Titicaca, Andes	—	—	2.5	28	—	—	7
Schöhsee, Germany	15	4.5	1.0	1.8	0.03	0.2	8
World ave.	≈40	35	10	10	0.9	0.8	9
Sacramento, Calif.	—	6.3	2.9	—	<1	0.4	9
Truckee, at km 10	110	9	4	5	2	>10	10

* References: (1,2) Goldman, various sources; (3) Goldman and Wetzel, 1963; Horne, 1975; (4) Macan, 1970 and Hamilton-Taylor and Willis, 1990; (5) Oglesby, 1978; (6) Itasaka and Koyama, 1980; (7) Richerson, et al., 1977; (8) Groth, 1971; (9) Livingstone, 1963; (10) McLaren, 1977.

cycle occurs when ferric precipitate reaches the sediments. Iron ore beds were deposited in ancient seas by this process. In many productive lakes the benthic region can become anoxic in summer. Once the lake sediments become anoxic, the $Fe^{3+} \rightleftharpoons Fe^{2+}$ equilibrium shifts to the right, releasing soluble ferrous iron. Unfortunately, the exact level of dissolved oxygen or redox potential E_h at which this equilibrium shifts is difficult to measure in lake sediments.

Much of the crystalline form of iron flowing into lakes from watersheds is unavailable. Lake Tahoe, which has very low levels of dissolved iron, has large particles of insoluble iron pyrite, or fool's gold, along its beaches. Crystalline iron, alone or mixed with clays and soils, may pass directly to the sediments without dissolution. The iron cycle consists of two major compartments, the particular fraction and the soluble fraction, which includes most colloidal iron. The

particulates are represented by iron contained in organic matter and hydroxides. As mentioned previously, phosphate is commonly considered an important precipitating agent of iron, and the two nutrients may scavenge each other from solution. Solubility considerations suggest, however, that if such scavenging occurs, it is not by the mechanism of direct precipitation but rather by an indirect process such as adsorption of phosphate on ferric hydroxide, as suggested by Mortimer (1971), or uptake of iron and phosphate by microorganisms, which Shapiro et al. (1971) observed at Lake Washington.

The soluble or colloidal compartment contains all the iron normally measured in soluble form. The hydrated ferric iron (symbolized Fe^{3+} for simplicity) occupies a central position in the system. It is in equilibrium with nearly every other iron species. In oxygenated waters, the oxidation-reduction reaction favors the ferric form

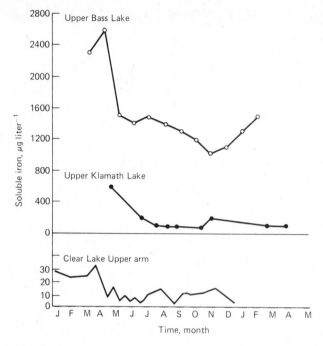

FIGURE 10-7 Seasonal cycles of dissolved iron in the upper mixed layers of three lakes. Upper Bass Lake (a small dimictic lake in Ontario, Canada), Upper Klamath Lake (mid-sized, very shallow, and polymictic, in Oregon), Clear Lake (a mid-sized polymictic lake in California). Notice the great differences in absolute quantities of soluble iron in each system but the generally similar pattern of lower soluble iron in summer. From McMahon (1969), Phinney and Peek (1960; cf Horne, 1975), Wurtsbaugh and Horne (1983).

(Elder and Horne, 1977). At pH levels encountered in most natural waters, the ratio of ferric to ferrous iron is near unity. This, coupled with the fact that ferrous iron does not easily form complexes, renders the ferrous contribution to the iron cycle small in oxygenated waters. Anoxic conditions and low redox potentials reduce ferric iron to the more soluble ferrous iron and alter the balance of the various fractions. In the hypolimnia of eutrophic lakes such conditions result in release of large quantities of ferrous iron.

Most animals acquire iron directly from their food, while phytoplankton must remove iron from solution or suspension. Perhaps the most intriguing problem concerning iron uptake is its possible role in algal competition. Little ionic iron is available in the oxygenated mixed layer of lakes, so most phytoplankton must either take up chelated iron directly or break the bond between iron and organic matter. Some algal species use only inorganic iron, others use chelated iron, and some use both. Nevertheless, all algae do not have an equal ability to take up chelated iron. Blue-green algae can gain a competitive advantage over other plankton by an extracellular secretion of powerful iron chelators called *siderophores* (Neilands, 1981; Hutchins et al., 1991). Iron deprivation in these blue-green algae induces hydroxamate chelators. Blue-green algae have this advantage because their chelators are stronger than those produced by competing algae (Groth, 1971). Bacteria also produce siderophores and, when growing on particles in lakes or on dead leaves in streams, may compete with algae for available iron. Extracts from blue-green algal blooms are sometimes toxic to other phytoplankton (e.g., Lefevre et al., 1952; Lange, 1971; Williams, 1971). The inhibition of competing algae by blue-greens may be the result of direct toxicity or iron limitation induced by the production of siderophores.

Seasonal Cycles Seasonal changes in the concentration of particulate iron are much smaller than those of soluble iron and often follow the rise and fall of the plankton. Figure 10-7 shows

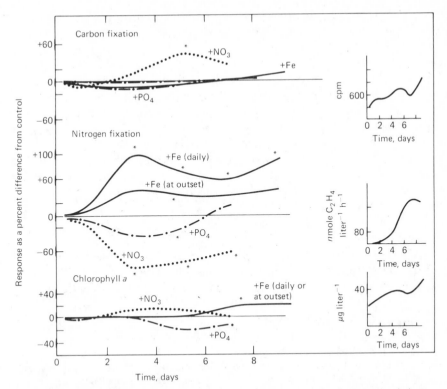

FIGURE 10-8 Stimulation of nitrogen fixation by addition of soluble iron to natural phytoplankton assemblages. The experiment was carried out at the end of the spring *Aphanizomenon* bloom in Clear Lake, California. The initial soluble iron concentration was 4 μg liter^{-1} and total filterable iron was 890 μg liter^{-1}. At this time the lake contained 80 μg liter^{-1} NO_3—N, 225 μg liter^{-1} NH_4—N, and 37 μg liter^{-1} PO_4—P 20 μg liter^{-1} Fe, 200 μg liter^{-1} NO_3—N and 100 μg liter^{-1} PO_4—P were added only at day 0. In the case of daily addition of iron, 20 μg liter^{-1} was added on each day. Small graphs show absolute levels of the control, large graphs percent difference from control, * = significance $P > 0.01$. Note that only iron, not nitrogen or phosphorus, stimulated nitrogen fixation and that photosynthesis and chlorophyll *a* were almost unaffected. c.p.m. = ^{14}C-uptake, in counts per minute. From Wurtsbaugh and Horne (1983).

seasonal iron cycles in several types of lakes. These lakes range in mean depth from 2.4 to 15 m and in area from a few hectares to over 17,000 ha. The lakes show large differences in absolute levels of soluble iron but have rather similar levels of particulate iron. At present one can only speculate that iron limitations and severe interspecific algal competition for iron may occur in those lakes with low levels of soluble iron. Where iron levels are high it seems unlikely that blue-green algae could chelate and thus make

unavailable all soluble iron (Fig. 10-7). As mentioned previously, stimulation of natural or pure algal cultures by iron has often been shown in the laboratory. Dramatic increases in nitrogen fixation can be produced by addition of iron to samples taken during blooms of the blue-green algae *Aphanizomenon* or *Anabaena* (Fig. 10-8). This is due to the need for iron in the nitrogenase enzyme and in the respiratory system of the heterocyst, which protects nitrogenase from denaturation by oxygen (Chap. 8). However, studies in enclosed vessels may overestimate iron limitation. Like phosphate limitation, iron deficiency may be satisfied under natural conditions by materials excreted by zooplankton.

Diel Variations   Since iron may play a role in interalgal competition, daily changes in its concentration are important. Iron levels are usually highest between noon and midafternoon (Mc-Mahon, 1969; Elder and Horne, 1978). In stratified lakes and rivers, animal excretion and lake mixing constitute the main sources of daily variations in iron levels. Inflowing rivers and atmospheric fallout of dust and rain may also contribute considerable quantities, but these do not fluctuate so rapidly. Diel vertical migrations of zooplankton, fish, and some algae change iron levels by uptake or excretion. Afternoon convec-

tion and wind mixing of the epilimnion may disrupt the thermocline, bringing hypolimnetic iron up from below (Chap. 5, Fig. 10-9).

Finally, mention should be made of one of the most familiar iron-related sights in nature—the rusty-brown iron deposits in small streams and marshes. These deposits are composed of iron oxide or hydroxide that forms when seepage from acid and anoxic areas such as peat bogs encounters the well-aerated water. These deposits are often made slimy by a covering of iron bacteria (Chap. 11).

TRACE ELEMENTS

Trace metals are important in aquatic ecosystems. However, technical difficulties involving the chemical form and biotic availability of the

FIGURE 10-9   Daily changes in concentrations of two soluble trace metals with depth. Note the low constant surface (0 to 8 m) values in the oxygenated epilimnion and the constant higher values in the anoxic hypolimnion. The variable levels at 12 m in the metalimnion may be due to the breaking of internal waves or leakage from the shoreline, where the stratified layer meets the lake bed. The lake is Perris Reservoir in southern California. From Elder et al. (1979).

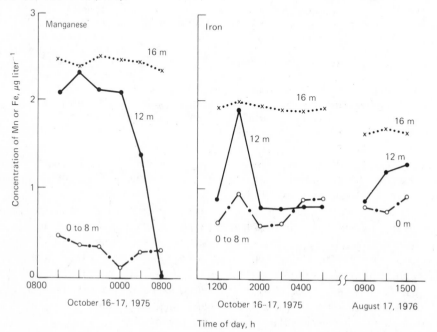

minute quantities present have hindered ecological interpretation (Table 10-3). Annual, seasonal, and daily variations in temperature, pH, dissolved oxygen, and the chelating capacity of the water may rapidly change both the absolute and biologically available quantities of most metals.

Nevertheless, some generalizations can be made regarding how these metals influence aquatic plant growth. First, trace metal limitations are most likely to occur in oligotrophic lakes, particularly those with small drainage basins, on basic or ultrabasic rocks. Micronutrient limitation in lakes was first discovered in Castle Lake, California, utilizing a then-new radiocarbon bioassay technique (Goldman, 1963; 1972). Second, the actual concentration of a trace metal often gives little information on its role as a limiting factor, as a result of algal luxury consumption, recycling, and the variation in the ability of organisms to extract chelated and unchelated forms. Third, effects of additions of one trace metal that stimulates growth are likely to reveal a spectrum of other elements that are very close to limiting plant growth at the time. When one metal is limiting it is likely that a few others are also approaching limiting levels. Physical and chemical availability of metals is often controlled by the same mechanism, such as the redox potential E_h at the sediment-water interface (Chap. 7). Living organisms are chiefly responsible for the cycling of copper, zinc, cobalt, and molybdenum, whereas redox potential in the sediments is more significant in the cycles of manganese and iron.

At the higher trophic levels there is no aquatic analog of the well-known specific nutrient deficiencies found in terrestrial systems. For example, the growth of cattle or sheep is commonly reduced by lack of cobalt, molybdenum, or magnesium even when grass is plentiful. In contrast, it is usually a simple lack of food that limits fish productivity in trace element-deficient oligotrophic mountain lakes. Trace element fertilization of lakes simply provides more plant food without relieving any obvious animal metal deficiency.

Toxic effects of trace metals on some animal populations in lakes are well known, particularly that of copper on young salmonids in unbuffered mountain streams (Sellers et al., 1975). Dramatic poisoning of streams by zinc, copper, and other metals in runoff from mining areas or chromium from industrial use are also well known (Whitton, 1970; Bryan and Hummerstone, 1971; Weatherley and Dawson, 1972).

In oxygenated waters the soluble forms of trace metals are present in microgram quantities and rarely exert toxic or stimulatory effects. One reason for this is the evolution of biotic mechanisms for uptake or chelation of metals. The presence of organic matter in all lakes, together with inorganic particulate debris, produces stable chelates of trace metals and prevents their precipitation as insoluble inorganic salts (Groth, 1971). Most organisms can accumulate metals far in excess of their immediate needs. The actual concentrations of dissolved metals found in the photic zone depend on the interplay between uptake by the phytoplankton, release by decay from sediments, and input from rivers. In stratified eutrophic lakes, decay and subsequent release of metals exceeds uptake, increasing the soluble metal content in the hypolimnia. Manganese and iron (Fig. 10-9) are easily released from anoxic sediment, while zinc, cobalt, molybdenum, and copper are less mobile.

Manganese

Manganese, whose cycling closely parallels that of iron (Fig. 10-9), is needed by plants for photosystem II, the oxygen-evolving process in photosynthesis. Animals and plants need manganese as a cofactor in several enzyme systems, including those involved in respiration and nitrogen metabolism. Manganese toxicity has been reported only in streams polluted by mine wastes.

Considerable effort has gone into determining the effects of manganese on aquatic algal communities since the early work of Guseva (1939). She suggested that blue-green algal blooms in a Russian reservoir were sometimes inhibited by naturally occurring levels of manganese. Later work by Patrick et al. (1969) suggested that this conclusion was also applicable to stream algae. Although there has been no successful repetition of these studies, it now appears that calcium normally prevents any measurable toxic effect. The levels of manganese (> 2 mg liter^{-1}) that were toxic in these laboratory experiments are larger than those usually encountered. In contrast, Goldman (1966) and Lange (1971) have shown that some algal populations increase with small manganese additions. In general, manganese plays a minor role in regulating the growth of algal populations in most lakes.

Zinc

Zinc serves as an activator in some enzymatic reactions and is a cofactor for the enzyme carbonic anhydrase. This enzyme catalyzes a critical rate-limiting step for carbon use in photosynthesis (Chap. 7). Apart from the normal flow of trace element-loaded sediment caused by land disturbance, the zinc plating of pipes, gutters, and culverts can add greatly to zinc levels in streams. As with most trace elements, serious limitation of phytoplankton growth by zinc deficiency, although known to occur (Goldman, 1965), has not been widely studied. In Lake Tahoe, only unchelated zinc is inhibitory to algal growth, while chelated zinc can be stimulatory (Elder, 1974). The qualities of soluble zinc produced by mining wastes are often large enough to decimate the flora and fauna of the receiving water in the vicinity of the discharge.

Copper

In phytoplankton, copper functions mainly as a metalloprotein component and is probably a catalyst. Enzymes concerned with nitrate transformations require the presence of copper. Copper forms the active center of the molluscan blood pigment hemocyanin. Despite the frequently low availability of lake copper, deficiencies of this metal have rarely been demonstrated (Goldman, 1965; Horne, 1975). Even in the case of eutrophic Clear Lake, California, stimulation was small and the onset of toxic effects rapid (Fig. 10-10).

Copper toxicity is well known and appears to exert its major effect on algae by interfering with the activity of enzymes situated on cell membranes (Steeman Nielsen and Wium-Anderson, 1971). This interference prevents cell division and leads to an eventual cessation of photosynthesis by product inhibition. Toxic effects are much more pronounced at lower trophic levels, especially in phytoplankton and zooplankton, than at higher trophic levels. As little as 0.1 μg liter^{-1} ionic copper can kill some algae in water with low chelation potential, and even in normal lakes, 5 to 10 μg liter^{-1} affects blue-green algae. In contrast, most fish are almost unaffected at 100 to 500 μg liter^{-1} copper. Even trout, which are very sensitive to metal poisoning, especially in soft waters, often survive levels of 30 μg liter^{-1}. The relative tolerance of fish to copper makes it possible to control nuisance algae with copper sulfate applications. The method has been used for over 60 years on some lakes, with no significant long-term changes in benthic animal populations. Algae may develop a resistance to copper, which often necessitates the use of other methods of algal control (Chap. 22). The major problem in the use of copper sulfate is its rapid loss from solution. At pH levels of 6 to 8.5, most ionic copper is lost by precipitation as the mineral malachite, which is hydrated copper carbonate ($CuCO_3 \cdot Cu[OH]_2$). Some loss of ionic copper by sorption or chelation by organic materials is probable. Low levels of copper (5 to 20 μg liter^{-1}) can persist in soluble form for several days, if not weeks (Elder and Horne, 1978b). If low levels of soluble copper are ionic, they will depress blue-green algal growth while not affecting other phytoplankton. However, in nature most copper is chelated and nontoxic and bears no apparent relation to algal growth patterns.

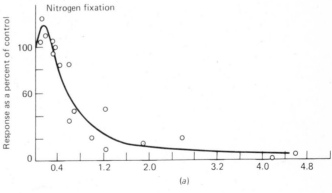

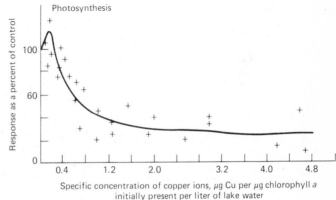

FIGURE 10-10 Effect of added ionic unchelated copper on photosynthesis and nitrogen fixation by the Clear Lake, California, phytoplankton population. Note the apparent slight stimulation response at very low additions and the rapid toxic effect soon after. From Horne (1975) and W. A. Wurtsbaugh and A. J. Horne, (1982).

Molybdenum

Molybdenum is needed for several enzymatic processes, particularly those involved in the nitrogen cycle, since molybdenum is part of the active center of nitrate reductase and nitrogenase enzymes (Chap. 8). Molybdenum deficiency, but not toxicity, for phytoplankton growth is well known. This may reflect the emphasis placed on this element, since it was the first micronutrient found to limit algal growth in the lakes (Goldman, 1960). In Castle Lake, California, a clear picture of its role has emerged. Bottle bioassays indicated that natural phytoplankton populations were limited by molybdenum at certain times of year (Fig. 10-11d). The main inflow of molybdenum is via springs that flow through an alder stand prior to entering the lake (Fig. 6-1). Since

these trees require molybdenum for nitrogen fixation as well as for nitrate reductase, virtually all the molybdenum is stripped from the groundwater inflows. Paleolimnological studies of the lake sediments (Chap. 20) indicate that in the past a larger molybdenum supply, presumably now eroded away, had provided adequate amounts of molybdenum.

In one of the first whole-lake experiments, molybdenum was added to increase the lake concentration to 7.7 μg liter^{-1} from less than 0.2 μg liter^{-1}. Most interesting were the responses of the higher trophic levels which could not be assessed adequately by bottle tests. Cladocerans increased ten-fold, and fish yields also exceeded the average of the preceding quarter century (Fig. 10-11a to c). A species change was observed after molybdenum addition to Castle Lake, when

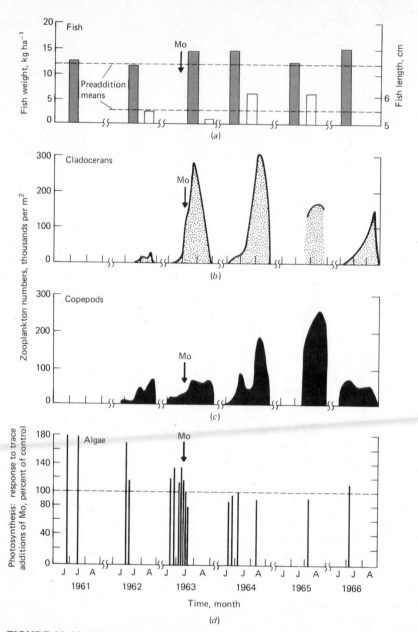

FIGURE 10-11 Changes in phytoplankton, zooplankton, and trout produced by addition of small quantities of a limiting trace metal, molybdenum, to Castle Lake, California. (*d*) Note immediate cessation of stimulation of photosynthesis by further additions of molybdenum in bottle assays, (*c*) delayed increase in populations of the longer-lived copepod zooplankton, but (*b*) almost immediate response for the rapidly reproducing cladoceran zooplankton, which were mostly *Daphnia rosea*. Despite natural year-to-year variations in cladoceran numbers, the prolonged increase over 4 years after molybdenum addition was probably due to the addition. (*a*) Note rapid response in fish catches or yield and increase in average fish length in years following molybdenum addition. This response by fish is similar to that found in fish ponds fertilized with nitrogen and phosphorus, where effects usually occur in the first year after addition and last for 3 to 4 years. Arrow indicates date of molybdenum addition to the epilimnion in July 1963. Lake eilimnion concentrations rose from less than 0.2 to 7.7 µg liter^{-1}, while hypolimnion levels remained at less than 0.2 µg liter^{-1}. Phytoplankton numbers and primary production (now shown) rose less dramatically in the years after molybdenum addition, presumably due to rapid grazing of the algae by the increased zooplankton crop.

TABLE 10-4

NUMBERS OF CELLS PER LITER OF THE MAJOR CASTLE LAKE PHYTOPLANKTON FROM JUNE 29, 1959, CULTURES INCUBATED FOR 5 DAYS WITH AND WITHOUT MOLYBDENUM

Species	Control	$+100$ mg liter^{-1}Mo
Dinobryon sertularia	99	255
Cyclotella menghiniana	401	301
Synedra radians	268	345
Total algae counted	1984	2376

Modified from Goldman et al., 1975.

the chrysophyte *Dinobryon sertularia* increased rapidly relative to other algae (Table 10-4).

Colbalt

Cobalt is needed in vitamin B12 or as a metal with which to synthesize that vitamin. Cobalt in vitamin B12 lies at the active center of four pyrrole rings in a fashion almost identical to magnesium in chlorophyll (Fig. 10-4) or iron in the blood pigment hemoglobin. Like molybdenum, cobalt has been shown to stimulate production in some oligotrophic lakes, and it is present in very small quantities in almost all lakes. The actual amounts in lakes are largely controlled by biological cycling.

Other Trace Metals

As bioassay experiments are more widely applied, it is likely that specific trace element responses will appear from a greater diversity of aquatic habitats. An example is the discovery of a specific requirement for selenium in the growth of the dinoflagellate *Ceratium* in Lake Kinneret (Lindström and Rodhe, 1977). Selenium, like arsenic, can be very toxic to cattle or birds at higher concentrations, especially in wetlands and warm-water reservoirs. In lesser amounts selenium is the co-factor in glutathione peroxidase which acts as an anti-cancer agent in mammalian cell membranes (Combs and Combs, 1986).

The physical and chemical structure of aquatic ecosystems forms the habitat for the host of organisms living in lakes, streams, and estuaries. These organisms are discussed in general terms in Chap. 11 and in more detail in subsequent chapters.

FURTHER READING

Egeratt, A. W. S. M., and J. L. M. Huntjens (eds.). 1975. "The Sulphur Cycle." *Plant Soil*, **43:**228 pp.

Goldman, C. R. 1960. "Primary Productivity and Limiting Factors in Three Lakes of the Alaska Peninsula." *Ecol. Monogr.*, **30:**207–230.

Goldman, C. R. 1972. "The Role of Minor Nutrients in Limiting the Productivity of Aquatic Ecosystems." *Symposium on Nutrients and Eutrophication*, pp. 21–33. In, G. E. Likens (ed.) American Society of Limnology and Oceanography, Special Symposia vol. 1.

Groth, P. 1971. "Untersuchungen über einige Spurenelemente in Seen" ("Investigations of Some Trace Elements in Lakes"). *Arch. Hydrobiol.*, **68:**305–375. (Summary in English)

Hamilton-Taylor, J., and M. Willis. 1991. "A Quantitative Assessment of the Sources and General Dynamics of Trace Metals in a Soft-Water Lake." *Limnol. Oceanogr.*, **35:**840–851.

Kellogg, W. W., R. D. Cadle, E. R. Allen, A. L. Lazrus, and E. A. Martell. 1972. "The Sulfur Cycle." *Science*, **175:**587–596.

Moore, J. M., and S. Ramamuorthy. 1984. *Heavy Metals in Natural Waters*. Springer-Verlag, New York. 268 pp.

Stewart, W. D. P. (ed.) 1974. *Algal Physiology and Biochemistry.* Botanical Monographs, vol. 10. University of California Press, Berkeley. See especially J. C. O'Kelley, "Inorganic Nutrients," chap. 22, pp. 610–635; W. M. Darley, "Silicification and Calcification," chap. 24, pp. 655–675; and E. A. C. MacRobbie, "Ion Uptake," chap. 25, pp. 676–713.

Whitton, B. A. 1970. "Toxicity of Heavy Metals to Freshwater Algae: A Review." *Phykos,* **9:**116–125.

CHAPTER 11

Organisms in Lakes, Streams, and Estuaries

OVERVIEW

The reader has been exposed to the physical and chemical nature of inland waters, and it is now appropriate to consider the plants, animals, fungi, and bacteria that give life and a great deal of interest to limnology. Here limnology diverges sharply from classical zoology and botany and assumes the more general view of the ecologist. The relationships of the components of the aquatic ecosystem may, in this approach, be considered of greater significance than their taxonomic status. Trophic relationships—which organisms are the producers, which the consumers, and which the recyclers—are of paramount importance. Recognition of the individual species, however, is likely to prove essential once the more general relationships are understood. This chapter, especially Tables 11-1 to 11-9, is intended as a reference for organisms mentioned in other chapters. Only those taxonomic groups most familiar to limnologists have been included.

In this chapter we will discuss viruses, bacteria, fungi and fungi-like organisms, algae, aquatic macrophytes, protozoans, rotifers, crustaceans (cladocerans and copepods), aquatic insects, worms and molluscs, fish, and finally amphibians, reptiles, aquatic birds and mammals.

INTRODUCTION

The compartmentalization of plants and animals into trophic levels in the aquatic ecosystem is very useful in understanding their general relationships (Chap. 15). Although the levels themselves are often not discrete entities, they provide an order that the limnologist finds convenient. If we consider the pyramid of biomass and energy in the aquatic system (Chap. 15), we see that most of the organic material resides at the level of the primary producers and that there is a progressive decrease at each successive level.

FUNCTIONAL CLASSIFICATION

Organisms can be classified at the functional level by their sources of energy, sources of carbon, and, in the case of some lower organisms, such as sulfur bacteria, the molecule that serves as the electron donor. Classified on the basis of their energy sources are the *phototrophs*, which derive energy directly from sunlight in photo-synthesis, and the *chemotrophs*, which utilize a chemical energy source. If the cell receives electrons from an organic compound it is an *organotroph;* if it derives them from inorganic matter it is a *lithotroph*. The prefix *litho-*, from the Greek word for stone, is also the root of the word *lithosphere*, which is the nonaquatic portion of the earth. Organisms are also classified on the basis of the type of carbon used for food. *Autotrophic* organisms utilize inorganic carbon dioxide to produce organic matter, and *heterotrophic* organisms depend on preformed organic carbon such as glucose or pyruvate.

The six terms—*phototroph* or *chemotroph, organotroph* or *lithotroph*, and *autotroph* or *heterotroph*—can be used in various combinations. For example, the base of most aquatic food chains is formed by algae and higher aquatic plants that use light energy, carbon dioxide as a carbon source, and the oxygen in water as the electron donor. They could be called photo-lithoautotrophs but are referred to by the short-ened term *photoautotrophs*. This is because the electron donor for almost all photosynthetic organisms is an inorganic compound.

Most heterotrophs use organic carbon both for energy and as an electron donor, while most autotrophs do not. For convenience the food chain is simply divided into autotrophs (plants and chemolithotrophic bacteria) and heterotrophs (some bacteria, fungi, and animals). Higher in the food chain are heterotrophic animals called *herbivores*, which utilize plant material for their growth, and higher-level heterotrophs, *carnivores*, which feed on the herbivores and, sometimes, each other. *Omnivores* eat both plants and animals and thus function at more than one trophic level (Chap. 15).

We begin with a discussion of the simplest communities of lakes and streams. With the exception of higher aquatic plants that can be cut or dragged from the depths by divers, the general methods for their collection, identification, and preservation are included here or in the three chapters that follow.

THE MAJOR GROUPS OF ORGANISMS

Viruses

The role of viruses in the aquatic environment has largely been associated with problems of public health. Such well-known diseases as hepatitis can be transmitted by ingestion of natural waters contaminated with the feces of infected people. Viruses are obligate intracellular parasites. They are very small, usually about 0.02 μm across, although some forms are 10 times that large. They can be seen individually only using electron microscopy. Viruses include phages, which attack only bacteria and blue-green algae. Viruses are usually identified by their protein shell or the disease they cause. Little is known about their role in limnology other than that cyanophages are associated with the decline of blue-green algae growing as periphyton or phytoplankton (Chap. 12). The use of cyanophages as an algal nuisance-control technique has been attempted, but blue-green algae may build up a resistance to the virus just as humans develop immunity to influenza virus. Presumably, virus attacks affect many aquatic organisms and may play an important role in their population dynamics. In the late 1980s a severe die-off of the common seal occurred in their breeding islands off northeastern Britain. The virus disease influenza was found to be the cause. The role of viruses is an area needing further stury.

Bacteria

Although there may be a million bacterial cells per cubic centimeter in the open waters of lakes and rivers, these constitute relatively low numbers when compared with bacteria in soil. Bacteria are unicellular organisms that can multiply very quickly by simple division but occasionally reproduce sexually. Most do not contain chlorophyll or carry on photosynthesis, although a special group of anoxic photosynthetic bacteria are found in some lakes and estuaries.

The cell wall of bacteria is composed of a mixture of acetylated sugars and amino acids called a *peptidoglycan*. When present in abundance in the cell wall, it is stained by a crystal violet dye-iodine complex that is not removable by alcohol. These bacteria are called *gram-positive*. If little peptidoglycan is present, the dye complex is easily removed by alcohol and the bacteria are referred to as *gram-negative*. This method is used extensively in identifying various groups of bacteria (Table 11-1). The gram-negative, gram-positive test is useful because the division produced is related to other, more important differences (Laskin and Lechevalier, 1977).

Bacteria have a great variety of shapes (Table 11-1), but small coccoid, rod-shaped, single, and chain-forming bacteria are the most common. Most taxonomic groups contain many examples of cocci, rods, and spiral forms. The limnologist is also likely to encounter bacteria embedded in thick mucus sheaths. A common example is *Sphaerotilus*, the ''sewage fungus,'' which is quite common in streams where organic matter is present and may become superabundant in polluted waters. Like some of the unicellular algae, many bacteria can swim by using hairlike flagella, which may be attached at either or both ends of the cell or all around the cell. Unfortunately, the shape of bacteria provides little insight into their role in aquatic ecosystems.

In addition to morphology, bacteria are classified by mode of nutrition or serology, which detects characteristic chemicals such as peptidoglycan. Bacterial filaments can rarely be seen by eye with a normal microscope but often can be seen as black hairlike extensions on aquatic organisms such as attached algae. Nevertheless, most bacteria are very small, between 0.2 and 5 μm long, and often appear only as dots when viewed under the highest power of the light microscope. Consequently, their ability to perform chemical transformations has become the standard method for identification and classification. Although this functional classification requires time-consuming procedures, it should be familiar to limnologists who are already acquainted with the functional role of higher organisms (Chaps. 15, 16). The nutritional requirements are found

by giving the bacteria a range of substrates and determining which promote growth and what products are released. Bacteria have very specific requirements for organic or inorganic nutrients and release characteristic products. For example, some can only convert acetate to carbon dioxide, some convert nitrite to nitrate, some require anoxic conditions, and some require light. Collectively, bacteria can mediate more chemical transformations than any other group of organisms. These include the nitrogen transformations such as nitrogen fixation, denitrification and nitrification, breakdown of cellulose, mineralization of carbon and sulfur, spoilage of food, and disease production in plants and animals. Selective breeding and genetic engineering concentrate on enhancing the transformations most useful to humans. Oil-degrading bacteria helpful in cleaning up oil spills provide a good example. A general bacterial classification, based on nutritional requirements, is Bergey's manual (Buchanan and Gibbons, 1974); a summary of the parts most useful to limnologists is given in Table 11-1. Oxygen plays a major role in this classification, because some bacteria require oxygen, others cannot tolerate it, and others, called *facultative* forms, can grow with or without it.

The main role of bacteria in nature is in the recycling of organic and inorganic materials. Heterotrophic bacteria cause decay and provide a nutritious layer for detritivorous animals feeding on decaying organic particles in rivers and lakes (Chaps. 15, 16). Bacteria sometimes produce outbreaks of disease that decimate the host populations. For example, the ''salmon disease'' in New England has been attributed to *Cutophage* spp., members of the gliding bacterial group (Table 11-1).

Chemolithotrophic bacteria found in the sediments or on particles suspended in natural waters are responsible for the oxidations of ammonia first to nitrite and then to nitrate, hydrogen sulfide oxidation to sulfate, and oxidation of ferrous (Fe^{2+}) iron to ferric (Fe^{3+}) iron (Table 11-1). They produce the familiar whitish yellow sulfur patches on rich organic mud flats of estuaries

TABLE 11-1

PARTIAL CLASSIFICATION OF THE BACTERIA COMMON IN AQUATIC HABITATS

Blue-green algae (cyanobacteria) are discussed with the algae (Table 11-3). They have much in common with both algae and bacteria.

Taxonomic division	Aquatic habitat	Substrate for energy, electrons or carbon	Example and some products
Requiring light			
1. Photolithotrophic or photoautotrophic		H_2S, CO_2	Green and purple sulfur bacteria, e.g., *Chromatium* ($H_2S \rightarrow S$)
2. Photoorganotrophic or photoheterotrophic	Dim, anoxic layer below thermocline in deeper lakes or mud surfaces in marshes and estuaries	Organics, CO_2	Purple, nonsulfur bacteria, e.g., *Rhodospirillum*
Not requiring light			
3. Gliding	Detritus, sediments, parasitic on other organisms, sulfur springs	Cellulose, chitin, H_2S	*Cytophaga* (cellulose, chitin) *Beggiatoa* ($H_2S \rightarrow S$)
4. Sheathed	Attached to rocks, logs, in flowing water	Organics	*Sphaerotilus*, the sewage fungus
5. Budding or appendaged	Streams, water pipes	H_2S, predatory on other bacteria	*Thiodendron* ($H_2S \rightarrow S$) *Caulobacter* (predatory)
6. Spiral or curved	Eutrophic fresh or saline water	Organics, N_2, predatory	*Spirillum* *Bdellovibrio* (predatory)
7. Gram-negative, oxic, rod- and cocci-shaped	Fresh, saline water, and living organisms	Organics, N_2, CH_4	*Azotobacter* ($N_2 \rightarrow$ org-N) *Methylomonas* ($CH_4 \rightarrow$ org-C)
8. Gram-negative, facultatively anoxic, rod-shaped	In plants, animal intestinal tracts, fresh or salt water	Parasitic, disease-causing in animals and plants	*Escherichia coli* (lactose $\rightarrow CO_2$)
9. Gram-negative anoxic	Anoxic sediments	SO_4, S, N_2, parasitic	*Desulfovibrio* (SO_4, $S \rightarrow H_2S$)
10. Gran-negative, chemolithotrophic	Oxic lake sediments, rivers, sulfur springs	Reduced N or S compounds	*Nitrosomonas* ($NH_4^+ \rightarrow NO_2$) *Nitrobacter* ($NO_2 \rightarrow NO_3$) *Thiobacillus* (H_2S, $S \rightarrow SO_4$)
11. Methane-producing	Anoxic hypolimnia, muds, marshes	CO_2	*Methanobacterium* ($CO_2 \rightarrow CH_4$)

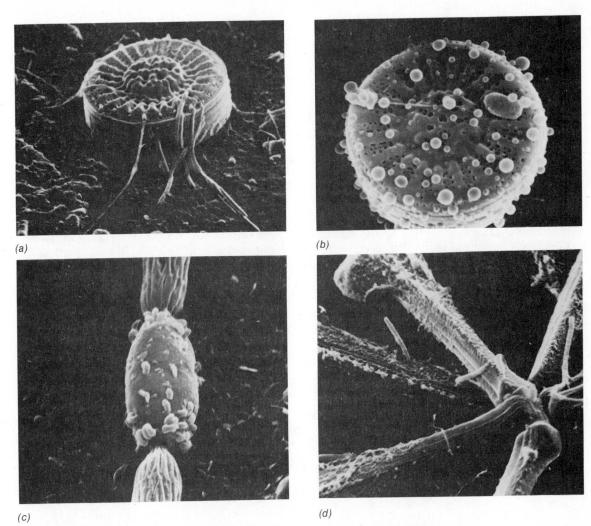

FIGURE 11-1 Microbes on dead and living phytoplankton. (*a*) Filamentous bacteria on the diatom *Cyclotella* from Lake Michigan. The algal cell is about 15 μm in diameter. (*b*) Coccoid bacteria on *Cyclotella* from Lake Tahoe. (*c*) Bacteria on the heterocyst of the blue-green alga *Aphanizomenon flos-aquae* from Clear Lake, California. Magnification ×9000. The bacteria are clustered around the junctions with adjacent vegetative cells; possibly these leak organic material. (*d*) Bacterial infection on the diatom *Asterionella* late in the spring bloom in Lake Tahoe. SEM pictures by H. W. Paerl.

or saline lakes and form the rust-colored gelatinous masses often found in streams.

Layers of chemolithotrophic purple photosynthetic bacteria are often found in anoxic conditions in lakes or on the mud surface of tide flats. Unlike algae, photosynthetic bacteria cannot tolerate oxygen. These bacteria are known for their ability to exist in platelike layers at very low light levels in or just below the metalimnion. The plate is usually found below the zone where algae are likely to grow. Photosynthetic bacteria occur in many productive lakes, particularly saline ones, and, because of their narrow vertical distribution, may go unnoticed during routine sampling. Cyanobacteria, procaryotic cells that produce oxygen in photosynthesis, are also called blue-green algae (see later in this chapter).

Little is known about the role and numbers of bacteria in aquatic ecosystems. The *coliform bacteria* that are particularly well known to public health officers and sanitary engineers are the facultative, gram-negative, rod-shaped, non-spore-forming ones that can ferment lactose. They are associated with sewage since many, but not all, are derived from the digestive tract of mammals. Although there will always be coliform bacteria present in natural waters, high levels provide evidence of water pollution from sewage.

Limnologists are becoming increasingly familiar with the morphology of bacteria due to the use of the scanning electron microscope (SEM). This method of observation has shown epiphytic bacteria apparently in the process of

digesting moribund diatoms (Fig. 11-1*a*, *b*) or growing on living blue-green algae (Fig. 11-1*c*). Unlike other plankters, most planktonic bacteria are in a resting stage. Of the millions of bacteria present in a cubic centimeter of water, only a few thousand, at most, are likely to be metabolically active. The remainder wait for a solid surface or suitable nutrient conditions to initiate enzyme activity. The physiological response can be rapid, and bacteria may grow unchecked until their food supply is exhausted. An example of the division between total and viable bacteria is given in Fig. 11-2 for relatively unproductive Windermere and more eutrophic Esthwaite Water in the English Lake District. Very few bacteria were viable in the oligotrophic lake relative to the more eutrophic one, but the total number of bacteria was similar in both lakes (Fig. 11-2). The presence of more viable bacteria in the epilimnion of Esthwaite Water than in that of Windermere correlates well with the number of phytoplankters. Similar results have been

FIGURE 11-2 Total and viable bacteria in a deep mesotrophic lake, (Windermere, North Basin) and a shallow more eutrophic lake (Esthwaite Water) during the summer stratification. Dashed line indicates short-term maximum in the epilimnion. Although the total bacterial numbers are similar in both lakes, note that numbers of viable bacteria are much greater in the eutrophic lake. Redrawn from Jones, 1977.

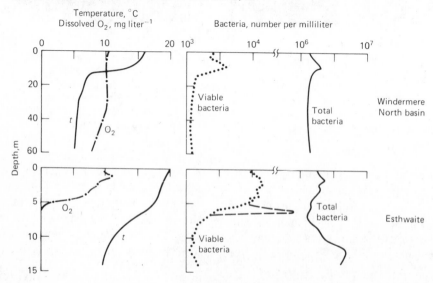

found in German lakes (Overbeck and Baben-zien, 1964) and a tropical lake in the Amazon region (Schmidt, 1969). In general, exponen-tially growing phytoplankton are relatively bac-teria-free, whereas slow-growing, dead or dying algae are rapidly attacked (Fig. 11-1). It has even been suggested that diatoms growing far from shore and organic substrates in the oligotrophic, tropical oceans are virtually bacteria-free.

Fungi and Fungilike Organisms

Like viruses and bacteria, the aquatic fungi par-ticipate in decomposition and recycling of veg-etable and animal matter. An obvious example,

known to fisheries biologists, is *Saprolegnia*, a frequent parasite of dying or injured fish. Spawned-out salmon may be completely encased in a white cocoon of *Saprolegnia*. Primitive par-asitic fungi such as chytrids are common in many lakes and may alter the species composition of spring algal blooms (Chap. 12).

All fungi have rigid cell walls and are either *saprophytic*, using organic substances for growth, or *parasitic* (Table 11-2). The thin film of bacteria and fungi present on virtually all sub-merged organic detritus is a major food source for river and lake invertebrates. Although most bacteria can use detrital cellulose, only fungi and a few bacteria possess the special enzymes that

TABLE 11-2

CLASSIFICATION OF FUNGI AND FUNGILIKE ORGANISMS COMMON IN AQUATIC HABITATS

Taxonomic division	Aquatic habitat	Example
Organism with true branching mycelium but a prokaryotic cell organization		
Actinomycetes (Actino-mycetales)	Damp leaves, streams, benthic sediments of lakes	*Actinoplanes* *Streptomyces* (odor-producing form)
Organisms with eukaryotic cells and often a true branching mycelium		
1. Phycomycetes: 　a. Chytridiomycetes 　　(water molds)		*Rhizophydium* (parasitic, single cell) *Allomyces* (saprophytic, fila-mentous)
b. Oomycetes 　　(water molds and 　　mildews)	Most fresh or saline waters, on living or dead animals or plants	*Saprolegnia* (parasitic on fish or their eggs) *Aqualinderella* (on fruits)
2. Ascomycetes and Fungi Imperfecti		*Cryptococcus* (aquatic yeast) *Dactylella* (captures nema-tode worms)
3. Basidiomycetes	Uncommon in free water, common on damp wood	*Aureobasidium* (from streams)

can break down lignin, which is the skeletal material of leaves. Fungi may digest the majority of plant cellulose and the chitinous skeletons of insects. Fungi grow and follow the bacteria in a second phase in the decomposition of detritus. True fungi and the Actinomycetales are classified by their sexual structures and shapes. In water the lower fungal orders, phycomycetes, some yeasts, and the Fungi Imperfecti are the most common (Table 11-2).

Green Plants: Algae and Macrophytes

Algae Shallow habitats may have extensive growths of higher aquatic plants, but algae dominate primary production in most aquatic ecosystems. They are present as free-floating phytoplankton (Fig. 11-3a,b) or attached algae (Fig. 11-4). The latter dominate the shallow areas of clear-water lakes and streams, and the former are most important in larger lakes and in the slowest

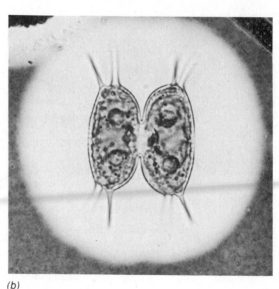

(b)

(a)

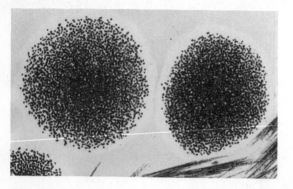

(c)

FIGURE 11-3 Common phytoplankton. (*a*) The colonial pennate diatom *Asterionella formosa,* which occurs in the spring and fall plankton of most moderately productive lakes (Chap. 12). Magnification ×520. (*b*) A representative of the summer plankton, the green alga *Xanthidium.* A ball of gelatinous, very hydrated mucus surrounds the cell but can be seen only if the background water is stained with india ink. These mucus balls are common in planktonic algae and may serve as protection against digestion when swallowed by animals. Magnification ×610. (*c*) *Microcystis aeruginosa* ×80. This colonial coccoid blue-green phytoplankton occurs in the summer and fall in more productive lakes. It is held together with mucus. Blue-green algae may form spectacular water blooms. All photographs by H. Canter-Lund.

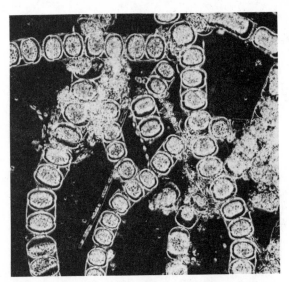

FIGURE 11-4 Attached algae. Long chains of the filamentous centric diatom *Melosira* scraped from rocks in San Francisco Bay. The chains are 20 to 40 μm in diameter. A long solitary pennate diatom is visible at bottom center, and bacteria, detritus, and broken cells compose the whitish amorphous areas on the right. This mixed assemblage is often called aufwuchs. Photograph by H. M. Anderson.

reaches of rivers. The algae, an extremely diversified group, are separated from higher plants more by what they lack than what they have. Photosynthetic algae lack roots, stems, and leaves. Algae may be unicellular, colonial, or filamentous. They can develop special reproductive cells, but rapid growth occurs by vegetative reproduction.

The primary classification of algae into different divisions is on the basis of pigment composition, how they maintain their energy reserve, cell wall composition, locomotory organs, and general structure (Table 11-3). The algae contain two main groups of pigments, chlorophylls and carotenoids. Chlorophyll is a complex molecule composed of four carbon-nitrogen rings surrounding a magnesium atom (Fig. 10-4). The loss of the metal atom produces the common

degradation product phaeophytin. Carotenoids are composed of linear unsaturated hydrocarbons called *carotenes*. The orange color of carrots is caused by this pigment and is the basis of the name. The red color of some zooplankton, salmon, and trout is derived from a high carotenoid diet. Chlorophyll *a* is the only form that can pass electrons, excited by light energy, to produce chemical energy in photosynthesis. All other pigments, including the widespread *b* and *c* forms of chlorophyll, carotenes, xanthophylls, and the less common phycocyanins, phycoerythrins, and phycopyrrins, are accessory pigments. They gather light in regions of the spectrum where chlorophyll *a* does not absorb light. The accessory pigments then pass electrons to chlorophyll *a*. This allows growth in the dim light deep in lakes, where most red and blue light is absent (Fig. 3-9*b*).

The cell walls of algae are composed of cellulose and other polysaccharides, silica, proteins, and lipids. All of these combine in various proportions to produce distinctive cell walls, which may form the basis for taxonomic classification (Table 11-3). Silicon compounds form the cell walls of diatoms. These frequently have beautiful and intricate ornamentation, which has added to the popularity of diatom taxonomy. The high-resolution light microscope and the scanning electron microscope (Fig. 10-2) reveal details of the three-dimensional structure of diatom shells or *frustules*. Taxonomists have classified over 10,000 species of diatoms on the basis of their frustules alone without the need to see the cells alive or preserved. The science of paleolimnology (Chap. 20) uses frustule classification because diatom shells may be the only recognizable algal cells that survive in the often acidic, bacteria-rich lake sediments. The concentrated deposits of marine diatoms now unlifted above sea level are called *diatomaceous earth* and are of commercial importance as an inert filtering substance for a variety of liquids. Swimming pool filters are traditionally packed with diatomaceous earth. Other algae have hardened but less

TABLE 11-3

CLASSIFICATION OF ALGAE COMMON IN AQUATIC HABITATS

Name and typical color	Most common aquatic habitat	Common morphology and locomotion	Cell wall* composition and major pigment	Examples
1. Diatoms (golden-brown) Bacillariophyta	Oceans, lakes, rivers, estuaries; attached or planktonic	Usually microscopic, filamentous, or unicellular	Opaline silica	*Asterionella* *Melosira* *Nitzschia* *Navicula*
2. Green algae (grass-green) Chlorophyta	Lakes, rivers, estuaries; planktonic or attached	Microscopic or visible; filamentous colonial, or unicellular; some are flagellated	Cellulose	*Cladophora* *Oocystis Ulva*
3. Dinoflagellates (red-brown) Pyrrhophyta	Oceans, lakes and estuaries; planktonic	Microscopic; unicellular or small chains; all are flagellated	Cellulose (when present), some silicated forms	*Peridinium* *Ceratium*
4. Blue-greens (blue-green) Cyanophyta	Lakes and oceans; planktonic or attached	Microscopic or visible; usually filimentous; some can float and glide	Mucopeptide (amino sugar + amino acids)	*Anabaena* *Nostoc* *Phormidium* *Oscillatoria*
5. Chrysophytes (yellow- or brown-green) Chrysophyta	Lakes, streams, oceans; planktonic	Microscopic; unicellular, or colonial; some are flagellated	Pectin, sometimes silicified or cellulosic	*Mallomonas* *Dinobryon* *Tribonema*
6. Cryptomonads (various colors) Cryptophyta	Lakes; planktonic	Microscopic, unicellular, flagellated	Cellulose	*Rhodomonas*
7. Euglenoids (various colors) Euglenophyta	Ponds, lakes, oceans; planktonic	Microscopic, unicellular, flagellated	Proteinaceous pellicle	*Euglena*
8. Red algae Rhodophyta	Oceans, estuaries; lakes, streams; attached	Visible or microscopic; colonial or unicellular	Cellulose + gels	*Gigartina* *Batrachospermum*
9. Brown algae Phaeophyta	Oceans, estuaries; attached, free-floating	Visible, often long fronds	Cellulose + gels	*Gracilaria* *Sargassum*

* Not all listed are true cell walls but have a similar function.

long-lasting shells. The dinoflagellates, for example, include armored forms that have several distinctively ornamented plates (Fig. 11-7b).

Many planktonic algae have the ability to move. The most common swimming device is one or more flagella, whiplike structures containing contractile fibrils. Flagella serve as oars or like a ship's propeller, depending on the type of organism. Large dinoflagellates, such as *Peridinium* or *Ceratium* (Fig. 11-7b), are able to migrate very rapidly in response to changes in light, while most flagellates, for example, the small chrysophyte *Mallomonas* or *Euglena*, appear to swim randomly. Many otherwise nonmotile forms, such as diatoms and attached filamentous green algae, may have flagellated sexual gametes. Some pennate diatoms and filamentous blue-green algae have the ability to move by gliding when next to a solid surface. All planktonic blue-green algae contain vacuoles, minute air-filled sacs that can be created or collapsed (Fig. 12-3). This alters their buoyancy and allows them vertical movement in the water column (Fig. 12-2). Motile forms have the obvious advantage of being able to adjust their position to optimize the availability of light and nutrients. This has the disadvantage, however, of using up a portion of their available energy.

The green algae contain chlorophyll *a* and *b*, carotenes, and some xanthophylls, but they lack the phycobilins. Their photosynthetic storage is in the form of microscopically visible structures called *pyrenoids*, which consist of starch plates surrounding a protein core. The presence of starch is the basis for the commonly used starch-iodine test. The cell walls consist of an inner cellulose and outer pectinaceous layer. Frequently green algae are flagellated for one phase of their life cycle.

Blue-green algae possess chlorophyll *a*, β-carotene, and a number of unique xanthophylls and phycobilins, particularly phycocyanin-c, which gives them a distinctive blue-green color. Glycogen granules serve as their main energy store, together with globules of lipid. Granules containing cyanophycin, a polypeptide consisting of argenine and aspartic acid, provide a unique storage of nitrogen. The cell wall of blue-green algae is made of mucopeptides similar to those contained in bacteria, and many species are surrounded by a gelatinous sheath or matrix (Fig. 11-3*c*). Sexual reproduction is very rare in blue-green algae, and vegetative reproduction can be more rapid than in most other phytoplankton.

The diatoms contain chlorophyll *a* and *c*, carotene, and a few xanthophylls, but lack phycobilins. They store their energy as fat and oil in large globules and sometimes as chrysolaminarin, a polysaccharide. The cell wall is made of silica embedded in a pectinaceous matrix and is constructed of overlapping halves called *valves*. This gives the diatoms a pillboxlike structure (Fig. 11-1*a*, *b*). They have no flagella except during sexual reproduction, when uniflagellated spermatozoids may be produced.

Other algal classes also contribute to the diversity of the freshwater plankton flora. Examples include the dinoflagellates *Peridinium* and *Ceratium*, which become very abundant in some temperate lakes (Figs. 11-7*b*, 12-13). Most freshwater planktonic algae are photoautotrophic, and a good deal of effort in limnology has been directed toward quantitative estimation of the energy flows associated with their photosynthesis (Chap. 15).

Algae that grow on submerged rocks, plants, or debris in lakes and streams are often called *periphyton* (meaning "on plants"), but are best referred to as *attached algae* (i.e., on any substrate) (Fig. 11-4). These algae are most commonly green or blue-green or diatoms. Among the attached diatoms, unicellular pennate forms dominate over filamentous centric ones. The golden-brown color of rocks in streams and lakes is often due to a film of diatoms, while green or blue-green algae make up the long, often brilliant green, filamentous streamers. Anglers wading in streams know that algae-covered rocks are slippery! Attached algae occur in all streams, but growth is restricted in shaded areas. In sunny areas productive streams may have luxuriant growth of the blanket weed *Cladophora*. In terms of functional or visible catagories, this filamentous green alga is a *mesophyte*, intermediate between true higher plants or *macrophytes* and diatoms or other small algae, referred to as *microphytes*. Submerged higher plants and mesophytes provide a substrate for dense *epiphytic* diatom growth. Historically, less attention has been paid to the ecological role of attached algae relative to the more easily studied phytoplankton, but in situ methods for measuring the productivity of periphyton are now available (Marker, 1976a; 1976b).

Macrophytes   Large plants, the aquatic macrophytes, may dominate in wetlands, shallow lakes, and streams. Most aquatic macrophytes are flowering plants (angiosperms), but aquatic ferns, mosses, liverworts, and even the large algae of the Charophyceae group may be abundant in particular habitats.

Macrophytes are classified by their habitat since they comprise such a diverse taxonomic group. The major division is based on their attachment by roots to a solid substrate. The two divisons, free-floating and rooted, are common to lakes, rivers, marshes, and estuaries (Table 11-4). Rooted macrophytes may have all or part of their vegetative and sexually reproductive parts above the water or may be completely submerged (Fig. 11-5). Many have some emergent leaves or flowers for only a short time. Rooted plants have the advantage of being able to mine the littoral sediments for nutrients as well as re-

TABLE 11-4

CLASSIFICATION OF AQUATIC MACROPHYTES COMMON IN AQUATIC HABITATS

Aquatic habitat	Taxonomic group*	Examples
Free-floating		
1. Subtropical, tropical lakes, slow streams	MA MA F	*Pistia* (water lettuce) *Eichhornia* (water hyacinth) *Salvinia* (water fern)
2. Temperate ponds and backwaters	F MA	*Azolla* (water fern) *Lemna* (duckweed)
Rooted		
1. Temperate marshes, lake and stream edges	MA DA MA	*Phragmites* (giant reed) *Rorippa* (watercress) *Scirpus* (bulrush)
2. Tropical marshes and rivers, lakes/ edges	MA DA	*Papyrus* (reed) *Victoria* (water lily)
3. Ponds, slow streams	DA MA DA DA	*Nuphar* (water lily) *Potamogeton* (pond weed) *Ceratophyllum* (coontail) *Myriophyllum* (milfoil)
4. Estuaries	MA MA	*Zostera* (eel grass) *Ruppia* (widgeon grass)
5. Deep in unproductive lakes; also near lake edges	L A A B	*Isoetes* (quillwort) *Chara* (stonewort) *Nitella* (stonewort) *Fontinalis* (willow moss)

* MA = monocotyledenous angiosperm (angiosperms are higher, or flowering, plants): DA = dicotyledenous angiosperm; F = fern; L = Lycosida; B = moss; A = large algae.

(a)

(b)

FIGURE 11-5 Aquatic macrophytes. These large plants may be completely or partially submerged or almost fully emergent from the water. (*a*) Typical above-water view of a mostly submerged macrophyte along the protected shore of a small lake. The sexual parts are above water for fertilization. (*b*) Underwater view of the same stand shows the bare sediment and the very dense stand of plants in this very transparent karst lake in Plitvice, Croatia-Slovania. These stands are valuable cover for young fish and invertebrates.

moving them directly from the water. They remove nutrients, particularly phosphorus, from the sediment and return them to the surrounding water through excretion or decomposition (Chap. 9). The epiphytic algae are likely to be the most immediate beneficiaries of this process, since they are in direct contact with plant surfaces. Rooted macrophytes do not always use the roots to supply nutrients. Their role as attachment organs is important in streams and along wave-swept shores.

The most striking feature of an aquatic macrophyte assemblage is the distinct zonation as one moves from land to progressively deeper water. One or two species will occupy a band at each depth, although variations in the type of substrate and exposure to waves may interrupt the regularity of distribution (Fig. 11-6). Macrophytes can cover the entire lake bed if the water is shallow and transparent. Even deep lakes with sparse phytoplankton may be sufficiently clear that light reaches the bottom.

All freshwater angiosperms are restricted to shallow water, and growth at depths greater than about 10 m may be prevented by an inability to compensate for the increased pressure. Angiosperms are also not found much below 2 percent of surface illumination. Their place is taken by totally submerged lower plants (Fig. 11-6). These species appear to be shade-adapted to the dim blue-green light characteristic of the deeper waters in unproductive transparent lakes (Fig. 3-8*b*).

A typical member of this deep community is the primitive and cosmopolitan club moss, the quillwort *Isoetes*, which grows up from the bottom sediments of clear mountain lakes in spiky clumps. Also common are mosses, the charophyte algal genera *Chara* and *Nitella*, and mesophytic algae. *Chara* is known as skunk weed in the United States because of the strong smell of some species. In both deep and shallow lakes it often becomes enveloped by a calcium carbonate crust, which may protect it from excessive solar radiation and animal grazing. Species of *Nitella* together with aquatic mosses such as

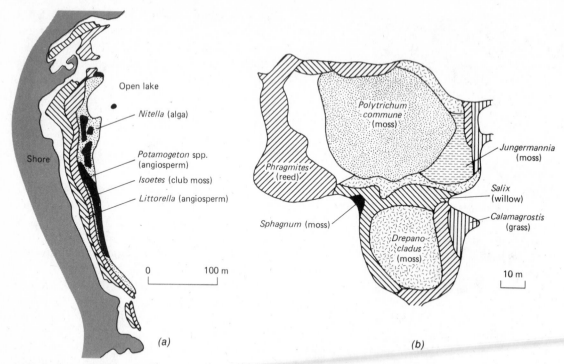

FIGURE 11-6 (*a*) Zonation of rooted aquatic macrophytes in wetlands in relatively unproductive Windermere. The more primitive Charophyte alga *Nitella* and the primitive club moss *Isoetes* (quill-wort), extend into deeper water than *Littorella* (shoreweed). The long stems of potamogeton (pond-weed) permit growth in deep water. There is no emergent, rooted vegetation on this wind-swept, rocky shore. Redrawn and modified from Pearsall and Pennington (1973). (*b*) Zonation of rooted macrophytes in a shallow, naturally acid lake (pH = 4.2), lake Ao-numa, Honshu, Japan. As in Win-dermere the primitive mosses occupy the deepest zones and submerged and emergent angiosperm reeds occupy the lake margins. Redrawn from data provided by Yamamoto, Kata, and Kashimura, Takai University, Japan.

Sphagnum and *Fontinalis* and occasionally the liverwort *Marchantia aquatica* are also shade-adapted. The aquatic mosses in particular survive only where there is a lack of grazing and an absence of competition from angiosperms. Most mosses are unable to use bicarbonate and prefer fast-flowing streams, where atmospheric carbon dioxide is abundant (Chap. 16). Some mesophy-tic algae grow at extraordinary depths. In very transparent Lake Tahoe, one can observe the green alga *Gongrosira* covering rock surfaces like green paint even at 160 m. Growth in the very low light at this depth may be subsidized by facultative heterotrophy.

Emergent monocotyledonous angiosperms are the dominant macrophytes in marshes and along many stream courses. Wetlands represent the transitional zone between land and water, and plants growing in coastal zones may have a cyclic exposure to fresh and salt water through tidal intrusion (Chaps. 18, 19). Where wave action does not uproot plants, many temperate lakes have extensive littoral stands of macro-phytes. These are frequently growths of *Phrag-mites australis*, reeds that make excellent roof thatch. Other common freshwater-rooted plants include cattail or reed mace *Typha*, the American bulrush *Scirpus*, and *Carex*, the sedge. In the tropics enormous stands of emergent plants, especially papyrus, noted in biblical times along the Nile Delta and once used to make paper, serve to buffer lakes and river systems from the inflow of nutrients and sediments. In saline waters the widgeon grass *Ruppia*, the eel grass *Zostera*, and the alkali bulrush *Scirpus robustus* are food for ducks, geese, and other animals.

One of the most important of the emergent macrophytes is cultivated rice, which contributes most of the caloric intake of the world's population. Wild rice, the aquatic grass *Zizania aquatica*, is native to shallow northern lakes of the United States and Canada. It was an excellent and important food for the original native tribes and is now cultivated as a gourmet item. Another delicious plant is the dicotyledonous angiosperm watercress (*Rorippa nasturtium-aquaticum*), found in permanent and temporary streams and springs where cool well-oxygenated waters flow. It is cultured extensively for salad.

If algal concentrations or sediment turbidity are too high, higher plants may be shaded out. Fertilizing to promote an algal bloom can be prescribed for macrophyte weed control in farm ponds. Among the rooted macrophytes, which have much of their foliage at or near the surface, are the highly successful monocotyledonous pond weeds, *Potamogeton*. These are found in temperate waters of both high and low fertility. Rooted floating plants are typically the more advanced dicotyledonous angiosperms with well-developed leaves. Water lilies of the genera *Nymphaea* or *Nuphar* are well-known examples. The giant water lily, *Victoria*, of the Amazon and Paraná river systems of South America is a spectacular representative of this growth form. The underside of the leaf is protected from gazing animals by sharp spines and its shape and flotation assured by an intricate series of rigid gas-trapping cells. Most lakes, ponds, and streams have some representatives of dicotyledonous angiosperms and most have common names. Dense beds of water milfoil (*Myriophyllum*) and coontail (*Ceratophyllum*) are food for muskrat and their seeds are eaten by birds. An interesting turnabout in the food chain is provided by the carnivorous bladderwort, *Utricularia*, which, like Venus's flytrap, catches small animals in pouches to supplement its nitrogen supply.

There are relatively few pelagic or free-floating macrophytes. This may be because they require rather fertile water and are subject to stranding in large lakes when exposed to wind or water-level fluctuation. The free-floating water fern *Salvinia* spp. and the monocotyledonous angiosperms, water cabbage *Eichornia crassipes* and water lettuce *Pistia stratiotes*, may completely cover the surface of even very large water bodies in the tropics and subtropics and produce a variety of water management and public health problems. In Lake Kariba, Africa, a third of the reservoir was once covered by over 10 billion (10^{10}) *Salvinia* plants. In temperate and subtropical regions much smaller free-floating plants, such as the duckweed *Lemna*, a monocotyledonous angiosperm, and the fern *Azolla*, completely cover the shallow wind-protected areas of ponds, irrigation ditches, and backwaters. *Azolla* contains the symbiotic nitrogen-fixing blue-green alga *Anabaena azollae* that helps give the combined plant system value as cattle feed and as fertilizer for rice fields. The suspended roots of *Lemna* may be covered with nitrogen-fixing bacteria. *Lemna* and *Azolla* appear yellow-green, but late in the growing season *Azolla* may have a red coloration.

Most aquatic macrophytes are not used for food, as their common name *waterweed* implies (Mann, 1988). However, the seeds of the angiosperms are a favored food for many birds, and the shelter provided by their dense foliage is often vital for small invertebrates and the eggs and young of fish. Some macrophytes break down rapidly and contribute to the detritus pool. For example, 80 percent of the nitrogen in leaves and stems of watercress is returned to the stream within 3 weeks of the plants' deaths in autumn. Throughout the world, rooted macrophytes are managed for fisheries enhancement or flood con-

TABLE 11-5

CLASSIFICATION OF PROTOZOANS COMMON IN AQUATIC HABITATS

Name	Aquatic habitat	Examples
1. Flagellates	Lakes, oceans; some parasitic forms	*Synura* * (Chrysomonad) *Ceratium* * (Dinoflagellate) *Euglena* * *Oikomonas*
2. Ciliates	Ponds, streams, detritus; also parasitic forms	*Paramecium* *Vorticella* *Ichthyophthirius* (parasitic on fish)
3. Amoeboid	Testate and naked forms in most waters; also parasitic	*Difflugia* *Globigerina* (Foraminifera) *Actinosphaerium* (Radiolaria) *Vampyrella* (algal parasite)
4. Sporozoans (all endoparasitic)	Aquatic organisms	*Henneguya* (on fish) *Plasmodium* (human malaria)

* Photosynthetic forms are also classed as algae (Table 11-3).

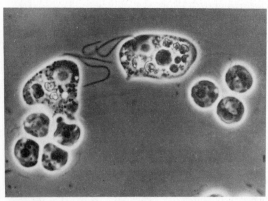

(a)

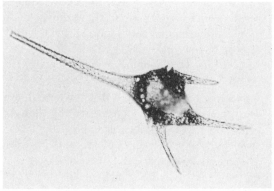

(b)

FIGURE 11-7 (*a*) Flagellated protozoans of the *Pseudospora* type, which are invading the colonial green algal *Paulschultia*. Magnification ×685. (*b*) The large photosynthetic dinoflagellate protozoan *Ceratium*, a common genus in lakes, and the open ocean (magnification ×265). The central groove, which holds the flagellum, four long spines, and the small armored plates, is visible. This genus can be photosynthetic. Photographs by H. Canter-Lund.

trol. Dense growths of macrophytes effectively dam swamps and rivers, sometimes increasing the depth of a river fourfold. In this way, macrophytes assist in spreading flood waters onto the surrounding land to increase its fertility and provide additional areas for fish and amphibians to feed and spawn. However, the water lost by wetland plant evapotranspiration may reduce water supplies downstream.

Protozoans

These unicellular organisms range in size from a few microns to 5 mm long. Protozoans are found in almost all aquatic habitats (Table 11-5) and tend to be most abundant in waters where organic matter, bacteria, or algae are abundant. Farm ponds that receive drainage from manure heaps and even antarctic pools near seal wallows teem with rapidly moving protozoans. Benthic algal felts in lakes or vegetation and rocks in slow-moving streams are also good sites for protozoans. Due to the wide dispersal of resting stages, most genera and even some species are found worldwide. Protozoans move slowly, using amoeboid motion, or rapidly, using flagella or cilia. Their classification is largely based on locomotion (Table 11-5).

Protozoan ecology has been rather neglected, perhaps because many are soft-bodied and difficult to preserve. An exception occurs in some saline lakes and the oceans where sediments consist of the remains of the calcified or silicified skeletons of radiolarians and foraminiferans. The well-known freshwater ciliate *Paramecium* is a particularly common form in temporary pools. Some species of this genus may contain live cells of the green alga *Chlorella*, which are an integral part of the animal's metabolism. *Vorticella*, an attached filter-feeding ciliate, is probably the most familiar protozoan encountered in detritus from streams or ponds. Protozoans feed on detritus and also consume free-living bacteria, fungi, yeasts, algae, and other protozoans (Fig. 11-7*a*).

Some protozoans are strictly parasitic. Ex-

amples are the ciliate *Ichthyophthirius*, which causes white pustules on freshwater fish, the orange-colored *Vampyrella*, which feeds on algae, and *Plasmodium*, which causes human malaria. Some flagellated protozoans, such as *Ceratium* or *Peridinium* (Fig. 11-7*b*) can photosynthesize and are sometimes classified with the algae (Chap. 12). Protozoans that parasitize freshwater phytoplankton may modify algal species composition. Similarly, protozoans may alter the composition of zooplankton or fish communities. In other cases they may merely attack sick or dying individuals. An example of probable protozoan infestation on an adult copepod zooplankton is shown in Figure 11-8.

Rotifers

Rotifers are often as small as the larger ciliated protozoans and also inhabit a wide range of aquatic habitats. Much is known about the biology of laboratory cultures but, perhaps because

FIGURE 11-8 Infestation of a copepod, probably by protozoans, the tulip-shaped organisms under the animal's body. Photograph by M. L. Commins.

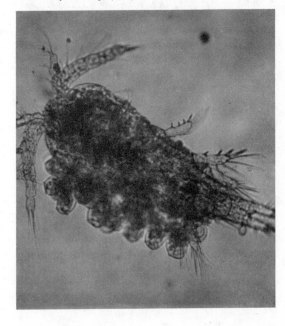

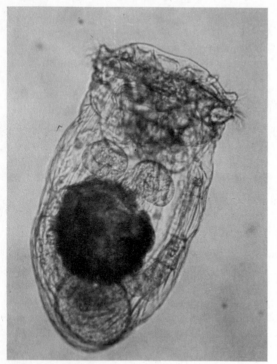

(a)

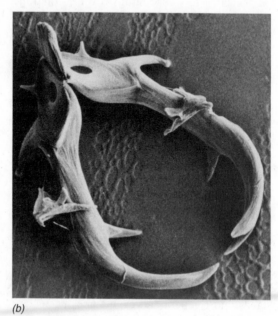

(b)

FIGURE 11-9 Planktonic rotifers. Most rotifers are herbivorous, but (*a*) shows a relatively large predatory rotifer, *Asplanchna*. Its body consists of a nonrigid sac topped by a ring of cilia, which provides good mobility. Only in a few species does the ring of cilia resemble rotating wheels for which the group is named. The large dark area in the center of the body is the gut and the circular object is an egg (most rotifers are female). (*b*) The antlerlike structures, called *trophi* (much enlarged here), are located just below the ring of cilia. Trophi are hard and their pointed ends assist *Asplanchna* to grasp its prey. Photographs by M. L. Commins.

of their small size, these metazoans are still somewhat neglected in limnology. The taxonomic and life histories of rotifers are reviewed in Hutchinson (1967), Ruttner-Kolisko (1972), and Pennak (1978).

There are over 1800 species of rotifers; many are cosmopolitan and most occur only in freshwater. The majority are sessile, but rotifers also form an important part of the zooplankton community in lakes, although many pass through coarse plankton nets. They usually dominate the zooplankton in rivers. Most rotifers have a crown of cilia, which is used both for movement and

for drawing in suspended particles (Fig. 11-9). Food is captured and macerated by hard structures called *trophi*. A few predatory species can extend this structure outside the body to penetrate a prey and suck out its contents. Some rotifers, such as *Asplanchna*, are permanently planktonic, but most attach to solid substrates with their foot and creep in leechlike fashion. The rotifer body is protected by a cuticle that may be thickened to produce a distinctly ornamented *lorica*. Rotifers are usually classified by the distinctive shape of their trophi and lorica (Table 11-6).

(a)

(b)

Plate 1 *(a)* Spirit Lake in Washington State was much enlarged in 1980 when a huge mud slide dam followed the eruption of the Mt. Saint Helens volcano. Millions of trees were killed and several thousand can be seen floating in the lake (white area at upper right). This lake is deep blue because it is oligotrophic (Chap. 3) but the hue has been slightly enhanced by using a polarizing filter. *(b)* An Antarctic coastal lake, Heyward Lake, Signy Island. This small shallow lake often becomes free of ice for only a few days. It is also oligotrophic but has a thick, slow-growing felt of blue-green algae (cyanobacteria) characteristic of systems exposed to intense solar radiation that damages plankton in shallow water.

(a)

(b)

Plate 2 *(a)* Lake Baikal, Siberia is the oldest and deepest lake in the world. Its study requires large boats including bow-loading vessels that allow disembarkation in remote beaches where there are no jetties. It is still quite oligotrophic but the area near the major inflowing river is eutrophic. *(b)* Crater Lake in Oregon is one of the most oligotrophic lakes in the world due to the very small drainage area, mostly the rim of the volcanic crater in which it formed. The color has been brought out by using a polarizing filter (photograph by G. Maiii).

(b)

(a)

(a)

Plate 3 *(a)* Glacial flour formed by ice grinding rock produces the brown muddy color of the Athabasca River seen here near its source in southern Canada. The large amount of suspended sediment scours the rocks of attached algae and clogs fish gills. *(b)* Glacial flour and very cold water draining from a glacier enter Lake Louise, Canada and, being denser than the lake water, plunge below it forming a distinct line between the brown inflow and the blue-green lake water.

Plate 4 *(a)* The aptly named Reflection Lake in Yosemite Valley, California is occasionally almost filled in with sediment which is eroded away leaving a shallow lake where emergent macrophytes can grow (lower right). *(b)* A dystrophic lake in the Marble Mountain wilderness of northern California is stained with humic acids draining from the surrounding coniferous forest (Chap. 6).

(b)

Plate 5 *(a)* This marsh in Oregon is similar to many throughout the world. Emergent cattails, growing in a few centimeters of water, enclose slightly deeper water dominated by floating duckweed, filamentous green algae, and rooted macrophytes such as water lilies with floating leaves. The water is slightly brown with humic acids. *(b)* A Cyprus swamp in the Florida Everglades shows the buttress roots characteristic of the species. These trees are smaller than most and allow light to penetrate to the ground where grasses grow. The wet and dry hydroperiod makes this swamp more productive than permanently flooded wetlands (Chap. 17).

(b)

(a)

(a)

(a)

(b)

Plate 7 *(a)* A small white submersible, here being boarded by Dr. Goldman, is used for deepwater surveillance in Lake Tahoe along with *(b)* a smaller, remotely operated, vehicle seen near a submerged tree stump indicating that the lake was once much shallower.

Plate 8 *(a)* Large waterfalls such as Murchison Falls on the White Nile in Uganda block the upstream migration of fish into Lake Victoria. This reduces the fish diversity downstream (Chap. 17). *(b)* An artificial barrier was built at this narrows on the El Cahon River in Honduras when a dam was constructed in the 1980s. The high sediment load is due to erosion upstream where slash and burn agriculture has destroyed most vegetation cover (Chap. 6).

(b)

(a)

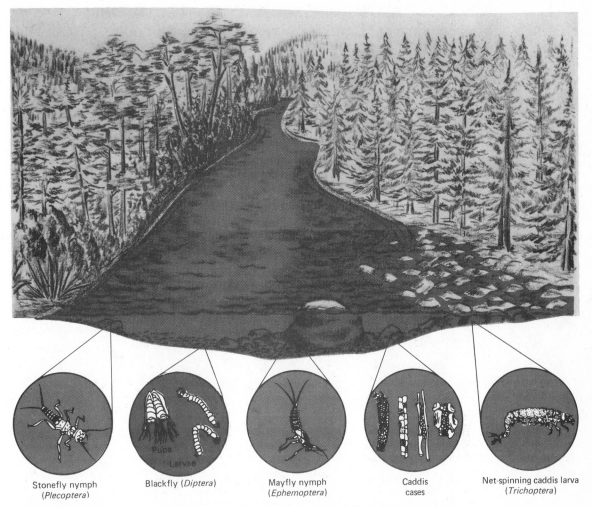

Stonefly nymph
(*Plecoptera*)   Blackfly (*Diptera*)   Mayfly nymph
(*Ephemoptera*)   Caddis
cases   Net-spinning caddis larva
(*Trichoptera*)

FIGURE 11-12   The major groups of stream insects. Most of the benthic insects in streams are larval forms, called *nymphs*, which do not resemble their adult flying forms. Most stream invertebrates are only 1 or 2 cm long. The mobile ones are flattened to resist the water current and hide from predatory fish during the day. At night they emerge to graze on algae or on each other (Fig. 16-20). The fixed forms, such as the blackfly, Simuliidae, or the net-spinning caddis fly, live in protected cracks or other places where predators are few.

geon were often considered pests because they interfered with fishing gear during capture of other species. In San Francisco Bay similar problems caused migrating sturgeon to be caught in large numbers, stacked like cordwood on the

beaches, and left to rot. Sturgeon are now protected in San Francisco Bay, and the population is slowly increasing there.

The closely related paddlefish *Polyodon,* once abundant in the Mississippi River drainage of

TABLE 11-8

CLASSIFICATION OF BENTHIC INVERTEBRATES COMMON IN LAKES AND STREAMS

Taxonomic group	Common aquatic habitat	Food/feeding method	Examples
1. Turbellaria (flatworms)	General	Carnivores	*Dugesia*
2. Nematoda (round worms)	General	Carnivores, herbivores parasites	*Dolichodorus*
3. Annelida Oligochaeta (segmented worms)	General	Sediment grazers	*Tubifex* (red worms)
Hirudinea (leeches)	General	Carnivores, detrivores	*Haemopis* (horse leech)
4. Mollusca Gastropoda (snails)	General	Grazer	*Limnaea* (pond snail) *Planorbis* (ramshorn snail)
Palacypoda (bivalves)	Streams	Filterers	*Anodonta* (swan mussel)
5. Crustacea Malacostraca (crayfish, amphipods)	General	Detrivores	*Gammarus* *Astacus*
6. Insecta Plecoptera (stoneflies)	Well-oxygenated waters	Mostly omnivores	*Nemoura* *Isoperla*
Odonata (dragonflies)	Ponds, streams	Raptorial carnivores	*Libellula*
Ephemeroptera (mayflies)	General	Mostly scrapers, grazers	*Baetis* *Ephemerella*
Hemiptera (water bugs)	General	Beaked carnivores, herbivores	*Notonecta* (backswimmer) *Gerris* (water strider)
Megaloptera (hellgrammites, alderflies)	General	Carnivores	*Sialis*
Trichoptera (caddis flies)	General	Mostly filterers, scrapers	*Limnephilus* *Hydropsyche*
Coleoptera (beetles)	Pools	Raptorial carnivores	*Dytiscus* (diving beetle)

TABLE 11-8

CLASSIFICATION OF BENTHIC INVERTEBRATES COMMON IN LAKES AND STREAMS *(Continued)*

Taxonomic group	Common aquatic habitat	Food/feeding method	Examples
Diptera (two-winged flies)	Pools	Carnivores	*Culex* (mosquito)
	Lakes	Raptorial carnivores	*Chaoborus* (phantom midge)
	Fast-flowing water	Filterers	*Simulium* (blackfly)
	General	Filterers, scrapers, carnivores	*Chironomus* (bloodworm, true midge)

North America, comprised a significant portion of the commercial river fishery of the central United States. In the same general habitat are found a single species of bowfin, Amidae, and numerous representatives of gars, *Lepisosteidae*, which are covered with an armor of primitive scales.

Among the progressively more advanced bony fish, the great stocks of shad and herring, Clupeidae, are best known from marine areas but have several freshwater representatives, such as the gizzard shad and goldeye herring. The salmon family, Salmonidae, includes the lake-dwelling trout and whitefish, of great commercial value, in northern lakes. The pike, Esocidae, and perch, Percidae (Chap. 14), are circompolar in distribution (Fig. 11-13). They are valued as food and are important in lakes as predators. The minnow family, Cyprinidae, has many representatives in Europe, North America, and Asia (Fig. 11-14) and dominates China's fresh waters. The Cyprinidae include the carp, originally native to Asia, which have long been utilized for aquaculture and are greatly valued as food in many countries. The carp's ability to endure poor water quality makes it a natural survivor in polluted situations. Introductions in Europe and North America have made it widespread. The freshwater suckers, Catostomidae, are close relatives

of the carp and are widespread in North America (Fig. 11-13). Although very bony, they are excellent food if properly prepared. They, like members of the salmon and minnow families, have round, cycloid scales. The family Centrarchidae (Fig. 11-14) is among the most successful of modern North American fishes. It contains the black basses, sunfish, and crappies, which, like the perch family, have ctenoid scales. Both families are prized as sports fish, but some species overpopulate artificial lakes. A similar family, Cichlidae, which includes the numerous species of *Tilapia*, is extremely abundant and important as food in Africa, South and Central America, and India (Fig. 11-14).

Pacific and Atlantic salmon, shad, and smelt are *anadromous* fish. Feeding in fertile areas of the ocean, salmon grow to large adults, which must return to freshwater streams to spawn. In so doing, the Pacific salmon, which die after spawning, carry in their bodies nutrients from the sea to unproductive lakes and streams where their progeny will eventually hatch. These species may be introduced to lakes where they are able to complete their life cycle by spawning in the lakes' tributaries and spending their adult life in the lake in the same manner that their marine relatives spend theirs in the sea. Fish that live in fresh waters but must go to the oceans to spawn

(Text continued on p. 221.)

TABLE 11-9

TAXONOMIC CLASSIFICATION OF FISH REFERRED TO IN THIS TEXT

Only some of the more than 300 families of freshwater and marine fish are listed.

Taxonomic classification	Selected examples	Particular references In this text
	Agnatha (jawless fish)	
Order: Petromyzoniformes Family: Lampreys (Petromyzonidae)	Sea lamprey, *Petromyzon fluviatilis* Brook lamprey, *P. branchialis*	Changes in Great Lakes fisheries, Chap. 14
	Gnathostoma (jawed fish)	
Order: Acipenseridae Family: Sturgeons (Acipenseridae)	Lake sturgeon, *Acipenser fluvesens*	Changes in Great Lakes fisheries, Chap. 14
Paddlefish (Polydontidae)	American paddlefish or spoonbill cat (*Polydon spathula*)	Plankton feeding, Chap. 16.
Order: Anguilliformes Family: Eels (Anguillidae)	Freshwater eel, *Anguilla anguilla*	A catadromous fish, Chap. 16.
Order: Clupeiformes Family: Herrings (Clupeidae)	Alewife, *Alosa pseudoharengus*	Introduced to Great Lakes fishery, Chap. 14
Order: Salmoniformes Family: Salmon, trout, whitefish, chub, char and greyling (Salmonidae)	Kokanee salmon, *Onchorhynchus nerka* Chinook or king salmon, *O. tshawytscha* Trout, *Salmo salar* Lake whitefish, *Coregonus clupeaformis* Blackfin cisco or chub, *C. nigripinnis* Bloater, *C. hoyi* Lake herring, *C. artedii* Lake trout, *Salveleneus namaycush*	Top predators in many cold lakes and rivers, Chap. 14. Changes in Great Lakes fisheries, Chap. 14
Family: Smelts (Osmeridae)	Rainbow smelt *Osmerus eperianus* (mordax)	
Family: Pike (Esocidae)	Pike, *Esox lucius*	Population dynamics in Windermere, Chap. 14
Order: Cypriniformes Family: Minnows, carp (Cyprinidae)	European carp, *Cyprinus carpio*	Introduced to North America and Great Lakes fisheries, Chap. 14.

TABLE 11-9

TAXONOMIC CLASSIFICATION OF FISH REFERRED TO IN THIS TEXT *(Continued)*

Only some of the more than 300 families of freshwater and marine fish are listed.

Taxonomic classification	Selected examples	Particular references In this text
	Gnathostoma (jawed fish)	
	European roach, *Rutilus rutilus*	Food-chain dynamics in River Thames, Chap. 15
	Bleak, *Alburnus alburnus*	
	California roach, *Hesperoleucus symmetricus*	Feeding in rivers, Chaps. 14, 16
	European minnow, *Phoxinus phoxinus*	
	European chub, *Squalius cephalus*	
Family: Suckers (Catostomidae)	Tahoe sucker, *Catastomus tahoensis* Mountain sucker, *C. platyrhynchus*	Feeding and distribution in lakes, Chap. 14, and river ecology, Chap. 16
Family: North American catfish (Ictaluridae)	Channel catfish *Ictalurus punctatus*	
Order: Cyprinodontiformes Family: Killifishes, pupfish (Cyprinodontidae)	Desert pupfish, *Cyprinodon nevadensis*	Saline habitats, Chap. 21
Order: Gasterosteiformes Family: Sticklebacks (Gasterosteidae)	Three-spined stickleback, *Gasterosteus aculeatus*	
Order: Mugiliformes Family: Mullet (Magilidae)	Grey mullet, *Mugil cephalus*	Breeding migrations to estuaries, Chap. 19
Order: Perciformes Family: Temperate basses (Percichthyidae)	Striped bass, *Morone saxatilus*	Introduction to San Francisco Bay, Chap. 19
Family: Sea basses (Serranidae)	White bass, *Roccus chrysops*	Feeding methods in lakes, Chap. 14
Family: Sunfish (Centrachidae)	Sunfish, *Lepomis* spp. Large-mouth black bass, *Micropterus salmoides*	Food webs, Chap. 15, introduction to Lake Gatun, Chap. 14
Family: Perch (Percidae)	Perch, *Perca fluviatilis*	Year class survival in Windermere, Chap. 14
Family: Archerfish (Toxotidae)	Archerfish, *Toxotes jaculator*	Special feeding methods, Chap. 14

TABLE 11-9

TAXONOMIC CLASSIFICATION OF FISH REFERRED TO IN THIS TEXT *(Continued)*

Only some of the more than 300 families of freshwater and marine fish are listed.

Taxonomic classification	Selected examples	Particular references In this text
	Gnathostoma (jawed fish)	
Family: Cichlids (Chchlidae)	Tilapia, *Tilapia* spp.	Phytoplankton feeding, Chap. 14, and tropical lakes, Chap. 21
Family: Icefish (Channichthyi- dae)		"Bloodless" fish, Chap. 21
Order: Scorpaeniformes Family: Sculpins (Cottidae)	Miller's thumb, *Cottus gobio* Piute sculpin, *C. beldingi*	Resource partitioning in streams, Chap. 14
Order: Gadiformes Family: Cod (Gadidae)	Burbot, *Lota lota*	Great Lakes fisheries, Chap. 14

Modified from Lagler et al., 1977.

///// Cyprinodonts (killifish)

▓▓▓ Catostomids (suckers)

\\\\\ Esocidae (pike)

FIGURE 11-13 World distribution of three common groups of fish. The catostomids, or sucker family, are mainly confined to North America. In Africa and the tropical coast of Asia, suckers are replaced by cyprinodonts (killifish). The two families overlap in the southwestern United States. In contrast the pike are a cold-water circumpolar group. (Redrawn and modified from Lagler et al., (1977).

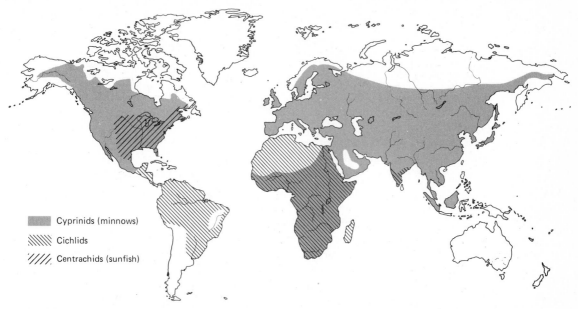

Cyprinids (minnows)

Cichlids

Centrachids (sunfish)

FIGURE 11-14 World distribution of three more common groups of fish. Minnows (cyprinids) are widespread throughout most of the world. The centracids or sunfish, such as the crappie or black bass, are confined to the central and southeastern United States, although they have been widely introduced to warm lakes elsewhere. The cichlid family is common over most of Africa and South America and is famous for rapid speciation after an initial species invades a new lake (Fig. 14-7). Redrawn from Lagler et al., (1977).

are called *catadromous;* the eel, Anguillidae, which returns from both Europe and North America to spawn in the waters near Bermuda, is the best known example. After hatching, their larvae are carried by the Gulf Stream to the shores of North America and Europe, where they ascend the rivers as elvers to grow to maturity in fresh water. Both elvers and adult eels are highly prized as food and are extensively cultered in Japan.

Since anadromous or catadromous fish must move between fresh water and salt water, they are specially equipped metabolically to adjust their salt balance, or *osmoregulate.* Estuaries usually provide the transitional zone for a more gradual adjustment to salinity changes (Chap. 17). Freshwater fish entering salt water must be able to eliminate salts effectively to remain *hypotonic* to their environment, while saltwater fish

entering fresh water must conserve the salts in their body fluids to remain *hypertonic* to their new, less-saline habitat. Except for sharks and their allies, which maintain a high urea concentration in the blood, the bony fish balance salt uptake and loss with their gills and kidneys. Some additional salt loss occurs in marine fish through feces.

Amphibians, Reptiles, Birds, and Mammals

The amphibians require water in their early life stages and are therefore inseparably tied to the aquatic habitat. Even the terrestrial salamanders found in moist habitats beneath logs and leaves must return to water to reproduce. Newts, salamanders, and frogs inhabit the water's edge, and their young spend their preadult period beneath the surface. The mud puppy, *Necturus*, with external gills at the neck, spends its entire life in midwestern streams of North America in fairly active competition with benthic fish. The stream angler often captures them when fishing with worms.

Reptiles are able to leave water, since their amniotic eggs do not need external water and their impervious skin retains body fluids in terrestrial and even desert environments. Many reptiles, however, remain closely associated with the water. In Central America, a light-footed lizard, the Jesus lizard, can actually run across the surface of the water. Small snakes are common predators of fish and amphibians in weedy streams and ponds. *Natrix*, known as the water snake in America and the grass snake in Europe, often delight the limnologist with their graceful swimming motion. Among the more dramatic examples of aquatic snakes is the Amazonian giant anaconda, whose size and strength is legendary. Major carnivorous reptiles in tropical rivers and lakes include the caimans of South America, a number of species of the more widely distributed crocodiles, and American alligators.

Although feeding mainly on fish, larger individuals also take small to moderate-sized mammals, including an occasional human. In a sense, crocodiles are to a limnologist what man-eating sharks are to the oceanographer—they provide a certain element of danger and excitement during the study of tropical habitats. In fact, because of the value of their hides, they are an endangered species almost everywhere.

Perhaps the best-documented attack of a crocodile on limnologists occurred during one of the expeditions of Daniel Livingstone on Lake Chishi, Zambia. He had set out in a rubber boat powered by a small outboard motor. In the middle of this large, shallow lake, an enormous Nile crocodile, *Crocodilus niloticus* (Fig. 11-15), suddenly attacked the bow of the boat from beneath. The bow chamber collapsed, and despite blows from the aluminum oars wielded by Livingstone and a kick from his companion Richardson, the giant reptile maintained the attack. The creature finally climbed on top of the disabled craft and drove the limnologists into the water. From the size of the crocodile, estimated to be a meter

FIGURE 11-15 Several very large Nile crocodiles, *Crocodilus niloticus*, at rest near the plunge pool below Murchison Falls on the River Nile, Uganda.

across the back, both men might well have been recycled into the aquatic food chain had it not been for the crocodile's apparent fixation on sinking the rubber boat. As they swam toward shore, the crocodile was last seen still atop the boat (Richardson and Livingstone, 1962). An explanation for this aggressive behavior was provided from observations in a marsh near Lake Chishi, where a wooden scow 4 m long, also powered by an outboard motor, was repeatedly attacked by Nile crocodiles. They appeared to be defending their territory from the noisy craft in an area where they had not been hunted (Jackson, 1962).

Wetlands are the traditional nesting and feeding grounds for many species of water fowl. They exhibit a great variety of feeding activities and adaptations, since they feed at every level of the aquatic food chain. Specific examples are referred to throughout this text. The various herons and egrets stalk their prey on long legs, while the tropical fish eagle, fish hawk, and osprey

pluck living fish when any venture near the surface. Among the most interesting avian fish predators are the kingfishers and Arctic terns that hover over the water and dive to capture minnows and young salmon during their migration to the sea. Whether straining algae out in flamingo fashion (Fig. 11-16) or pecking along the shore in search of snails and small crustaceans, the diversity of bird life associated with the aquatic environment provides another realm of interest for limnologists. Perhaps the most truly aquatic birds are grebes and cormorants, which, like penguins, obtain food by directly pursuing and capturing fish under the water. The cormorant literally flies through the water. In rivers and streams the water ouzel also uses its wings to swim as it moves from rock to rock in the fast-flowing rapids.

Mammals have many representatives associated with inland waters. Much of the early exploration of North America was carried out in search of new beaver-trapping grounds, since

FIGURE 11-16 A small part of the huge flock of lesser flamingoes, *Phoenicopterus* (= *Phoeniconais*) *minor*, feeding on the blue-green alga *Spirulina* and benthic diatoms (Tuite, 1981) in alkaline Lake Nakuru, Kenya. The bird's bill is specially adapted to remove algae while the head is inverted (Jenkin, 1936).

this animal had been hunted to extinction in much of Europe. Their luxuriant pelts once formed an important part of the New World's currency. Closely associated with beavers are muskrat and mink and their South American relatives, the coypu, which are also highly valued for their fur. Muskrats abound in marshy areas, along small streams, and particularly in irrigation ditches. Like the beaver, they operate through the winter, under the ice, and live in bank burrows. Beavers are limnologically important as they create their own aquatic environment throughout the northlands of the New World. Their small ponds often provide the only relatively still water in upland areas.

Although seals are usually considered marine, endemic populations of the freshwater seal, *Phoca (Pusa) sibirica*, exist in Lake Baikal, Siberia, and another species is found in Lake Iliamna at the base of the Alaskan peninsula. Otter have representatives in both the Old and New Worlds. They seem to play as much as they hunt for fish, and make excellent pets. Among the larger mammals, the hippopotamus has a role in the freshwater ecology of many African lakes and marshes (Fig. 11-17). They consume enormous quantities of terrestrial grasses around the lake, fertilize the nearshore waters with their excrement (Horne and Viner, 1971), and keep waterways open in the shallower portions of their habitat. During periods of drought or overpopulation they may denude the shore zones and accelerate erosion. They are considered by some limnologists to be even more dangerous than crocodiles, and both authors have had their boat in Lake George, Uganda, attacked by these impressive herbivores. Elephants, cape buffalo, and bison make a great deal of use of water, and in North America and Africa some ponds owe their origins to their wallowing.

Like the seal, the manatee is a truly aquatic mammal inhabiting areas of North, Central, and South America as well as Africa. They are frequently found in clear streams or estuaries and consume higher aquatic plants. A number of attempts have been made to utilize their grazing abilities to control aquatic plant infestations, but their slow reproduction and susceptibility to injury by boats have greatly limited the success. Their numbers have declined drastically since they were extensively harvested for food, and they are now considered endangered animals.

Having considered the broad range of bacteria, fungi, plants, and animals, the next three

FIGURE 11-17 African hippopotami in a *Pistia*-covered pool near Lake George, Uganda. These animals are normally out of the water only during darkness, but this shallow, muddy pool allowed them to show more of themselves than the limnologist usually sees.

chapters provide more detail on phytoplankton and periphyton, zooplankton and zoobenthos, and fish and fisheries. In these chapters we have selected a few examples from among the enormous diversity that characterizes aquatic environments.

FURTHER READING

Bold, H. C. 1985. *Introduction to the Algae: Structure and Reproduction.* Prentice-Hall, Englewood Cliffs, NJ. 662 pp.

Brinkhurst, R. O., and D. G. Cook (eds.). 1980. *Aquatic Oligochaetes.* Plenum, New York. 529 pp.

Holm, L. G., L. W. Weldon, and R. D. Blackburn. 1969. "Aquatic Weeds." *Science,* **166:**699–709.

Hutchinson, G. E. 1975. *A Treatise on Limnology,* vol. III: *Limnological Botany.* Wiley, New York. 660 pp.

Jones, J. G. 1971. "Studies on Freshwater Bacteria: Factors Which Influence the Population and Its Activity." *J. Ecol.,* **59:**593–613.

Laskin, A. I., and H. A. Lechevalier. 1977. *Handbook of Microbiology,* Vol. I. *Bacteria* 757 pp. Vol II. *Fungi, Algae, Protozoa, and Viruses,* 874 pp.

Mitchell, D. S. 1969. "The Ecology of Vascular Hydrophytes on Lake Kariba." *Hydrobiologia,* **34:**448–464.

Pennak, R. W. 1989. *Freshwater Invertebrates of the United States,* 3d ed. Wiley, New York. 628 pp.

Round, F. E. 1988. *Algae and the Aquatic Environment.* Biopress, Kendal, England. 460 pp.

Russell-Hunter, W. D. 1968, 1969. *A Biology of Lower Invertebrates* (1968), 181 pp. *A Biology of Higher Invertebrates,* (1969), 224 pp. Macmillan, New York.

Ward, H. B., and G. C. Whipple. 1959. In W. T. Edmondson (ed.), *Freshwater Biology,* 2d ed: Wiley, New York, 1248 pp.

Ward, J. V. 1992. *Aquatic Insect Ecology. 1. Biology and Habitat.* Wiley, New York, 438 pp.

Willoughby, L. G. 1969. "A Study of the Aquatic Actinomycetes of Bleham Tarn." *Acta Hydrobiol. Hydrographia Protistol.,* **34:**465–483.

CHAPTER 12

Phytoplankton and Periphyton

OVERVIEW

Phytoplankton are the ''grass'' of lakes and oceans, and most species have worldwide distribution. They are small, free-floating algae ranging in size from the single-celled picoplankton, which are less than 5 μm in diameter, to colonial forms the size of peas. Most phytoplankton are not visible to the naked eye but when concentrated are responsible for the characteristic greenish color and reduced transparency of some lake waters.

Phytoplankton in temperate regions usually grow in a series of pulses or blooms. Growth in blooms is based on rapid vegetative reproduction, with slower sexual reproduction occurring only under unfavorable environmental conditions. The first blooms are initiated in spring by the increase in sunlight, and autumn growth is terminated as light decreases late in the season. During the summer, nutrient limitation and zooplankton grazing reduce phytoplankton concentrations. In the tropics and warm low-latitude temperate lakes, growth is continuous when sufficient nutrients are available. In polar regions where sunlight and ice-free periods are brief, there is only a single short bloom. The annual growth cycle of each species is further modified by nutrient availability, the degree of thermal stratification, algal movement, interalgal competition, zooplankton grazing, and parasitism by protozoans, fungi, bacteria, and viruses. Algae have evolved various strategies to overcome nutrient depletion and grazing. These include production of special extracellular enzymes that release chemically bound nutrients and also enzymes within the cell to enhance uptake of low concentrations of nutrients. Some phytoplankton swim or change cell density to reach more favorable light or nutrient conditions. Certain algae form resting stages to survive unfavorable conditions, and others reduce zooplankton grazing by producing toxins or protective gelatinous coats. Large size and ability to reproduce faster than zooplankton can consume them are other methods of survival. Grazing and parasitism delay the time of maximum algal density and may also change species composition to favor unpalatable species such as blue-green algae.

Holoplankton, algae that are always present in the plankton, include the diatoms *Asterionella, Fragilaria,* and *Tabellaria.* They dominate the spring bloom in lakes because they grow faster than competing algae. Blooms may be slowed by zooplankton and protozoan grazing or by infestations of chytrid fungi. Growth eventually stops after thermal stratification because diatoms deplete the nutrients in the epilimnion. The limiting nutrients may be silica (SiO_2), needed for diatom cell walls, phosphorus, nitrogen, or even trace metals, depending on the geographical and geological location of the lake. Diatoms have an advantage over other phytoplankton because a silica cell wall requires much less energy to synthesize than a cellulose wall.

Meroplankton, algae that are sometimes present in the plankton, include the common diatom *Melosira,* dinoflagellates, and some blue-green algae. All meroplankton must have some form of resting stage in the sediments to survive non-bloom periods. In stratified lakes *Melosira* succeeds because it is present in large numbers in the winter plankton. Live cells are resuspended from the sediments during fall or spring overturn. *Melosira* has a low growth rate but takes advantage of the high nutrient levels in early spring and benefits from low levels of competition and grazing. Suspension of heavy filaments of this centric diatom depends on continual vigorous mixing. A few days after thermal stratification, and well before nutrients are depleted, healthy *Melosira* cells sink to the bottom and form resting stages.

Meroplanktonic *blue-green algae (cyanobacteria)* such as *Aphanizomenon, Anabaena,* and *Microcystis* are most common in eutrophic lakes in the warm waters of summer and fall. They overwinter as akinetes, sporelike resting stages. Although blue-green algae grow more slowly than diatoms at low temperatures, they reproduce faster at higher temperatures. Planktonic blue-green algae succeed because they regulate their position in the water column to the depths most favorable for growth. This occurs by a two-step process: (1) production of relatively permanent minute *gas vacuoles* that give a slight positive buoyancy in starved cells; and (2) photosynthetic production of dense carbohydrate during the day, which acts as *ballast* to cause sinking. The bal-

last is used up overnight and the algae float to the surface in the morning to resume the cycle. Floating near the surface shades out competing algae. Large colonies rise or sink much faster than single filaments, and large colonies of blue-greens dominate the summer–fall plankton in eutrophic lakes. Large size and the presence of toxic chemicals that deter feeding reduce losses to zooplankton. A few genera of blue-green algae, such as *Aphanizomenon,* can fix dissolved atmospheric N_2 gas. All other algal groups and many blue-greens lack this ability. Blue-green blooms decline if their flotation fails, if they are stranded on the shore or destroyed by summer sunlight, or if they deplete an essential nutrient. Rapid destruction of large blooms may also occur from cyanophage virus or cytrid fungus attack.

Dinoflagellates, such as *Peridinium* and *Ceratium,* generally grow best in summer and fall because they can actively swim to favorable light and nutrients. The algae are positively phototactic and may form reddish brown surface patches, called *red tides.* Dinoflagellate nutrient requirements are complex and may include organic substrates. Their populations may decline due to zooplankton grazing, competition from other algae, and possibly nutrient depletion.

The cycles of other algae in the plankton are not well understood. Chlorophyte, chrysophyte, cryptophyte, and euglenophyte algae often dominate the reduced summer plankton due to an ability to take up nutrients at low levels and to maintain their position by swimming. In some lakes they also exist below the thermocline and at great depths. Very small algae, the picoplankton, may dominate the oligotrophic waters of the open ocean and a few unproductive lakes.

The spatial distribution of phytoplankton is uneven for almost all species. Surface patches or streaks of blue-green algae or dinoflagellates are often visible in oceans and eutrophic lakes. Rapid reproduction produces a patch of algae only if the growth rate exceeds turbulent dispersion. Uneven grazing by zooplankton can also produce patches. Horizontal patches and vertical layers are also produced by active motion by the algae as they attempt to optimize their light and nutrient conditions.

Attached algae or *periphyton* grow on submerged rocks, mud, and vegetation. Only pennate diatoms, filamentous greens, and blue-greens are common members of the periphyton. Pennate diatoms and blue-greens move over the substrate by gliding, but filamentous greens are fixed. Attached algae follow the cycles of the material on which they grow. Aquatic vegetation dies in winter while storms move rocks and stir sediments. Like phytoplankton the periphyton have seasonal cycles but are more likely to maintain year-round populations if the substrate is stable. Grazing, especially by aquatic insect larvae and snails, is important in regulating periphyton biomass. Much of the interest in periphyton is in their colonization of new sites, which follows a pattern akin to that in terrestrial vegetation where small first colonizers are gradually shaded out by taller species.

In this chapter we discuss measurement of phytoplankton and periphyton; algal movement in water; seasonal cycles, spatial variation, and patchiness of phytoplankton; the relative success of major phytoplankton groups; and the gliding motion and seasonal cycles of periphyton.

INTRODUCTION

Found in all lakes, slow-flowing rivers, estuaries, and oceans, phytoplankton are probably the most common photosynthetic organisms on the planet. They are the ''grass'' of lakes and seas and most species have a worldwide distribution. Some phytoplankton are even found in slow-flowing rivers and quiescent backwaters. Phytoplankton are small, free-floating algae ranging in size from 1 to 5 μm across (picoplankton) to over 100 μm in diameter (large net plankton). Rarely visible to the naked eye, large clumps of phytoplankton range from tiny green specks to colonies the size of lawn clippings. One species forms a colony

as large as a baseball. Dense accumulations of phytoplankton of any size are commonly detected by the yellow-green color they impart to otherwise blue lakes.

Phytoplankton, like terrestrial plants, are seldom distributed completely at random due to variations in reproductive patterns, microhabitat preferences, or grazing. Most have an uneven distribution despite the fact that they are constantly mixed by water movement. The seasonal variations so obvious in the growth of terrestrial plant communities are just as apparent in the phytoplankton (Fig. 12-1). However, the continuous annual accumulation of biomass in the trunks and branches of forest trees has no counterpart in plankton. All phytoplankton biomass is active and photosynthetic, while much of the forest biomass serves only to support the photosynthetic leaves. Like grass, almost all phytoplankters are dependent on a single season's growth or a physical redistribution of resting stages to reach their annual maximum. Following a bloom, phytoplankton biomass is reduced to almost nothing. Virtually all the dynamic features of lakes—color, clarity, trophic state, water chemistry, the taste and odor of the water, animal plankton and fish production—depend to a large degree on phytoplankton. This chapter focuses on temperate and Mediterranean climates; special aspects of tropical, polar, and alpine phytoplankton are covered in Chap. 21. Physiological adaptations to overcome low nutrient levels are discussed in Chaps. 8, 9, and 15.

MEASUREMENT

Phytoplankton samples in the epilimnion are best collected with a tube sampler or small sampling bottle that encloses water at a given depth. Either method collects all phytoplankton, regardless of size. Where only large algae are of interest, plankton nets are adequate. However, in some oligotrophic lakes more than 90 percent of the phytoplankton will pass through even the finest mesh nets. More detailed instructions on sam-

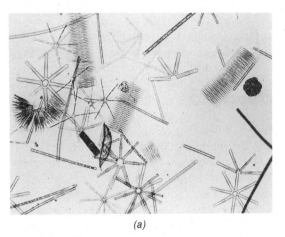
(a)

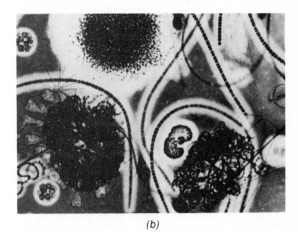
(b)

FIGURE 12-1 Phytoplankton from (*a*) the early spring bloom and (*b*) fall blooms in a mesotrophic lake, the South Basin of Windermere, England. See also Fig. 11-3. (*a*) The dominance of the colonial pennate diatoms, *Asterionella* (slender stars), *Fragilaria* (comblike), *Tabellaria* (stout stars), and filamentous diatoms (*Melosira*) typical of spring blooms (Fig. 12-6). (*b*) The condition in October just before overturn. The plankton is dominated by large colonies of blue-green algae, but diatoms and green algae are also present. Photographs by H. Canter-Lund.

pling are given in *IBP Handbook No. 12* (Vollenweider, 1969) and *Limnological Analysis* (Wetzel and Likens, 1991).

An integrated water sample that contains a representative sample of phytoplankton may be collected with a flexible tube open at both ends. It is lowered through the water column and sealed at the top, usually by bending it double. The entire sample is then recovered by hauling the tube to the surface, using a rope attached to the lower end. Alternatively, the tube can be attached to a pump that continually draws up water from selected depths. A fluorometer may be connected to the flow of water from the tube. This instrument measures the photons emitted by even low levels of chlorophyll *a* pigment excited by light of a particular wavelength. Fluorescence can be calibrated to give a continuous record of living phytoplankton, but its use has limitations in eutrophic systems where chlorophyll *a* exceeds about 10 μg liter^{-1}. At high cell densities, underestimates result from light absorbed by overlapping cells. The light emitted per unit of chlorophyll *a*, called the *fluorescent yield,* varies with the physiological state of the phytoplankton. This variation requires frequent recalibration of the fluorometer against known chlorophyll *a* standards. Algae can also be detected with a submarine turbidity meter, which measures the intensity of a horizontal beam of light as it is lowered through the water. High light extinctions are often due to dense algal concentration (Baker and Brook, 1971), but interference by organic debris or muddy water is a major drawback.

Remote sensing is another method of measuring the surface layer of algae over large areas. This technique usually involves airplanes or satellites equipped with specialized cameras. Limnologists can obtain useful data with a camera in a small airplane or even from nearby mountains (Wrigley and Horne, 1974). Algae and other vegetation reflect certain specific wavelengths (Fig. 3-7). The best results to date have been achieved from eutrophic lakes using the near-infrared band (700 to 800 nm). Striking details of horizontal distribution of algae are revealed using this method of aerial synoptic sampling (Fig. 5-3).

Microscopic identification and counting of natural populations of phytoplankton is difficult to perform with a high degree of accuracy. Although algae are best identified alive, this is rarely possible. Consequently, methods have been developed for preservation, most frequently with iodine, formalin, gluteraldehyde, mercuric chloride, or chloroform. Iodine, usually prepared as Lugol solution, offers the double advantage of making cells heavy enough to settle out for counting and preserving any flagellae. Settling chambers are an excellent method of concentrating the normally dilute algal populations of lakes for microscopic examination and counting (Lund, Kipling, and LeCren, 1958). Small cells may settle so slowly that alternative concentration techniques are required.

Sufficient samples should be taken to determine daily and seasonal vertical and horizontal variations in numbers, particularly for motile dinoflagellates, blue-green algae, and ciliates. The standard technique to account for spatial distribution is *synoptic sampling,* where many samples are taken as rapidly as possible over the entire lake or estuary. Sample collections are normally scheduled for soon after dawn and should take less than 2 hours. They often involve the use of several high-speed boats or even helicopters. In contrast, diel collections require staying in one or more stations over 24 hours and collecting every 1 to 3 hours. Combined diel and synoptic sampling produce a very good picture of the short-term plankton dynamics in lakes and estuaries.

The problem of quantitative sampling of periphyton from natural substrates is only partially solved. They can be scraped, washed, or scrubbed from plants and rocks and collected from sediments by removing a sediment core. A toothbrush, wash bottle, and tweezers can remove most algae, even from cracks in rocks. For collection underwater, a brush mounted inside a syringe barrel is used to scrub the surface and the dislodged periphyton are then sucked into the syringe. Once removed, however, the separation of algae from other detritus is tedious. On sediments, most pennate diatoms will move onto a clean surface provided for them, and this is an excellent method of estimating in situ populations. In most cases investigators circumvent the problem by placing artificial substrates in the water and removing them at intervals afterwards. Almost any substrate—glass slides, clay tiles, or plastic rods—seems to work well. The material, size, and shape can be designed to fit the investigator's requirements. While the method is precise and simple, the species composition and biomass may differ from natural substrates.

ALGAL MOVEMENTS IN WATER

Although phytoplankton are largely at the mercy of water currents, most are slightly heavier than water and tend to sink (Walsby and Reynolds, 1979). Phytoplankton move by swimming or changing their density. For the smaller phytoplankton viscous forces are important and the Reynolds number is low (Chap. 4). Thus the sinking of phytoplankton due to gravity is very slow compared to the descent of a small stone. Sinking is slowed down by viscous drag on cell walls and reversed by upward turbulent mixing. Turbulent downward mixing also occurs. Some periphyton can move across the substratum, but most have less need of motion since they are attached to the substrata and exposed to a moving layer of water.

Algae deplete the nutrients in the water immediately around them, resulting in a diffusion shell through which fresh nutrients must pass. At these small dimensions and low Reynolds number the water is more viscous and the rate of supply or transport of nutrients through the diffusion shell is affected by cell motion. When the cell moves relative to the water, the diffusion shell becomes somewhat stretched and thinner, allowing more rapid contact with a fresh nutrient supply. This is similar to the way the windshield

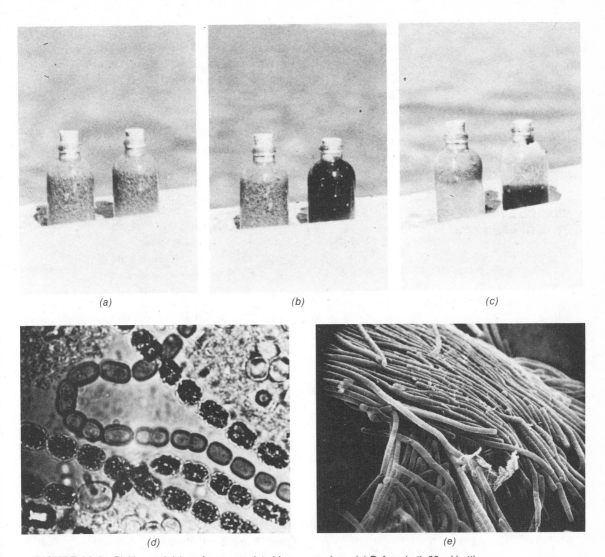

(a)   *(b)*   *(c)*

(d)   *(e)*

FIGURE 12-3 Sinking and rising of gas vacuolate blue-green algae. (*a*) Before, both 60-ml bottles contain equally distributed algae. (*b*) Immediately after collapse of gas vacuoles (right-hand bottle). The squashing of the vacuoles was caused by applying a pressure of about 4 atm by gently hammering the cork into the bottle to simulate the osmotic pressure caused by small-molecular-weight sugars produced by photosynthesis. The dark (green) color is due to the lack of reflection of white light when gas vacuoles collapse. (*c*) Thirty seconds after pressure was applied, the control algae have floated to the surface and those with collapsed vacuoles have sunk. This experiment indicates the strong permanent positive buoyancy found in most colonial populations and mimics natural diel changes in some genera (see text). This algal population was composed mostly of *Microcystis, Aphanizomenon* flakes, and *Anabaena* from Clear Lake, California. Large colonies (*e*) increase rising or sinking speeds. (*d*) Photomicrograph made using color infrared film showing filaments of *Anabaena* with intact gas vacuoles (filaments above and below) and with vacuoles collapsed (central clear filament). Infrared light is reflected by the gas vacuoles (Fig. 3-7). Also visible is a heterocyst (large clear cell at lower left). Photograph by H. M. Anderson. (*e*) SEM photograph of a bundle of *Aphanizomenon* filaments in typical flake form ($\times 370$). Photograph by H. W. Paerl.

availability of nutrients. The directional photo-tactic movement of dinoflagellates and ciliates gives rise to spectacular red tides in oceans and lakes. Their movement allows access to optimum light, temperature, and nutrients. In addition, mobile phytoplankton can shade out competing algae as well as rooted higher plants in shallow lakes. The energy requirements for this type of swimming, discussed later in this chapter, are high.

SEASONAL CYCLES OF PHYTOPLANKTON

Phytoplankton are subject to strong seasonal influences. In the temperate and polar zones there is great contrast between summer and winter, and in the tropics between rainy and dry seasons. Algae respond to this constant rearrangement of the physical and chemical structure of their environment with characteristic population fluctuations. A typical composite picture of seasonal cycles of biomass and species composition in the temperate zone is given in Fig. 12-4.

There are three obvious features of the seasonal cycle: the large spring diatom bloom, the smaller irregular summer peaks of various flagellates, and the large autumnal bloom of diatoms, blue-green algae, and dinoflagellates (Fig. 12-1a, b). The term *bloom* simply indicates relatively large amounts of phytoplankton. Blooms occur when cell numbers greatly exceed their annual average or background concentrations or when a certain level is reached, for example, 5 million cells per liter. A bloom is also evident when algae color the water. Figure 12-4 describes a typical seasonal bloom pattern, but there are lakes where other algal types replace those shown and there are seasonal cycles where peaks of algal abundance are less pronounced. We describe well-known examples of spring, summer, and fall blooms and trace some of the causes. Reviews on seasonal variation of phytoplankton by Lund (1965), Morris (1980), Harris, (1986), Fogg and Thake (1987), and the Societas Inter-nationalis Limnologiae (1971) are listed in the further readings at the end of this chapter.

Changes in phytoplankton numbers (dC/dt) can be expressed by the following conceptual equation:

$$\frac{dC}{dt} = \frac{dP}{dt} C - (S + G + Pa + D) \quad (2)$$

where C = algal cell concentration

$\frac{dP}{dt}$ = rate of photosynthesis

S = sinking out of algae to below the photic zone

G = zooplankton grazing

Pa = parasitism or disease

D = natural death or senescence

Each of these factors is considered here, but it is important to realize that it is not yet possible to solve the above equation because S, G, Pa, and D have rarely been measured in natural plankton. Changes in both phytoplankton biomass and species succession are of more than academic interest. Increases in algal biomass can produce more of some fish species but may eliminate others by robbing the hypolimnion of dissolved oxygen. Increases in the "wrong" species of algae, for example blue-green scums, can destroy the potential of a lake or reservoir for recreation or as a drinking water supply. With increasing human population and a limited number of lakes and reservoirs, understanding the seasonal succession of the phytoplankton is essential for limnologists and water managers alike.

At one time it was thought that the phytoplankton seasonal cycles were a relatively simple series of algal successions of limited relevance to community dynamics or the food web (Smayda, 1980). Modern techniques that allow the comparison of field and laboratory results, especially those using mesocosms, has changed the outlook so that phytoplankton ecology has become an exciting area of limnology. We describe how several different types of algae dom-

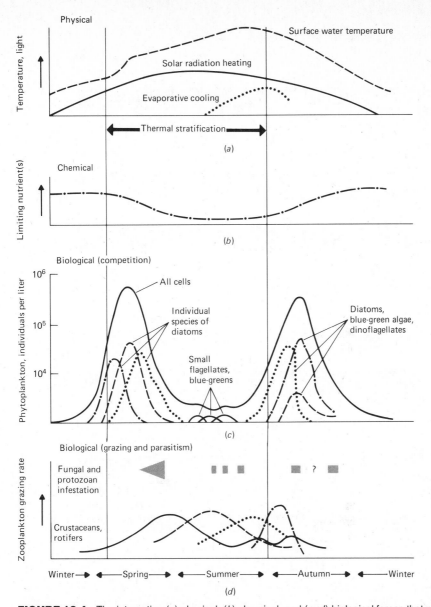

FIGURE 12-4 The interacting (*a*) physical, (*b*) chemical, and (*c*, *d*) biological forces that regulate phytoplankton seasonal cycles. The spring bloom is caused by a physical effect, the increase of sunlight and solar heating. High growth rates occur only after thermal stratification, since unstratified plankton mix through the entire water column and receive insufficient light. Stratification cuts off the supply of nutrients from the hypolimnion, and one or more elements may successively or alternately limit daily growth. The rising temperature increases zooplankton grazing rates and microbial parasitic attacks. Both of these may decimate spring blooms. Diatoms in spring enjoy high nutrients, adequate light, and, at least initially, low grazing and predation. Zooplankton select diatoms and avoid large algae, some of which are toxic. The decline of the spring diatom bloom is due to grazing and/or nutrient depletion. Small summer blooms of large blue-green algae or rapidly reproducing small flagellates chemically deter, avoid, or outgrow predation, and nutrients recycle rapidly at low concentrations. The summer bloom is comprised of algae that can survive grazing and parasites as well as low nutrient(s). Destratification in the fall due to evaporative cooling increases nutrients: light is still adequate, but the higher temperatures allow zooplankton grazing and perhaps parasitism to play a larger role. Thus large algae such as blue-greens and dinoflagellates, as well as diatoms, are present. The fall bloom is caused by the descent of the thermocline, bringing nutrients to those algae that can survive grazing.

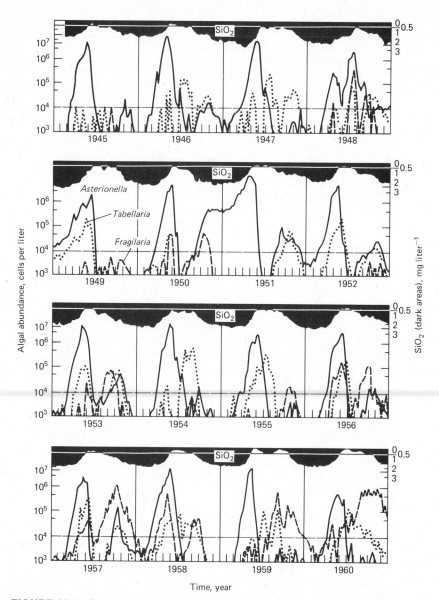

FIGURE 12-5 Seasonal changes in the limiting nutrient, silica, and in the major diatom genera in the North Basin of Windermere, 1945–1960. Solid line = *Asterionella formosa,* dashed line = *Fragilaria crotonensis,* dotted line = *Tabellaria flocculosa* var. *asterionelloides,* black = dissolved silica in surface waters. Note the regular seasonal cycles in most years. Modified from Lund, (1964).

inate the lake biota and then deduce some reasons for their relative success.

The Spring Bloom of a Holoplanktonic Diatom: *Asterionella formosa*

Holoplankton (*holo* = ''totally'') are algae that are always present in the plankton, as distinct from *meroplankton,* which spend some of their life cycle in a dormant form, usually in the sediments. Most open ocean algae are holoplanktonic, while lake and coastal forms may be either holoplanktonic or meroplanktonic.

Asterionella is a common diatom in the spring bloom of temperate lakes throughout the world (Figs. 12-1*a,* 12-5, 12-6). The spring bloom provides grazing for zooplankton, which in turn, feed young fish during the crucial posthatching period. The conditions necessary for initiation of a bloom of a holoplanktonic such as *Asterionella* may be summarized as follows: sufficient light and nutrients and freedom from severe parasitism and grazing. The increasing sunlight in spring, not temperature rise, remains the key force, just as it is for the spring growth of land plants.

A problem in describing algal blooms arises from the use of the term *growth rate,* which is often inferred from the rate of population increase in the lake. Although very rapid cell division rates do occur, the lake population may actually rise quite slowly. During periods of rapid growth, losses from increases in sedimentation, grazing, and parasitism tend to create the fairly uniform increase in population numbers actually observed.

Asterionella continues to increase and dominate the spring population as long as it has the necessary light, nutrients, and freedom from predation. Its dominance over potential competition from other diatoms, such as *Fragilaria* and *Tabellaria,* or blue-green algae, such as *Oscillatoria,* is maintained because *Asterionella* can grow faster than the competing algae under these conditions. In addition, *Asterionella,* like many algae, has the ability to store one of the major growth-limiting nutrients, phosphorus, in a nontoxic form. As much as 100 times the amount needed for cell structure and function can be stored as polyphosphate granules by the process of ''luxury consumption'' (Chap. 9). *Asterionella* can reduce phosphate in lakes to very low levels, and the population can be sustained on stored phosphorus for a considerable time even when external phosphate is apparently limiting.

FIGURE 12-6 The spring bloom of the holoplanktonic diatom *Asterionella* in the North Basin of Windermere in relation to the critical limiting nutrient silica. The similar diatom *Tabellaria* is uncommon and sporadic, and *Fragilaria* is usually found later in the year (see Fig. 12-7 for exceptions). Note that the maximum bloom population in the water is 500 or 2000 times that of the winter population (exceptionally, 50,000 times). This is typical for holoplankton, which must have fast growth rates (high μ) to increase from a small overwintering inoculum and to survive grazing. Redrawn from Lund (1964) and Heron (1961).

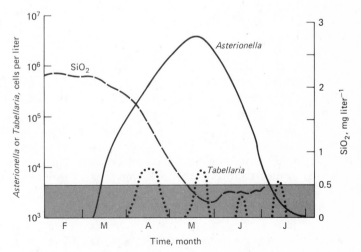

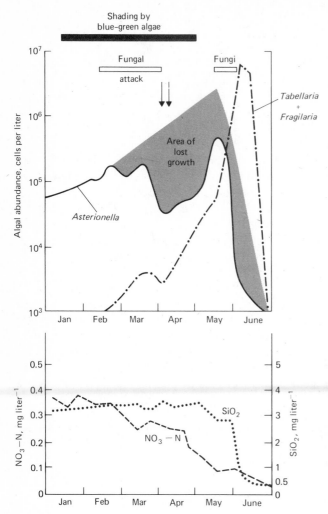

FIGURE 12-7 Interaction of physical, chemical, and biological factors in a diatom spring bloom. See Fig. 12-4 for simplified version. ($\downarrow\downarrow$ = floods). The cytrid fungi infestation is species-specific and here is confined to *Asterionella*, thus the slower-growing competing diatoms *Tabellaria* and *Fragilaria* become more abundant than normal. Floods wash out and thus reduce all algae. The nutrients nitrate and silicate have no effect until SiO_2 reaches low levels (0.5 mg liter^{-1}). Shading by blue-green algae, *Oscillatoria*, hinders a rapid start to the diatom bloom since *Oscillatoria* floats near the lake surface. Based on Lund (1949; 1950).

The role of nitrogen as a limiting element in some blooms of *Asterionella* appears to be small. As in most temperate climates, rain falls in the English Lake District all year, and nitrate is continually fed to the lake via rivers. Silicon, which falls from 3.0 to 0.5 mg liter^{-1} (as SiO_2), is believed to play the major role in limiting the *Asterionella* bloom in Windermere (Fig. 12-6).

Without parasitism, *Asterionella* will grow faster than competing phytoplankton such as *Fragilaria*. However, the situation changes when parasitism favors competing algae (Fig. 12-7). Important phytoplankton parasites include primitive single-cell aquatic fungi called *chytrids*, which are host-specific (Chap. 11). Chytrids attach to one member of an *Asterionella* colony (Fig. 12-8). The fungi penetrate algal cells using their pseudopodia, eventually killing them. The parasites then form spores that are released to the water to infect other cells. Chytrid attacks, like many other infectious epidemics, occur when a large number of individuals live close

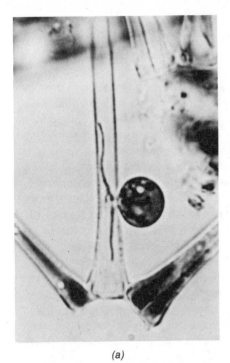
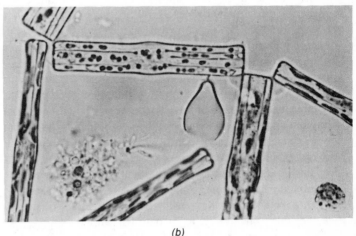

(a)   (b)

FIGURE 12-8 Predation of the spring diatom bloom by cytrid fungi. (*a*) *Zygorhizidium affluens* infecting *Asterionella*. The young sporangium of this primitive fungus has two internal rhizoidal threads, which have digested most of a diatom cell. The two adjacent ones are still alive and still full of cell material (×1900). (*b*) The dehisced sporangium (empty cell case) of *Chytridium versatile* on a *Tabellaria* colony (×800). When the fungus was present, the rhizoidal threads destroyed one individual but, again, adjacent cells are still alive as shown by their large chloroplasts. Photographs by H. Canter-Lund.

together, as occurs during the spring bloom. While *Asterionella* is infected, its population growth rate is reduced to below that of other algae, such as *Tabellaria* and *Fragilaria,* which then overtake the *Asterionella* population (Fig. 12-7). Nevertheless, when *Asterionella* eventually recovers from the chytrid infection, it may once again outgrow other plankton algae so long as nutrients remain plentiful.

Diatoms also compete with other types of algae. In Windermere there is competition for light between diatoms and the blue-green alga *Oscillatoria*. In its colonial filamentous form *Oscillatoria* is holoplanktonic in Windermere and Esthwaite Water and overwinters in moderate

numbers even under the occasional ice cover. *Oscillatoria* blooms can shade *Asterionella*, reducing growth (Fig. 12-7) but when the *Oscillatoria* populations decrease, *Asterionella* resumes vigorous growth.

An important consideration in phytoplankton ecology is the dilute nature of the cell suspension in lakes compared to those grown in culture flasks. Optimal light and high nutrients enable laboratory cultures to reach 10^9 (1 billion) or even 10^{10} cells liter^{-1}. Under natural conditions in lakes, 10^7 cells liter^{-1} may be the maximum for any one species. At typical lake phytoplankton densities, there are sufficient light and nutrients for *Asterionella* and *Oscillatoria* to coexist. Coexistence of this sort occurs in many algal populations.

Algal blooms generally end quite suddenly (Figs. 12-4, 12-5). The possible reasons for bloom decline are physical (no light), chemical (lack of nutrients), or biological (grazing). There is no shortage of light when *Asterionella* declines in summer, and this species can grow at temperatures from 0.5 to 24°C. However, higher temperatures promote higher growth rates, which increase nutrient consumption. The effect of grazing by zooplankton or parasitism is apparently negligible for *Asterionella* in Windermere, although this may not be true for other lakes. Nitrogen and phosphorus are not below critical levels inside the cell, and Lund (1950) found in the English Lake District that silicon is the critical factor which eventually limits the bloom of *Asterionella*. The role of silicon as a limiting nutrient is confined to diatoms, because the cell wall is made from silica (SiO_2; Chap. 10). Silica, a form of opaline glass, is not readily recycled in lakes; fresh supplies come from river inflows in winter. The amount of dissolved silica in early spring after stratification determines the maximum spring diatom population, assuming another nutrient does not become limiting first. When silica drops below 0.5 mg liter^{-1} in Windermere (Fig. 12-7), growth of *Asterionella* stops. Below this level the enzyme uptake systems in this species are unable to extract silica from the water. *Asterionella* blooms decline rapidly because each cell requires a minimum level of about 140 pg (picogram $= 10^{-12}$ g) of silica per cell. Cells continue to divide even without sufficient silica, but the resultant daughter cells have thin walls and die. In some English lakes, this chemical factor, rather than physical conditions, grazing, or competition, terminates the *Asterionella* bloom in late spring.

Asterionella in the English Lake District provides a good example of silicon as a growth-limiting element. Other diatoms, for example the common marine diatom *Sketetonema*, have more flexible requirements for silica and can tolerate

a thinner cell wall. *Asterionella* populations may be controlled in some lakes by other factors as well. For example, lake residence time (Chap. 2), nitrate, and phosphate levels can be important, and the rule that *Asterionella* growth stops at 0.5 mg liter^{-1} SiO_2 is not true in all lakes. In other lakes in England, nitrogen, competition with *Stephanodiscus,* parasitism, or physical factors may limit growth before lack of silica at the 0.5 mg liter^{-1} level occurs (Hutchinson, 1957).

In the Laurentian Great Lakes and many other temperate zone waters, phosphate limits phytoplankton growth in unpolluted diatom-dominated areas (Figs. 9-5, 15-9), while silica or nitrogen may play a similar role in the more eutrophic waters. Regardless of which factor limits growth at any one time, the interaction of the three structural elements—physical (light), chemical, and biological (chytrid predation and competition from other diatoms and blue-green algae)—makes the spring bloom of *Asterionella* in the English lakes a valuable case study in limnology.

The Spring Bloom of a Meroplanktonic Diatom: *Melosira italica*

Melosira is a large chain-forming diatom abundant in many lakes and estuaries. The seasonal cycle we describe here is derived from studies of warm monomictic English lakes; it has many features in common with cycles in dimictic or polymictic lakes elsewhere in the world. Various species of *Melosira* are common in lakes as varied as Siberian Lake Baikal, African tropical Lake Tanganyika, and temperate Lake Biwa, Japan (Skabitchewsky, 1929; Kozov, 1963; Mori and Miura, 1980). We choose this cycle because of the detailed studies carried out over the last 30 years by Lund (1954; 1971).

The bloom cycle of the meroplankton *Melosira* in the English lakes (Fig. 12-9) is quite different from that of *Asterionella*. *Melosira* is a winter-spring species most abundant in the plankton from October to May; its numbers peak

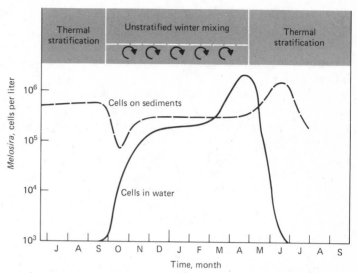

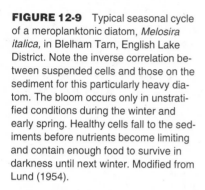

FIGURE 12-9 Typical seasonal cycle of a meroplanktonic diatom, *Melosira italica,* in Blelham Tarn, English Lake District. Note the inverse correlation between suspended cells and those on the sediment for this particularly heavy diatom. The bloom occurs only in unstratified conditions during the winter and early spring. Healthy cells fall to the sediments before nutrients become limiting and contain enough food to survive in darkness until next winter. Modified from Lund (1954).

well before the annual spring maximum of *Asterionella.* Despite light conditions that are unfavorable to growth, the increase of *Melosira* in the fall is more rapid than that of *Asterionella* in spring. This is due to a massive resuspension of resting cells from the sediments. Without any growth, *Melosira* numbers rapidly rise to 100,000 times that of the nonbloom population, and during winter there is little loss to grazing parasitism.

Comparing the cycle of *Asterionella* (Fig. 12-6) with that of *Melosira* (Fig. 12-9), one can see that the sudden large increase in numbers of *Melosira* in autumn coincides with the breakdown of the summer thermal stratification. Simultaneously, the number of *Melosira* cells in the lake sediment decreases by about 200 times. In fact, the number of cells in the sediment is inversely related to that in the plankton (Fig. 12-9). The cells first found after the fall overturn are visibly distinct from the later winter-spring population and are accompanied by fungal threads characteristic of bottom deposits. *Melosira* is a heavy diatom with a thick silica cell wall and cannot remain in the plankton without vigorous mixing. Holomictic stirring (Chap. 4) occurs in mon-

omictic lakes throughout the winter, which keeps *Melosira* suspended. Despite the high nutrient levels, the lack of light slows growth rates. In spring, light provides the necessary energy for increased photosynthesis and growth. In dimictic lakes with winter ice cover, *Melosira* must wait until after ice-out for holomictic stirring and growth to begin. Resuspension of *Melosira* in very deep monomictic lakes, such as Loch Ness, Scotland, is also delayed until early spring, when the lakes may finally mix top to bottom.

Growth of *Melosira* in spring is slow relative to *Asterionella* and other holoplankton. One winter cell of *Melosira* can multiply to only about 200 before the bloom ceases. In contrast, *Asterionella* increases by 500 to 2000 times each spring. Before nutrients become limiting, the *Melosira* bloom declines when thermal stratification cuts off deep mixing. The heavy *Melosira* cells then sink through the thermocline during the first period of calm weather (Fig. 12-9).

Melosira survives anoxic conditions in the lake sediments for up to 2 years, while other algae usually die. Because *Melosira* cells drop to the bottom early in the season, they are healthy and not nutrient-depleted. These cells then form a physiological resting stage with a low respiratory rate biochemically akin to a spore. Their low oxygen demand enables *Melosira* to survive virtually anoxic conditions in the sediments of eutrophic lakes.

Although *Melosira* is unlikely to experience a nutrient shortage before stratification occurs, if a lake is destratified by artificial mixing, nutrient depletion could occur. This was demonstrated by Lund (1971), who induced nutrient depletion by mixing and caused mass deaths of *Melosira* cells. He concluded that continual year-round mixing prevented many healthy resting cells from reaching the sediments to supply the innoculum for the next season's bloom.

In the English Lake District chytrid fungal infections and zooplankton grazing do not influence the seasonal cycle of *Melosira*. *Melosira* is larger than most chain-forming diatoms and is not ingested by most zooplankton. In some estuaries, however, waves produce shearing forces that break up long diatom chains, which are then more easily ingested by zooplankton.

Because the sediment supplies all the cells of meroplanktonic algae for initiating the next year's spring bloom, the size of one year's maximum can influence the seed population the following year. Late winter storms, if severe, may mix deeper into the sediment and increase the percentage of cells resuspended regardless of the last season's maximum. In the deepest lakes, sediment may be disturbed only in years of the strongest winter storms. Large winter floods can bury sunken populations with sediment or wash out suspended algae. Since cells do not grow at this time, they do not replace themselves. The resulting lower spring innoculum in turn produces a smaller spring crop.

Eutrophic polymictic lakes with continual vigorous wind mixing and ample nutrients should provide ideal conditions for one or more of the many species of the genus *Melosira*. However, there are few naturally eutrophic lakes with continuous large supplies of all nutrients.

Seasonal Cycles of Blue-Green Algae

Blue-green algae (cyanobacteria) are generally less important as food for zooplankton than are most other algae, although there are exceptions, particularly in some tropical waters. Like thistles left alone by cows in a grassy field, blue-green algae are weeds among the more nutritious populations of diatoms, dinoflagellates, and green algae. Most zooplankton are deterred by the size or taste of blue-green algae and either ignore them or, if collected, soon reject them from their feeding apparatus.

Blue-green algae cause unsightly algal scums on eutrophic lakes and shade out other algae and macrophytes that contribute more to the fishery. A blue-green algal bloom in a lake is often the first obvious sign of cultural eutrophication. For this reason, it seems paradoxical that blue-green algae are often abundant when nutrient concentrations are low. Cultural eutrophication and the inflow of sewage distort nutrient cycles; it is better to consider the interaction of blue-greens with pollution using applied limnology and lake management techniques (Chap. 22).

Most blue-green algae blooms occur in the late summer or autumn (Fig. 12-4), although spring blooms and year-round growths are known. Blue-green algae in lakes may be holoplanktonic or meroplanktonic, but since many species form spores meroplankton is probably more typical. We will discuss spring and fall blooms of two types of blue-green algae: those like *Aphanizomenon* and *Anabaena* that often fix N_2 and those like *Microcystis* and *Oscillatoria* that cannot fix N_2. All of these algae contain gas vacuoles and regulate their buoyancy.

The Spring Blue-Green Bloom

Polymictic Clear Lake, California, has a small overwintering population and a large, almost unialgal, spring bloom of *Aphanizomenon,* a summer bloom of *Anabaena* followed by *Microcystis,* and an *Aphanizomenon* bloom in early

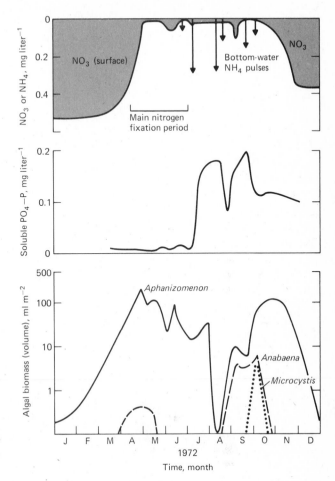

FIGURE 12-10 Spring and fall blooms of the blue-green algae *Aphanizomenon, Anabaena,* and *Microcystis* in warm unstratified Clear Lake, California, in relation to the cycles of nitrogen and phosphorus. Note that N_2 fixation allows continued spring growth after nitrate is used up (see also Fig. 8-2). Ammonia is low at this time. Phosphorus is always naturally in excess in this lake, which is surrounded by easily eroded soils (Chap. 2). Ammonia released from the sediment in summer is a result of the decomposition of the spring bloom. Ammonia stimulates the growth of the non-N_2-fixing *Microcystis*. Nitrogen is not the only reason for the success of these three blue-green algae, which form large colonies and show considerable buoyancy regulation. Redrawn from Horne (1975).

winter (Fig. 12-10). Crose Mere is a warm monomictic, stratified lake in England (Fig. 12-11), and many lakes in the United States have a similar pattern.

The large spring *Aphanizomenon* population in eutrophic Clear Lake initially dominates because of gas vacuole buoyancy. Nutrients are plentiful at this time, but rain and muddy inflows make the lake turbid in winter. Thus only floating algae can get enough light to grow in the early spring. When nitrate and ammonia are depleted, growth of *Aphanizomenon* continues unabated into early summer due to N_2 fixation and the

continued shading out of competing algae. The necessary phosphorus is supplied from zooplankton recycling and from the sediments. In Clear Lake and most other lakes, parasitism or animal grazing of blue-greens is unimportant in regulating bloom size or timing. Growth of *Aphanizomenon* ceases in summer, probably due to a lack of soluble iron needed for N_2 fixation (Figs. 10-8, 12-12) and the intense sunlight that kills this alga when near the surface. *Aphanizomenon* forms large-radius flakelike colonies that can float rapidly to the surface (Fig. 12-2a, 12-3). Other eutrophic lakes, such as Upper Klamath

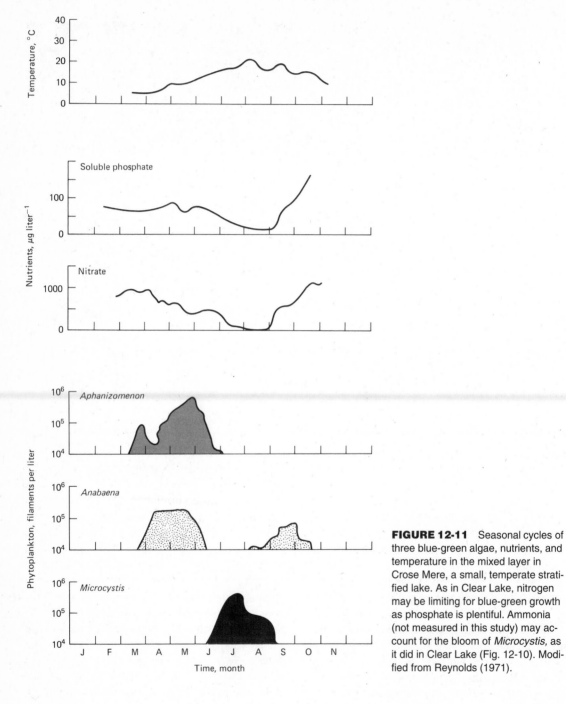

FIGURE 12-11 Seasonal cycles of three blue-green algae, nutrients, and temperature in the mixed layer in Crose Mere, a small, temperate stratified lake. As in Clear Lake, nitrogen may be limiting for blue-green growth as phosphate is plentiful. Ammonia (not measured in this study) may account for the bloom of *Microcystis,* as it did in Clear Lake (Fig. 12-10). Modified from Reynolds (1971).

Algal genus	Suggested controlling factors					
Aphanizomenon	1 Algal buoyancy 2 Low sunlight 3 Water turbidity	1 Buoyancy	1 Nitrogen fixation 2 Lack of grazing	1 Lack of Fe 2 Light induced death	1 Buoyancy	1 Algal buoyancy 2 Low light
Anabaena	1 Low sunlight 2 Water turbidity	Poor buoyancy relative to *Aphanizomenon*	?	Lack of Fe	Nitrogen fixation	? 1 Low light 2 Water turbidity
Microcystis	1 Low sunlight 2 Water turbidity	Lack of NH₄		Rate of supply of NH₄		1 Low light 2 Water turbidity

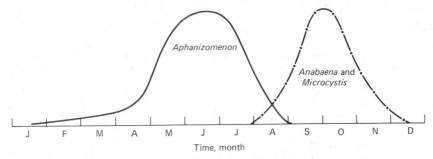

FIGURE 12-12 Suggested factors controlling the blue-green algal blooms in Clear Lake, California. Note that many factors interact to regulate the bloom and that these factors change over the seasons. Modified from Horne (1975).

Lake, Oregon, and Smith Lake, Alaska, have a winter ice cover but quickly become warm in spring. In these lakes, spring blue-green blooms after ice-out are often preceded by a short period of diatom growth before the water warms up. Periods of low surface temperatures (4 to 8°C) in spring provide well-illuminated turbulent conditions that favor diatom growth over that of blue-greens.

In late spring or early summer, nutrients in eutrophic lakes become limiting for blue-green algae despite their advantages of gas vacuoles and luxury phosphorus consumption. The nutrients most likely to become depleted are nitrogen, phosphorus, and iron. Which of these becomes depleted first differs from lake to lake, but because it comprises 5 percent of the cell nitrogen is often the first nutrient to be depleted in natural or culturally eutrophic lakes. Under such circumstances, blue-green algae often fix N_2 gas.

The role of N_2 fixation in lakes, including Clear Lake, was described in Chap. 8. We need only mention here that N_2 fixation allows *Aphanizomenon* to continue growth when it has depleted the winter accumulation of nitrate. Figure 12-10 shows the close correlation of *Aphanizomenon* growth, N_2 fixation, and the decline of nitrate. Also correlated is an increase in heterocysts, which are the actual site of N_2 fixation. The ability to fix N_2 allows *Aphanizomenon* to extend its period of dominance and increase its maximum standing crop above that which could be sustained by the nitrate in the lake.

The very dense spring-summer bloom of *Aphanizomenon* in Clear Lake declines rapidly in midsummer, probably from a lack of iron. The enzyme that carries out nitrogen fixation contains iron, and in this lake concentrations of soluble iron are particularly low (Fig. 10-7), whereas phosphate supplies from animal excretion and from the sediments are high (Fig. 9-3c). Cessation of growth does not explain the decline of a population that is not grazed or parasitized. One possibility is death by overexposure to sunlight. Damage to the photosynthetic apparatus by sunlight in oligotrophic high-altitude or high-latitude lakes occurs in all phytoplankton, not just blue-greens. The initial effect of high light is a bleaching of the chlorophyll and then destruction of the DNA in chloroplasts by ultraviolet light. This short-wavelength light penetrates only a short distance in lakes, so surface blooms are most affected. Death is probably due to the photooxidative disruption of the cells followed by lysis and disintegration. As explained previously, blue-greens can modify their buoyancy to maintain themselves close to optimal light intensities. Normally they sink down to avoid high midday light. However, buoyancy regulation requires the synthesis of sugars or carbohydrate ballast, which are supplied only by active photosynthesis. When nutrient depletion reduces photosynthesis, the algae lose the ability to sink and are trapped at the lake surface. This occurs in midsummer in Clear Lake when the sun is at its maximum and a rapid destruction of surface algae by sunlight can occur. Two hours of sunlight can destroy as much as 80 percent of the *Aphanizomenon* population (Horne and Wrigley, 1975). The *Aphanizomenon* population of Upper Klamath Lake, Oregon, has an adequate nutrient supply and survives summer conditions without the spectacular mortality found in Clear Lake. Presumably this results from a more continuous nutrient supply in this very shallow lake and the consequent ability to photosynthesize and regulate buoyancy.

The Late Summer-Autumn Blue-Green Bloom

Fall blooms of blue-green algae are common in many temperate lakes (Figs. 12-4, 12-11, 12-12). In Clear Lake, the spring bloom is followed by late summer-autumn blooms of *Anabaena* and *Microcystis*. Unicellular *Microcystis* aggregates into large clumps in a firm mucus matrix and containing up to a million cells. It is a major nuisance species and is of particular interest because it cannot fix N_2 gas. The two factors explaining its abundance are increased animal and bacterial recycling of ammonia in summer and, again, shading out of other algae.

Blue-greens may possess very efficient mechanisms for the uptake of nutrients at low concentrations. In warm lakes, almost all planktonic blue-green algae can compete successfully with other species for nutrients. When nitrogen limits summer growth, *Microcystis* is dependent on ammonia supplied by animal and bacterial excretion in the water or sediments. Recycling via the microbial loop (Chap. 15) and internal loading from the shallow sediments account for much of the nutrient needs of *Microcystis,* even when the free concentration of nutrients is very low. Large populations cannot be created by recycling the small pool of euphotic-zone nutrients, so a bloom of *Microcystis* must be supplied partially by ammonia from the anoxic sediments. In stratified lakes nitrogen is supplied to the epilimnion from the lowering of the thermocline in autumn (Chap. 4). The amount of ammonia released in two contrasting basins of Clear Lake is different. The ammonia level in the bottom waters, which soon mixes into the euphotic zone, is much greater in one basin than in the other, and the size of the *Microcystis* bloom correlates well with the larger benthic releases of ammonia.

Horizontal transport by the wind is an advantage unique to blue-greens in all seasons. The great buoyancy of flakes of *Aphanizomenon,* large coils of *Anabaena,* and clumps of *Microcystis* carries them to the very surface of the water on calm mornings, where they form dense patches only a few centimeters thick. These patches often move with the wind at a much higher speed than the rest of the water column. The physical mechanism for this differential transport is not clear, but the patch water is warmer than its surroundings. An infrared videotape of the water surface in eutrophic lakes on a calm morning indicates a complex series of moving plumes and patches of warmer and colder waters. After a few minutes, algae are transported to a position over a different deep water mass (Figs. 5-3, 5-4). If a colony then sinks using buoyancy regulation or is mixed down by the wind, it reaches a new water mass, which may provide a better source of nutrients. Horizontal movements of surface algae and the ability to rise and sink are unique advantages because little energy is required for either process.

Dinoflagellates and Red Tides

Unlike the blue-green algae, dinoflagellates can quickly regulate their position by swimming. Dinoflagellates are usually large phytoplankton and can move at speeds of meters per hour. They are phototactic, and normally swim up to the surface in the morning for photosynthesis and then down again in late afternoon. During a dinoflagellate bloom, these movements result in surface masses in lakes, estuaries, and the ocean that are clearly visible to the naked eye. These blooms, called *red tides* but actually more brown or vermilion, are occasionally spectacular.

In Clear Lake a red tide of *Peridinium pernardii* formed a dense band some 20 m wide and about 40 km long near the shore in spring (Horne et al., 1971). This bloom was caused by a combination of late floods that retarded the growth of its spring competitor *Aphanizomenon* and a period of calm sunny weather that warmed the nearshore lake sediments. Heating the mud increases the bacterial release of nutrients and growth factors such as vitamins, which are essential for dinoflagellate growth but not necessary for most other phytoplankton. It is possible that organic nutrients released from the warm sediments could be used directly by *Peridinium,* since some dinoflagellates can feed in both autotrophic and heterotrophic modes.

Dinoflagellate blooms are not well understood in most lakes or oceans, but considerable knowledge has been gained from some rather unusual lakes in the Austrian Alps (Fig. 21-10) and the desert Lake Kinneret (also known as Lake Tiberias or Sea of Galilee). *Peridinium* blooms are common and quite regular in Lake Kinneret (Berman and Rodhe, 1971) and may reach nuisance levels in spring (Fig. 12-13a) at the nearshore surface (Fig. 12-13b). In Lake Kinneret, as in Clear Lake, California, there is interalgal competition in spring between *Peridinium* and *Microcystis.* Though the mechanisms may not be the same in all lakes, the species that blooms first prevents the bloom of the other. Unlike marine red tides, whose initiation is still largely a mystery, some freshwater red tides can now be predicted with near certainty (Serruya and Pollingher, 1971). Dinoflagellate and ciliate red tides also occur in estuaries, but the salt wedge produces some unique conditions that do not apply in lakes. The movements, physiology, and physical processes that concentrate and dissipate red tides in estuarine waters are described in Chap. 19 (Seliger et al., 1970; Fig. 19-14).

SPATIAL VARIATIONS: VERTICAL AND HORIZONTAL PATCHINESS

Vertical Variations

Almost all phytoplankton show vertical variations in abundance through the euphotic zone, despite mixing by wind and waves. There are usually more phytoplankton in the surface layers because there is more sunlight there. For diatoms, green algae, and small flagellates, vertical variations are usually small except at the density gradient of the thermocline. Here sinking cells accumulate and provide a concentrated source of food for zooplankton, bacteria, and fungi. A typical vertical distribution of a diatom species in unstratified waters is shown in Fig. 12-14a, and a rare example of almost uniform distribution is shown for isothermal waters during the summer season in Fig. 12-14b.

A very different picture is presented by motile algae, which form concentrated thin layers near the thermocline. One good example of such mi-

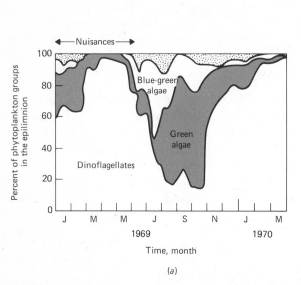

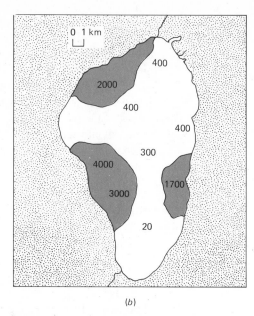

(a)   (b)

FIGURE 12-13 Temporal and spatial distribution of dinoflagellate "red tides" in Lake Kinneret. (a) Seasonal distribution of phytoplankton. Note the dominance of dinoflagellates (mostly *Peridinium*) and the virtual absence of diatoms (dotted area) in this warm, well-stratified Mediterranean lake. The color of dense surface patches in spring is easily seen, and they may become nuisances for beach users. (b) Horizontal distribution of *Peridinium* cells (shaded areas, in cells ml^{-1}) in March 1970. Note the extreme horizontal patchiness of these algae. Both figures after Berman and Rodhe (1971).

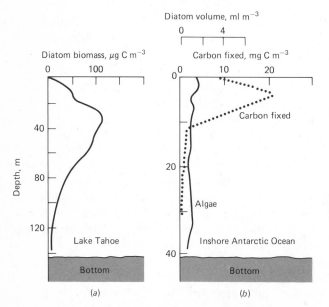

(a)   (b)

FIGURE 12-14 Vertical distribution of phytoplankton. Changes in biomass with depth for two diatom species in the photic zone of unstratified systems. (a) Uneven distribution of *Cyclotella ocellata* in Lake Tahoe in April 1976. In this transparent lake, 20 to 60 m may be the optimal depth for growth at this time and primary production shows a similar vertical profile (Fig. 15-12). Redrawn from Lopez and Richerson (unpublished). (b) Uniform distribution of the giant chain-forming diatom, *Biddulphia striata*, in very well-mixed antarctic waters. Even though primary production peaks near the surface, the constant storms (winds up to 160 km h^{-1}) and the very cold summer water (0°C) mix the water column continuously and maintain a rare uniform diatom distribution. Redrawn from Horne et al. (1969).

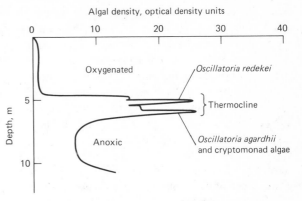

FIGURE 12-15 Vertical distribution of motile phytoplankton: cryptomonads and blue-green algae in a very strongly stratified kettle lake. Note the thin plates of dense algae concentrations, which may be only a few centimeters thick. Such concentrations can occur only around the thermocline, where turbulence is minimal. Redrawn from Baker and Brook (1971).

crostratification is shown in Fig. 12-15 for blue-greens and cryptomonads in Josephine Lake, Minnesota. These blue-greens grow best near the thermocline in lakes with anoxic hypolimnia, where oxygen is low but carbon dioxide and nutrients are high. Algae in these dense microlayers must often grow in dim light; they compensate for this by producing more pigments that cover a wider range of wavelengths than near-surface algae. Some microlayers in the metalimnion are very stable and are not disturbed even by vigorous surface mixing. Figure 12-16 shows

the changes in the vertical distribution of the alga *Anabaena circinalis* in Crose Mere, England, that occurred over only a few days (compare with Fig. 12-11). In small lakes like Crose Mere or even large ones, surface scums frequently wash up on shore, dry out, and die.

Horizontal Variation

Remote sensing reveals the detailed patterning of the horizontal patchiness by algal reflectance in the invisible near-infrared band. The intricate swirls, plumes, and simple blocks of reflected

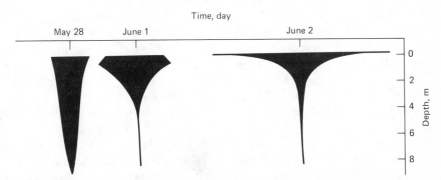

FIGURE 12-16 Short-term changes in vertical distribution of *Anabaena circinalis* in Crose Mere, England. Diagrams represent "cylindrical curves." The horizontal axis at each depth corresponds to the cube root of the number of colonies recovered at that depth. Note that the volume of algae per unit area of surface is about the same for each day; that is, this surface accumulation cannot be ascribed to growth. It is simply due to the existing algae floating to the surface in a calm period. Redrawn from Reynolds (1971).

light are shown in Figs. 5-3 and 5-4. Surface algal concentrations shown in these aerial photographs of Clear Lake, California, vary by factors of 100 within 1 m and 10,000 over less than 1 km. It is probable that similar complex patchiness occurs for other types of algae in near-surface phytoplankton in many water bodies. However, it is more difficult to detect the patterns that occur deeper in the water column.

Although surface patches may be advantageous for blue-greens, this is not the case for most other phytoplankton. High concentrations of algae attract herbivorous zooplankton just as windrows of seaweed and debris in the oceans attract fish, birds, and sea snakes. If algae growth is faster than zooplankton grazing, or if turbulent diffusion does not erode it away, the patch will expand. If, as is usually the case, water turbulence is much greater than can be overcome by growth, the patch is dissipated. Only patches more than 1 km across are likely to persist for several days in lakes. Both light and strong winds affect the patchiness of blue-greens in Clear Lake. On calm nights, very distinct patterns are observed on the surface. By the following morning, day nocturnal winds destroy the surface patterns (Horne and Wrigley, 1975).

Horizontal patterns of blue-green algae are not always ephemeral. Under some conditions, patches can persist for more than a few hours, even for weeks. In Lake Rotongaio, New Zealand, the influence of a small hill and a regular wind pattern resulted in a surface chlorophyll concentration that was much higher than in the rest of the lake (Fig. 12-17). Patchiness is not always an advantage. In Lake Rotongaio at this time the phytoplankton was an almost unialgal population of a small species of *Anabaena*, making its biochemical ecology easier to study than for mixed populations. The cells in the patch were physiologically distinct and relatively unhealthy. For example, the algae inside the patch had much lower rates of photosynthesis per chlorophyll *a* than those outside the patch. The most likely reason was nutrient depletion, because the

patch did not mix with the nutrients in the rest of the lake. In this small lake, the inflowing stream from nutrient-rich springs has a considerable effect on the nutrient cycles. Such horizontal spatial heterogeneity may be more common than is realized, since few measurements of such conditions have been made. Such situations can be studied using repeat remote sensing (Fig. 5-3).

THE RELATIVE SUCCESS OF THE MAJOR PHYTOPLANKTON GROUPS

As in most environments, the dominance of one group of algae is the result of multiple factors. We have discussed the competitive advantages of size, shape, type of movement, use of nutrients, and resistance to sinking, predation, and disease. In addition, each of the major groups of phytoplankton has unique characteristics of energy use and a form of chemical defense. All of these advantages may change in importance with season or in different lakes. Here we discuss energy and chemical defenses and then consider all of the competitive factors to arrive at a logical reason for the success of each major group in the plankton.

Energetics: The Cell Wall

The construction of the cell wall in phytoplankton represents a major investment of metabolic energy. In most phytoplankton the cell wall makes up 50 percent of the cell mass. Green algae and dinoflagellates have a cell wall made of cellulose, a high-molecular-weight glucose polymer. The glucose is manufactured by energy-demanding reduction of CO_2 to the —CH_2—units that comprise most of the cellulose molecule. Blue-greens have a cell wall made of peptidoglycans, such as muramic acid, glucosamine, and other amino acids. This synthesis is even more energy-demanding than cellulose synthesis. In contrast, the cell wall of the diatom, the frustule, is made by polymerization of soluble SiO_2 (actually $Si(OH)_4$) in the water. Very

(a)

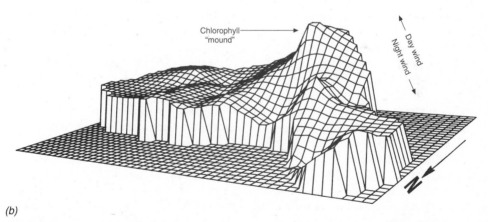

(b)

FIGURE 12-17 Long-lived horizontal patchiness in a small lake. (*a*) Aerial photograph of a Lake Rotongaio in New Zealand, situated very close to the much larger Lake Taupo. The photograph showns small tree-covered hills (dark areas in midleft). (*b*) Projection of the surface concentrations of the blue-green alga *Anabaena,* from the same perspective as the aerial photograph. The large "mound" of chlorophyll (up to 194 μg liter^{-1}) would be present in the same place in the lake (see arrow). The interactions of the regular reversal of the day and night winds and the hills caused the patch and also did not allow it to disperse. The eventual result was that the algae became relatively unhealthy, probably due to nutrient depletion. Lake Rotongaio is eutrophic and the surface appears uniformly opaque. Lake Taupo, however, is oligotrophic, and its bottom sediments appear as dark and light areas. Modified from Horne and Commins (1989).

TABLE 12-1

ENERGY REQUIRED FOR CELL WALL CONSTRUCTION

The differences are important for interalgal competition. Values are for individual members of the phytoplankton or periphyton community. Note that the energy needed for a diatom cell wall is more than 12 times less than that needed for potential competitors, such as green or blue-green algae. It is not surprising that diatoms are the most abundant aquatic algae in most lakes and upwelling areas of the ocean where the weight of the silica frustule is compensated for by turbulent mixing. Species without cell walls (some ciliates and flagellates) are not at competitive advantage since they must maintain shape by pumping out water with their contractile vacuoles (Table 12-2). 1 pW = 10^{-12} W.

Process	Energy required, pW
Cell wall construction (per molecule C or Si)	
Cellulose (most algae)	2.5
Peptidoglycan (blue-greens)	3.4
Silica (diatoms)	0.11
Protein (gas vacuoles)	4.8
Lipid (cell membrane)	6.0

Modified from Raven 1982; 1984; Werner, 1977.

little extra energy is needed to deposit SiO_2. Because the cell wall is such a large structure, energy efficiency in its synthesis is important in the competitive struggle.

The relative amount of energy needed for some cellular processes is shown in Table 12-1. Diatoms need about 12 times less energy than other algae for constructing cell walls. Given adequate SiO_2, diatoms should outcompete other phytoplankton on an energy basis. This is apparently the case, since diatoms are by far the most common algae in both fresh and saline waters. About 25 percent of the world's net primary production comes from marine diatoms, which thus rank equally with pine forests and the grasslands of the terrestrial ecosystem (Werner, 1977).

Energetics: Swimming and Buoyancy

Diatoms and blue-green algae have a competitive advantage in terms of the energy required for moving within the water column. The active swimming of large phytoplankters such as dinoflagellates requires large amounts of energy (Table 12-2). In contrast, the energy required for the vertical movement of blue-greens is small, especially for those species that use carbohydrate ballast to balance more permanent gas vacuoles. Diatoms do not swim, and they have relatively small changes in density.

Diatoms are favored in turbulent waters, but in the stable, stratified conditions of warm lakes they may sink below the metalimnion. Under these conditions, blue-greens are favored and, in fact, often dominate. Dinoflagellates are also common under these conditions. They are strong swimmers, able to travel several meters in a few hours. Dinoflagellates are phototactic, and they swim to the surface during the day to obtain light energy. At night they sink or swim to the sediments or hypolimnion to obtain nutrients. Although they must expend a great deal of energy to move so far each day, there is little competition from other algae groups in late summer and fall, so a relatively energy-intensive strategy is successful. Blue-greens are also found in these conditions but, especially if phosphorus is limiting, even their ability to fix N_2 is of little use. Thus in the autumn in many lakes and in tropical

TABLE 12-2

ENERGY REQUIRED FOR MAINTAINING CELL SHAPE IN CELLS WITH NO CELL WALL AND FOR CELL MOTION

If they did not pump out excess water, cells in fresh water without rigid cell walls would swell up and burst. The osmotic pressures are: 2 osmoles m^{-3} (fresh water), 80 osmoles m^{-3} (inside the algal cell), and > 100 osmoles m^{-3} (seawater).

Process	Energy required, pW
Osmotic balance	
Contractile vacuole (fresh)	3.4
Contractile vacuole (marine)	<3.4
Cell motion	
Flagella (50 $\mu m\ s^{-1}$)	0.00024

Modified from Raven 1984.

oceans dinoflagellates dominate the phytoplankton.

Energetics: Light

Phytoplankton exist in a mostly gloomy world, with only occasional flashes of higher light when they are swirled to the surface on a sunny day. The average light experienced by a planktonic algae (Fig. 3-7) ranges from darkness to about 400 $\mu E\ m^{-2} s^{-1}$ (E = Einstein). In comparison, terrestrial plants receive up to 1800 $\mu E\ m^{-2} s^{-1}$.

The different groups of algae have characteristic responses to light, thus competition for the available light and the ability to use a fluctuating light source can play a role in the dominance of one group of phytoplankton over another. As shown in Table 12-3, growth for most phytoplankton begins at around 5 to 7 $\mu E\ m^{-2} s^{-1}$. Green algae begin to photosynthesize at somewhat higher light, at 21 $\mu E\ m^{-2} s^{-1}$. At higher light intensity (39 to 47 $\mu E\ m^{-2} s^{-1}$), blue-greens and dinoflagellates reach their maximum photosynthetic

TABLE 12-3

MAXIMUM AND MINIMUM LIGHT ENERGY REQUIRED FOR GROWTH (μ) FOR DIFFERENT ALGAE GROUPS

Photoinhibition occurs when light intensity curtails photosynthesis and is shown for the onset on photoinhibition. Note that diatoms do well in both low and moderately high light regimes. Photoadaptation, which occurs when algae are exposed for some hours to one light regime, can alter the values given below, which are for general comparative purposes.

Phytoplankton group	Growth rate (μ)		Onset of photoinhibition, μE
	μ_{min}, $\mu E\ m^{-2} s^{-1}$	μ_{max}, $\mu E\ m^{-2} s^{-1}$	
Blue-greens	5	39	>200
Dinoflagellates	7	47	233
Diatoms	6	84	86
Greens	21	211	>250

rates. Diatoms do not achieve peak photosynthesis until 84 $\mu E\ m^{-2}\ s^{-1}$. Green algae can use up to 211 $\mu E\ m^{-2}\ s^{-1}$, but this exceeds the light normally available in the epilimnion. The range of light that can best be used by diatoms, 6 to 84 $\mu E\ m^{-2}\ s^{-1}$, is best suited to that normally found in the mixed layer of temperate lakes and oceans. Diatoms dominate in these situations for much or all of the year (Fig. 12-5).

Outside of temperate waters, phytoplankton are sometimes exposed to higher light intensities. For example, solar radiation is intense in tropical climates, where thermal stratification is more pronounced. High sunlight intensity also occurs during polar and alpine summers. Here, photoinhibition, akin to sunburn in humans, depresses and may even stop photosynthesis. This process has received much attention recently because photoinhibition is due in part to ultraviolet rays, which could increase if the world's ozone layer is depleted. Of importance for interalgal competition is the fact that the onset of photoinhibition begins at different intensities for each of the algal groups (Table 12-3). Diatoms are the first to be inhibited, at 86 $\mu E\ m^{-2}\ s^{-1}$, an intensity just above that of the intensity for maximum growth. In contrast, blue-greens, dinoflagellates, and greens all can tolerate at least 200 $\mu E\ m^{-2}\ s^{-1}$ before photosynthesis begins to be inhibited. These three groups tend to dominate in warmer lakes where sunlight is intense.

RESISTANCE TO ZOOPLANKTON GRAZING: CHEMICAL DEFENSES

Phytoplankton are the main food supply for herbivorous zooplankton. The larger cladoceran species, such as *Daphnia,* are particularly effective at filtering particles. When abundant in late spring, zooplankton can strain the entire lake epilimnion volume in only a few days. They may remove almost all of the smaller algae, which results in a spring "clear water" phase. Larger greens and blue-greens are little affected. Since phytoplankton can neither move away from gra-

zers nor construct large protective structures to deter grazing, their situation is analogous to that of many terrestrial plants. It is not surprising that the similar solution of chemical deterrence has been evolved as a defense to grazing in both environments. Some shrubs and plants synthesize bitter alkaloids that are distasteful to grazers such as deer, while grasses rely on a fast growth rate to survive grazing. In the phytoplankton, blue-greens and possibly dinoflagellates synthesize compounds that are distasteful or even toxic to herbivorous zooplankton. In contrast, diatoms and small flagellates usually have high reproduction rates.

Experiments have been devised in which a zooplankter is held in place and exposed to water containing various types and sizes of blue-green algae. The larger algal colonies are too big for cladocerans, such as *Daphnia,* to take inside their carapace. Smaller colonies of blue-greens are collected in the animal's food groove but usually rejected (Burns et al., 1989). In contrast, similarly sized diatoms, flagellates, and yeast particles are eaten. Tests conducted with free-swimming zooplankton confirm these findings. Even if ample food is supplied, some blue-greens, especially *Microcystis,* will reduce the filtering rate of *Daphnia* and some other cladocerans (Fig. 12-18).

Blue-greens manufacture a whole range of toxic or unpleasant tasting compounds, including the *Daphnia* filtering inhibitor, a toxin that is poisonous to cows and pigs that drink water from eutrophic lakes, and taste and odor substances that render drinking water supplies unpalatable to humans (Chap. 6). These toxins are normally contained inside the algae cell and are released into the water only when the cells are eaten, decompose, or lyse. The zooplankton feeding inhibitor is not the same compound as the other toxins, since some strains of *Microcystis* that would kill mammals do not impair feeding in *Daphnia* (Lampert, 1987). It is also dissimilar to the taste and odor substances, such as geosmin and methyl-isoborneol (MIB). These two com-

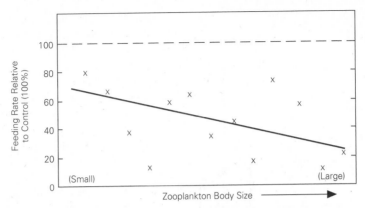

FIGURE 12-18 Effect of a toxic strain of the blue-green algae *Microcystis* on the feeding rates of 13 species of cladoceran zooplankton. The results are shown as a percentage of the control (100 percent), which is the feeding rate on the green algae *Scenedesmus* in the absence of the blue-green. The feeding mixture was 9:1 *Scenedesmus:Microcystis,* 1.0 mg liter^{-1} total carbon. Note that the largest species (*Daphnia magna* and *Daphnia pulex*) filtered only 10 to 20 percent of the control, while the smallest species (*Ceriodaphnia* and *Bosmina*) filtered 70 to 80 percent of normal. Considerable variation in this relationship occurs; the line shown is only an approximate trend. Greatly modified from Lampert (1987).

pounds are synthesized by blue-green algae and some actinomycete fungi, but their purpose, if any, remains unknown. However, when the cells decay the substances are released into the water and are the most common cause of unpleasant taste and odor in drinking water.

Although the feeding inhibitor substance is very effective against larger cladocerans, such as *Daphnia,* it is ineffective against most other zooplankton. Other cladocerans, such as *Bosmina,* rotifers, and copepods, may be unaffected and often coexist with dense blooms of blue-greens. In the extreme case, the copepod *Thermocyclops hyalinis* eats and survives well on a diet of the blue-green alga *Microcystis* in the very eutrophic tropical Lake George in Uganda. In addition, not all strains of a potentially toxic species of blue-green alga are actually toxic. Figure 12-19 shows the variable inhibition of the same amount of different strains of *Microcystis* on *Daphnia* filtration rates. It is clear that the chemical defenses of the three major blue-green genera (*Microcystis, Aphanizomenon,* and *Anabaena*) are only partially responsible for their success in lakes.

ATTACHED ALGAE: THE PERIPHYTON

Attached algae, also known as periphyton, coat virtually any submerged surface. The slippery "slime or scum flora" of underwater rocks is the bane of the angler's life but provides nutritious food for snails, some fish, and aquatic invertebrate larvae. Periphyton grow on rocks, mud, vegetation, jetty pilings, and boat hulls in lakes, rivers, estuaries, wetlands, and the ocean. Together with other microbes such as bacteria, fungi, protozoans, and small metazoans, attached algae make up the aufwuchs community that is the climax state for submerged surfaces. Periphyton have been neglected relative to phytoplankton because they are more difficult to collect quantitatively. More studies have been carried out recently, especially in regard to their role as food for grazing invertebrates and as ex-

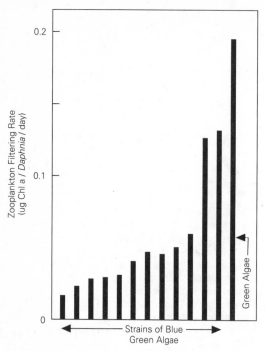

FIGURE 12-19 Different toxicity of 12 strains of the blue-green alga *Microcystis* inferred from the filtering rate of the large cladoceran zooplankter *Daphnia magna* as compared with a nontoxic food, the green alga *Scenedesmus*. Note that some strains have little effect while others are so highly inhibitory to the zooplankter that it would soon die. Modified from Nizan et al. (1986). Toxic strains of *Microcystis* are common in lakes, but the toxicity varies greatly over time and space as well as from lake to lake. However, it is an obvious advantage to the algae if it is avoided by large cladocerans, the most efficient filter feeders in eutrophic lakes.

of water body and in conditions that range from the most oligotrophic to the most eutrophic. The numbers and species vary considerably from site to site, but the most nutrient-rich waters do not always contain the most periphyton, since competition for sunlight between phytoplankton and periphyton may favor the floating species. Shading explains why periphyton are rare in eutrophic, turbid Clear Lake, California, but common in the more transparent waters of Borax Lake, located between two of the arms of Clear Lake (Wetzel, 1964). Alternatively, competition for nutrients may favor attached algae. This finding is used in lake management to increase water transparency. In the small streams of city parks, applied limnologists add rocks or macrophytes to provide additional surfaces for periphyton. These then remove soluble nutrients, to the detriment of phytoplankton growth in downstream lakes and ponds. Periphyton and aufwuchs coatings, also called biofilms, can be used in industrial processes, including sewage treatment and nutrient stripping.

Periphyton cause fouling of ships' bottoms, which reduces their speed and increases fuel consumption. For centuries copper solutions or copper strips were used on marine ships to prevent fouling. The technique depends on the antifoulant being soluble enough to discourage the biofilm but not soluble enough to dissolve over the ship's voyage. Over the last 20 years, antifouling paint containing tributyl tin has been used successfully and has replaced copper on racing yachts and submarines. Unfortunately, tributyl tin continues to be released from docked boats and is so toxic that entire estuaries have been polluted, with consequent loss of some animal species. This paint has now been banned in some regions.

Motion of Attached Algae or Periphyton

Common attached algae are large filamentous greens such as *Cladophora* and *Ulothrix*. These are fixed in one place, and only the tiny swimming and planktonic sexual zoospores can move.

perimental tools to determine the extent of nutrient and toxic pollution. Periphyton are influenced by nutrient levels but are able to extract nutrients from both productive and unproductive lake waters.

Only pennate diatoms, filamentous greens, and blue-greens are common members of the periphyton. Pennate diatoms and blue-greens move over the substrate by gliding, but filamentous greens are immobile. Periphyton are very adaptable. They are found in almost every type

Fixed sites such as rocks and branches are a disadvantage in lakes and streams if they are overturned by fish or storms. In estuaries, mud is continually resuspended and may cover immobile intertidal algae. If this happens to green algae they will die. Pennate diatoms and filamentous blue-green algae, which can move, are common in these unstable conditions. Their motion is called *gliding* and is possible only if the alga is in contact with a solid substrate, such as a rock or sediment particle.

Gliding in pennate diatoms is shown most dramatically on the sand or mud of estuaries. Here a golden "blush" of diatoms occurs every day at low tide. To photosynthesize at low tide but to prevent being washed away at high tide, the diatoms move in and out of the sediment, sometimes traveling several millimeters each day. The silicon shell or frustule of pennate diatoms has characteristic slits or pores on both sides, called *raphes*. Through these pores the diatom excretes polysaccharide mucilage that sticks to the substrate and pushes the diatom along. The rigid frustule provides the firm surface against which to push away from the substrate. A good analogy is a caterpillar tractor that continually leaves its tracks behind while producing new ones at the raphe (Harper, 1977). The speed of these diatoms ranges from 0.2 to 35 μm s^{-1}, which is about a million times slower than a typical lake shore or river current (10 to 200 cm s^{-1}).

Diatoms and most algae live their life at low Reynolds numbers (R_e). The R_e of a typical pennate diatom is about 10^{-4} because they are very small and move very slowly. At these scales any motion is controlled only by viscous forces, since turbulence does not occur (Chap. 4). Observed under the microscope, the jerky back-and-forth gliding of diatoms is not a smooth motion the word *gliding* implies. Because only viscous forces operate, there is no inertia. Acceleration and stopping are therefore virtually instantaneous. Cessation of the secretion of mucus will instantly stop forward motion (Edgar, 1979). The energy needed for mucus production might seem too great for survival in a competitive environment. Edgar (1982) calculated that for a diatom to move at 10 μm s^{-1}, only about 5×10^{-12} W of energy per cell, or about 5 percent of the available power, is needed to overcome the frictional shear resistance to motion. Of course additional energy is needed to synthesize the mucus. Given sunlight to produce glucose, however, synthesis of polysaccharides such as polyuronic acids is not very costly to the cell.

Gliding in blue-green algae occurs by a different process. Fibrils in the cell wall contract and provide the motive force. Gliding speeds are comparable to those of pennate diatoms, at about 1 to 10 μm s^{-1}. Under the microscope the process does not appear smooth but is much less jerky than that of pennate diatoms. The long filaments appear to wave and sometimes spiral as they move over the substratum. Most of the blue-greens that coat the sediments of lakes and streams can glide and may thus gain both additional light exposure and access to new nutrient supplies just above the sediments. In addition, they can move out of silt layers deposited by storms. Some benthic gliding species such as *Oscillatoria princeps* and *Phormidium* are so successful that they become severe nuisances in reservoirs, where they produce taste and odor compounds.

Seasonal Cycles of Periphyton

Like phytoplankton, periphyton show seasonal cycles. However, the relative importance of the controlling variables is somewhat different. Modifying the phytoplankton growth equation [Eq. (2)] for periphyton, we have:

$$\frac{dC}{dt} = \frac{dP}{dt} \cdot C - (G + Pa + D) \qquad (3)$$

Where cell concentration (C), grazing (G), infections, parasitism and disease (Pa) and cell death (D) are defined as in Eq. (1).

In Eq. (3), grazing, especially by aquatic insect larvae, is obviously more important in reg-

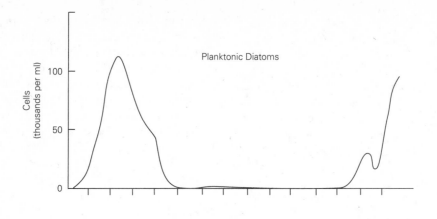

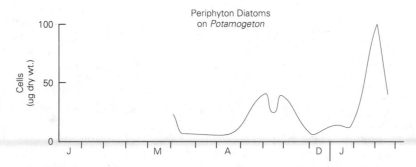

FIGURE 12-20 Seasonal cycles of diatom periphyton and diatom phytoplankton in a shallow lake, Hickling Broad in eastern England. In this example, the maximum periphyton population occurred during the minimum phytoplankton biomass. The attached algae grew on a submerged macrophyte, *Potamogeton*. The slightly brackish lake received some domestic and agricultural runoff, and both algal communities are severely nitrogen-limited in summer. Modified from Moss (1981).

ulating periphyton biomass than it is in regulating phytoplankton biomass. There are two reasons for this difference. First, sinking has been removed from the equation, thus all remaining independent variables become more important. Second, it is mechanically more efficient to scrape or graze a two-dimensional layer of periphyton than to filter algae from a three-dimensional planktonic environment. In unproductive oligotrophic lakes, this increase in efficiency can be the difference between success and failure

for grazers. In productive eutrophic wetlands, the increased efficiency of two-dimensional grazing can give rise to some of the most productive systems on earth.

It is less easy to generalize the typical periphyton seasonal cycle than that of phytoplankton. Figure 12-20 compares the seasonal cycles of periphyton and phytoplankton in the same lake. The seasonal cycles for several populations of periphyton in different habitats is depicted in Fig. 12-21. In general, light is still a strong con-

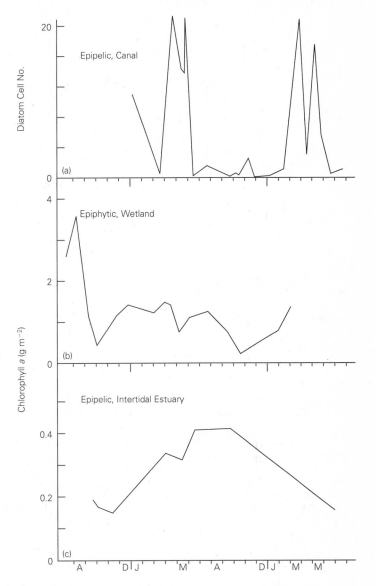

FIGURE 12-21   Seasonal cycles of periphyton in (*a*) a slow-moving canal water, (*b*) a wetland, and (*c*) an estuary. Most of the algae were pennate diatoms. The canal populations growing on mud showed a strong seasonal cycle but with different timing from that shown in Fig. 12-21. In this canal, the water velocities are more like those in a lake than those in a river. In contrast, the eutrophic wetland and the estuary had much more constant populations through the year. Even so, a winter minimum occurred, most likely due to low light. Note that although algal abundance is lowest in winter, moderate populations are present for much of the rest of the year. The periphyton grew on the macroalga *Chara* in the wetlands and on the intertidal sediment in the estuary. Modified from Round (1973), Horne and Roth (1989), and Gregg and Horne (unpublished).

trolling variable and most periphyton show minimum populations in the winter. As in lakes, diatoms tend to be more common in the cooler spring period and blue-greens more common in summer. Large filamentous green algae, such as *Ulothrix* and *Cladophora*, are common attached forms in slow-moving streams and on rocks in the littoral zones of lakes. *Cladophora*, also known as blanket weed, is a summer species, and *Ulothrix* is most common in spring. Both genera may quickly disappear if they are heavily grazed by aquatic insects and snails. The summer periphyton may be reduced to a remnant population of one or two species that can withstand

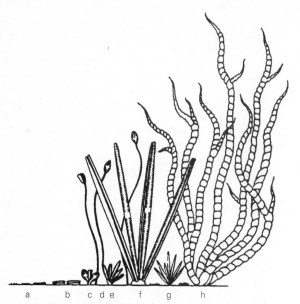

FIGURE 12-22. An idealized succession of periphyton as they colonize a new substrate. Small bacteria are soon joined by small pennate diatoms, such as *Navicula,* that are prostrate on the surface. *Navicula* species may be only 10 to 20 μm long. From then on new species must occupy the space away from the surface, just as bushes and trees grow above grasses in terrestrial vegetational succession. Large diatoms such as *Synedra* may be 100 to 300 μm long and grow at right angles to the surface. Green algae such as *Stigeoclonium,* over 1 mm long, then come to dominate much of the surface. Finally, long strands of the green alga *Cladophora,* some of which are over 1 m long, smother most of the original colonizers. However, *Cladophora* itself is big enough to support many species of pennate diatoms, which begins the colonization cycle anew. a = attached bacteria, b = *Navicula meniscus* (prostrate attachment and mucilage coat), c = *Gomphonema parvulum* (short stalks), d = *G. olivaceum* (long stalks), e = *Fragilaria vaucheriae* (rosette, mucilage pads), f = *Synedra acus* (large rosette, mucilage pads), g = *Nitzschia* sp. (rosette, mucilage pads), h = *Stigeoclonium* sp. (upright filaments). Modified from Hoagland et al. (1982).

grazing and reduced nutrient concentrations. Some deep clear lakes, estuarine mudflats, and wetlands ponds may have large standing crops of attached algae for most of the year (Fig. 12-21 *b, c*). This longer domination by one type of algae has no counterpart in the plankton, which changes continually.

Colonization of Substrata by Periphyton

Major storms and heavy grazing can completely scour or clean the stream substratum and require recolonizing. The same result may occur in lakes following strong wave action. There is a well-defined succession of aquatic microbes that colonize new surfaces. Within minutes the surface begins to be coated with dissolved amino acids and other soluble organic compounds deposited by electrostatic forces. Within hours a coating of bacteria begins to form, and within days periphyton are present. The algal succession begins with low-profile diatoms and climaxes with an upper story of long-stalked and rosette diatoms together with filamentous green and blue-green algae (Fig. 12-22). Recent studies indicate that the larger species absorb enough light to impair the growth of those beneath. Overall, the succession of periphyton is very like that of terrestrial plants invading a piece of bare ground. The main difference is that the algal invasion is complete within weeks or months, while the terrestrial invasions may take many years.

The disappearance of the periphyton film or mat occurs by grazing, sloughing, or death. In oligotrophic Lake Tahoe, large mats of decaying periphyton are found along parts of the shoreline in spring. They create a nuisance but represent only a fraction of the underwater carpet of stalked diatoms that coat the lake bed due to nutrient release due to human activities in the watershed. A good example is the large mats of *Cladophora* that were a common sight on Lake Erie's public beaches during its most eutrophic phase in the 1960s.

Phytoplankton and zooplankton are sometimes confused taxonomically (Table 11-5), but in ecological terms the answer is quite clear: algae are the producers and zooplankton the consumers. In Chap. 13 we discuss how the animal plankton and benthos adjust to changes in their

(a) *(b)*

(c) *(d)*

FIGURE 12-23 Some of the common periphyton and associated organisms that occur in successions shown in Fig. 12-21. (*a*) Flexibacterial trichomes, which colonize submerged surfaces in days. (*b*) Coccoid bacteria joined by strands. (*c*) A medium-sized pennate diatom, *Amphipleura pellucida,* which glides over the surface and colonizes in about a month. (*d*) A rosette of a fixed pennate diatom, *Synedra acus,* a large diatom characteristic of the "mature" climax of the periphyton colonization. Note the tiny, by comparison, pennate diatom, *Gomphonema parvulum* (arrow), which forms a "'lawn" understory layer. Courtesy of K. D. Hoagland.

phytoplankton and periphyton food supply and to predation from fish.

FURTHER READING

Boney, A. D. 1975. *Phytoplankton.* Institute of Biology Study 52. Crane, Russak, New York. 116 pp.

Carr, N. G. and B. A. Whitton (eds.). 1973. *The Biology of Blue-Green Algae.* University of California Press, Berkeley. 676 pp.

Edgar, L. A. 1984. "Diatom Locomotion." *Prog. Physiol. Res.,* **3**:47–88.

Fogg, G. E., and B. Thake. 1987. *Algal Cultures and Phytoplankton Ecology.* 3d ed. University of Wisconsin Press, Madison. 269 pp.

Fogg, G. E., W. D. P. Stewart, P. Fay, and A. E. Walsby. 1973. *The Blue-Green Algae.* Academic Press, London.

Harris, G. P. 1986. *Phytoplankton Ecology: Structure, Function, and Fluctuations.* Chapman & Hall, London. 384 pp.

Hutchinson, G. E. 1957. *A Treatise on Limnology, vol. 2: Introduction to Lake Biology and the Limnoplankton.* Wiley, New York. 1115 pp.

Lund, J. W. G. 1965. "The Ecology of the Freshwater Phytoplankton." *Biol. Rev.,* **40**:231–293.

Morris, I. (ed.). 1980. *The Physiological Ecology of Phytoplankton.* University of California Press, Berkeley. 625 pp.

Round, F. E. (ed.). 1988. *Algae and the Aquatic Environment.* Biopress, Bristol, England. 460 pp.

Societas Internationalis Limnologiae. "Factors That Regulate the Wax and Wane of Algal Populations." Symposium no. 19. 1971. *Mitt. Int. Ver. Theor. Angew. Limnol.* 318 pp.

Werner, D. (ed.). 1977. *Biology of Diatoms.* University of California Press, Berkeley. 498 pp.

Vincent, W. F. (ed.). 1989. "Dominance of Bloom-Forming Cyanobacteria (Blue-Green Algae)." *N. Z. J. Marine Freshwat. Res.,* **21**:361–542.

CHAPTER 13

Zooplankton and Zoobenthos

OVERVIEW

The main components of lake zooplankton are the microzooplankton, composed of protozoans and rotifers, and mesozooplankton crustaceans, which include cladocerans as well as cyclopoid and calanoid copepods. In certain lakes macrozooplankton such as larvae of the insect *Chaoborus* or the opossum shrimp *Mysis* are abundant. In temporary ponds fairy shrimp occur in early spring, while in salt lakes brine shrimp may be the only animal plankton. Most zooplankton are about 0.5 to 3 mm long; the majority feed on algae or clumps of bacteria from 1 to 15 μm in diameter. Cyclopoid copepods and rotifers may devour other zooplankton. Large zooplankton range from up to 500 per liter in eutrophic lakes to less than 1 per liter in the most oligotrophic waters.

Adaptations of zooplankters to the aquatic habitat include active movement, rapid reproduction, small size, vertical migration to deep water during daylight, and shore avoidance. Zooplankton are often transparent, which reduces predation by fish. Some have spines to provide protection from invertebrate predators. Rapid parthenogenetic reproduction reduces the impact of predation and permits some zooplankton to exploit fast-growing algal blooms. Cladocerans and rotifers are more abundant in summer, when there is more food. Copepods and opossum shrimp are generally perennial, with active overwintering populations. Many cladocerans and rotifers have resting stages and resistant eggs that overwinter in the sediments or are transported by wind or birds to colonize new habitats. Zooplankton are the main link between small phytoplankton and larger carnivores, primarily young fish. Zooplankton excretion recycles nutrients, and this may be the main source of nitrogen and phosphorus during thermal stratification. Most zooplankton feed by grasping larger prey or sweeping algae and bacteria from the water and concentrating this food for ingestion by filtration through bristle-covered thoracic limbs. The distribution and abundance of zooplankton is determined by the amount of food and extent of predation.

Zoobenthos spend most of their lives in or near the sediments. They are often pigmented and wormlike and include a diverse group of small animals such as insect larvae, crustaceans, worms, and mollusks. Benthic invertebrates, which dominate the biomass of streams and rivers, are discussed in the chapter on flowing waters. The benthos is patchily distributed and difficult to sample quantitatively. Zoobenthos transform fine particulate detritus into protein and, in turn, are consumed by fish and wading birds. Like zooplankton, they recycle nutrients by their excretion. Feeding mechanisms range from those of clams, which filter out algae, bacteria, and detritus, to insect larvae, which seize other animals, or oligochaete worms, which ingest bottom sediments. The distribution and abundance of zoobenthos is primarily determined by the availability of dissolved oxygen and bottom type. The presence and absence of specific species has been valuable in the classification of lake trophic levels. The most dense and diverse zoobenthos populations are found in the sediments above the thermocline and along the lakeshore, where turbulence provides oxygen and food. Below the thermocline, zoobenthos are less abundant because temperatures are low, oxygen concentrations may be reduced, and the substrata tends to be more uniform. Because of the low oxygen level, only a few specialized organisms, such as chironomid midge larvae, exist in the profundal zone of eutrophic lakes.

In this chapter we discuss zooplankton—measurement, population structure, feeding, and reproduction—and zoobenthos—profundal and littoral habitats, adaptations to varying oxygen supplies, feeding, and life cycles and mass emergence.

INTRODUCTION

Crustacean zooplankton are small, semitransparent organisms that, along with the pelagic protozoans and rotifers, comprise most of the freshwater animal plankton (Fig. 13-1*a, b*; Figs. 11-7 to 11-11). The larvae of marine benthic crustaceans, mollusks, and worms are conspicuous components of zooplankton in estuaries and the sea. In fresh waters this is not the case. True zooplankters are independent of the lakeshore or bottom and inhabit all depths if oxygen conditions are suitable. Some species occupy the nearshore zone, often in association with higher aquatic plants and the littoral substrate. Others have resting stages that enable them to reappear suddenly after extended periods of absence. *Daphnia,* the common ''water flea,'' has an overwintering resting stage, the *ephippium,* which is produced in summer or fall as the adult population dies off.

Freshwater zooplankton populations in the pelagic zone are usually characterized by only a few dominant species. This is in marked contrast to the diverse assemblages of pelagic marine ecosystems, where there may be more than 50 species of copepods as well as many species of planktonic mollusks, annelids, radiolarian protozoans, tunicates, and medusae. The pelagic region of the few very large lakes, perhaps because of their greater size, may have as many as 25 crustacean species. Typically in a single lake there are a few species of cladocerans, one to three copepod species, and three to seven species of rotifers at any one time. Protozoan zooplankters are very diverse but have received relatively little attention. The transparent ''phantom'' midge larvae of *Chaoborus* are the only truly planktonic insects. Close relatives of the mosquitos, they are voracious predators and are planktonic only at night. The littoral zone of most lakes has a diverse assemblage of copepods, cladocerans, rotifers, and protozoans, with many species strictly sessile and others exhibiting a life style alternating between benthic and planktonic.

MEASUREMENT OF ZOOPLANKTON

Despite many years spent improving plankton nets, the problem of quantitative sampling of zooplankton has not been completely solved. Early biologists such as Ernst Haeckel took qualitative zooplankton samples by dragging through the water a net made of the same silk bolting cloth used to sieve flour. Modern methods use

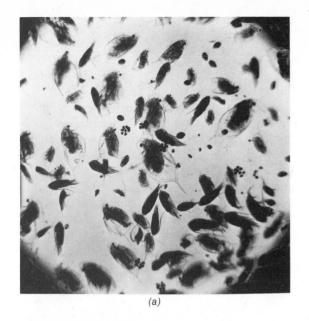

(a)

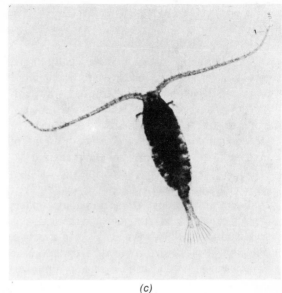

(c)

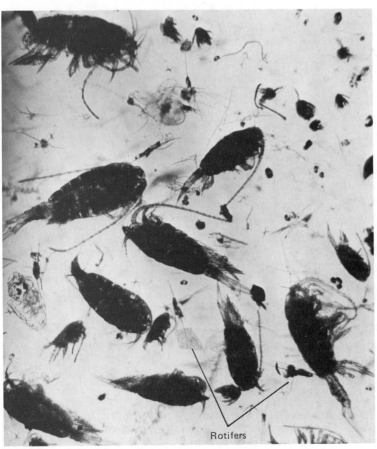

Rotifers

(b)

FIGURE 13-1 Zooplankton from (*a*) a productive lake, Clear Lake, California, and (*b*) an unproductive one, Lake Tahoe. The pictures represent organisms as normally seen after collection by net tows, which may damage some individuals, and preservation with formalin, which causes the antennae to fold down alongside the body. The dominance of cladocerans over copepods typical of productive lakes in summer is shown. (*b*) Some of the dozen or so moult stages of copepods and a few rotifers. Copepods usually outnumber cladocerans in unproductive lakes (Fig. 13-5*a*). Cladocerans disappeared from Lake Tahoe after the introduction of mysid shrimp (Fig. 13-13). In both, large colonial algae are just visible, indicating the approximate upper limit of size of herbivorous zooplankton food. Most algae eaten are smaller than those shown here. (*c*) A copepod with antennae in a typical position when seen alive. Photographs by M. L. Commins and G. W. Salt.

267

the same principle but with more advanced and robust materials. The objective is to obtain a representative animal sample from a known volume of water. Most nets, traps, or pumps fail either to collect all the organisms or to measure the volume of water filtered, or both. Some of the larger, stronger swimmers avoid capture.

Nets of various kinds are employed for both horizontal and vertical tows (Fig. 13-2a, b). They strain the larger zooplankters and phytoplankters from the water and are normally hauled at a speed of about 0.3 to 0.5 m s^{-1}. In practice, selection of mesh size involves a compromise. A larger mesh of 200 μm or greater minimizes clogging with algae in more productive waters but will lose many of the smaller forms. The smallest mesh, of 80 to 100 μm, will clog rapidly. Phytoplankton sampling techniques are required to retain the minute rotifers or juvenile stages of copepods and cladocerans. The entrance to the net may be restricted to provide a larger filtering area of the net surface relative to the water entering the net. A ratio of at least 40:1 for net opening to filtering area reduces the back pressure that builds up within the net but this may still generate a shock wave that warns zooplankton ahead. Since all nets are subject to clogging as organisms or detritus accumulate in the

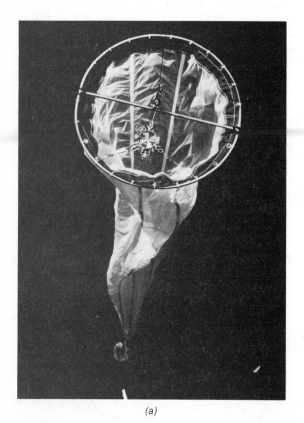

(a)   (b)

FIGURE 13-2   A large zooplankton net (a) in the lake and (b) just after a haul. Note the flow meter in the net opening in (a) and the weighted cod end in (b), where the sample accumulates. Such large nets are used in oligotrophic waters, but much smaller ones are adequate for more productive lakes. Photograph (a) by R. Richards.

mesh, sampling efficiency is highest at the start of the tow but steadily declines as the tow continues. For quantitative sampling, nets have a flow meter at the throat that measures the actual volume of water passing through (Fig. 13-2a).

Large-volume clear plastic plankton traps are lowered at a high speed and closed quickly. Avoidance by the stronger swimming zooplankton can still be a problem when zooplankton are sparse and the number collected by traps is often statistically inadequate. Integrated water samples taken with plastic vertical tubes or even garden hose are particularly useful for slow-moving zooplankton in shallow lakes. Pumping from specific depths has been employed because it has the advantage of sampling continuously with sufficient intake velocity to reduce escape. Still, distant zooplankton will swim against the current where it is weak, reducing the sampling efficiency. Nets mounted on benthic sleds, mechanical dredges, or direct collection by divers may be required to sample amphipods and other zoobenthos associated with the lake sediments. Sleds and dredges are difficult to operate quantitatively but may be the only way to collect large numbers of organisms near the bottom. The use of remotely operated vehicles (ROVs) in positioning sampling equipment or actually seeing and counting zooplankton by video-linked computer shows considerable promise for clear waters.

Variable-frequency echo sounding is used for detecting dense concentrations of zooplankters, which, like fish, form *deep scattering layers* (Fig. 14-3). High-speed plankton samplers such as the Hardy plankton recorder were developed for marine work and can be towed routinely along sea lanes or across large lakes by commercial ships.

Field sampling errors invariably exceed subsampling errors, so it is advisable to sample a large volume of water and then subsample before counting. Subsampling may be done with a piston pipette or a mechanical plankton splitter. Zooplankton are usually easier to identify soon after collection than after extended storage, even in neutralized formalin, where they gradually lose both color and shape. A binocular dissecting microscope is convenient for identifying and counting most individuals, although rotifers and small or juvenile stages of copepods and cladocerans require higher magnification.

ZOOPLANKTON POPULATION STRUCTURE

Much of the fascination in the study of lakes lies in understanding the structure and dynamics of zooplankton populations in both space and time. The zooplankton community of copepods, cladocerans, and rotifers is usually composed of five to eight dominant species and several rarer forms. Factors such as oxygen, light, temperature, water movements, food, disease, competition, and predation influence the number of species found and their abundance. Low pH, for example, reduces both diversity and numbers. Diel vertical migrations, discussed later, are an obvious response to predation. Selective predation on one zooplankter increases the chances for population growth for others. Zooplankton suffer from diseases and parasites, but few studies have documented the quantitative significance of this type of attack (Fig. 11-8).

The more species of fish that are present in a lake, the greater the number of zooplankton species that are likely to occur. Why this relationship holds is not clear, but a reduction in interspecific competition for phytoplankton might be involved. Another explanation is merely that a habitat suitable for a variety of fish is also suitable for a variety of zooplankton. There also tends to be a direct relationship between number of species and the area of the lake. Large oligotrophic lakes have more species than smaller lakes; for example, the Great Lakes have about 25 species of crustaceans (Patalas, 1969). Small lakes may have as few as 2 to 5 species of crustaceans, and not all of these will be found in the plankton at any one time.

Size-Selective Predation, Trophic Cascades, and Cyclomorphosis

Large zooplankton dominate when zooplanktivorous fish are absent but are soon eliminated if fish predators are introduced. Fish can easily see the pigmented eye spot or the dark gut contents of zooplankton but may be unable to see the body and carapace, which are often virtually transparent. The importance of *size-selective predation* on zooplankton community structure has been clearly demonstrated (Hrbachek, 1962; Brooks and Dodson, 1965). Brooks and Dodson documented a dramatic shift from predominantly large-bodied zooplankters to small-bodied species following the introduction of the planktivorous alewife *Alosa pseudoharengus,* which selectively feeds on larger zooplankton. This research led to an exiting phase in experimental zoology that continues today. It explains the relative abundance of large and small zooplankton as a function of selective predation by fish and predatory zooplankton (Dodson, 1974; Hall et al., 1976). The basic concept of *size-selective feeding* is that fish usually select the more visible, large zooplankton such as *Daphnia rosa,* allowing for a relative increase in the smaller species. The *size-efficiency hypothesis* explains why larger zooplankton (longer than 1 mm) tend to dominate in the absence of strong size-selective predators such as fish. When fish are not present large zooplankton dominate because they have a smaller ratio of basal metabolism to overall respiration than do smaller zooplankton. The efficiency of large size is common to all animals and explains why, for example, small mammals such as voles must feed every few hours while elephants can go for days or even weeks without food. In addition, large zooplankton are able to utilize a larger size range of algal particles, and their large size offers some protection from invertebrate predators such as *Chaoborus* or cyclopoid copepods.

Size-selective predation by fish and zooplankton grazing on algae (Porter, 1973) are critical for the *trophic cascade* concept (Carpenter et al., 1985). This theory argues that the fish, zooplankton, and algal communities are interlinked and changes in large fish will affect everything down to algae and nutrients. If we consider the trophic pyramid from the top down, we can see that if piscivorous fish are reduced, their prey—zooplanktivorous fish—would increase. This predation, in turn, reduces herbivorous zooplankton, leading to an increase in phytoplankton. Finally, available nutrients decrease as they are taken into algae (Fig. 13-3). On the other hand, if piscivorous fish increase, then zooplanktivorous fish will decrease, herbivorous zooplankton will expand and graze down the phytoplankton. Available nutrients will increase. Starting from the bottom of the trophic pyramid, the nutrient changes, as occur when sewage is diverted from a lake, are thought to control algae, zooplankton, and fish. Cascading trophic interactions have been demonstrated in lakes of various sizes, including Lake Michigan (Scavia et al., 1986), and appear to be most common in oligotrophic systems (Carpenter 1988; Carpenter and Kitchell, 1988). The trophic cascade is generally weaker in eutrophic systems (McQueen et al., 1986; Benndorf et al., 1988), but Vanni et al. (1990) found strong effects in eutrophic Lake Mendota, Wisconsin, following a massive die-off of planktivorous fish. This concept is used in *biomanipulation,* a modern method of algae nuisance control. Biomanipulation of food webs to improve water quality in lakes is receiving considerable attention (Shapiro and Wright, 1984; Benndort, 1988; Carpenter, 1988; Carpenter and Kitchell, 1988; Vanni et al., 1990).

The trophic cascade is part of the *top-down, bottom-up concept* by which limnologists can explain many population changes (Fig. 13-3). Top-down, bottom-up theory states that ecosystems are structured on the one hand by their nutrient base, such as total internal and external nutrient loading, and on the other by the types of top predators present. At the population level, *Daphnia,* for example, would be controlled by

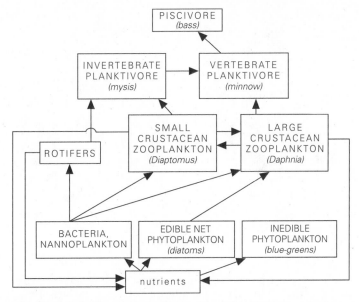

FIGURE 13-3 The trophic cascade in lakes. This idealized conceptual "top-down" model assumes that the effect of changes in the top predators cascades all the way down the trophic pyramid to the lowest (nutrient) level. Modified from Carpenter et al. (1985). It is the opposite of the "bottom-up" concept that assumes changes in nutrients flow up the pyramid, eventually affecting fish abundance. Typical members of each compartment are indicated, but it should be remembered that sometimes the animals may be omnivorous. For example, rotifers may eat inedible blue-green algae or minnows may eat small zooplankton if larger ones are scarce. Using experimental mesocosms, McQueen et al. (1986) demonstrated that changes at the top or bottom must be quite large to pass across trophic levels, and even then may only reach part way up or down the trophic pyramid.

interactions with the higher level (zooplanktivorous fish) through mortality and interactions with lower trophic levels (algae) through natality changes.

Like all crustaceans, including marine crabs and lobsters, freshwater crustaceans are surrounded by a rigid shell or *carapace*. It has long been observed that some herbivorous zooplankton show marked seasonal changes in the shape of the carapace (Brooks, 1946). For example, the head of *Daphnia* may be rounded or have a spike-shaped helmetlike appearance. The ventral or tail region may also develop a long spine of varying length (Fig. 13-4a, b). These changes in

carapace shape are called *cyclomorphosis*. As the name implies, the shape may change with season in a cyclic fashion. Since crustaceans molt many times in their lives, the degree of cyclomorphosis may vary from young to old individuals. Spatial variability in cyclomorphosis is also common; *Daphnia* populations in one lake may have a spiked helmet while those in a nearby lake have a rounded head. Cyclomorphosis is thought to be caused by various environmental factors, including temperature and turbulence, but recent work indicates that most changes can be accounted for by predation.

After certain invertebrate predators are intro-

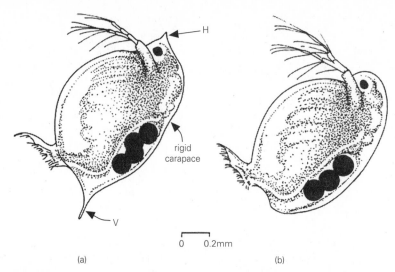

0   0.2mm

(a)   (b)

FIGURE 13-4   Chemomorphosis in zooplankton. The presence of invertebrate predators causes chemomorphosis-characteristic changes in the shape of the rigid shell or carapace—in many zooplankton, including *Daphnia ambigua* shown here. (*a*) Adults exposed to the invertebrate predator *Chaoborus* have spines both on the head (helmet, H) and a ventral spine (V) at the opposite end. (*b*) Adults not exposed to the predator show no spines. Based on Hebert and Grewe (1985). The dotted area represents the body and feeding legs, the black spot is the eye, and the round hatched spots are eggs, since almost all *Daphnia* are females. It may appear that these spines are poor defensive weapons but they are sufficient to make it awkward for *Chaoborus* to grasp and hold *Daphnia,* which has a powerful escape mechanism in its upper limbs. These give it the "hopping" motion from which *Daphnia* derives its common name, water flea. If the predator cannot hold it firmly, the animal will simply pull away to safety.

duced to a culture of *Daphnia,* newly moulted individuals possess more spines. The effect is the same even if only an extract of the predator is added. Morphometric change due to a chemical clue released by the predator is called *chemomorphosis* (Fig. 13-4). Gilbert (1966) showed that a similar spiny response occurs in the rotifer *Brachionus calyciflorus* when a predatory rotifer, *Asplanchna,* is present. Spines are not formed in the absence of predators, since spine production requires energy that would otherwise be used to improve individual reproduction (Walls and Ketola, 1989).

Spatial Variation: Vertical Migrations and Littoral Avoidance

Large zooplankton in lakes and oceans migrate vertically over the diel (24-hour) cycle. Diel ver-

tical migration is believed to be a strategy to avoid predators that rely on sight feeding. Many zooplankton spend the daylight hours in the aphotic zone and migrate to the surface at night to feed. The activity is common in a variety of aquatic environments and is exhibited by organisms ranging in size from barely visible freshwater crustacean zooplankton to marine squid over 10 cm long. It is not surprising that there are several explanations for this phenomenon. In deep, stratified lakes macro- and mesozooplankton segregate at different levels during the day and at night. This leads to a much more defined and mobile distribution than occurs with phytoplankton. Optimal depth for migrating zooplankton varies with season, time of day, species, life stage, and trophic state of the lake.

Vertical migration by planktonic crustaceans

is often less pronounced in shallow lakes and is most common for larger species or life stages. Microzooplankton such as rotifers, protozoans, and smaller life stages show little regular vertical migration. Larger zooplankton respond to changes in light intensity by swimming upward in the evening and downward at dawn. Very large species, such as the opossum shrimp, *Mysis relicta,* swim at speeds up to 1.7 cm s^{-1} during the evening hours, preying on other, smaller zooplankters as they go. Most freshwater copepods and cladocerans swim at about half the speed of *Mysis.* During thermal stratification, these smaller zooplankters pass through the thermocline to graze in the epilimnion during the darker hours, thus reducing their exposure to predation by *Mysis.* They retreat from the light to the cool hypolimnetic waters by day. In the ocean, a whole industry of night fishing depends on this migration. Squid that have swum to the surface to feed on migrating zooplankton are drawn to lights like moths to a flame. Once alongside the boats they are easily netted.

A typical vertical distribution of four different species in Lake Tahoe is shown in Fig. 13-5. The opossum shrimp, *Mysis relicta,* avoids warm near-surface water and always remains below the thermocline. The copepods *Diaptomus* and *Epischura* migrate upward at night into the warmer surface waters where they avoid nocturnal predation from *Mysis* and have a richer supply of algae. Using an alternative strategy, *Diaptomus nauplii* remain deep in the cold water, below the peak of *Mysis* abundance. The overall result is that prey species tend to distribute themselves to reduce their losses to predation.

Predation also stimulates vertical migration in some shallow lakes. Peter and Tuesday Lakes are small, low-elevation kettle lakes in Wisconsin where extensive biomanipulation experiments involving addition and removal of planktivorous fish were carried out over several years (Carpenter et al., 1987). When fish predation in these two lakes was low, vertical migration patterns in *Daphnia* were weak and variable. In contrast, when fish predation was increased by

adding planktivorous minnows, within a few weeks regular vertical migration became the norm (Fig. 13-6). Although the thermocline in Tuesday Lake is at only 3 m, it is too dark for fish to see zooplankton in the hypolimnion. This lake's low transparency is due to staining by humic acids from the surrounding pine forest.

Some diel vertical migrations are not due to light or predation. In Lake Constance, a deep, mesotrophic lake near the Alps in Germany, starvation was the main factor (Geller, 1986). Most zooplankton in this lake did not migrate during the spring phytoplankton bloom, despite peak invertebrate predation pressure. Only when the phytoplankton bloom had crashed did regular vertical migrations occur. The migrations in Lake Constance can best be explained on the basis of the animal's energy budget. Phytoplankton are most common in the warm epilimnion, where zooplankton filtering and feeding rates are also higher.

One drawback of this behavior for zooplankton is that respiration increases with temperature, and in summer can use up more energy than increased feeding can supply (Chap. 15). The imbalance is most pronounced when food is scarce. If the zooplankton remain in cold water they respire less but have no access to the phytoplankton in the epilimnion. During vertical migration they spend some time in cool water and some in warmer water. One might expect, however, that feeding and respiration rates would adjust quickly to the ambient temperature. If so, there would be no net energy advantage to migration. In fact, rapid acclimation to higher temperature does occur for feeding and filtering but not for respiration. When poikilothermic (cold-blooded) animals are cold-adapted, they are able to spend a short time at higher temperatures without a rise in their respiration rate. Zooplankton can make short forays into warmer water without losing their low temperature advantage. In this manner they increase their efficiency in utilizing the food by diel vertical migrations. Since the light at the maximum depth of zooplankton mi-

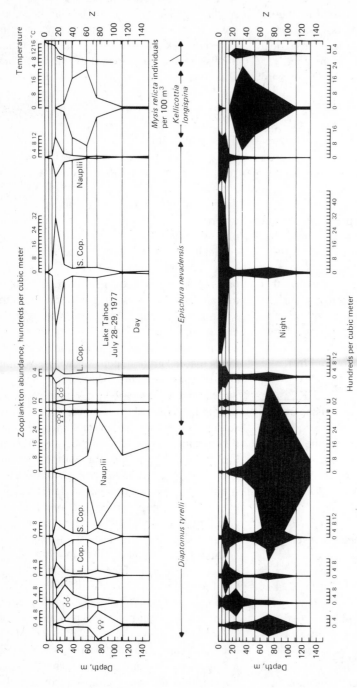

FIGURE 13-5 Day and night vertical distributions of several growth stages of four species of zooplankton in Lake Tahoe. Similar distributions of different species occur in most lakes. Temperature is indicated by Θ; the thermocline is at about 20 m. Note the daily migration of *Epischura* copepodites from 20 m in the day to the surface at night and the very different positions of females (♀), males (♂), copepodites, and nauplii of the other calanoid copepod, *Diaptomus*, which may reflect temperature preferences. *Mysis*, the opossum shrimp, migrates to 300 m during the day so is not shown in the upper figure. Note that the scale for *Mysis* differs by an order of magnitude from the rest. The four species shown constituted the entire lake zooplankton in 1977. L. Cop = large copepods, S. Cop = small copepods. From Roth and Goldman (unpublished).

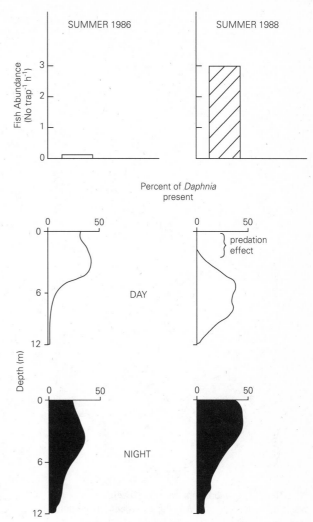

FIGURE 13-6 The effect of predation by planktivorous fish (minnows) on the vertical migration of *Daphnia* in Tuesday Lake, a small lake in northern Wisconsin. Note that the zooplankton remained in the warmer, food-rich epilimnion in 1986, when minnows were virtually absent. In contrast, zooplankton showed regular migrations and shunned the epilimnion in 1988, when minnows were introduced. The zooplankton then remained in the cool dark hypolimnion during the day. Redrawn and modified from Dini and Carpenter (1991).

gration in Lake Constance is adequate for fish to see zooplankton, predation cannot be the dominant cause of vertical migration.

Horizontal patchiness is a normal feature of zooplankton populations (Fig. 13-7). Some planktonic forms exhibit *littoral avoidance*—they make horizontal migrations away from the lake edge. The spatial separations due to vertical and horizontal migration provide an important element of structure to aquatic ecosystems (Chap. 2).

In other cases, a combination of predation and competition may control the zooplankton horizontal numbers and population structure. In studies of two cladocerans in a Japanese mountain lake, Ogochi Reservoir, it was found that *Daphnia* dominated the zooplankton near the dam but *Bosmina* predominated at the shallow end (Urabe, 1990). *Daphnia* was able to outcompete *Bosmina* near the dam, where food was limiting. At the upper end of the reservoir there was more food and both species might have

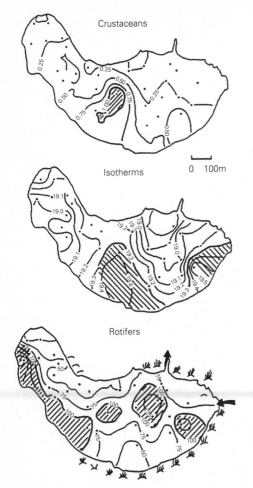

FIGURE 13-7 Horizontal variation in zooplankton abundance. Numbers of individuals per liter for two common groups, crustaceans (mostly nauplii and *Bosmina,* intervals of 0.25 individuals liter^{-1}) and rotifers (*Keratella,* intervals of 25 individuals liter^{-1}), in the early morning in the epilimnion of eutrophic Lake Rotongaio in New Zealand. Also shown are the surface temperature contours, although there was only a difference of 0.6°C over the entire lake and temperature was not related to zooplankton abundance. Note that, as in many eutrophic lakes, small rotifers are numerically more common than crustaceans. The rotifers and crustaceans show littoral avoidance and tend to cluster near the lake center, although some rotifers have been blown to the eastern edge by the morning breeze. Shaded areas show highest zooplankton concentrations and temperatures. Dots indicate sampling points; arrows show inflow and outflow streams. Modified from Horne and Commins (1989).

been expected to prosper. However, a greater abundance of planktivorous fish that selectively ate *Daphnia* gave rise to the dominance of *Bosmina.*

ANNUAL AND SEASONAL VARIATIONS

Zooplankton-Phytoplankton Interdependence

The overall features of annual changes in biomass for zooplankton and phytoplankton in temperate lakes are quite similar; this is well illustrated in Lake Lucerne, Switzerland (Fig. 13-8a, b). Because the water in this large lake takes some time to heat up and stratify, the "spring" bloom actually peaks in July and consists of diatoms, green flagellates, and some crysophytes. It is nonetheless similar in principle to the May spring diatom bloom in Lake Windermere shown in Fig. 12-5. In Lake Lucerne (Fig. 13-8) the interactions of the primary producers, the herbivores and the carnivores, are obvious. The repeated overgrazing of photosynthetic stock in the lake and its recovery when grazing declines have exact parallels in the familiar television saga of wildebeest and zebra grazing and migrating up and down the East African Plains. Here the huge herds of animals eat all of the grass and within a few weeks must move on or starve. In eutrophic lakes, zooplankton can filter the entire hypolimnion in a few weeks and soon eat most of the phytoplankton. Unable to leave the lake, zooplankton then die or form resting stages.

Overwintering populations consist of small numbers of adult and immature copepods, which grow slowly since phytoplanktonic food is scarce and the water is cold. Cladocerans such as *Daphnia* are rare because they overwinter in the sediments in a resting state, or *diapause,* which is analogous to the resting cells of the meroplanktonic alga *Melosira* discussed in Chap. 12. Protozoans and rotifers are also uncommon in

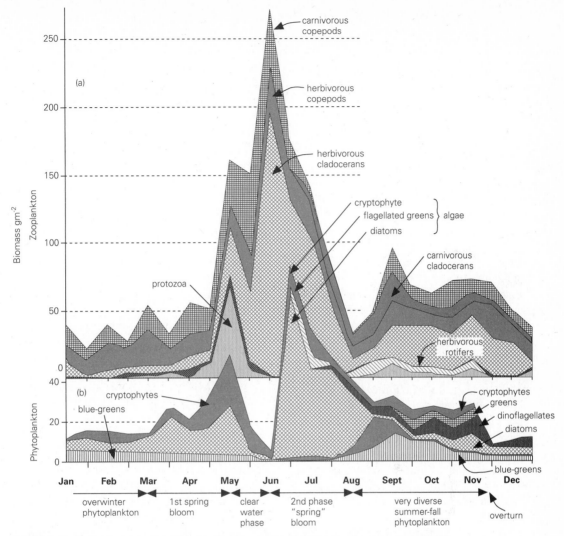

FIGURE 13-8 Seasonal cycles of (*a*) zooplankton and (*b*) phytoplankton in a large mesotrophic temperate lake, Lake Lucerne in Switzerland. Numbers are stacked curves so that, for example, the peak biomass of carnivorous copepod peak is at about 260 g m^{-2}, that of herbivorous copepods is about 230 g m^{-2}, and so on. (Note that the two scales are different.) The most obvious features are (1) the low overwintering biomass of copepods, (2) the spring bloom of nanophytoplankton (mostly cryptophytes) in April–May, followed by (3) a bloom of herbivorous cladocerans, whose overgrazing induces (4) a dramatic "clearwater phase" in June, in which phytoplankton reach an annual minimum and herbivores also decline slightly. (5) The twin annual peaks of phytoplankton and zooplankton in July are comprised of fast-growing diatoms and, as a result of grazing pressure, inedible algae (flagellated greens), which profit from nutrients recycled by the mass of herbivorous zooplankton. At this time the carnivorous zooplankton, mostly copepods, actually make up the largest single group biomass, although the numbers of these large individuals are much less than the herbivores. (6) The decline in edible phytoplankton causes the herbivorous cladocerans to switch from parthenogenetic to sexual reproduction. This results in resting eggs and decreases the coupling between zooplankton and phytoplankton in July–August. (7) Large carnivorous cladocerans dominate a diverse zooplankton for the rest of the stratified period. This figure uses biomass and thus deemphasizes the large numbers of small protozoans and rotifers, which play a large role in nutrient recycling in summer and autumn. Modified from H. Burgi (personal communication).

the winter plankton, but their cysts and resting eggs are present in the sediments.

In spring, as the lake temperature increases, zooplankton become more active. There is a fairly linear relationship between the rate of feeding and temperature, so that growth increases rapidly as the water warms, as long as there is sufficient food. It should be remembered that often dense zooplankton in the Antarctic Ocean carry out their entire life cycle at about zero degrees centigrade and that food supply, rather than temperature, is the ultimate limiting factor for zooplankton. The spring-early summer phytoplankton bloom of nutritious cryptophytes and diatoms (Fig. 13-8b) results in high zooplankton fecundities, often the greatest noted during the entire season. The resulting high birth rates, together with the hatching of rotifer and cladoceran resting eggs and protozoan cysts, results in a dramatic increase in the number of zooplankton (Fig. 13-8a). Protozoans, rotifers, and cladocerans increase more rapidly than copepods due to their very short period of juvenile development. Copepod eggs also hatch in spring, but their maturation rate is much slower.

The net result is a rapid spring increase in the number of cladocerans, rotifers, and protozoans with a slower rise in copepods (Fig. 13-8a). Cladocerans and rotifers in temperate lakes in late spring can increase their biomass by a few percent each day. Because of their small size the changes in rotifers are not very obvious in Fig. 13-8; this is discussed later. Protozoans can probably grow even faster, but there is little in situ information on these small animals. The average size of individual crustacean zooplankters also increases at this time, making them more important as grazers than their numbers would suggest. One reason for this is that large zooplankton filter much more water and remove many more phytoplankton than a similar biomass of small zooplankton.

As mentioned in Chap. 12, grazing by large numbers of zooplankton in spring creates a phase of low phytoplankton numbers in early summer in most lakes (Fig. 13-8b; Sommer et al., 1986). This is called the *clearwater phase* because the lake water is often at its most transparent. Only large, indigestible algae remain, and they absorb little light relative to a similar mass of small particles (Chap. 3). In Fig. 13-8b, the clearwater phase in Lake Lucerne is followed by a second spring-early summer phytoplankton bloom. This does not always happen in other lakes; often the clearwater phase is followed directly by the lower populations of the diverse summer phytoplankton.

The spring-summer peak is the most prominent feature of the zooplankton seasonal cycle. When expressed as numbers of individuals, this peak is usually dominated by herbivorous cladocerans composed of one or more species of *Daphnia*. Other cladocerans, such as *Bosmina*, are also common. Cladocerans also exhibit a smaller autumn bloom, but one that is much less well-defined. The smallest group, the protozoans, peak in May in Lake Lucerne, just before the *Daphnia* bloom. The peak shown in Fig. 13-8a is based on biomass and underepresents the large numbers of small protozoans present. Carnivorous rotifers such as *Asplanchna* are also most common in the early spring and summer, when their prey are most available. Both predatory and herbivorous copepods are most abundant in the early part of the *Daphnia* bloom and in the autumn, when their food supplies are also maximal. In contrast, the predatory cladocerans such as *Leptodora* are common only from midsummer through autumn (Fig. 13-8). Finally, herbivorous rotifers are found mostly following the summer minimum in this lake. They can feed on algae and bacteria that are too small or toxic for cladocerans or copepods. In other lakes the cycles may differ considerably; for example, in dimictic lakes some rotifers reach their peak abundance in winter under ice cover.

After the zooplankton maximum the remaining sparse phytoplankton is mostly composed of large and hard-to-digest green and blue-green algae or small phytoflagellates, such as the cryp-

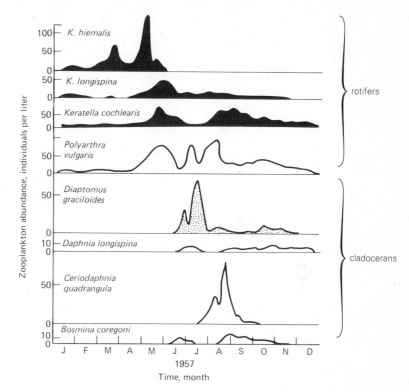

FIGURE 13-9 Seasonal cycles of major zooplankton in temperate Lake Erken, Sweden. Note how the different species of *Keratella*, the calanoid copepod *Diaptomus*, and the cladocerans *Ceriodaphnia* and *Bosmina* peak at different times of year. Modified from Nauwerk (1963).

tophytes (Fig. 13-8). In particular, the blue-greens are often actually toxic or at least are rejected by zooplankton (Burns et al., 1989). However, Lake Lucerne is not very eutrophic and does not exhibit large blue-green blooms. When the fecundity and numbers of the spring zooplankton decline to low levels they are replaced by a smaller group of different species adapted to feed on summer phytoplankton. This succession is illustrated for the rotifer *Keratella* and other genera of zooplankton in Lake Erken, Sweden, in Fig. 13-9.

Other Factors Influencing Zooplankton Seasonal Cycles

Competition and environmental variables are important in determining the speciation and seasonal abundance of zooplankton in some lakes. For example, in the English Lake District large annual changes in the populations of limnetic

crustaceans have occurred over the last 20 years (Fig. 13-10). In mildly eutrophic Esthwaite Water (Tables 21-1, 21-2), two cyclopoid copepods, *Cyclops abyssorum* and *Mesocyclops leuckarti*, coexist in widely varying numbers. The less common *Cyclops* exhibited several years of very small populations followed by dramatic increases in the 1960s, when its numbers almost equaled those of *Mesocyclops* (Fig. 13-10).

These variations seem to have no connection with the variations in the phytoplankton but may be part of a long-term population change. The English Lakes, like most mountain lakes, were created by retreating glaciers about 10,000 years ago in much cooler climatic conditions. *Cyclops abyssorum* is probably an ice age species that is gradually being replaced by the warm-water *M. leuckarti*. These two species now coexist in only 3 of 18 lakes in the English Lake District. A

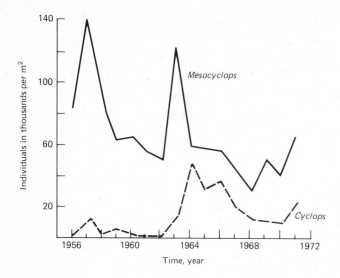

FIGURE 13-10 Effect of long-term climatic change and competition between species on the mean annual totals of the two cyclopoid copepods, *Cyclops abyssorum* and *Mesocyclops leuckarti*, in Esthwaite Water, English Lake District, from 1956 to 1971. Note the large variation from year to year. From Smyly (1978).

possible mechanism for the replacement is interspecies predation on the nauplier or copepodid instars. These two adaptable copepod species have similar life cycles but are different in body size, periodicity, and vertical distribution. Both species can switch from an herbivorous diet to a carnivorous one in the immature copepodid stages (Fig. 13-17). If copepodids of one species grew faster than the other they could switch to a carnivorous diet earlier and prey on the slower-growing species. Since cooler water favors *C. abyssorum* and *M. leuckarti* favors warmer water, the size of the summer population would depend on whether the spring weather was warm or cold.

Top-down and bottom-up food chain influences can act simultaneously to alter the zooplankton seasonal cycles and population structure over several years. The seasonal cycles of several species of two common zooplankton genera, the cladoceran *Daphnia* and the calanoid copepod *Diaptomus,* are shown in Fig. 13-11 for Lake Washington, near Seattle. *Diaptomus ashlandi* was the dominant species from 1972 to 1975, when five species of *Daphnia* were present in low numbers. In 1976 a remarkable change occurred: two species of *Daphnia* suddenly increased. *Diaptomus,* though still common,

showed a reduction in peak numbers from 200 per liter in 1973–1974 to 50 per liter by 1976.

The reasons for the sudden increase in *Daphnia* in Lake Washington involve interactions at all trophic levels. Prior to 1965, *Daphnia* populations were low, due to grazing by an opossum shrimp *Neomysis. Neomysis* decreased after 1965, due to an increase in fish predation. In modern terms this would be a top-down effect. Between 1965 and 1975, *Daphnia* was not able to take advantage of reduced *Mysis* predation pressure due to mechanical interference in its feeding. This bottom-up effect was caused by an abundance of the blue-green alga *Oscillatoria rubescens,* whose long filaments are collected during feeding but then rejected. This process uses energy that would otherwise go to growth and reproduction. By 1975 restoration of the lake had progressed so far that *Oscillatoria* was no longer present in sufficient amounts to prevent the increases in *Daphnia* (Fig. 13-11).

Changes in population may occur for reasons other than temperature or competition. For example, following trace element fertilization of Castle Lake, California, with molybdenum, *Daphnia rosea* and *Diaptomus novamexicanus* increased dramatically (Fig. 10-11). The cladoceran response to an increase in algal growth was

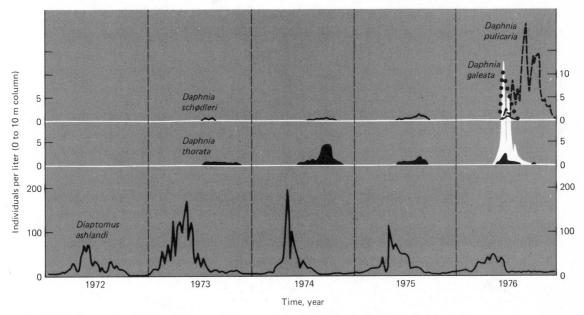

FIGURE 13-11 Top-down and bottom-up effects on the seasonal and year-to-year variations of a zooplankton population dominated by a calanoid copepod, *Diaptomus,* and various species of the cladoceran *Daphnia.* Note how two *Daphnia* species suddenly invaded the plankton in 1976 and the differences in scales. The lake is Lake Washington, Seattle. The bottom-up effect was indirectly due to a large decrease in nutrient input and the top-down effect to changes in fish stocking (see text). *Daphnia ambigua* (not shown) was present only in 1972 and 1973. Redrawn from Edmondson and Litt (1982).

almost immediate, since their generation time is about 14 days. The copepod *Diaptomus* responded by producing large numbers of eggs and showed an order-of-magnitude increase when these eggs hatched the following year. An increase in trout yield due to increased zoobenthic production occurred for several years after the fertilization (Fig. 10-11).

Competition between different zooplankters causes the patterns of seasonal abundance of the large predatory rotifer *Asplanchna priodonta* in small, productive Donk Lake in Belgium (Fig. 13-12). Two main peaks in abundance usually occur in early spring and in autumn, but maximum populations vary greatly from year to year. These seasonal patterns may be due to interaction between *Asplanchna* and large filter-feeding zooplankton such as *Bosmina* and *Daphnia.* There is apparently little direct food competition;

Asplanchna feeds mostly on other rotifers, such as *Keratella* as well as on phytoplankton. However, *Keratella* may be outcompeted for food by *Bosmina,* since both feed on small algae and bacteria, and thus not be available for consumption by *Asplanchna.*

A top-down predation effect was also responsible for a dramatic population shift of the zooplankton in oligotrophic Lake Tahoe. In this case the opossum shrimp *Mysis relicta* was introduced as a forage food for juvenile lake trout. It was thought by the fisheries authorities that *Mysis* would feed on detritus and thus not affect the zooplankton. However, given the opportunity, *Mysis* acted as a predator (Fig. 13-5). Introduced in the 1960s, *Mysis* increased dramatically by the early 1970s, but the cladocerans *Daphnia pulicaria, D. rosea,* and *Bosmina longirostris* disappeared from the pelagic zone (Fig. 13-13).

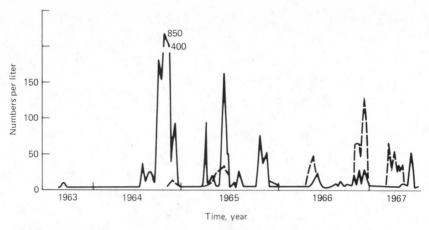

FIGURE 13-12   Seasonal cycles of the predatory rotifer *Asplanchna priodonta* in Donk Lake, Belgium, at two stations (dashed and continuous lines) in this small (43-ha; 20-acre) lake. Note that if only one station had been sampled, a decline could have been shown from 1964 to 1966. Actually no such trend occurred. Modified from Dumont (1972).

Predation by *Mysis* and another introduced species, the Kokanee salmon, *Oncorhynchus nerka,* combined to produce the cladoceran decline. *Bosmina* now coexists with *Mysis* only in relatively shallow Emerald Bay, where primary productivity may be high enough to allow *Bosmina* to offset predation with a higher birth rate than is possible in the oligotrophic pelagic zone (Morgan, 1980).

Seasonal fluctuations in zooplankton are, like those of phytoplankton, less dramatic in the tropics than in temperate regions. However, the numbers of some species of tropical zooplankton may vary seasonally over two orders of magnitude, especially in deeper tropical lakes. Polar and alpine zooplankton tend to show more seasonal variation, primarily because the short season includes only a spring peak, even though it may actually occur in summer.

FEEDING

Most zooplankton are filter feeders on suspensions of mixed bioseston composed of algae, bacteria, and detritus. Filtering rates increase with temperature, which is most apparent in temperate lakes in spring. In other climates, zooplankton have adapted to filter at temperatures ranging from 0°C in alpine or polar regions to over 35°C in tropical lakes.

Food Quality and Selection

Food quality is important, and zooplankton are discriminating in their food selection. Diatoms, small flagellates, and many small green algae are the preferred food sources. Long-term observations show that severe zooplankton declines occur when populations of diatoms and small flagellates shift to large greens, colonial and filamentous blue-greens, or dinoflagellates (Russell et al., 1971; Reid, 1975). Studies with *Daphnia* fed on *Chlorella* show that the age of phytoplankton cells can also be important in determining their nutritional value and older cells may even be toxic. In addition to the quantity of available food, nutritional value, such as variations in carbohydrate-to-protein ratios, lipid composition, and vitamin and trace element content, is reflected in the species composition and condition of the phytoplankton. This, in turn, determines the standing crop and recruitment of zooplankton.

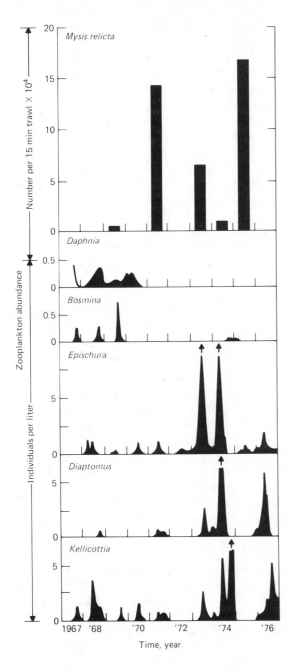

FIGURE 13-13 Effects of predator introduction on the seasonal cycles of zooplankton in Lake Tahoe. Note how the *Daphnia* (*D. rosa* and *D. pulcaria*) and *Bosmina longirostris* populations decreased drastically, while the copepods *Epischura nevadensis* and *Diaptomus tyrelli* and the rotifer *Kellicottia longispina* increased after the introduction of the predatory opossum shrimp *Mysis relicta*. Redrawn and modified from Goldman et al. (1979).

erally avoided by most zooplankton. Large blue-green algal colonies are too big to enter the filtering apparatus of cladoceran zooplankton such as *Daphnia*. Small filaments are physically ejected from the food groove. Ejection requires considerable energy in some species (Porter and McDonough, 1984). Because of their taste (DeMort, 1986), smaller blue-green algal filaments are either often rejected or not filtered. Arnold (1971) examined the grazing of the cladoceran *Daphnia* on cultures of small colonies of various planktonic blue-green algae and concluded that they are not only rejected but if eaten are poorly digested. These conclusions based on laboratory work have been confirmed for *Daphnia* in mesocosm and field studies and with other cladocerans, such as *Bosmina* (Burns, 1987; Haney, 1987; Lampert, 1987). Even the presence of blue-green algae can suppress the feeding of cladoceran zooplankters, probably due to the production of toxins by the algae (Fulton and Paerl, 1987; Burns et al., 1989).

Grazing influences the succession of phytoplankton species, which gradually change from a largely edible group of cells in spring to predominantly inedible ones, such as blue-green algae, in summer.

Blooms of blue-green algae such as *Microcystis* may be held in check through removal of the smallest colonies by grazing (de Bernardi et al., 1981). Certain large green and blue-green algae, particularly those with durable cell walls and gelatinous sheaths, may pass unharmed through the guts of zooplankters and even gain some nutrients from their host during passage (Porter, 1976).

An increase in zooplankton filtration rates in spring can slow down or even halt the spring

It is important to realize that not all of the available phytoplankton are eaten, and of those ingested some are not digested. In temperate climates, blue-green algae (cyanobacteria) are gen-

algae bloom. Because the major food source for herbivorous zooplankton is the ubiquitous diatom population, grazing pressure is also likely to change diatom species composition and numbers. The importance of grazing by zooplankters on phytoplankton density is illustrated by the pioneering *grazing theory* of Harvey (1937). Beginning with 100 algal cells, after six divisions there are 6400 cells. If, however, 10 percent is grazed off between divisions, only 3410 cells result, which amounts to a reduction in the potential population size by almost half. In Lake Washington in late spring each zooplankter can filter the algae from several milliliters of lake water per day. In this case the number of algae removed is approximately the same as the rate of primary production, so zooplankton grazing keeps the algal population constant.

Feeding and Filtering Techniques

Crustacean zooplankton employ various feeding methods. Their antennae and thoracic limbs differ considerably in shape and size, providing a different filtering capacity for different species. This reduces interspecific competition for food and permits the simultaneous existence of several quite similar types of animal. Figure 13-14 illustrates the feeding method and filtering appendages of *Daphnia*. The legs of cladocera such as *Daphnia, Ceriodaphnia,* and *Bosmina* bear hairs and setae used to filter particles which are then collected in the ventral food groove and moved to the mouth. The water around zooplankton has a low Reynolds number and is viscus. In this environment the setae-bearing appendages act like solid paddles and actually filter particles out only in the "final squeeze" close to the animal's body. *Polyphemus* and *Leptodora* are raptorial cladocerans, which are predatory on other cladocerans, copepods, protozoa, and rotifers.

Calanoid copepods create a current by flapping four pairs of feeding appendages. Their second maxillae seize particles prior to filtering them (Koehl and Strickler, 1981). Calanoids filter out particles from about 5 μm to over 100

μm in size. Some, such as *Diaptomus shoshone,* are opportunist predators and alternate between suspension feeding and predation. Many cyclopoid copepods are raptorial feeders on the young stages of their own species, those of other copepods, and rotifers.

Rotifers such as *Keratella, Filinia*, and *Brachionus* are omnivorous genera, whereas *Asplanchna* is largely predatory. Rotifers use their anterior ring of cilia to direct particles to the mouth (Fig. 11-9). Unlike the cladocerans and copepods, which actually filter particles from the water, rotifers sediment particles inside their body walls. Because of their small size, rotifers feed on smaller particles than most cladocerans and copepods—nannoplankton, bacteria, and detritus up to about 15 μm in diameter. Predatory rotifers such as *Asplanchna* draw small organisms into their mouths by using the water current from their cilia and then seize them with their trophi or mouth parts (Fig. 11-9). Food selection by zooplankton has been extensively reviewed (Kerfoot, 1980; Lampert, 1985).

The *filtration rate* or *grazing rate* is the volume of ambient medium per unit time that is cleared of particles. The *feeding rate* is the quantity of food actually ingested per unit time. Both feeding rate and filtering rate are affected by cell or detritus concentration. The feeding rate is usually proportional to food concentration up to a saturation point where the ingestion rate limits feeding. In general, the filtering rate of zooplankton increases with the square of the body length and also increases with temperature to an optimal level before declining. This varies with species and with acclimation temperature (Burns, 1969). Mechanisms of zooplankton feeding were elegantly investigated in situ by Haney (1973), who added ^{32}P-labeled yeast in a special chamber.

Although cladocerans are adversely affected by blue-green algae, some small copepods and rotifers actively feed on them. This occurs in temperate lakes but is more pronounced in warmer waters. In shallow tropical lakes, some species of zooplankton, fish, and flamingos have adapted to consume blue-greens. Copepods, such

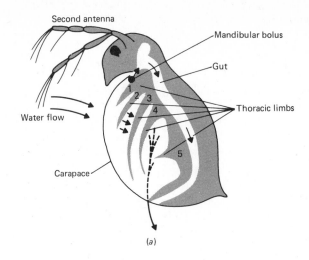

(a)

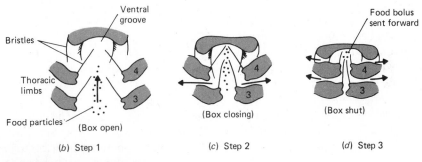

(b) Step 1　　　　(c) Step 2　　　　(d) Step 3

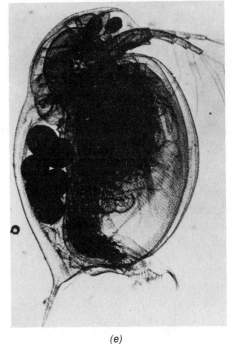

(e)

FIGURE 13-14 Feeding in the cladoceran *Daphnia*. The fast-filter pump used is a "box" formed by the body and carapace and the third, fourth, and fifth thoracic limbs. (*a*) When the limbs move out, food particles, carried in by a current of water, move into the box (*b*). As the limbs close in, particles are retained by the bristles as water is squeezed out (*c*) and particles are trapped, and swept up toward the mouth (*d*). Rejected particles are expelled through the lower carapace. The bristles overlap and are feathered for maximum food retention. (Modified from Russell-Hunter, 1969.) Laminar flow predominates at the small dimensions of the bristle apertures. The limbs sweep the water like solid paddles rather than filters and in copepods may act as grabs which only separate particles from water during the final squeeze (Koehl and Strickler, 1981). (*e*) The "box" of the carapace (light stippled area) and the body and limbs. Several dark eggs are also visible inside the carapace.

as *Bockella* and *Thermocyclops,* feed by grasping the blue-green algae rather than filtering them.

Nutrient Recycling by Zooplankton

The nutrients in the epilimnion and hypolimnion of lakes are increased by zooplankton excretion. In addition, grazing down of the algae results in lower rates of nutrient uptake. Metalimnetic oxygen depletion (Fig. 7-7) often results from zooplankton respiration when animals congregate there to feed (Shapiro, 1960). Ammonia and orthophosphate excreted in the euphotic zone are directly available for primary production and can constitute a substantial fertilization (Hargrave and Green, 1968; Johannes, 1968; Axler et al., 1981). Excretion of nutrients by zooplankton may have direct (Lehman, 1980) or indirect effects (Roth and Horne, 1981) on algae. Recycling of nutrients in the water column is enhanced by the presence of microzooplankton, such as protozoans. These small and often neglected zooplankton are major participants in the *microbial loop* in both marine and freshwater systems. Since the development of new optical and cell fixation techniques, research on the microbial loop has challenged some traditional views of the food web. The microbial loop focuses on the use of dissolved organic matter accidentally released by algae or excreted by zooplankton. Algal cells are not very ''watertight'' and lose photosynthetic material, especially under conditions of stress such as high sunlight. These extracellular products of photosynthesis, such as glycolic acid, are then used by planktonic bacteria, which are in turn consumed by heterotrophic flagellate and ciliate zooplankton. The microbial loop recycles organic matter that would otherwise be lost. This is considered in more detail in Chap. 15.

REPRODUCTION

That zooplankton are adapted to maximize utilization of the short-lived phytoplankton blooms is well illustrated by their life cycles and reproductive strategies (Figs. 13-15 to 13-18). Under favorable conditions rotifers and cladocerans have a life cycle of only a few days, so they are capable of producing many generations each year (Fig. 13-15a). They are thus termed *multivoltine.* Some copepods are multivoltine, but most copepods and mysids are *univoltine*—they produce only a single generation each year. They grow relatively slowly because several molts are required before sexually reproductive adults are produced (Fig. 13-17). Multivoltine zooplankton reach full size and begin to reproduce early in relation to their life expectancy. Most of the food they assimilate in their lifetime goes into egg production rather than growth of individuals. In contrast, univoltine lake copepods and benthic insects spend most of their lives and energy in growing to sexual maturity. Thus growth in more highly developed organisms takes a larger percentage of the total food than is utilized in egg production. Therefore, multivoltine rotifers and cladocerans increase rapidly when food is available (Fig. 13-8a), with their numbers rising almost as fast as those of phytoplankton (Fig. 13-8b).

Rotifers and cladocerans can avoid the time-consuming process of finding a mate by reproducing rapidly through *parthenogenesis.* In this process the ovum develops without fertilization of the egg and only females are produced (Fig. 13-15). Although the life cycles of rotifers and cladocerans are ecologically similar, they are quite different cytologically (Fig. 13-15a, b).

After production the fate of the eggs varies. Most rotifers carry their eggs but some quickly release them, and a few, such as *Asplanchna,* brood them internally. Female cladocerans usually carry their eggs inside their carapace. Female cyclopoid copepods carry eggs in paired sacs attached to the abdomen (Fig. 13-16). Calanoid copepods typically have an unpaired egg sac, but a few genera, such as *Epischura* and *Limnocalanus,* shed their eggs one at a time into the water.

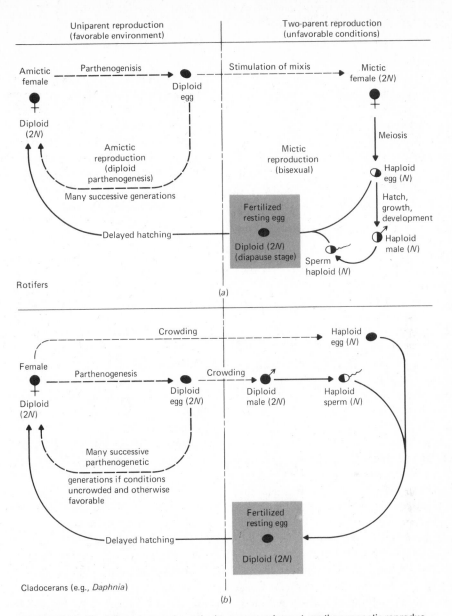

FIGURE 13-15 Life histories of zooplankton were uniparent, parthenogenetic reproduction is important. The cycles of (*a*) rotifers and (*b*) cladocerans such as *Daphnia* appear similar but are very different genetically. Both groups use parthenogenetic reproduction when conditions favor rapid growth, e.g., during phytoplankton blooms. In rotifers sex determination has a chromosomal basis; females are diploid (2N), and males are haploid (N). In cladocerans, as in most higher animals, sex is determined by the familiar XX chromosome (female) and XY (male). In both groups under favorable conditions diploid females produce diploid eggs which hatch into more diploid females without the ovum having to be fertilized by a male. Thus exact copies are produced. Under stress of crowding, temperature, photoperiod, or diet changes, males or haploid eggs are produced and sexual reproduction occurs. The fertilized resting eggs produced have a greater genetic variability to survive possible new conditions in the following years. For more details see Edmondson, 1955; Gilbert and Thompson, 1968; King, 1972.

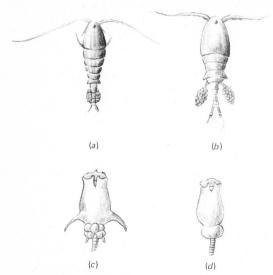

(a)   (b)

(c)   (d)

FIGURE 13-16 Zooplankton and their eggs: (a) calanoid copepod; (b) cyclopoid copepod; (c) the rotifer *Brachionus,* with summer eggs; and (d) *Brachionus* with single autumn egg. Modified from drawings by H. Anton.

Unfavorable conditions, particularly declining temperatures, crowding, and changes in diet or photoperiod, cause parthenogenesis to cease (Fig. 13-14), and males as well as females are produced by sexual reproduction. The resulting eggs are usually thick-walled and resistant to desiccation and cold. This has an obvious advantage for the zooplankton of temporary ponds, who must survive long periods without water. Copepods always reproduce sexually (Fig. 13-17). However, they can produce resting eggs, and under stress copepodids may enter a benthic resting stage.

Population Dynamics

A study of population dynamics requires knowledge of intrinsic rates of growth, birth, and death. Rates of *natality* (birth) and *mortality* (death) in natural populations reflect the seasonal dependence of zooplankton on food quantity and quality, predation, and physical and chemical fluctuations. For example, food supply greatly affects the number of eggs produced by zooplankton. Birth (*b*) and death (*d*) rates together determine the instantaneous rate of growth in numbers (*r*) of a population, according to the general formula $r = b - d$. The exponential rate of growth per day over a short time interval is estimated from *r* and is easily calculated from the weekly population data by the equation

$$r = \frac{\ln N_{t_1} - \ln N_{t_0}}{t_1 - t_0}$$

where N_{t_1} = number of individuals at time t_1
N_{t_0} = number at t_0
$t_1 - t_0$ = length of time in days between the two sampling intervals

(For more details, see Edmondson, 1974a; 1977). The major assumptions are that population changes are exponential between any two sampling dates and demographic rates are constant during the sampling interval. Although these assumptions may not always be realistic for natural populations, they are necessary to make the mathematics of the equations tractable. An example of the population dynamics of the common cladoceran *Daphnia* in a lake is given in Fig. 13-18.

While *r* is simply estimated from weekly population estimates, the data required for the calculation of *b* and *d* are more difficult to obtain. Birth rate *b* is an estimate of the number of new individuals born to the population each day. Like *r*, it is an instantaneous, exponential rate. The calculation of *b* requires weekly estimates of egg numbers and the density of females. In most zooplankton species, eggs are carried by the female and are easily identifiable if separated after collection. Eggs can also be counted within egg cases or brood pouches (Fig. 13-16). Sedimentation of unfiltered samples is an accurate way to estimate zooplankton, eggs, and rotifer densities.

Assuming that eggs and females are counted accurately, the instantaneous birth rate, in new individuals per day, is calculated as follows:

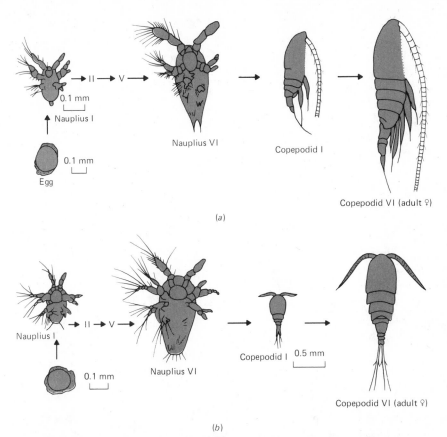

(a)

(b)

FIGURE 13-17 Life cycles of copepods. Freshwater copepods always produce sexually fertilized eggs. The free-swimming larva that hatches from the egg does not look like a small adult, as do young rotifers and cladocerans. It is known as a stage 1 nauplius and has three anterior pairs of appendages. There are 11 subsequent molts, in each of which there is an increase in size and development of the appendages. The final stage is the adult; the first six are nauplii and the last six are copepodids since the change at nauplius Vi is greater than other between-molt variations. (*a*) The calanoid copepod *Diaptomus vulgaris*. (*b*) The cyclopoid copepod *Cyclops strenuus*. Note scale changes. Redrawn from Ravera (1953). There are considerable variations in the general pattern of metamorphosis among the groups of copepods.

$$b = \ln\left(\frac{E}{D} + 1\right)$$

where E = egg ratio = number of eggs divided by number of females
D = egg development time, days.

The egg ratio is easily computed from samples, but D must be determined experimentally. Con-veniently, variation in egg development time within a population is determined almost totally by temperature. Egg development time varies inversely with temperature, and it is preferable to determine D for individual populations. Egg development time can be estimated in the laboratory by isolating a group of 50 to 100 females with eggs at a temperature similar to the environment at the time and depth of capture. A

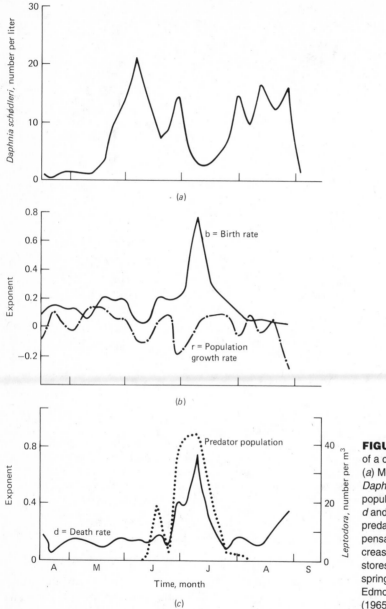

FIGURE 13-18 Population dynamics of a cladoceran herbivore in summer. (*a*) Measured changes in numbers of *Daphnia schoderi*. (*b*) Birth rate *b* and population growth rate *r*. (*c*) Death rate *d* and numbers of the large cladoceran predator *Leptodora* in July. Some compensation for losses occurs from an increase in birth rate, which eventually restores the *Daphnia* population to its spring level. Redrawn and modified from Edmondson (1974). Data from Wright (1965).

graph of percent unhatched eggs versus time is extended to the point where no eggs remain unhatched. The resultant time is an estimate of *D* at that temperature (Edmondson, 1965). Alternatively, individual eggs can be followed from the time of their production to hatching. The major difficulty in calculating *D* for zooplankton is estimating the average temperature to which the egg is exposed. In lakes, water temperatures change during the development of the eggs. Zooplankton are rarely evenly distributed with depth and usually migrate vertically through layers of various temperatures on a seasonal or daily basis (e.g., Fig. 13-5). Egg temperature may be estimated by using an average egg depth, calculated maximum and minimum egg development times (Goldman et al., 1979), or a more exacting approach that takes into account zooplankton vertical distributions, migrations, and the volumes of water strata of different temperatures (Prepas and Rigler, 1978). Once D is known, b can be calculated from the egg ratio and r is determined from weekly population measurements. The instantaneous death rate d is then calculated by subtraction, since $d = b - r$.

Taken together, estimates of r, b, and d greatly expand an analysis of zooplankton population dynamics. Birth rates can be influenced by food supply as well as temperature and are therefore useful indicators of relationships between zooplankton and their food (Frank et al., 1957; King, 1967). An analysis of death rates can establish relationships between zooplankton and higher trophic levels or the influence of major environmental fluctuations on zooplankton populations. Although the above discussion on population dynamics has been directed toward zooplankton, a

similar approach may be applied to the zoobenthos of lakes, streams, estuaries, and even wetlands (Erman and Erman, 1975).

THE BENTHIC ENVIRONMENT: ZOOBENTHOS

The benthic environment can be divided into two distinct habitats, the *littoral* and the *profundal*. The littoral zone shows large daily as well as seasonal variations of physical and chemical factors. In contrast, the profundal zone is below the thermocline and is physically and chemically uniform, except for the summer decreases in oxygen in mesotrophic and eutrophic lakes.

The Profundal Zone

The community structure of the profundal zone of lakes is relatively simple, with only four main groups of macroinvertebrate benthic organisms present. These are oligochaete worms, amphipods, insect larvae (a few chironomid midges and the transparent ''phantom'' midge larvae, *Chaoborus*), and sphaerid and unionid clams (Fig. 13-19). Oligochaetes are a cold-water group; only a few species live in permanently warm lakes and rivers in the tropics (Timm,

FIGURE 13-19 Lake benthos in the profundal zone. This habitat has a monotonous low diversity of animals, and abundances are usually low relative to the more productive littoral zone. Note that the amphipods and the phantom midge, *Chaoborus* (not shown), inhabit the surface muds, together with the small fingernail clams (Sphaeridae, not shown). These animals disturb only the upper 1 to 3 cm of sediment. The tube-dwelling chironomid midge larvae also mix little sediment. In contrast, oligochaete worms and large deposit-feeding unionid clams mix sediments thoroughly down to about 10 cm. Modified from Fisher (1982).

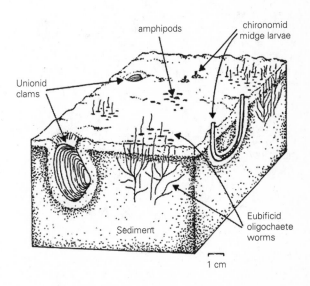

1980). The amphipod crustacean *Monoporeia affinis,* together with another occasional member of the benthos, the mysid shrimp *Mysis relicta,* dominate much of the profundal benthos in the Great Lakes and other northern cold-water lakes. Insects are represented predominantly by many species of chironomid larvae, which are specialized for habitats ranging from the most oligotrophic, such as the bottom of Lake Superior, to the most eutrophic, including sewage outfalls. In Lake Baikal, Siberia, an endemic chironomid was collected at over 1300 m. Occasionally, as in Lake Erie, the burrowing mayfly *Hexagenia* may dominate some areas of the profundal zone, provided oxygen is high. In oliogotrophic Lake Tahoe, where dissolved oxygen is always high, the stonefly *Capnia lacustra* is found at 80 m. Freshwater clams and mussels are more common in the littoral zone and in rivers, but some species, such as the unionid *Anodonta,* are found at depths of 30 m in Lake Michigan.

The patchy physical and chemical nature of the substratum strongly influences the structure of the benthic community. In Lake Geneva, Lang (1989) showed that small mounds of sediment, called *pillows,* were inhabited by very different oligochaete worm populations than nearby trenches. Underwater videotapes show that some fish, such as the burbot in Lake Superior, may create their own burrows in the mud (Boyer et al., 1989).

The Littoral Zone

Diversity, density, and productivity are high in the littoral zone (Figs. 13-20, 13-21, Tables 13-1 and 13-2). Most types of insects, snails, worms, crustaceans, and fish occur in these shallow, well-mixed waters. For example, there are 52 species of aquatic insect larvae in the littoral zone of Lake Mendota, Wisconsin, but only 2 to 3 insect species at 20 m in the profundal zone (Ward, 1992). Although not strictly benthic, the shallow, transparent zones of lakes where aquatic macrophytes are abundant (Fig. 11-5, Plate 4a) have a benthic community associated with the shelter and detritus provided by these larger plants. An individual *Potomogeton* plant about 50 cm high can contain as many as 555

JUNE PLANT

CHIRONOMIDS
(LARVAE): 177 INDIVIDUALS

NAIDIDS: 143 INDIVIDUALS

OTHERS: 235 INDIVIDUALS

TOTAL: 555 INDIVIDUALS

AUGUST PLANT

CHIRONOMIDS
(LARVAE): 69 INDIVIDUALS

NAIDIDS: 22 INDIVIDUALS

OTHERS: 292 INDIVIDUALS

TOTAL: 383 INDIVIDUALS

50 cm

FIGURE 13-20 High abundance of animals in macrophytes in the littoral zone. The additional surface of aquatic macrophytes greatly increases the habitat for otherwise benthic animals, most of which move freely between the two habitats. In small Eau Galle Lake, Wisconsin, a single pondweed (*Potomogeton*) had a surface area of about 280 cm^{-2} and provided habitat and a food supply of aufwuchs for hundreds of chironomid midge larvae and naidid worms as well as colorful water mites (Hydracarina), nematode worms, ostracods, *Hydra,* and gastropod snails. Modified from Beckett et al. (1992). Similar habitats based on the large alga *Chara* may contain up to 350,000 rotifers and about 500,000 tiny nematodes per liter of water amongst the algal filaments. (Horne and Roth, 1988).

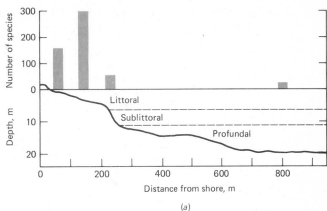

(a)

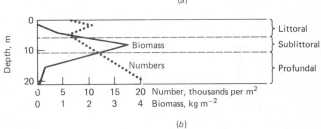

(b)

FIGURE 13-21 Distribution of zoobenthos in eutrophic Lake Esrom, Denmark. The near shore zone has (*a*) high species diversity and (*b*) low total numbers compared to the low diversity and high numbers of organisms in the almost stagnant low-oxygen environment of the profundal zone. Oligotrophic lakes with high oxygen levels in the sediments show higher diversity in the profundal zone. Redrawn and modified from Jónasson (1978).

individual larger animals, such as chironomid larvae and naiad worms (Fig. 13-20). The area provided by such macrophyte "forests" can be enormous. For example, Losee and Wetzel (1988) estimated that macrophytes provide 10 times more surface area than benthic sediments in small, hardwater Lawrence Lake, Michigan. Large, deep lakes, in contrast, have much more extensive profundal than littoral zones. The profundal zone of Lake Baikal constitutes at least three-quarters of the total sediment area.

At the lake edge the continual turbulence produced by waves and currents imparts an energy subsidy for the biota by providing a stream of food particles and oxygen. The productive littoral and sublittoral areas are most affected by

TABLE 13-1

TYPE OF FEEDING OF ZOOBENTHOS IN RELATION TO DEPTH IN LAKE ESROM, DENMARK

Approximate values in numbers of organisms per unit area or weight as a percentage of total. Note the absence of herbivores and grazers in the deeper, darker waters.

Zone	Herbivores and grazers		Filterers		Detritivores		Carnivores	
	No.	Wt.	No.	Wt.	No.	Wt.	No.	Wt.
Surf and littoral	30	40	26	46	32	7	13	7
Sublittoral	0	0	63	99	30	1	7	1
Profundal	0	0	20	16	70	72	10	12

Modified from Jónasson (1978).

TABLE 13-2

DISTRIBUTION OF ZOOBENTHOS IN LAKE BAIKAL, SIBERIA

The lowest biomass occurs in deeper zones, as in shallow, eutrophic Lake Esrom (Fig. 13-21a, b) and absolute quantities are about 100 times less in Baikal. Taken as a whole, Baikal has only 5 to 6 g m^{-2} of zoobenthos. Where there are extensive shallow areas, zoobenthos thrive by using the littoral zone algae and macrophytes to supplement their diet of phytoplankton.

Open lake regions		Area of extensive shallows	
Depth, m	Zoobenthos, g m^{-2}	Depth, m	Biomass, g m^{-2}
0–20	25–30	0–50	30
20–70	20–25	0–100	20
70–250	10–15	0–250	22
250–500	3–5		
>500	1–2		

Modified from Kozhov (1963).

diffuse chemical pollution from inflows, which tend to follow the shoreline. The effect of reducing nearshore benthos by poisoning or smothering the animals with sediment often has a particularly damaging effect on fish stocks, since many open-water species feed and reproduce in the littoral zone.

The structure of benthic invertebrate communities is also affected by fish and can be considered in the cascading trophic interactions concept mentioned earlier. For example, in both the pelagic and profundal regions of a previously fishless lake, densities of the dominant macroinvertebrates declined after cutthroat trout *Oncorhynchus clarki* were introduced (Luecke, 1990). Formerly, pelagic *Chaoborus* instars burrowed into the profundal sediment by day; after the trout introduction they migrated to the surface only at night. *Chaoborus* can detect fish predators by chemical clues (Tjossem, 1990). The introduced trout selectively consumed the larger benthic invertebrates, but were apparently unable to exploit invertebrates effectively where cover was provided by the rocky littoral substratum. In contrast, feeding by bluegills and yellow perch can change the abundance and composition of sheltered littoral invertebrates (Gilinsky, 1984; Post and Cucin, 1984; Mittelbach, 1988), per-

haps due to the greater suction afforded by their mouth morphology (Lauder and Liem, 1981) or a difference in their saltatory search patterns (O'Brien et al., 1986) relative to the cutthroat's cruising search pattern.

Adaptation to Varying Oxygen Supplies

In addition to supplying food, turbulence in the littoral zone provides oxygen. The high rates of feeding, respiration, and growth in the warm shallow waters are possible only if ample oxygen is available. For example, the surf-zone amphipod *Gammarus pulex* has a high oxygen requirement for its activity, which is linearly proportional to the amount of dissolved oxygen (Fig. 13-22). In contrast, a typical member of the profundal benthic community of eutrophic lakes, the chironomid midge *Chironomus anthracinus,* shows a curvilinear relationship between respiration and dissolved oxygen. Its activity remains constant until low oxygen levels are reached; 75 percent of maximum respiration is possible even at very low oxygen levels (Fig. 13-22). Profundal species may experience very low oxygen levels in the muds during summer, and the ability of *C. anthracinus* to feed at low oxygen levels is due to hemoglobin (Fig. 10-4) present as its blood pigment. Hemoglobin carries more oxygen than

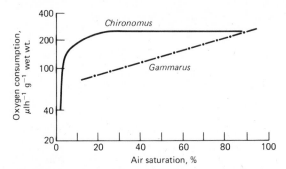

FIGURE 13-22 Adaptation to benthic environments. Zoobenthic activity as measured by oxygen consumption (respiration) can be related to dissolved oxygen (percent air saturation) in the water for two animals from contrasting benthic habitats. Note the linear relationship between dissolved oxygen and activity for the amphipod *Gammerus pulex,* which lives in the well-oxygenated littoral zone. This can be compared with the curvilinear relationship for *Chironomus anthracinus* from the stagnant low-oxygen profundal zone. The ability to have constant activity over a large range of oxygen concentrations down to low values allows *Chironomus* to utilize the low-oxygen habitat denied to *Gammarus.* For example, a drop from 90 to 30 percent air saturation does not affect the activity of *Chironomus* but substantially reduces that of *Gammarus.* Redrawn and modified from Jónasson (1978).

that found in simple solution in the blood fluids. In addition, the pigment in *Chironomus* has a special mechanism for binding the oxygen, which allows it to pick up and unload oxygen over the small range of oxygen levels found in the sediments of eutrophic lakes. In contrast, most kinds of hemoglobin can load oxygen only at high concentrations and unload only at low concentrations.

ZOOBENTHOS FEEDING

In the littoral zone all types of feeding are represented, from carnivory to grazing. If there are submerged aquatic plants they are often coated with bacteria, periphyton, nematodes, rotifers, and protozoans. Grazing snails, chironomid larvae, mayflies, and small fish consume this food supply. In the profundal zone the benthos has

two main sources of food: algae falling from the photic zone and detritus in the sediments. In addition, there are a few active predatory midges, such as *Chaoborus* and *Procladius.*

The dependence of zooplankton on the seasonal changes of phytoplankton was described earlier in this chapter, and a very similar relationship occurs with zoobenthos. In the profundal zone macroinvertebrates feed on the sunken spring bloom and mostly starve for the rest of the year. They are able to do this because they can store large quantities of lipids and the cold temperature reduces their respiration. Diatoms are a particularly important food source for the profundal benthos, because they are heavy, sink quickly, and reach the bottom relatively intact. The arrival of the diatom bloom on the sediments is correlated with a spurt of growth in profundal macroinvertebrates (Fig. 13-23). A similar relationship occurs between chironomids and dinoflagellate plankton in a high alpine lake (Pechlaner et al., 1972). Diatoms are an important source of fatty acids and are generally a high-quality, high-energy food for benthic invertebrates. The preference for algae over detritus is shown in eutrophic Lake Vallentunasjon in Sweden, where the diatom *Melosira* provides 49 percent of the carbon requirements of the midge larva, *Chironomus plumosus* (Johnson et al., 1989). Carbon from microbial detritus supplies only 11 percent, which is similar to the organic carbon content of the sediments.

Other zoobenthic invertebrates are true detritivores (Table 13-1). In the food web they convert low-quality, low-energy detritus into better-quality food for higher trophic levels, such as fish and crayfish. For example, the oligochaete worm *Tubifex* ingests rich mud and detritus. After this is digested and assimilated the worm has increased the energy content from 20 cal mg^{-1} (as wet detritus) to 950 cal mg^{-1} (worm tissue; Ivlev, 1939).

Food rather than space may limit growth in the profundal benthos, which can lead to *resource partitioning* when two species live in the

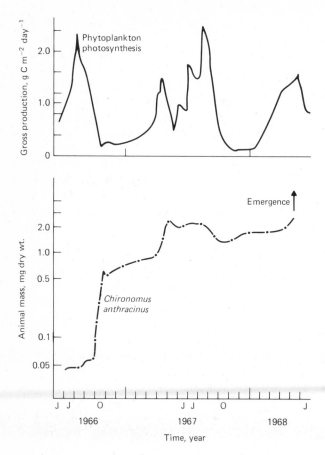

FIGURE 13-23 Growth and life cycle of the profundal midge larvae, *Chironomus anthracinus*, in Lake Esrom, Denmark, in relation to its main food supply. The spring bloom of the diatom *Asterionella* in the epilimnion is particularly important, but these algae must sink to the lake bed before they can be gathered by this deposit-feeding chironomid species. Food is normally scarce and rapid growth in the first year occurs for only limited periods: just after the autumn overturn and following the spring diatom maximum (the main spurt of growth). In the second year only relatively small fluctuations in weight occur. Some larvae can get enough food to emerge in 1 year but most require 2 years. Redrawn from Jónasson (1978).

same habitat. For example, two species of *Chironomus* often occur together in the sediments of eutrophic lakes. *C. anthracinus* forages as a deposit feeder and ingests relatively low-quality detrital food. *C. plumosus* is a suspension feeder that ingests high-quality detrital matter such as undecayed algae (Johnson et al., 1989).

ZOOBENTHOS LIFE CYCLES AND MASS ADULT EMERGENCE

Most benthic organisms have only one generation per year, but in some cooler climates they may live longer. The life cycle is partially controlled by food availability. In addition, the life cycle for many species must be timed so that the adult emerges into the air to mate at the proper season (Fig. 13-23). For the most common forms, such as chironomids, the adult midges emerge, mate, and lay their eggs in summer following the spring algal bloom. However, in cold Alaskan tundra ponds as much as 7 years may pass between egg and adult emergence. Presumably, growth occurs for only a few weeks each year.

Life histories in the other three common benthic invertebrates groups vary. *Chaoborus,* like most of the related chironomid species, normally has only one generation per year. Fingernail clams live and reproduce for several years and, of course, have no emergent stage. In the more productive littoral zone the clam life cycle is shorter than in the profundal zone. The life cycles of oligochaete worms are difficult to measure, because after breeding the reproductive organs are reabsorbed and the adult is indistinguishable from an immature form. A further complexity is that oligochaetes are keyed out taxonomically by the form of the mature sexual organs and details of the internal structure. The latter is lost in preserved specimens and thus single species have not been followed over time.

The number of adult midges emerging in early summer can be enormous. A particularly good example of mass emergence occurs in Lake Myvatn, Iceland. *Mý* is the Icelandic name for midges, and the adults form dense black columns at the lake edge that can be seen miles away (Lindegaard and Jonasson, 1979). The swarms are composed of *C. islandicus* and *Tanytarsus gracilentus,* which feed among the abundant *Cladophora* algae growing on the bottom of this shallow, eutrophic lake. In shallow lakes the whole lake bed is equivalent to the littoral zone. The production of these midges has sustained a large duck population and even a wild duck egg industry for centuries (Gudmundsson, 1979). Other benthic organisms also emerge in massive swarms. In Clear Lake, California, billions of adults of the small gnat *Chaoborus* may emerge on warm evenings and darken street lights. In central Africa near Lake Malawi, ''Kungu cakes'' made of compacted masses of adult *Chaoborus* are eaten by the indigenous residents.

Many zoobenthos do not spend their entire larval existence in the sediments. The predatory gnat *Chaoborus* usually is found in the sediment during the day and at night becomes planktonic, feeding on rotifers and small crustaceans. To avoid fish predation in daylight, *Chaoborus* larvae in eutrophic lakes descend to the low oxygen levels near the lake bed or burrow into the mud (Fig. 13-24). *Chaoborus* is as well-adapted for respiration at low oxygen levels as is *Chironomus* (Fig. 13-22). In oligotrophic lakes, *Chaoborus* larvae are uncommon because these unproductive waters provide no anoxic refuge from predation.

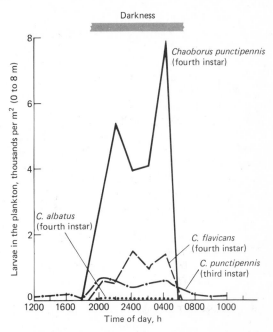

FIGURE 13-24   Diel migrations of three species of the predatory gnat, *Chaoborus,* the only true plankonic insect. This example is in Frains Lake, Michigan, in May. Fourth instar larvae remain in benthic darkness during the day and swim up to feed only at night. They accumulate at about 2 to 5 m in this small dimictic lake. Modified from Roth (1968).

We have discussed the primary and secondary trophic levels of phytoplankton, zooplankton, and zoobenthos. In Chap. 14 we consider the highest trophic level, the fish, which have a variety of roles in lake structure. Many rivers, lakes, and estuaries studied by limnologists have been preserved from total destruction through the efforts of anglers and their organizations, but unfortunately the average limnologist is often poorly informed about the fish and fisheries.

FURTHER READING

Brinkhurst, R. O. 1974. *The Benthos of Lakes.* Macmillan, New York.

Burns, C. W., D.J. Forsyth, J. F. Haney, M. R. James, W. Lampert, and R. D. Pridmore. 1989. ''Coexistence and Exclusion of Zooplankton by *Anabaena minutissima* var. *attenuata* in Lake Rotongaio, New Zealand.'' *Arch. Hydrobiol., 32*:63–82.

Capblancq, J., and H. Laville. 1972. ''Etude de la productivité du lac de Port-Bielh, Pyrenees centrales.'' pp. 73–88. In Z. Kajak and A. Hillbricht-Ilkowska (eds.), *Productivity Problems of Freshwaters.* PWN, Warsaw-Krakow.

Carpenter, S. R., J. F. Kitchell, and J. R. Hodgeson. 1985. ''Cascading Trophic Interactions and Lake Productivity.'' *Bioscience, 35*:634–639.

Cook, D. G., and M. G. Johnson. 1974. ''Benthic Macroinvertebrates of the St. Lawrence Great Lakes,'' *J. Fish. Res. Board Can., 31*:763–782.

Edmondson, W. T. 1974. ''Secondary Production.'' *Mitt. Int. Ver. Angew. Limnol., 20*:229–272.

Jónasson, P. M. 1978. ''Zoobenthos of Lakes.'' *Verh. Int. Ver. Limnol., 20*:13–37.

Jónasson, P. M. 1990. ''Energy Budget of Lake Esrom, Denmark.'' *Verh. Int. Ver. Limnol., 24*:632–640.

Hall, D. J., S. T. Threlkeld, C. W. Burns, and P. H. Crowley. 1976. ''The Size-Efficiency Hypothesis and the Size Structure of Zooplankton Communities.'' *Ann. Rev. Ecol. Syst., 7*:177–208.

Havel, J. 1986. ''Predator-Induced Defences: A Review.'' pp 267–279. In W. C. Kerfoot and A. Sih (eds.). *Predation: Direct and Indirect Impacts on Aquatic Communities.* New England Press, New Hampshire.

Kajak, Z. 1988. ''Considerations on Benthos Abundance in Freshwater, Its Factors and Mechanisms.'' *Int. Rev. Ges. Hydrobiol. Hydrogr., 73*:5–19.

Kerfoot, W. C. (ed.). 1980. *Evolution and Ecology of Zooplankton Communities.* American Society of Limnology and Oceanography Special Symposium, vol. 3. University of New England Press, New Hampshire. 793 pp.

Kerfoot, W. C. and A. Sih (eds.). 1987. *Predation: Direct and Indirect Impacts on Aquatic Communities.* University of New England Press, New Hampshire. 386 pp.

Lampert, W. (ed.). 1985. ''Food Limitation and the Structure of Zooplankton Communities.'' *Arch. Hydrobiol., 21.* 497 pp.

Lampert, W. 1987. ''Laboratory Studies on Zooplankton-Cyanobacteria Interactions.'' *N.Z. J. Marine Freshwat. Res., 21*:483–490.

Lampert, W. 1989. ''The Adaptive Significance of Diel Vertical Migration of Zooplankton.'' *Funct. Ecol., 3*:21–27.

Lewis, W. M. 1979. *Zooplankton Community Analysis: Studies on a Tropical System.* Springer-Verlag, New York. 163 pp.

McQueen, D. J., J. R. Post, and E. I. Mills. 1986. ''Trophic Relationships in Freshwater Pelagic Ecosystems. *Can. J. Fish. Aquat. Sci., 43*:1571.

Porter, K. G. 1977. ''The Plant-Animal Interface in Freshwater Ecosystems.'' *Am. Sci., 65*:159–170.

Porter, K. G., E. B. Sheer, B. F. Sheer, M. L. Pace, and R. W. Sanders. 1985. ''Protozoa in Planktonic Food Webs.'' *J. Protozool., 32*:409–415.

Resh, V. H. and D. M. Rosenburg (eds.). 1984. *The Ecology of Aquatic Insects.* Praeger, New York, 625 pp.

CHAPTER 14

Fish and Fisheries

OVERVIEW

Fish are masters of the turbulent aquatic environment and dominate the trophic pyramid in most lakes, streams, rivers, and estuaries. Their large size and voracious appetites greatly influence the biological structure of aquatic ecosystems. Competition for food results in *resource partitioning* of the available food among fish species and their young. Specialized modes of feeding allow fish to use different parts of the planktonic habitat, and some have adapted to feed on small benthic animals or browse on aquatic vegetation. Almost all lake fishes are planktonic in their early life stages and feed on small zooplankton, small benthic animals, or aufwuchs on submerged plants and rocks. Most *planktivorous* fish eat only zooplankton since few can subsist on phytoplankton alone. Larger, carnivorous fish, called *piscivores,* eat smaller fish, including members of their own species. *Detritivorous* fish digest bacteria, fungi, and protozoans living on particles of detritus or mud, although they inevitably also ingest nutritious insect larvae and worms along with the detritus. In flowing waters invertebrates are the major food items. Many fish are opportunistic feeders, and even the larger carnivores can sometimes be found with algae, detritus, or mud in their stomachs.

The great mobility of fish enables them to make large spatial movements in response to changes in the distribution of resources such as food, cover, or spawning habitat or to escape dangers such as predators, lack of oxygen, or unsuitable temperatures. Fish show definite habitat preference and many have fixed home ranges for feeding, breeding, or avoidance of predation. These locations change markedly with season or time of day and are usually associated with submerged structures such as macrophytes, overhanging vegetation, temperature, light, or chemical gradients. Species such as pike, perch, trout, or carp usually live in one part of the lake or river and breed in another, while a few species migrate considerable distances to breed. Anadromous fish, such as salmon, shad, and smelt, spawn in streams but mature in the ocean, while the many species of eel are catadromous; they mature in freshwater but return to the sea to reproduce.

The seasonal cycles of fish in lakes are less dramatic than those of plankton. Because most

299

fish live for many years, the total biomass may be fairly constant from year to year, but there is usually considerable variation in the size of the various year classes. The success or failure of a year class or *cohort* depends on the interaction of environmental factors and predation. Larval and juvenile fish are very vulnerable to predation, and their growth rate depends on water temperature and food supply. For cold-water fish such as pike or trout, warm summers enable young of the year to reach a larger size by their first winter. At this size they are much less vulnerable to predation. For other species, inter- and intraspecies competition for food, cannibalism, and predation also play a role. Particularly in rivers, but also in lakes, floods and droughts alter the availability of sites for reproduction and feeding.

Native fish stocks are often damaged by overfishing and introductions of exotic fish esteemed by anglers. Various sport fish and the European carp have been moved far beyond their original ranges and have changed the entire trophic structure in many aquatic systems. A sad example of cultural impact is found in the Laurentian Great Lakes, where the two premium salmonid species, locally called lake trout and whitefish, were decimated by commercial fishing and by the construction of a canal that allowed the invasion of a large parasitic sea lamprey. These stresses were compounded by introductions of the marine alewife, rainbow smelt, and European carp, which may have reduced the stocks of other salmonid species. The alewife, in particular, became superabundant and spectacular, smelly die-offs occurred along some lake beaches in the 1960s. Long-term stocking of large exotic and native salmonid piscivores has been partially successful in restoring the ecological balance and alewife stocks have declined. In the Great Lakes emphasis is now placed on sport fishing for introduced fish, particularly Pacific salmon.

Many fish have great commercial value, and it is unfortunate that most human modifications of streams, estuaries, and lakes reduce fish populations. Dams prevent spawning migrations and block important upstream food supplies but do provide new lake fish habitat. Flood control measures that straighten channels, clear snags, and remove riparian shade often destroy both instream habitat and off-stream wetlands. Many fish depend on the flood plain wetlands for breeding or feeding. Pollution in the watershed and littoral zone together with hypolimnetic deoxygenation due to eutrophication are also major causes of fishery declines. Organic and heavy metal pollution have raised concentrations of contaminants in some fish flesh to levels where they are unsafe for human consumption. The standing crop of fish is related to the nutrient supply and, for example, may decrease as total phosphate loadings are decreased by sewage treatment. The potential fish production is related to the *morphoedaphic index* (total dissolved solids divided by mean depth) and reflects the greater availability of nutrients in shallow hardwater lakes. In lakes and reservoirs, careful management, including stocking of young fish, may maintain or even increase fish yields over those of the original system, but this usually involves considerable change from the original species composition.

In this chapter we discuss measurement of fish, feeding and resource partitioning, distribution and habitat preferences, seasonal population changes, tropical river fishes and the importance of the flood plain, decline and partial recovery of the Great Lakes fishery, the effects of water developments, fisheries management, and new reservoirs.

INTRODUCTION

Fish occupy several different levels of the aquatic food chain and comprise over 40 percent of the earth's vertebrate species. Excluding the great value of the water itself, fish are the main product harvested from inland waters. Sports fishers represent a formidable body of public opinion in favor of maintaining the quality of fresh waters. In the United States alone, about 30 million people, or 12.2 percent of the population, purchased sport fishing licenses in 1989. Despite their importance, fish are only now being seriously considered in limnological investigations. Fishery biologists recognize that fish yield is a function of the whole-lake or stream production process. Limnologists, in turn, are increasingly aware that fish can be extremely effective in altering both the structure and function of primary and secondary components of the lake or stream system. The importance of fish in altering the average size and species composition of zooplankton and zoobenthos populations was discussed in Chap. 13. The relationships between light, nutrients, and primary production are reasonably well understood but seldom used as a basis for prediction of fish production (Melak, 1976). This is due in part to the complexity of the food web, since fish often feed at several trophic levels. The task of integrating fish yield, primary and secondary productivity, growth, mortality, competition, and population dynamics with basic limnological parameters is a challenge for the modern fishery biologist.

Although fish are almost ubiquitous, some groups of lakes do not normally contain fish. Examples are mountain lakes where it is physically impossible for fish to pass upstream over large waterfalls that guard the lake. In many of these beautiful lakes fish stocking has completely changed the original situation, even in national parks. There are no fish in Antarctic lakes and some arctic lakes and most ephemeral and vernal pools are also fishless.

One problem with discussions on fish and fisheries is the use of the same common name for entirely different fish. This is particularly true in North America, where the European-derived words *roach, chub,* and *herring* are used to describe similar-looking but taxonomically distinct New World species. The taxonomy of fish is covered in general terms in Chap. 11. We attempted to avoid name confusion by the use of both common and scientific names in Table 11-9. The complex taxonomy of fish has been simplified to cover only those referred to in the text. A few general remarks and Figs. 11-13 and 11-14 will also assist the reader. We make frequent reference to five families of fish: minnows, suckers, ciclids, sunfish, and pikes. The minnow family, Cyprinidae, is found in Europe, Asia, North America, and Africa. The sucker family, Catostomidae, is particularly abundant in North America and is closely related to the minnows. The cichlid family is abundant in Africa and South and Central America but is replaced by its ecological equivalent, the sunfish family (Centrarchidae), in North America. The pike family, Esocidae, is widespread throughout the east and north of North America and in northern Europe and Asia but is absent elsewhere.

MEASUREMENT

Fishery studies involve collection and identification of the species present, age determination, growth rates, habitat preferences, and population structure. Collecting procedures are summarized in Table 14-1. Modern sampling techniques can be very effective if their limitations are recognized and the underlying assumptions in their use not violated. In particular, trends in population size can be followed over time.

Nylon nets are the most common method of fish collection. The simplest approach is seining, where a long, fine-mesh net is worked toward shore. Losses are reduced during seining if the net contains a cod end, which is a finer-mesh, sacklike extension from the midportion of the net to the end. Gill nets placed at various depths capture fish by their gills when they attempt to pass through the mesh. A disadvantage of gill nets is that most fish are killed and other nontarget species, such as otters and diving ducks, trapped and drowned. Fyke nets or hoop nets are particularly appropriate for the live collection of migrating fish in streams and small rivers. They are fixed-trap nets with funnel-like throats

TABLE 14-1

SUMMARY OF SOME OF THE MAJOR SAMPLING DEVICES AND TECHNIQUES USED IN FISHERY RESEARCH

Key: 1 = active sampler, 2 = passive sampler, qV = can quantify fish density per unit volume, qA = can quantify fish density per unit area, Dv = provides information on vertical distribution, P = gives higher precision estimates of density and abundance, B = provides specimens for measurement and identification, DB = dual beam and split beam echo sounders can estimate the size distribution of fish and macroinvertebrates, BO = behavioral observations, species identification. Not shown here is radiotracking or mark and recapture techniques which follow the movements of individual fish.

Habitat	Sampling gear	Results and uses
Limnetic zone	Midwater trawls	1, qV, Dv, B
	Purse seines	1, qV, B
	Gillnets	2, Dv, B
	Hydroacoustics	1, qV, qA, Dv, P, DB
	Underwater video	1, Dv, BO
Littoral zone	Gillnets	2, B
	Electroshockers	1, B
	Trapnets	2, B
	Beach seines	1, qA, B
	Poisons (rotenone)	1, qA, B
	Underwater video	1, qV, qA, Dv, BO
	Scuba	1, qV, qA, Dv, BO
Profundal zone	Bottom trawls	1, qA, Dv, B
	Gillnets	1, Dv, B
	Trapnets	2, Dv, B
	Underwater video	1, qA, Dv, BO
	Scuba	1, qA, Dv, BO
Lotic systems	Electroshockers	1, ~qA, B
	Poisons	1, ~qA, B
	Gillnets	2, B
	Fyke/hoop nets	2, qA, B
	Scuba/snorkeling	1, ~qA, B
	Hydroacoustics	2, qV, qA, P, BO

through which the fish enter but have difficulty exiting (Fig. 14-1). Small or large otter trawls are used to sample mid- or near-bottom water and require an engine powerful enough to overcome the drag of the net, which must be towed at moderate speed. *Electrofishing,* a technique employed in nature by electric eels and a few tropical catfish, is particularly useful in streams and shallow regions of lakes. A portable generator or battery supplies current and develops an electric field between positive and negative electrodes held in the stream (Fig. 14-2) or suspended from a boat (Larimore et al., 1950). Alternating current electronarcotizes any fish passing between the electrodes. Direct current attracts fish toward the positive (anode) pole, where they are netted. If the voltage is not too high and care is taken in handling, both large and small fish taken by electrofishing revive fairly quickly when returned to the water. The fish can be identified, weighed, measured, tagged, and then returned to the water without

(a)

FIGURE 14-1 Fyke or hoop nets set in a stream to assess the population of migrating fish. (*a*) Taken in a coastal stream to assess steelhead movement to spawning grounds after a storm. A great advantage of fyke and the similar hoop nets over gill nets is that the fish can be released unharmed. Other fish moving within their home range or to spawn are also captured. Note the long "wings" on either side of the main net that allow the entire stream to be fished. Fyke nets must be tended every day and are prone to be damaged or even completely buried under debris in floods, as this one was a few days after the picture was taken. Photograph courtesy of M. L. Commins. (*b*) Hoop nets drying after use in eutrophic Tjeukemeer Lake in the Netherlands.

(b)

harm. With practice, loss rates as low as 5 percent can be attained. Migrations and movements are studied by tagging or fin clipping and then subsequent collection of fish. The mark-and-recovery technique of population estimation may be applied to most kinds of animals. For example, individual crayfish are marked by cauterizing their carapace with small dots or numbers, which last through several molts.

Rotenone, long used by native inhabitants of the Amazon basin, is used for management and estimation of total fish populations. This substance is prepared from the roots of *Derris* and other native plants and, when added to water, blocks oxygen metabolism in fish. Most fish arrive gasping at the surface, where they can be collected with a dip net. In streams fish are carried downstream and collected by a seine placed

FIGURE 14-2 Electrofishing in a stream. The small direct current draws semiparalyzed fish toward the anode, where they are easily collected in a hand net, identified, weighed, measured, and then returned to the water. The method works well unless there are many snags or thick vegetation where fish cannot be seen. If the fish are handled gently, it is possible to re-fish the same sites and collect very similar numbers, ages, and diversity of fish as those caught a few days earlier. This photograph was taken in the Santa Ana River drainage in Southern California.

below the poisoned reach. In large lakes "cove" rotenone application in bays separated from the lake with nets gives the best estimate of fish composition and abundance. Rotenone is used to remove nongame fish, often called rough, coarse, or trash fish, before establishment of a sport fishery for trout or bass. This technique should be used with caution because indiscriminate application may further reduce endangered fish species. Because of its mode of action, rotenone kills most invertebrates as well as fish. The importance of these nongame fish and invertebrates should not be underestimated; they often serve as food for sport fish and recycle nutrients for primary and secondary production.

Hook-and-line fishing is a slow but valuable means of sampling fish populations and a dili-gent angler willing to use a variety of baits and hook sizes throughout the year can collect most of the species present.

Hydroacoustic assessment of pelagic fish and crustaceans using sophisticated echosounders can give a precise estimate of population abundance, especially for temporal and spatial distribution (Fig. 14-3a, b). Because the response is instantaneous, dynamic vertical and horizontal patterns can be followed. Midwater trawls are usually employed in conjunction with hydroacoustics to determine the species composition of the observed echoes.

Mark and recapture methods identify fish by tags, clipped fins, or subcutaneous magnetically coded wires. It is possible to equate the number of marked fish (M) in a population (N) to the number of marked fish recaptured (R) in a subsequent sample containing C total fish. For the simplest estimate $N = MC/R$ (Ricker, 1975).

Once caught, fish can be identified from taxonomic keys or, if they are unusual or from a remote part of the world, sent to a specialist for identification. The limnology student should consult the comprehensive treatment of ichthyology by Lagler et al. (1977). Collections of type specimens are also available in some of the major museums, and the local curator of fish is usually both interested and helpful in identification.

Fish scales contain growth rings, which, like tree rings, are used to determine the age and growth rate of many fishes. Species without scales can usually be aged using cross sections of vertebrae, spines, or otoliths (calcareous ear stones). Tetracycline injection, which provides a distinct mark on the otolith, is very effective in lake trout aging studies.

FEEDING AND RESOURCE PARTITIONING

Fish are often the only important large aquatic predators, and results of their feeding can be dramatic. For example, one small fish can eat hundreds more zooplankton than the largest

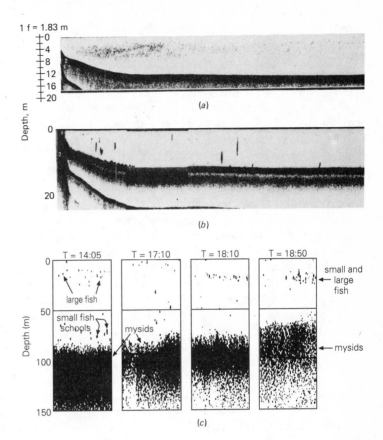

FIGURE 14-3 Echo-sounding charts, which detect fish by reflection of sound waves from their gas bladders. (*a*) Schools of clupeid fish indicated by dark dots between 2 and 6 m in the Great Rift Lake Tanganyika, Africa, at night. Note the concentration of fish near the lake edges. (*b*) Similar chart for midday, showing only a few fish remaining in the water column (thin, black blobs). Modified from Balon and Coche (1974). (*c*) Acoustic record of diel movements of kokane salmon in Okanagan Lake, British Columbia, Canada. Small dots are individual large fish or schools of small ones. The dense bands are Mysid shrimps. Note that at 14.05, large kokanee remained above 50 m while smaller ones schooled below 50 m, in darkness and away from predation. As the afternoon merged into dusk, the small kokanee moved up above 50 m, where there is more zooplankton food. Predatory mysids also moved up, but later in the day. Modified from Levy (1991).

predatory zooplankter. The impact of fish on zooplankton community structure in waters with fish versus those without fish is illustrated in Fig. 13-6. Feeding may be conveniently divided among *pelagic* fish, which feed in open water, and *littoral* and *benthic* fish, which feed at the lake edge or on the bottom of lakes and streams. Pelagic feeding is either *planktivorous* or *piscivorous*. Benthic and littoral feeding is often more generalized and can include grazing on aquatic plants as well as ingestion of bottom debris (*detritivorous* feeding) or ingestion of benthic invertebrates. In flowing waters, some fish eat drifting invertebrate larvae, some pluck insect larvae and crustaceans from the substrate, some feed on detritus in pools, and others seize emerging adult insects.

In general, pelagic fishes are associated with surface waters, and some feed exclusively in the top few centimeters. One example is the common North American mosquito fish, *Gambusia affinis.* An extreme and fascinating example is the tropical forest archer fish, *Toxotes jaculator,* which is able to dislodge its prey from adjacent terrestrial vegetation with a jet of water from its mouth. The white bass, *Morone (Roccus) chrysops,* feeds on zooplankton; it has been observed to take *Daphnia* trapped in windrows produced by Langmuir spirals from the lake surface (Fig. 5-14). The surface-feeding habits of trout and various members of the sunfish family also make them excellent targets for surface fishing with fly and plug.

Planktivorous fish, including some shad, herring, whitefish, or minnows, feed almost exclusively on zooplankton all of their lives. Even large predators like pike and lake trout depend on tiny rotifers, protozoans, and zooplankton in their early life stages. The success of a particular year class may depend on the abundance of these small food items immediately after hatching, when the yolk sac has been absorbed and the juveniles must quickly find other food. Some smaller planktivores pick out an individual zoo-plankter and swallow it, while larger fish engulf a whole patch of zooplankton. Feeding is directed by vision, rather than vibrational or chemical clues. This was demonstrated in a fascinating study by Rudy Strickler and others who created a laser hologram of a *Daphnia*. Fish struck at this light image and tried to eat it. Large fish strain out animal plankton by using gill rakers, protrusions on the gills that hold back particles prior to swallowing. Many pelagic species, such as the whitefish, *Coregonus* spp., have very fine gill rakers and can filter very small prey. As was discussed in Chap. 13, selective predation by fish tends to shift the zooplankton community to smaller species. One mechanism for this change is that the coarse gill rakers of large fish allow the smaller zooplankton to escape.

Although most planktivorous fish feed on zooplankton, a few species utilize phytoplankton. A large minnow, the Sacramento blackfish, *Orthodon microlepidotus,* once the dominant fish in lowland California, feeds partially on phytoplankton. In central Africa, the cichlids *Tilapia nilotica* and *Haplochromis nigripinnis* subsist predominantly on large colonies of the plank-tonic blue-green alga *Microcystis aeruginosa.* They do this by secreting extra acids into the stomach once the algae have been ingested. Without this acidity, blue-green and gelatinous green algae pass through most fish guts undigested. Stomach acidity in vertebrates drops to about pH 2 during digestion of proteins but is lowered to 1.4 in this species (Fig. 14-4). The acid must be released only after food is in the stomach, because undiluted acid would destroy the stomach walls. The low pH assists in breakdown of the blue-green algal cell wall, which, unlike most algal walls, contains amino acids suitable for incorporation into fish protein. Nitrogen is typically in short supply in most tropical lakes, and this unusual feeding method may allow *Tilapia* to dominate the planktivorous fish populations in some tropical lakes. In some African lakes entire fishing industries are based on this white-fleshed fish.

A variety of benthic fish feed principally on the organisms associated with the lake or stream bed. For these fish *detritus*—dead leaves, twigs, and other organic debris—is often the major source of food. Detritus is covered with a living film of bacteria, fungi, protozoans, small insect larvae, and worms. This covering, rather than the original matter, provides the food for detritivorous fish. Small stones are sometimes ingested to help grind up detritus into an easily digestible paste. Almost all fish occasionally ingest detritus, either accidentally or when it is present in the stomach of their prey. The importance of detritus is illustrated by the fact that in some African rivers the most important detritivores decline dramatically downstream of dams that cut off the supply of riverine detritus.

The sucker family, Catostomidae, and some of the freshwater catfish, Ictaluridae, have particularly well-adapted ventral mouths, which are useful in ingesting detritus and insects from the bottom. The highly successful carp also has a mouth well-adapted for feeding on the bottom. The Parana River, in Argentina, contains enormous numbers of the large sabalo, *Prochilodus platensis,* gut-content analysis of which reveals only clay and sediment particles. It appears likely that this fish digests bacteria, fungi, and organic material attached to the clay particles. Other bottom feeders include sturgeon and sculpins, which feed on small insects attached to rocks and weeds.

A few species, such as white amur, also

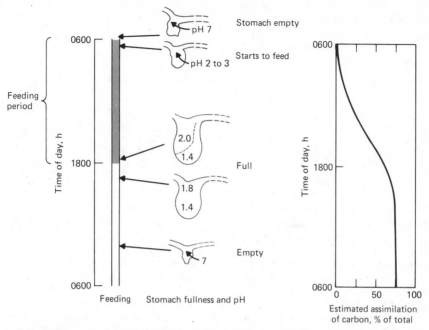

FIGURE 14-4 Feeding and digestion of the blue-green alga *Microcystis* by the planktivorous tropical fish *Tilapia*. Note the extreme acidity of the lower stomach, which enables breakdown of the normally resistant peptidoglycan cell wall. The feces of this fish are turned brown by the acid; when no acid is excreted the feces are green. The stomach returns to a neutral pH when the fish is not feeding. Modified from Moriarty et al. (1973).

known as the grass carp, feed on aquatic vegetation and are often planted to control nuisance weeds in recreational lakes. To prevent uncontrolled spreading of this species, which is native to the Amur River in China, only a sterile form is allowed in North America. The roach, *Rutilus rutilus,* a cyprinid, apparently feeds exclusively on filamentous algae, but careful examination of the gut contents usually shows invertebrates ingested along with the algae.

Resource Partitioning

Although some fish are omnivorous, others are very specialized in their selection of food. This is an illustration of *resource partitioning,* which states that the fish eat only some portion of the available food and thus avoid too much direct competition with others. For example, several

kinds of fish can graze the bottom of a lake or stream by selectively removing a single organism or vegetation type. In Castle Lake, California, two species of trout, the brook trout, *Salvelus fontinalis,* and the rainbow trout, *Salmo gairdneri,* have partitioned the food supply. The brook trout feed mainly on the bottom, taking chironomid and dragonfly larvae, while the rainbow trout feed near the surface, depending on terrestrial organisms in summer (Fig. 14-5) (Swift, 1970; Wurtsbaugh et al., 1975). Another example of resource partitioning involving many species is shown for Lake Tahoe in Fig. 14-6a. A similar division of food resources occurs in streams where the largest, most aggressive carnivores, such as trout, pick off the drifting insects below riffles or banks of submerged vegetation. Smaller fish, such as sculpin and dace, catch

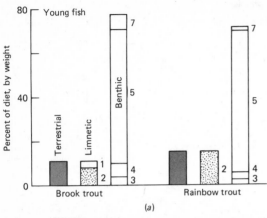
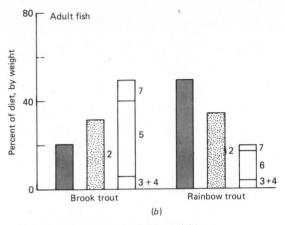

FIGURE 14-5 Resource partitioning in lakes between two species of young and adult trout. (*a*) Young native brook trout, *Salvelinus fontinalis,* lived near the lake bed and fed mostly on benthic animals. The young of the rainbow trout, *Salmo gairdneri,* had a more pelagic habitat but still fed mostly on benthos. (*b*) The adults maintained habitats similar to those of their young stages but changed food preferences. Young, but adult, rainbow trout switched to mainly terrestrial food in summer and fed much less on benthos. Adult brook trout increased their consumption of cladocerans. These data are from mesotrophic Castle Lake, California. Shaded = terrestrial origin; dotted = limnetic; white = benthic; 1 = copepods; 2 = cladocerans; 3 = chironomid larvae; 4 = chironomid pupae; 5 = mayfly larvae; 6 = dragonfly larvae; 7 = other benthos. Modified from Wurtsbaugh et al. (1975) and Swift (1970).

benthic invertebrates in the shallow water of the riffles, while suckers sort the detritus at the bottom of the pools (Fig. 14-6*b*). In some African lakes one species may rapidly evolve into a ''flock'' of many different species, each of which utilizes different food resources (Fig. 14-7).

DISTRIBUTION AND HABITAT PREFERENCES

Except in their very early planktonic life stages, fish are masters of the turbulent water environment and actively select sites for feeding, breeding, and resting. Unfortunately most fish behavior cannot be easily seen, but the advent of radiotelemetry tracking combined with patient underwater observation and statistical analysis of catch data has provided new information on fish behavior, including habitat preferences.

Many fish in lakes show strong preferences for a habitat that includes a diverse collection of submerged and emergent macrophytes. Chemical and biological features of littoral habitats have been shown to be directly correlated with variety and numbers of fish. For example, in Lake St. Clair, Michigan, the abundance and diversity of 29 species of fish was investigated in relation to the habitat quality of the littoral zone (Table 14-2). Samples included species from both natural areas (mostly yellow perch, cyprinids, and killifish) and areas disturbed by pollution and eutrophication (mostly centrachids, especially rock bass). The important aspects of the submerged vegetation were the surface area of the plants, density of the animal inhabitants, and species richness (Table 14-2). The increased diversity of this plant habitat in Lake St. Clair supports a great diversity of insect larvae and snails that are food for the fish. In addition, the rich aufwuchs layer coating most submerged vegetation feeds small juvenile fish, which find refuge from predation and cannibalism.

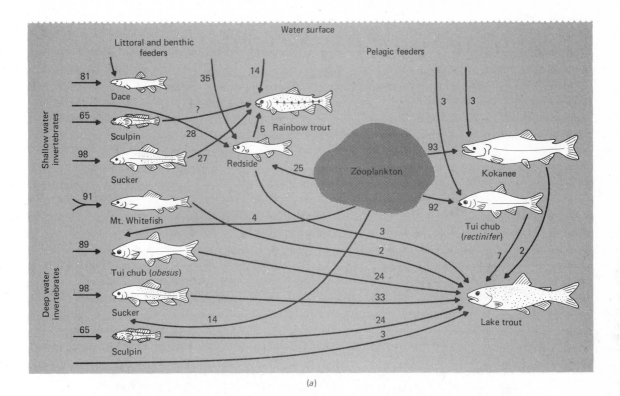

(a)

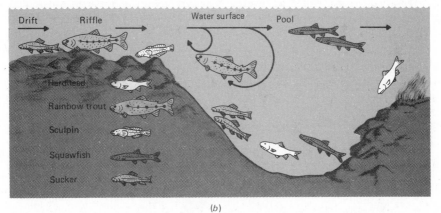

(b)

FIGURE 14-6 Resource partitioning by lake and stream fish. (*a*) Feeding interactions in oligotrophic Lake Tahoe. Note how the total lake food supply of zooplankton and deep or shallow zoobenthos is partitioned between the various fish types. The division into littoral and pelagic, and surface
and deep water is typical of most lakes and oceans. Young and adult fish usually have different prey
requirements. Numbers next to arrows are percent diet by volume. Modified from Moyle (1976), Miller
(1951), and Cordone et al. (1971). (*b*) Feeding interaction in a mountain stream in the northwestern
United States. Note that trout feed on drift invertebrates above and below a riffle; sculpins and small
suckers feed in the shallow riffle areas and among boulders. Larger fish browse on detritus and
submerged plants in pools, and some feed on drifting invertebrates not taken by the more aggressive
trout. Redrawn and modified from Moyle (1976).

FIGURE 14-7 Adaptive radiation: species of the genus *Tilapia* and one species of another genus adapted for various forms of feeding in Lake George, Uganda. Shown are the very specialized phytoplanktivorous form *T. nilotica,* which feeds on the blue-green alga *Microcystis,* and other species that feed in benthic, offshore and nearshore zooplanktivorous habitats.

The Lake St. Clair data show that the fish prefer certain types of littoral habitat. They also indicate that some fish have a definite home range. Studies using radio transmitters attached to larger fish have shown this to be true for many individuals, but with differences between the sexes and even within one sex. Diel and seasonal movements of walleye, an important sport fish in Marion Reservoir, Kansas, were followed after surgically implanting ultrasonic tags in the abdominal cavity. The female walleye established definite home ranges of 10 to 90 ha (5 to 40 acres) and moved from them only to spawn in the littoral zone (Fig. 14-8). Males were more nomadic and made circuits of the lake over periods of weeks. At least one male repeatedly held station at a fixed spot, a brush pile. Marion Reservoir has some areas of flooded timber but has few of the rocky ledges, islands, and channels that would add diversity to the habitat. Under such conditions, more fidelity to a particular area of the lake would be expected. Not all fish show such home range behavior. In another study in the same reservoir, Prophet et al. (1991) failed to find any seasonal up- and down-lake migrations or a home range for populations of striped bass-white bass hybrids.

Even though larval fish are members of the plankton, they are soon large enough to select the most favorable habitat. A study of the distribution of fish larvae between 4 and 19 mm long living in either macrophyte beds or an open

TABLE 14-2

HABITAT PREFERENCES

Correlations between abundance and diversity (species richness) between 29 species of fish and several measures of habitat quality in the littoral zone of Lake St. Clair, Michigan. The data is expressed as the percent of total fish variance explained by individual habitat variation. In this type of study only a small amount of variation can usually be explained by each variable; some yet unknown factors play a role. Note that the most fish abundance changes (13 percent of total variance) were associated with changes in the area of plant surface, presumably because that provides both refuge from predation and a place where macrofaunal food such as insect larvae and snails can also live (correlation with food, i.e. phytomacrofauna density = 9 percent of total variance). Highest fish biodiversity was associated with the highest submerged plant diversity (30 percent of total variance), probably because more ecological niches are provided by many different plant species. Values shown in bold are statistically significant at $P < 0.05$. Water quality variables such as transparency, dissolved oxygen, and temperature were not significantly related to the abundance or diversity of the fish.

Habitat variable	Fish species richness, % of total variance	Fish abundance, % of total variance
Macrophytes		
Surface area	**14**	**13**
Diversity	**30**	8
Phytomacrofauna		
Density	6	**9**
Diversity	**10**	<1
Water quality		
Transparency	-1	-3
Dissolved oxygen	-6	**-8**
Temperature	<-1	<-1

Modified from Poe et al., 1986.

stream channel indicated considerable selection of habitat (Table 14-3). Although the swimming ability of the smallest larvae was limited, the macrophyte beds were much preferred in the daylight and less so at night. This horizontal drift migration is similar to the zooplankton migrations and occurs for the same reasons: to avoid predation in the day and to reach more food at night. Even after the larval or fry stage, the distribution and habitat preference of small or juvenile fish is influenced by predation risk. In the presence of the predatory largemouth bass, small bluegills were found to remain in the cover of macrophytes and feed under suboptimal foraging conditions while larger bluegills fed at higher rates on zooplankton in the open waters. When predators were absent, the smaller bluegills emerged from the weeds and joined the larger fish to feed on the offshore zooplankton. This resulted in higher feeding and growth rates. In addition, the hunting efficiency of the largemouth bass was reduced as the density of macrophytes increased (Savino and Stein, 1982). Thus the smaller, vulnerable bluegills traded lower feeding and growth rates for greater protection from predators. In another example, juvenile rainbow trout were confined to feeding in nearshore habitats with complex cover, despite the higher densities of *Daphnia* offshore, because of the high risk of predation from brown

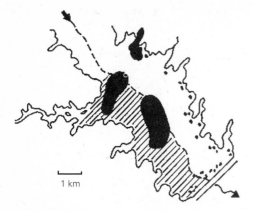

1 km

FIGURE 14-8 Habitat preference in lake fish. The home range for three female and one male walleye, as measured by ultrasound radiotracking, are shown in black in a Reservoir in Kansas. The small uppermost range contains two individuals. The cross-hatched area is where trees were left uncut to provide habitat and the dotted line is the thalweg (old river channel). Note that the fish remain in the physically more diverse areas (snags, old trees, and littoral regions with inlets) except for spawning in the littoral zone at the dam or on the northern shore (black dots). Modified from Prophet et al. (1989).

trout *Salmo trutta,* large rainbow trout, and birds (Tabor and Wurtsbaugh, 1991).

Temperature and oxygen conditions also regulate fish distribution and habitat preferences. There is a wide variety of thermal tolerances both among species and between life stages (Jobling, 1981). Three convenient categories are cold-water, cool-water, and warm-water fishes (Fig. 14-9), and juveniles often prefer temperatures that are several degrees warmer than adults of the same species. Taken together, these different thermal preferences act to segregate species with different thermal tolerances during summer stratification, and can either enhance or reduce competition for other resources, depending on whether they concentrate similar species in more limited areas or separate potential competitors. In winter, many species move to deeper water and exhibit much lower activity and feeding due to their lower metabolic rates (Magnuson et al., 1979; Fig. 14-9).

Temperature and oxygen gradients can interact to exclude fish from all or a fraction of a

TABLE 14-3

HABITAT SELECTION IN LARVAL FISH

The day and night distribution of larval fish (4 to 19 mm) between macrophyte beds and open channels for Steel Swamp, part of the Savannah Rivers system in South Carolina. Even though they are still weak swimmers, the tiny fish avoid the open channel in the day; some venture out in the night when predation is low. Even so, most of the 17 species of fish preferred the macrophytes at any time of day or night. The most common larvae were minnows and sunfish. Data are given in CPUE (Catch Per Unit Effort; number of fish per 5-minute pump sample). In terms of total numbers, the highest CPUE = 2876 fish.

Fish group	Fish abundances in open channels		Fish abundance in macrophyte beds	
	Day	Night	Day	Night
Total	0.14	3.93	38.19	67.2
Pike	0.00	0.00	0.02	0.08
Cyprinids	0.04	1.63	19.79	22.08
Chubsucker	0.02	0.13	6.04	13.00
Pigmy sunfish	0.00	0.13	5.50	14.88
Centrachids	0.00	0.13	2.87	2.54

Modified from Paller, 1987.

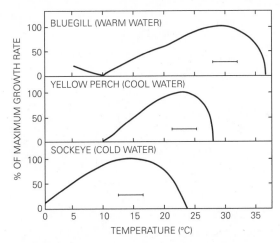

FIGURE 14-9 Thermal habitat preference. The relationship between thermal niche and body growth is shown for warm-, cool-, and cold-water fish and assumes that food is not limiting. Note that there is a gradual rise from cool to optimum (shown by bar) but that temperatures above optimum soon become lethal. This has important consequences for thermal pollution in summer or in tropical waters, when lethal and normal seasonal high temperatures are not far apart. Redrawn from Magnuson et al. (1979).

water body. Oxygen-temperature squeezes are a common problem in eutrophic, warm-water reservoirs and some natural lakes. In these cases the hypolimnion initially becomes anoxic at the bottom in summer and the depth of anoxia gradually rises through the season while the thermocline falls (Fig. 7-8). Temperatures in the epilimnion and metalimnion can approach or exceed lethal limits while dissolved oxygen falls below usable concentrations (4 to 5 mg liter^{-1}) in the hypolimnion. An example is the striped bass, which was excluded from large regions of Lakes Texoma and Whitney due to lethal levels of temperature, dissolved oxygen, or both (Farquhar and Gutreuter 1989; Mathews et al., 1989).

Fish vulnerable to predation use a combination of cover and light levels to minimize their exposure to sight-feeding predators. In shallow, eutrophic Clear Lake, California, tidewater silversides *Menidia beryllina* migrate from cover

in littoral areas to feed in the zooplankton-rich epilimnion offshore at dawn, but they return to the shorelines in the morning before they are satiated (Wurtsbaugh and Li, 1985). The silversides could fill their stomachs if they remained offshore longer, but they apparently minimize daylight exposure to offshore piscivorous fishes. Similar tradeoffs occur with pelagic species. Juvenile sockeye salmon *Oncorhynchus nerka* and the landlocked adult kokanee, which is the same species, stay in the darker deep waters during the day and ascend to feed for a short period in the zooplankton-rich epilimnion at dusk and dawn. Juveniles thus limit their exposure to sight-feeding predators by feeding when light is just sufficient to detect zooplankton but dark enough to minimize the probability of detection by predators (Fig. 14-1*b*; Eggers, 1970; Clark and Levy, 1988). In contrast, the older, less vulnerable kokanee feed all day in the lighted epilimnion.

SEASONAL POPULATION CYCLES

Unlike plankton, most fish are present year round, and seasonal changes in fish biomass reflect increases in the size of individuals as well as their abundance. Of more interest are the large variations that occur in the sizes of individual year classes. The year class, or *cohort,* is the group of fish that was hatched in a particular year. In the case of lake trout, which may live as long as 20 years, there will be 15 to 20 year classes present at any one time, but there are progressively fewer individuals in the older age classes (Fig. 14-10). Individuals of other species, such as the mosquitofish, live for only 2 years and there are therefore only 2 year classes. It is interesting that sometimes unusually large numbers of a particular year class survive and continue to dominate the population for several years. The members of each cohort can generally be distinguished from each other by their length (Fig. 14-10).

Few long-term records of fish population structure are available, but in Windermere fre-

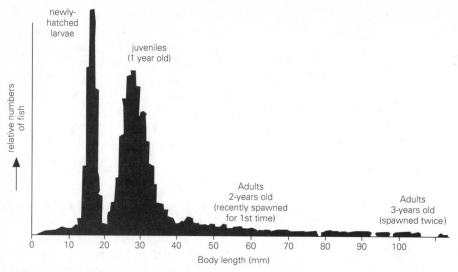

FIGURE 14-10 Size and age class structure in fishes. When the numbers are plotted against the length of each individual, the several peaks indicate the different year classes or cohorts. These data are for a medium-sized piscivorous fish, the bullie or Toitoi, *Gobiomorphus cotidians,* in oligotrophic Lake Taupo, New Zealand. Note the large numbers of recently hatched larval fish and 1-year-old juveniles but the much smaller numbers of 2- and 3-year-old adults. Most length-frequency curves for fish show a similar pattern. In this species it indicates that the main mortality occurs in the second winter. Note also that any mortality, such as fishing or piscivory, that selects larger fish (here 2 to 3-year-olds) would soon deplete the spawning stock. This may have happened in the Great Lakes salmonid fishery in the 1960s. Modified from Stephens (1983).

quent gill net collections between 1942 and 1972 were made for two common fish, the large piscivorous pike, *Esox lucius,* and a smaller predator, the perch, *Perca fluviatilis.* The pike and near relatives of the perch are holarctic and are abundant in lakes and streams in northern North America. These fishes can survive up to 20 years, and specimens of all ages can be found in the lake. However, very few survive beyond 8 years and most are sexually mature at 2 to 3 years. Thus the majority of the adult population belongs to only a few successful cohorts. Fish produce far more eggs than are required to replenish the population, since most of the young die or are eaten in the first year. In this lake over a 20-year period the strongest pike year class was 7 times as large as the weakest, and the perch varied 400-fold between maximum and minimum year classes (Fig. 14-11).

Perch and pike spawn once per year, in spring.

Perch attach strings of sticky eggs to submerged aquatic vegetation and stones, while pike spawn in shallow, weedy areas. The young fry feed on protozoans and rotifers and soon graduate to small insect larvae and crustaceans. Both grow quickly; perch reach about 8 cm in length after 1 year and pike may exceed 20 cm by fall. In 1963 the 4-year-old cohort dominated the perch population (Fig. 14-12). This cohort was the 1959 year class, and it continued to dominate all age classes even in 1966, when it had reached an age of 7 years.

There are two factors involved in the long-term dominance of abundant year classes: the initial survival of a large hatch and the factors that allow its continued success. Before pursuing this discussion of perch year class success, we will consider the contrasting case of pike in Windermere. Pike year classes have more stability than those of perch; no one year class dominated

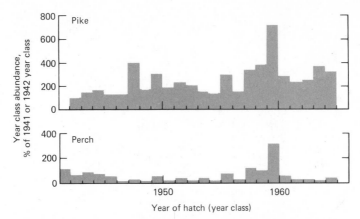

FIGURE 14-11 Reproductive success in fishes. The abundance of each year class for pike and perch in Windermere North Basin for the years 1941 to 1964. Note that only a few classes of perch are very successful. Pike year classes are generally more successful but a few are very successful. Note also that back-to-back successful year classes do not occur, perhaps due to cannibalism. The height of the bar each year is a percentage of the value of fish that hatched (for perch in 1941, for pike in 1942). Samples were collected almost weekly throughout the winter months. Redrawn mainly from Kipling and Frost (1970).

from 1941 to 1964. The abundance of perch and pike year classes in this cool, relatively oligotrophic lake has been attributed to temperature. A warm summer enables the cold-blooded fish to feed faster and grow more quickly, as for zooplankton. An index of the effect of temperature on growth conditions incorporates the increase in temperature above 14°C during the summer period (May to September). For example, if the average epilimnetic temperature for one day is 17°C, then the index scores 3 (that is, $17 - 14 = 3$). The cumulative number for the whole summer is the temperature index. When this index is plotted against the relative abun-

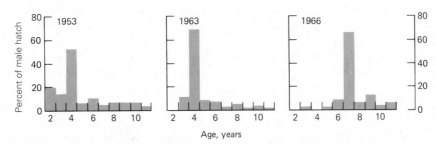

FIGURE 14-12 Effect of a successful year class: cohort dominance over time. Age distribution of male perch in Windermere North Basin in 1953, 1963, and 1966. Values are expressed as a percentage of the estimated total male population. Note the persistence and dominance of the 1959 year class in 1963 (4 years old) and 1966 (7 years old). For comparison, 1953 data are shown (the 1949 year class dominated). In this lake cannibalism and other factors reduce the frequency of successful year classes. Modified from LeCren (1958) and Kipling (1976).

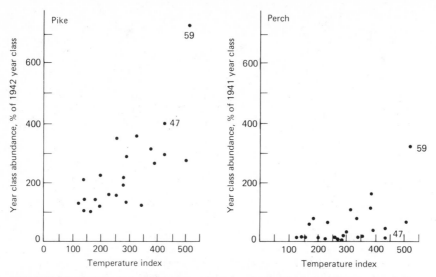

FIGURE 14-13 Effect of warm years on fish abundance. Year-class abundance of pike and perch in Windermere North Basin relative to temperature index for 1941 (perch) or 1942 (pike) to 1964 (see text). Note the dominating effect of higher temperatures in summer, a high index in the success of pike. In this case warmer water probably produced more algae and invertebrates so the juvenile pike could feed and reach the winter at a size at which predation was not important. In most first winters, when growth stops, predation is a major cause of death (see also Fig. 14-9). For perch only the warmest years, such as 1959, produced high numbers for that year class, since other factors usually control year class abundance. The year class abundance was estimated each winter so that about 6 to 9 months had passed from hatching to collection of the first year cohort. Modified from LeCren (1958) and Kipling (1976).

dances of the year classes for both fish, a relationship is shown for both pike and perch (Fig. 14-13).

Temperature controlled the major variation in year class strengths for this pike. Other factors, such as the number of adults at the time of egg hatching or the biomass of adult females that laid the eggs, showed no significant correlation with year class abundance. Older pike are cannibalistic on pike smaller than about 20 cm long. In warm years, many more young are able to exceed this critical size by fall and thus avoid predation by larger fish during the winter.

In the case of perch, the relationship with temperature occurs only in some of the warmest years. The unusually warm 1959 season, as well as being a great wine year in Europe, produced a large class of perch, whereas the warm 1947 season was a complete failure for that year class. Therefore other factors must modify the influence of temperature. These factors are the biomass of mature female perch, availability of suitable spawning areas, food supply for the fry, total biomass of perch more than 1 year old, cannibalism, predation by pike and fish-eating birds, and occasional winter ice. The most abundant perch year classes were produced when there were relatively few breeding perch; the weakest year classes occurred when perch were most common. Thus there were always sufficient eggs, but cannibalism may have effectively reduced the numbers of young fish. In Windermere, and perhaps in many cool temperate lakes, the pike year class abundance is determined primarily by temperature during the first few months of life, but perch appear to be controlled by more complex factors.

As mentioned above, fish are extremely vulnerable to a variety of dangers during their early life stages. Due to their high fecundity, a small change in the proportion of offspring that survive the critical early life stages translates into large differences in the abundance of year classes that can persist over their life span. Survival is positively correlated to body size. Larger larval and juvenile fish can feed on a larger suite of prey sizes and types, can move more widely to search for prey and suitable environmental conditions, and are vulnerable to fewer predators (Miller et al., 1988). Larval fish are generally transparent and occupy either pelagic or extremely shallow littoral habitats until they metamorphose as juveniles into a small version of their adult form. One way to avoid early predation is to avoid the planktonic egg sac stage. This is the case with many trout and salmon, which produce some of the largest eggs among fishes. Their larvae, called *alevins,* develop into fully formed fish (25-mm fry) while still in the gravel of the spawning tributaries. The fry either migrate to lakes or to the ocean immediately after emerging from the gravel or stay in the relatively safe environment of the stream (from a few weeks to 3 years) until they are large enough to avoid predation in larger waters.

The preceding sections have described how biotic and abiotic factors influence abundance, growth, survival, and distribution of fish in lakes. In addition, the fish themselves influence the community structure of the waters they inhabit (Carpenter, 1988; Northcote, 1988). These cascading trophic interactions are described in Chap. 13 (Fig. 13-3).

TROPICAL RIVER FISHES AND THE IMPORTANCE OF THE FLOOD PLAIN

Most of the largest rivers are in tropical climates. Their fish populations are still only lightly fished and reveal things not apparent in the highly modified rivers of the developed world. The number of fish species in tropical rivers is very high. There are about 1300 species of fish in the entire Amazon system, and over 85 percent are either siluroids (catfish) or characoids (Lowe-McConnel, 1986). However, in comparison to the large number of species, the density of fish is usually not very high. Characoids are laterally compressed open-water fish from a few centimeters to 1 m in length. In terms of diet, the different species range from fruit eaters to mudsuckers to the notorious carnivores, such as the piranha. Some of the larger species are harvested for food and export by the local population. The Amazon catfish of the central basin can also be a fierce piscivore and, although not a match for the 250-kg Mekong catfish, can weigh up to 30 kg. Younger large catfish and smaller catfish species feed on zooplankton.

Fish dynamics in tropical rivers illustrate the importance of the flood plain. In temperate and arctic rivers fish do not feed and breed in the flood plain to the extent they do in tropical rivers, although they may venture there on occasion. In the dry season all fish in the Amazon are confined to the main stem, the tributaries, or the flood plain (*varsia*) lakes. In the flood season allochthonous fruits, seeds, and terrestrial arthropods are abundant and attract fish species that utilize this food. Some fruit eaters, including large fish, build up fat stores that can support them until the next flood. Most Amazon fish, including piscivores, are very mobile and migrate both to and from the varsia during the flood season.

The dependence of some fish on the flood plain is shown in the Niger River in Africa, where there are two major groups of fish (Mochokidae and Moromyridae) that together contain 44 species. Of these, 18 species migrate to breed on the flood plain. Of the 16 species found in muddy areas of the river main stem, all but 2 breed in the flood plain. In contrast, of the 14 species found in rocky, clearwater main stem channels, only 1 breeds in the flood plains. Such a division suggests a distinct group of fish that can take advantage of the flood plain but live alongside others that benefit only indirectly, if at all, from floods. Presumably long droughts are a great risk for flood plain breeders, but one that is compensated for by the greater productivity of the flooded areas. The seasonal growth during flooding and cessation in dry periods is obvious from the condition index (Fig. 17-8). The growth patterns are comparable to the winter-summer growth fluctuations in temperate fish, but in the tropical rivers temperatures are high (>25°C) and more constant.

The advantages of flood plains are considerable. Worldwide, the catches of fish can be related to the flood plain area by the relationship:

$$\text{Catch (kg)} = 5.5 \times \text{Flood plain area (ha)}$$

(Welcomme, 1976). Like the productive coastal mangrove swamps with their protective stilt roots, vulnerable eggs and larvae in the flood plain can develop with a low density of predators (fish and human) in the extensive vegetation-clogged flood plain. In this way they can reach a size at which predation is less of a threat before they return to the main stem.

Not all fish use the flood plain for spawning, since they are deterred by the low dissolved oxygen that results from vegetation rotting in the tropical heat. Many characoids migrate laterally to the flood plain early, feed, and then return to the turbulent and well-oxygenated main stem to breed. They may then return to flooded areas to feed again. Other Amazon characoids feed in the flooded varsia and then migrate upriver at low waters to spawn. The Amazon basin is unusually flat and lacks hydraulic barriers such as big waterfalls, thus almost any type of fish migration is possible: fish move from tributaries to main stem (and vice versa), from main stem to the flooded varsia (and vice versa), and even to and from the estuary. Of course, any future dams, barrages, or heavily polluted sections will hamper these annual wide-ranging fish migrations.

THE DECLINE AND PARTIAL RECOVERY OF THE GREAT LAKES FISHERY

Modification of lakes and rivers for navigation often has unexpected consequences. Development of the St. Lawrence waterway provided a nearly 3000-km connection between the Great Lakes and the North Atlantic Ocean. Opening of the first Welland Canal in about 1830 and a second canal 100 years later allowed the invasion of the sea lamprey, *Petromyzon marinus,* and the alewife, *Alosa pseudoharengus,* into the upper Great Lakes. Both have caused serious fish management problems. For several years, mass mortalities of the alewife littered summer beaches with tons of rotting fish, and the population explosion made this species the most abundant fish in Lake Michigan in terms of both weight and numbers (Fig. 14-14*b*).

Although sea lamprey occur naturally in Lake Ontario, the Niagara Falls prevented their passage into Lakes Erie, Huron, Michigan, and Superior until completion of the Welland Canal. They began their invasion of Lakes Huron and Michigan in the 1930s, and in 1946 they were found in Lake Superior (Fig. 14-14). The sea lamprey is a very effective predator and can grow to over 70 cm in length. In the Great Lakes it grows only to 42 to 48 cm long and 130 to 270 g, depending on the salmonid food supply (Houston and Kelso, 1991). It feeds by attaching to large fish with its suckerlike mouth, rasping a hole through the body wall, and extracting the fish's internal fluids. A single individual will consume almost 9 kg of fish in its lifetime. The appearance of the lamprey was coincident with the decline of the salmonid fishery in lakes Michigan, Huron, and Superior (Fig. 14-14*a*).

The story of the decline of several major fish species in the Great Lakes provides an excellent example of the complex structure of aquatic ecosystems. More complete explanations have been given by Baldwin (1964), Smith (1968), Beeton (1969), and Christie (1974). The major commercial fish in the Great Lakes were all members of the salmonid family (Table 11-9), including the

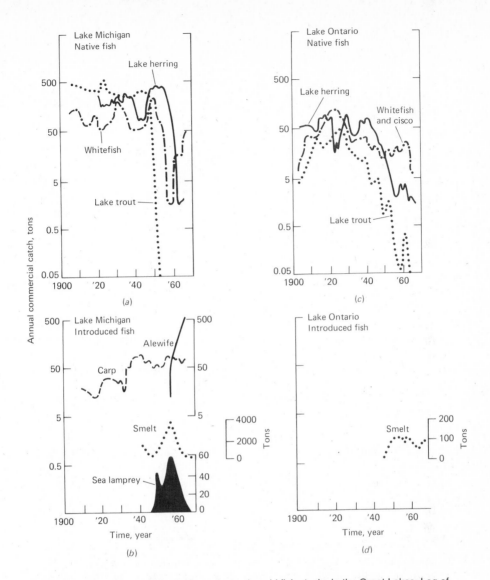

FIGURE 14-14 Decline of native premium salmonid fish stocks in the Great Lakes. Log of commercial fish catches for (*a*) native stocks and (*b*) introduced species in Lake Michigan, which is above Niagara Falls and originally was isolated from sea lampreys and alewives. Similar data (*c, d*) are shown for Lake Ontario, which is below Niagara Falls and has always been connected with the natural habitat of the sea lamprey and alewife. Both of these species entered the Upper Great Lakes in 1920–1930 via the Welland Canal, and smelt were introduced at about the same time (carp were introduced earlier). Note the rapid decline in the largest, most valuable fish (lake trout, whitefish, lake herring, and cisco, all in the salmon family). The combined pressures of overfishing of the breeding stock and sea lamprey predation on the smaller remaining individuals destroyed the fishery. The enormous biomass of smelt, alewife, and carp (note scale change) also had effects. Smelt and alewife compete for zooplankton with the lake herring; bottom-grubbing carp destroy the littoral breeding grounds of whitefish. Note the recovery of whitefish in Lake Michigan when commercial fishing was restricted and the lamprey population was decreased by poisoning. The increase in smelt and alewife is due to the decline of the large predators that were the target of the commercial fishery. This situation has now been partially reversed (Fig. 14-15). Note also the switch to carp fishing as the other stocks collapsed. Modified from Beeton (1969) and Christie (1974).

pelagic lake trout, *Salivelinus namaycush,* and an inshore fish, *Coregonus clupeaformis,* usually called whitefish. The smaller deep-water coregonids, collectively called cisco, include *Coregonus artedii,* referred to as lake herring. The lake trout, a large fish that grows to about 50 cm long, was a mainstay of the century-old commercial fishery in the Great Lakes until the 1940s. The very rapid decline of this species occurred more or less simultaneously in all five lakes during 1945 to 1955 (Fig. 14-14*a, c*). The decline was initially attributed entirely to predation by the sea lamprey. However, it occurred in Lake Michigan at a time when lampreys were relatively uncommon (Fig. 14-14*a, b*) and in Lake Ontario where lampreys had always been present (Fig. 14-14*c, d*). Obviously, factors in addition to lamprey predation were involved.

In the Great Lakes, fishing pressure was concentrated on the larger fishes. Unfortunately, these were the same size class preferred by the sea lamprey. Lampreys do not usually kill larger fish by occasional parasitic feeding, but mortality is severe if smaller individuals are attacked or larger fish are repeatedly attacked. The lake trout is unusual in that it becomes sexually mature at 6 to 7 years of age, after it has reached a large and commercially desirable size. Some other fish mature earlier and begin to reproduce at a size below the harvestable limit. By taking virtually all of the large fish, both commercial fishing and the lamprey were exploiting the entire breeding population. Commercial fishing had already placed heavy stress on the breeding populations of trout, and the extra predation due to the lamprey's introduction may have tipped the balance toward collapse of the fish stock as the lamprey population exploded after the initial introduction. The trout might have better survived lamprey predation without fishing pressure, since the two species have apparently coexisted for centuries in Lake Ontario.

Due to the number of intermediate-sized but sexually immature trout and a possible increase in fishing effort or efficiency, fish catches remained constant in the Great Lakes (Table 14-4) while the numbers of reproductive adults probably declined rapidly. Eventually, with the almost complete loss of the breeding stock, the fishery suddenly collapsed and failed to recover (Fig. 14-14*a, c*). Though an occasional successful year can restock the population, as in the case of perch in Windermere (Fig. 14-11), there is a point at which there are insufficient adults re-

---

TABLE 14-4

THE SUDDEN DECLINE IN CATCHES OF PREMIUM SPECIES (LAKE TROUT, WHITEFISH, LARGER CISCO) IN ALL THE GREAT LAKES COMBINED

The catches now are considerably less than in the 1900–1920 period and contain large proportions of smaller fish such as yellow perch, rainbow smelt, and alewife, as well as smaller cisco. These fish cost more to catch and sell for less than the premium species.

Decade	Premium species as a % of total	Total catch, thousands of tons per decade
1900–1909	77	77
1910–1919	77	61
1920–1929	80	54
1930–1939	78	61
1940–1949	73	54
1950–1959	67	52
1960–1969	45	52

Modified from Christie (1974).

maining to influence future stocks. Since the decline of the lake trout, extensive electrocution of adult lampreys and poisoning of larvae in breeding streams has reduced their numbers (Fig. 14-14*b*). A gradual buildup of natural predators and diseases also may have established a degree of natural lamprey population control (Fig. 14-14*b*). In addition, since commercial fishing for lake trout has been restricted and artificial stocking has been carried out, the populations have shown some recovery.

A decline in commercial catch of whitefish, *Coregonus Clupeaformis*, lake herring, *C. artedii*, and a smaller *Coregonus* species called *cisco* (Fig. 14-14*c*) occurred at about the same time as that of the lake trout (Fig. 14-14*a, c*). In this case overfishing and lamprey predation combined with other environmental pressures may have been responsible for the decline. Rainbow smelt, *Osmerus mordax*, were introduced into the Great Lakes from Crystal Lake, Michigan, in the 1920s to 1930s, and huge stocks rapidly developed in the shallower areas of Lakes Michigan and Huron. The commercial catches of 2000 to 4000 tons annually in the late 1950s in Lake Michigan can be compared to yields of only 500 tons of trout, whitefish, and lake herring (Fig. 14-14*a, b*). Smelt are planktivorous feeders that, because of their enormous numbers, compete for food with the young of native fish. In most lakes, including Lake Michigan, the smelt contributed to the decline of lake herring stocks (Fig. 14-14*a, b*). The smelt may have had little direct effect on whitefish, since large populations of both species coexisted in some of the other Great Lakes (not shown in Fig. 14-14).

The rapid increase in the alewife population in Lake Michigan in the 1960s (Fig. 14-14*b*) could also have been responsible for the decline of the lake herring, because both eat similar zooplankton. Once again, the decline of the herring fishery in Lake Ontario (Fig. 14-14*c*), where the alewife has always been present, shows the crucial role of overfishing salmonid stocks already pressured by competition and lamprey predation (Regier and Lotus, 1972). The alewife increase in Lake Michigan occurred between 1950 and 1960. The rise is probably exaggerated by the relative lack of fishing for alewife before the mid-1950s (Fig. 14-14*b*). It is interesting to speculate why the alewife was not very abundant prior to this time. The small alewife spends much of its life in open water. Alewife increased as the larger deep-water predators, such as lake trout and burbot, *Lota lota,* declined.

The demise of the whitefish and cisco (Fig. 14-14*a, c*) must be largely attributed to a mixture of overfishing and lamprey predation. In the case of the whitefish, the introduction of carp (Fig. 14-14*b*) may have accelerated the decline by physical interference rather than resource competition. Whitefish spend more time in the littoral zone, in contrast to the open-water ciscos, and the presence of large numbers of bottom-grubbing carp may have interfered with whitefish breeding. Other factors influencing the general decline of the Great Lakes fisheries include pollution, harbor construction, dredging of rivers and bays used for spawning, and the intentional introduction of a variety of exotic trout and salmon.

Finally, mention should be made of the fishing strategies used in the Great Lakes prior to 1970, after which commercial fishing was restricted and mostly replaced by sport fishing. When stocks of one large species declined in the 1950s, commercial fishers naturally put more effort into catching the remaining stocks of large fish as well as beginning to fish for smaller fish. Some idea of the direct effects of fishing is shown for a coregonid, the blackfin cisco, *C. nigripinnis,* which was virtually exterminated by overfishing long before the entry of lampreys. The lake sturgeon, a large long-lived fish not subject to severe lamprey predation, was also reduced to a remnant population by excessive fishing.

Several successive species of cisco were overfished. Starting with the largest, *C. artedii* and *C. nigripinnis,* both reaching 40 cm, the fishery progressed down to the smallest, the bloater, *C. hoyi,* which is about 20 cm long. In addition, the fishery switched in part from a profitable high-quality product for human consumption to a less valuable fish meal industry that uses carp and alewife as well as indigenous small fish.

Restoration of some aspects of the Great Lakes fishery has been primarily due to pressure from sport fishers, who prefer to catch lake trout and other large species. An extensive stocking program focusing on lake trout, sturgeon, and two non-native salmon species was begun after the declines of the 1960s. The populations of the non-native salmon increased dramatically, and they are now the main large salmonid sport species. Lake trout stocking was also successful, although this fish has had only very limited success in reproducing in the lakes. Encouraging news is that the increased population of these larger piscivores has reversed some of the earlier trends. One consequence is a dramatic decline in the numbers of alewife in all of the Great Lakes, including Lake Superior (Fig. 14-15). However, the swing to large piscivores may now have gone too far. Due to the popularity of the salmon fishery, managers were pressured to increase stocking rates continually. Stewart et al. (1981) warned that these stocking rates and consequent food demands on small fish would exceed the productive capacity of their prey (primarily alewife and rainbow smelt). Because some of the stocked salmonids were relatively long-lived (Chinook salmon 4 to 7 years, lake trout up to 60 years), the maximum forage demand of these piscivores was not fully exerted for several years. Under the high salmonid stocking rates, this "predatory inertia" could accumulate beyond the sustainable limits of the forage populations (Stewart and Ibarra, 1991). Ironically, managers are now working to reduce the predation pressure to sustain the exotic forage base of alewives. There is even an Alewife Protection Society.

Other Fishery Declines

Other great fisheries have suffered the same fate as the Great Lakes native fish, and for many of the same reasons. In particular, overfishing of the largest individuals as well as decline in the overall stock is found worldwide. For example,

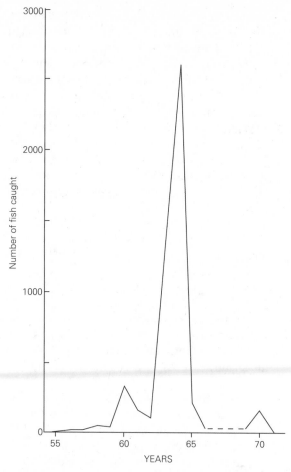

FIGURE 14-15   Rise and fall of the introduced zoo-planktivorous fish: the alewife in Lake Superior. Note the peak populations in the early 1960s and the current lower populations. A similar population change occurred in the more eutrophic lakes, such as Lake Erie and Lake Ontario (O'Gorman and Schneider, 1986). These data show a top-down, trophic cascade effect. The increase in alewife was mostly due to reduction in predation by the large native salmonids following overfishing (Fig. 14-14). The decrease is due to increased predation after heavy stocking of exotic and native piscivorous salmonids. Dotted line = no data. Modified from Bronte et al. (1991).

in the Volga River in Russia, the numbers and size of the largest individual fish have declined during the twentieth century. The most important fish is the beluga, the enormous Volga sturgeon. The largest individuals weighed almost 1300 kg and produced the best caviar in the world. Their decline can be attributed to two main factors: overfishing and spawning ground destruction. The beluga once made its way from the land-locked Caspian Sea 2000 km upstream to spawn in the upper reaches of the Volga. Due to reservoir construction, there is now only 580 km of undammed river. The commercial catch has dropped from 27,000 tons in 1910 to only 5000 tons in the 1970s.

In the Mississippi, the largest fish, the paddle-fish, has also become quite rare, once again most probably due to overfishing and inundation or canalization of its natural river habitat.

EFFECTS OF WATER DEVELOPMENT: DAMS AND FLOOD CONTROL

Water development throughout the world has had a profound effect on inland and estuarine fisheries. The construction of levees and artificial channels, removal of riparian vegetation, and draining of marshes for flood control is commonplace despite the inevitable loss of fish habitat. Breeding grounds, such as swamps flooded in spring, help to maintain high fish production in the river system but are usually the first to be drained and lost forever, since they can be turned into valuable, flat agricultural land. The loss of the riparian corridor removes shade, thus greatly increasing water temperature, and also eliminates a major source of food. Many fish feed on terrestrial insects that accidentally fall into the water from the overhanging vegetation, and the leaves that fall in provide a source of organic detritus for benthic invertebrates.

Innumerable stream systems have been modified in their upper course by dams converting riverine areas to impoundments. In Lake Baikal, Siberia, the establishment of a hydroelectric dam raised the water level and placed spawning areas below optimum depth for the most important coregonid fish present. Most dams designed for hydropower or flood control change the timing and temperature of the water released. Demand for electricity to power air conditioners in sum-

mer results in high flows that increase the frequency and intensity of bed scour downstream. Although good for white-water rafting in summer, this can lead to an impoverished benthic invertebrate food supply for fish. In winter when power is not needed or if flood control is required downstream, the lower releases may not be adequate to clear silt from spawning gravels or keep open river channels. However, if the water is diverted to consumptive use for agriculture or distant city supplies, there will be lower flows in spring and summer as well as an overall decrease in total discharge. The consequent decrease in the wetted area of stream reduces the amount of habitat for fish and invertebrates, which may then show a permanent decrease. Water diversion also diverts both eggs and young fish from the system. In extreme cases irrigation projects may dry up streams that once ran year-round and can result in the partial or complete extinction of lakes such as the huge Sea of Aral in Russia (Chap. 3) or Walker Lake, Nevada that is now only a quarter of its 1890 size.

FISHERIES MANAGEMENT

Even quite small dams with only a few feet drop are formidable blocks to either upstream or downstream migration. Nonetheless, while effectively destroying one kind of habitat, they create another and, as discussed later, overall productivity and biodiversity may change, even increase. Some properly regulated reservoirs may provide excellent year-round flows and cool hypolimnetic waters immediately below the dam to improve the spawning opportunities for cold-water fish such as salmon. Many dams, including the large complex of Tennessee Valley Authority dams, are now run with the health of the river fishery in mind. The extensive Shasta Dam system ($V = 8$ km^3) on the Sacramento River in northern California, although cutting off extensive reaches of spawning gravels upstream, has improved downstream rearing areas with a continuous flow of cold water during the summer

Management approaches to overcoming fisheries problems include stream improvements, spawning area enhancement, and reservoir level fluctuations. Streams can be improved both through the removal of blocks to migration and by the construction of fish ladders. The removal of obsolete small dams has improved fish habitat in many rivers, especially in the northeastern United States. The development of gravel spawning stretches below reservoirs or in tributary streams has compensated for some losses. Unfortunately, fish ladders usually do not perform up to expectations, and adult fish may require truck transport around dams. Although adult salmon may be taken through a dam by elevator fish ladders or truck, the young when migrating downstream are often unable to find their way through the still waters of the reservoir or are killed in the turbines. These young fish can also be trucked directly from hatchery to below dams. Air narcosis (a form of diver's bends) can also kill salmonid fish below high dams (Chap. 7). Both oxygen and nitrogen contribute to this effect, and while as little as 7 percent supersaturation may cause narcosis, measured values to 43 percent are not uncommon below dams. Modification of the spillway to divert water horizontally rather than vertically in the deep afterbay pool has reduced the narcosis problem considerably, especially in the Columbia River. Many lakes throughout the midwestern and western United States are crowded with enormous numbers of tiny centrarchids in which inter- and intraspecific competition restricts growth. In reservoirs the water level can be lowered in the spring as a means of stranding some fish nests, increasing the size of the remaining individuals.

Stocking fish grown in fish hatcheries has long been a standard management practice throughout the world where angler demands are high but is less satisfactory than enhancing conditions for natural reproduction. Exotic species have been introduced on a worldwide basis and are at best a mixed blessing. Rare or endangered species may be eliminated by the introduction of an exotic form that rapidly takes over the habitat. The carp and the mosquito fish are large and small fishes, respectively, that have displaced native species in many places but which also survive where many of the native species cannot.

In their original state many streams and rivers had huge log jams along much of their length. These were semipermanent and stretched for hundreds of meters in some cases. On the Willamette River in Oregon, jams were even included on early maps. Log jams barred navigation, even for the canoes of the European settlers, and were soon cleared with explosives. On the lower Red River in Louisiana, a log jam known as the Great Red River Raft extended for 160 miles in the 1800s and even had trees growing on the surface (Bartlett, 1984). This jam took 6 years to demolish using specially designed battering ram vessels. Although such jams block navigation, it is unlikely that fish find them much of a hindrance, since there are always small channels, especially at high water.

Anglers often remove smaller log jams and snags that obstruct them when they are wading along a stream. Federal and state agencies remove log jams and large snags that impede navigation, particularly at low water levels. However, snags and jams perform a vital role in providing a back eddy where fish can rest out of the main current. The absence of such resting places is a major reason that fish cannot migrate up lined concrete drainage channels, even when there is plenty of clean water flowing down them. The value of snags as sites of higher invertebrate biomass and drift that are a major source of fish food is shown in Fig. 14-16. In this study of a low-gradient warm-water stream in Georgia, a very small area of snags supported most of the invertebrate drift and provided over half of the prey for four of the eight most common fish species. In cooler waters there is a linear relationship between the number of snags and the number of young salmonid fish in the stream. Snags in lakes perform many of the roles of

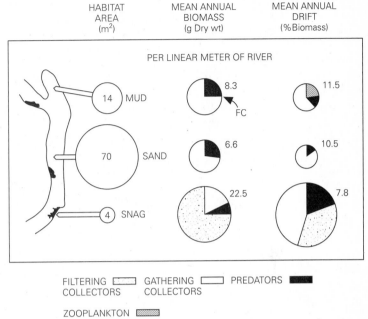

HABITAT AREA (m^2) MEAN ANNUAL BIOMASS (g Dry wt) MEAN ANNUAL DRIFT (%Biomass)

PER LINEAR METER OF RIVER

14 MUD   8.3 FC   11.5

70 SAND   6.6   10.5

4 SNAG   22.5   7.8

FILTERING COLLECTORS   GATHERING COLLECTORS   PREDATORS

ZOOPLANKTON

FIGURE 14-16. The value of woody snags (submerged trees) for invertebrate and fish production in rivers. Over the year, 60 percent of the invertebrate biomass and 78 percent of the nocturnal drifting invertebrates were supported by the snag habitat, which, however, constituted less than 5 percent of the total habitat area. Virtually all of the filtering species were confined to the snag region. In contrast, the most common habitats (sand and mud) provided little support for invertebrates and the fish that feed on them. Modified from Benke et al. (1985). Snags also provide turbulent eddies in which fish can rest out of the main current.

snags in streams. Fisheries managers are now replacing some of the former snags and not removing ones that form naturally as trees or large branches fall into streams or wash down into lakes.

The Morphoedaphic Index, Lake Fertilization, and Bioenergetic Models

The productive potential of fisheries is linked to the trophic state of waters supporting them. The *morphoedaphic index* (MEI; Ryder, 1965) is a simple but very useful way to make a first approximation of the potential standing crop or yield to the fishery from a lake or reservoir. The MEI is simply the concentration of total dissolved solids (TDS, in mg liter^{-1}) divided by the mean depth, $\bar{z}$ (in meters) of the water:

$$\text{MEI} = \text{TDS}/\bar{z}.$$

The MEI, when applied appropriately, provides a very useful estimate of potential fish yield (yield per area = Y/A) or standing crop based on two easily measured variables (TDS and mean depth):

$$\log_e (\text{Y/A}) = f + 9 \log_e(\text{MEI})$$

or

$$\log_e(\text{Y/A}) = f + g \log_e(\text{MEI}) + h \log_e(\text{MEI})^2$$

where *f*, *g*, and *h* are empirical constants used depending on whether the water is a reservoir or natural lake and the climatic zone of the water body (Oglesby, 1982).

The limnologist may be of particular assistance to the fisheries biologist through controlled fertilization of infertile waters. With the increase in eutrophication of most natural waters, this is more likely to be a tool in aquaculture than in general fish management. However, in certain environments, trace element deficiency can be relieved at minor cost with a resulting increase in the production of trout (Fig. 10-11). Salmon managers in British Columbia, Canada, routinely fertilize oligotrophic lakes to enhance primary productivity, zooplankton density, and thus juvenile sockeye salmon populations where the young salmon utilize these nursery lakes for 1 or 2 years before migrating to the ocean (Hyatt and Stockner, 1985; Stockner, 1987). As more is learned about the structure of aquatic food chains, it may be possible to tailor fertilization or nutrient removal to enhance specific portions of the food chain that go directly into fish production.

The effect of reductions in nutrients following sewage treatment can result in a dramatic decline in fish stocks. In a decade-long, multireservoir study Yurk and Ney (1989) showed that fish stocks were strongly correlated with total phosphorus (Fig. 14-17). In this case the phosphorus loadings to the lakes were reduced by 50 to 80 percent after precipitation of phosphate at the sewage treatment works. Nitrogen loadings are not affected by the process and were therefore probably unchanged.

Bioenergetic models such as that of Hewett and Johnson (1987) measure consumption rates by fish coupled with data or models of the population dynamics of fishes. This allows researchers and managers to quantify interactions among trophic levels, identify potential bottlenecks to production of desirable species, and examine critical processes affecting recruitment, production, and community structure. Using this approach, Stewart et al. (1981) predicted that the number of piscivorous salmonids stocked in Lake Michigan would exceed the ability of the forage fishes to sustain them. Their predictions were confirmed a decade later, with critically low populations of alewives and other forage fishes and reduced growth and productivity by the salmonids (Kitchell and Crowder, 1986; Stewart and Ibarra, 1991). Bioenergetic models give managers a way to predict the consequences of population manipulations to the community structure of the perturbed water body.

Effects of Introducing Exotic Predators

Unexpected fisheries management problems have occurred following the introduction of ex-

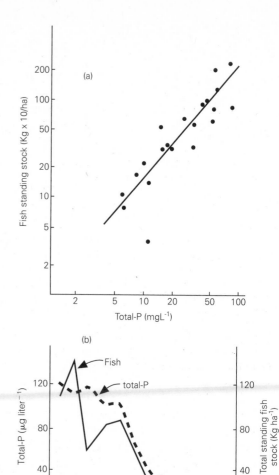

FIGURE 14-17 Fish and nutrients: effects of major, long-term decreases in phosphorus loading on fish standing stocks. (a) Log-log regression of lake total phosphorus and fish stocks for 22 reservoirs in Southern Virginia following sewage treatment that reduced phosphorus loading by an average of 51 percent. Over an 11-year period the standing stock of fish also declined significantly ($P < 0.001$; $R^2 = 0.75$; i.e., 75 percent of the decline in fish can be attributed to the decline in phosphorus). In many individual reservoirs the total fish stock to phosphorus regression is poor but is improved if the same fish species are compared. (b) Smith Mountain Lake, where total phosphorus fell by 79 percent, resulting in a total fish standing stock decline of 76 percent. Note how well the two decline curves follow each other over the years ($R^2 = 0.66$, or 66 percent; $P < 0.03$). Modified from Yurk and Ney (1989).

otic species in a variety of fresh waters around the world. The usual reason for introductions is to provide a large fighting fish for anglers. In addition, there are often accidental or unofficial introductions of non-native fish. After completing a fishing session, anglers often tip out the contents of the bait bucket into the water. Bait fish are basically any small fish and may include the young of many species shipped across continents with no concern for accidental introductions. Careless bait disposal accounts for the presence of the eastern green sunfish in very isolated streams in the southern Californian coastal regions, which have only one or two native fish species.

In Central America the intentional introduction of the piscivorous sunfishes, largemouth bass, and black crappie has raised havoc with the native fishery in Guatemala's Lake Atitian. A similar introduction of an Amazon River cichlid, the peacock bass, to Gatun Lake in Panama (Zaret and Paine, 1973) has altered the trophic structure of the entire system (Fig. 14-18). An unexpected side effect has been an increase in mosquitoes that carry malaria. The loss of mosquito larvae predators, most notably the topminnow *Melaniris,* to predation by the peacock bass may be responsible for a general increase in mosquitoes.

Fish managers and limnologists should try to maintain stocks of native fish. New introductions of exotic fish or invertebrates should be made with caution, and then only after very careful study.

Fish Kills

Water quality remains of prime importance in the management and conservation of fish resources. A common cause of changes in water quality is the increase in nutrients that cause eutrophication. Early stages of nutrient enrichment increase fish production while altering species composition to favor less desirable fish. One of the most serious effects of eutrophication in lakes is the depletion of oxygen in the hypolimnion. This results in the loss of deep-water spawning grounds, summer habitat for cold-water species, and the elimination of some benthic invertebrates utilized for food. Rivers, streams, and estuaries often show fewer undesirable effects of increased productivity but, again, less desirable fishes may predominate as eutrophication progresses.

If there are no oxygenated refuges, eutrophication can result in *summer fish kills.* The increased algal population falls to the lake bed, where bacterial decomposition depletes dissolved oxygen in the hypolimnion. Kills occur when oxygen is depleted from unstratified lakes at night or during a windless day. *Winter fish kills* occur when oxygen is depleted under a cover of winter ice and snow. Inflow of water with low dissolved oxygen from peat swamps may also produce winter fish kills. The cause of these kills was found by fisheries biologists, who were among the first to make extensive use of the Winkler method of measuring oxygen dissolved in water. Fish kills resulting from industrial pollution are sufficiently dramatic to raise a public uproar against the polluter. Reports of fish kills in the United States have greatly increased in recent years, but it is not clear whether this is a real trend or an artifact of reporting procedures.

Chemical and Thermal Pollution

Chemical pollution or low oxygen levels may destroy fish populations or block migrations. The high biological oxygen demand of poorly-treated sewage can reduce dissolved oxygen to levels that stop the upstream migration of salmon in rivers. Similar affects occur from unionized ammonia (Table 8-3) discharged from some sewage treatment plants and agricultural lands. Oxygen reduction is often more difficult for fish to overcome than thermal effects. Oxygen levels below 5 mg liter^{-1} can block migration of coho salmon even though they were undeterred by river temperatures of 23°C, well above the normal limits for this fish. The River Thames in England (Chap. 22) and the River Clyde in Scotland had a variety of fishes that formerly migrated through the main river and estuary. By blocking migra-

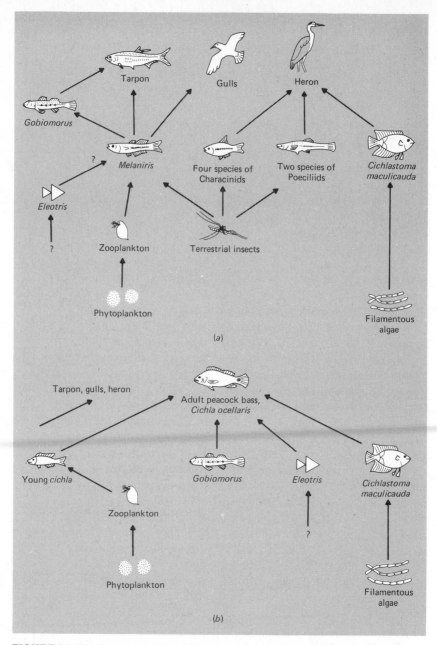

FIGURE 14-18 Food web effects of the introduction of exotic predators. The peacock bass, *Cichla ocellaris,* a sport fish, was introduced into Gatun Lake, Panama. (*a*) The postulated system prior to bass introduction with about 12 fish species, including the valuable top fish predator, the tarpon. Also present were several other higher predators, including gull (terns), heron, and kingfishers. (*b*) After the bass introduction 11 fish species were drastically reduced and only 2, including *Cichlastoma,* increased. The role of some common small fish, such as *Eleotris,* is unknown. Losses shown in higher predators are from semiquantitative observations. Redrawn and modified from Zaret and Paine (1973).

tion, pollution can have an effect upstream as well as downstream from the source of pollution (Maitland, 1974).

Aquatic organisms concentrate pollutants within their bodies without necessarily being affected. Although humans are remarkably resistant to many potential poisons, they face increasing levels of dangerous substances concentrated by favorite food organisms. Pacific salmon, introduced in the Great Lakes for sports fishing, have at times been considered a health risk if regularly consumed because of high concentrations of chlorinated hydrocarbons such as polychlorinated biphenyls (PCBs). Striped bass in the Hudson River have also been put out of bounds for human consumption due to an elevated level of PCBs in their flesh. The pollutant was derived from the waste from a factory that manufactured electrical transformers which used this oil as an insulator. Fortunately, the abundance of striped bass does not appear to be greatly affected by PCBs. Similarly, methyl mercury derived from extensive use of metallic mercury in a variety of industries has contaminated the aquatic food chain. The problem is exacerbated because PCBs, methyl mercury, and the now-banned insecticide DDT are concentrated through successive levels of the food chain to the point where large predatory fish may contain hazardous levels in their fat.

An example of the concentration of chlorinated hydrocarbons in the aquatic food chain is provided by Clear Lake, California. The high fertility of this lake supports a very productive recreational fishery as well as one of the few remaining lake commercial fisheries in the United States. Since the mid-1940s the lake has been the site of numerous attempts to control the Clear Lake gnat, *Chaoborus astictopus*. First, the newly invented insecticide DDD, a derivative of DDT, was used. Predatory fish such as largemouth black bass and catfish attained high levels of DDD and its derivatives in their fat (Hunt and Bischoff, 1960). The elegant western grebe *Aechmophorus occidentalis,* presumably feeding

on these contaminated fish, declined catastrophically and took years to recover after DDD use ceased. Although the fishes seemed little affected, the older individuals among the predatory species, particularly catfish, showed a high pesticide level in their tissues and were not recommended for human consumption. The Clear Lake example served to alert the public to the dangers of persistent pesticides (Carson, 1962; Rudd, 1964).

Fish can also be used as sensitive measures of pollution. Because fish are sensitive indicators of many aspects of water quality, they are used in bioassays to determine the toxicity of industrial chemicals or municipal effluents. Originally these tests involved only measuring acute toxicity. For example, a cage of sticklebacks can be placed in 100 percent effluent in the lake or in the laboratory. Modern laboratory tests employ young of more than one species to measure sublethal effects, including changes in metabolism or behavior. These give a much better estimate of the potentially harmful effects of low levels of pollutants, although great care is needed to obtain unambiguous results.

Waste heat may, under some circumstances, increase growth rates of some fish but may be lethal to others. The most pronounced effects of thermal pollution occur in rivers where power plants utilize a large fraction of the flow for once-through cooling. A good example is the Wabash River, a typical large Mississippi drainage river, where up to two-thirds of the river volume is used for cooling the power station turbines in the autumn low-flow period. The fish are dominated by gizzard shad, which feed on vegetation, detritus, and zooplankton; also important are carp, catfish, three species of redhorse, and the sauger. The large number of species commonly present (about 20) allows the use of a composite diversity index to demonstrate effects after power station construction. Laboratory studies predict the effects of various temperatures on individual species (Gammon et al., 1981). Diversity, density, and biomass of the fish community de-

TABLE 14-5

DECLINE IN PRODUCTIVITY IN THE SURFACE WATERS OF A NEW RESERVOIR, DWORSHAK RESERVOIR, NORTH IDAHO, IN THE FIRST 3 YEARS AFTER FILLING

The lake is 80 km long. Numbers are expressed as a percent of 1972 values except for photosynthesis, where 1973 is the base year. Little change in levels of NO_3^- or soluble PO_4^{3-} occurred.

	1972	1973	1974
Phytoplankton total numbers	100	2–70	9
Photosynthesis	—	100	28
Zooplankton:			
Copepods	100	40	30
Cladocerans	100	70	46

Modified from Falter, 1977.

creased where the river temperature rose to 28 to 32°C near the outfall. Even at these high temperatures there was no direct mortality of the large adult carp, channel catfish, sauger, or redhorse, although the latter two selected lower temperatures when available. After dilution the river temperature was elevated only 1 to 4°C for about 6 km downstream, but even this small change affected the fishes. The composite index, which is based on numbers, biomass, and diversity, showed a decrease below the power plants.

NEW RESERVOIRS

New reservoirs typically go through an early period of high fish production soon after they are filled and then decline to a much lower level of productivity (Table 14-5). This high initial pro-

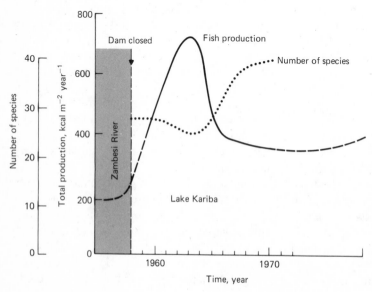

FIGURE 14-19 Effects of new reservoirs on fish abundance and diversity. Fish production and species numbers in the Zambezi River before and after the creation of a very large reservoir, Lake Kariba ($V = 156$ km³). Note the rapid rise in production after dam closure and its similarly rapid fall to about preimpoundment levels after a few years (see also Table 14-5). Diversity increased from 28 to 41 as fish from the upper river found suitable niches as the lake environment replaced the very swift waters of the original Zambezi. Modified from Balon and Coche (1974).

ductivity is due to flooding of terrestrial plants and nutrient-rich soil. It is followed by a decline in basic fertility as nutrients are lost by outflow of the nutrient-rich hypolimnetic water and by sedimentation. Unfavorable species composition may also limit the harvest of fish from a reservoir. For example, the lake formed by Kariba Dam on the Zambesi River in Africa did not produce the protein formerly harvested from the now-flooded valley (Harding, 1966), although recent data are more encouraging (Fig. 14-19). The Niger River in Nigeria has been dammed to form Kainji Lake (Table 2-1), which has large fluctuations in water level. Preimpoundment studies of fisheries in the river and the associated swamps were compared with postimpoundment catches 2 years after damming. Although the populations had not stabilized, a rise in predatory fishes in the reservoir was attributed to an increase in small forage fish (clupeids). Cichlids of the genus *Tilapia,* which were not numerous in the river, increased, but below the dam the total catch declined as detritivores lost their food supply (Blake, 1977).

Chapters 11 to 14 have introduced the biological world of lakes, in particular the algae, the invertebrates, and the vertebrate fish. In Chap. 15 we cover some important interactions that involve all trophic levels. Nutrient uptake kinetics, primary production, interspecific competition theory, the microbial loop, and mixed-layer nutrient cycling all play their part in determining the dynamic overall biological structure of the lake ecosystem.

FURTHER READING

Allen, K. R. 1951. "The Horokiwi Steam: A Study of a Trout Population." *Bull. Mar. N.Z. Fish.,* **10:**1–238.

Balon, E. K., and A. G. Coche (eds.). 1974. "Lake Kariba: A Man-Made Tropical Ecosystem in Central Africa." *Monogr. Biol.,* **24.** 767 pp.

Barbour, C. D., and J. H. Brown. 1974. "Fish Species Diversity in Lakes." *Am. Nat.,* **108:**473–489.

Berra, T. M. 1981. *An Atlas of the Distribution of the Freshwater Fish Families of the World.* University of Nebraska Press, Lincoln. 197 pp.

Carpenter, S. R. (ed.). 1988. *Complex Interactions in Lake Communities.* Springer, New York.

Carpenter, S. R., J. P. Kitchell, and J. R. Hodgson. 1985. "Cascading Trophic Interactions and Lake Productivity." *Bioscience,* **35:**634–639.

Carpenter, S. R., and J. F. Kitchen. 1988. "Consumer Control of Lake Productivity." *Bioscience,* **38:**764–769.

Christie, W. J. 1974. "Changes in the Fish Species Composition of the Great Lakes." *J. Fish. Res. Board Can.,* **31:**827–854.

Fryer, G., and T. D. Isles. 1972. *The Cichlid Fishes of the Great Lakes of Africa: Their Biology and Evolution.* Oliver & Boyd, Edinburgh. 641 pp.

Lagler, K. F., J. E. Bardach, R. R. Miller, and D. R. M. Passino. 1977. *Ichthyology.* 2d ed. Wiley, New York. 506 pp.

Magnuson, J. J. 1962. "An Analysis of Aggressive Behavior, Growth and Competition for Food and Space in Medaka, *Oryzias latipes* Pisces (Cyprinodontidae)." *Can. J. Zool.,* **40:**313–363.

Magnuson, J. J., L. B. Crowder, and P. A. Medvick. 1979. "Temperature as an Ecological Resource." *Am. Zoologist,* **19:**331–343.

Marshall, N. B. 1966. *The Life of Fishes.* Universe Books, New York. 402 pp.

Miller, T. J., L. B. Crowder, J. A. Rice, and E. A. Marshall. 1988. "Larval Size and Recruitment Mechanisms in Fishes: Toward a Conceptual Framework." *Can. J. Fish. Aquat. Sci.,* **45:**1657–1670.

Moyle, P. B., and J. J. Cech. 1988. *Fishes: An Introduction to Ichthyology,* 2d ed. Prentice-Hall, Englewood Cliffs, NJ.

Northcote, T. G. 1988. "Fish in the Structure and Function of Freshwater Ecosystems: A 'Top-Down' View." *Can. J. Fish. Aquat. Sci.,* **45:**361–379.

Oglesby, R. T. (ed.). 1982. "The Morphoedaphic Index: Concepts and Practices." *Trans. Am. Fish. Soc.* (Special Section) **111:**133–175.

Rawson, D. S. 1952. "Mean Depth and the Fish Production of Large Lakes." *Ecology,* **33:**513–521.

Ricker, W. E. 1975. *Computation and Interpretation of Biological Statistics of Fish Populations.* Department of Environment Fisheries and Marine Service, Ottawa, Canada. 382 pp.

Ryder, R. A. 1965. "A Method for Estimating the Potential Fish Production of North-Temperate Lakes." *Trans. Am. Fish. Soc.,* **94:**214–218.

Scavia, D., G. L. Fahnenstiel, M. S. Evans, D. J. Jude, and J. T. Lehman. 1986. "Influence of Salmonine Predation and Weather on Long-Term Water Quality Trends in Lake Michigan." *Can. J. Fish. Aquat. Sci.,* **43:**435–443.

Schreck, C. B., and P. B. Moyle (eds.). 1990. *Methods for Fish Biology.* American Fisheries Society, Bethesda, MD.

Shapiro, J., and D. I. Wright. 1984. "Lake Restoration by Biomanipulation: Round Lake, Minnesota, the First Two Years." *Freshwat. Biol.,* **14:**371–383.

Stewart, D. J., and M. Ibarra. 1991. "Predation and Production by Salmonid Fishes in Lake Michigan, 1978–88." *Can. J. Fish. Aquat. Sci.,* **48:**909–922.

Stockner, J. G. 1987. "Lake Fertilization: The Enrichment Cycle and Lake Sockeye Salmon (*Oncorhynchus nerka*) Production." pp. 198–215. In H. O. Smith, L. Margolis, and C. C. Wood (eds.). *Sockeye Salmon* (Oncorhynchus nerka) *Population Biology and Future Management. Can. J. Fish. Aquat. Sci.,* **96.** 486 pp.

Spigarelli, S. A. (ed.). 1990. "Fish Community Health: Monitoring and Assessment in Large Lakes." *J. Great Lakes Res.,* **16:**403–469.

Vanni, M. J., C. Luecke, J. F. Kitchell, and J. J. Magnuson. 1990. "Effects of Planktivorous Fish Mass Mortality on the Plankton Community of Lake Mendota, Wisconsin: Implications for Biomanipulation." *Hydrobiologia* **200/201:**329–336.

Werner, E. E., J. F. Gilliam, D. J. Hall, and G. G. Mittelbach. 1983. "Experimental Tests of the Effects of Predation Risk on Habitat Use in Fish: The Role of Relative Habitat Profitability." *Ecology,* 64:1540–1548.

Wootton, R. J. 1990. *Ecology of Teleost Fishes.* Chapman & Hall, London.

Wurtsbaugh, W. A., and H. Li. 1985. "Diel Migrations of a Zooplanktivorous Fish (*Megidis beryllina*) in Relation to the Distribution of Its Prey in a Large Eutrophic Lake." *Limnol. Oceanogr.,* **30:**565–576.

CHAPTER 15

Food-Chain Dynamics

OVERVIEW

Energy and nutrients are transferred through successive trophic levels. Photosynthesis provides the basic food for herbivorous animals, which are then eaten by the carnivores. Energy is a convenient measure of this transfer but oversimplifies the situation. Organisms require a balanced diet of essential elements or preformed organic molecules, such as amino acids and vitamins, as well as a minimum amount of energy. Nutritive value is not equivalent to energy content. Most of the energy and nutrients acquired by one trophic level are lost as heat or excretion, with only a small amount retained for growth. Based on energy, the efficiency of transfer to the next higher level varies from 2 to 40 percent, depending on age and level in the food chain. The most generalized concept of biomass or energy transfer is the *ecological pyramid*. At the broad base is a large plant biomass; herbivores make up the middle; and a small group of carnivores is supported at the top.

Many aquatic organisms are omnivorous, which makes it difficult to measure transfers of energy or nutrients between trophic levels. In fact, *trophic levels* are an idealized concept. The varied choices of food are best described in a *food web,* which is derived from qualitative measurement of the contents of animal guts. When the amounts and types of food utilized by each organism are known, a *dynamic food web* can be constructed.

The efficiency of aquatic food webs is enhanced by the ability of some small organisms to recycle organic matter. This pool of ''soluble detritus'' is the basis of the *microbial loop*. Dissolved organic matter and small suspended particles provide food for bacteria, heterotrophic microflagellates, and ciliates. These tiny organisms feed larger zooplankton and small fish. The original source of soluble detritus is autotrophic primary production by large phytoplankton and small picoplankton. The microbial loop is most important in large oligotrophic lakes where the biomass of larger nutritious algae such as diatoms is low. It also plays a role during the midsummer phytoplankton minimum in more eutrophic lakes.

Microbes in the epilimnion also mineralize particulate and soluble detritus, releasing inorganic nutrients for phytoplankton growth. This *nutrient regeneration in the mixed layer* is most important during the nutrient depletion in summer, when it can supply 5 to 10 percent of daily phytoplankton requirements. This small supply of nitrogen and phosphorus is one of the reasons algae are able to grow slowly at very low nutrient concentrations.

An alternative to studying the entire and complex food web is to measure changes in subcompartments of the system. Stable or radioactive isotopes are frequently used to trace the flow of nutrients or biomass over short distances in the food web. The rate of transfer of essential substances can be measured by using additions of limiting nutrients to pure cultures or natural populations of bacteria and algae. These studies enable the researcher to find biochemical constants such as the maximum growth rate (u_{max}) and to measure the plant's ability to take up nutrients at low levels (K_m). The constants vary with species and are useful in explaining phytoplankton seasonal cycles as well as predicting changes when nutrient levels change.

In this chapter we discuss measurement, nutrient and energy flow in food webs, the microbial loop and nutrient regeneration in the mixed layer, growth kinetics and the prediction of phytoplankton competition, isotopic tracers in food webs, and primary productivity.

INTRODUCTION

Food-chain dynamics are more complicated than such subjects as light, temperature, or the distribution of the various species of organisms. The difficulty stems from our inability to extrapolate accurately from laboratory studies to natural plant growth or animal feeding rates. In the laboratory, large animals such as fish can rapidly consume a variety of prey. In contrast, under more natural conditions the choice of prey is limited and feeding rates are considerably lower than those observed in the laboratory. In nature, avoidance of predators and the availability of cover also reduces feeding rates. In this chapter

we discuss general physiological factors, such as nutrient uptake, the efficiency of energy transfer between trophic levels, and the microbial loop. A physiological approach extends the traditional ecological methods that rely on analysis of gut contents or decrease in prey species numbers through grazing or predation. Food chains, when reduced to flow diagrams, provide a simplified view of the dynamic structure of the aquatic ecosystem.

MEASUREMENTS

At the base of the food chain, changes in the rate of photosynthesis can be related to changes in light, nutrients, and a variety of other environmental factors. The various elements present in plant tissue are easily measured and show the nutrients available to herbivores at the next trophic level. Further, they may provide clues as to the nutrient factors limiting plant growth. Another approach to plant dynamics is to measure the plant's response to additional nutrients in growth experiments. Transfer of energy and nutrients have been considered between trophic levels. A similar approach can also be applied to evaluate transfer efficiency for one species between one generation and the next. For aquatic animals the number and condition of eggs and young can indicate the food and energy transferred to the next generation.

To study food webs limnologists measure the energy or nutrient content of individual organisms. In addition to these static values it is often possible to measure the rate at which animals and plants take up nutrients. These kinetic investigations often involve radioactive and stable isotopes as tracers. Some of the naturally occurring isotopes or metals, such as ^{15}N, copper, and selenium, may act as *biomarkers*. They are most useful in large food webs or in field experiments where additions are undesirable and may contaminate the ecosystem.

Details of the most commonly used techniques to measure biomass and nutrients are given in the *IBP Manuals* 8 (Golterman et al., 1978) and 12 (Vollenweider, 1969), by Parsons et al. (1984), and in the latest APHA volume. The energy content of individuals or whole populations is measured by combustion in a bomb calorimeter. The energy found at each trophic level can then be used to determine energy flow. Used alone, this approach is limited, because the limnologist is as much concerned with the nutritive value of the food as with its energy content. It is difficult to make the measurements needed to construct even a simple food web, and con-

structing a complete dynamic food web is an even harder task.

NUTRIENT AND ENERGY FLOW IN FOOD WEBS

Before attempting food-chain studies, year round measurements of the numbers and biomass of the major groups of organisms are needed. An *ecological pyramid* is made by lumping organisms into general functional groups by their feeding habits, for example, carnivores, herbivores,

FIGURE 15-1 Biological pyramids of numbers or biomass, energy, and food value for a typical temperate lake in summer and winter. Note that only values in summer make a real pyramid. Also note the thicker upper part of the pyramid for mass or food in winter. This is due to the death of most lower organisms in winter, while larger organisms such as fish and larger copepods survive mostly on stored food reserves and metabolize slowly at the low temperatures. The quantitative values are for illustrative purposes only but are of the correct order of magnitude for some lakes.

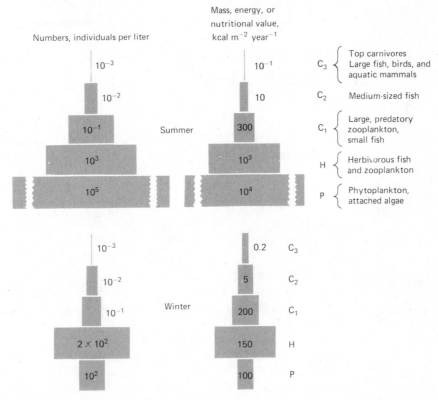

primary producers, or detritivores (Fig. 15-1). More refined measurements, which include splitting the biota into functional groups, such as mayfly-eating fish, algal-scraping insects or snails, or heterotrophic bacteria, allow assembly of a *food web* (Fig. 15-2). Finally, knowledge of actual amounts of energy and nutrients passed between each small functional group will allow construction of a *dynamic food web* (Figs. 15-3, 15-4).

Biological pyramids are derived from measurements of the numbers or biomass of organisms present at each season of the year: primary producers form the bottom level (P; e.g., the diatom *Asterionella*), herbivores or grazers are included in the second level (H; e.g., the zooplankton *Daphnia*), and primary carnivores that graze on small herbivores make up the next level (C_1; e.g., zooplankton such as the rotifer *Asplanchna* or young fish). If present, secondary or tertiary carnivores form the apex of the pyramid (C_2 to C_4; e.g., adult piscivorous fish such as lake trout, birds, and otters). Figure 15-1 shows summer and winter pyramids for a typical temperate lake. Normally numbers of organisms or biomass decrease as one moves up to higher trophic levels.

FIGURE 15-2 Qualitative food web for the Truckee River, California. Solid lines indicate measured pathways. Broken lines are assumed pathways derived from the other studies in adjacent waters. Note the omnivorous feeders (e.g. dace, trout, sculpin) using more than one trophic level. Most herbivores prefer microscopic diatoms to large filamentous green and blue-green algae.

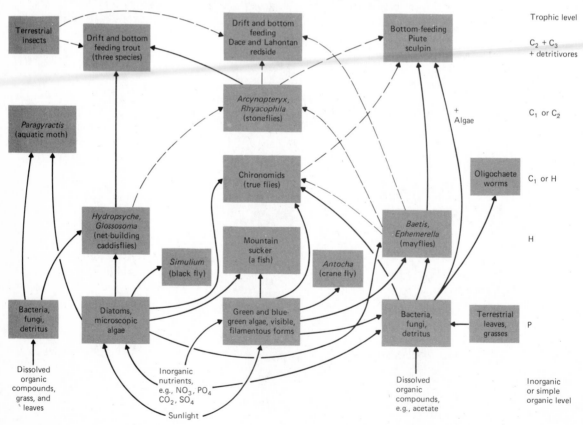

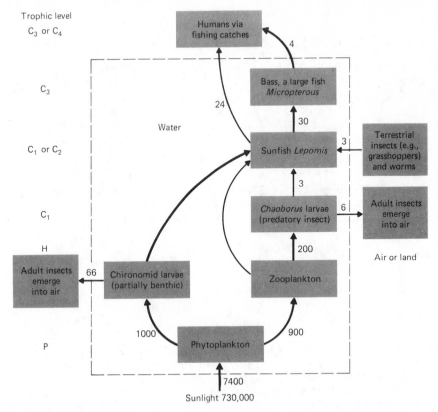

FIGURE 15-3 Dynamic food web for a small lake managed for fish production. The management simplifies the food web by reducing the habitat for competing animals or plants. Values shown are in kilocalories per square meter per year uncorrected for losses in respiration or assimilation. Heavy lines indicate the most important pathways. Note that even in this system the omnivorous feeding habits of the sunfish and people make a calculation of trophic-level efficiency difficult (see Table 15-2). Also note that a large part of the higher trophic-level production was lost to the air as adult chironomid flies. Redrawn from Odum, 1971, who originally modified data from Welch, 1967.

In winter the pyramid may be inverted, with only a few primary producers relative to grazers and carnivores. As discussed in previous chapters, this reflects reduced animal feeding rates and light-limited photosynthesis. During cold periods most small cladocerans and rotifers form resting stages and are absent from the plankton. Those remaining are the larger copepods and their young, which feed and metabolize slowly in the cold water.

A typical food web developed from studies on the Truckee River in the Sierra Nevada mountains of California is shown in Fig. 15-2. Samples for analysis of benthic invertebrates and attached algae were taken simultaneously on the same rocks. The algae and invertebrates were counted and the guts of common grazing insects were removed and dissected to find which algae were being consumed. Fish stomach contents were examined for their choice of prey. To simplify Fig. 15-2, the individual species are lumped into genera or feeding classes. This is also the logic be-

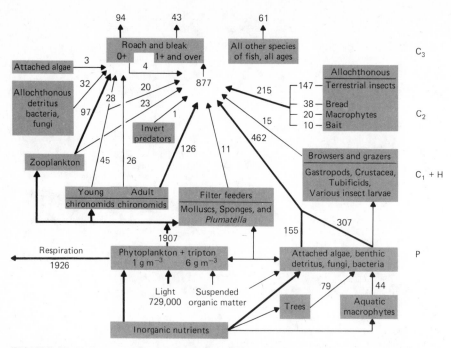

FIGURE 15-4 Dynamic food web for a natural system. Energy flowchart for the River Thames below Kennet mouth. In general, primary producers are shown at the bottom, invertebrate animals in the center, and fish at the top, but to avoid complex networks of arrows, sources of attached algae, detritus, and allochthonous materials are shown in two places. Heavy arrows indicate the largest channels of energy flow. Note the twin flow of energy to fish from low quality attached algae and high-quality animal food from terrestrial insects and adult chironomids. Energy input from dissolved organic matter was not measured directly. Redrawn from Mann et al., 1972.

hind the functional classification of the structure of stream animal communities proposed by Cummins (1973; Chap. 16). Food webs sometimes reveal food preferences (Table 15-1). For example, in the Truckee River the uncommon pennate diatom *Cocconeis* is frequently eaten by net-spinning caddis fly larvae. In contrast, the common pennate diatom *Nitzschia* is eaten less frequently than would be expected if the animals were not selective (Table 15-1). Similarly, rainbow trout preferentially select caddisfly larvae (Fig. 15-2).

Efficient transfer of energy and nutrients from one trophic level to the next is important for biological success. Although this figure varies considerably, an average of 10 percent of energy is transferred from one trophic level to another. The maximum efficiency of energy transfer in young, actively feeding animals is about 30 to 40 percent and is limited by their ability to convert food protein to body protein. In general, the higher the level in the food chain the greater the energy and nutrient content of the food items consumed. Thus fish eating smaller fish or zooplankton gain more calories per unit weight of food than do herbivorous fish or zooplankton, which extract energy from plant and detrital material. The efficiency of energy transfer is thus understandably higher as one proceeds up the food chain.

TABLE 15-1

INGESTION OF DIFFERENT BENTHIC DIATOMS BY COMMON BENTHIC INSECTS IN A CALIFORNIA STREAM

+ = taken in preference; 0 = no preference shown; − = under utilized; total = rating of the group. The diatoms were scraped from the same rocks and gravel area from which the insects were collected. The differences shown could be due to active selection by the insects in the case of the grazers or to a differential drifting of the algae in the case of the filterers.

Insect herbivore	Genus of diatom eaten						
	Gomphonema	Navicula	Cymbella	Cocconeis	Epithemia	Diatoma	Nitzschia
Glossosoma	+	−	0	+	0	−	−
Baetis	0	−	0	+	0	−	−
Heptagenia	−	0	−	+	0	−	−
Ephemerella	−	0	0	+	0	−	−
Chironomidae	+	+	+	−	+	0	−
Total	0	−1	0	+3	+1	−4	−5

Unpublished data from A. J. Horne and P. W. Johnson.

The energy used in hunting, avoidance of predation, and uptake of very dilute nutrients is lost for growth and reproduction. Reproduction considerably lowers the overall efficiency of transfer from adult to adult of the next generation. For mammals the average value is only 2 to 5 percent, but it may range as high as 20 to 25 percent for fast-growing poikilothermic zooplankton. Much of this difference is due to the necessity of maintaining a constant body temperature in warm-blooded animals.

For centuries, fish farmers have increased production in fish ponds. These ponds have greatly reduced biodiversity and consequently have higher efficiencies than more diverse natural aquatic systems. The fish pond shown in Fig. 15-3 was managed to increase the harvest of sunfish and bass. In this artificial system the efficiency of energy conversion between trophic levels is easy to calculate. The values obtained (Table 15-2) show that the average conversion may exceed 10 percent between trophic levels. As noted above, energy conversion efficiency increases from light to algae to herbivores to primary carnivores to the top predator (bass).

A dynamic food web was measured during the International Biological Program studies on a lowland river, the Thames, in England (Fig. 15-4). Because of the relatively slow flows, large size, and high nutrient loadings, this river has a community structure that combines major elements of both lakes and rivers. It has an important plankton community, as occurs in lakes, but also the large allochthonous contribution typical of flowing waters (Chap. 16). Figure 15-4 illustrates the complex interactions between nutrients, bacteria, and the various trophic levels of algal primary producers, grazing insects, other invertebrates, and, finally, the primary and secondary carnivores. In evaluating this figure keep in mind that *trophic levels* is an abstract concept useful in recognizing interactions and patterns within food webs. Organisms may spend part of their time at one trophic level and part at another. The many links in the food web allow most herbivores and carnivores to utilize more than one food source.

In the Thames, light provides 7×10^5 cal m^{-2} y^{-1} of energy for phytoplanktonic growth. The efficiency of conversion of light to plant material in the river is roughly 0.3 percent, a typical value for most photosynthetic organisms.

TABLE 15-2

ENERGY CONVERSION IN A FISH POND

The system is managed for optimal production of bass and sunfish by reducing the complexity of the food chain. Even so, only a tiny fraction of the original solar energy reaches the fish. The majority sustains the lower links in the food chain (Fig. 15-3).

	Annual production, kcal m^{-2}	% efficiency of transfer
Light	730,000	—
P : phytoplankton	7,400	1
H : zooplankton		
+ chironomids	1,900	26
C$_1$: *Chaoborus* larvae		
+ sunfish	550	29
C$_2$: sunfish		
(on *Chaoborus*)	3	
C$_3$: bass + people		
(on sunfish)	54	11
C$_4$: people		
(on bass)	4	

In turn, the primary producers in the river provide about 1900 cal m^2 y^{-1} for direct use by herbivores. The diet of herbivores is supplemented by allochthonous detritus from tree leaves, aquatic macrophytes, and aufwuchs, which provide only 460 cal m^2 y^{-1}. Table 15-3 confirms, as expected, that the efficiency of energy conversion in the Thames is greatest at higher trophic levels.

As mentioned earlier, it is difficult to be precise about energy-transfer efficiency. Depending on how one partitions the potential food, efficiencies can range from 2 to 24 percent (Table 15-3). For example, if chironimid larvae acted as carnivores their efficiency was 24 percent, but if they consumed only plant material the value dropped to only 2 percent. Since no analysis of gut contents was made in this study, actual efficiencies are unknown, but plant material is often a main source of food for chironomid larvae (Table 15-1).

Zooplankton are uncommon in fast-flowing rivers but in the slow-flowing River Thames they constitute a major energy source for fish such as the roach. Other minnow family members, such as the bleak, consume periphyton and benthic diatoms, but chironomids and terrestrial insects also supplement their diet. These insects provide high-protein food with a well-balanced amino acid content.

As indicated for bleak in the Thames, as well as in most lakes, rivers, and oceans, the consideration of energy transfer alone oversimplifies food relationships. Although the many different plant species shown in Table 15-4 have a similar caloric content, there are large variations in their relative amounts of protein, phosphorus, potassium, and other minerals. Thus some plants are better-quality food than others. Animals are less variable in their protein-to-energy ratio. The digestibility of food is also important, since diet items such as crayfish require almost as much energy to digest as they yield to the fish that consume them.

THE MICROBIAL LOOP AND NUTRIENT REGENERATION IN THE MIXED LAYER

Long neglected, microbes such as viruses, bacteria, fungi, and tiny heterotrophic flagellates and

TABLE 15-3		

VARIOUS WAYS OF LOOKING AT FOOD-CHAIN ENERGY CONVERSION IN THE RIVER THAMES, BELOW THE ENTRY OF THE RIVER KENNET

Note that C_2 fish must acquire most of this high-quality food from allochthonous sources, since the river cannot provide enough to maintain measured growth. This food is mostly terrestrial insects, worms, and chironomids from surrounding ponds. Also, the four cyprinid fish common in this river are quite omnivorous and take food from several levels depending on season, prey availability, and age class of the fish.

Trophic level	Annual production, kcal m^{-2}	% efficiency of transfer*
Light	729,000	
P:		
Plants, mostly phytoplankton	2,369	0.33
H:		
Herbivores/grazers, filtering organisms	191	8.1
H + C_1:		
Young chironomids (primary carnivores),	45	2–24 (average 11)
		0.1
Leeches	1.7	~0.1
Allochthonous fish food, terrestrial insects, etc.	215	n.c.
Adult chironomids	152	6–64 (average 29)
H + C_1 + C_2:		
Fish	198	19

See Fig. 15-4 for energy food webs.
* Annual production of trophic group per annual production of food.
n.c. = not calculated since food source is unmeasured terrestrial material.

ciliates may play a key role in the epilimnion of lakes and oceans. As part of the microbial loop, their growth on otherwise unavailable organic nutrients provides food for larger zooplankton and fish. Microbial decomposition of dead matter regenerates inorganic nutrients for algae growth.

The Microbial Loop

Initial attempts to construct complete food webs, such as that in Fig. 15-4, were made in the 1970s during the International Biological Program. In the planktonic environment, these studies indicated some problems with the traditional energy flow diagram of phytoplankton to zooplankton to fish. In particular, there was sometimes too little algal productivity to support the measured increases in animal biomass. This was most evident in oligotrophic lakes and the open sea, es-

pecially in summer. In part the imbalance was due to the neglect of the very small nannoplankton and picoplankton, which pass through the nets and filters used to collect the larger phytoplankton. In addition, there was no clear idea of the role played by tiny organisms such as microflagellates and the larger ciliates. These plankton, which are often heterotrophic, may be present in very large numbers.

The planktonic food web differs from terrestrial webs in that most dead particulate matter and detritus sinks to the lake bed and is unavailable to planktonic bacteria or small detritivors for at least that season. However, *soluble detritus* composed of *dissolved organic matter* (DOM) and very small organic particles remains dissolved or suspended for long periods. The main sources of soluble detritus are algal exudates

TABLE 15-4

QUANTITIES OF SELECTED CHEMICAL SUBSTANCES AND CALORIC CONTENTS OF SEVERAL SPECIES OF AQUATIC MACROPHYTES

Values for all constituents except tannins were obtained for samples from a single lake and should be subject to a minimum of between-site variation.

Species	Protein*	Non-cell wall constituents	Tannins	% dry weight Ash (minerals)	Phosphorus	Potassium	Caloric content, kcal g^{-1} dry wt.
Typha latifolia	4.0	34.7	2.1	7.5	0.14	2.65	4.26
Hydrotrida carolinensis	10.5	60.6	2.5	—	—	—	4.06
Brasenia schreberi	10.9	70.4	11.8	7.6	0.14	0.99	4.03
Utricularia inflata	11.4	59.3	—	14.0	0.12	1.98	4.02
Nelumbo lutea	12.1	56.9	9.2	8.8	0.19	2.27	4.23
Myriophyllum heterophyllum	13.5	63.0	3.2	12.2	0.16	1.25	3.96
Eleocharis acicularis	14.1	—	2.0	11.2	0.24	2.86	4.26
Najas guadalupensis	14.4	—	1.4	12.8	0.15	3.49	3.92
Nymphaea odorata	14.6	58.1	15.0	8.1	0.18	1.28	4.18
Ceratophyllum demersum	17.1	53.1	1.9	14.9	0.26	4.01	3.91
Nuphar advena	21.6	68.5	6.5	10.6	0.40	1.88	4.32

Modified from Boyd and Goodyear (1971).
* Protein—sum of amino acids

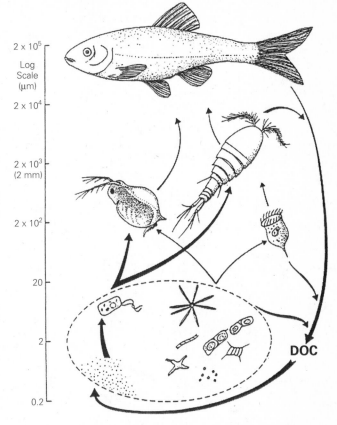

FIGURE 15-5 The microbial loop. Soluble organic matter, known as extracellular products of photosynthesis (ECPP), continually leaks from phytoplankton cells. Small fragments lost during feeding and organic matter from fish and zooplankton excretion together with ECPP form a pool of "soluble detritus" analogous to the particulate detritus of rivers and terrestrial ecosystems. Soluble detritus is used by small heterotrophs (bacteria, microflagellates, and ciliates) and returns to the main food web when they are consumed by larger grazers, such as the cladoceran *Daphnia,* rotifers, "herbivorous" copepods, and even very small fish. In this way organic matter is not lost from the planktonic habitat. It becomes important in summer when low inorganic nutrient levels reduce the productivity of larger phytoplankton (Fig. 12-4). Heavy lines show microbial loop. Modified from Fenchel (1988) with ideas from Porter (1988), Geller (1991), and Geller et al. (1991).

known as *extracellular products of photosynthesis* (ECPP). Contributions to the soluble detrital pool are also made by microbial decomposition, animal excretion, and fragments lost when fish and zooplankton feed. The energy and nutrients in soluble detritus are utilized by bacteria, heterotrophic nannoflagellates, and ciliates. These small organisms form part of a *microbial loop* when they are consumed by larger filter feeders such as *Daphnia,* rotifers, copepods, or even small fish (Figs. 15-5, 15-6). The importance of the microbial loop varies between lakes but is of more consequence in large oligotrophic lakes and the open ocean than in eutrophic situations.

Quantification of the microbial loop required the development of techniques to identify and measure the activity of bacteria and tiny heterotrophic microflagellates. The actual counting is done using epifluorescence microscopy. In this method, active cells take up a fluorescent dye and are easily distinguished from inactive or dead cells as well as detritus. Isotopic tracers, such as the radioactive tritium-labeled amino acid thymidine, can be used to monitor bacterial production just as ^{14}C is used for phytoplankton productivity measurements. Stable isotope tracer methods, such as ^{15}N-labeled cell exudates, require expensive mass spectrometers. Here, phytoplankton are grown with ^{15}N nitrate as a nutrient source, after which the ^{15}N-labeled ECPP produced is separated from the cells by filtration. The labeled ECPP is added to water containing bacteria and flagellates. The amount of ^{15}N label

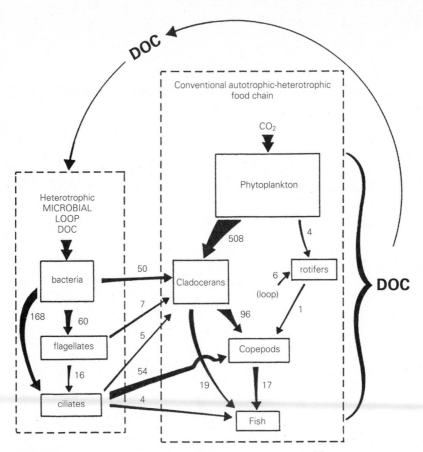

FIGURE 15-6 Carbon flow chart, showing the microbial loop during the midsummer phytoplankton minimum. Although the conventional CO_2-phytoplankton-zooplankton fish pathway still dominates the food web, in this period of low inorganic nutrient concentrations and relatively low phytoplankton production some zooplankton depend on the microbial loop for survival. The microbial loop (left) is the bacteria-microflagellate-ciliate part of the food web that utilizes dissolved organic carbon (DOC), which is not directly available to other plankton. Note that 60 percent of carbon obtained by rotifers and 36 percent of that used by copepods is derived from the microbial loop. Large zooplankton (copepods) graze on loop ciliates while small zooplankton (rotifers) mostly eat loop bacteria. In contrast, the numerically dominant cladocerans (80 percent of larger zooplankton biomass) collect about 90 percent of their carbon food from the autotrophic phytoplankton and only 10 percent from the loop. The phytoplankton at this time is usually dominated by tiny nannoplankton, rather than large diatoms such as *Asterionella*. Note also that fish at this time eat more copepods than the more abundant cladocerans so are more dependent on the microbial loop than might appear at first sight. This example is from Lake Kinneret in the Middle East. Box sizes represents relative biomass (e.g., rotifers and flagellates were uncommon) and size of arrow indicates size of carbon transfer. Numbers on arrows indicated estimated carbon flow (g C m^{-2} day^{-1}). Losses to respiration and cannibalism are ignored here. Modified from Berman (1988).

they incorporate gives a quantitative estimate of that part of the microbial loop. All of these methods have drawbacks, and some links in the microbial loop are still only estimates needed to prepare mathematical models of total productivity in the mixed layer (Fig. 15-6).

Nutrient Generation in the Mixed Layer

Summer in thermally stratified lakes is usually characterized by depletion of one or more limiting nutrients. Nevertheless, a small plankton population is able to grow. As just described, zooplankton can be supported by organic matter recycled in the microbial loop. *Nutrient regeneration in the mixed layer* is a parallel mechanism by which algae and bacteria interact to recycle inorganic matter to support the small summer phytoplankton crop.

Microbial remineralization of organic matter produces new and recycled nutrients, and most studies have been directed toward nitrogen and phosphorus. *New nutrients* are those that recently arrived from the inflowing rivers or rainfall together with those already present. New nitrogen is also produced by biological N_2 fixation. *Recycled nutrients* are those recently excreted by zooplankton and fish. Aquatic animals excrete both inorganic and organic matter, and some organic compounds are then mineralized by aquatic bacteria. Dead material, which is primarily the remains of phytoplankton, is decomposed by both bacteria and fungi. Recycled nitrogen and phosphorus are important in the epilimnion of some temperate lakes in summer or in the tropics. In contrast, the large spring algal bloom of temperate lakes and the brief algal blooms of the polar zones are mostly supplied with new nitrogen.

The importance of nutrient recycling in the epilimnion is illustrated in Castle Lake, California. In this small lake, there are no major stream inflows, and groundwater seepage and rainfall are low in the sunny subalpine Californian climate (Fig. 6-1). In summer dissolved inorganic nitrogen (DIN: nitrate, nitrite, ammonia) is very low, usually below 10 μg liter^{-1}, but dissolved

organic nitrogen (DON) averages almost 20 times as much. DON also contains organic carbon, and this serves as a source of energy to heterotrophic organisms. Most DON is not readily available to bacteria. However, by adding glutamate labeled with ^{15}N tracer as well as ^{14}C label, the rates of the heterotrophic processing of DON and dissolved organic carbon (DOC) can be estimated under the most favorable situation. About 5 percent of phytoplankton nitrogen requirements are supplied by bacterial mineralization of the soluble detritus pool (Zehr et al., 1985). This is equivalent to a daily rate of about 1 μg N liter^{-1} and is thus about 10 percent of that available for algae growth in the epilimnion of this mesotrophic lake. Similar studies can be made of phosphorus regeneration (Suttle and Harrison 1988), and similar contributions to the mixed layer have been found. In oligotrophic situations, the rates are often similar but the contribution of microbial mineralization is proportionately larger.

GROWTH KINETICS AND THE PREDICTION OF PHYTOPLANKTON SPECIES COMPETITION

The phytoplankton ecologist often needs to know how algae will respond to different nutrient concentrations. Which algae will dominate as the nutrient conditions change? This problem is interesting in itself but is also important in such applications as predicting the effect of changes in the nutrient loading that occur when sewage treatment plants are constructed or improved. There are several approaches to determining the outcome of this *resource competition* between species, a subject obviously of interest to both aquatic and terrestrial biologists. Most general ecological texts cover this topic (e.g., Begon et al., 1986). Some aspects of most concern for phytoplankton are based on the graphical-mechanistic approach of Tilman (1982) and others (Smith, 1983). Recently, an entire edition of *Limnology and Oceanography* (Vol. 36, No.

3, 1991) was devoted to aspects of control of phytoplankton productivity and species diversity in the ocean.

Under steady-state conditions only one factor can limit the growth rate of an algal cell at any one instant. The limiting factor can be a nutrient, light, temperature, or the maximum growth rate. This limiting-factor concept, or law of the minimum, is often called *Liebig's law*. When light or nutrients decrease, the plants that require the lowest concentrations are most likely to succeed. Although Liebig's law is a useful concept, it is an oversimplification when applied to a diverse assemblage of phytoplankton. Different species have different optimum values for nutrients, light, or temperature, so that at any one time more than a single factor will limit population growth even though only one factor limits each individual. For example, in the case of nitrogen and phosphorus, colimitation by both of these elements is the most frequent result in bioassay experiments (Fig. 9-8). The law of the minimum finds its best application during a bloom dominated by a single species.

Growth Kinetics

The *substrate-growth curve* is widely applied in microbial kinetic studies in lakes and estuaries. This technique involves measuring the growth of natural or laboratory cultures of phytoplankton or bacteria at several different nutrient concentrations. After incubation, the differences in growth between treatments is usually apparent. If all nutrients are added at the start of the test, it is called a *batch culture*. If nutrients are added continuously and the overflow volume removed, it is called a *chemostat* or *continuous-flow culture*. Growth (μ) can be measured in different ways using, for example, cell counts, spectrometric or fluorometric estimates of chlorophyll *a*, or ^{14}C uptake. The nutrient or substrate (S) added at various levels must be growth-limiting, and all other nutrients, light, and temperature maintained at optimum levels. Under ideal conditions a progressive increase in growth will be produced, with increasing nutrient levels up to the saturation point (Fig. 15-7). The equation describing such growth is:

$$\mu = \frac{\hat{\mu} S}{K_s + S}$$

where μ = measured growth rate
S = substrate (nutrient) concentration
$\hat{\mu}$ = maximum growth rate
K_s = half saturation constant, that is, the substrate concentration at which half the maximum growth rate occurs (Fig. 15-7)

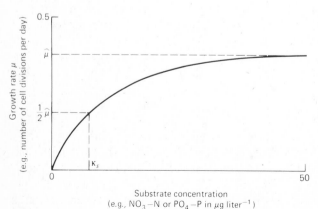

FIGURE 15-7 The theoretical nutrient-uptake growth-rate curve (Substrate-growth or Monod curve). Growth proceeds to $\hat{\mu}$. At $1/2\hat{\mu}$ the dotted lines show how K_S is derived. In practice, the equation is rewritten as $S/\mu = (1/\hat{\mu})\, S + K_S/\hat{\mu}$ to give a straight-line graph of the type $y = mx + c$. S/μ is then plotted against S and K_S obtained from the intercept of $K_S/\hat{\mu}$ since $\hat{\mu}$ is known. This plot is more accurate than any other transformation. Dowd and Riggs, 1965.

Note that $\hat{\mu}$ and K_s are, in principle, fixed intrinsic properties of the species and remain constant, while μ and s change with environmental conditions. Examples of these values for nitrogen and phosphorus for several phytoplankton are given in Tables 8-2, 9-3, and 10-2. The equation also assumes a steady-state condition, which can be achieved only with continuous-flow laboratory cultures.

The substrate-growth method works with most organisms and is easy to carry out. In its simplest form the batch method requires only a few flasks and a routine growth-measuring technique. Pioneering methods developed by Eppley and Thomas (1969) and others on algal, inorganic nutrient kinetics, and by Wright and Hobbie (1966) on organic, bacterial kinetics are now common in studies of phytoplankton.

Prediction of the Outcome of Algal Species Competition

As nutrients wax and wane between spring and fall, phytoplankton with different $\hat{\mu}$ and K_s values respond differently. The following examples for two competing species of phytoplankton (referred to as species 1, species 2, and so on) cover most possibilities.

1. $\hat{\mu}_1 = \hat{\mu}_2 = 0.4$ cell divisions per day
   $K_{s,1} < K_{s,2}$
   where $K_{s,1} = 5$ μg liter^{-1} substrate
   $K_{s,2} = 15$ μg liter^{-1} substrate
2. $\hat{\mu}_3 > \hat{\mu}_2$
   where $\hat{\mu}_2 = 0.4$ cell divisions per day
   $\hat{\mu}_3 = 0.6$ cell divisions per day
   $K_{s,3} = K_{s,2} = 15$ μg liter^{-1} substrate
3. $\hat{\mu}_4 > \hat{\mu}_2$
   where $\hat{\mu}_2 = 0.4$ cell divisions per day
   $\hat{\mu}_4 = 0.5$ cell divisions per day
   $K_{s,4} > K_{s,2}$
   where $K_{s,4} = 24$ μg liter^{-1} substrate
   $K_{s,2} = 15$ μg liter^{-1} substrate

These conditions are plotted in Fig. 15-8. Which species of the pair will eventually become dominant at 10 and 50 μg liter^{-1} of substrate? The graphs show that for case 1, species 1 outcompetes species 2 at lower nutrient levels but at higher levels they are equal competitors. For case 2, species 3 always outgrows species 2. For case 3, the most interesting, species 2 wins at low substrate levels but at about 40 ug liter^{-1} species 4 starts to dominate. Examples for laboratory pure cultures of a blue-green alga and a diatom are shown in Fig. 15-9.

Prediction of the Outcome of Species Competition in Lakes

Because $\hat{\mu}$ and K_s are fixed attributes of an algal species or at least a genetic race within a species, we can predict the outcome of changes in any nutrient concentration for any algal species if $\hat{\mu}$ and K_s are known. Diatoms have a high maximum growth rate and a high K_s relative to many algae and require high concentrations of nutrients for growth. Therefore, diatoms bloom in spring and fall, when nutrients are high (Fig. 12-4). In summer, when nutrients are low, a fast growth rate is less advantageous than the ability to take up nutrients at low concentrations (low K_s). Blue-green and flagellated algae owe their success in part to their ability to grow slowly at low nutrient levels. Of course, many other factors, such as grazing, parasitism, sinking, and active swimming, modify the final outcome of phytoplankton competition during the year (Chap. 12).

The results of interalgal competition can be predicted only if differences in the maximum growth rate, $\hat{\mu}$ or K_s, are large and constant and the same factor remains limiting. As mentioned earlier, a whole spectrum of factors may limit growth during a single day as well as through the year. For example, phytoplankton may start the season with an ample, well-balanced supply of nutrients but deplete one more rapidly than the others. Although only one nutrient can limit cell growth at one instant, over longer periods the balance in the supply of nutrients is also important. It is thus convenient to discuss their availability in terms of the *resource ratio* or ratio

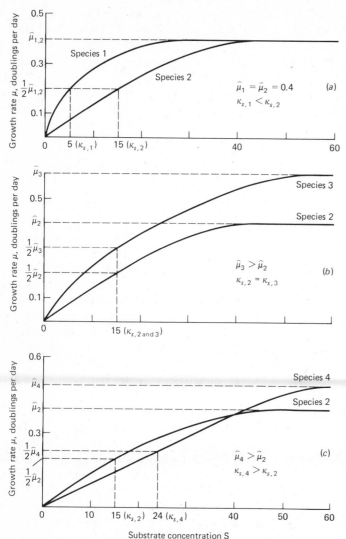

FIGURE 15-8 Three idealized examples of competition between algae with different half-saturation constants (see text for more details). Note the different results in overall growth at 10 and 50 μg liter^{-1} substrate for the different species. Note that phosphate or ammonia is shown as the growth-limiting substance, but in real systems, the limiting factor could also be NO_3, SiO_2, Fe, CO_2, or light. Note that at approximately 50 μg liter^{-1} the enzyme systems are fully saturated and growth rate predominates over uptake kinetics. Note that in the bottom graph species dominance changes with substrate concentration. This type of competition occurs each year as nutrient levels decrease in spring.

of actual, or potentially limiting nutrients, such as nitrogen, phosphorus, or silica.

The resource ratio approach to *resource competition* was tested experimentally for two algae, *Asterionella formosa* and *Cyclotella meneghiniana*. Both of these diatoms are common in lakes and have similar maximum growth rates ($\hat{\mu}$) at nutrient saturation. In contrast, they have different growth kinetics, with *Asterionella* out-

growing *Cyclotella* when phosphate is low. When silica is low the opposite is true. As the ratio of available nutrients, Si:P, changed from more than 90 to less than 90, laboratory growth studies predicted that *Asterionella* will be outcompeted by *Cyclotella* (Fig. 15-10). Resource competition of this sort has been used to explain the observed diatom community structure in Lake Michigan (Fig. 15-10), where Si:P in sum-

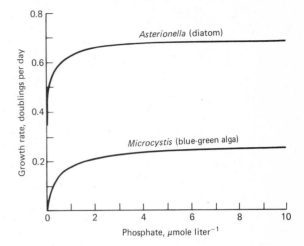

FIGURE 15-9 The substrate-growth curves for laboratory cultures of two common planktonic algae. Note that the diatom easily outgrows the blue-green alga under the conditions of this experiment; i.e., temperatures are moderate (20°C), silica is plentiful, and light is quite high (100 fc). At half this illumination or with low silica, neither the blue-green alga nor the diatom would have any distinct advantage. Redrawn from Holm and Armstrong, 1981.

mer ranges from less than 1 near inflowing rivers to greater than 100 in pelagic waters. Similar studies based on N:P have been used to predict the dominance of blue-green algae in lakes (Smith, 1992). Growth rates and resource competition also result directly from changes in physical variables such as light, temperature, and pH. The availability of many substances, particularly CO_2, is also influenced indirectly by acidity (Fig. 7-3). Carbon dioxide is most available

FIGURE 15-10 Effect of changes in the ratio of silicate to phosphate on the outcome of competition between two diatoms, *Asterionella formosa* and *Cyclotella meneghiniana*. The shaded areas represent ratios at which one or another species should dominate as ascertained by kinetic studies on pure cultures of each species and by long-term laboratory experiments on mixtures of the two. The black line shows measured proportions of *Cyclotella* vs. Si:P ratios in Lake Michigan. The agreement between laboratory prediction and field data is imperfect, especially at low Si:P ratios. Considering all the other factors which contribute to algal growth (Chap. 12), prediction from kinetic parameters alone is quite good. Redrawn and modified from Tilman, 1978, Kilham and Tilman, 1979.

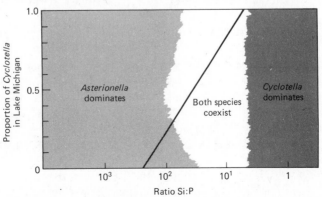

at low pH and is the only carbon fraction used by many higher plants and algae. Lowering the pH experimentally in lake mesocosms altered the species composition of phytoplankton (Shapiro, 1973). In unaltered mesocosms where the pH was 8 to 9, blue-green algae dominated the phytoplankton. One reason for their success is that they can use bicarbonate as a carbon source and have a lower K_s for CO_2 than do the other phytoplankton. Acid was added to other enclosures. More CO_2 was available at this lower pH; green algae and diatoms increased while blue-green algae decreased. The higher K_s for CO_2 of green algae and diatoms was not a disadvantage at lower pH.

ISOTOPIC TRACERS

Radioactive or stable isotopes of biologically important elements are routinely used to trace the pathway of nutrients from one trophic level to another. For example, ^{14}C is widely used to measure photosynthesis and ^{15}N and ^{32}P are used to determine uptake of N_2, NH_4, NO_3, and PO_4. Their use is essential when changes in natural concentrations are too low to be measured accurately. An entirely different use is to label one trophic level and follow the tracer to other levels. Using this method there is no doubt as to the origin and amounts of the element transferred. Unfortunately, carbon, the most abundant element of organic material, cannot be used this way due to its loss in respiration and recycling.

As mentioned in the section on microbial loops, ^{15}N can be used to show nitrogen flow through several trophic levels. When $^{15}N_2$ gas is added to a mixed assemblage of mosses, grasses, and the nitrogen fixing alga *Nostoc,* the gas can be fixed only by the algae. Experiments on a community growing in coastal wetlands showed that the grasses and mosses also became labeled with ^{15}N (Stewart, 1967; Horne, 1972). Obviously, nitrogenous material from *Nostoc* had been lost by excretion or decay and picked up by the other plants.

The isotope ^{15}N is an especially useful tracer

for natural systems because it is stable and non-radioactive and presents no radiation hazard (Preston, Stewart, and Reynolds, 1980). The radioactive isotopes ^{32}P and ^{13}N decay too rapidly for long-term experiments, and elements such as ^{99}Mo and ^{33}S are needed in such small amounts or have such short half-lives that they are less reliable tracers for most food web studies. The dangers associated with radioactive isotopes, especially those that emit strong radiation, preclude their large-scale use in nature.

PRIMARY PRODUCTIVITY

Measurements of photosynthesis or primary productivity are essential in food-chain studies. The daily and seasonal carbon flow forms the base of the annual food pyramid and can be used to estimate maximum production at higher trophic levels. The *sustainable yield* of a fishery, for example, can be estimated from measurements of primary production (Steele, 1974). Changes in photosynthetic rates show the almost instantaneous effect of perturbations of nutrients, toxicants, or physical changes in the environment. Biomass changes could be used but are relatively insensitive except over long periods. Primary productivity is related to the rate of change in biomass of various lake phytoplankton species according to the following equation (de Amezaga et al., 1973).

$$\text{Primary productivity} = \sum_{i=1}^{m} a_i \frac{db_i}{dt}$$

Where b_i = the biomass of species i, a_i is the coefficient of the species i contribution to primary productivity and m is the number of species. Cell counts, chlorophyll a levels. ATP, total organic or inorganic carbon, pH, or oxygen can also be used to measure changes in plant growth. In practice, changes in oxygen and uptake of the radioisotope ^{14}C are widely used (Figs. 15-11, 15-12).

The *light-and-dark-bottle method* uses changes in dissolved oxygen to estimate net and gross community metabolism in eutrophic

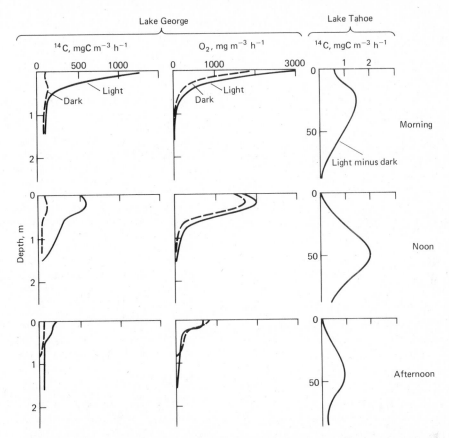

FIGURE 15-11 Diurnal changes in gross primary productivity with depth for two contrasting lakes, productive Lake George, Uganda, and unproductive Lake Tahoe. Primary productivity was measured with both the ^{14}C and the O_2 light- and dark-bottle methods in Lake George, but only the ^{14}C method is sensitive enough for Tahoe. In the productive tropical lake, respiration (dark-bottle results) almost equals photosynthesis, producing high gross but low net productivity values. Note that despite the different methods and differences in absolute gross production of over 3 orders of magnitude, the daily and depth patterns are similar. Productivity peaks near the surface in the early morning, a subsurface peak may be produced around noon, and a smaller morning-type peak is produced in the afternoon. These lakes were well illuminated with continuous sunshine at the time of measurement. In climates with more rain, wind, and cloud cover in summer, these patterns may be less obvious. From Ganf and Horne, 1975; Tilzer and Horne, 1979.

waters. This method, which measures both respiration and photosynthesis, measures oxygen changes that occur in both light and opaque bottles during an in situ incubation of several hours (Fig. 7-2). The incubation period can be as short as 30 minutes in highly productive waters and as much as 24 hours in mesotrophic systems. In productive waters loss of carbon dioxide or increases in oxygen can be measured directly in the water column to give an estimate of whole-lake photosynthesis.

In practice, one takes three sets of samples. A sample is measured for intial oxygen content (I) at the start of the experiment. The light (L) and

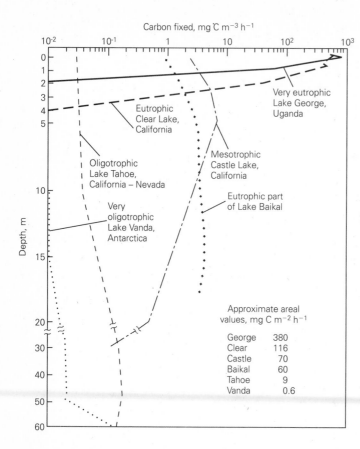

Carbon fixed, mg °C m⁻³ h⁻¹

FIGURE 15-12 Primary production in six contrasting lakes. Very oligotrophic and permanently ice-covered Lake Vanda, Antarctica, oligotrophic Lake Tahoe, mesotrophic Castle Lake, California, eutrophic Clear Lake, California, and very eutrophic Lake George, Uganda. Primary production can vary widely over the surface of very large lakes. The culturally eutrophic section of oligotrophic Lake Baikal is also shown. Note the log scale for primary productivity. Productivity per unit volume is very different between the lakes, but on an areal basis there is less difference due to the deeper photic zones of the more transparent lakes. To use this dilute algal crop, zooplankton require great expenditure of energy to filter the large volumes of water. Areal values are from the literature; the curves are on specific, not necessarily average, days. Redrawn from Goldman (1968a; 1968b), Goldman and Wetzel (1963), Ganf and Horne (1975), Tilzer and Horne (1979) and Goldman (unpublished).

dark bottles (*D*) are incubated for some time and then their oxygen content measured. Net productivity is *L* minus *I*, gross productivity is *L* minus *D*, and respiration is *I* minus *D*.

For unproductive waters or short incubations, the sensitivity of the $^{14}CO_2$ method using the light-and-dark-bottle technique is required. The isotope is added in the form of sodium carbonate or bicarbonate, which rapidly disperses through the inorganic carbon pool (Fig. 7-4). The addition of labeled carbon increases total carbon by an insignificant amount. After a short incubation, the water is filtered and the radioactivity contained in the phytoplankton measured with a Geiger-Muller counter or a scintillation counter. [For details on primary production, see Wetzel and Likens, (1991), Vollenweider (1969), or Goldman (1960; 1968a; 1968b).] The radioactiv-

ity (disintegrations per minute; dpm) of the filter as well as that added initially and the total inorganic carbon level in the water ($\Sigma^{12}C_i$) are needed to calculate the primary productivity, which can be expressed by the equation:

$$^{12}C \text{ fixed} = \frac{(^{14}C, \text{ light dpm}) - (^{14}C, \text{ dark dpm})}{^{14}C, \text{ dpm added}} \times \Sigma\ ^{12}C_i \times BA \times 1.06$$

where *BA* = bottle aliquot correction factor

1.06 = isotope discrimination factor, since the heavier isotope ^{14}C is taken up approximately 6 percent more slowly than ^{12}C

TABLE 15-5

DIEL VARIATIONS IN EXTRACELLULAR RELEASE OF PHOTOSYNTHETIC PRODUCTS (ECPP) BY PHYTOPLANKTON IN CONTRASTING LAKES, VERY UNPRODUCTIVE LAKE TAHOE (SECCHI DISK ~ 30 m) AND PRODUCTIVE LAKE GEORGE, UGANDA

The values for Lake George are given for several depths on one day and those for Tahoe for various days throughout the growth period. Note the regular increase in surface ECPP in Lake George as the day progresses. In Tahoe, note the low ECPP during the most favorable growth period (June) and the high releases at night. For both lakes, ECPP is an important component of primary production which is directly usable by bacteria. Units are in percent of total carbon fixation.

Lake, date	Depth	Morning		Noon		Afternoon	Night	Day average
		0700–1000	1100–1230	1300–1400	1500–1600	1700–1900		
Eutrophic Lake George, Uganda, March 26, 1968	0–8 cm	7	20	27	40	34		26
	15–23 cm	9	13	18	27	37		21
	30–40 cm	23	20	22	44	57		33
	50–60 cm	45	29	36	50	45		41
	150 cm	54	45	24	29	26		36
	Depth av.	28	25	25	38	40		31
		0600–1000	1000–1400		1400–1800		1800–0600	
Oligotrophic Lake Tahoe, 1975:	April	14	12		15		42	17
	June	6	8		5		18	7
	July	13	15		13		13	16
	Sept.	11	9		10		45	10

Modified from Ganf and Horne (1975), and Tilzer and Horne (1979).

The general distribution of primary production in the water column is illustrated in Fig. 15-12 for several lakes with different trophic states: permanently frozen Lake Vanda and monomictic Lake Tahoe, which are oligotrophic lakes, compared with mesotrophic Castle Lake, eutrophic Clear Lake, and very eutrophic Lake George, Uganda. The higher production per unit volume is particularly evident. Note that if the productivity is measured per unit area of surface, as is normal in terrestrial studies, there is often less difference between oligotrophic and eutrophic lakes. The long photic zone of the clearer lakes partially compensates for their low production per unit volume. The higher production per unit of surface area of eutrophic lakes is shown in the inset in Fig. 15-12. Remember that, in contrast to the land, most of the world's aquatic net primary production occurs in the cold waters of upwelling areas and polar or subpolar seas, not in the tropics. Some tropical lakes have very high gross primary production, but because of elevated respiration rates net production is low. Rates of primary productivity for a variety of lakes and estuaries are given in Figs. 7-2, 19-6, 22-6, and Tables 18-3 and 19-1.

Both the oxygen and ^{14}C methods have been very useful, especially in eutrophication studies (Fig. 22-6). There are a few drawbacks, mostly due to the enclosure of a small volume of water in the incubation bottle. The major problems in ^{14}C studies are due to nonphotosynthetic dark uptake and the release of soluble extracellular products of photosynthesis (ECPP) to the medium. Dark uptake is related to respiration and is subtracted from light uptake. Although ECPP is usually less than 10 percent, under some circumstances it may amount to as much as 95 percent of total production (Anderson and Zeutschel, 1970). Some soluble ECPP values are shown in Table 15-5.

Because primary production measurement requires much time and effort, attempts have been made to use mathematical models that require only a few, more easily measured variables

(light, chlorophyll, and the extinction coefficient of the water). The method is most useful where there are many lakes, as in Alaska, Canada, Minnesota, or Wisconsin. Photosynthesis can be modeled with an equation of the form developed by Talling (1970):

$$\Sigma_a = n \frac{P_{max}}{K_e} F\left(\frac{I_0'}{I_k}\right)$$

where Σ_a = photosynthesis or carbon fixed per unit area

n = population density (e.g., in mg chlorophyll a m^{-3})

P_{max} = photosynthetic rate at light saturation, which must be determined empirically using a lake water sample

K_e = average light extinction coefficient (Chap. 3)

I_0' = incident light intensity

I_k = light intensity for P_{max}

F = function of the ratio I_0'/I_k

Using this model, only one measurement of photosynthesis and chlorophyll may be required, since the other values remain relatively constant. Unfortunately, there are many problems with the model due to algal patchiness (Figs. 5-3, 12-13, 12-14, 12-15). Changes in P_{max} with chlorophyll, variations in the physiology of the algae, and horizontal variations in K_e, limit the model's usefulness. Nevertheless, the method provides a useful approximation of photosynthesis if a complete study is impractical. It has also stimulated theoretical studies of light and photosynthesis (Margalef, 1965; Rodhe, 1965; Vollenweider, 1965; Tilzer et al., 1975).

Rivers, wetlands, and estuaries, discussed in Chaps. 16 to 19, are very different from lakes. Even limnologists who will work exclusively with lakes can benefit greatly from a better knowledge of flowing waters, wetlands, and estuaries. For example, most lakes receive water via rivers and streams and may have substantial wetlands around their perimeter.

FURTHER READING

Berman, T. (ed.) 1988. "The role of Microorganisms in Aquatic Ecosystems." *Hydrobiologia,* **159,** special issue. 313 pp.

Berman, T. 1990. "Microbial Food Webs and Nutrient Cycling in Lakes: Changing Perspectives." pp. 511–526. In M. Tilzer and C. Serruya (eds.). *Large Lakes: Ecological Structure and Function.* Brock/Springer, New York.

Butler, E. I., E. D. S. Corner, and S. M. Marshall. 1969. "On the Nutrition and Metabolism of Zooplankton. VI. Feeding Efficiency of *Calanus* in Terms of Nitrogen and Phosphorus." *J. Mar. Biol. Assoc. U.K.,* **49:**977–1001.

Carpenter, S. R. (ed.) 1988. *Complex Interactions in Lake Communities.* Springer-Verlag, New York. 283 pp.

Geller, W., R. Berberovic, U. Gaedke, H. Muller, H-R. Pauli, M. M. Tilzer, and T. Weisse. 1991. "Relations among the Components of Autotrophic and Heterotrophic Plankton during the Seasonal Cycle 1987 in Lake Constance." *Verh. Int. Ver. Limnol.* **24:**831–836.

Goldman, C. R. 1969. "Photosynthetic Efficiency and Diversity of a Natural Phytoplankton Population in Castle Lake, California." pp. 507–517. In *Prediction and Measurement of Photosynthetic Productivity.* Proceedings IBP/PP Technical Meeting. Trebon, Czechoslovakia.

Ivlev, V. S. 1963. "On the Utilization of Food by Plankton-Eating Fishes." *Fish. Res. Board Can.* Translation Series no. 447. 17 pp.

Jassby, A. D., and C. R. Goldman. 1974. "Loss Rates from a Lake Phytoplankton Community." *Limnol. Oceanogr.,* **19:**618–627.

Mann, K. H., R. H. Britton, A. Kowalczewski, T. J. Lack, C. P. Mathews, and I. McDonald. 1972. "Productivity and Energy Flow at All Trophic Levels in the River Thames, England," pp. 579–596. In Z. Kajak and A. Hillbricht-Ilkowska (eds.). *Productivity Problems of Freshwater.* PWN, Warsaw-Krakow.

Mullin, M. M., and P. M. Evans. 1974. "The Use of a Deep Tank in Plankton Ecology. II. Efficiency of a Planktonic Food Chain." *Limnol. Oceanogr.,* **19:**902–911.

Porter, K. D. 1988. "Phagotrophic Phytoflagellates on Microbial Food Webs." *Hydrobiologia,* **159:**89–98.

Riemann, B., and M. Sondergaard. 1986. *Carbon Dynamics in Eutrophic, Temperate Lakes.* Elsevier, Amsterdam. 284 pp.

Steele, J. H. 1974. *The Structure of Marine Ecosystems.* Blackwell, Oxford. 128 pp.

Stockner, J. G. and K. S. Shortreed. 1989. "Algal Picoplankton Production and Contribution to Food-Webs in Oligotrophic British Columbia Lakes." *Hydrobiologia,* **173:**151–166.

Strickland, J. D. H., O. Holm-Hansen, R. W. Eppley, and R. J. Linn. 1969. "The Use of a Deep Tank in Plankton Ecology. I. Studies of the Growth and Composition of Phytoplankton Crops at Low Nutrient Levels." *Limnol. Oceanogr.,* **14:**23–34.

Teal, J. M. 1957. "Community Metabolism in a Temperate Cold Spring." *Ecol. Monogr.,* **27:**283–302.

Winberg, G. G. 1970. "Energy Flow in the Aquatic Ecological System." *Pol. Arch. Hydrobiol.,* **17:**11–19.

CHAPTER 16

Streams and Rivers

OVERVIEW

Streams and rivers are closely linked to their catchments or watersheds. The relatively fast-flowing water and the input of organic matter from the drainage basin are the two factors that most set apart rivers and streams from lakes. Secondary production in streams is often dependent on leaves, twigs, grasses, fruits, and fallen insects all of terrestrial origin. This *allochthonous* material may contribute almost all of the organic matter to shaded streams. Where sunlight can penetrate, attached algae, higher aquatic plants, and mosses produce *autochthonous* organic matter. True plankton is common only in deep, slow-moving stretches of rivers or behind dams. Unlike lakes, benthic invertebrates, especially insect larvae, constitute the bulk of the invertebrate fauna, while fish dominate the vertebrates. All biota in streams are influenced by the unidirectional current and are adapted accordingly. Flowing waters are referred to as a lotic environment, in contrast to the standing or lentic habitat of ponds and lakes. The lotic habitat is subdivided into two zones: the cool, shallow, and often stony bottomed stream and the warmer, deeper, silty bedded river. Streams consist of clear water flowing over shallow gravel *riffles* separated by deeper pools that collect organic debris. Rivers are muddier, larger, and deeper and usually lack riffles and pools.

Water motion is the dominant environmental feature, since it controls the physical structure of the streambed. Current velocity in concert with the underlying geology provides a variety of possible substrate sizes, from silt to boulders. This, in turn, influences the amount of benthic biomass, since fist-sized stones usually provide the most favorable habitat for algae and invertebrates. The discharge (volume per time) and the current (distance per time) determine the amount of suspended material that is transported. *Floods* and the smaller *spates* are events of major importance in the lotic environment. Typical winter or spring floods uproot plants but most animals can avoid this regular disturbance. Atypical summer floods are unpredictable and often completely denude streams of benthic biota. The annual range of stream and river temperatures is 10 to 20°C, which is similar to that found in lakes, but diel (24-hour) changes are much greater than in lakes. Although large rivers do not change in temperature very much on a daily basis, a small unshaded stream may heat up 10°C on a hot summer's day and cool by the same amount at night. Temperature increases caused by clearance of the *riparian corridor* of streamside trees and bushes usually reduces the abundance of fish and benthos. This, in addition to erosion control, is a good reason for leaving buffer strips along the edges of streams when harvesting timber or clearing land for agricultural use.

The chemical composition of streams is affected by their irregular discharge. Most streams and rivers have a maximum discharge during winter rains or spring snow melt. Most particulates are carried in from the watershed and others are scoured from the riverbed during highest discharges. These particles carry most of the annual flux of such nutrients as phosphorus and iron as well as organic debris. High discharges also transport much of the annual load of soluble nutrients, such as nitrate and silica. Streams fed by snow or glacial melt show large diel variations in discharge. Streams fed by springs have a more uniform discharge and also a more constant nutrient concentration.

The rock type predominating in the drainage basin affects the vegetation and hence the quality of allochthonous matter. *Soft-* or *acid-water* streams flow over hard granitic, slate, or sandstone rocks, which release few nutrients. In this situation terrestrial vegetation is likely to be composed of *Sphagnum,* other mosses, and coniferous forests, which have relatively low productivity and produce limited allochthonous material. *Hard-water* streams are formed on more easily broken down limestones or sedimentary rock and are usually surrounded by highly productive deciduous trees or grasslands. Such watersheds provide both allochthonous material and ample nutrients for high autochthonous production. Aquatic fungi and bacteria process dead allochthonous and autochthonous material, collectively called *detritus,* which is eaten by other stream dwellers. Microbial decomposition requires ample supplies of inorganic nutrients, particularly nitrogen, to break down detrital organic carbon. Only the microbial coating on the detritus is digested. It is more nutritious than the cellulose-rich debris, which may actually cycle several times through animal guts before its disappearance. Transformation of leaves and woody matter is assisted by a succession of *functional groups* of stream invertebrates. *Shredders,* such as crayfish, tear leaves into smaller fragments; *collectors,* such as midge larvae, filter out small particles including shredder feces; *grazers,* such as caddisfly larvae, eat both small fallen particles and attached algae. Invertebrate and fish predators complete the food chain. The net result is a transformation of organic matter, starting with large particles in the headwaters and ending as fine refractory particles and dissolved organic compounds in the lowland river. *Drift* is composed of detritus, algae, and invertebrates carried along by the current. Most drift occurs at night, and both fish and invertebrates feed heavily on this resource.

The range of aquatic habitats, from the small stream to the river, is encompassed in the *river continuum concept.* This idea is based on the sources of allochthonous organic matter that fall into or grow in the stream. The concept envisions a cascade, or continuum, of highly nutritious organic matter from large leaves and grasses in the upper watershed streams to the refractory fine-particulate detritus in the larger rivers. This concept explains why the invertebrate population is dominated by shredders in small streams and why collectors or filterers gradually increase downstream. Grazers should be most common in mid-sized streams, since attached algae are most common in this region. The continuum is not completely fixed in time or space but shows seasonal variations.

In this chapter we cover measurements in streams and rivers, the definition of streams and rivers, the lotic environment, nutrients, soft-water and hard-water streams, organic compounds, allochthonous and autochthonous food webs, the river continuum concept, drift, and fish.

INTRODUCTION

Streams can never be considered by themselves because the role of adjacent land is always crucial. This "landscape" modifies the chemistry of the drainage water before it reaches a lake or ocean. The distinction between lakes and streams is evident in their formal names, *lentic* (calm) and *lotic* (flowing). Although lake waters are by no means still, the slowest currents in rivers are about the maximum found in lakes. The faster currents and frequent dependence on *allochthonous* ("outside the system") primary production are the other major factors distinguishing rivers from lakes.

The distinction between streams and rivers is similar to that between ponds and lakes; they are ill-defined words in common usage. It is useful to separate streams and rivers so long as the definitions are not applied too rigorously. In common usage, *streams* are small and often have steep gradients, while *rivers* are large and usually have low gradients at lower elevations. Despite appearances, the average current in rivers is more rapid than in small tributary streams.

The main part of the river, through the lowland plains, is subject to more human pollution than upstream. An example of a damaged and partially restored river, the Thames, is given in Chap. 22. Most towns, industries, farmers, and even individual citizens have long regarded rivers as dumping grounds for their waste; only recently has progress been made toward restoring rivers in urban and industrial areas.

MEASUREMENT

The physical and chemical limnology of streams or rivers is usually measured by similar methods to those for lakes. Discharge in small streams may be measured by direct collection at a culvert. For larger streams, a V-notch weir or Paschall flume is used, which can be calibrated so that the height of the water corresponds to the discharge. *Discharge* is water flow expressed as volume per unit time (e.g., cubic meters per second) and *current* is distance traveled per unit time (e.g., centimeters per second). Where no calibrated structures are available, discharge is estimated from current measurements. Today most current meters use the electromagnetic effect of the water flow over a small bullet-shaped device containing the sensors. The speed of the current is measured at 5 to 10 equally spaced sites across the stream, with the meter held about one-third of the way from the bottom. The depth at each reading and the stream width allow calculation of the discharge using special tables. The method requires the selection of a fairly uniform cross-section.

The entire microscopic attached community of streams is termed *aufwuchs*. This community of bacteria, fungi, algae, and small animals can grow luxuriantly almost year-round. The aufwuchs community is collected by scraping rocks, aquatic plant surfaces, or submerged logs. Artificial substrates such as tile, brick, or inert plastic tubing may be placed in streams to study aufwuchs accumulation. The in situ effects of biostimulatory substances or toxicants can be measured using artificial substrates and diffusers that allow soluble chemicals to pass slowly into the water. Large stream plants, generally flowering angiosperms, are collected by cutting or uprooting both the stems and the often extensive root systems. The extent of streambed plant cover can be estimated with transects or photography.

Benthos in water more than a meter deep can be obtained either by diving or using mechanical samplers. However, virtually all studies and most techniques have been restricted to shallow water. The most widely used device is the *Surber sampler,* which covers a 1-ft square (about 930 cm^2). Benthic organisms dislodged by manual disturbances in the square are trapped in an extended

(a)   (b)

FIGURE 16-1   (*a*) The Surber sampler used for collecting benthic invertebrates in a stream. Water flow is from right to left. (*b*) The entire sampler on land, showing the rigid brass square that is pressed into the substrate when under water.

downstream net (Fig. 16-1). Small rocks are turned over in the water to release benthos, and larger rocks and those with cracks and holes are removed for the retrieval of invertebrates on shore. There are several drawbacks to the Surber sampler. Small animals and most algae are lost through the large mesh, and invertebrates that live deeper in the gravel are not collected. Smaller meshes can be used but tend to clog rapidly. The Surber sampler is also restricted to shallow waters that do not flow over the top of the net. This may be overcome by using a taller system, such as a *Hess sampler,* which can be employed in up to 1 m of water. Considerable replication of samples is essential for adequate estimation of invertebrate numbers, since they are very heterogeneous (Cummins, 1975; Resh, 1979). A comprehensive description of the sta-

tistical methods available for the analysis of benthic invertebrate data is given in Elliott (1973). Benthic invertebrates in streams may complete several, one, or only part of a generation each year. In addition, some benthic organisms may require a true resting stage or diapause to complete their life cycle, while others spend many months as inconspicuous eggs. Many hatch and spend the summer as aerial adults. The net result is that insect numbers in rivers appear highly variable through time. Their populations can be estimated if their life cycles of hatching, egg laying, and resting stages are known.

Recent studies have extended the range of benthic invertebrates deeper into the streambed than the few inches usually sampled. In coarse gravels this zone may extend well away from the river. This region, called the *hyporheic zone,* is defined as still flowing slowly (centimeters per hour) and has a chemical composition similar to that of the stream water. It is thus distinct from the true ground water, which moves much more slowly (centimeters per year) and in which most chemical constituents have been altered by microbes or sorbed onto soil particles. Surprising numbers of small insect larvae have been detected up to several hundred yards from the open water (Hynes, 1972; Stanford, 1988).

The collection of fish and other free-swimming organisms is discussed in Chaps. 13 and 14. A classification of streams based on 13 easily measured variables, such as width, substrate, and maximum and minimum temperatures, was proposed by Pennak (1971). This system remains useful for comparing streams in different regions.

STREAMS AND RIVERS

Streams are zones where a rapid flow of shallow water produces a shearing stress on the streambed, often resulting in a rocky or gravel substratum covered by oxygen-saturated water. However, many lowland streams have muddy beds. For purposes of definition, the stream waters usually have an average monthly mean temperature less than 20°C, except in tropical climates. Many streams are shaded by trees, which considerably reduce solar heating. Deeper *pools* of relatively slow-moving water are separated by *riffles* of shallow, turbulent water passing through or over stones or gravel of a fairly uniform size (Fig. 16-2). Intermediate areas of moderate current often found in larger streams and rivers are termed *runs*. Riffles make excel-

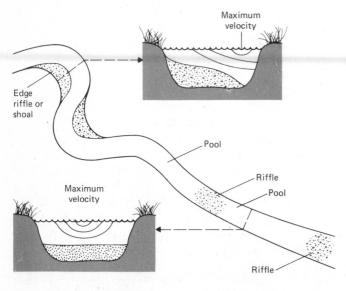

FIGURE 16-2 Water flow and the major structural components of a stream. Note the alternating pools and riffles. A major feature of the riffle is that water flows through the gravel as well as over it. This enables fish eggs and small benthic invertebrates to obtain the oxygen they need while being protected from predation by larger organisms such as fish.

FIGURE 16-3 The alternation of pools and riffles in the Truckee River, California. Riffles usually occupy a smaller area than pools but are more productive.

lent sites for stream surveys. They are actually the "larder" of the lotic environment, containing the majority of the stream's benthic invertebrates (Fig. 16-3). Stones in sunlit riffles are often covered with algae and mosses, which are the main in situ primary producers. In contrast, the pools, which usually cover several times the area of the riffles, contain different, less dense biota living among a mixture of stones and fine-grain sediments. A characteristic feature of pools is the accumulation of decaying terrestrial debris. Pools and riffles support higher plants called *aquatic macrophytes,* but rarely will the whole streambed be covered (Gessner, 1955; 1959).

River waters are deep and generally sufficiently turbid to prevent light penetration to the riverbed. This, together with rapid current in some transparent rivers, such as the Brooks River in Alaska, restricts the growth of aquatic macrophytes. These become important only at the edge, where they provide fish breeding sites and refuges for smaller organisms. Autochthonous

primary production is carried out by true phytoplankton, typically centric diatoms, and by blue-green algae in warmer climates. In contrast to streams, rivers may reach mean monthly temperatures in excess of 20°C. Shading by vegetation is usually small due to their larger width. Deep rivers generally have a small gradient and shear stress on the bed is low. This condition produces muddy, debris-laden sediments, and riffles are absent. The average current, as well as discharge, becomes greater as the overall size increases so that river waters move faster than streams, despite their lesser slope. Eddies behind rocks and snags in stream pools whirl water around but delay its downstream passage. These types of obstructions are minor in rivers. The passage of much of the stream water through riffles is necessary for the oxygenation of the under-rock habitat and imposes a frictional drag on the water. The proportionately smaller fraction of water in frictional contact with the bed in rivers and the generally smoother bed also account the more rapid flow in rivers.

THE LOTIC ENVIRONMENT

Discharge

Annual patterns of stream flow determine many of the physical and biological properties of lotic systems. Discharge is dependent on rainfall, catchment geology, area, bed slope, and dam control by vegetation, beavers, and, most important, humans. For detailed discussions of river flow, physics of stream channel interactions, and turbulence, the reader is referred to major texts such as those by Leopold et al. (1964), Morisawa (1968), Hynes (1972), and Fischer et al. (1979). As in lakes, water movements in streams are not uniform. Currents vary from highest just below the surface near the stream center to lowest at the streambed and along the bank (Fig. 16-2). This distribution is the basis for the current-measuring methods discussed earlier. There are areas of high and low flow around submerged objects, and river bends produce both turbulent and quiet areas.

Seasonal and daily variations in discharge are important in river and stream ecology. For example, high mountain streams show their greatest discharge during midafternoon snow melts in late spring and lowest discharges after freezing at night (Fig. 16-4). Most important from both the biological and physical points of view are the very high discharges, known as *floods*, if the water overflows the banks, or *spates* if the high water stays within the banks. When in flood,

scouring and bank-eroding effects are much larger than during normal discharge. Most biota avoid floods either by migrating to calm backwaters or by having life cycles that are terrestrial or aerial at these times. When floods occur at unusual times, the fauna may be severely depleted and require several years to recover. Salmon ascend rivers during periods of high discharge because there are few shallow water barriers. Flooding in streams carry large amounts of suspended material (Fig. 16-5), which is deposited downstream in lakes, rivers, or flood plains. Severe floods are detrimental to smaller biota if they leave only inhospitable large rocks, but smaller spates remove excessive silt from gravels and produce better environments for fish eggs, benthic invertebrates, and algal production.

In rivers, floods are generally less destructive, stirring the already silty bottom and spreading it over the flood plain. This cannot occur if the river has been canalized, levied, or dammed. Floods may benefit some areas, such as the lower Nile, by adding fertile mud to the fields. This process has now been greatly reduced on the Nile by the Aswan High Dam in Egypt, where the reduction of the sediment load has caused the Delta of the Nile to recede from the Mediterranean. Since phosphate and most metals are generally transported as particles, flood transport is important to the phosphorus budgets of unpolluted lakes (Fig. 16-6). Nitrogen, which is largely transported in dissolved forms, is affected more

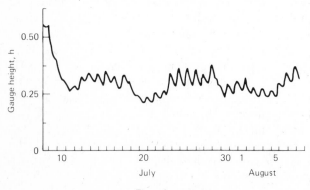

FIGURE 16-4 Daily changes in stream discharge in a stream fed by snowmelt. The relationship between gauge height h and discharge Q is given by $Q = h^b$, which indicates an exponential increase in Q with increase in h. Thus the changes in discharge in this example would be much more extreme than they appear.

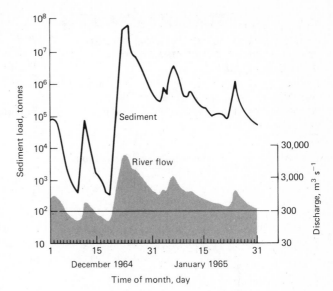

FIGURE 16-5 Relationship between discharge and sediment load for the Eel River, in northern California. This river, like the Yellow River in China, carries much more sediment than most rivers, partially due to natural erosion in the headwaters. The general effect is similar in most flowing waters. Redrawn from Waananen (1970) and Beaumont (1975).

by the volume of water discharged than by current (Table 16-1, Chap. 8).

River and Stream Order

Rivers and streams are also classified by their order (Strahler, 1957). Low-order streams are small and have no larger tributaries, and high-order streams or rivers have tributaries of intermediate order. An example is shown in Fig. 16-7. The smallest trickles and rivulets are first-order streams. When two first-order streams join they become a single second-order stream. No increase in order occurs if more lower-order

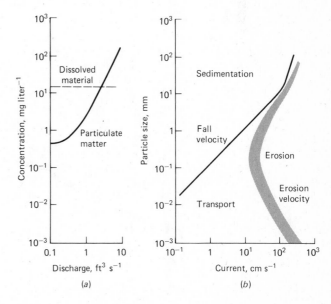

FIGURE 16-6 The relationship of discharge, current, and the concentrations and transport of soluble and particulate materials. (*a*) A small stream in a heavily wooded part of the northeastern United States in which most particulate matter moves only at highest discharges. This phenomenon is shown for a different stream in Fig. 16-11. Modified from Likens et al. (1977). (*b*) Erosion and deposition of a uniform material, such as a sandy bank, for all flowing waters. Note that the size of the particle, as well as the water current, controls how easily it will be eroded. Modified from Morisawa (1968).

TABLE 16-1

GROSS ANNUAL OUTFLOW OF DISSOLVED AND PARTICULATE MATTER IN A SMALL WOODLAND STREAM

Figures are given as a percentage of the total of that element. Note that most phosphorus and all iron moves in the particulate form, while nitrogen and silicon move mostly as dissolved forms.

Element	Particulate fraction, %	Dissolved fraction, %
P	63	37
N	3	97
Si	26	74
Fe	100	0
S	0.2	99.8
C	32	68
Na	3	97
K	22	78
Ca	2	98
Mg	6	94
Cl	0	100
Al	41	59

Modified from Likens et al. (1977).

streams join a higher-order stream. Two second-order streams joined create a third-order stream, and the process continues to still higher orders. The Mississippi River, for example, reaches 12th order before it reaches the ocean (Fig. 16-7).

Temperature

The temperature of most streams is lowest in the uplands and becomes gradually warmer in the lower reaches. Even arctic rivers are warmer in the lowland; for example, the Brooks River, in Alaska, approaches 15°C in summer. High mean temperatures in many rivers restrict the spread of some organisms. Streams may have daily temperature variations of up to 10°C, which are normally greatest in level, rocky, unshaded zones (Fig. 16-8). These large diel changes are normally found above the tree line or where the stream shrinks to the center of its channel. Clearance of streamside vegetation increases water temperature and, together with the loss of tree root habitat, can cause dramatic reductions in fish

FIGURE 16-7 Stream order nomenclature. Streams of equal order move to the next order when they merge. The smallest streams (first-order) become second-order by merging, but to become third-order they must join another second-order stream (see Strahler, 1957).

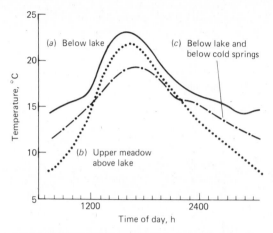

(a) Below lake

(c) Below lake and below cold springs

(b) Upper meadow above lake

Time of day, h

FIGURE 16-8 Daily variation in average summer temperatures for three reaches of Martis Creek, California, a small, partially shaded mountain stream. Note the typical large diel (24-hour) variation of more than 10°C in all reaches. A lake in the same area would show only 1 or 2°C diel change in temperature. Surface discharges from a lake to the stream heats up the section below the lake (a) relative to an unshaded meadow section above the lake (b). Cold springs reduce temperature (c) to below that initially present prior to lake heating. Redrawn from McLaren et al. (1979).

production (Bingler and Hall, 1975). Such clearances of the riverside, or *riparian,* vegetation are now illegal in many areas. Rivers show smaller daily temperature variations since their large volume and heat capacity buffer change. Average stream temperature is not necessarily the same as that of the microhabitats occupied by benthic invertebrates and fish, which may hide in the gravel or near cold springs. The effect of shading is shown in Fig. 16-9, which illustrates the increase in temperature resulting from a few meters of unshaded meadow followed by a decrease in temperature when the stream reenters a shady zone. The amount of cooling found after entering shade depends on the type of stream. Where groundwater inflows are small relative to stream volume, back radiation and conduction to the streambed produce the cooling (Burton and Likens, 1973). Where groundwater or side stream

inflows are large, they exert the major cooling effect (Brown, 1970).

The amount of radiant heat retained by a stream can be expressed by the equation

$$T = \frac{HA}{Q}$$

where T = temperature rise (°F)
H = heat flux (BTU ft^{-2} min^{-1})
A = area (ft^2)
Q = discharge (ft^3 sec^{-1})

This equation applies to streams with gravelly beds, which are highly permeable to water and where the heat of both water and gravel is distributed by water movement. In streams flowing over rock beds some solar radiation is lost by conduction to the earth and less heating of the water occurs. Rocky streams lose more heat than gravelly ones, which increases the likelihood that *anchor ice* will form in winter (Chap. 19).

Cool water released from the hypolimnion of reservoirs can be deleterious to the growth of fish or rice crops. On the other hand, if well-oxygenated, these releases of cool water are beneficial for salmon spawning or trout fisheries in warm climates. Shady streams are poor environments for primary production. Once shade is cleared primary production may increase, but not always usefully, since unpalatable benthic algae may coat the streambed. It is wise stream management practice to leave a buffer strip of original vegetation about 30 m wide to reduce erosion, prevent temperature increases, and preserve the benthos (Erman et al., 1977).

NUTRIENTS

The chemistry of rivers and streams in relation to the distribution of biota is often overshadowed by physical considerations. Some nutrients such as nitrate and silicate, are largely present in soluble form, whereas others, such as phosphate, are associated with the particulate phase (Table

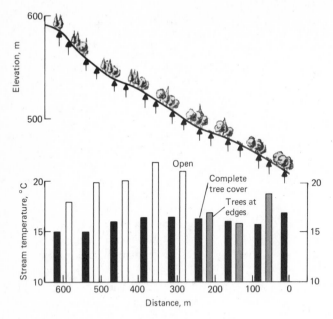

FIGURE 16-9 Effects of shade on the temperature of a small stream in midsummer at midday on a sunny day. Black bars represent stream temperatures under dense tree cover; open bars, temperature in unshaded reaches; and hatched bars, effect with trees in a strip only 10 m wide on each side of the stream. Arrows show where temperatures were taken. Note the rapid increase and decrease of up to 5°C in less than 50 m. That the decrease is due to the immediate shading effect is shown by the similar temperature reduction given by full forest and the small buffer strip only 10 m wide. On cloudy days the fluctuation in temperature was reduced to 1.5°C. The effect is mostly due to the heat stored in streambed rocks. The trees by this stream in the Hubbard Brook ecosystem were cut as part of an experiment. Normally such a regular pattern of shade and open water would not occur. From Burton and Likens (1973).

16-1). In the Hubbard Brook ecosystem, a wooded area in New Hampshire, 97 percent of the nitrogen and 74 percent of the silicon was carried in soluble form as nitrate or silicate. In contrast, only 37 percent of phosphorus was transported in soluble form. These proportions vary with season, climate, discharge, floods, and geology of the watershed. In Ward Creek, a small subalpine stream in the western United States, soluble phosphate dominates at low discharges but makes up only a few percent at high discharge (Fig. 16-10a). The effect of floods on particle transport is indicated in Figs. 16-5 and 16-6.

The seasonal variation in major nutrients is shown for Ward Creek in Fig. 16-10. This pattern is typical for many streams with a large seasonal increase in discharge from snow melt. Extreme cases, where the stream may freeze in winter, are discussed in Chap. 21. In streams fed by snow melt, there is a large daily fluctuation in discharge and thus nutrient transport (Fig. 16-4). Most large rivers show little daily variation in flow or nutrient transport but peak once each year

during the annual flood. This is especially evident in tropical rivers, such as the Amazon, Nile, Niger, and Congo (Chap. 17).

Variations in nutrient discharge are subdued in streams fed by ground water. For example, Wraxall Brook, a chalk stream in southern England, has fairly constant nitrate levels throughout the year, but there are some peaks (Fig. 16-11). Nitrate levels were once probably more stable and the peaks may now be due to fertilizer from adjacent fields. Ground water usually has a long residence time and a more constant nutrient content than surface water (Table 16-2). The beneficial effect of springs on stream biota in alpine and polar regions is discussed in Chap. 21. The buffering effect of underground reservoirs provides the constant temperature and chemical composition of springs of worldwide economic importance to the brewing, whiskey, and bottled water industries.

Year-to-year variations in nutrients in most streams (Fig. 16-12) are more pronounced than in lakes, since in lakes the large volume dilutes the effect of inflows. Even in undisturbed sys-

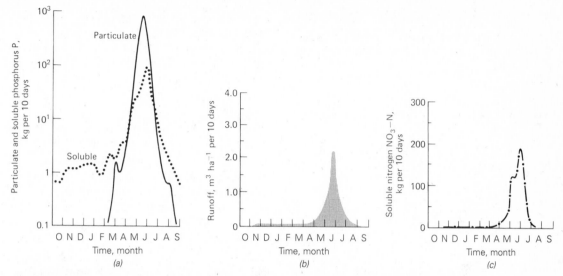

FIGURE 16-10 Flux of nitrogen and phosphorus relative to water flow in Ward Creek, California, a subalpine stream fed mostly by snowmelt. Most phosphorus (*a*) moves in the particulate form and nitrogen as soluble nitrate, as is the case for most streams (Table 16-1). The spring-summer melt (*b*) in June increases the flux of particulate phosphorus (note log scale) much more than nitrate. In this example particulate phosphorus carried during the high melt discharges increased 10,000 times, but nitrate and soluble phosphate increased only 100 to 200 fold. This difference is due to high discharges that carry particulate material eroded from banks or resuspended in pools; soluble nitrate is carried in more constant concentrations during all discharges (Fig. 16-6). Redrawn from Leonard et al. (1979).

tems the causes of year-to-year changes in nutrients in streams and rivers is not well understood. A combination of many factors in the watershed controls nutrient flux. In the case of nitrate, the sources and sinks of nitrogen in the watershed are dominated by levels of nitrate and ammonia in rainfall, biological nitrogen fixation and denitrification, freezing and thawing of soil,

natural fires, erosion, recycling by vegetation, and retentions by the humus layer. Some of these effects are shown for the Hubbard Brook ecosystem in Fig. 16-12. Here a gradual increase in nitrate in rainfall is apparently responsible for an increase in nitrate levels in the stream. There is, however, no direct correlation between stream nitrate levels and the measured inflows of nitrate

FIGURE 16-11 Concentration of nitrate and discharge in Wraxall Brook, a small chalk stream fed by groundwater springs. Note the relatively small seasonal changes in nitrate and, to a lesser extent, discharge. Nitrate levels are higher than in most lakes, where 0.5 to 1.0 mg liter^{-1} are typical maximum values (Tables 8-2, 19-1 and Figs. 8-6, 12-11). Redrawn from Casey (1977).

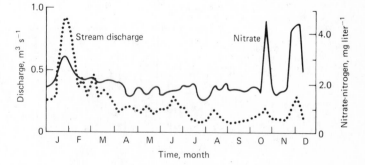

TABLE 16-2

ANNUAL MEANS AND RANGES IN THE LEVELS OF NITRATE IN HOLLYBUSH SPRING, A CHALK SPRING

Year	Nitrate concentration, mg liter^{-1}		No. of samples
	Mean	Range	
1968	5.36	5.11–5.96	8
1969	6.00	5.10–6.96	52
1970	5.54	4.96–6.10	52
1971	5.47	4.72–7.48	52
1972	5.14	4.61–5.56	51
1973	5.27	4.56–5.74	51

From Casey (1977).

during any single year. The two largest peaks of nitrate are related to years when unusually severe frosts occurred when the soil was not insulated with a blanket of snow. This caused freezing and thawing of the upper soil, which increased release of nitrate to the stream (Fig. 16-12).

In almost all cases the soil horizon containing humus is an important reservoir of nitrogen for the watershed and can temporarily reduce and even reverse the flow of nitrate. The lack of any correlation between nitrate in 12 rivers in England and nitrate added as fertilizer is shown in Table 16-3. At most only half and usually only one-third of nitrogen added to agricultural land finds its way into crops. The rest is lost to ground water or rivers, is denitrified, or is held in the humus. Some nitrogen is taken up by plant growth, and this could interfere with correlations such as those shown in Table 16-3. However, in many streams and rivers nitrate is often so abundant (Table 16-4) that biological uptake removes only a small fraction (Casey, 1977). This is not the case in most alpine and arid-zone streams, where nitrogen is in short supply and biological uptake further reduces its concentration. Phosphorus probably undergoes similar large modification by the watershed, but due to absorption of phosphate onto soils (Chap. 9) little is released to streams, except by erosion. Soluble phosphate concentration in unpolluted rivers is usually less than 0.01 mg liter^{-1} PO$_4$—P and often only 0.001 mg liter^{-1}.

The concept of the limiting nutrient is not as

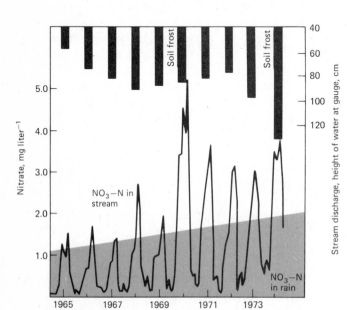

FIGURE 16-12 Year-to-year variation in seasonal patterns of nitrate concentration in Hubbard Brook, a small creek in a heavily wooded watershed in the northeast United States, as related to nitrate in rainfall and in the stream. The nitrate increases more or less proportionately with discharge (black bars at the top). The increase in nitrate in rainfall (shaded area at bottom) over the 20 years apparently appears as an overall trend but does not account for the high values in 1969–1970 or 1973–1974. These unusually high levels of nitrate from the watershed might be due to nitrate released by severe frosts that increased the freeze-thaw cycle in the surface soils. Redrawn and modified from Likens et al. (1977).

TABLE 16-3

EFFECT OF THE WATERSHED ON FLOWS OF NITROGEN INTO RIVERS IN ENGLAND

Most values are for the period 1953–1967. The nitrate purchased for fertilization has been correlated with nitrate levels in the rivers concerned. Note the negative, positive, and lack of correlations in the various watersheds. Although much of the nitrate in these rivers is almost certainly derived from fertilizers, there is not often a direct correlation even over quite long time periods (Fig. 16-12).

River	Significant ($P < 0.1$) correlation coefficients
Dee	−0.89
Rother	+0.90
Severn	+0.75
Stour	+0.71
Devon	+0.52
Wensum	+0.52
Twelve other rivers including the Thames	No significant correlation

Modified from Tomlinson (1970).

clear in streams as in lakes. Although some nutrients are present in very small concentrations in some streams, most rivers are rich in accumulated nutrients (Table 16-4). Certainly many animals and plants increase downstream of large influxes of nutrients, such as those from agricultural or domestic waste discharges. Nonetheless, sometimes such increases do not occur, and even in pristine mountain streams thick felts of algae may cover the rocks in spring or summer.

Increases in stream fertility can rarely be ascribed to the effect of any single nutrient. The lower trophic levels, primary producers and saprophytes, are less affected by low nutrient concentrations in flowing waters than in lakes. A major reason for mobility in lake algae is to "stretch" the diffusion shell (Chap. 12) and allow more rapid access to scarce nutrients. Adapting this idea to stream plants and animals, it can be seen that running water provides a permanently stretched diffusion shell so that even nutrients in low concentrations are available. For example, the most rapidly moving lake phyto-

TABLE 16-4

NUTRIENT CONCENTRATIONS IN RIVERS AND STREAMS

The highest nitrate, ammonia, and soluble phosphate values are found in rivers polluted with agricultural drainage and sewage. The unpolluted maximum concentrations are probably nearer 5.0 mg liter^{-1} for NO_3—N and 0.01 mg liter^{-1} for PO_4—P. Minimum values for nitrate and maximum values for phosphate and sulfate are usually found in arid areas, such as East Africa or the southwest United States. Maximum nitrate and minimum phosphate concentrations are often found in temperate areas, such as northern Europe or the northeastern United States. Values for rivers are world averages and examples are from most major watersheds (see tables in Chaps. 8–10). Values for streams are from a less extensive data base and are only illustrative.

Nutrient	Typical value, mg liter^{-1}	Range
Rivers		
Nitrate (NO_3)	1.0	0.003–7.0
Ammonia (NH_4)	0.05	0.005–10.0
Silica (SiO_2)	9	1.4–35
Soluble phosphate (PO_4)	0.1	0.001–1.0
Sulfate (SO_4)	20	0.4–290
Streams		
Nitrate (NO_3)	0.5	0.003–5
Ammonia (NH_4)	0.04	0.005–1.0
Silica (SiO_2)	6	0.5–20
Soluble phosphate (PO_4)	0.002	0.001–0.013
Sulfate (SO_4)	8	0.3–20

plankton travels less than 5 m h^{-1} and most travel much more slowly. A similar cell as part of a filament attached to a rock in a stream with water current of about 50 cm s^{-1} would experience more than 300 times the water contact of the most rapidly moving lake plankton.

Soft-Water and Hard-Water Streams

Soft- and hard-water streams are defined by the chemical composition imposed on them by the watershed rocks. Hard waters are rich in calcium, magnesium, carbonate, and sulfate and a slightly

TABLE 16-5

THE FACTORS INVOLVED IN THE PRODUCTION OF HARD-WATER STREAMS, WHICH ARE OFTEN ALKALINE AND NUTRIENT-ENRICHED, AS COMPARED WITH SOFT-WATER STREAMS, WHICH ARE USUALLY ACID AND NUTRIENT-DEPLETED

Factor	Soft/Acid	Hard/Alkaline
Watershed	Sandstone, sedimentary, or metamorphosed rock with slow weathering rates. Little chemical breakdown to buffer the rainfall which is acidic. Stream waters produced are poor in calcium and are acidic.	Alkaline sedimentary rock (e.g., limestone or chalk), which is rapidly weathered by rain to yield stream water rich in calcium and slightly alkaline.
Vegetation of watershed	Acid-tolerant plants (e.g., *Sphagnum*) where waterlogged and coniferous forest soil result in slow decomposition of litter by microbes. In the tropics, e.g., the Amazon basin, ion exchange is tightly controlled by efficient recycling so that nutrient washout is slow.	Deciduous woodlands typically have higher input of nutrients from rock weathering and a greater loss of organic matter to streams. Microbial decomposition in the leaf litter is rapid.

alkaline pH, whereas soft or acid waters are low in these constituents (Chap. 10). The chemistry of the drainage basin also affects the amounts and nutritional value of allochthonous and autochthonous organic matter (Table 16-5). It is reasonable to assume that hard and soft water also correspond to nutrient-rich and nutrient-poor. The soils in hard-water drainages supply more nutrients such as nitrogen and phosphorus than soils in soft-water regions. For example, N_2 fixation by blue-green algae (cyanobacteria) is much more common in alkaline areas. Productive watersheds contain dense stands of terrestrial vegetation, some of which falls into streams. The higher nutrient content of the waters also assists microbes to process the carbonaceous detritus. Consequently, invertebrates and fish are generally more abundant in hard waters. Acidification of lakes and streams can occur following deposition of residues derived from the burning of fossil fuels (Chap. 6). This rapid increase in acidity has decreased fish in some lakes and streams.

Some benthic invertebrates that are particularly dependent on a single element may be restricted to hard waters. Mollusks and some crustaceans, for example, require large amounts of calcium to construct their shells. Despite this need, low calcium levels in soft-water streams do not necessarily limit these organisms, since their growth and thus their annual demand for calcium is low (Young, 1975). In soft or acidic waters, such as high mountain lakes in granitic basins, reduced shell thickness may result from low calcium concentrations. One of us recalls that aquatic snails in Brooks Lake, Alaska, were so thin-shelled that they could scarcely be handled without breaking.

Organic Components and Detritus

The dead organic matter in streams plays a larger role than in lakes and has been divided into fractions based on size and solubility. These fractions are useful in describing the food chain in flowing waters and form the basis of the river continuum concept described later in this chapter. They include allochthonous organic particles, such as entire dead leaves, twigs, bark, and fruits. This input is termed *coarse particulate organic matter* (CPOM) and consists of particles larger than 1 mm in diameter. In contrast, *fine particulate organic matter* (FPOM) has particle sizes less than 1 mm. *Dissolved organic matter* (DOM), leached from soils or particulates, is also present together with excretory products of stream animals. Once in the stream, CPOM is degraded by animal and microbial action to FPOM and DOM. Most benthic invertebrates gain little nutritive value from CPOM until it has undergone considerable microbial modification. The changes are similar to those that occur in composting and require considerable supplies of inorganic nutrients, particularly nitrogen (Kaushik and Hynes, 1971), since protein nitrogen in leaves and dry grasses is withdrawn to storage in the plants before leaf fall occurs.

Allochthonous and autochthonous organic matter in streams and rivers soon becomes coated with bacteria and fungi, which impart a distinct slimy feel. This coating is the main food for stream invertebrates that cannot digest cellulose and lignin, the main components of CPOM. The enzyme cellulase is found in many bacteria and fungi and breaks down cellulose in plant cell walls. In general, bacteria cannot break down the lignin-rich polymers that are the main structural components in plant tissue. Just as in terrestrial systems, this breakdown is accomplished by fungi. One of the most common aquatic fungi, the Hyphomycetes, have unique triradiate spores adapted to adhere to leaves and twigs even in swirling stream waters. These fungi possess low-temperature enzyme systems that work well during winter, when leaves are most abundant.

The coating of bacteria and fungi is the nutritious part of detritus. Invertebrate feeding on detritus has been likened to a dinner plate, where the unmodified leaf forms the plate and the microbial coating is dinner. After ingestion, digestion, and excretion the now clean dinner plates (CPOM fragments) become recoated with microbes and eaten again by other, smaller invertebrates. The fragments become smaller and smaller until they are finally reduced to FPOM and DOM. It may take passage through many animals to complete the process.

FOOD WEBS

The key to understanding the ecology of streams is knowledge of the food web (Figs. 15-2, 15-4). Invertebrates dominate the stream benthos and fish the open water. Fish are rarely seen because they feed at dusk and dawn and hide under overhanging plants or rocks in the daylight. However, even casual observation of the underside of rocks in a stream reveals caddisfly larvae and snails, and further examination reveals a great variety of insect larvae in various stages of development. Apart from insects, only oligochaetes, nematode worms, crustaceans, and mollusks are abundant in the stream benthos. For extensive discussions of the role of benthic invertebrates in running water, the reader is referred to Hynes (1972) and Macan (1974). In typical stream riffles, the species vary but the organisms appear rather similar throughout the world, due to the process of convergent evolution. Among the largest organisms are the insect orders Trichoptera (caddisflies), Plecoptera (stoneflies), Ephemeroptera (mayflies), Odonata (dragonflies), oligochaete worms, and some snails (Mollusca). On rocks and branches in swifter currents, such as waterfalls or the raceways of dams, the larvae of blackflies (Simuliidae) are often abundant and may be the only invertebrates present. Suspended bacteria, often dislodged from decaying matte, are common in streams and constitute a major food supply for blackfly larvae.

As in lakes and on land, benthic food webs in streams are constructed from measurements of individual biomasses of stream organisms and of

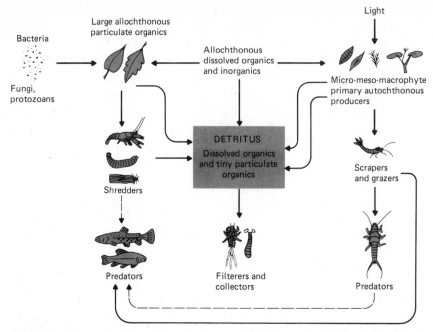

FIGURE 16-13 The functional roles of benthic invertebrates in streams. The crucial role of detritus is shown by its position at the center of the diagram. Fish, larger carnivorous stoneflies, and grazers on attached algae are the only organisms not directly involved with detritus. The detritus pool contains fungi, bacteria, and small protozoans, which continually convert the inedible cellulose and lignin of detritus into food for the invertebrates using nitrogen and phosphorus dissolved in the water. For further details of the functional roles of the organisms see Table 11-8. Modified from Cummins (1974).

the transfer rates between trophic levels. These values are interlinked by known or assumed predator-prey relationships. The feeding techniques of benthic invertebrates are *grazing,* or scraping of microbes on solid surfaces; *shredding* of CPOM; *collecting* or *filtering* of drifting FPOM; and *predation.* These groups constitute the four *functional groups* of the benthic invertebrate community (Fig. 16-13).

Grazing on attached algae, bacteria and fungi, and small animals such as rotifers is readily observed in snails but is also common in benthic insects, such as caddisflies and mayflies. Grazing on pennate diatoms may be supplemented by direct consumption of mosses. As mentioned earlier, higher aquatic plants are not normally eaten directly, but the rich covering of periphy-

ton on their leaves and stems provides a nutritious food source for various grazing animals (Fig. 16-14). Stem-mining insect larvae, such as chironomids, are an exception and exist entirely on macrophyte tissues. Fish with suckerlike mouths graze algae from rocks and are particularly abundant in small, sunlit streams.

Shredding is necessary because leaves and twigs are too big for ingestion by most stream dwellers. Following the surface coating by microorganisms, CPOM is then shredded by larger invertebrates. Some stoneflies, amphipods, and crayfish bite or tear whole leaves and ingest the fragments, many of which are then dropped or partially digested and defecated (Fig. 16-13; Mathews and Kowaicezwski, 1969; Cummins et al., 1973; Cummins, 1974).

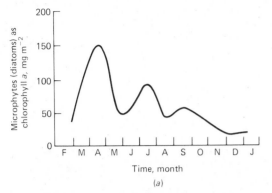

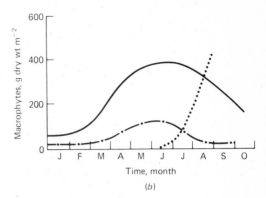

FIGURE 16-14 Seasonal variation in microphyte diatoms, expressed as chlorophyll *a*, and macrophytes in the hard-water chalk stream ecosystem of Brere Stream, England. Note the large and typically irregular seasonal variations in microphyte chlorophyll on the flint rocks (*a*). This contrasts with the regular rise of three macrophytes (*b*). The differences are probably due to lack of direct grazing by benthic invertebrates on macrophytes and continual grazing on the microphyte algae. In (*b*) the solid line represents water buttercup or crowfoot (*Ranunculus penicillatus*); dotted line, watercress (*Rorippa nasturtium-aquaticum*); dashed line, another water buttercup or crowfoot (*R. calcareus*). Redrawn and modified from Westlake et al. (1972) and Marker (1976a).

Collectors and fiterers remove any suspended particles from the water. They collect FPOM of living bacteria and algae that have been dislodged from their substrate. Filtration can require a good deal of energy if water is sucked in and expelled, as occurs in clams. More passive mechanisms are used by midge larvae, which hold feathery fanlike structures into the current and retract them when they are full of particles. Some caddisfly larvae spin long nets that catch FPOM from the current, allowing the larvae to remain hidden. Although they do not feed by filtration, the ubiquitous deposit-feeding worms that burrow in the sediment of pools and under rocks also depend on deposits of FPOM.

Predators include invertebrates such as stonefly larvae and dragonfly nymphs. However, usually the most dominant carnivores in the stream environment are fish. Often neglected are bird predators, such as the dipper and heron.

The Allochthonous Food Chain

The typical stream with its overhanging trees is too shady for photosynthesis for most of the year. It derives most of its energy from the watershed outside the stream, and thus allochthonous detritus dominates the carbon and energy budgets. Metabolism in shaded woodland streams is dominated by heterotrophic organisms, principally fungi, bacteria, and small invertebrates. The overall detritus-based community uses more oxygen than it produces. This is well-illustrated in New Hope Creek, which flows through deciduous woodland in North Carolina. A considerable oxygen debt is incurred when the tree cover is complete, but in spring, when trees are without leaves, there is a near balance between oxygen production and respiration (Fig. 16-15).

Although streams can be productive environments, decay and recycling of plant material in water is always slow relative to that on land. Leaves or logs stored underwater by beavers for their winter feed or by humans for commercial timber show little decay because fungi do not grow without good supplies of oxygen. The low solubility of this gas in water (Chap. 7) slows decomposition. In addition to leaves and other plant detritus, there is also a considerable living allochthonous contribution from the land. Caterpillars, flies, earthworms, crickets, and other

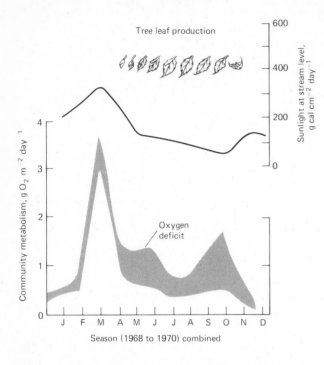

FIGURE 16-15 Metabolism of New Hope Creek, North Carolina, a woodland stream in the eastern central United States. For most of the year this type of stream is heterotrophic; that is, community respiration is greater than photosynthetic oxygen production. The shaded area represents the oxygen deficit or degree of heterotrophy. The upper boundary of the shaded area represents respiration and the lower boundary photosynthesis. The resulting deficit must be made up by in-stream aeration. This heterotrophy is due to the lack of light (upper curve) for photosynthesis when the trees leaf and block out light to this small stream, which is overshadowed by the riparian vegetation. Rivers and streams with less vegetation in dry or alpine areas do not show as much heterotrophy. Redrawn and modified from Hynes (1975).

insects fall from overhanging vegetation or, during rains, are washed from the soil to be consumed by fish and larger invertebrates. This contribution may sometimes be large. One of us counted over 100 large caterpillars that fell in one afternoon onto a 10-m stretch of stream beneath a willow tree. In the tropics the constant supply of fresh, nutritious blossoms and fruits is a major allochthonous food source (Fittkau, 1964).

The Autochthonous Food Chain

Not all streams are heavily dependent on terrestrial food sources. In streams where there are both sunlight and a suitable substratum autochthonous primary production in the stream itself plays a major role, as it does in lakes. Such conditions occur in the semiarid areas of Alaska, northwest America, and other dry regions and in the treeless uplands of northern Europe and Asia. Earlier research overemphasized the role of allochthonous production and underestimated

autochthonous primary production (Minshall, 1978). Often algae are overlooked simply because they are eaten almost as fast as they reproduce and never build up to visible mats. In unshaded streams and rivers the main primary producers are usually attached algae, which coat the rocks and submerged logs. Pennate diatoms such as *Nitzschia* and *Gomphonema* are more common than centric forms and are responsible for the distinct yellow cast of rocks in mountain streams. Filamentous green algae such as *Ulothrix* and *Cladophora* may stretch for more than a meter from their moorings and are more common than single-cell forms. Blue-green algae such as the filamentous *Phormidium* cover muddy silt and *Nostoc* form gelatinous brown blobs on rocks. Both of these algae can be very common in some streams, and *Nostoc* and *Rivularia* can fix considerable amounts of N_2 as well as CO_2. For convenience, small, usually unicellular attached algae, such as diatoms, are called *microphytes*. The larger green and blue-green algae with some chain-forming diatoms are easily visible with the naked eye and are called *mesophytes.* Large higher aquatic plants are termed *macrophytes* (Chap. 11). A typical distribution of micro-, meso-, and macrophytes is shown for a subalpine river in Fig. 16-21. In small streams deciduous riparian vegetation may shade out plant growth except in early spring (Fig. 16-15). Thus abundant growth of plants is usually confined to large, shallow rivers or streams above the tree line.

Macrophytes in rivers are usually confined to the river banks due to turbid water or substratum suitable for rooting. The highly prized trout chalk streams in England contain dense masses of macrophytes such as *Ranunculus,* the water crowfoot (Fig. 16-14). Enormous numbers of attached diatoms and small animals such as mayfly larvae are found in the shelter of these dense growths. As they become detached from the plant the larvae fall prey to fish waiting in the downstream eddy. In some streams, much of the food chain may be based on the existence of detritus produced by macrophytes. Attached algae growing on rocks, logs, leaves, and stems of larger aquatic plants may form the main diet of grazing benthic invertebrates. In contrast, higher plants in streams are seldom directly eaten although manatee and grass carp do eat macrophytes. Phytoplankton and zooplankton are minor components of undisturbed lotic ecosystems. This is not the case where the currents are much reduced by dams or locks, such as on the Mississippi, the Thames in England, or the Dnieper in the Republic of Russia. Here, true phytoplankton occurs because the residence time of the water is longer than the time required for cell division (Fig. 15-4). Dinoflagellates and ciliates are rare, presumably because their vigorous swimming ability is of no use in turbulent, shallow water.

THE RIVER CONTINUUM CONCEPT

Streams and rivers are complex habitats, in large part because they change from small trickles in the headwaters, to streams, and, finally, to large rivers in the lower flood plain. Over the years, several attempts have been made to provide some generalizations applicable to flowing waters. Early investigators divided the river into reaches based on characteristic types of fish. For example, in Europe Schindler (1957) described the cold, well-oxygenated mountain stream as the brown trout-bullhead reach and the still cool but downslope region as the grayling-minnow-dace reach. The deeper, warmer, more turbid upper river was the barbel-perch reach, the lowland river was the bream-carp reach, and the estuary was the flounder-stickleback reach. Of course, not all streams and rivers fit these generalizations and the fish species are often different in different geographic regions.

Better understanding of lotic dynamics showed the limitations of this approach and gave impetus to the *river continuum concept* (Vannote et al., 1980). This approach is based on stream order (Fig. 16-7), type of particulate organic matter, and type of benthic invertebrates present. It envisions that the coalescing network of streams in the drainage basin forms a continuum of physical gradients and associated biotic adjustments. The river continuum concept states that the structure and function of the benthic invertebrate community, from headwaters to river mouth, is strongly regulated by the gradient of allochthonous and autochthonous organic matter. The relative importance of most of the major functional invertebrate groups, shredders, grazers, collectors, and predators gradually changes downstream with the food supply (Figs. 16-16, 16-17). For small streams of order 1 to 3 flowing in wooded areas, high inputs of large allochthonous organic particles, CPOM, constitute the food supply for large shredders such as crayfish and some stoneflies. In turn, FPOM produced by the CPOM users dominates the central-lower river (orders 4 to 7). Inputs of coarse material from the riparian zone in the headwaters declines. The sediment collectors or open water filtering species, such as the larvae of midges and caddisflies,

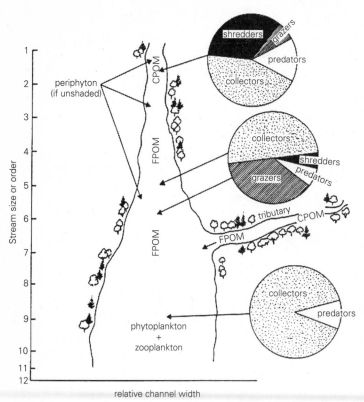

FIGURE 16-16 The river continuum concept. The relative abundance of functional groups of benthic invertebrates (collectors, shredders, grazers, and predators) changes from headwaters to river mouth (Fig. 16-17). Coarse particulate organic matter (CPOM) consisting largely of leaves and twigs is supplied in the upstream regions, where riparian vegetation dominates small streams. Downstream CPOM contributions are small relative to the size of the river, leaving only fine particulate organic matter (FPOM). The river continuum hypothesis suggests that benthic invertebrates change downstream in response to changes in the food supply, as indicated by the CPOM:FPOM ratio. Note that shredders of CPOM are confined to headwaters and grazers of periphyton and bacteria mostly thrive in mid-sized rivers, where light can reach the substratum. Collectors are always abundant but totally dominate in large rivers. Modified from Vannote et al. (1980).

feed on FPOM. As streams become larger the supply of allochthous CPOM progressively decreases and so FPOM decreases as well. However, autochthonous primary production by attached algae and macrophytes provides some CPOM for grazers, which are likely to be more important in middle-order streams. Finally (orders 8 to 12), only the refractory part of the FPOM and dissolved organic matter (DOM) remain, since they are not a suitable food for most aquatic organisms. In unwooded regions where there is more sunlight, autochthonous production by attached algae feeds the grazer/scraper population of snails and caddisflies, even in lower-order streams (orders 1 to 3). This group also feeds on the surface of larger CPOM fragments.

The relative importance of grazers and collectors is predicted to change if the river continuum concept is correct. The shredders are expected to

be common only in the lower-order streams (orders 1 to 3) and the grazers to be most abundant in the middle-order waters (orders 4 to 7; Figs. 16-16, 16-17). Collectors that filter out FPOM are expected to be present throughout the stream, since some CPOM will be transformed to FPOM even in the headwaters. However, their relative abundance is predicted to be greatest in the large, higher-order streams (order 5 and greater). In contrast to the other functional groups, predators, always relatively uncommon, are predicted not to be favored by decreases in the CPOM:FPOM ratio.

Considerable effort has gone into determining the applicability of the river continuum concept to stream-river systems in general. Most work has been done in small streams (orders 1 to 4), and there is evidence that the concept applies in general terms for numerous streams and rivers

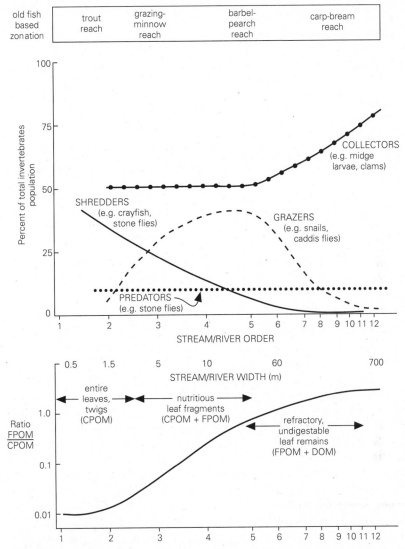

FIGURE 16-17 The river continuum concept. (*a*) The older concept based on typical fish. (*b*) An idealized representation of the relative abundance of types of benthic invertebrates (collectors, shredders, grazers, and predators) from headwaters to river mouth. Compare with real data in Figs. 16-18 and 16-19. (*c*) The ratio of coarse particulate organic matter (CPOM) to fine particulate organic matter (FPOM) increasing downstream as entire leaves, twigs, grass blades, and fruits are eaten and recycled by the invertebrates and microbes. Modified from Vannote et al. (1980). DOM = dissolved organic matter.

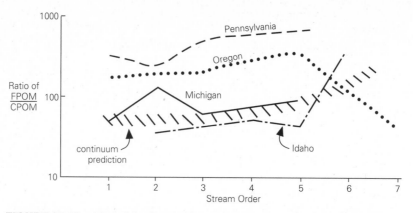

FIGURE 16-18 A test of the river continuum concept. The downstream increase in the ration of FPOM to CPOM as predicted by the hypothesis (cross-shaded line) and as determined in four rivers spread across the northern United States. Note that the agreement is generally good for two sites and passable for the other two. The effect is even more apparent for the amount of CPOM (not shown), which decreases exponentially downstream as predicted by the continuum concept. Modified from Minshall et al. (1983).

in temperate climates (Hawkins and Sidell, 1981; Minshall et al., 1983; 1985; Townsend and Hildrew, 1988). However, some exceptions are apparent (Ward, 1986; Ryder and Scott, 1988) and require modification of the original hypothesis. Minshall et al. (1983) studied the distribution of particulates, benthos, attached algae, primary production, and respiration in four streams (orders 1 to 7) in Michigan, Pennsylvania, Idaho, and Oregon. These data were compared with the predictions of the continuum hypothesis. The results for these different climatic regimes were in general agreement with the predictions of the river continuum concept. One important finding was the dominance of the smallest ultra-FPOM (UFPOM < 50 μm), which made up the majority of both deposited and transported organic matter. However, the ratio of coarse to fine particles followed the predicted pattern (Fig. 16-18), primarily due to an exponential decrease in CPOM downstream. The continuum hypothesis predicts that attached algae and primary production will increase downstream. This was supported in the work of Minshall et al. (1983), who also found that shredders were most abundant in the head-

waters. The importance of collectors generally increased downstream but varied considerably with season and site. Grazers did not follow the predictions of the continuum concept and were most abundant in the upper reaches in summer and lower reaches in autumn.

As an overall guide, the continuum concept is supported by other studies that indicate local effects on the distribution of benthos. The influences of leaf detritus, discharge, and temperature on the distribution of the benthos in an English river is shown in Fig. 16-19. In this study the importance of fish as predators or competitors with the large invertebrate shredders was measured using enclosure experiments. The overall results seem to confirm the continuum hypothesis in low-order streams. The hypothesis has not been tested in tropical or arctic streams, and desert streams may prove to be exceptions due to the lack of allochthonous material.

DRIFT

The annual changes in the resident benthic invertebrate population are complicated by drift

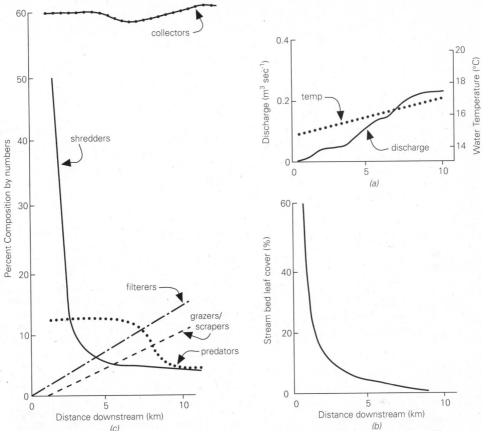

FIGURE 16-19 Application of the river continuum concept to a lower-order stream. (*a*) Physical variables: discharge substitutes for stream order. (*b*) Availability of allochthonous leaves on the streambed. (*c*) Distribution of shredders, filterers, collectors, grazers, and predators. General agreement with the river continuum concept is shown (shredders decline, grazers, and filterers increase). Note that the predicted increase in collectors and decline in grazers at higher-order streams (> 7) is not applicable here. Further downstream trout replace the only shredder, a stonefly larvae, as the top predator, but experiments with mesocosms (Chap. 1) indicate that the decrease in shredders is not due to fish predation. Modified from Townsend and Hildrew (1988).

(Fig. 16-20) and by hatching and emergence of species that have flying adult stages. These include the majority of the benthic insects, such as stoneflies, mayflies, and caddisflies, but not the various worms and mollusks. Drift, which contains many small living organisms and pieces of detritus, is the major food of many stream fish and invertebrates. It includes clumps of bacteria, algae, detritus, other aquatic and terrestrial invertebrates, and fragments of vegetation. In fishery-related contexts, drift may refer only to free-floating invertebrates. The larvae of many caddisflies spin remarkable funnel-shaped nets for collecting drift. Most stream dwellers, however, use the bristles on their legs or mouthparts as filters and scrape off and eat the particles they collect. The collection of drift food by most stream insects is not simply a matter of remaining stationary and waiting, because diurnal variation in drift and exposure to predation complicate their feeding.

Much drift consists of small insect larvae that

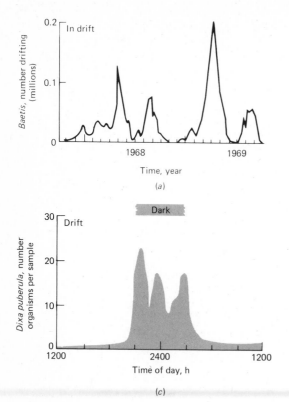

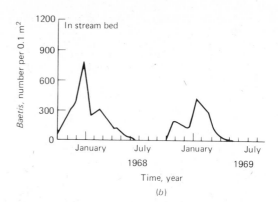

FIGURE 16-20 Examples of invertebrate drift. (*a*) Drifting of the mayfly larvae, *Baetis bicaudatus*, compared with (*b*) numbers in the streambed in the Temple Fork of the Logan River, Utah. This stream is less than 4 m wide at the sampling station shown. The drift is a major food for fish. Redrawn and modified from Pearson and Kramer (1972). (*c*) Diel variation in the drift of the larvae of the midge *Dixa puberula* in Wilfin Beck, a stony stream in the English Lake District. Note the rapid onset of drift as night falls. This reduces predation by fish that depend on sight to detect their food. Redrawn from Elliott and Tullett (1977).

FIGURE 16-21 Longitudinal distribution of animals and plants relative to temperature. There are cold springs between stations 3 and 4 and warm surface discharges from a reservoir above station 6 in Martis Creek, a small mountain stream in California. For diel variation in this stream see Fig. 16-8. Black bars represent the most common organisms in each taxonomic grouping, such as mayflies for benthic invertebrates and brown trout in the fish group. Shaded bars are the second most common. Letters indicate the actual organisms present (see key below). Note the predominance of brown trout in the cooler sections and the Tahoe sucker in the warmer sections. This corresponds to their known temperature preferences. There is no obvious relationship between fish and their food (benthic invertebrates for trout and other carnivores and algae for the others). Mayflies are little changed downstream, but chironomids (Diptera) dominate below the reservoir, where their food of detritus and lake planktonic algae is washed. The microphytes in general, especially the small pennate diatom *Navicula*, are not favored by this reservoir discharge. Microphytes have been replaced as the primary autochthonous producers below the reservoir by the mesophyte green filamentous alga *Cladophora*, the emergent macrophyte *Ranunculus*, the water buttercup, and submerged plants such as the pond weed *Elodea* (not shown here). The mesophyte *Nostoc* favors the faster-flowing middle sections of this creek, while the other common mesophyte, *Cladophora*, prefers the slower upper reaches, in common with the habitat preferences of the macrophytes. The large contribution of the irregularly distributed mesophytes and macrophytes to the detritus pool is obvious at station 6. Fish are plotted as weight, but if those that were too small to catch using conventional electrofishing (Chap. 14) were accounted for, smaller fish such as Lahontan redside would be more apparent. Fish: bt = brown trout, *Salmo trutta*; rt = rainbow trout; ct = cutthroat trout, *S. clarkii*; ts = Tahoe sucker, *Catostomus tahoensis*; ms = mountain sucker, *C. platyrhynchus*; sd = speckled dace (minnow), *Rhinichthys osculus*; lr = Lahontan redside (minnow), *Richardsonius egregius*; ps = Paiute sculpin, *Cottus beldingi*. Benthic invertebrates: m = mayflies (Ephemeroptera); d = true flies or Diptera; c = caddisflies (Trichoptera); r = other types. Microalgae, mostly diatoms: Na = *Navicula*; Ni = *Nitzschia*; c = *Cymbella*; g = *Gomphonema*; r = other types. Mesophytes (green and blue-green algae): c = *Cladophora*; n = *Nostoc*. Macrophytes (higher aquatic plants): wb = water buttercup, *Ranunculus*. Redrawn and modified from Horne et al. (1979).

move to new habitats by releasing their hold on the substrate. A good example is shown for a mountain stream in Utah in Fig. 16-20a. The quantities of total drifting material are sometimes astonishingly large; millions of individual animals may pass one spot in a single night. Invertebrate drift normally occurs at night (Fig. 16-20c), probably to avoid predation by sight-de-

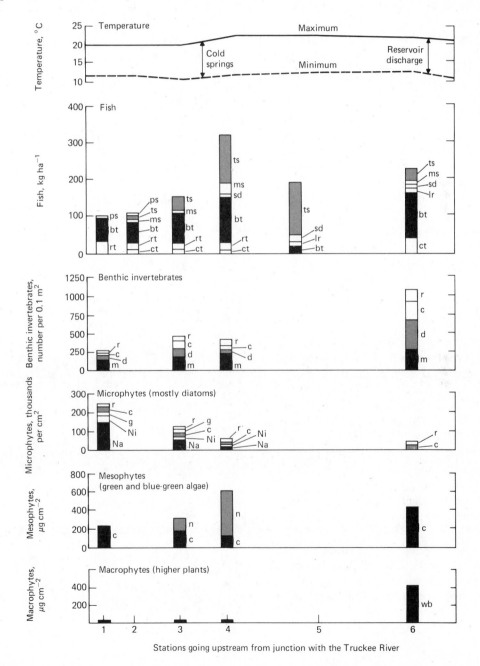

pendent fish. Many insects gradually drift downstream during their lives and, when they emerge for a brief aerial existence, fly back upstream to lay their eggs. Mayflies (Ephemeroptera, from *ephemeral,* meaning ''short-lived'') and some other insects may live only a matter of hours after emergence, which limits their flight range.

Most predation occurs in daylight, since many fish and carnivorous insects hunt by sight. The result is that herbivores feed near or under stones and emerge to drift or feed in more exposed places at night. Some insects possess special structural adaptations to prevent them from being dislodged by the current and becoming edible drift. The flattened bodies of stoneflies and mayflies and the hooks at the ends of their legs are adaptations to swift water. The Simuliidae (blackflies) are particularly good at holding on, and they are usually abundant in torrential sites such as waterfalls or rapids where few predators can feed effectively.

FISH

Fish are an important component of most stream biota. They are also specially adapted for the currents normally encountered in their chosen habitat. Both stream and lake fish are considered in Chap. 14. The distribution of fish is influenced by physical habitat and the presence of other animals and plants, particularly those used for food and shelter. Fish may be territorial in streams and rivers and often remain in one small reach for most of their lives. The distribution of several trophic levels, including fish, is given for a western mountain stream in Fig. 16-21. The distribution of six fish species was unrelated to food sources such as microphytes, mesophytes, higher plants, or benthic invertebrates but was related to temperature. Two of the three trout species were found in the cooler water downstream from cold springs, and minnows (Cyprinidae) and suckers (Catostomidae) dominated just below the warm surface outflow of a shallow

reservoir. Food was not a limiting factor here, but in other streams there may be more direct relationships between food supply and fish distribution. In larger streams and rivers collection becomes more difficult at all trophic levels and a general ecological role is ascribed to each functional group of fish in the stream (Fig. 14-5) much as that for invertebrates (Fig. 16-13).

Where the river first encounters the influence of the sea, the limnologist finds the physical boundary of the science. Estuaries are common waters for limnologists and marine biologists alike, and this seaward limit of the river provides the basis for Chap. 17.

FURTHER READING

Barnes, J. R. and G. W. Minshall (eds.). 1983. *Stream Ecology: Application and Testing of General Ecological Theory.* Plenum, New York.

Blum, J. L. 1956. ''The Ecology of River Algae.'' *Bot. Rev., 22*:291–341.

Cummins, K. W., R. C. Petersen, F. O. Howard, J. C. Wuycheck, and V. I. Holt. 1973. ''The Utilization of Leaf Litter by Stream Detritivores.'' *Ecology, 54*:336–345.

Cummins, K. W., G. W. Minshall, J. R. Sidell, C. E. Cushing, and R. C. Petersen. 1984. ''Stream Ecosystem Theory.'' *Verh. Int. Ver. Limnol., 22*:1818–1927.

Hynes, H. B. N. 1972. *The Ecology of Running Waters.* University of Toronto Press, Toronto. 555 pp.

——— 1975. ''The Stream and Its Valley.'' *Verh. Int. Ver. Limnol., 19*:1–15.

Kaushik, N. K., and H. B. N. Hynes. 1971. ''The Fate of Dead Leaves That Fall Into Streams.'' *Arch Hydrobiol., 68*:465–515.

Likens, G. E., F. H. Bormann, N. M. Johnson, D. W. Fisher, and R. S. Pierce. 1970. ''Effects of Forest Cutting and Herbicide Treatment on Nutrient Budgets in the Hubbard Brook Watershed Ecosystem.'' *Ecol. Monogr., 40*:23–47.

Likens, G. E. 1984. ''Beyond the Shoreline: A Watershed-Ecosystem Approach.'' *Verh. Int. Ver. Limnol., 22*:1–22.

Lock, M. A., and D. D. Williams (eds.). 1981. *Per-*

spectives in Running Water Ecology. Plenum, New York.

Merrit, R. W., and K. W. Commins (eds.). 1984. *An Introduction to the Aquatic Insects of North America.* 2d ed. Kendall-Hunt, Dubuque, IA.

Minshall, G. W. 1978. "Autotrophy in Stream Ecosystems." *Biocience,* **28:**767–771.

Minshall, G. W., R. C. Petersen, K. W. Cummins, T. L. Bott, J. R. Sedell, C. E. Cushing, and R. L. Vannote. 1983." "Interbiome Comparison of Stream Ecosystem Dynamics." *Ecol. Monogr.,* **53:**1–25.

Moore, J. W. 1976. "Seasonal Succession of Algae in Rivers. I. Examples from the Avon, a Large Slow-flowing River." *J. Phycol.,* **12:**342–349.

Mordukai-Boltovskoi, P.D. (ed.). 1979. "The River Volga and Its Life." *Monogr. Biol.,* **33.** 473 pp.

Omernik, J. M. 1976. "The Influence of Land Use on Stream Nutrient Levels." U.S. EPA-600/3-76-014. Corvallis, OR. 68 pp. plus appendix.

Pennak, R. W. 1971. "Towards a Classification of Lotic Habitats." *Hydrobiologia,* **38:**321–334.

Pfeifer, R. F., and W. F. McDiffett. 1975. "Some Factors Affecting Primary Productivity of Stream Riffle Communities." *Arch. Hydrobiol.,* **75:**306–317.

Resh, V. H. 1979. "Sampling Variability and Life History Features: Basic Considerations in the Design of Aquatic Insect Studies." *J. Fish Res. Board Can.,* **36:**290–311.

Stanford, J. A., and A. P. Covich (eds.). 1988. "Community Structure and Function in Temperate and Tropical Streams." *J. North Am. Benthol. Soc.,* **7:**261–529.

Swale, E. M. F. 1969. "Phytoplankton in Two English Rivers." *J. Ecol.,* **57:**1–23.

Vannote, R. L., G. W. Minshall, K. W. Cummins, J. R. Sedell, and C. E. Cushing. 1980. "The River Continuum Concept." *Can. J. Fish. Aquat. Sci.,* **37:**130–137.

Ward, J. V., and J. A. Stanford (eds.). 1979. *The Ecology of Regulated Streams.* Plenum, New York. 398 pp.

Waters, T. F. 1972. "The Drift of Stream Insects." *Ann. Rev. Entomol.,* **17:**253–272.

Whitton, B. A. (ed.). 1975. *Studies in Ecology, vol. 2: River Ecology.* University of California Press, Berkeley. 725 pp.

Wiley, J. M., and S. L. Kohler. 1984. "Behavioral Adaptations of Aquatic Insects." pp. 101–133. In V. H. Resh and D. M. Rosenberg (eds.). *The Ecology of Aquatic Insects.* Praeger, New York.

CHAPTER 17

Big Rivers and Their Flood Plains

OVERVIEW

In desert and tropical rain forest alike, the productivity of big rivers largely depends on the growth of higher plants in the flood plain. The dynamic interaction of river and flood plain gives rise to the *flood pulse concept* in contrast to the river continuum concept, which applies best to streams and small rivers. Flooding in large rivers is a predictable, annual event, and both river and land organisms adapt their life strategies accordingly. The aquatic-terrestrial transition zone forms a slow, *moving littoral habitat,* where large amounts of organic carbon are temporarily available for the detrital food web. In contrast, the habitat in the main stem of large rivers is usually one of strong currents and water turbid with suspended inorganic silt. Consequently, autochthonous (within-river) primary production is light-limited and low, despite a usually adequate supply of nitrogen and phosphorus. Thus big rivers depend on allochthonous (external) inputs of organic carbon, primarily from aquatic plants. In the smaller streams an influx of leaves and grass from terrestrial habitats provides ample material, but the stream continuum model predicts that all usable food will have been extracted when the stream reaches river proportions. Big rivers are all of a higher order (orders 7 to 12) and need additional sources of organic carbon to be productive. Some big rivers do not receive this external carbon and are unproductive as well as low in species diversity. Overall, river productivity in tropical and temperate zones is similar, but arctic rivers tend to be less productive. Antarctica lacks rivers.

Almost all large rivers show a single, strong annual discharge peak, and their productivity and fisheries are dependent on this regular inundation of the flood plain. Big tropical rivers, such as the Amazon and the Mekong, have extensive and productive flood plains and contain several hundred species of fish. Warm temperate rivers, such as the Mississippi, with a moderately large flood plain, have a few hundred species of fish. In contrast, big rivers, such as the Colorado or the Murray-Darling in Australia, that flow through deserts or canyons or have very small flood plains typically contain only a few dozen indigenous fish species.

The ratio of the discharge volume to drainage area divides big rivers into four general groups. Those with high ratios are tropical rain forest rivers, where evaporation is balanced by rains and by inflow from tributaries all the way to the sea. At the other extreme, desert rivers, with smaller ratios, lose much of their original volume by evaporation and in lower reaches the few tributaries provide little water.

In the tropics the flood plain contains a unique flora of specially adapted aquatic grasses and macrophytes, which form "floating meadows." An abundance of fruits, seeds, and leaves as well as trapped terrestrial invertebrates are eaten by fish and mammals that follow the rising waters inland. These *lateral migrations* from the river main stem to the flooded plain are distinct from the more familiar *longitudinal migrations* up and down the main stem. In temperate rivers, floods function to replenish seasonal wetlands with silt and give adult fish feeding and spawning access to productive wetlands and backwaters. In these fertile nurseries, their young can grow quickly before returning to the main river. In arctic big rivers, the timing of the flood and scouring ice fragments eliminate the use of the main stem as a refuge for larger organisms unless they migrate long distances to lakes or the ocean. However, large rivers are famous for extensive longitudinal fish migrations, which are prevented only by hydraulic barriers such high waterfalls or dams. Trips of several hundred kilometers are common and are usually made to spawn after feeding in flood plains, lakes, backwaters, or the sea. Conditions different from those favored by adults are required by young fish, and this justifies the energetically costly upstream migrations. These nursery areas have favorable food supplies, oxygen, or temperature conditions, and ample cover and less predation on the juveniles.

Most large rivers in the temperate zone have been modified for many years by the construction of dams. This turns them into a series of lakes, with the free-flowing river restricted to reaches between the dams. Although few species have become extinct, prized large migratory salmon and sturgeon have lost access to much of their spawning areas and have declined in abundance. In tropical and arctic regions most dams

have been constructed in the last few decades. Dams also eliminate the annual flood and reduce the amount of particulate matter passing downstream for the detritus-based food chain.

In this chapter we consider measurement, definitions, the annual flood plain inundation, the Amazon, the Colorado and other desert rivers, the Mackenzie and other arctic rivers, and the Mississippi and other temperate rivers.

INTRODUCTION

During the nineteenth century large rivers fired the imagination of European explorers and wealthy adventurers. The spectacular waterfalls (Plate 8A) give an indication of their enormous force and energy. Fifty years ago, Burton and Speake successfully searched East Africa for the source of the Nile, while others attempted to traverse the Amazon from mouth to source. These travels, combined with Huckleberry Finn's rafting on the Mississippi and Livingstone's Congo River reports, were once the only sources of limnological data. Most knowledge of flowing waters comes from studies in small, shallow, wooded streams in the temperate zone. Controlled experiments, the essence of modern limnology, are often impossible in big rivers. Nevertheless, studies in the larger North and South American rivers and some in Asia, Australia, and Africa have now been carried out (see Further Reading). In addition, the construction of large dams has provided a form of experimental manipulation in flow patterns. Finally, the flood pulse concept (Junk et al., 1989) provides a new, theoretical understanding of the subject.

In Chap. 16 we used the conventional divisions of streams (rhithron) and rivers (potomon) with some success. In particular, the older convention of the cooler, well-oxygenated (trout) stream comprising the small low-order headwater stream and the warmer muddy (carp) stream for the lower reaches are useful concepts. The river continuum hypothesis extended this approach to the cascade of allochthonous matter from large leaves, grass stems, and twigs consumed by shredding insects and crustaceans in the headwaters down to fine particles consumed by detritus feeders in the lower reaches. Closer examination of a worldwide sample of flowing waters indicates that some headwater streams may be warm and muddy, especially in flat landscapes. Similarly, the lower reaches of rivers do not fit all aspects of the river continuum. This is especially true for larger rivers (greater than 7th order). Any organic matter passed down tributaries (less than 6th order) to the big river will consist of fine particulate organic matter and large tree trunks. These are of little nutritional value to most river organisms, although *iliotrophic* (mud-eating) species, such as the sabalo of South American rivers, may benefit from bacteria that coat some of the deposited fine material. Big river productivity actually depends on local allochthonous matter, in particular the flood plain, which is inundated regularly each year.

In this chapter we examine the big rivers of the world, defined as those over 2000 km long. Because the productivity of big rivers is so closely tied to their seasonally flooded margins, they resemble some of the seasonal wetlands discussed in Chap. 18. We consider a generalized big river and then discuss four contrasting types: the fully tropical Amazon, the semidesert Colorado, the temperate Mississippi, and the arctic Mackenzie. Examples from other large river systems are given when appropriate.

MEASUREMENT

A combination of standard lake and stream methods, described in other chapters, is the basis for the study of large rivers. However, two other factors must be considered. First, the study of big rivers, like that of large lakes and the ocean, can be dangerous and frequently requires large, robust, and often expensive equipment. For example, a useful big river boat costs about $600,000 (1993 U.S.) and requires a professional crew. Thus team research becomes desirable to

spread costs, and multiauthored papers are the common method of publication. For example, the average number of authors per publication referred to in this chapter is 3.2. The average for the whole text is 1.7. Second, many big rivers are located far from centers of limnological expertise, thus equipment reliability is more important than sophistication.

THE DEFINITION OF BIG RIVERS

The usual criteria for defining large rivers are length, discharge, and drainage area. A recent volume on the subject suggested that length greater than 2000 km defines a river (Davis and Walker, 1986). Very long rivers with part of their watercourses in semidesert conditions (e.g., the Nile, Colorado, Murray-Darling) have much lower discharge than long rivers that flow entirely in tropical rain forests (e.g., the Amazon, Zaire-Congo) or cold arctic climates (e.g., the Ob, Mackenzie). These contrasts can be expressed in the discharge:area ratio. This ratio (Table 17-1) indicates a clear distinction between the tropical rain forest rivers (ratio $> 0.45 \times 10^{-3}$) and desert rivers ($< 0.05 \times 10^{-3}$). In the rain forest as much as half of the evaporating water is returned to the river as local rainfall. In contrast, evaporated water is permanently lost to dry desert air. Other rivers lie between these extremes.

An alternative is a more functional approach to define big rivers. The stream continuum concept suggests that rivers larger than the 7th order lack adequate supplies of nutritious particulate organic matter to support a detritus-based food chain. Another and related characteristic that separates big rivers from other flowing waters is their low autochthonous primary productivity. Large rivers are almost always turbid with clouds of sediment that are continually resuspended by the strong currents and carried seaward by their great discharges (Chap. 16; Fig. 16-5, 16-6). Big rivers have low transparencies with secchi depths of only 1 to 100 cm and potential euphotic

TABLE 17-1

DISCHARGE-DRAINAGE BASIN RELATIONSHIP FOR SOME LARGE RIVERS

Rivers fall into four groups based on the ratio of discharge volume (km^3) and drainage area (km^2). Discharges are estimates of the original unmodified flows.

River	Discharge (D), $km^3 \, y^{-1}$	Drainage Area (A), $km^2 \times 10^6$	Ratio (D/A), $\times 10^{-3}$
Tropical rain forest (ratio $>0.45 \times 10^{-3}$)			
Amazon	5,500	7	0.79
Zaire	1,800	4	0.45
Mekong	4,800	0.78	6.1
Wet temperate or subtropical (ratio 0.2–0.4×10^{-3})			
Rhine	70	0.22	0.32
Parana	730	3.2	0.23
Uruguay	124	0.37	0.34
Moderately dry, all climates (ratio 0.1–0.2 $\times 10^{-3}$)			
Mississippi	560	4.8	0.12
Mackenzie	333	1.8	0.19
Niger	220	1.1	0.19
Volga	238	1.3	0.18
Desert rivers (ratio $< 0.05 \times 10^{-3}$)			
Colorado	18	0.6	0.03
Nile	90	3.0	0.03
Murray-Darling	22	1.1	0.02
Orange-Vaal	12	0.65	0.02

zones (Z_{eu}) of 5 cm to 3 m, and in most cases less than 1 m. In contrast, most lakes have Z_{eu} values of > 5 m and many are > 10 m. It is important to note that turbidity in big rivers is *abiotic turbidity* and that the chlorophyll *a*-secchi disc relationship (Fig. 22-1) is not applicable. In shallow streams, small rivers, and flood-plain wetlands, turbidity does not reduce photosynthesis very much because they are so shallow that light penetrates most of the water column. In contrast, big rivers are both deep ($Z = 10$ to 20 m, even 70 m) and turbid. Consequently, the few phytoplankton in big rivers spend most of

their time in darkness, and sediments scour attached algae from rocks. The fluctuating water levels and mobile sediments of big rivers do not provide a good habitat for most macrophytes. Finally, the few big rivers flowing through hard-to-erode granitic rocks and forest are "black waters"—acidic and colored with humic substances draining infertile leached soils. This combination of low pH and low nutrients further reduces primary production by both algae and macrophytes. Examples are the Rio Negro (Black River), the major tributary to the Amazon (Fig. 17-1), a tributary of the Mackenzie River

FIGURE 17-1   Aerial photograph of the junction of the Amazon and its main tributary, the Rio Negro. The "black" waters of the Rio Negro are stained brown with humic acids leached out of the poor soils. The water color contrasts with that of the "white" water Amazon, which is almost milky with suspended sediments that are typical of most big rivers. Due to the higher current speed and velocity of big rivers, they can carry much more sediment than streams. Photograph by J. Melak.

draining peaty "muskeg bogs" in the Arctic, and some small tributaries in the Mississippi drainage.

As a result of restricted photosynthesis in the river, the higher trophic levels, including fish, must be sustained by allochthonous material. If there is low input from the surroundings, these large rivers will be depauperate in both fish abundance and diversity. The dependence on allochthonous inputs is similar to that of small wooded temperate streams (Fig. 16-15), but the leaf fall from overhanging vegetation is hardly sufficient to sustain large rivers up to 20 km wide.

Because of the swift currents big rivers carry large quantities of sediments. The sediments are of two kinds: a permanently suspended *wash load* and the temporarily suspended material called the *bed load*. The heavy particles of the bed load bounce along the bottom and during floods big rivers will move boulders as large as houses.

THE FLOOD PLAIN

In higher-order rivers flood plain vegetation compensates for both low in-river primary production and the lack of usable detritus. Allochthonous sources include fresh dead leaves, fruits, and seeds from terrestrial plants and terrestrial insects. In addition, isolated pools and wetlands in the flood plain contain stems and seeds of living aquatic plants, aufwuchs on submerged surfaces, and planktonic and benthic aquatic invertebrates. This food is available to fish from the main stem of the river as they follow the water rising onto flood plain. As the floods recede organic matter from the flood plain is carried to the river and supports detritus feeders during the low flows of the dry season.

Soluble plant nutrients are present in large amounts in most flood waters (Table 17-2), with additional supplies leached or flushed from the flooded soils. In tropical and warm climates, enormous growths of floating macrophytes, rooted aquatic grasses, and other plants occur on the flood plain. Periphyton and aufwuchs soon cover many of the newly wetted surfaces. In the calmer, shallow waters of the flood plain's temporary lakes, phytoplankton bloom as nutrients rise, and zooplankton blooms soon follow. Molluscs, oligochaetes, and a variety of aquatic insects also increase. Large numbers of terrestrial insects, trapped by the flood waters, add further to the food supply for invading fish. In cooler climates flooding plays a lesser role but is still important in fish reproduction and the maintenance of seasonal wetlands. The tropical flood plain provides some fish a protected place to feed and perhaps spawn. It is also a food-rich habitat for juvenile fish. In temperate and polar climates plant growth in the flood plain is less spectacular or absent. Riparian growth along the shoreline is dependent on flooding to eliminate competitors that cannot germinate in the short dry periods.

The extent of the flood plain depends on the river's discharge and relative flatness of the basin. The Amazon has perhaps the most favorable

TABLE 17-2

SOME MAJOR NUTRIENTS IN BIG RIVERS

Ammonia is rarely measured but may not be insignificant (e.g., 340–760 mg liter^{-1} in the Volga). Note that values are usually quite high compared with lakes, certainly enough to support good phytoplankton blooms. These usually do not occur since the high turbidity of most rivers causes light limitation of photosynthesis. Values in μg liter^{-1}, nd = no data.

River	NO$_3$—N	PO$_4$—P	References
Niger	1100–6300	500–3100	1
Orange-Vaal	300–1400	30–100	2
Colorado			3
Mackenzie	600	16	4
Parana	>500	<100	5
Volta	0–5000	20–160	6
Volga	50–4000	1–250	7
Nile	10–1000	1–40	8
Mississippi	700–3000	40–440	9
Amazon			
White water	4–15	15	10
Clearwater	<1	<1	10
Blackwater	36	6	10
General means			
Africa	170	nd	10
Europe	840	nd	10
North America	230	nd	10
South America	160	nd	10

(1) Welcomme, 1986; (2) Cambray et al., 1986; (3) Day and Davies, 1986; (4) Brunskill, 1986; (5) Bonetto, 1986; (6) Petr, 1986; (7) Payne, 1986; (8) Rzóska, 1976; (9) Fremling et al., 1989; (10) Payne, 1986, Forsberg et al., 1988.

morphometry for maximum flood plain development; about 55,000 km^2 of its drainage area is flooded annually. This is about the size of Lake Michigan. In contrast, the Darling River in Australia and the Colorado in the United States have almost no flood plain in most years and flood only after exceptionally heavy rains.

What do the flood plains of large rivers look like? In the dry season the flood plain of the Amazon main stem consists of quite dense tropical rain forest interspersed with semipermanent lakes. On the Niger River in Africa the interior delta is in tropical woodland steppe—extensive dry grasslands dotted with shrubs and trees. In the desert sections of the Nile or the Darling in Australia there are no trees, and the Nile's internal delta, the Sudd, is a vast stand of papyrus

and *Phragmites* swamp. The lower Nile in Egypt and the Mekong River in Vietnam have had a flood-water-dependent, cultivated flood plain for millennia. Northern temperate river flood plains such as the Mississippi are characterized by blackwater forest of cypress trees and tupelo. In the Arctic the flood plain is a maze of peat bog lakes, seasonal wetlands, and clumps of stunted willow and alders.

In the wet season the open water area of the flood plain is much more extensive, with only tree tops visible in some tropical flood plains and only the higher hummocks above water in arctic areas. In temperate flood plains flood waters are less than 1 m deep, leaving most trees and shrubs above water. In big rivers flooding is usually predictable, since the very size of the catchment dampens the effects of single storms. Typically the rain will fall in the steep headwater regions over 1000 km from the main stem flood plain. The seasonal rainfall pattern in the wetter parts of the vast drainage basins produces an annual cycle of flooding and drawdown, which is characteristic of large rivers. There is only one high-water period, and the resulting flooding can persist for several months.

Flooding is used as a clue for biological activity from fish spawning to seasonal aquatic plant growth. This is especially important in tropical environments, where clues such as temperature and day length are similar year-round. E. P. Odum used the term *pulse stabilization* and the idea was recently generalized to most large rivers in the *flood pulse concept* (Junk et al., 1989), the counterpart to the stream continuum concept for smaller river and streams (Vannote et al., 1980). As the name suggests, the flood pulse is the dynamic aspect of flooding. It is the principal driving force in the existence, productivity, and interactions of the major biota in river-flood plain systems. Flooding creates an aquatic-terrestrial transition zone (ATTZ). High production in the land-water interface is important to most flooded regions, even small ones (Wetzel, 1990). In lakes the littoral zone is more productive than other zones (Chap. 2); by analogy with lakes, the ATTZ can be thought of as a *moving littoral zone* (Fig. 17-2). In large rivers, the ratio of the ATTZ moving littoral zone to permanent water is much greater than in most lakes or oceans.

Both aquatic and terrestrial organisms can adapt to the alternating wet and dry conditions caused by flooding. This predictable condition can lead to high productivity in rivers, but in small streams unpredictable flooding reduces the opportunity to adapt life strategies to take advantage of the ATTZ. Primary production in the ATTZ is greater than in either the main river or the isolated lakes and wetlands that remain as the floods recede. Fish yields are related to the amount of accessible flood plain but exact relationships are hard to determine, since other factors, such as fishing pressure, affect the catch of fish. Nonetheless, in a study of the Mississippi drainage, 55 percent of the variation in average fish catch was attributed to the flood plain (bottom-land, hardwood forest) in combination with fishing effort and latitude (Rissotto and Turner, 1985).

Few large rivers pass through permanent lakes, except at their headwaters. The Athabasca River in Canada flows into Lake Athabasca ($A = 7900$ km^2) but sediment transport has produced natural levees so high that the river will soon bypass the lake. Instead of lakes, large *internal* or *central deltas* are quite common and very important for the biota of many big rivers (e.g., the Niger and Nile in Africa). These seasonal lakes and wetlands along the river's course dampen discharge fluctuations and also considerably alter the chemical composition (Chap. 18).

THE AMAZON

The Amazon is the largest of all rivers in terms of both discharge and drainage area (Tables 17-1, 17-4). It is also one of the longest (Day and Davies, 1986). Although rainfall averages of 2 m y^{-1} in the Amazon, this is not unusually high. For example, rainfall on temperate watersheds such as the English Lake District is 2.5 m of rainfall, and almost 4 m falls in the central massif (Pearsall and Pennington, 1973). However, the vast size of the Amazon drainage basin and its flat lower drainage basin make it unique. Although it is not always typical of large water-courses, the Amazon has generated many of the ideas about the dynamics of big rivers. Most important is the concept of the importance of the flood plain to the fishery and general river production. The flood plain of the Amazon is called the *varsia*. For most of its length the Amazon is a 2- to 20-km-wide turbid (white-water) river

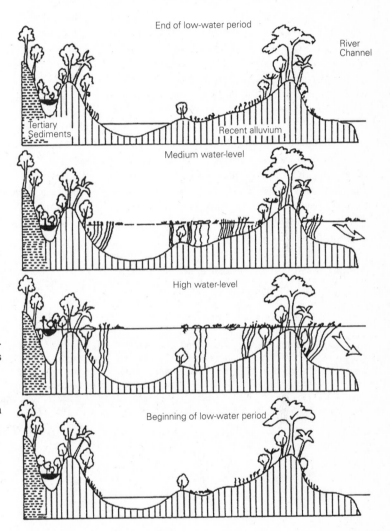

Levée

End of low-water period

River Channel

Tertiary Sediments

Recent alluvium

Medium water-level

High water-level

Beginning of low-water period

FIGURE 17-2 The moving littoral zone, or ATTZ (aquatic terrestrial transition zone), characteristic of big rivers as they flood and subside. This diagram from the middle Amazon shows both the floating meadow at medium and high water level, flood plain varsia lakes, and decay of the aquatic vegetation in the dry season. The ATTZ is the main transfer area for terrestrially derived fruits and insects to fish (as water rises) and aquatic plants to terrestrial insects and microbes (as the soil dries out). See also Fig. 17-7. Modified from Junk (1986).

flowing in a broad flood plain 20 to 100 km across. Small varsia lakes dot the landscape. There are numerous clearwater tributaries draining the surrounding tropical rainforest. The largest of these is the Rio Negro, which, although relatively transparent, is stained the color of tea by tannins and lignins (Fig. 17-1). Its dark ap-

pearance relative to the white water main stem gives it its name.

Productivity and the Amazon Food Chain

The light-limited, nutrient-rich white-water river and its nutrient-depleted, acidic clearwater tributaries are unproductive, whereas the flooded varsia is extremely productive. The Amazon River is an unsuitable habitat for both rooted and floating aquatic macrophytes as well as for planktonic and attached algae. The ever-shifting and abrasive sandy bed combines with water level fluctuations of 10 to 15 m, which discourages most macrophytes. Temporary submerged sand banks up to 8 m high occur in the deep main stem of the river. Here, macrophytes would either be periodically dried out or not find a stable substratum in which to root. The deep, muddy water restricts photosynthesis by phytoplankton, and scour reduces aufwuchs growth. However, for most of the year, "great rafts of aquatic plants can be seen floating downriver" (Junk, 1986). These plants are presumably washed out of the varsia.

The main stem of the Amazon, excluding the mountainous, cooler Andean headwaters, is sit-uated in a tropical rain forest. As with many tropical forests, the soil is poor and thin because the underlying granite rock does not decompose into a very fertile soil. In addition, efficient internal recycling on the forest floor releases few nutrients or organic detritus to the river (Table 17-2).

The productive flood plain contains not only forest but many permanent lakes and swamps, which merge with the overflowing river water. Because the middle reaches of the Amazon are so flat (mean slope $= 1$ or 2 cm km^{-1}), river-bank overflow occurs easily. Rains are greatest between December and April in the distant upper catchment, but the resulting high waters only reach the main stem between May and August (Fig. 17-3).

In the early flood stages, the overflowing waters become enriched with nitrate and phos-

FIGURE 17-3 Rainfall and river height for the Amazon at Itacoatiara about 150 km downstream of Manaus (see map, Fig. 17-9). Note that due to the size of the drainage basin, the flood peak in the lower Amazon is a few months later than peak rainfall. The single flood is characteristic of large rivers, because their great volume buffers the effect of storms on any single tributary. The actual rainfall in the Amazon (average about 2 m) is similar to that in many lake districts, for example the English Lake District (2.5 m). It is the low evaporation in the humid climate together with rainfall that drops back in the drainage basin which keeps the Amazon the largest river in the world. Modified from Smith (1981).

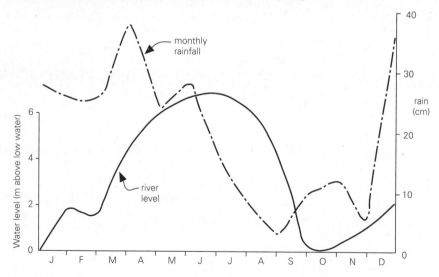

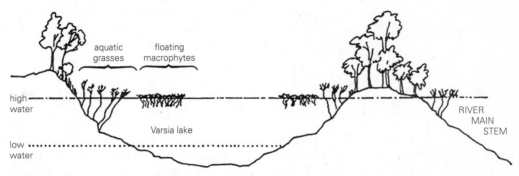

FIGURE 17-4 A floating meadow formed by aquatic plants as the Amazon forest floods dry land. Some of the aquatic grasses, such as *Paspalum fasciulatum,* may grow up to 15 m long and become stranded on the tree tops as the water drops. Others, such as the floating macrophytes *Pistia* and *Eichhornia* (water hyacinth), flourish in the much-expanded varsia lakes. Modified from Junk (1970).

phate leached from the forest floor. Utilizing this nutrient supply, large free-floating plants form a community unique to the tropics—the *floating meadow* (Fig 17-4). The growth of this community relative to the flood stages is shown in Fig. 17-5. The water cabbage (*Pistia*), the water hyacinth (*Echhornia*), the water fern (*Salvinia*), and the duckweed (*Lemna*) are carried from the small permanent lakes to the rest of the varsia. Rooted aquatic grasses, particularly *Echinocloa*

and *Paspalum,* keep up with the rising flood water by greatly elongating their stems to as much as 15 m. An idea of the scale of the Amazon floods and aquatic grass growth is seen in Fig. 17-6, which shows masses of aquatic grass stranded in the trees 10 m above the ground when the floods retreat. Submerged macrophytes such as coontail (*Ceratophyllum*) and the famous water lily *Victoria amazonica,* with its huge floating leaves, also grow well in the shallower

FIGURE 17-5 Growth of the major rooted plant species in the Amazon flooded forest relative to the water level. Most growth occurs in the rising water. The productivity of terrestrial plants in the region is much lower than that of the varsia and flood plain vegetation (Table 17-3). Modified from Junk (1986).

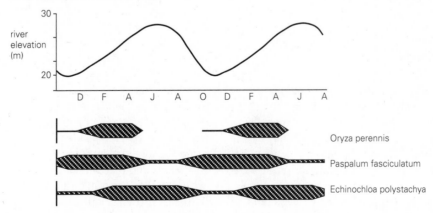

FIGURE 17-6 Aquatic grasses in the Amazon flood plain stranded in the tree tops. The scale of big river floods can be seen: the grasses are about 10 m from the forest floor. The grass will decay or be eaten by terrestrial insects such as grasshoppers before the next flood. Photograph by J. Melak.

areas. Many of these plants become overgrown with attached algae and aufwuchs to provide food for such grazers as snails and aquatic insect larvae. The rapidly reproducing rotifer and cladoceran zooplankton consume the blooms of phytoplankton, bacterioplankton, and other particles dislodged from the flooded forest.

The varsia lakes, which become nutrient-depleted in the dry season, become more fertile as they receive nutrient-rich flood waters (Forsberg et al., 1988). Depending on the amount of sediment that floods in along with the soluble nutrients, phytoplanktonic primary production may increase rapidly or be delayed until light penetration improves as the sediment settles. Unlike many tropical lakes, the varsia lakes are not dominated by blue-green algae (cyanobacteria). Instead they contain a more varied algal assembly. This may be due to the relatively small fetch and abundance of sites for periphyton, since tree tops are still above water and there are many submerged sites for aufwuchs growth. Many of the strategies for dominance in blue-green algae depend on vertical and horizontal motion in stratified, nitrogen-depleted open water (Chap. 12). In the varsia, horizontal drift (Fig. 5-3) could be

a disadvantage and move the floating blue-greens into the shade of the trees or onto the shore.

The Amazon with its varsia tends to be more productive than many big rivers. It belongs in a group of rivers with large flood plains and high fish species diversity that includes the Parana or Rio de la Plata in South America, Zaire or Congo River in West Africa, and the Mekong in southeast Asia. Estimates of the annual production of algae, grasses, and higher plants in Amazonian varsia and nonvarsia sites during wet and dry seasons are given in Table 17-3. The contribution made by the aquatic grasses and floating plants (53 t dry wt ha^{-1}) is much greater than that of the dry season terrestrial vegetation (18 t dry wt ha^{-1}). It is likely that aufwuchs shows a similar response. In the dry season varsia lakes have been shown to produce a maximum of 10 t dry wt ha^{-1} (clearwater) and 3 t dry wt ha^{-1} (white waters). Wet season measurements are more difficult to obtain. Higher plants in nonvarsia habitats, such as the huge area of unflooded tropical rain forest produce relatively little organic matter (10 t dry wt ha^{-1}, as measured by leaf and litter fall to the forest floor; Table 17-4).

The large mass of aquatic macrophytes is not a major food source for larger animals. Some, such as the giant Victoria lily have a lower surface covered with sharp spines, which may deter herbivores such as manatees. In addition, few organisms outside their native habitat feed on the Amazon macrophytes. In fact, most of the pest weeds now causing problems in the world's lakes, reservoirs, and river backwaters have been spread out of the Amazon basin by accidental release from ornamental ponds and aquaria. The water hyacinth, *Echhornia,* is a good example. The main beneficiaries of the huge macrophyte production in the varsia are terrestrial grasshoppers, which eat the living plants and the microbes that decompose the plants after stranding by the receding flood water. Some floating macrophytes and associated plants float to the river, but these are not a large fraction of the varsian total. Using lignin as a tracer and the ratios of carbon iso-

TABLE 17-3

HIGH ANNUAL PRIMARY PRODUCTIVITY OF TROPICAL ALGAE, GRASSES, AND HIGHER PLANTS IN THE VARSIA (FLOOD PLAIN) UNDER FLOODED CONDITIONS AS COMPARED WITH PRODUCTION IN DRY CONDITIONS OR IN NEARBY, NONVARSIA TERRESTRIAL RAIN FOREST

All sites are situated in the Amazon Basin in the central river reach. Aufwuchs production has not been measured but probably exceeds that of phytoplankton.

Taxon	Production, t dry wt $ha^{-1} y^{-1}$	Growth season	Reference
Varsia grasses: aquatic			
Paspalum fasciculatum	45	Wet	1
Oryza perennis	10	Dry?	2
Varsia annuals: higher plants			
Salvinia auriculata	8*	Wet	1
Ludwigia densiflora	8	Dry	2
Nonvarsia rainforest leaf litter	10	All year	3
Varsia lakes: phytoplankton	?	Wet	4
Clearwater	10	Dry	5
White-water	3	Dry	6

References: (1) Junk and Howard-Williams, 1984; (2) Junk, 1986; (3) Adis et al., 1979; (4) Melak, pers. comm.; (5) Schmidt, 1973a; (6) Schmidt, 1973b.
* Although growth rates may be similar areal coverage is greater in the wet season.

topes, it was found that most of the coarse organic particles (> 63 μm) and the fine material (< 63 μm) originated in the upper watershed, not in the lower flat 2000 km (Hedges et al., 1986). Thus, through the terrestrial food chain, the varsia recycles most of the organic matter it produces (Fig. 17-7).

Fishes

There are about 1300 species of fish in the entire Amazon system (Table 17-4), and over 85 percent are either characoids or catfish (siluroids; Lowe-McConnel, 1986). In comparison with the high species numbers the density of fish is moderate. Characoids are laterally compressed open-water fish ranging from a few centimeters to 1 m in length. Diet range from fruit to mud to other fish. Even more so than temperate fish such as trout, Amazon fish utilize terrestrial food sources including fallen insects and fruit. Amazon catfish are piscivorous. Young large catfish and all life stages of smaller catfish species eat zooplankton. Amazon fishes are also discussed in Chap. 14.

Many Amazon fish benefit from the annual floods. They migrate from the main river to feed in the newly flooded varsia and then migrate again to breed elsewhere in the main stem of the river. Other fish breed in the varsia itself, and the young of these fish not only find ample food but may avoid density-dependent predation. When they move back to the crowded main stem these young fish may be large enough to avoid most

TABLE 17-4

FISH SPECIES RELATIVE TO RIVER LENGTH, DRAINAGE BASIN AREA, AND PRESENCE OF LARGE HYDRAULIC BARRIERS SUCH AS FALLS OR CATARACTS ON THE MAIN LOWER RIVER

Most of the upper branches of big rivers, off the river main stem, are in mountains and have waterfalls. Note that the climatic regime, and thus the flood plain contribution to the river, dominates over length or drainage area with regard to number of fish species.

River	Length, km	Area, km²	No. of fish species	Barriers
Tropical				
Amazon	6,440	6,500,000	1,300	No
Zaire (Congo)	4,670	4,000,000	669	Cataracts
Mekong	4,180	780,000	900	Cataracts
Parana	4,000	2,800,000	600	Falls
Volta	1,600	400,000	122	Rapids
Niger	4,170	1,100,000	134	Rapids
Zambezi	3,450	1,295,000	156	Cataracts
Temperate				
Mississippi	3,731	4,800,000	241	At 824 km
Rhine	1,320	220,000	—	Cataracts, fall
Volga	3,690*	1,300,000	82	No
Columbia	2,000	670,000	—	No[†]
Desert				
Nile	6,670	3,000,000	115[‡]	Cataracts
Colorado	2,300	600,000	32	Cataracts
Orange-Vaal	2,500	650,000	16	Yes
Murray-Darling	2,740	1,070,000	22	No
Arctic				
Mackenzie	4,210	1,800,000	52	No

* Reduced to 3530 km due to channel straightening.
[†] Upper 20 percent of watershed inaccessible to migratory fish.
[‡] Rises to 320 if hydraulically isolated lakes Victoria, Edward, George, Kioga, Albert, and Tana are included.

predators. This is also the case in other tropical rivers, such as the African Niger, where the internal delta floods in the same fashion as the varsia. The importance of the flood plain for the reproduction of some fish families is shown in Fig. 17-8.

The varsia was created over 15,000 years ago by sedimentation of the old steep river valley as the sea level rose. The extent and importance of the flood plains in the Amazon has varied considerably over the last million years. At one time most of the Amazon basin was a huge lake, thus

the fish and other organisms in the varsia are opportunists that, like estuarine species (Chap. 19), survive in lesser numbers in their base habitat (main river) and exploit new habitats such as the flood plain by rapid reproduction when conditions are favorable.

Comparison of the Amazon with Other Tropical Rivers

The Amazon is bigger and has a smaller elevation change over its length than many other tropical rivers. Once past the headwaters there are

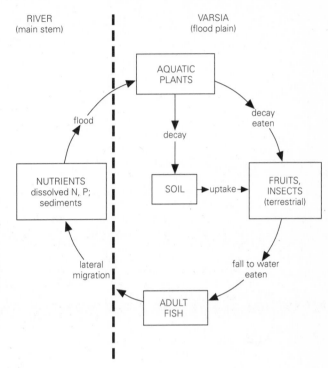

RIVER (main stem)

VARSIA (flood plain)

AQUATIC PLANTS

flood

decay eaten

decay

NUTRIENTS
dissolved N, P;
sediments

SOIL →uptake→

FRUITS, INSECTS (terrestrial)

lateral migration

fall to water
eaten

ADULT FISH

FIGURE 17-7 Nutrient cycles in the Amazon and its flood plain (the varsia). The rising water releases nutrients from the newly flooded soils. These, together with sediments and dissolved nutrients carried by the flood water, stimulate growth of aquatic algae and macrophytes. These plants, in turn, decay on the flood plain, feeding terrestrial insects and microbes, and supply the soil with nutrients. River fish swim into the varsia with the rising water and feed on terrestrial fruits, leaves, and insects that grew using the nutrients left by the previous year's floods. Once replete with food the fish normally return to the river and breed at once or after upstream or downstream migration to spawning grounds as far away as 2000 km.

no waterfalls or rapids as the wide river flows through an area of low geological relief. Nevertheless, the Amazon has much in common with the Zaire (Congo) and Mekong rivers, even though they have occasional rapids. These three rivers have a high ratio (> 0.45) of discharge to drainage area (Table 17-1) and large numbers of fish species. Like the Amazon, the Zaire has a very large discharge, as might be expected for a system flowing latitudinally in tropical rain forest. Although it is very flat for most of its lower reach, the Zaire has white-water rapids near its entry to the sea. Some tropical rivers, such as the Parana or White Nile, have huge waterfalls on some tributaries, which form complete hydraulic barriers to fish migration (Plate 8A).

Flood-plain wetlands vary considerably from one tropical river to another. In the Amazon the flood plain is dominated by the interconnecting varsia lakes, while in the Pantenal, 500 km to the south, the flood plain is bone dry at low flow

and a single sheet of water in the wet season (Welcomme, 1988).

THE COLORADO RIVER

In stark contrast to the Amazon is the Colorado, which flows for 2300 km through western North America. Although about half as long and draining about 9 percent of the area drained by the Amazon's watershed (Table 17-1), the Colorado's discharge is only 0.3 percent of the Amazon's flow. The dry, almost desert regions through which the Colorado flows for much of its length have very low rainfall and there are no important tributaries. This is very different from the Amazon rain forest, continually recharged by tributaries all the way to the ocean (Fig. 17-9).

The Colorado has cut some of the deepest canyons in the world. The Grand Canyon in the Arizona desert is the most famous. Canyons obviously have very restricted flood plains (Plate

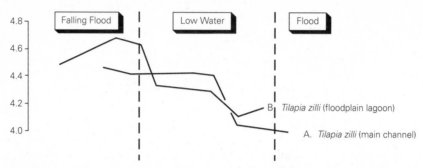

FIGURE 17-8 Big river fish benefit from feeding in the flood plain. The condition factor (weight in kilograms divided by length in centimeters) for *Tilapia* in the flood plain compared with the same species in the main channel. The flood plain fish have the best condition and accumulate fat reserves at the end of the flood period. The condition of the main stem fish is little affected by water level but is generally lower than in the flood plain fish. Often these species are opportunists and will use the flood plain but can survive droughts at lower numbers in the perennial main stem. This example is from the internal Central Delta of the River Niger in West Africa, situated about half way along the river's length. Modified from Daget (1957) and Welcome (1986).

6B), consequently there is a very limited supply of nutritious allochthonous food. Before sections of it were dammed, the Colorado was one of the muddiest of rivers and autochthonous primary production was limited to attached algal growth on a few rocky riffles. Only occasional side canyon areas are suitable for riparian tree growth.

The hypothesis that the flood plain is vital for fish development is borne out by the low fish diversity in the Colorado. There are only 32 native species of fish in the Colorado, contrasting with 1300 in the Amazon and 900 in the Lower Mekong River in Asia (Table 17-4). Another desert river, the Murray-Darling system in Australia, has low fish diversity, with only 22 native species. The Colorado's discharge may have been even lower in the past, and selective extinction of some fish has occurred. Unlike the Amazon, Nile, Congo, Parana, and other rivers in wetter regions, the Colorado is isolated, with no possibility of fish recolonizing from other rivers.

Although now altered by huge dams and reservoirs, the original Colorado contained some regions with small flood plains (up to 1 km wide) as well as backwaters. Gallery forests of cotton-

wood trees, reeds, and rushes were present in some flatter areas toward the estuary. Today, little or no water reaches the estuary in most years. In the regulated river below the dams, incense cedar grows where floods once washed trees away. Now and in times past the fish apparently still depended on the annual floods, as they do in the Amazonian ecosystem. The surviving fish now present in shorter undammed areas produce good year classes (Chap. 14) in years of higher discharges and poor ones in low-flow years.

Fish in desert rivers such as the Colorado do not breed or feed on the flood plains. Instead, they utilize hydraulically isolated backwaters in the side canyons, which become nursery areas for the young fish after the higher water opens up and recharges them. When these backwaters are permanently connected with the main stem, as occurs following dam construction, adult fish gain access and eat the young fish. This situation has become worse following stocking of the river with non-native species. Unlike the Amazon, long fish migrations were not common even in the original Colorado River (Stanford and Ward, 1986). This was probably due to the scarcity of

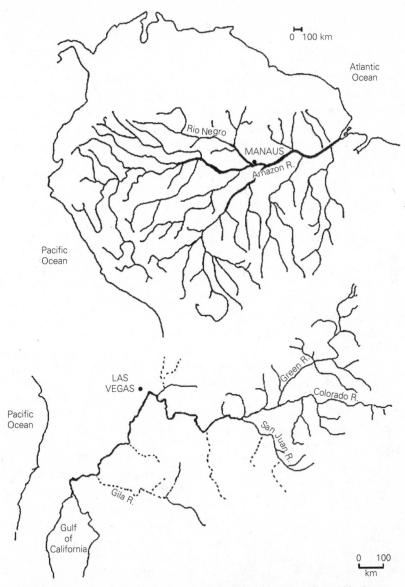

FIGURE 17-9   The drainage basin and tributaries for two very different big rivers:
the tropical Amazon and the desert Colorado. Once away from the headwaters, tributaries to the Colorado are few and ephemeral (dotted lines). In contrast, the Amazon
has numerous permanent tributaries right up to its mouth. The contrast in the drainage
basin area to discharge ratio that results from the effect of tributaries is shown in
Table 17-1.

calm backwaters, food, and spawning grounds anywhere along the river. Also in contrast with the tropics, the aquatic environment in the original Colorado was severe and highly variable. Very hot summer water temperatures alternated with cold winter temperatures, and the water was both salty and very muddy year-round. Much of the river consisted of long turbulent rapids, the remnants of which are now popular with whitewater rafters. Lack of zoobenthos in the sandy, shifting river bed forced fish to feed in the few areas where attached algae, insects, or snails were present. Together, these constraints produced a simple food chain comprising a few endemic species of minnows and suckers. Only three species were important in the lower main stem of the river—squawfish, bonytail chub, and razorback sucker. Swift currents favored these large fish, one of which developed a pronounced vertical hump that increased stability (Fig. 17-10). The main piscivore, the squawfish, reached 2 m long and weighed up to 45 kg. It was called the *white salmon* and once ran in large numbers during spawning. This occasional mass gathering

FIGURE 17-10 The Colorado Razorback sucker, *Xyrauchen texanus*. The knife-edged hump may be an adaptation to provide stability by acting as a dorsal keel in the swift currents. Desert rivers lack many snags and fallen trees that provide eddies to shelter fish in other rivers. Photograph by Gordon Mueller, USBR, Denver, Colorado.

of fish belies the fact that the original Colorado was an unproductive system compared to the big tropical or temperate rivers with their large flood plains.

The Colorado now discharges to the ocean only after the largest floods such as that of 1983. One reason for this is that more than 10 years of discharge is stored in the reservoirs behind Hoover Dam (Lake Mead) and in Lake Powell. Lake Mead has the distinction of being the largest reservoir in the United States. All of the water in the Colorado River is appropriated for agriculture and drinking water in the surrounding states of the United States and Mexico. The warm, fast-flowing sections have almost all been flooded, and cold hypolimnion releases do not favor native fish. The strenuous hike to the bottom of the Grand Canyon in the national park reveals a relatively clear and cold river, not the muddy warm torrent of yesteryear. Introduced fish such as rainbow trout have become common almost everywhere. Lack of habitat and especially predation on young native fish by introduced species have greatly reduced or eliminated the original inhabitants. Managing reservoir releases to isolate native fry in backwaters has produced more native fish, which, as adults, often compete well with the introduced species.

Comparison of the Colorado with Other Desert Rivers

Other rivers with desert lower sections include the Murray-Darling in Australia, the Orange-Vaal in Southwest Africa, the Zambesi in East Africa, and the Nile in Northeastern Africa. All of these rivers have a very low ratio of discharge to drainage basin area (0.02 to 0.03×10^{-3}; Table 17-1). As in most arid zones, these rivers have also been extensively dammed and diverted. The Orange-Vaal, in particular, loses almost as much of its flow to irrigation as does the Colorado. All have small flood plains and a low fish diversity (Table 17-4). Some of these rivers differ from the Amazon as well as the Colorado in that they contain large natural hydraulic barriers to fish migration. Spectacular examples are Murchison Falls on the Upper White Nile (Plate 8A) and Victoria Falls on the Zambezi.

The lower Nile is even more poorly supplied from its lower tributaries than the Colorado. Neither Egypt nor Sudan has sufficient rainfall to provide much runoff, and only the upper 56 percent of the 3 million km^2 drainage area normally feeds water to the river. Excluding the species in the tropical, hydraulically separate lake systems in the upper reaches, the fish diversity of the Nile is quite low (115 species). If the lakes near the source of the Nile are included, for example Lake Victoria, the species diversity for the entire river would rise to over 300 species. The original Nile had some quite large flood plains in its lower reaches, for example north of the Aswan Cataract, and reed beds grow in the large internal delta (Sudd). Many of these important sources of organic carbon have now been much reduced.

The Colorado is now highly regulated, and all of its water is used for agriculture or human consumption. The Murray River in Australia, although originally much slower-flowing than the Colorado, is also totally regulated for the same uses. Increased salinity and reduction of prized native fish such as the murray cod (Murray) and squawfish (Colorado) have occurred. Blue-green algae blooms are now a problem in the Murray due to its shallow reservoirs. The very deep Colorado reservoirs are oligotrophic and do not have this problem.

THE MACKENZIE RIVER

This arctic river is 2700 km long and flows almost directly north to south over 15° of latitude from its origins in the Athebasca Glacier in the western Rocky Mountains of Canada to the Arctic Ocean (Table 17-1). The Mackenzie is different from both the tropical Amazon and the desert Colorado in that much of its boggy catchment basin is underlain by permafrost in summer and is completely frozen in winter. The watershed contains a mixture of tundra to the north

and subboreal pine, birch, and aspen forest to the south.

The hallmark of all big rivers is high turbidity, but the Mackenzie is even more cloudy than most due to the presence of fine *glacial flour* (Plates 3a, b). This material, derived from the grinding of rock by glaciers, remains suspended from source to mouth. The high turbidity, very coarse sediments, and strong current restrict autochthonous primary production except at low discharge. In addition, nutrient concentrations are quite low (Table 17-2). When flows are low, attached filamentous blue-green algae dominate the biomass and together with diatoms can coat the rocks and sediments. The benthic invertebrate community is similar to that of cold-water streams and consists of fine suspended detritus feeders, such as blackflies and hydropsychids, shredders, scrapers such as the mayfly *Baetis,* and predatory stoneflies (Barton, 1986). The short summer and late flood season puts a premium on species that can reproduce quickly. The high turbidity does not seem to affect the fish seriously, perhaps because glacial flour is less abrasive on the gills than other suspended sediments.

The river discharge is greatest in June and July. Except in the internal and estuarine deltas, flooding is restricted by natural levees. In contrast to warmer regions, there is poor growth of riparian bank vegetation, and high sediment loads maintain the levees. There is some input of allochthonous debris (twigs and leaves) but no equivalent of the varsia contribution. Aquatic grasses and macrophytes are not important.

Like the Amazon, the Mackenzie main stem is quite flat, and there are no serious hydraulic barriers to fish migration. Long migrations do occur but mostly to and from the estuarine delta or to and from large lakes on smaller tributary rivers. Because the flood plain is unproductive or made inaccessible by natural levees, fish in the Mackenzie breed in the river or in lakes, not on the flood plain. There are relatively few fish species in the Makenzie (52; Table 17-4), which suggests a low overall food supply. The major fish species are a typical North American cold-water assemblage, including 10 coregonids, 10 salmonids, pike, and 12 minnow species. Although the numbers of individuals may sometimes be high, they represent the accumulated growth of many years and fishers can easily decimate the stock. An important adaptation to the highly variable environment of the Arctic is that most of these fish are long-lived, which enables them to survive several bad breeding years.

The Mackenzie is unusual in that the main stem passes through two large lakes. The system is very young, and where it flows into Lake Athabasca the river has already converted the area into a shallow marsh, the Peace-Athabasca Delta. This area is probably the most important wetland in North America for nesting waterfowl and is used primarily by birds following the Central and Mississippi flyways. This vast internal delta (3800 km^2) consists of a mature boggy area and a zone where sediments are still being deposited. In former times the spring melt increased discharge from the Peace River and reversed the outflow from Lake Athabasca, which then flooded out over the low-lying delta. Ice dams in the channels during spring breakup assisted the flooding. After snowmelt the river discharge declined and the delta slowly drained. The result of the flooding was the establishment of a series of pulse-stabilized seasonal wetlands of high productivity as well as the replenishment of ponds in perched basins. As in the Amazon and Colorado, a predictable and regular flood was necessary to maintain the river wetlands.

Unfortunately, much of this ecosystem was destroyed by the creation of the Bennett Dam on the Upper Peace River in 1967. Discharges decreased and the river height fell by 3 m, which prevented flooding of the delta in spring. Within a few years the surface area of the perched basin lakes was reduced by 40 percent and less productive willows and meadow plants invaded the seasonal wetlands. Muskrat numbers fell to less than half because few marshes had enough deep water to allow overwintering in this harsh climate. Shallow lakes tend to freeze to the bottom leaving no room for the muskrats.

Comparison of the Mackenzie with Other Arctic Rivers

The discharge of the Mackenzie is moderate for its drainage basin, and the ratio of the two (0.19 $\times$ 10^{-3}) is similar to those of the Mississippi, Niger, and Volga Rivers (0.17 to 0.19 $\times$ 10^{-3}; Table 17-1). It is difficult to collect data on big rivers in cold climates, and little comparative information with other rivers is available, except for fish harvesting. The rivers draining central north Canada toward Hudson Bay are similar to the Mackenzie and are fed by the short spring melt. The flood pulse in these rivers is often large but soon recedes, which gives little time for fish to exploit the ATTZ (Roy, 1989).

In arctic rivers the meltwater floods contain ice fragments that scour the flood plain and retard plant production in what is already a short growing season. The small effect of the flood plain on North American arctic rivers is reflected in the fact that they are generally poor in organic carbon in comparison to temperate and tropical rivers. Of course, the tundra and taiga have few of the grasses and trees that grow so well in the flood plains of the large rivers in temperate and tropical regions. Arctic rivers have a high percentage of anadromous fishes, possibly because adult fish have few places to overwinter. Additional information from the big arctic rivers of Siberia (the Ob, Lena, and Yenisei) are needed to make further generalizations.

THE MISSISSIPPI

The sediment-laden ''Old Muddy'' of the pioneers drains almost 13 percent of the North American continent, including 31 U.S. states and two Canadian provinces (Fremling et al., 1989). Here we emphasize the large lower river formed from three major tributaries: the upper Mississippi, Missouri, and Ohio. Unlike most big riv-

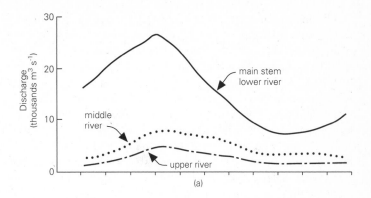

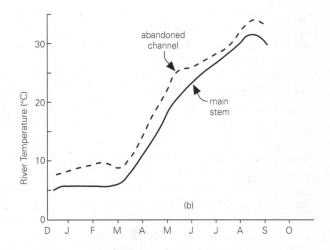

FIGURE 17-11 Physical features of the Lower Mississippi River. (*a*) The regular and predictable single flood event in large rivers is well illustrated by the lower river, which rises about 11 m in a normal year. Much smaller peaks occur in the upper reaches. (*b*) Temperatures in the Mississippi reach tropical values in summer, and tropical weeds such as water hyacinth are common, especially in the slow-moving backwaters. The abandoned channel, a few kilometers from the main channel, is always warmer. Higher temperatures speed larval fish development. Modified from Fremling et al. (1989) and Beckett and Pennington (1986).

ers, the Mississippi's headwaters drain gentle slopes or alluvial plains, rather than high mountain ranges. The river falls only 440 m over the 3731 km from its source near Lake Itasca, Minnesota, to the Gulf of Mexico near New Orleans. The headwaters extend for the first 824 km; the Upper Mississippi, by now a 9th- and 10th-order river, covers 1148 km and the Middle Mississippi adds another 314 km. The main stem, or Lower Mississippi River, is formed after the confluence of the three tributaries and stretches 1570 km from the mouth of the Ohio River to the sea.

As in other large rivers, flooding is a regular and predictable event in the lower reaches. The large peak in the discharge curve occurs in March and April in the lower river, in marked contrast to the small peaks in the upper reaches (Fig. 17-11*a*). Although mighty floods occurred on this river prior to the installation of flood control structures in the 1930s, the dry areas to the west and evaporation reduce the amount of discharge per unit drainage to well below that of the tropical rivers (Table 17-1). The original Mississippi drained forested areas to the north or east and prairie grasslands to the west. The major floods occurred when the snow melt and spring rains in all three tributary watersheds, especially the Ohio, came together in the main stem. The

Mississippi main stem, which may be as much as 2.5 km wide, has formed a very wide flood plain replete with oxbow lakes, abandoned channels, and swamps. The natural flood plain covers 90,000 km^2 in a valley that is about 1000 km long and 40 to 200 km wide. At the height of the exceptional floods of 1927, almost 70,000 km^2 was flooded. Due in part to these floods, the river is now regulated to reduce flooding, and the current flood plain extends over only 10,000 km^2. Nonetheless, floods have not been completely eliminated; in 1973 high waters inundated almost 50,000 km^2 of the lower Mississippi Valley.

Modifications to the river began in 1727 and continue to this day. The modern Mississippi is primarily modified for flood control and navigation with 11 flood control dams, most of which are below the nine glacial lakes in the upper reaches. The natural banks have been stabilized; there are over 2500 km of levees in the main stem alone. Flow patterns have been changed by dredging, diking off side channels, and using wing dams to scour a deep channel for navigation. Needless to say, these modifications have had a major effect on the river biota.

The river is in the temperate region, but because it flows north to south and is in the interior of a large continent, the water experiences a wide range of temperatures. Even in the lower reaches temperatures vary from 5 to 35°C; surprisingly, temperatures do not vary much from main stem river to sheltered backwater (Fig. 17-11b).

Productivity

The original role of allochthonous matter cannot be ascertained directly, since the river is now excluded from 90 percent of the original flood plain. Even so, carbon input from the watershed is important. For example, the carbon budget for one pool on the upper river gives a phytoplankton to aquatic macrophytes to flood plain ratio of 1:8:40. This indicates that the flood plain still dominates the carbon flow in the upper river. In the lower river dams and the smaller flood plain

have increased the relative and absolute contribution of phytoplankton.

As in most large rivers, the concentrations of inorganic nutrients are high and do not limit algal growth (Table 17-2). Prior to modification, it is unlikely that large amounts of plankton could have survived in the turbid main stem of the Mississippi, but the formerly extensive flood plain lakes and quiet backwaters must have provided good sites for phytoplankton and zooplankton growth. The lower river is now a series of shallow navigation pools that provide the environment for substantial phytoplankton blooms.

Fortuitously, the new impoundments have created much new riparian habitat, which benefits from the stabilized water levels. The warm summer in the Mississippi Valley (Fig. 17-11b) supports a considerable growth of aquatic macrophytes and algae. As this plant material rots the finer particles are carried to the main stem, especially after summer thunderstorms. Once in the river, the organic particles become food for the mass of detritus feeders such as clams and the filter-feeding insect larvae that abound in the lower Mississippi. Where natural banks remain, they are dominated by clay-burrowing mayflies and hydropsychid caddisflies (Beckett and Pennington, 1986).

Somewhat neglected in the organic carbon budget of big rivers is the role of ultra-large particulate matter, mostly tree trunks and branches. As an indication of the scale of this allochthonous contribution in the Mississippi, over 200,000 logs were removed from the lower 1600 km of the river as navigation hazards and many more passed to the sea unnoticed (Harmon et al., 1986).

Fishes

There are 241 fish species in the Mississippi, placing it between the tropical rivers and the stressed desert and arctic systems (Table 17-4). About 195 of these species are found in the main stem. The diversity of the Mississippi fish population is apparent when it is considered that there are only 600 freshwater fish species in the entire North American continent.

By analogy with other big rivers, the abundance and diversity of the fishes in the Mississippi depends on the size of the flood plain. Since only 10 percent of the flood plain is now flooded each year, there has probably been a considerable loss in fish biomass. This loss of flood plain can be reversed only by curtailing river navigation and human activities in the flood plain. Thus current efforts to maintain a productive and diverse fish and invertebrate population focus on enhancing the most valuable aspects of the remaining flood plain, particularly fish breeding areas.

The original river contained numerous backwaters, which were important for fish production and as nursery habitats. They included tributary channels and both oxbow lakes and abandoned meanders, which were connected with the river during the flood period. Unfortunately, many backwaters were drained in the 1920s and the remaining backwaters are threatened with siltation and eutrophication. Several fish species breed in backwaters made accessible by the flood water and their young move to the main stem as the water drops. Again, access to isolated backwaters is important for the year class strength of the fish. Equally important is the role of the seasonally flooded wetlands in the migration and breeding of waterfowl.

The fish now found in the Lower Mississippi have been divided into four main groups based on a synoptic survey of a 100-km stretch near Greenville, Mississippi. These communities are abandoned river channels and natural banks, which were always present, and dike fields and revetted banks, which were constructed over the last 100 years (Fig. 17-12). Although the flood plain lakes and abandoned channels are very val-

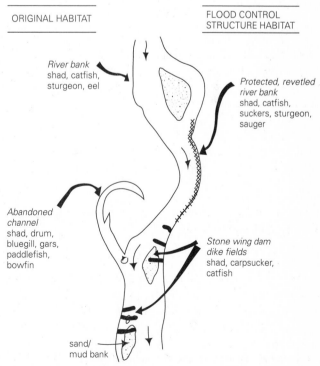

FIGURE 17-12 Fish preferences for original and constructed habitat in the lower Mississippi. Note that some ancient species, such as the paddlefish, bowfin, and gar, are not able to use the constructed areas and require natural banks or abandoned channels. With the managed river, these are no longer being created. Others, such as shad and catfish, are at home in most or all of the habitats. A revetment (shown by xxxx) is an erosion barrier often made of large angular concrete, which has some of the habitat features of a tree stump. The stone dikes or wing dams (thick lines) divert water toward the main channel and usually have mud or sand banks (shaded areas) around them. Modified from Beckett and Pennington (1986).

ORIGINAL HABITAT

FLOOD CONTROL STRUCTURE HABITAT

River bank
shad, catfish,
sturgeon, eel

Protected, revetted
river bank
shad, catfish,
suckers, sturgeon,
sauger

Abandoned
channel
shad, drum,
bluegill, gars,
paddlefish,
bowfin

Stone wing dam
dike fields
shad, carpsucker,
catfish

sand/
mud bank

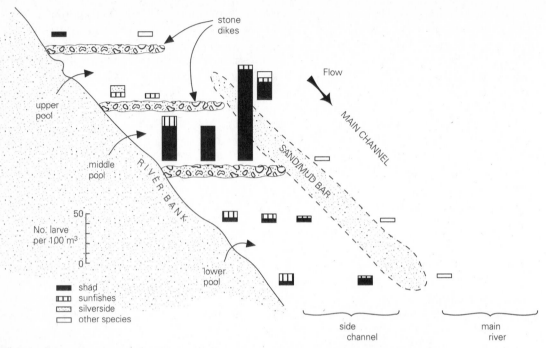

FIGURE 17-13 Utilization of an artificial habitat by young fish in the modern highly modified lower Mississippi. Stone dikes or wing dams were constructed to close off secondary channels to the main current and stabilize point bars (mud or sandbanks) so that the main channel is more easily navigable by large barges. As expected, most small fish prefer the quiet pools created by the dike construction. Different larval species are found in the pools and the main river. Modified from Beckett and Pennington (1986).

uable fish habitat, the new dike field structures are used by juvenile fish as a refuge from the artificially fast-flowing main channel (Fig. 17-13).

Comparison of the Mississippi with Other Temperate Rivers

The big temperate rivers in Europe include the Danube, the Rhine, and the Volga. Like the Mississippi, all are highly modified by dams. The Volga has seven major and several minor reservoirs spaced along its 3500 km length. Only the lower 580 km of the Volga remains undammed, but even here discharge is regulated by upstream reservoirs. Most of the original flood-plain veg-

etation has been inundated, but emergent and submergent macrophyte beds in shallow waters are a partial replacement. The best stands are in the Ivankovo Reservoir, where the water level fluctuations are small. The Mississippi has a very similar ratio of discharge to drainage basin area to the rather different Mackenzie and Niger rivers as well as the more similar Volga River (Table 17-1). The Rhine, in contrast, has more water for the size of its drainage basin. One difference between the Mississippi and some other highly modified rivers such as the Colorado and the Amu Darya in Uzbekistan is that there is little reduction in the flow of the Mississippi due to water diversion for agriculture.

Both the Mississippi (241 species) and the Volga (82 species) have retained their original fish diversity. Species dominance, however, has changed to favor slow-water and lake species and away from migratory swift-water fish. In some cases there have been invasions of introduced species that thrive in the plankton-rich eutrophic reservoir water. The exotic planktivores *Osmerus* and *Clupeonella* now dominate Volga reservoirs, and species with similar requirements thrive in Mississippi impoundments. Of considerable commercial importance is the decline of the caviar industry on the Volga and Mississippi drainages. The decline is due to the effect of dams and overfishing of the largest individuals.

In this chapter we discussed the flood plains of big rivers with particular regard to their role in the organic carbon budget of the river and its fish. Flood plains are, however, but one type of wetland, and not all wetlands are so closely associated with river systems. In Chap. 18 we turn to the more familiar marshes, swamps, bogs, and fens.

FURTHER READING

Axler, R., L. Paulson, P. Vaux, P. Sollberger, and D. H. Baepler. 1988. "Fish Aid: The Lake Mead Fertilization Project." *Lake Res. Man.,* **4:**125–135.

Barton, D. R. 1986. "Invertebrates of the Mackenzie River System." pp. 473–492. In B. R. Davies, and K. F. Walker (eds.). *The Ecology of River Systems.* Junk, The Hague. 793 pp.

Conservation 2001. 1986. Fairfield Osborn Symposium. Rockefeller University, New York.

Davies, B. R., and K. F. Walker (eds.). 1986. *The Ecology of River Systems. Junk,* The Hague. 793 pp.

Dodge, P. D. (ed.). 1989. Proceedings of the International Large River Symposium. *Can. Speak. Pub. Fish. Aquat. Sci.,* **106.**

Harmon, M. E., J. R. Franklin, F. J. Swanson, J. D. Lattin, S. V. Gregory, N. H. Anderson, S. P Cline, N. G. Aumen, J. D. Sidell, G. W. Lienkaemper, K. Cromak, and K. W. Cummins. 1986. "Ecology of Course Woody Debris in Temperate Ecosystems." *Adv. Ecol. Res.,* **15:**133–302.

Hedges, J. I., W. A. Clark, P. D. Quay, J. E. Richy, A. D. Devol, and U. de M. Santos. 1986. "Composition and Fluxes of Particulate Material in the Amazon River." *Limnol. Oceanogr.,* **31:**717–738.

Junk, W. J., P. B. Bailey, and R. E. Sparks. 1989. "The Flood Pulse Concept in River-Floodplain Systems." In P. D. Dodge (ed.). Proceedings of the International Large River Symposium. *Can. Speak. Publ. Fish. Aquat. Sci.,* **106.**

Mordukhai-Boltonvski, P. D. 1979. *The River Volga and Its Life.* Junk, The Hague. 473 pp.

Pearsall, W. H., and W. Pennington. 1972. *The Lake District.* Collins, London. 320 pp.

Roy, D. 1989. "Physical and Biological Factors Controlling the Distribution and Abundance of Fish in the Hudson/James Bay Rivers." In P. D. Dodge (ed.). Proceedings of the International Large River Symposium. *Can. Speak. Publ. Fish. Aquat. Sci.,* **106.**

Rzoska, J. (ed.). 1976. *The Nile: Biology of an Ancient River.* Junk, The Hague. 417 pp.

Vannote, R. L., G. W. Minshall, K. W. Cummins, J. R. Sidell, and C. E. Cushing. 1980. "The River Continuum Concept." *Can. J. Fish Aquat. Sci.,* **37:**130–137.

Welcomme, R. I. 1976. "Some General and Theoretical Considerations on the Fish Yield of African Rivers." *J. Fish Biol.,* **8:**351–364.

Wetzel, R. G. 1990. "Land Water Interfaces: Metabolic and Limnological Regulators—The Edgardo Baldi Memorial Lecture." *Verh. Int. Ver. Limnol.,* **24:**6–24.

Welcomme, R. I. 1988. "Concluding Remarks I: On the Nature of Large Tropical Rivers, Floodplains, and Future Research Directions." *North. Am. Benthol. Assoc.,* **7:**525–526.

CHAPTER 18

Wetlands

OVERVIEW

Wetlands are diverse in both form and function and include marshes, swamps, bogs, fens, mosses, muskeg, mires, and vernal and ephemeral pools. The definition encompasses the salt marshes and mangrove swamps of sea coast and estuary, the freshwater marshes of the prairie, the flood-plain swamps of rivers, and the littoral zone marshes of lakes. Wetlands are an *ecotone,* the transitional zone between land and water, and they combine characteristics of both environments besides having some unique characteristics of their own. The heterogeneous wetland habitat consists of permanent or seasonal shallow water dominated by large aquatic plants and broken into diverse microhabitats. Waterlogged soils are usually anoxic, and this has profound consequences for higher plants whose roots need oxygen. These conditions permit the growth of only specially adapted plants and trees together with mosses and attached algae; their presence is used in the legal definition of wetland. Adaptations of higher plants to anoxic soils include transfer of oxygen from leaves to roots via interconnected interior spaces (*lacunae*) and small adventitious ''air'' roots growing on the trunk (*pneumatophores*). Anoxia also changes the chemical state and biological availability of nutrients and toxicants in soils.

Wetlands are divided into four groups based on the dominant large vegetation, source of water, and presence or absence of peat. *Marshes* are characterized by emergent other aquatic macrophytes, whereas *swamps* are dominated by trees. Acidic *bogs* are characterized by a low species diversity, few higher plants, and an abundance of the peat-building *Sphagnum* moss. The more alkaline *fens* are often species-rich and contain both mosses and aquatic macrophytes. Marshes and swamps are fed by ground and river waters, which can be either rich or poor in nutrients; bogs, in contrast, always depend on mineral-poor rainwater. Fens are typically supplied by mineral-rich ground water. Bogs, fens, and many marshes are characteristically underlain by thick peat deposits. Swamps are often poor in peat deposits, which are flushed out by floods or oxidized in the dry seasons. As with lakes, wetlands vary in nutrient supply and biological productivity; some are among the most productive sites on earth and others are aquatic biological deserts. The main wetland types differ in rates of primary production in the order marshes >

swamps > fens > bogs. Most wetland plants are not directly eaten by most herbivores, thus the detritus pathway characterizes the food web. In nutrient-rich and unshaded wetlands algae provide a direct food source for small grazing animals.

The presence or absence of a dry period separates wetlands into the functional categories of seasonal and permanent wetlands. Bogs and fens are always wet but swamps and marshes may be flooded permanently or only seasonally. *Seasonal wetlands* are characterized by a dry period when all or most of the area reverts to terrestrial status. The wet-dry cycle releases nutrients from soils, and during the wet period productivity can be very high. Most of the organic matter produced in the flooded period is decomposed in the well-oxygenated dry season so organic deposition is low. Algae, aquatic grasses, a few other plants, insect larvae, and other small organisms that can survive the rigorous environmental fluctuations often become superabundant. Migratory birds that breed in seasonal wetlands feed on the dense but short-lived explosion of the insect population.

Permanent wetlands are usually found in river deltas, the margins of ponds and lakes, tidal estuaries, and flat areas in the mountains. They are characterized by large, long-lived trees and tall reeds that tolerate the permanently waterlogged soils. These wetlands also provide cover and breeding grounds for birds, fish, reptiles, and mammals. Permanent wetlands are usually less productive than seasonal wetlands but are net accumulators of organic matter, since decomposition is slow under conditions of permanent anoxia.

Wetlands alter the hydrology of streams and rivers by impeding water flow and enhancing sediment deposition. Most important, bacteria and plants in wetlands can transform inflowing ammonia, nitrate, and phosphate into organic forms, which are later released downstream as detritus. However, inorganic nutrients are also released downstream, often at a different season than when they entered. Marshes, in particular, are being considered as waste treatment facilities and show the greatest potential for "polishing" or removal of low amounts of contaminants in already treated wastes.

Although apparently transient features of the landscape, wetlands represent a relatively long-lived ecological continuum between the states of dry land and open water. Like lakes, they are permanent features unless the water regime or inorganic sediment inputs are substantially altered. Many wetlands rapidly accumulate their own organic matter when first formed, but further accumulation above the water surface is prevented by oxidation. The waterlogged soils prevent succession to terrestrial vegetation.

Drained or reclaimed wetlands form ideal sites for farms and cities. In addition, peat deposits are mined for a low-grade fuel and bedding for garden plants. Wetlands are a threatened resource: vast areas have been drained for agriculture and urban needs. Only recently has recognition of their value as wildlife feeding and breeding areas led to protection and restoration.

In this chapter we discuss characteristics and history of wetlands, losses, measurement, wetland types, structure, adaptations to anoxia, the lacunae system, nutrient fluxes, productivity, food chains, and protection and restoration.

CHARACTERISTICS AND HISTORY OF WETLANDS

Today, the preservation of wetlands is considered important by both scientists and the public. Therefore, considerable thought has gone into distinguishing wetlands from other aquatic and terrestrial habitats. This has been most pronounced in North America and Europe, where laws have been designed specifically to protect wetlands. The characteristics of shallow water, saturated soil, and dominance by vegetation adapted to waterlogged conditions define wetlands. In contrast to the official definitions, everyone has their personal vision of a wetland, whether it is a cattail bed swaying in the wind around a small pond, a vast coastal salt marsh thick with flocks of waterfowl, or the shady wooded thickets beside a stream. In this chapter we concentrate on freshwater, nontidal wetlands not directly associated with running water. River flood plains and the riparian habitat of streams are covered in Chaps. 16 and 17. The tidal salt and freshwater marshes and mangrove swamps of estuaries are considered in Chap. 19. Some biological features of wetlands plants, such as shoreline zonation in the sheltered areas of lakes, are presented in Chap. 11.

The scientific study of wetlands is difficult, and much remains to be discovered. One reason is that wetlands are the most physically and chemically heterogeneous of all the major aquatic ecosystems (Fig. 18-1). In seasonal marshes, short stretches of shallow open water, dense growths of submerged and emergent macrophytes, and organic sediments all occur in close proximity. Even small organisms can readily move between compartments. Anoxic mud may be close to submerged photosynthetic plants where the water is supersaturated with oxygen. Nutrients may be scarce in the open water but plentiful in the sediments. Further, conditions can change rapidly with the seasons, over a day, or even hourly. In contrast, some permanent wetlands appear monotonous, with wide swaths of a single species of moss, reed, or tree. Although not quite as uniform as they seem, especially if the microbial and insect populations are considered, wetlands certainly require a different approach. The recent interest in all types of wetlands has substantially increased the number of specialized publications. A good general reference work on wetlands is provided by Mitsch and Gosselink (1993), and their management is the focus of Gangsted's work (1986). Also available are edited volumes on wetlands as waste-treatment systems (Hammer, 1989) and on macrophyte assessment (Dennis and Isom, 1984).

Wetlands are of considerable economic importance. They can be highly productive, with

(a)

(b)

FIGURE 18-1 Wetland types. (*a*) The Florida everglades. The seasonally flooded marsh (dominated by sawgrass) meets the edges of a seasonal cypress swamp. Note the buttressing of the lower tree trunks. (*b*) A seasonal marsh in California, showing the heterogeneous spatial arrangement of shallow open water, emergent cattails, and bulrush. Submerged plants were common but are not visible here.

large crops of algae, macrophytes, trees, and aquatic invertebrates. This food supply and the cover and isolation from terrestrial predators provided by reed beds encourages nesting and rearing of waterfowl such as geese and ducks, which are highly valued by hunters, bird watchers, and politicians alike. Over 10 million ducks alone are shot for sport each year in the four main U.S. flyways, and the majority breed in the northern wetlands of Canada and Alaska. Following flooding, fish from large rivers and lakes make lateral migrations into wetlands to feed and breed. Wetlands also serve as a natural buffer between land and water by acting as a sponge for sediments and nutrients, holding back inflowing matter. Finally, wetlands are now valued for their intrinsic aesthetic value and as distinct ecosystems for research by limnologists and ecologists alike.

Loss of Wetlands

Wetlands that once occupied large areas of the temperate zone are a rapidly vanishing habitat. In the southeastern United States, swamps and marshes were once a major feature of the coastal plains (Fig. 18-2), but many have been altered or eliminated. Changes in a small section of one

of these marshes—a pocosin marsh in North Carolina—since the 1700s is shown in Figs. 18-3*a* and *b*. Now a productive farm area bordered with pine plantations, the original marsh survives only on the fringes of the ocean, among recreational cottages. Drainage ditches and subsurface tile drains, a process originated by the Dutch in the 1600s, became the standard procedure for drying out land for arable farming and grazing. Most wetlands were destroyed by this process of reclamation, which may seem inexplicable today, but in former times marshes were unpopular, even with some biologists! Linnaeus, the Swedish inventor of biological taxonomy in the sixteenth century, said of a local marsh, "Never could a priest describe hell worse than this." He

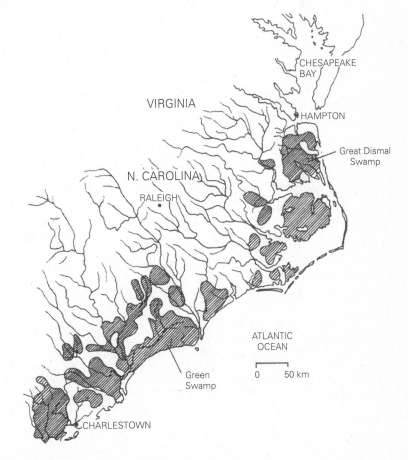

FIGURE 18-2 Wetlands in the southeastern United States. About half of the wetlands in the lower 48 states have been drained, almost all for agricultural use. Many of these, including the Great Dismal Swamp of Virginia, were familiar obstacles to the settlement of the early pilgrims, and many mature stands of large cypress trees were not logged until early in the twentieth century.

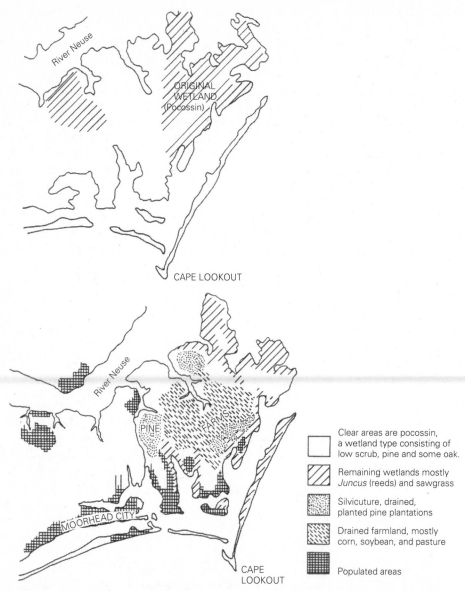

FIGURE 18-3 Changes in two types of wetland in North Carolina since 1700. Pocosin wetlands consist of low scrub, pine, and some oak and are less frequently flooded than the lower-lying wetland, which contains mostly reeds (*Juncus*) and sawgrass. (*a*) Original disposition of the wetlands based on early maps. (*b*) The situation in 1970, as determined by remote sensing. Note that the main pocosin stands have been replaced by drained farmland and pine plantations. Only the marginal marshes next to the sea remain. The area is a popular resort, with many summer homes scattered along the shores.

was probably referring to one aspect of the high productivity of seasonal wetlands—swarms of biting mosquitos and midges, not to be taken lightly. One of us recalls dispatching 50 mosquitos with a single swat in an Alaska tundra bog. Humans are not the only organisms affected. In summer, arctic caribou herds run for miles to immerse themselves in the Arctic Ocean and temporarily escape mosquito bites. At the other end of the world, one of the subtle pleasures of antarctic limnology is the absence of biting flying insects in summer in the small wetlands that dot the antarctic coast and islands.

In other cases wetlands were drained to eliminate disease, primarily malaria, yellow fever, and sleeping sickness. Drainage during the construction of the Panama Canal is a well-known example. In areas where large wetlands still remain, the resident human population is often at subsistence level, and both humans and animals are subject to insect-borne disease. Flood control is another reason for draining marshes, since the drag of the vegetation on the water reduces the current velocity and causes the waters to spread out and flood the surrounding land. An example of new flood control strategies conflicting is the Florida Everglades, the largest freshwater wetland in the United States, which consists of seasonal cypress swamps, emergent macrophyte marshes, and aquatic grasslands (Plate 5b). Earlier this century, flooding of farmland and small towns in the upstream northern drainage was reduced by the construction of flood control channels to divert water east to the Atlantic Ocean away from the former route south through the Everglades to the Gulf of Mexico. The entire region is now in dire straits because it lacks adequate freshwater flows.

Wetlands were most often drained for agriculture, because the rich organic peat deposits form the richest and deepest soils. In Africa, the lower Nile once was surrounded by vast areas of papyrus marsh, but after 5000 years of reclamation—since the time of Pharaohs—this useful plant is virtually extinct in Egypt. Further up-

stream, on the Upper Nile, lies a giant papyrus marsh called the Sudd. It is larger than the state of Maine and awaits only the cessation of a local war before it, too, will be partially drained for agriculture. In the United States, the Great Black Swamp, which guarded the southeastern inflow to Lake Erie, was drained and farmed in the 1800s (Fig. 18-4a). The fertile farms of eastern England were created 400 years ago by draining the great tidal marsh, The Wash (Fig. 18-4b), and the site where King John became bogged down and lost his crown jewels is now probably a potato field. Three crops a year can be raised in the 280,000 ha (700,000 acres) of the inland, tidal estuarine marsh comprising the Sacramento Delta in California. This region, with its giant 5-m-high tules (*Scirpus*) reeds, was drained and leveed less than 100 years ago.

Acidic peat bog soils make poor farmland, but the peat has many uses. For example, when dried, peat makes a passable slow-burning fuel. Peat is also an excellent plant bedding material. In Europe, many peat bogs have been dug up over the last few hundred years. Although this has resulted in the loss of the peat bogs they have often been replaced by shallow, often dystrophic lakes. Most of the lakes in the large area of southeastern England called the Norfolk Broads and lakes in northern Holland are flooded medieval peat diggings. The ancient *Sphagnum* bogs of Minnesota, Siberia, Scandinavia, and Ireland are major sources of peat for fuel and gardening.

The loss of many wetlands has prompted an environmental movement to preserve what remains and even to create new wetlands. The losses have been so extensive that some countries, such as The Netherlands, have essentially no bogs left. Concerned wetlands ecologists have spearheaded environmental groups, nicknamed *peatniks,* to preserve what is left in other regions, especially Ireland. A recent concept that has led to preservation, restoration, and creation of wetlands has been their use as pollution control systems. These can function for municipal wastewater, urban storm runoff, and agricultural

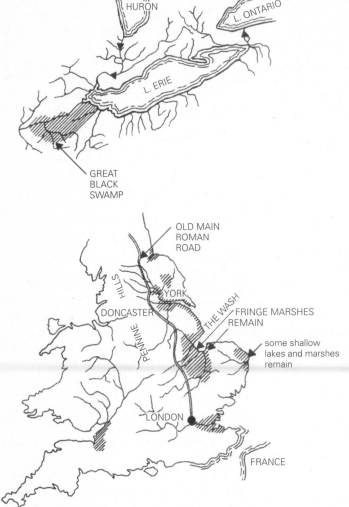

FIGURE 18-4 Losses of wetland habitat. (*a*) Former site (cross-hatched) of the Great Black Swamp, a very large swamp at the east of Lake Erie and drained for agriculture in the 1800s. It protected the lake from the direct inflow of part of the local watershed and would have reduced the loading of particulate-associated matter such as phosphate. (*b*) Decrease in wetlands in England since Roman times (approx. 60 to 400 A.D.). Hatched areas indicate the original areas of marsh. Note how the old Roman road had to skirt wetland to the east and hills to the west. These wetlands remained intact and a refuge for rebels after the Norman conquest (1066 A.D.) but were drained in the 1600s and now are now highly productive row crop farmlands. The tiny remnant marshes hug the coast of The Wash, a large bay in the southeast.

drainage. Knowledge of the types, structure, and function is essential for proper management of wetlands, whether for preservation or use in wastewater treatment.

MEASUREMENT

Sampling of wetlands usually employs a variety of methods originally developed for other aquatic and terrestrial systems. The main difficulty is getting representative samples in an environment that is spatially heterogeneous. Wetlands usually include several different habitat types, such as emergent plants, submergent plants, floating plants, benthos, trees, shrubs, and open water. Furthermore, there is spatial variability within each habitat. The best solution to such a patchy distribution is to employ stratified random sampling by dividing the wetland into zones of open water, submerged vegetation, emergent vegetation, and so on. Even so, it is difficult to be certain that one organism, such as a common midge larva, has not strayed in from another nearby habitat. Because collection and identification of invertebrates is time-consuming, it may be best to sort small, detritus-colored insect larvae while they are still alive and moving. To determine biomass, collection of both aboveground and below-ground parts of aquatic macrophytes is necessary. Although this is labor-intensive, it is important since about half of the biomass of cattails, for example, is found in the roots and bulky rhizomes.

Remote sensing is an ideal method to survey the larger plants and animals in wetlands, although submerged vegetation is less easily identified. Because wetland plants tend to form large stands of one species they may be mapped by standard color infrared aerial photography. It is essential to have sufficient ground truth for accurate calibration of remotely sensed images.

TYPES OF WETLANDS

Although no sharp dividing line exists between the types of animals and plants in wetlands and those in open waters or land, grouping organisms often aids in understanding their ecology. Here we use function and structure to group wetlands. The functional groups are *seasonal wetlands* and *permanent wetlands.* Structural groups, based on dominant type of vegetation, water source, and formation of peat, are *swamps, marshes, bogs,* and *fens.*

Seasonal and Permanent Wetlands

Seasonal wetlands dry out in most summers. This is essential for maintaining their astonishingly high productivity. It is more the presence of relatively short but very high peaks of usable productivity, rather than high total annual production, that makes seasonal wetlands so valuable for breeding birds, fish, amphibians, and insects. High rates of primary production occur in spring, when they are needed by young animals. This is particularly important for birds, which must obtain sufficient protein for egg white production

in the short period prior to laying. The seeds and winter vegetation that sustain birds through the winter are not an adequate source of high-quality protein for egg production.

Seasonal wetlands are typically found in unshaded open areas when low emergent and submergent plants combine with algae to make full use of the spring sunlight. Many aquatic animals are eaten in the wet season, with the survivors migrating to other habitats when the water dries up.

In temperate and tropical climates the shallow waters of seasonal wetlands are choked with aquatic plants. Some of this vegetation, especially the seeds, are available to aquatic creatures. Most plants, however, remain and decompose in the dry season to produce a rich particulate organic base for the next season's detritivores. In the decomposition process some inorganic nutrients are released to the soils; these are flushed out during the initial flooding. In all climates the most productive seasonal wetlands have submerged vegetation coated with thick layers of aufwuchs. This is composed of periphytonic algae, bacteria, and protozoans that are fed on by smaller insect larvae. These epifloral layers contain the major producers of usable primary production in many seasonal wetlands. The shallow water often overlies an abundant assemblage of benthic worms and insect larvae, although diversity is reduced by the anoxic conditions. In seasonal wetlands containing trees, such as the cypress or gum tree swamps of the southern United States, reduced light restricts the growth of aquatic plants. These wetlands are less productive because much fixed carbon is held in tree trunks and branches.

Permanent Wetlands

Permanent wetlands form the ecotone or transitional zone between land and water. They are generally less productive than seasonal wetlands, and some are very unproductive. Sediment decomposition and nutrient recycling is slowed by the small amount of available oxygen, and if conditions are acidic peat deposits accumulate. Permanent wetlands in temperate and tropical climates are generally dense stands of a few species of reeds, grasses, or specially adapted trees. In cool, wet, alpine, or polar climates higher plants are generally scarce and the wetland is composed of infertile and acidic peat bogs of *Sphagnum* and other moss species.

Marshes, Swamps, Bogs, and Fens

Structural classification of wetlands is based on three dominant features: presence of dominant plants, amount of peat, and source of water. Although these are adequate descriptions, their application in the field is sometimes complicated by different uses of the same terms (Table 18-1). In this text we use *marshes, swamps, bogs, and fens* (Plates 5a, 5b, and 6a). *Marshes* (Fig. 18-5) are dominated by emergent aquatic macrophytes, such as reeds and sedges, and have submerged or floating macrophytes, such as pondweeds and waterlilies. A major distinguishing feature of marshes is the absence of trees and shrubs. Marshes often accumulate peat and have an external source of water, such as overflow from streams and rivers or ground water (Table 18-2). *Swamps* (Fig. 18-6) do contain large trees and shrubs, but a variety of aquatic macrophytes grow in the more open sunlit areas. Swamps generally accumulate little peat and, like marshes, usually have an external source of water. *Bogs* (Fig. 18-7) accumulate peat and are dominated by acidophilic mosses and sedges. They have few or no trees or aquatic macrophytes. Bogs have little or no external water inflow and are dependent on a high water table replenished by rainwater. Bogs are also given local names, such as *muskeg* in Canada and Alaska and *moors, mosses,* and *mires* in Europe. *Fens* have some characteristic of both bogs and marshes. They are distinguished by a mineral-rich groundwater source and a more alkaline (higher) pH than bogs.

The two sets of classifications—seasonal and

TABLE 18-1

SUMMARY OF THE FEATURES OF MARSHES, SWAMPS, BOGS, AND FENS

Almost all wetlands are slightly acidic due to the anoxia of flooded soils. As well as direct river inflow, marshes and swamps may receive water from river overflows during floods and from ground water. These terms are a simplification of the wide and historical literature on wetlands, and some European classifications may not fit exactly to the terms listed here.

Name	Typical emergent (submerged) macrophytes	pH	Water source	Organic matter (peat)
Marsh	Cattails, reeds, tules (water lilies, pondweeds)	5.1–7.0	River	Yes
Swamp	Cypress, tupelo (water lilies)	3.0–7.0	River	Little
Bog	*Sphagnum* (none)	3.6–4.7	Rain	Lots
Fen	Mosses, sedges (cottongrass, willowswater)	5.1–7.6	Ground	Yes

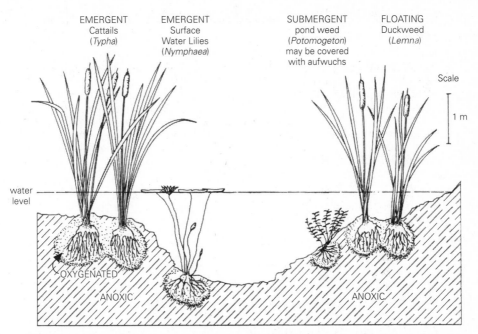

FIGURE 18-5 Cross section of a marsh. Marshes are characterized by emergent and/or submergent macrophytes, with an attached microbial community (aufwuchs). Trees are absent. Note that the soils and sediments are anoxic except for the small zone around the root hairs. Where there is sufficient light, the stems and leaves of submerged macrophytes provide surfaces for the attachment of nutritious aufwuchs, which is grazed by insect larvae, shrimp, and snails. When eutrophication of marshes occurs, the overgrowth of periphyton can shade and eventually kill submerged higher plants, to the detriment of small zooplankton and fish that use the plants as a refuge from predation (Chap. 20). Compared with other wetlands, the vertical profile of a marsh is moderate (see scale), and large variations in water level are not common.

permanent wetlands; marshes, swamps, bogs, and fens—can be combined to describe almost all existing wetlands. For example, the flooded rain forest or varsia of the Amazon and much of the Florida Everglades are seasonal swamps. The vast blanket bogs of Minnesota are permanent bogs. The small vernal pools found in many regions are seasonal marshes. The huge papyrus growths on the Nile and similar tropical rivers are permanent marshes. The reed and sedge growths that fringe many lakes and ponds are also permanent marshes. The extensive stands of cypress trees in the southeastern United States (Fig. 18-2) are seasonal swamps in at least some

years, since the seeds of these trees require dry conditions for germination.

STRUCTURE OF WETLANDS

The essence of a wetland is shallow water: wetlands form in shallow topographic depressions and lakes and ponds occupy the deeper ones. A very shallow water column allows ready access of oxygen to the sediments, where heterotrophic, oxygen-demanding processes often dominate over oxygen-producing, photosynthetic ones. Shallow water also permits even short-legged birds to reach benthic prey. Emergent aquatic

TABLE 18-2

NUTRIENTS AND ORGANIC MATTER IN WETLANDS

Hydraulic residence time indicates the flow of nutrients as well as water through the system and is roughly related to the fertility of the wetland. However, the main instantaneous source of nutrients is the sediments, which are much more similar in nutrients between wetland types than are inflows. The wide range of the productivity to biomass (P:B ratio) is due to the death and decay of most marsh plants each year rather than a very large difference in primary production (Table 18-3). Marsh plants thus have a low biomass relative to the long-lived trees in swamps that give a high, almost constant biomass. Swamps do not accumulate much peat, while in bogs almost all organic matter is retained as acid peat.

Name	Hydraulic residence time (days)	Ca^{2+}, mEq liter^{-1}	% Org matter (peat)	Soil N, g m^{-2}	P:B ratio
Marsh	4	6–13,000	39–75	1340	1.2
Swamp	0.4	—	Small	1300	0.07
Bog	70	13–160	90–100	500	0.1
Fen	5	200–500	10–95	—	—

Modified from Mitsch and Gosselink (1993).

plants generally require only a few centimeters of water and most submergent ones can survive only a couple of meters of immersion. Bottomland swamps, such as the cypress forests of the Mississippi, flood only to a depth of 30 cm to 1 m (Fig. 18-6). Germination requires that light reach the sediments, thus wetland vegetation is effectively confined to shallow water.

The three-dimensional structure of a marsh is determined by the presence or absence of large aquatic plants, whether emergent or submergent. The submerged stems and leaves of large macrophytes provide an extensive surface in the otherwise featureless mixed water layer (Fig. 18-5). The increased productivity of wetlands relative to lakes (Table 18-3) is partially due to these additional solid surfaces. In the temperate marsh, shallow water with dense clumps of tall cattails (*Typha*) or common reed (*Phragmites*) are interspersed with patches of deeper open water. The shallow margins of the pools may be fringed with bulrushes (*Scirpus*). The shallow open water is often filled with water lilies or submerged macrophytes such as the pondweed, *Potomoge-*

ton. This provides well-illuminated surfaces for aufwuchs growth. The macrophytes themselves are often of little direct food value, and grazing snails, shrimp, and small fish depend on the attached microbes for sustenance. Without the surfaces provided by the stems and leaves of macrophytes, the system is more a pond or small lake than a true wetland. Unlike in lakes, phytoplankton are not the main primary autochthonous producers of most wetlands. Their place is taken by the macrophytes themselves and periphyton such as mobile pennate diatoms and large green and blue-green algae.

Along with direct consumption of living macrophytes and algae, the other main pathway for autochthonous production in wetlands is the detrital food chain. Dead parts of stems and leaves of wetland plants fall to the sediments. Here detritus may accumulate as peat, be swept away by floods, or be shredded and decomposed and enter the detrital food chain. In the former two cases, in situ decomposition is low and the detritus pathway is not dominant. The detritus pathway dominates the metabolism of the sediments; if

A SWAMP (Cypress, Willow)

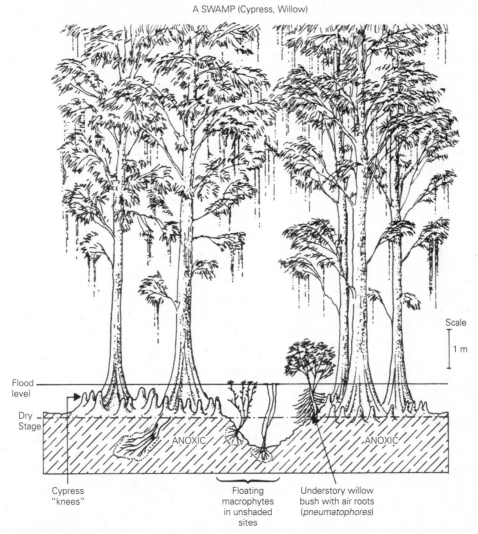

Scale

1 m

Flood level

Dry Stage

ANOXIC   ANOXIC

Cypress "knees"

Floating macrophytes in unshaded sites

Understory willow bush with air roots (*pneumatophores*)

FIGURE 18-6 Cross section of a cypress-willow swamp with lichen (Spanish moss) hanging from the branches. Swamps are characterized by the presence of trees and shrubs. Emergent and/or submergent macrophytes are mostly confined to sunlit areas. As with marshes, the soils and sediments are anoxic except for the small zone around the root hairs of macrophytes. The "knees" of the cypress trees are not a major source of root oxygen. In contrast, the pneumatophores (adventitious roots) are an oxygen source for willow, tupelo, and some other types of swamp trees during flood periods. In estuaries, mangrove trees use adventitious roots at high tide (Chap. 19). Compared with other wetlands, swamps have a high vertical profile that enables parts of them to remain above water even when flood waters rise over 1 m (see scale).

A BOG

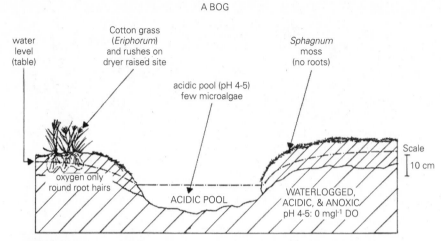

FIGURE 18-7   Cross section of a *Sphagnum* bog. This moss, and the peat it lays down, dominate most bogs—along with a few other acid-tolerant mosses such as *Polytrichum commune.* More rarely, higher acid-tolerant plants such as cranberry are dominant. The water table is actually raised a few centimeters above the soil surface by the capillary action of the dead lower moss accumulation. Open water is represented only by small yellow-brown pools rich in humic acids. Only a few species of algae and invertebrates can tolerate the acid conditions. On slightly better drained hummocks, a few higher plants, such as the pretty cotton grass or rushes, can find a roothold in the anoxic waterlogged ground. Compared with other wetlands, bogs have a small vertical profile (see scale) and are never covered by standing or running water, as are swamps or marshes.

algae are few the entire wetland may be considered a detritus-based system. Many well-shaded wetlands, such as dense swamps and thick reed beds, are almost totally detritus-based. Where storm flows carry large amounts of allochthonous dead leaves and other organic matter, it may be trapped and processed in the wetland.

Wetlands often exist without stands of large macrophytes if the water is very shallow, very acidic, or temporary. The water may, in fact, be completely filled with small plants. For example, a peat bog consists almost entirely of living and dead *Sphagnum* moss, with open water confined to depressions (Fig. 18-7). A few acidophilic plants, such as cotton grass (*Eriophorum*), cranberry (*Vaccinium*), or the carnivorous pitcher plant (*Darwintonia*), grow rooted in the spongy moss where the ground rises a few centimeters, enabling their roots to develop.

Ephemeral pools exist in many places and, as their name suggests, have brief aquatic lives of a few weeks to months. They may be 5 to 10 cm deep, and photosynthetic organisms are represented only by attached algae (Fig. 18-8). The small volume of water is well heated daily, and a few species of insect larvae can feed on the algae, microbes, and ostracods growing rapidly at the high temperatures.

Vernal pools (from *ver,* the Latin for "spring") are favorite sites for spring field trips by biology classes. These seasonal wetlands have some characteristics of ephemeral pools but persist longer. Algae are often outcompeted by a few species of rapidly growing submergent and emergent macrophytes (Fig. 18-8). A restricted zooplankton fauna consisting of protozoans, rotifers, freshwater fairy shrimps, and chydorids can complete their development in the short time

TABLE 18-3

PRIMARY PRODUCTION IN WETLANDS

A wide range of trophic states is found in wetlands. In general, the order of productivity is marshes > swamps > bogs and fens (fens are nonacid peatlands with a supply of mineral-rich ground water). As in lakes, increases in nutrient supply in any wetlands increases the primary production. In addition, the length of the hydroperiod, especially the provision of a dry period that allows oxygenated recycling of nutrients, usually results in a more productive system. Thus productivity in seasonal wetlands > permanent wetlands in most cases.

Wetland type	Net primary production, g dw m^{-2} y^{-1}	Biomass present, g dw m^{-2} y^{-1}	N loading, g m^{-2} y^{-1}	P loading, g m^{-2} y^{-1}	Mineral cycle	Flood period
Freshwater marsh						
Average	2,000	46	22		Closed	Long
Eutrophic						
Fringe reeds	6,000	—	—	—	Open	Short
Nutrient-polluted seasonal	22,000	20	600	120	Inflow	
Oligotrophic (prairie pothole)	1,000	——	—	—	Open Closed	Long
Freshwater swamp						
Average	870	52	900	—	Open	Variable
Eutrophic seasonal (nutrient-rich)	1,750	—	—	—	Seasonal	
Oligotrophic (continuous flooding)	250	—	—	—	No	Long
Freshwater bog						
Average	560	53	0.8	—	Closed	Long
Eutrophic (nutrient-rich)	1,900	—	—	10	Closed	Long
Oligotrophic	100	3	—	0.1	Closed	Long
Freshwater fen						
Average		—	—	—	Closed	
Eutrophic	340	—	—	—	Closed	Long
Oligotrophic	—	—	—	—	Closed	Long

Modified and expanded from Mitsch and Gosselink (1993).

available. They often become superabundant, primarily due to the lack of fish predators and aquatic competitors. In the benthos, dense populations of insect larvae, including large predatory species such as tabanid horsefly larvae, provide a feast for small wading birds. Often vernal pools are home to rare and endangered plants and animals, including lilies and newts. For most of the year, vernal pools are dry and appear very similar to a terrestrial meadow. Vernal pools are becoming endangered habitats, as these flat areas are favorite sites for summer homes and other developments (Fig. 18-8).

THE LACUNAE SYSTEM

One characteristic of wetlands is that the soil is permanently or temporarily saturated with water.

FIGURE 18-8 A vernal pool. This seasonal mountain wetland emerges from the snow in spring and dries up within a few weeks or months—too short a time for large aquatic macrophytes to grow. Fast-growing aquatic grasses thrive in the shallow water and add to primary production from algae. Organic detritus from the previous dry period is also used. Only in the wetter years do frog tadpoles have time to pass through their aquatic stage before the water evaporates. For much of the rainless summer the ground is bone dry and the above-ground plants die back.

The ecologically significant feature of saturated soils is the rapid onset of soil anoxia following flooding (Figs. 18-5 to 18-7). Water contains little oxygen relative to that in a similar volume of air, so decomposing aquatic plants soon deplete the dissolved oxygen supply (Chap. 7). The lack of oxygen, in turn, prevents the invasion of the wetland by most higher plants, especially trees, since few tree roots can survive anoxic soils.

If rooted plants are to grow in waterlogged anoxic soils they must be able to supply oxygen to the roots. The adaptations of higher plants to saturated soils include pressurization of the interior spaces (the *lacunae*) of stems and roots. The design of the lacunae system is different for each species, but the common feature is that lacunae occupy most of the space in the leaves and stems in both submergent and emergent forms (Fig. 18-9). To prevent waterlogging if the plants are damaged by grazing or abrasion, watertight diaphragms at intervals along the lacunae act as bulkheads. The gas-filled lacunae also give buoyancy and hold the plant near the surface light.

In emergent or floating plants, pressure in the

FIGURE 18-9 The internal lacunae (or aerenchyma) of submerged aquatic plants, which occupy much more space (up to 60 percent) than any gas-filled spaces in terrestrial plants (about 5 percent). Submerged aquatic plants have little need for the supporting lignin and cellulose structures that comprise the bulk of the stems and leaves of land plants. During photosynthesis the interconnected lacunae permit oxygen to diffuse down to the root hairs. The buoyancy imparted by the gas also helps the plant to float. (*a*) Cross section of a petiole (flower stem) of the water lily *Nymphaea*. (*b*) Cross section of the midrib of a leaf of the common submerged pondweed *Potomogeton*. (*c*) Cross section of a leaf of *Zostera*, a common estuarine "sea grass." Shaded area indicates photosynthetic tissue; dark central region, the xylem and phloem that carries inorganic nutrients from roots to leaves. Modified from Sculthorpe (1967).

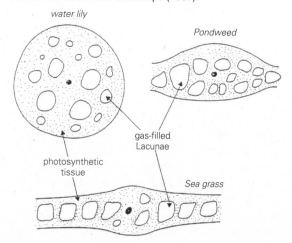

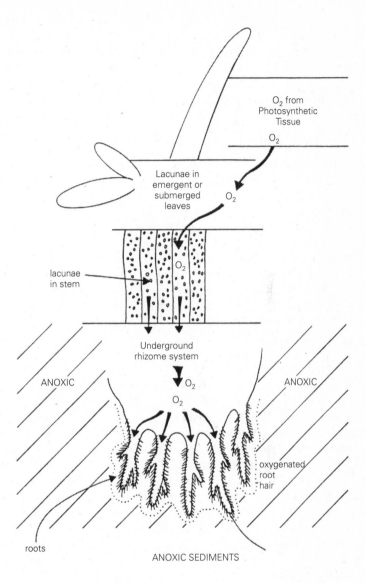

O₂ from
Photosynthetic
Tissue

O₂

Lacunae in
emergent or
submerged
leaves

O₂

lacunae
in stem

O₂

Underground
rhizome system

ANOXIC

O₂

ANOXIC

O₂

oxygenated
root
hair

roots

ANOXIC SEDIMENTS

FIGURE 18-10 The functioning of the lacunae system, which transfers oxygen down from the leaves to the root hairs in wetland plants. The system is found in submerged and emergent plants and distinguishes true wetland higher plants. Small mosses and algae lack true roots, and *Sphagnum* moss characterizes peat bogs. The gas pressure in the leaf may exceed 1.2 atm and contain over 50 percent oxygen. Oxygen is vital if the root hairs are to remain alive and take up nutrients from the soil water, since most higher plants cannot remove nutrients at the low concentrations found in open water.

lacunae is generated by sunlight heating leaves and oxygen produced as a byproduct of photosynthesis. As a result of the higher pressure, oxygen diffuses down the pressure gradient to the root hairs via the interconnected leaves and stems (Fig. 18-10). Root hairs need the energy derived from oxygenated respiration to carry out the process of active transport and uptake of nutrients against a concentration gradient in the soil. Gas pressures of 1.2 atm have been recorded inside the lacunae of *Egeria* (Brazilian elodea) during periods of active photosynthesis (Angelstein, 1911). Not all the interior gas is oxygen, which ranges from as little as 7 percent to as much as 30 to 55 percent by volume.

The importance of lacunae is demonstrated by the restricted habitat available for plants that do not possess these structures. Wetland plants are common in still waters, but most members of one group of aquatic plants, the Podostemacea, are restricted to highly oxygenated, fast-flowing water. These submerged plants have no lacunae and die if the water around them becomes stagnant, as sometimes occurs in droughts.

Because the water supports most of the weight of the plant, the strong and bulky lignin and cellulose support structures of terrestrial plants are not needed in submerged plants. They are still essential in above-ground stems and leaves in wetland plants, such as cattails or *Phragmites* reeds. These tougher stems of emergent aquatic macrophytes are filled with lacunae to oxygenate the roots. The air in the lacunae makes the stems buoyant, and they have been used for millennia to construct rafts and small boats, in Lake Titicaca and the River Nile. They were used by the Pomo Indians of Clear Lake, California up to 1900.

The large trees characteristic of swamps do not have a lacunae system. The root system thus functions only in the dry periods in seasonal wetlands; under flooded conditions the root hairs switch to the less efficient anoxic respiration. The low efficiency reduces annual productivity, but that may be unimportant as competition from other trees is prevented by the waterlogged soils. In species that dominate freshwater and estuaries swamps (cypress, tupelo, willow, mangrove), *pneumatophores* (adventitious or air roots; Fig. 18-6) grow out from the trunk near the water line, where they have access to well-oxygenated water. These small, delicate roots cannot survive continued desiccation in the dry season or abrasion by debris in floods, but they easily regrow.

Most smaller aquatic plants have shallow root systems that extend only a few centimeters into the mud. This reduces the distance over which any gases must be transported, and this region is the first to be oxygenated in dry periods. Floating species such as duckweed (*Lemna*), water hyacinth (*Eichhornia*), and water fern (*Azolla*) are not dependent on soils at all. They obtain oxygen as well as nutrients directly from the water using

their smaller roots, which cannot penetrate the soil. When stranded on the shore these species usually die; in fact, stranding is one of the most successful and least environmentally damaging control methods for moderate infestations of floating weeds in reservoirs.

NUTRIENT FLUXES IN WETLANDS

Nutrients can increase, decrease, or be transformed as they pass through a wetland. In general, wetlands act as *sinks* or accumulators for silt particles and soluble inorganic nutrients but *sources* for dissolved and particulate organic matter. Suspended silt is deposited in wetlands because the current is slowed by vegetation blocking the path of direct water flow. In time, silt is incorporated into the root zone. Nutrients present in the silt are used by roots of higher plants, but almost none can take up significant amounts of soluble nutrients via the leaves. Declines in soluble nutrients from open water are attributable to uptake by attached algae growing on leaves and stems of submerged plants and by the roots of floating plants, such as water hyacinth and duckweed. If conditions favor phytoplankton growth they will remove nutrients, although phytoplankton is not characteristic of many wetlands. Floating macrophytes that remove nutrients via their roots are confined to more eutrophic waters.

Wetlands act as chemical transformers. *The dominant effect of wetlands is to transform substances from inorganic nutrients to soluble and particulate organic compounds.* Inflowing nitrate and ammonia, as well as soluble phosphates, are taken up by the vegetation and transformed into microbial or plant matter. During growth, and especially after death and decay, soluble organic compounds containing nitrogen and phosphorus are released and flow downstream during high water when the hydraulic head permits discharge. The amount of material transformed by wetlands varies considerably. In large winter floods most water simply passes unchanged over the top of the dormant vegetation. In a small summer flood most of the water may remain in the wetland for weeks and may be highly modified by the time it exits. The hydraulic residence time of wetlands is intermediate between that of small lakes (months-years) and that of streams and rivers (minutes-hours). The relationship of water residence time to other factors is shown in Table 18-2.

In acidic bogs there is little input of nutrients, and these are rapidly stripped for plant growth. The filaments of *Sphagnum* in particular act as an ion-exchange resin, and basic ions such as calcium replace hydrogen in the matrix. The resulting water released downslope is acidic because it contains excess hydrogen ions and lacks balancing basic ions. Bog discharges are characterized by a low pH and the yellow-brown peaty stain of lignins, tannic and humic acids.

Inflowing nutrients from rain, rivers, or ground water usually supply only a small part of the annual supply of nitrogen and phosphorus used by the higher plants. Bacterial decomposition of the peat supplies the rest and is most important for nitrogen and sulfur compounds. Both nitrogen and sulfur may be entirely lost from wetlands systems by denitrification to N_2 or H_2S gases (Chaps. 8, 10). These processes are also important in the global recycling of nitrogen and sulfur and are a main mechanism for reducing the eutrophication potential of waters that flow to lakes via wetlands (see below). Phosphorus, nitrogen, iron, and silica may also be trapped as insoluble compounds or as peat. However, the efficiency of denitrification in natural wetlands is not known, partially due to technical difficulties. Phosphorus removal in wetlands is also not well understood; since phosphorus cannot be lost in a gaseous phase, its uptake and storage may depend on the types of plant present.

In contrast to the usual role of wetlands as a sink for soluble nutrients, very large swamps may decompose organic matter brought into the system by the river. For example, as the Nile flows through the vast papyrus swamps of the Sudd it becomes richer in phosphate and ammonia (Talling, 1957). Release of soluble iron is also favored by the acidic conditions in tropical wetlands. Even though tropical soils are slightly alkaline, the peat deposits of tropical swamps are acidic, anoxic, and harbor-dense microbial communities in the upper sediments. This promotes the release of soluble inorganic nutrients, especially iron and ammonia (Fig. 10-5).

Cypress trees and reeds are the dominant vegetation in many swamps and marshes and often shade the water surface to such a degree that growth of algae and floating and submerged aquatic plants is limited. A study of the shaded river wetlands in the Appalachicola River in Florida showed that, although there is some net loss, most of the nutrients which enter the wetlands also pass through (Elder, 1985). In contrast, in open wetlands where nutrient supplies are high and sunlight can reach the water, attached algae can strip out large amounts of the incoming nutrients. Because algae can double their population in only a few days, the inflowing nutrients can be rapidly incorporated into the food chain.

PRODUCTIVITY IN WETLANDS

Although generally considered to be rich ecosystems, wetlands are not always very productive. Some nutrient-rich seasonal wetlands are among the most productive systems on earth, but acid bogs are aquatic deserts (Table 18-3). The major differences between productive and unproductive wetlands are the nutrient supply and the existence of a wet-dry cycle. Although the freshwater marshes can be ranked by average primary production in the order (1) seasonal > permanent or (2) marshes > swamps > fens > bogs, there is considerable overlap in these classifications. Primarily due to the energy subsidy provided by the tide and the influence of the ocean, tropical mangrove swamps and their temperate equivalents, the coastal salt marshes, have a higher primary production (Chap. 19). Production in the river flood plain or riparian zone (Chap. 17) is intermediate between freshwater swamps and freshwater marshes.

As would be expected, in wetlands such as swamps and marshes primary production is generally higher when more nutrients are available. Usually the limiting nutrients are nitrogen in swamps and marshes and phosphorus in bogs. However, as in many lakes, it is likely that the nutrient actually limiting production will vary, with both nitrogen and phosphorus playing limiting roles during different seasons. In addition, some of the more common terrestrial limiting nutrients, such as potassium, are more important for higher plants. Algae do not require potassium in nearly such large amounts as do higher plants.

Marshes occupy the most eutrophic end of the wetlands productivity spectrum. If the below-ground parts of some emergent macrophytes are taken into account, the productivity of freshwater marshes is very high. A rough average for freshwater marshes is 2000 g dw m^{-2} y^{-1} (approx. 1000 g carbon m^{-2} y^{-1}; Table 18-3), much more than that of a typical lake and about the same as the primary production of most eutrophic lakes. The fringe reed marshes of some artificial fish ponds are reported to reach 6000 g dw m^{-2} y^{-1}, which is similar to that of heavily fertilized farm crops. This figure includes the extensive and usually unavailable below-ground rhizomes and roots of plants such as cattails and *Phragmites.* Because the above-ground parts of plants in a marsh die each winter, the productivity to biomass ratio (P:B) is quite high (1.2; Table 18-2).

Kesterson Marsh is an extreme example of a wetland made very eutrophic by nutrient additions. The agricultural drainage that supplied all the water for this marsh contained about 100 mg $liter^{-1}$ NO_3 and 20 mg $liter^{-1}$ PO_4, 100 to 1000 times more than that found even in flooding rivers. Fertilization produced enormous growths of algae of two kinds—the macrophyte algae *Chara,* which grows to over 1 m high, and the periphyton algae that grew on it. Emergent plant biomass was similar to that of other marshes,

since only one crop per year is possible. Under these superenriched conditions, primary production was estimated to be about 10 times more than that of the average marsh (Table 18-3). In contrast, prairie pothole lakes, which receive only relatively low concentrations of nutrients from a small watershed, may be 50 percent less productive than the average marsh. It should be remembered, however, that high primary production does not always lead to high secondary or tertiary production.

The average primary production of swamps is 870 g dw (dry weight) m^{-2} y^{-1}, about half that of marshes (Table 18-3). This is still enough for swamps to be considered rich ecosystems, as their valuable large timber stands attest. The large long-lived trees represent a large biomass component relative to marshes, and even though the productivity of the two differs by only a factor of 2 to 3 the P:B ratio is very low for swamps (0.07; Table 18-2). Swamps respond to inflow from a nutrient-enriched river with increases in the overall growth rate of trees. In the southern United States, addition of sewage resulted in a doubling of primary production from about 1000 g dw m^{-2} y^{-1} between similar cypress swamp domes (Brown, 1981). Phosphorus loading was about 10 g dw m^{-2} y^{-1}, compared with approximately 0.5 g dw m^{-2} y^{-1} in more unpolluted cypress swamps. In more hydraulically isolated swamps, phosphorus loadings of about 0.1 g dw m^{-2} y^{-1} produced only a low biomass production of 500 g dw m^{-2} y^{-1}. Similar but lesser effects could be expected from the more normal fluctuations in the nutrient supply from the watershed rivers.

Bogs and fens are at the unproductive end of the trophic spectrum of wetlands. Since low-nutrient rainwater is the main water source in bogs, productivity is low. Because most bacteria do not function well under acidic conditions, recycling is limited by the acidity of the peaty substrate. For example, decomposition removed only 5 to 10 percent of the surface plant matter from the upper layers of a *Sphagnum* bog in southern England (Clymo, 1965). In terms of decomposition, the half-life of leaves and stems of small higher plants in a Michigan bog was 1.5 to 8.4 years (Chamie and Richardson, 1978). Thus in contrast with lakes, which efficiently recycle nutrients in the mixed layer, little of the deposited organic matter is recycled in a newly formed or expanding bog. The P:B ratio in bogs is low (0.1; Table 18-2), mainly due to the low productivity, because biomass is high. There is a large amount of peat in many wetlands and *Sphagnum* does not die each winter. The most impoverished bogs are known as raised bogs, because their growth pattern elevates the mosses above the water table. In this position they receive only rain falling directly onto them and cannot reach down to the slightly richer water in contact with the soil or decaying plant fragments. In these raised bogs as little as 100 g dw m^{-2} y^{-1} (approx. 50 g carbon m^{-2} y^{-1}) is produced.

Fens are relatively rich in minerals supplied by ground water, but this source is not a good supply for all the nutrients needed for plant growth. The ground water is usually hard (rich in Ca, Mg, and carbonate; Chaps. 10, 20) but often low in nitrate and phosphate. Thus primary production is somewhat less than that in swamps and marshes (Table 18-3).

The effect of drying on wetlands is the other factor that increases productivity. As for large river flood plains (Chap. 17), seasonally wet habitats tend to be more productive than permanent ones with the same nutrient supply, since recycling of nutrients is more efficient when oxygen can occasionally penetrate the sediments. This is illustrated in the case of cypress swamps, which range from permanently flooded to seasonally flooded to drained areas. Seasonally flooded swamps are more productive than similar swamps with other hydroperiods (Fig. 18-11).

Increased production is correlated with the evolution of communities adapted to each *hydroperiod*. Hardwoods and cypress or tupelo (gum tree) dominate the seasonal wetlands. In the permanently flooded areas pure swamp cypress

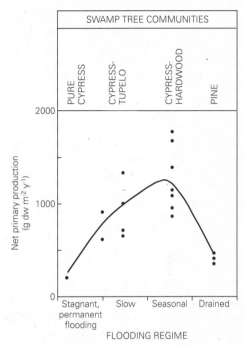

FIGURE 18-11 Effect of seasonal or occasional drying on productivity in swamps. The stagnant, permanent water of the pure cypress swamps reduces primary production to about 20 percent of that found in seasonal swamps with similar hardwood trees. The inefficiency of anoxic respiration in the roots is the main cause of the differences, since the oxygen transfer system to the roots cannot supply as much oxygen as would diffuse through dry soil. Note that unnaturally drained swamps are also relatively unproductive. Modified from Mitsch and Ewel (1979) and Canner and Day (1982).

flourishes, and in the drier regions pines are more common.

The abundance of the most common organisms at all trophic levels in Kesterson Marsh is shown in Table 18-4. This marsh, which was a permanent wetland at this time, consisted of pools of water filled with the macroalgae *Chara* and its associated aufwuchs separated by dense stands of tall cattails and shorter clumps of alkali bulrush. In the shallow water where it grows in monoculture, cattails were by far the best producers of biomass (over 8 kg m^{-2}). The shallower, almost dry areas contained pure stands of alkali bulrush, but this smaller plant contributed less biomass (about 1.5 kg m^{-2}). In the submergent habitat the *Chara* and aufwuchs each contributed about the same amount of biomass as the alkali bulrush.

The secondary production of some marshes can be very high. For example, some of the 17 common aquatic animals in Kesterson Marsh were extremely abundant (Table 18-4). Over 7000 chironomid midge larvae were present in 1 m^2 of submerged vegetation, and twice as many were sometimes found in the benthic ooze. In terms of the larger predators, almost 100 dragonfly larvae m^{-2} were found in the dense and fertile matrix formed by the submerged vegetation.

Cattails are not a very good habitat for the aquatic stages of insects, and most of the aquatic insect biomass lived in the submerged epifaunal habitat of the *Chara* or in the benthos. Nevertheless, in comparison to the plant biomass, that of the aquatic insects was very small—less than 20 g m^{-2}, or only about 0.2 percent of the total plant biomass. Most of the plant biomass was destined to become peat. Since this marsh was well supplied with nutrients and a productive water bird habitat, the inefficiencies of permanent wetlands as producers of secondary and tertiary trophic levels are evident. In a eutrophic lake the biomass ratio of animals to plants might be as high as 30 to 40 percent, with the phytoplankton continually being grazed at high rates (Chap. 15). Where Kesterson Marsh dried out in summer and the dead matter was decomposed, however, the ratio of plant biomass, mostly attached algae, and herbivorous animals was similar to that of a lake.

PRIMARY PRODUCTION OF WETLANDS VERSUS LAKES

Wetlands have some characteristics of terrestrial vegetation, which is more productive in general than aquatic vegetation. Even though a raised bog has an extremely low production value for wetlands, it is much greater than that of oligotrophic lakes. For example, annual production of a raised bog is similar to that of mesotrophic subalpine Castle Lake, California (40 to 50 g C m^{-2} y^{-1}), and the midwestern hard-water lake Lawrence Lake, Michigan (29 to 45 g C m^{-2} y^{-1}; Wetzel, 1983). The reason is that most lakes are extremely dilute solutions of well-mixed water where even phytoplankton exist more due to lack of competition than to adaptation to the planktonic environment. In addition, the light regime in water is less suitable for maximal growth than that in wetland or terrestrial systems (Tilzer, 1990). This is well illustrated by considering the total global primary production. The most extensive aquatic habitat on earth is the open ocean, which covers 71 percent of the earth's surface but contributes only 30 to 50 percent of primary production (Parsons et al., 1984).

Natural rainwater is almost always low in nutrients compared with river or ground water, so wetlands such as bogs that are dependent on rain are unproductive (Table 18-3). However, in many areas rainwater is increasingly contaminated with nitrogen and sulfates from the combustion of fossil fuels (Chap. 6). Rain also may contain dust particles blown from dry soils cleared of protecting vegetation for agriculture. In these cases, the productivity of the bog may rise and changes in species composition analogous to those in lakes during eutrophication may occur.

FOOD CHAINS

The detritus pathway is considered the most common route for organic matter transfer in wetlands (Mitsch and Gosselink, 1993). Detritus is discussed earlier in this chapter and detritus-based food webs are discussed in Chap. 16. Most nonalgal organic production in marshes, swamps, and bogs is not edible until processed by a whole host of insects and microbes. In this regard the wetlands food web is similar to that of a stream.

TABLE 18-4

HIGHEST MONTHLY AVERAGE NUMBERS AND EQUIVALENT BIOMASS FOR COMMON ORGANISMS IN A 50-ha (100-acre) SECTION OF KESTERSON MARSH, A VERY EUTROPHIC CALIFORNIAN CATTAIL-ALGAE WETLAND IN 1986–8

Ranking by numbers. This combination of biota will not occur at the same time since plants are most abundant in summer and die in winter, while many insects are most abundant in winter since they form aerial stages to mate in summer and also avoid the more extreme conditions of seasonal marshes. Aufwuchs consisted of diatoms, microbes, and small animals such as nematodes and rotifers. The common names for some of these organisms are: *Chara,* skunkweed or stonewort; chironomid, midge; Tabanid, horsefly; ephydrid, brinefly; Corixid, water boatman; nymphs and adults combined; Ephemeroptera, mayfly; stratiomid, flowerfly; Syrphid, rat-tailed maggot; Ceratopogonid, biting midge; Dytiscid, diving beetle; *Berosus* and Hydrophylid, water beetles. Very large flocks of blackbirds roosted and nested in the cattails but fed mostly in nearby pastures and only a few emerging insects were taken. lar = larvae, ad = adult.

Taxon	Biomass, g dry wt m^{-2}	Numbers, no. m^{-2}	Food habits
Emergent habitat			
Cattail	8570	—	Emergent macrophyte
Alkali bulrush	1920	—	Emergent macrophyte
Tricolored blackbird		0.02	Insects from fields
Redwing blackbird	—	0.2	Insects from pasture
Marsh harrier		0.000004	Predator on birds/mammals
Submergent habitat			
Chara	1592	—	Submerged macroalgae
Aufwuchs	1657	—	Microalgae-microbe mix
Submerged epifaunal habitat			
Chironomid larvae	0.95	7141	Aufwuchs grazers
Ceratopogonid larvae	0.01	2987	Predators/engulfers
Dytiscid larvae	0.83	1584	Piercing predators
Ephydrid larvae	0.5	810	Grazer on aufwuchs
Damselfly nymphs	2.81	220	Predators on chironomids
Dytiscid adults	0.31	208	Piercing predators
Berosus larvae	0.82	197	Piercing herbivores
Syrphid larvae	2.15	144	Detritus collectors
Hydrophylid ad	0.39	101	Grazers/collectors
Dragonfly nymphs	0.37	91	Predators on chironomids
Corixids	0.11	91	Herbivores
Hydrophilid larvae	0.07	64	Predators
Tabanid larvae	0.69	59	Piercing predator
Ephemeroptera larvae	0.01	11	Grazers
Stratiomyid larvae	0.13	5	Collectors/gatherers
Berosus adults	0.03	5	Collector/gatherers
Benthic habitat			
Chironomid larvae	7.08	15,356	Grazers on aufwuchs

Data from Horne and Roth (1989).

In spite of the high primary production of many wetlands, they may not produce large crops at higher trophic levels. It is important to distinguish *total production* from *usable production* for higher trophic levels. Much organic matter in wetlands is never used by insects, fish, and birds. The main reason is that in permanent wetlands most of the annual production of organic matter accumulates as peat. In seasonal wetlands microbial recycling of detritus releases most inorganic nutrients back to the plant roots for the next year's growth. In contrast, most of the primary production in larger lakes is used as food in the upper waters; little sinks untouched to the lake sediments. A notable exception in wetlands is the crop of seeds from macrophytes, which is often a favorite food of water birds. For example, the small seeds of the submerged macrophytes *Ruppia* and *Zanichellia* as well as those of the alkali bulrush are sought by ducks and coot. *Ruppia*'s common name—*widgeon grass*—reflects this.

The wetland food web differs from the examples given in Chap. 15 (Figs. 15-2 to 15-4) in several ways besides peat accumulation. Very small animals, such as nematodes and rotifers, play a more important role in the dense vegetation stands of wetlands (Mitsch and Gosselink, 1986). For example, several hundred thousand nematodes and rotifers per liter were found in water strained from the submerged vegetation in

FIGURE 18-12 The food web in a marsh. Heavy solid lines indicate food pathways established by gut content analysis; dashed lines, probable pathways based on literature data; dotted lines without arrows, emergence of aerial adult insects from aquatic immature stages. Note that the key intermediate organisms are the larvae of chironomid midges. This marsh was dominated by cattails and bulrush (emergent), *Chara* (a submerged macroalgae but similar in function to a submerged macrophyte such as pondweed), and periphyton microalgae (as aufwuchs). Data are from Kesterson Reservoir, an inland and somewhat saline wetland in the Central Valley of California. However, the taxa of the animals and plants found there are typical of those in most freshwater wetlands. Modified from Horne and Roth (1989).

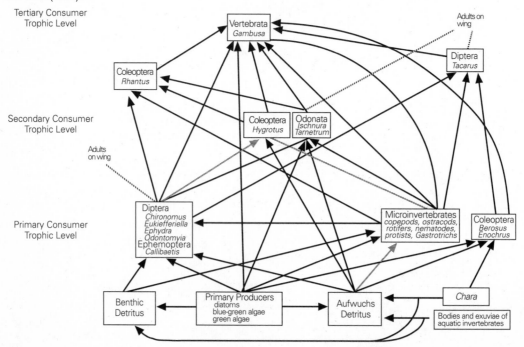

eutrophic Kesterson Marsh in California. This compares with only a few hundred rotifers per liter found in eutrophic lake water. An idea of the complexity of a marsh food web is shown in Fig. 18-12. This semiquantitative representation encompasses only the submergent contributions to the system and the central role of the most common insect larvae, the chironomid midges, and their predators (labeled secondary consumers). Also evident is the complex web of dependence common to most food chains (Chap. 15).

The inedibility of almost all of the vegetative parts of emergent and some submergent aquatic plants modifies the food web relative to typical terrestrial and aquatic examples. The poor food value of wetland plants serves as a protection against grazing by larger animals and fish. Terrestrial plants fill their leaves with toxic alkaloids to protect against browsing by deer and caterpillars. Some wetlands plants, such as fresh watercress, employ chemical warfare but most are so difficult to digest that even ruminants find it difficult to extract enough energy from them. There are some exceptions; for example, in prairie ponds in the United States, muskrats are thought to feed on the dominant macrophyte, cattails, and eventually eliminate these plants. However, this process takes many years and is also correlated with periodic droughts, when much aquatic vegetation dies back and is recycled back into the food web. Some large grazers, such as Florida manatee, eat submerged plants, but they select only a few species.

Although many marshes are considered to have a detritus-based food chain, a recent study on seagrass meadows indicates that other routes are available (Kitting, 1984). In most wetlands the main grazing species—snails, shrimps, or insect larvae—feed at night or in dense cover to avoid sight predation by fish and birds. Thus for most of the daylight hours, when human observers usually work, it appears that the main grazers are in the benthos, presumably feeding on the detritus. Kitting found that the grazers made sufficient identifiable sounds when feeding that he could use underwater microphones to identify

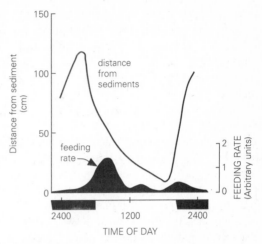

FIGURE 18-13 Frequency and distribution of a snail grazing on the attached microbial community (aufwuchs) in a tidal marsh, determined by sound using underwater hydrophones (Fig. 19-13). This method allows quantitative study of grazing, which is deterred by predators in daylight and disturbed by flash photography. Different groups (snails, shrimps, and so on) have a distinct sound as they rasp and bite at their food. Snails feed over 24 hours but venture out along the macrophyte stems only under the cover of darkness. Modified from Kitting (1984).

and record their activities. He found that a whole host of grazers moved up from the benthos onto the aufwuchs-rich plant stems as night fell (Fig. 18-13). Living algae are a better food than detritus and are preferred if they can be obtained without undue risk of predation.

PROTECTION AND RESTORATION

There is little use in recreating a malarial swamp or flooding an urban area or productive farmland unless it can be demonstrated that the net result is beneficial. It may not be obvious to the general public why anyone would wish to create a wetland that may be smelly, inaccessible, and insect-ridden. In principle, if not always in practice, it is quite simple to preserve an existing wetland or create a new one. The process requires little more than provision of the appropriate hydraulic conditions and possibly the replanting or encouragement of wetland vegetation. The tenacity of many wetlands species is attested to by their classification as weeds for removal or poisoning in ditches and shallow lakes where they interfere with drainage and recreation. In fact, numerous wetlands have been created simply by flooding the site.

The recreation of all aspects of a wetland is not so easy as just growing some wetland plants. In particular, some original or desired species may be very difficult to establish. At present much research is directed toward solving such problems as how big a wetland is needed for the permanent success of a desired species; how the wetland should be partitioned between seasonal and permanent water; how to control the access of humans and dogs, especially during the breeding season; whether more emphasis should be placed on protection of the rare species to the detriment of the more common ones, which are more important in the overall food chain; and how catastrophic events, such as the 100-year flood, should be simulated in constructed wetlands.

Wetlands situated near towns and cities usually require extensive management. Disease vectors continue to be a serious problem in wetlands, especially during summer. In estuaries and marshes, the cycling of sulfur can result in the emission of malodors such as hydrogen sulfide (Chap. 10). These are a nuisance to the local public and can easily reach the level at which public health is endangered. Diseases transmitted by insect vectors such as mosquitos and biting gnats are typically controlled by draining shallow stagnant water or with insecticides. The introduction of fish such as the mosquitofish (*Gambusia*), which prey on insect larvae, has been successful in many cases. Hydrogen sulfide emissions are more difficult to cure. None of these alternatives, however, is appropriate for a truly natural wetland.

The decline in wildfowl, especially those hunted for sport, has created an economic interest in preserving remaining wetlands. Organizations such as Ducks Unlimited have purchased large numbers of small wetlands in the United States and Canada and claim to have produced millions of additional waterfowl.

When a river mixes with the saline water of the ocean it forms an estuary. Wetlands play a very important role in estuaries and are equally threatened there too. Study of estuaries is common to limnology and marine biology alike, and this seaward limit of the river provides the basis for Chap. 19.

FURTHER READING

Dennis, W. M., and B. G. Isom. (ed.). 1984. *Ecological Assessment of Macrophyton: Collection, Use, and Meaning of Data.* American Society of Testing Materials, Special Technical Publication no. 843. Philadelphia. 122 pp.

Elder, J. F. 1985. "Nitrogen and Phosphorus Speculation and Flux in a Large Florida River-Wetland System." *Water Resour. Res.,* **21:**724–732.

Ellenbroek, G. A. 1987. *Ecology and Productivity of an African Wetland System: The Kafue Flats, Zambia.* Junk, The Hague. 267 pp.

Garstang, E. O. 1986. *Freshwater Vegetation Management.* Thomas, Fresno, CA. 377 pp.

Good, R. E., D. F. Wigham and R. L. Simpson (eds.). 1978. *Freshwater Wetlands: Ecological Processes and Management Potential.* Academic, New York.

Hammer, D. A. (ed.). 1989. *Constructed Wetlands for Wastewater Treatment: Municipal, Industrial, and Agricultural.* Lewis, Chelsea, Michigan. 831 pp.

Hook, D. D. 1988. *The Ecology and Management of Wetlands.* Vol. 1. *Ecology of Wetlands.* 592 pp. Vol 2. *Management, Use, and Value of Wetlands.* 394 pp. Timber Press, Portland, OR.

Kitting, C. L. 1984. "Selectivity by Dense Populations of Small Invertebrates Foraging among Seagrass Blade Surfaces." *Estuaries,* **7:**276–288.

Mitsch, W. J., and J. G. Gosslink. 1993. *Wetlands.* Van Nostrand Reinhold, New York, 722 pp.

Richardson, C. J., and P. E. Marshall. 1986. "Processes Controlling Movement, Storage, and Export of Phosphorus in a Fen Peatland." *Ecol. Monogr.,* **56:**279–302.

Sculthorpe, C. D. 1967. *The Biology of Vascular Plants.* Edward Arnold, London. 610 pp.

Verry, E. S., and D. R. Timmons. 1982. "Waterborne Nutrient Flow through an Upland Peatland Watershed in Minnesota." *Ecology,* **63:**1456–1467.

CHAPTER 19

Estuaries

OVERVIEW

An estuary is a partially enclosed body of water of variable salinity, with a freshwater inflow at one end and sea water introduced by tidal action at the other. The dominant features of an estuary are variable salinity, tidal action, a salt wedge or interface between salt and fresh water, and often large areas of shallow, turbid water overlying mud flats and salt marshes. They are complex and very productive water bodies. Estuaries have a lower species diversity of both plants and animals than lakes, rivers, or oceans, but a few species may be very abundant.

Nutrients are supplied to the estuary from the sea, the inflowing river(s), and adjacent marshes. Small detritus particles and dissolved organic matter in the river flocculate at the saltwater-freshwater interface to form clumps that settle more rapidly and serve as food for filter-feeding animals. More detritus is produced in estuaries than in lakes but some is continually lost to the ocean. Tidal motions provide an energy subsidy by bringing food to sessile organisms such as oysters—the most economically valuable product in many estuaries. Large, productive salt marshes develop in the waterlogged salty soil between high and low tide levels in temperate climates. In the tropics, mangrove swamps are the equivalent of these salt marshes. In polar regions ice fragments scour away most intertidal growth, resulting in lower productivity. The shallow, well-mixed waters of most estuaries are ideal sites for high rates of photosynthesis and secondary production. The various habitats—stable mud flats, scoured channels, expanses of deeper water, and salt marshes or mangrove swamps—effectively compartmentalize the biota into size and age classes. Juvenile stages of many commercially important ocean fish and crustaceans depend on this productivity and diversity of habitat for rapid growth and protection. Some adult marine fish and crabs spawn at sea and the eggs and larvae are carried into the estuary, where the young spend most of their early life. Other marine species return directly to the estuaries to spawn, and some, such as salmon, tarry only briefly in the estuary before proceeding upstream to spawn in the headwater streams.

INTRODUCTION

Tides and variable salinity make the structure of estuaries more complex than that of streams, rivers, or stratified lakes. The large number of interacting physical (marsh, mud flat, channels, open water, shoreline) and biological components (benthic micro- and macroalgae, zoobenthos, salt marsh vegetation, phytoplankton, zooplankton, and nekton) make the overall food web very complex. Even physical measurements become more complex, since the study of water movement in estuaries must take into account two different salinity layers and tidal fluctuations.

One reason for studying estuaries is that they support commercially valuable fish and shellfish. Unfortunately, this seafood harvest is threatened because larger estuaries are sites of harbors and ports, which affect the biota through dredging and pollution. Because some of the concepts formulated through the study of lakes and rivers are inapplicable to estuaries, it is important to become familiar with estuarine limnology.

In this chapter we discuss variable salinity and the salt wedge, trophic status, the biota, and tropical estuaries.

MEASUREMENTS

Sampling in estuaries involves a combination of methods used in lakes and rivers. Sediment, benthos, and plankton can be collected using standard limnological techniques with some differences due to the salinity of estuaries. To avoid corrosion, steel clips and instruments must be replaced by stainless steel, brass, or plastic components. Since estuaries are tidal, water currents are often sufficiently strong to measure using relatively insensitive cup-type flow meters. In deeper, open areas more sensitive instruments designed for oceans or lakes may be required. Salinity is easily measured by conductivity using a portable salinometer. Salinity, a measure of the dissolved solids present in 1 kg of filtered seawater after oxidation of organics, is usually expressed in parts per thousand, written as ppt or $^0/_{00}$. Sodium chloride dominates the total dissolved solids, and full-strength seawater has a

salinity of about 35 ppt. Salinity falls gradually from the sea to the upstream limit of the estuary, which is considered fresh water at about 0.5 ppt. Note that seawater has a different ionic composition than water from most inland saline lakes. These athalassohaline (non-sea salt) lakes are derived from the evaporation of fresh water (Chap. 21) and have relatively greater quantities of calcium, magnesium, and sulfate.

In most estuaries considerable areas of mud, which are often cut by deeper channels, are exposed at low tides. A shallow-draft, propellerless "jet" boat is best for sampling the mud flat zones at high tide but is usually unstable for rough open water. Sampling the mud flats at low tide requires special footwear, such as mud skis or snowshoe-type "mud striders" to prevent sinking.

VARIABLE SALINITY AND THE SALT "WEDGE"

Variable salinity is the most characteristic feature of estuaries. Salinity at one place changes daily with tides, and tidal excursion can be up to 5 to 10 km in large estuaries. Attached organisms such as mussels and seaweeds experience a wide range of salinities every day. Salinity also changes dramatically with the seasons. The head of the estuary is the least saline, but during the low flows of summer may experience almost full-strength sea water. Conversely, in winter, floods of fresh water may reach the mouth of the estuary. In many larger estuaries, upstream dams damp out extreme natural fluctuations in discharge. For example, between 15 and 40 percent of the freshwater flow of the San Francisco Bay estuary is diverted out of the watershed for agricultural and domestic use. Freshwater rarely ever now reaches the former estuary of the Colorado River in the Gulf of Mexico. In contrast, only about 3 percent of the freshwater inflow into Chesapeake Bay is used consumptively. In the Saint Lawrence River the overall volume of freshwater discharge to the estuary is unchanged by dam operations. Peak flows are, however, displaced from spring to winter to meet needs for electrical power. Because undiluted fresh water kills most estuarine organisms, occasional floods are essential to allow more freshwater species to become reestablished.

Where fresh and salt water meet, the resulting mixture is called *brackish water,* defined as having a salinity between 0.5 ppt and that of full-strength sea water. The length of the estuary, if defined as the zone of brackish water, varies depending on the volume of river flow relative to the size of the estuary and the strength of the tide. In an extreme case, the Amazon River in Brazil, the freshwater flow is so large that sea water never penetrates upriver. In the days of the early European explorers ships were able to take on fresh drinking water from this enormous discharge well out of sight of land. In West Africa the heavy inland rains periodically increase river flow so that the salinity of the coastal waters of the Gulf of Guinea are reduced to 27 ppt some 50 km offshore. In this case, and in the similar case of the inshore waters of the Gulf of Mexico, the whole coastal zone assumes some aspects of an estuary. At the other extreme, where a small stream flows into a large sunken valley, the estuary may be only a few hundred meters long. The rest of the estuary will then be an arm of the sea mostly enclosed by land. Thus the relative dominance of fresh- or saltwater discharges combines with morphometry to establish the unique characteristics of an estuary.

To survive variable salinities, organisms must be *euryhaline* (i.e., tolerant of a wide salinity range) and be equipped with special physiological mechanisms to eliminate salt. This *osmotic regulation* is needed because the body fluids of all organisms are similar in chemical composition and thus in ionic pressure. Marine fish and other organisms that live in salt water are *hypotonic* because they contain less salt than their surroundings and must gain water and excrete salt. Freshwater organisms are *hypertonic* and conserve salt by excreting water from which salt has been removed in the kidney. The constantly varying salinity of estuarine waters requires both types of osmotic regulation in the same animal. Such a physiological and anatomical flexibility is unusual; most species avoid osmotic changes or periodically switch systems as needed. For example, salmon and eels convert their osmoregulation from hypotonic to hypertonic, or vice versa, as they migrate between salt and fresh water. Salmon remain for a period above or below the estuary while their osmoregulator functions are reorganized. Most estuarine inhabitants cannot osmoregulate very well but survive because they either avoid salinity changes or their cells tolerate changes in internal salinity that would kill most other organisms. Since few species of bacteria, fungi, algae, higher plants, invertebrates, or fish can live in brackish water, the flora and fauna of estuaries tend to be poor in species relative to the adjacent habitats of the river and the ocean (Figs. 19-1, 19-2). In particular, insects are virtually absent in estuaries, as they are in the sea. Estuarine organisms are mostly of marine origin, and many common forms can survive in the coastal ocean. This is necessary because over geological time estuaries are not very permanent limnological features.

Where salt water and fresh water meet, the denser salt water sinks below the lighter fresh river water. The salinity-density effect dominates over any temperature-density effect. The result, called a *salt wedge,* is a permanent feature of most estuaries (Fig. 19-3). The salt wedge is not fixed in place but moves up and down the estuary with the daily tides. It moves seasonally down the estuary with high winter flows and up the estuary during the period of low summer discharge. Horizontal and vertical profiles of a salt wedge are shown in Fig. 19-4. The wedge is considerably modified by the degree of wind mixing and the shape of bottom topography. The saltwater-freshwater interface can be almost vertical, as occurs in the Thames Estuary in England. Here a large tidal range and low freshwater discharge combine with windy conditions

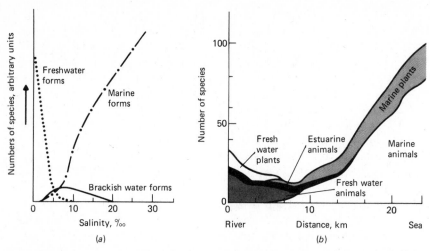

FIGURE 19-1 Low species diversity in estuaries relative to marine and fresh waters. (*a*) Simplified diagram: note that there are few true estuarine organisms but that many marine species can use the saltier regions. Modified from Barnes (1974) and Remane and Schlieper (1971). (*b*) Numbers of animal and plant species along the Tees Estuary, England. Marine animals are much more diverse in the ocean than plants such as seaweeds and account for much of the difference in diversity. Although there may be few true estuarine species, organisms such as oysters can be very abundant and commercially valuable. Modified from Alexander, Southgate, and Bassendale (1935).

to create strong mixing. Alternatively, large freshwater flows, such as those found in the Mississippi delta, cause a pronounced horizontal wedge.

As the fresh water moves seaward, there is a corresponding counterflow of saline bottom water upstream (Fig. 19-4). The upstream movement of bottom water is vital for the retention and recycling of organic detritus. The transport of young larvae, such as crabs and oysters, from the open sea to the upper parts of an estuary is also dependent on this bottom countercurrent.

The saltwater-freshwater interface is more than just an interesting physical phenomenon: it provides an excellent site for the precipitation or *flocculation* of organic and inorganic particles. A common technique in chemistry is to add a salt to a solution to precipitate an otherwise soluble compound. This "salting out" occurs continuously at the salt wedge interface. River silt particles of 4 to 60 μm diameter flocculate into much larger clumps when the fresh water meets the mass of cations, such as Na^+ and Mg^{2+}, in sea water. Flocs may further sorb soluble inorganic and organic compounds such as phosphates and the dissolved organic matter (DOM) common in rivers (Chap. 16). The resulting large particles fall to the bed of the estuary and may form mounds visible to divers. The particles are often supposed to be held in a *nutrient trap* by the counterflow currents in the salt wedge (Fig. 19-4). If the flocculated particles remain for more than a few hours near the salt wedge, bacterial growth provides a concentrated food source for both planktonic and benthic animals. The zone of highest benthic animal production is often associated with the salt wedge. The wedge moves up and down the length of the estuary, carrying planktonic organisms and fish, which also benefit from high productivity.

The average net accumulation over the sea-

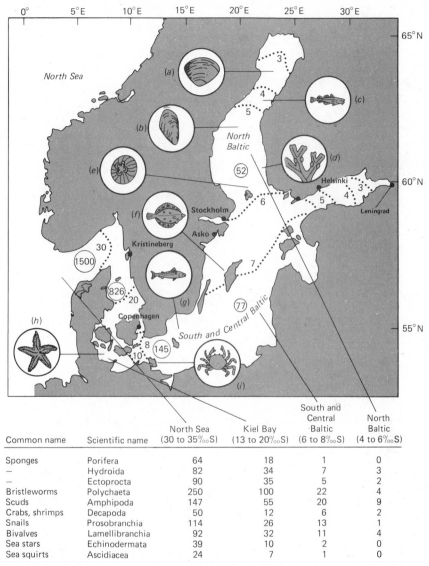

Common name	Scientific name	North Sea (30 to 35‰S)	Kiel Bay (13 to 20‰S)	South and Central Baltic (6 to 8‰S)	North Baltic (4 to 6‰S)
Sponges	Porifera	64	18	1	0
—	Hydroida	82	34	7	3
—	Ectoprocta	90	35	5	2
Bristleworms	Polychaeta	250	100	22	4
Scuds	Amphipoda	147	55	20	9
Crabs, shrimps	Decapoda	50	12	6	2
Snails	Prosobranchia	114	26	13	1
Bivalves	Lamellibranchia	92	32	11	4
Sea stars	Echinodermata	39	10	2	0
Sea squirts	Ascidiacea	24	7	1	0

FIGURE 19-2 Effect of brackish water in reducing biodiversity. In this example from the Baltic Sea, salinity ranges from less than 3 ppt to almost full-strength seawater, at 30 ppt (dotted lines indicate the isohaline fronts). There are only 53 macrofaunal species in the slightly saline upper estuary of the North Baltic, but 1500 species are found in the North Sea at the mouth of the estuary (numbers in circles indicates species number). Letters indicate distribution limits for some common marine species: a = the clam *Macoma baltica*; b = the mussel *Mytilus edulis*; c = cod fish; d = the brown macroalgae *Fucus vesiculosus*; e = the "jellyfish" *Aurelia aurita*; f = the flatfish; g = mackerel; h = the starfish *Asterias rubens*; i = the shore crab *Carcinus meanas*. The table shows the general distribution of some individual groups of organisms. Redrawn and modified from Jansson and Wulff (1977), Barnes (1974), and Remane and Schlieper (1971).

(a)   (b)

FIGURE 19-3 (*a*) The salt wedge in San Francisco Bay as outlined by inflowing turbid water during high winter discharges of the Sacramento River (upper center). The white coloration is the lighter, muddy fresh water, which will reach the open ocean through the Golden Gate at the lower left. The South Bay (on the lower right), having no direct river inflow, remains more saline (darker). The gradation in color from dark in the open ocean to very light upstream corresponds to decreases in surface salinity (Fig. 17-4). Photograph from 20,000 m, by NASA. (*b*) The salt wedge in winter as it appears looking seaward from a nearby hillside opposite the Golden Gate Bridge (far center), which is the connection with the sea. As in (*a*) the fresh water (grey) forms a tongue down the center of the Bay, isolating more saline water nearshore (darker zone) and also near the ocean (faintly darker). As these photographs show, salt wedges are more complex than most diagrams can indicate.

sons of organic detritus from flocculation and sinking of silt or dead grass and leaves has been estimated to average about 2 mm y^{-1}. Both marine and fresh waters contribute to this rich source of food for common detritus-feeding organisms, including flatfish, crabs, oysters, clams, and polychaete worms. The detritus also serves as a refuge from predation and as a buffer to salinity changes. While overlying water may vary from almost fresh to salty, the interstitial water has less variation (Fig. 19-5). Even very soluble compounds, such as nitrates, are only slowly exchanged from the interstitial mud to the overlying water. The slow exchange permits organisms such as marine clams to survive occasional floods of fresh water. Estuarine mud is continually resuspended by the tide until it is lost to the sea or settles among salt-tolerant vegetation.

EUTROPHIC ESTUARIES

Estuaries are among the most productive systems in the world (Table 19-1). The reason for this is best represented in terms of physical and chemical energy subsidies (Odum, 1971). The energy subsidy in estuaries may be usefully contrasted with lakes as follows:

1. Tidal action brings nutrients and food to the organism, saving energy that would otherwise be expended in searching or capture.
2. The mixing of large quantities of sea water with fresh water causes flocculation into larger particles used by zooplankton and filter-feeding benthos.
3. The shallow water and dark mud exposed at low tide is easily heated by the sun, increasing nutrient recycling through bacterial decay and accelerating the growth of benthic animals.

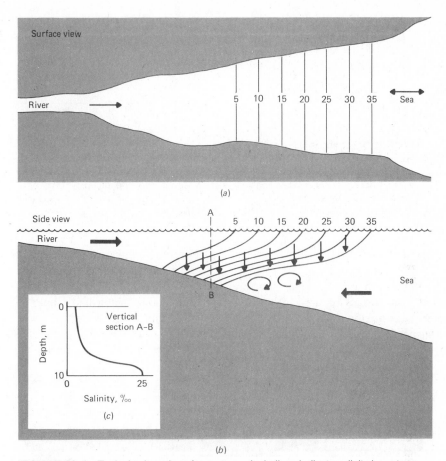

FIGURE 19-4 Typical salt wedge of an estuary. Isohalines indicate salinity in parts per thousand (*a*) at the surface or (*b*) with depth. Note the upstream flow of dense salt water counterbalancing the seaward flow of river water. The thin vertical and circular arrows indicate precipitation and sedimentation of particles in this brackish water zone. (*c*) The very sharp density gradient, or picnocline, which is much stronger than any thermocline, resists vertical mixing by the wind except in very shallow areas, such as mud flats exposed at low tide. There are other types of salt wedges possible, and isohaline profiles can be more or less vertical than those shown in (*b*). The same estuary may appear very different throughout the year (see Fig. 19-15 for examples from Chesapeake Bay). Modified from Barnes (1974).

4. Estuaries are usually shallow and gain much of their food from allochthonous sources, such as mangroves and salt marshes. These particles tend to be recycled by tidal action rather than lost to the sediments, as commonly occurs in stratified lakes.

5. The mere presence of the adjacent sea tends to reduce extremes in temperature.

Although many estuaries are very eutrophic, some are unproductive. In meromictic fjords, for example, the salty bottom water and sediments

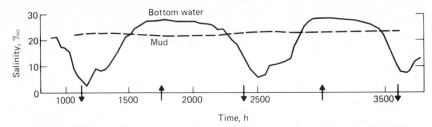

FIGURE 19-5   Changes in the salinity of estuarine bottom water and in the interstitial waters of the underlying mud over the tidal cycle. ↑ = high tide, ↓ = low tide. Note that although the salinity of the bottom water ranges from almost fresh to nearly full-strength seawater, that of the mud remains constant at about 22 ppt. The mud thus provides a refuge from osmotic pressure fluctuations for large and small burrowing organisms such as clams, crabs, and polychaete worms. Modified from Mangelsdorf (1967).

act as a nutrient trap, and mixing with the ocean is restricted by a sill of rock (Chap. 20). Productivity is also low in estuaries in polar climates, where the intertidal zone is scoured by ice and if the water is virtually opaque with large amounts of suspended glacial flour (Chap. 3; Fig. 19-8, Plate 3).

The back-and-forth motion of the tide provides an economical way to create and maintain a food supply. In lakes, animals and phytoplankton must swim or sink to find new food sources or nutrients (Chaps. 12, 13). In rivers, nutrients are supplied by the current to fixed organisms, but the biota is in constant danger of being swept away (Chap. 16) or, alteratively, the food supply may pass without being captured. Only in the estuary are nutrients and plankton moved back and forth and slowly passed out into deep water. It is thus not surprising that many fish and crustaceans spawn or at least spend their juvenile

TABLE 19-1

PRODUCTIVITY OF ESTUARIES AS COMPARED TO OTHER AQUATIC AND TERRESTRIAL AREAS

Net carbon production was converted to gross energy values, where necessary, by multiplying by 20.

Site	Gross primary production, kcal m^{-2} y^{-1}	Total for the world, 10^{11} kcal y^{-1}
Estuaries and reefs	20,000	4
Tropical forest	20,000	29
Fertilized farmland	12,000	4.8
Eutrophic lakes	10,000	—
Eutrophic seasonal wetlands	10,000	—
Unfertilized farmland	8,000	3.9
Coastal upwellings	6,000	0.2
Grassland	2,500	10.5
Oligotrophic lakes	1,000	—
Open oceans	1,000	32.6
Desert and tundra	200	0.8

Modified from Odum (1971) with additions from Goldman and Wetzel (1963), Goldman (1981), and Horne and Roth (1989).

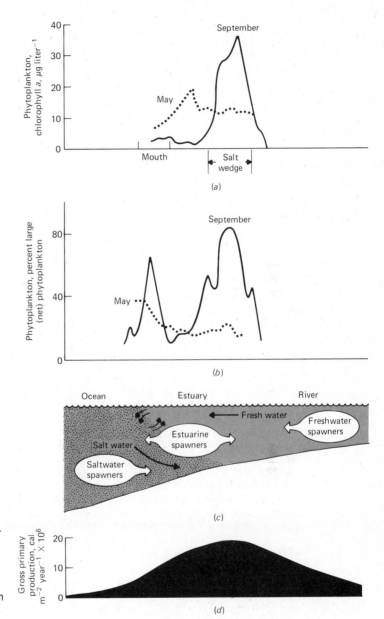

FIGURE 19-6 Spatial correlation between phytoplankton biomass and productivity and fish reproduction. Many fish spawn so that their young are carried by water currents to the salt-wedge region, where phytoplankton productivity and zooplankton biomass is greatest. Almost all fish feed on zooplankton when young. The general applicability of the concept is indicated by the fact that (a) and (b) are from San Francisco Bay while (c) and (d) are from the Hudson River, which flows through New York. Modified from Cloern (1979) and Hall (1977).

stages in estuaries. In most estuaries land or vegetation dampen the wave action. In contrast, the open sea coast or exposed beaches of large lakes are subject to pounding surf, which reduces productivity.

Surrounding marshes or mangrove swamps and submerged aquatic vegetation such as the sea grass, *Zostera,* provide an abundance of autochthonous organic matter in the estuary. Piles of decaying weeds along the shoreline often provide visual evidence of the abundance of large detritus. In the open water high rates of autochthonous input may occur from photosynthesis by planktonic and semiplanktonic algae and macroalgae or seaweeds (Fig. 19-6). Although estuaries are often turbid with suspended silt, their shallow depth usually permits planktonic algae adequate light for growth. Thick-walled pennate diatoms play a more important role in estuarine production than in most lakes. These heavy diatoms would be lost through the thermocline of most lakes but in an estuary are easily resuspended by frequent tidal action and mixing of the water column.

The efficient use of the high primary production by higher trophic levels is what makes estuaries such a valuable resource to humans. A vital element of estuarine structure is the separation of the resources into discrete compartments. The enclosure of open pasture lands in the 1700s in England greatly increased the productivity of farmland by preventing overgrazing. Similarly, shallow water in tidal marshes and mud flats exclude large fish and prevents overgrazing of young fish, shrimps, and large zooplankton that live there (Fig. 19-7). Protection from large predators together with the constant supply of food from algal and marsh plant debris makes estuaries an excellent refuge for the eggs or juvenile stages of most of the major *forage, sport,* and *commercial fish* and *shellfish.* It is a pity that these intertidal mud flats and marshes are sometimes considered unsightly. They are frequently filled in to become sites for airports, oil refineries, harbors, and marinas. Such developments destroy the base of the food chain on which the fishery depends.

THE BIOTA

In estuaries the physical compartmentalization of the biota in the mud, shallows, marshes, or mangroves (Fig. 19-7) is more pronounced than in large lakes or the ocean, where planktonic processes dominate the system. Constant tidal flooding waterlogs the soil between high and low tide with salty water. Only a few groups of specialized wetland plants have evolved to tolerate the extremes of the habitat. In places such as southwestern England or eastern Canada tidal fluctuations may exceed 10 m, which results in huge areas covered with one or two species of short

FIGURE 19-7 The use of the several physical compartments of the estuary as a nursery ground for fish and shellfish. Many estuarine fish, shrimps, mollusks, and crabs move to the constant salinity of the open sea to breed and lay their eggs. After hatching, young fish and the several larval stages of crustaceans drift around in the ocean plankton for weeks to months before entering the estuary. In the estuary larvae drop to the bottom and ride the countercurrent (Fig. 19-4) upstream to shallow or marshy areas. Some fish move to the freshwater rivers to breed and some breed in the outer estuary. All utilize the very high primary production, high temperatures, and protection from predation afforded by the estuarine nursery grounds to grow rapidly during their first year. From an idea by Odum (1971).

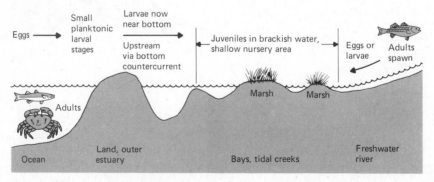

FIGURE 19-8   Complex arrangement of channels, mud flats, and open water in a tidal salt marsh on the Bradley River, in southwest Alaska. The winding channels increase the area of this type of habitat over straight channels. Large stands of one species of reed cover most of the marsh. The central portion shows the main river channel and mud banks. The many physical compartments provide refuges for small fish and shellfish.

FIGURE 19-9   Edge of a small reed bed on Chesapeake Bay. Colonization of the hard clay by these plants increases the diversity of habitat. The lower tidal range in this region (about 60 cm) reduces the intertidal area to insignificance compared with other regions, where tidal amplitude may reach 10 m (Fig. 19-8), but extensive subtidal sea grass beds in Chesapeake Bay (not visible in this picture) provide many of the habitats needed for fish breeding and protection of the young.

reeds or grasses. Figure 19-8 shows an example from western Alaska. The plant beds are intersected by an extensive network of steep-sided muddy drainage channels. Great care should be taken in such salt marshes, which can be crossed safely only at low tide. One of the authors and his grandfather narrowly escaped a Devon estuary when trapped by a fast-moving tide.

Marsh Plants, Seaweeds, Phytoplankton, and Intertidal Microalgae

Common plants such as *Spartina,* the cord grass, or *Carex,* a sedge (Chap. 11), provide a major source of primary production that is usually cycled into the estuarine food chain as debris after the plants have died (Figs. 19-9, 19-10). Reeds and salt-marsh channels provide excellent sites for attached algae, particularly diatoms and green and blue-green algae, which are grazed directly by snails and small animals or eaten as detritus when they become dislodged or die. The net productivity of this marsh-mud higher plant-algae system is unusually high when compared with other aquatic and terrestrial environments (Table 19-1). Much of the ecology of salt marshes is similar to that of the freshwater wetlands discussed in Chap. 17, but the tidal action provides an intermediate habitat between seasonal and permanent wetlands.

Most of the larger plant inhabitants of salt marshes are long-lived perennials, which may survive for up to 50 years. They become established on bare ground from seeds or small pieces of living plant. The long-lived, tough under-

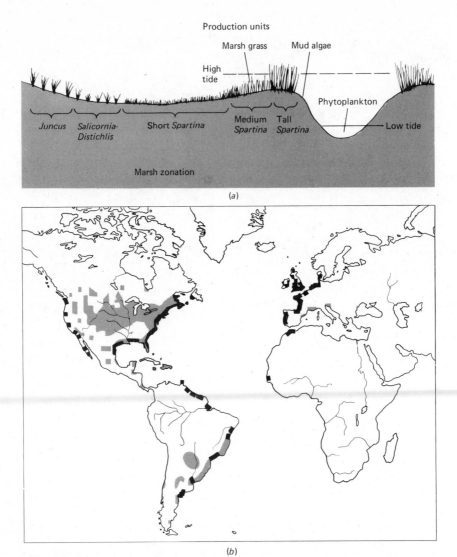

(a)

(b)

FIGURE 19-10 (a) Zonation of a *Spartina*-dominated salt marsh in Georgia and (b) the worldwide distribution of this genus of cordgrass (black = complex of marine species; shaded = freshwater species). Note the different ecotypes of the same species, *S. alterniflora,* in the Georgia marsh. There are short, tall, upper tidal, and lower tidal forms, each with its own productivity, associated epiphytes, and animal communities. Similar *Spartina* communities are found throughout the temperate areas of the world and in some parts of the tropics. Mangrove trees replace grasses and reeds in many tropical estuaries (e.g., Figs. 19-19, 19-21), and there are virtually no estuaries in desert areas, such as the northwest coast of Africa or the west coast of South America. Modified from Odum (1971) and Chapman (1977).

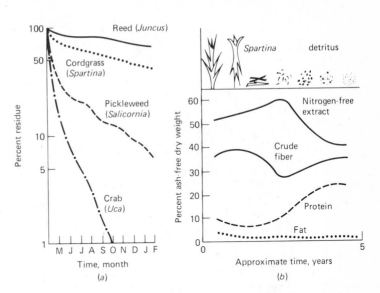

FIGURE 19-11 Decomposition of salt-marsh plants and animals. (*a*) The very slow degradation of estuarine grasses and reeds compared to the rapid decay of animal remains, such as those of crabs. (*b*) The changes in various nutritive components of *Spartina* as it decays. The colonization by bacteria and fungi as the detritus becomes smaller results in the typical increase in protein shown here (dashed line), which makes detritus such a good food source. Modified from Odum and de la Cruz (1967).

ground stems spread vegetatively, but the aboveground portions usually die in winter. The marsh maintains much of its physical integrity because the decay rate of marsh plants is slow relative to that of animal matter (Fig. 19-11). A strong winter structure is essential if the marsh is to avoid destruction of its sediment base by winter storms. In turn, the tall stems provide cover for birds and small mammals. The seeds and stems of macrophytes, some of which depend intermittently on fresh water, are important in the diet of some estuarine animals, especially the large flocks of geese and ducks that migrate annually along the coasts of the major continents. Estuarine marshes are frequently managed by wildlife agencies to provide the most suitable plant foods for migrating waterfowl.

As the sediment builds up around the stems of the pioneer marsh plants such as *Spartina*, other plants with less tolerance for saline water begin to colonize the marsh. This leads to an obvious vertical zonation of marsh growth. Mud flats occupy the lowest level, *Salicornia* and *Spartina* the next, and reeds such as *Juncus* and *Scirpus* the next; eventually, less salt-tolerant grasses and shrubs dominate at higher levels. The

lowest zones often differ in elevation from the upper ones by only a few centimeters and can easily change due to natural fluctuations in rainfall and tidal action. Marsh zonation is particularly amenable to mapping by remote sensing using the characteristic infrared signature of the major marsh plant types. This method is used to define changes due to human activities, especially filling, waste disposal, freshwater diversion, and dredging.

Seaweeds or macroalgae are a common sight in estuaries, usually as patches of green sea lettuce, *Ulva*, on the mud flats, or as brown or red seaweed strands on rocks or piers. Some seaweeds are mostly subtidal and are seen only at extreme low tides. Their large size and rapid growth rate make them important contributors to the overall autochthonous production of some estuaries. Because estuarine macroalgae are difficult to measure quantitatively, there are much fewer data on their rates of production than are available for the phytoplankton. A distinct population of the 1-m-long red alga *Gigartina*, estimated at 100 to 1000 tons, moves within a section of the San Francisco Bay during the summer (Fig. 19-12). Extensive meadows of spe-

FIGURE 19-12 A common estuarine macroalga or seaweed, the red alga *Gigartina,* also known as *Turkish towel.* These large algae grow in shallow, muddy water attached to rocks or small pieces of shell, and in about 4 years reach full size (about 40 cm in this case). They provide shelter from predation for small fish and shrimp. The fronds are sites for the attachment of eggs for fish such as Pacific herring, and the industry for fresh herring roe (eggs) generates about $20 million annually in San Francisco Bay. Photograph by A. Nanomura.

cialized higher plants occur below low tide. These are the sea grasses, such as *Zostera* and *Ruppia* in cooler waters and *Thalassia* and *Poseidonia* in tropical waters. They bear crops of nutritious aufwuchs, and the annual die-off of sea grasses is a major contributor to the detritus pool. Benthic samples from the deep ocean trenches are sometimes dominated by partially

decayed sea grass fronds washed in from shallow areas. The feeding of snails and shrimps on the seagrass aufwuchs community is difficult to observe because these small animals feed at night to avoid predators. In fact, many workers believed they fed on detritus until Kitting (1984), in an ingenious experiment, used the sound emitted by snails and shrimps grazing on aufwuchs to identify both food and grazer (Fig. 19-13).

Phytoplankton in estuaries may have spring and fall blooms similar to those in nearby shallow lakes (Fig. 12-3). Two examples from temperate estuaries are shown in Fig. 19-14. In some estuaries there may be only a single large bloom. Turbid water together with river and tidal effects may account for this single peak of spring or fall production. Although a few estuaries exhibit dense algal blooms, eutrophication is not as great a problem as in lakes. This may be due to large benthic populations. Unlike most zooplankton, benthic filter feeders, such as mussels, persist over winter and need only the spring increase in temperature to accelerate their feeding rates. In addition, a 5-cm-long mussel can filter a liter of water in a few minutes while a typical 0.5-mm-long zooplankter requires weeks to filter the same volume. In estuaries with deeper stratified sections, however, increased algae growth due to nutrient additions from agriculture sewage has resulted in anoxia and losses in bottom-dwelling fish stocks. Chesapeake Bay and the Baltic Sea are examples of cultural eutrophication in estuaries; the Thames is an example of extreme pollution and partial recovery (Chap. 22).

As in lakes, the onset of estuarine algal growth is due to the increase in light in late winter or spring (Fig. 12-3). Cessation of estuarine phytoplankton blooms is sometimes due to nutrient depletion, but the effect is not as clear-cut as in lakes. The spatial heterogeneity of estuarine biota is compounded by tidal changes each day. Variations in phytoplankton and zooplankton biomass may be large, but one common feature is a maximum near the salt wedge (Fig. 19-6).

The types of planktonic, benthic, and attached

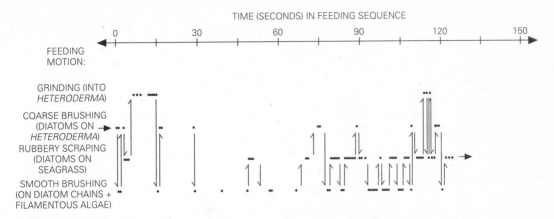

FIGURE 19-13 Underwater sounds made by shrimp and snails grazing on aufwuchs growing on seagrass beds. Sensitive hydrophones detect the different sound patterns in sufficient detail that the individual species of grazer and the food source can be identified (Fig. 18-13). Modified from Kitting (1984).

microalgae (excluding seaweeds or macroalgae) in estuaries are somewhat different from those in adjacent freshwater lakes or streams. The general estuarine rule of larger populations of fewer species applies. Diatoms are the dominant form, especially in cooler waters (Fig. 19-14). Green algae (Chlorophyceae) are often reduced to a few flagellated and attached forms, which may produce dense blooms. Finally, the benthic microalgal community is at least as important in most estuaries as it is in rivers and more important than in most lakes. This is simply due to the fact that ample light reaches the sediments in shallow estuaries and streams. Dinoflagellates and cil-

FIGURE 19-14 Seasonal variations of major types of estuarine phytoplankton. The phytoplankton is dominated by centric diatoms and, to a lesser extent, pennate diatoms. Diatoms usually comprise the majority of the phytoplankton in estuaries, although large ciliates and flagellates, including dinoflagellates, are occasionally abundant (Fig. 19-15). This data set is from the Lower Narragansett Bay, a large estuary on the east coast of the United States. Redrawn from Smayda (1957).

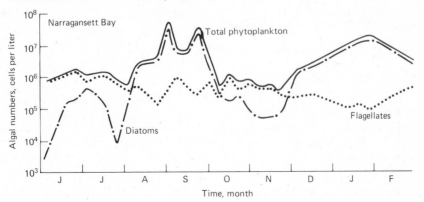

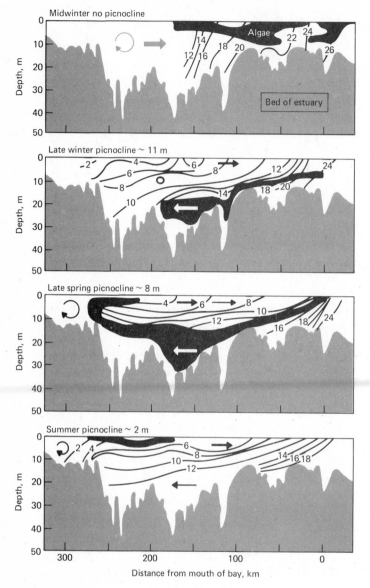

FIGURE 19-15 Growth and bloom of a dinoflagellate red tide in the Chesapeake Bay estuary. Black areas represent relatively high concentrations of *Prorocentrum mariae-lebouriae*; isohalines are every 2 ppt. Arrows indicate direction of water movement. Maximum densities range from 6×10^5 individuals per liter in winter to 4×10^6 during the surface red tides of summer. This motile phytoplankter is present near the surface at the mouth of the estuary in midwinter, when density stratification is weak and net freshwater outflow at any one depth is low. When snowmelt and rainfall increase freshwater outflow in later winter and spring, strong density stratification is established. Fresh water moves rapidly seaward and *Prorocentrum* rides the marine countercurrents upstream in deep channels below the main picnocline. The alga grows slowly at this time in the nutrient-rich but dimly lit depths. In late spring, *Prorocentrum* mixes vertically in the shallow, almost fresh upper estuary. It remains near the surface by positive phototaxis (Chap. 12) and produces dense surface blooms called *red tides* in summer. By late summer the main algal mass is gradually transported seaward again in the surface layer and mixed vertically near the estuary mouth when stratification ends in autumn. Modified from Tyler and Seliger (1978).

iates are common estuarine groups and sometimes become so dense at the surface that they form red tides (Chap. 12). Under certain hydrographic conditions they make daily vertical migrations between seaward-flowing upper layers and upstream-flowing deeper layers to maintain their position in the estuary. An example of di-

noflagellate migration has been well described for Chesapeake Bay (Fig. 19-15), and more spectacular examples are known from tropical waters (Seliger et al., 1970).

While dinoflagellates provide food for grazers, their importance to humans is related to paralytic shellfish poisoning (PSP). Some, but by no means all, estuarine and marine dinoflagellates produce a very powerful neurotoxin called *saxitoxin.* The common marine PSP-containing species, *Gonyaulax tamarensis,* is often carried into estuaries at flood tide, and *Prymnesium* is a true PSP-carrying estuarine form. The toxin is a three-ring heterocyclic compound containing several nitrogen atoms. Its effect on humans is similar to that of cobra venom. How this poison benefits the dinoflagellate is unknown, since it does not seem to deter shellfish feeding. In fact, the saxitoxin becomes concentrated in certain parts of the shellfish, including the muscle flesh, that comprise much of the edible body parts. Toxin production by dinoflagellates assumes special significance because estuaries are major sites for natural growth and mariculture of clams, mussels, and oysters. Although PSP is quite rare, almost every year a few people in North America die in agony from PSP after eating shellfish. Similar tragedies occur throughout the world.

A characteristic feature of most estuaries is shallow and well-mixed muddy waters. Under this vigorous mixing regime, phytoplankton and benthic microalgae are more difficult to distinguish than in lakes or the ocean. For example, in San Francisco Bay ($\bar{z} = 6$ m) a major diatom species, *Melosira moniliformis* (Fig. 11-4), is present in small chains in the plankton or on the sediments.

Intertidal microalgae, usually pennate diatoms, play a special role in estuaries. Their importance varies with the mean tide height, but in an estuary such as San Francisco Bay as much as one-third of the surface area of the estuary is exposed at low tide. Much smaller areas are exposed in Chesapeake Bay and very large amounts are exposed in the Bay of Fundy, Canada, and the Walden estuary in The Netherlands. The importance of intertidal microalgae lies in both their high biomass and their year-round persistence when compared with phytoplankton. For example, pennate diatoms may average up to 200 mg m^{-2} of chlorophyll *a* all year on intertidal mud flats, compared with an annual average of only a 1 to 10 mg m^{-2} for phytoplankton. Peak chlorophyll values on the mud flats may not differ much from average values, unlike phytoplanktonic chlorophyll. An example of the variation of intertidal chlorophyll and relative abundance of phytoplanktonic chlorophyll in an estuary is shown in Fig. 19-16.

Interstitial pennate diatoms remain in the sediment during high tides and emerge only when the substrate is exposed at low tide. These algae have an internal clock that tells them when daylight and low tide coincide. A beautiful golden-brown sheen of diatoms can appear in a few minutes as the tide recedes. The advantage of this strategy is that filter-feeding predators, such as clams, feed only when the substrate is submerged. The diatoms thus avoid exposure to predation. In addition, the diatoms glide by excreting a mucus (Chap. 12), which acts to bind the sediment and prevent erosion of the habitat by waves. On an English sandy shore it was shown that the beaches eroded much more in winter, when diatoms were not active, than in summer, when scanning electron microscopy provided visual evidence of soil binding by diatom exudates.

Zooplankton and Benthic Animals

In lakes zooplankton grazing is a dominant factor in phytoplankton seasonal cycles. In estuaries the benthos plays a much greater role. Zooplankton also follow the estuarine maxim of few species but abundance of individuals. Some forms, such as the copepod *Acartia,* which is common in the east and west coast estuaries of the United States, are mostly planktonic (Fig. 19-17). Others, such as the crustaceans *Corophium* and *Neomysis,* are at least partially benthic, perhaps because of the abundance of diatoms and detritus at the mud-water interface. Estuaries, like the open ocean, have no pelagic insects and copepods are more common than cladocerans.

Shallow estuaries with vigorously moving bottom water are physically similar to streams or lake littoral zones in that the zoobenthos population is large and influences the entire commu-

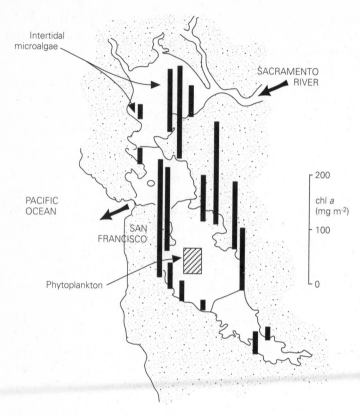

FIGURE 19-16 Biomass of intertidal microalgae in a temperate estuary compared with phytoplankton. The biomass of intertidal algae, mostly large pennate diatoms, is shown as the annual average for chlorophyll a for several sites in San Francisco Bay (black vertical bars). There is not much seasonal variation in biomass. The annual average for phytoplankton is relatively low (cross-hatched bar) and only during the spring bloom does phytoplankton biomass approach that found in some intertidal sites. The smaller phytoplankton value is due to greater grazing pressures as well as light limitation in the mixed layer in winter (intertidal algae are always exposed to light at low tide). From Gregg and Horne (unpublished) and Cloern et al. (1985).

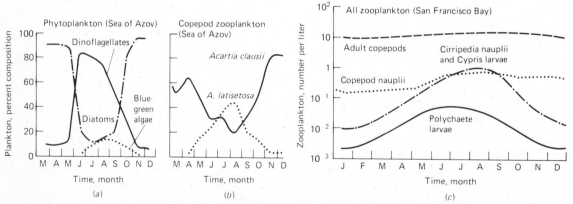

FIGURE 19-17 Seasonal cycles of zooplankton and phytoplankton in two estuaries. (*b*) *Acartia* spp., copepods common in many eastern American estuaries, may show peaks in summer or winter. This may be related to (*a*) phytoplankton food. (*c*) Estuarine benthos produces many larval stages (e.g., Polychaetes and barnacles) that have no counterpart in the freshwater zooplankton. Redrawn from Zenkevich (1963) and Storrs et al. (1966).

nity structure, including the plankton. The *infauna* contains most of the true estuarine benthic fauna and is dominated by relatively sessile types. Estuarine biodynamics are dependent on the huge populations of polychaete worms, clams, oysters, shrimps, and crabs living in or on the sediment. Benthic shrimp such as *Crangon* or the polychaete *Nereis* feed on debris in the mud and provide food for shore birds at low tide or larger fish during high tide. A sediment habitat reduces both bird and fish predation as well as salinity variation. Nevertheless, many birds are adapted to detect buried infauna, as can be seen any day along the shore where sandpipers, oyster catchers, and other long-billed birds feed as the tide recedes. The infauna of estuaries has fewer species than are found in the ocean sediments,

but these are often present in large numbers. This is illustrated in San Francisco Bay (Fig. 19-18) and other estuaries, such as the Baltic Sea (Fig. 19-2).

Most studies on estuarine benthos concern the *macroinfauna,* usually those that will not pass through a 0.5-mm mesh. Macroinfauna feed on littoral algae and sunken or flocculated autochthonous and allochthonous material that microbial action transforms to detritus. Some polychaete worms can burrow directly through the accumulated detritus, eating as they go, but others form characteristic tubes and pump detritus-filled water to feed. A pumping mechanism is also used by bivalves, which may live deep in the sediment, on the surface, or attached to rocks. Some snails graze directly on the mud surface,

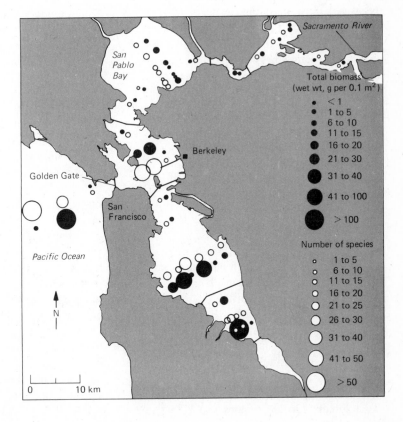

FIGURE 19-18 Species and biomass distributions for the benthic infauna (animals larger than 1.0 mm). Note the relatively few species present in most areas of San Francisco Bay, which, like many estuaries, has several different types of sediment. In many places one species comprises most of the biomass. That typical biomass values for estuarine infauna (20 to 100 g 0.1 m^{-2}) is far greater than that of the zooplankton. Modified from Nichols (1979).

and bivalves such as *Macoma,* the vacuum-cleaner clam, use a siphonlike tube to suck mud from around their buried position. Sedentary polychaetes use tentacles to collect the detritus. Finally, other estuarine dwellers, such as the amphipod *Corophium* and some crabs, pick out individual particles. Further discussions of estuarine macrofaunal feeding and the role of detritus are found in the texts by Barnes (1974) and Newell (1970).

The benthos in estuaries faces several problems during reproduction. Since the net flow of water is seaward, sedentary parents must get their eggs or motile larvae upstream to achieve dispersal from the home site. Many species accomplish this by using the bottom countercurrent, which moves upstream on the flood tide. The youngest planktonic larvae of the common American oyster *Crassostrea virginica* are uniformly distributed vertically, but older larvae actively seek the more saline, deeper water on flood tides. In this way they progressively move upstream. The young of many fish and shellfish, such as the Dungeness crab, *Cancer magister,* also employ the bottom countercurrent to move upstream. In Chesapeake Bay larvae theoretically could be transported upstream almost 10 km day^{-1} but it is doubtful that such efficient use of the currents is ever made.

Fisheries

The high quality and abundance of fish in and near estuaries is a result of the food and protection estuaries provide for the young (Figs. 19-6, 19-7, 19-11, Table 19-1). The ease of fishing in estuaries, relative to the open ocean, makes them very valuable when commercially important fish are present. Most of the ocean's harvest is caught close to shore and many of the fish in the catch depend on adjacent estuaries. For example, the Gulf Coast between Pascagoula, Mississippi, and Port Arthur, Texas, supplies about 20 percent of the total U.S. marine and freshwater fisheries catch. The Gulf catch is dominated by menhaden (*Brevoortia* spp.), considered an estuarine species. Gunter (1967) estimates that 97.5 percent

of the total commercial fish and shellfish catch of the Gulf states is directly dependent on estuaries at some stage in their life cycle. This is probably true in many areas of the world's oceans. Five of the six most important commercial fish and most sport fish in the United States are considered estuarine.

Large sport fish such as the striped bass (*Morone saxatilis*) require fresh water for spawning and estuarine marsh backwaters during the first few months after hatching. The Pacific herring, *Clupea harengus pallasii,* lay their eggs on estuarine grasses or seaweeds (Fig. 19-12). Many other fish, such as the Atlantic herring, *C. h. harengus,* spawn offshore in the constant conditions of the open ocean, but masses of their young migrate to the more fertile brackish waters of the estuary. Fish such as the menhaden, the grey mullet, *Mugil cephalus,* and most harvest shrimp (e.g., *Penaeiis setiferus*) breed similarly. Commercially important crustaceans such as the Dungeness crab and blue crabs, *Callinectes sapidus,* are also born at sea but grow to almost full size in the estuary (Fig. 19-7). Many adult mollusks, including the commercially important oyster, *Crassostrea virginica,* spend their whole life in and around the mud flats. Their young spend only a few months in the plankton before returning to the mud.

If estuaries are so productive, why do many species spawn at sea and only the young stages or adults frequent the estuary? The answer is that many organisms have not had time to adapt all of their life stages to the variable environment of estuaries. As mentioned previously, estuaries are relatively young, and most will vanish with the next ice age. In contrast, the open ocean is permanent and more constant than the estuary with regard to salinity, temperature, and oxygen content. Grey mullet swim far out to sea to spawn due to the high sensitivity of the eggs and larvae to changes in salinity. Thus the lower productivity of the ocean is compensated for by its chemical constancy. Most estuarine species can survive and breed in full-strength sea water off the coast, although their numbers may be lower. Be-

FIGURE 19-19 Large mangrove swamp on the Indian Ocean coast in tropical East Africa. The estuary is undisturbed by human activity and shows the typical estuarine dense growth of emergent plants, which occurs right up to the water's edge. (Compare with San Francisco Bay, Fig. 19-3.)

FIGURE 19-21 The dense maze of stiltlike roots of mangroves provides protection from large predators for small animals and a substrate for attachment of aufwuchs. This picture was taken near Miami Beach, Florida.

cause most estuarine organisms have marine origins, occasional freshwater floods during heavy rains maintain low diversity in estuaries compared to associated seas or rivers (Fig. 19-1*b*).

Birds are often ignored by limnologists, but in estuaries their importance is obvious. Vast flocks of geese, ducks, swans, and waders take refuge on the estuarine mud flats in winter. The economic value of recreational shooting of waterfowl is large and is an important consideration in the management of estuarine marshes. Large flocks of birds can substantially influence the population structure of estuarine mollusks, po-

lychaetes, and sea grasses. For example, wading birds have been estimated to reduce populations of the common clam *Macoma* by 4 to 20 percent annually. Large ducks and geese each may eat 3000 snails during a single low tide, but have a small effect on the vast shellfish resources of productive estuaries. The principal food of the brant goose (*Branta bernicla*) in estuaries is the eel grass, *Zostera marina,* and reclamation pro-

FIGURE 19-20 Estuary of the Congo (Zaire) River in west Africa, showing very large areas of mangrove swamps (hatched areas) in this relatively undisturbed estuary. In a temperate estuary, mangroves are replaced by extensive stands of reeds or other emergent vegetation. Redrawn from Eisma and Van Bennekom (1978).

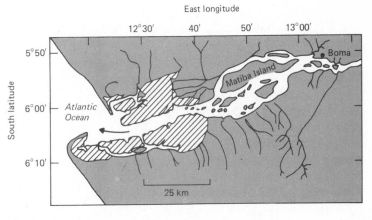

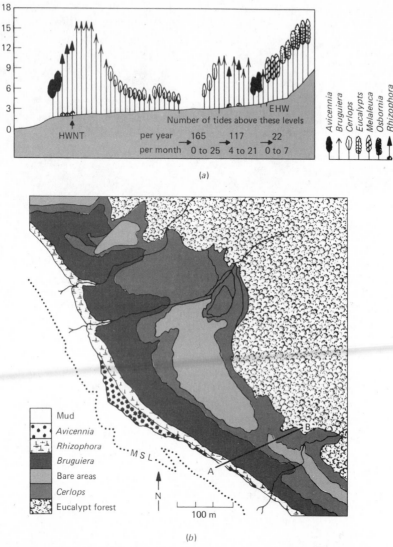

(a)

(b)

FIGURE 19-22 Zonation of mangrove species between sea and dry land on Magnetic Island, Australia. The amount of tidal exposure controls the species composition shown here. (*a*) EHW = extreme high water, HWNT = high water at neap (lowest) tide. The trees are drawn to scale; note considerable variation in height. (*b*) Map of the mangroves on the western shore. Notice the distinct zones in the mangroves and the bare area within the thickets of *Cerlops*. The landward fringe is so narrow that it does not show at this scale. The black line at lower right in (*b*) is the transect A–B shown in (*a*). MSL = mean sea level. Slightly modified from Macnae (1967).

jects that destroy the eel grass beds can decrease the bird's numbers. In a reversal of the usual roles, the bivalve, *Iscadium,* occasionally traps the toes and presumably drowns its major predator, the Clapper Rail, in San Francisco Bay (Morris et al., 1980).

TROPICAL ESTUARIES: MANGROVE SWAMPS

In hot climates the typical estuarine grass- or reed-dominated salt marsh of the temperate zone is replaced by low trees collectively called *mangroves.* The word may originate from *mangue,* a mixture of the Malay, Spanish, French, or Portuguese for "wood" and "grove" English for "a small wood." Several genera dominate mangrove swamps, but *Rhizophora, Avicennia,* and *Bruguiera* are common representatives. Mangrove swamps cover huge areas of the lowland tropics (Figs. 19-19, 19-20), and *Avicennia,* a cold-tolerant species, ranges as far north as Florida. Mangroves can tolerate salinities from full-strength seawater to fresh water and zero dissolved oxygen.

The ecological role of mangrove swamps is similar to that of salt marshes. They develop in waterlogged silt from upriver, which is continuously deposited and enriched by flocculation at the freshwater-saltwater interface. Mangroves grow rapidly and support large growths of attached animals and plants on their root system. These are exposed at each tide (Fig. 19-21) and are the most obvious feature of mangrove swamps at the water level. The roots form masses of stiltlike branches that grow away from the main trunk and can penetrate anoxic muds to obtain water and nutrients. The upper part of the roots supplies the necessary oxygen for the respiring root hairs below. Some mangrove species produce pneumatophores to assist in root oxygenation (Fig. 18-6).

Shallow water and the fencelike root system prevent large predators, such as fish or estuarine crocodiles, from entering the area enclosed by the trees. As in other marshes, the resulting refuge is an excellent rearing area for juvenile fish, shellfish, and reptiles. Crabs and their usually conically topped burrows are the most obvious animal feature of mangrove swamps at low tide, and as many as a dozen species may be present. Mangroves and the various crab species are zoned relative to seawater level. A typical transect through an Australian mangrove swamp relating plant types to tidal height is shown in Fig. 19-22.

Mangrove swamps are disappearing as they are cut down for charcoal or are drained and filled to provide industrial or residential sites. Oil exploration and production on major river deltas in the tropics, such as the Niger in Africa, threaten to pollute mangrove swamps. In many tropical countries, mangrove swamps are far more biologically productive than nearby oceans or the often arid land even a few hundred yards inland from high tide (Table 19-1). It would be much better to build behind existing swamps and cut only necessary access channels through the mangroves. In the long run, mangrove swamps are worth far more as natural aquatic farms for fish, shrimp, and crocodiles than as docks or factory sites.

FURTHER READING

American Fisheries Society. 1966. *A Symposium on Estuarine Fisheries.* R. F. Smith (Chairman). Special publication No. 3. 154 pp.

Barnes, R. S. K. 1974. *Estuarine Biology.* Edward, Arnold, London, and Crane, Russak, New York. Studies in Biology no. 49. 76 pp.

Champ, M. A., D. A. Wolfe, D. A. Flemmer, and A. J. Mearns. 1987. "Long-term Biological Records." *Estuaries,* **10:**181–275.

Chapman. V. J. (ed.). 1977. *Ecosystems of the World.* vol. 1. *Wet Coastal Ecosystems.* Elsevier, New York. 428 pp.

Coull, B. C. (ed.). 1977. *Ecology of Marine Benthos.* University of South Carolina Press, Columbia. 467 pp.

Day, J. W., C. A. S. Hall, W. M. Kemp, and A. Yanez-

Arancibia. 1989. *Estuarine Ecology.* Wiley-Interscience, New York. 558 pp. This multiauthored volume is designed as a textbook for courses on estuaries.

Day, J. W., and A. Yanez-Arancibia. 1990. "Lagoon-Estuary Ecosystems in Latin America." *Estuaries,* **13:**118–172.

Dyer, K., and R. J. Uncles. 1990. "Physical Processes." *Estuaries,* **13:**174–230.

Jefferies, R. L., and A. J. Davy (eds.). 1979. *Biological Processes in Coastal Environments.* Blackwell, Oxford. 684 pp.

Jorgensen, C. B. 1966. *Biology of Suspension Feeders.* Pergamon, New York. 357 pp.

Kennedy, V. S. (ed.). 1980. *Estuarine Perspectives.* Academic, New York. 533 pp.

Lauf, G. H. (ed.). *Estuaries.* American Association for the Advancement of Science, Washington. Publication no. 83. 757 pp. A multiauthored book with physical, chemical, and biological sections.

Livingstone, R. J. (ed.). 1979. *Ecological Processes in Coastal and Marine Systems,* vol. 10. Plenum, New York. 548 pp.

Monteleone, D. M. 1992. "Seasonality and Abundance of Icthyoplankton in Great South Bay, New York." *Estuaries,* **15:**230–238

Olansson, E., and I. Cato. 1980. *Chemistry and Biogeochemistry of Estuaries.* Wiley-Interscience, New York. 452 pp.

Orth, R. J., K. L. Heck, and M. P. Weinstein (eds.). 1984. "Faunal Relationships in Seagrass and Marsh Ecosystems." *Estuaries,* **7:**276–470.

Perkins, E. J. 1974. *Biology of Estuaries and Coastal Waters.* Academic, New York. 678 pp.

Ranwell, D. S. 1972. *Ecology of Salt Marshes and Dunes.* Chapman & Hall, London. 258 pp.

Skreslet, S. (ed.). 1986. *The Role of Freshwater Outflow in Coastal Marine Ecosystems.* Springer-Verlag, Berlin. 453 pp.

Wiley, M. L. (ed.). 1978. *Estuarine Interactions.* Academic, New York. 603 pp.

Wolfe, D. A. (ed.). 1986. *Estuarine Variability.* Academic, New York. 509 pp.

CHAPTER 20

Origin of Lakes and Estuaries, Eutrophication, and Paleolimnology

OVERVIEW

Water bodies are classified on the basis of the large-scale geological processes by which they were created. Almost all natural lakes and estuaries were formed by *tectonic, volcanic,* or *glacial forces.* Some of the oldest and deepest lakes have a tectonic origin, and some of the clearest and most recent are volcanic, but most lakes existing today were created by glacial action. The remainder resulted from landslides, river action, wind, meteorites, and animal activity. Increasingly important are artificial lakes and storage reservoirs.

Lake succession, from creation to destruction, occurs gradually for all but a few small lakes that quickly fill up with sediments or are destroyed by the same catastrophic processes which created them. Once the lake is created a biotic community becomes established. The lake progresses quickly to some trophic equilibrium, which then changes slowly but may oscillate back and forth as the climate varies. If the supply of nutrients is high, the lake is *eutrophic.* If nutrients are in short supply, the lake is considered *oligotrophic.* Eutrophic lakes are productive, turbid, shallow water bodies rich in algae and with considerable fluctuations in surface and benthic oxygen levels. Oligotrophic lakes are unproductive, often deep, with very transparent waters that are fully saturated with dissolved oxygen. Between these two extremes are *mesotrophic* lakes, which are moderately fertile. *Dystrophic* lakes are stained brown with humic acids and are usually unproductive. Estuaries, streams, and wetlands are generally more productive than lakes, primarily due to the energy subsidy provided by the water movement or the abundance of submerged solid surfaces.

Although lakes are geologically ephemeral, a few have existed for millions of years. Lake sediments are reservoirs of history; they record what has occurred in their watersheds, airsheds, and waters. The *paleolimnologist* reconstructs recent and ancient history by analyzing the plant and animal remains preserved in the sediments. Sediments are dated using natural or artificial markers such as ash from major volcanic eruptions or, more recently, radioisotopes from nuclear explosions. Some lake sediments contain alternate layers of dark and light sediment, called *varves,* which show winter and spring sediment inflows as well as the organic fallout from algae blooms. Pollen grains, plant fragments, organic carbon, pigments, diatom frustules, and remains of zooplankton, zoobenthos, and fish provide evidence of previous conditions.

This chapter discusses the origin of lakes, estuaries, and wetlands, lake trophic states and lake succession, eutrophication in flowing waters, cultural eutrophication, and paleolimnology.

ORIGIN OF LAKES

One method of classifying water bodies is by their origin. Lakes, streams, wetlands, and estuaries are formed through gradual or catastrophic geological events and usually are rejuvenated or become extinct through similar processes. Because lakes are ephemeral in the geologic sense, their geologic origin can be traced, the rate of "aging" measured, and an eventual disappearance predicted. The process may take a very long time. Lake Baikal in Siberia, for example, was formed 25 million years ago, yet it remains the world's deepest lake (Fig. 20-1, Plate 2a). This lake is located in a still-active rift valley and continues to widen at the rate of about 1 cm y^{-1}.

Most lake basins are created by gradual events, such as glacial activity or deformation of the earth's crust. A few result from rapid catastrophic geologic events, such as earthquakes, landslides, or volcanic eruptions. Occasionally a lake will vanish as quickly as it was created. For example, a lake in Alaska that formed due to a volcanic dam in the Valley of Ten Thousand Smokes, created by the Katmai eruption of 1913, was so short-lived that it was not named before the dam gave way and the lake emptied in a great flood. Mudslides following the recent explosive eruption of Mount St. Helens in Washington State created a much larger Spirit Lake (Plate 1a).

Lakes formed in one area are generally created by common natural events. It is therefore convenient to group them into *lake districts*. Although lakes in a given lake district have similar

FIGURE 20-1 Part of the steep, rocky shores of Lake Baikal, Siberia, a graben lake that is the oldest and deepest lake in the world. (See also Kozhov, 1963.) Although much of this blue-water lake is oligotrophic, the Selenga delta is culturally eutrophic due to disposal of sewage and other nutrient increases in the watershed.

characteristics, the different basin shapes distinguish them from one another (Chap. 21). A good example is the Great Lakes of North America. Although this system was formed by recent Pleistocene glacial activity, lakes Superior and Erie differ greatly from one another on the basis of water quality, basin morphometry, and biological productivity. The late Professor G. Evelyn Hutchinson, who noted that "it is this diversity in unity that gives the peculiar fascination to limnology," (Hutchinson, 1957) produced a very detailed classification of lakes based on the natural agent creating them. A simplified version of Hutchinson's system is presented here in the categories of tectonic agents, volcanic agents, glacially formed lakes, and others, including landslides, dissolving of limestone, natural coastline activities, organic accumulation, animal behavior, meteoritic impact, and excavation by rivers or the wind. Some lake types are illustrated in Fig. 20-2 and the color photographs in the center of this text.

Tectonically Formed Lakes

Tectonic lakes are formed by deep earth crustal movements, with the exception of volcanism. Most lakes formed tectonically are a result of

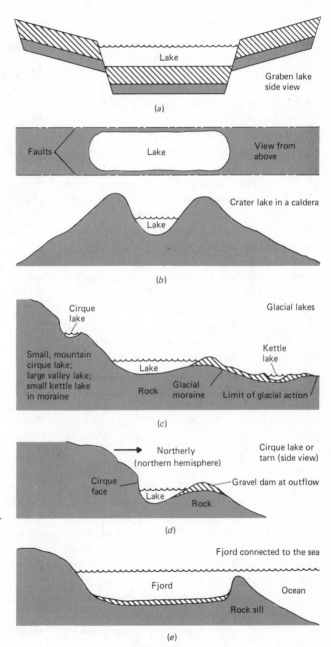

(a)

(b)

(c)

(d)

(e)

FIGURE 20-2 Sketches of the origins and present situations of the most common types of lakes. (a) A tectonically created graben lake formed by the sinking of land along faults. Examples include almost all the world's large, deep, old lakes. (b) A crater lake in a caldera inside a volcanic cone. Large and small examples are found in older volcanic regions throughout the world. (c), (d), (e) Glacial lakes and a marine fjord formed by the scouring action of glaciers in the recent geological past. These types of lake are very common in temperate areas and in mountains.

faulting. They may be one of two types: those associated with single faults and those associated with multiple faults, or *grabens* (Fig. 20-2a). Single-fault lake basins result from depressions brought about through tilting, while grabens are relatively large depressed areas located between adjacent faults. An example of a single-fault lake is Albert Lake in Oregon. Graben-fault basins are well-exemplified by Lake Tahoe and Lake Biwa in Japan. The huge Lake Baikal in Siberia

(Fig. 20-1, Plate 2*a*) and most large lakes in eastern Africa are *rift lakes*. Most old, deep lakes and many of the world's largest lakes were formed by tectonic action. The long chain of rift lakes in Africa comprises lakes Malawi, Tanganyika, Edward, Albert, and Turkana and the now marine Red Sea. They were all formed by one great fault during or before the Pliocene era, about 1 to 10 million years ago. Not all tectonic lakes are deep and relatively narrow, like Baikal. The size of the lake depends on the magnitude of the faulting and the amount of silting over the years since formation. The two smaller arms of Clear Lake, California, for example, are grabens but are only a few kilometers long and 10 to 12 m deep.

The second main type of tectonic lake arises from the uplift of portions of the sea floor. The shallow lakes of Florida were formed in this way. One of these, Lake Okeechobee, with an area of 1840 km^2, has the second largest surface area of any freshwater lake in the United States. The huge sub-Saharan Lake Chad changes shape with each season's rains and shrinks and expands dramatically as dry years are followed by normal or wet periods. The once marine Caspian Sea and the Sea of Aral (Chap. 3) were created by uplift of the sea floor.

A third type of tectonic basin is formed when the tilting, sinking or rising of the earth's crust reverses the existing drainage system. A good example is found in east Africa, where rising land reversed the flow of the Kafu River north of Lake Victoria. This flooded upstream valleys, creating Kioga Lake. Large Lake Victoria, Africa, and small Thurston Lake, California, and Lake Titicaca, high up in the Andes were formed by uplifting of the surrounding land. Variations on the same theme are the lakes produced by local subsidence or landslides following earthquakes. Reelfoot Lake, in Tennessee, was formed in 1811 along the Mississippi River by subsidence from a great earthquake. Other examples can be found in the southeastern United States. Lakes caused by subsidence over old coal

FIGURE 20-3 A lake created by large-scale earth movement, Slide Lake, Wyoming, was formed about 70 years ago when part of a hillside (center, marked by light-colored bare area) slid across the river in the valley. A dam was formed (right), which, although partially eroded in the first few years, has stabilized to form a large lake.

mines are common in Britain. A landslide created the aptly named Slide Lake, Wyoming, in 1925 (Fig. 20-3).

Volcanically Formed Lakes

Lakes created by volcanic activity are found in many parts of the world. Perhaps the best-known type is the *crater lake* (Plate 2*b*). *Calderas* form in volcanic cones after the magma has been ejected (Fig. 20-2*b*). A prime example is Crater Lake, Oregon, which is only 10 km across but over 600 m deep (Plate 2*b*). Smaller crater lakes form when the volcano becomes dormant. Examples are Crater Butte Lake in Mount Lassen National Park, California, and Lake Mahega, Uganda (Fig. 20-4). The Eifel district of Germany contains numerous craters formed by underground explosions producing deep lakes with low rims. Other examples are found in the Auvergne district of France, the base of Mount Ruwenzori in central Africa, and Big Soda Lake in Fallon, Nevada.

Lakes associated with volcanic action but not with craters are created by the damming of a

FIGURE 20-4 A small crater lake, Lake Mahega, Uganda. This is one of many shallow, alkaline lakes in this region. These lakes may appear brown, red, purple, or black and have secchi depths of only a few centimeters. Thus not all crater lakes are as transparent and deep as Crater Lake, Oregon.

FIGURE 20-5 A typical glacially formed lake, Lake Hawea, New Zealand. The mountains in the background formed the main basin. The foreground is a side bay probably formed by a small glacier moving into the picture.

valley by lava. Examples are Snag Lake in Lassen National Park, California, parts of Clear Lake, California, and many Japanese lakes. Lakes may also develop from basins formed in the lava due to differential cooling following an eruption. Examples are Lake Mývatn in Iceland and Yellowstone Lake in Yellowstone National Park. Sometimes volcanic action may alter a lake created by other forces. For example, although Lake Tahoe is in a graben basin, the outflow rim was established by a lava flow.

Glacially Formed Lakes

Glacial activity has been the most important lake-creating force over the last few millennia. Most of the world's lake basins, including the Great Lakes, were formed during the Pleistocene era, when glaciers covered much of the earth (Figs. 20-2*c-e*, 20-5). The lakes filled with water as the glaciers melted and shrunk. The famous lake districts, the Great Lakes, the Wisconsin lakes, the English and Scottish lake districts, the Experimental Lakes Area in Ontario Canada, and the Scandinavian and Alpine lakes are all dom-

inated by glacial lakes. Less well known are glacial lake districts in southern New Zealand, the Himalayas, and polar regions.

A common and often very beautiful type of glacial rock-basin lake is the *cirque lake* (from the French term *cirque*, meaning "semicircle" or "amphitheater") (Fig. 20-2*d*). Cirque lakes are usually found at the head of glaciated valleys where the valley abuts the steep slope of a mountain. Cirque lakes are usually deepest near the cliff and shallow near the outlet. The water is dammed at the outlet by a low barrier of glacial debris called a *moraine*. Rock is eroded by the slow downhill movement of the glacier, aided by a continual freezing and thawing activity that fractures the rock. Rocks frozen into the ice form effective chisels. Most of the weight of the glacier is adjacent to the rock face, and the eroding force is greatest just below the cirque face. This explains why that region is usually the deepest point in the lake that forms when the glacier retreats.

A series of valley-rock-basin lakes occur connected by streams are called *paternoster lakes*. They derive their name from the rosary-bead-like arrangement of several lakes in a linear series. Numerous examples of these can be found in the mountains of North America, including a six- to seven-lake chain in Glacier National Park, Montana. The Sierra Nevada, the eastern side of the Continental Divide in Colorado, and the Bighorn Mountains of Wyoming also contain examples of paternoster lakes.

Fjords and *piedmont lakes* are two types of glacial rock-basin lakes. Fjords occur along glaciated coastlines and are typically deep and steep-sided. Hornindalsvatn, a fjord lake on the west coast of Norway, is completely separated from the sea and at 514 m is the deepest lake in Europe, ranking ninth on a worldwide scale. Fjords are generally associated with Norway, but other examples occur in Scotland, New Zealand, and North America. A limnologically important feature of many marine and estuarine fjords is the presence of a partial dam of rock or moraine near the mouth, which prevents full circulation with the ocean (Fig. 20-2e).

Piedmont lakes are formed by a descending glacier and are frequently large and deep. They are typically located at the foot of mountains. Good examples are Lago di Garda and Lago Maggiore in the Italian Alps. Another example is Lake Wakatipu on New Zealand's South Island, where a glacier excavated the basin to 69 m below sea level.

Some lakes are formed by the damming of streams by glacial moraines, which are the rocks and debris left behind after the glacier recedes. Big Cedar Lake, Washington, is an example of a lake formed between two terminal moraines, which mark the farthest advance of a glacier. In the United States probably the best examples are the well-studied southeastern Wisconsin lakes: Green Lake, Lake Winnebago, and Lake Mendota. Other good examples are the Finger Lakes of New York State, elongated lakes with a "rich legacy of limnological research beginning with the classical investigations of Burge and Juday in 1912" (Bloomfield, 1978). Melting of blocks of ice trapped in glacial moraine is thought to form *kettle lakes* (Fig. 20-2c). These lakes characteristically have very steep sides and are some-

times meromictic because of their small surface-to-volume ratio and because the wind fetch is small. Numerous kettle lakes occur in the eastern and central United States. The famous Walden Pond in Massachusetts is an example of a double kettle.

Cryogenic lakes, also known as *thaw* or *thermokarst lakes,* are formed in areas of perennially frozen ground, or permafrost. If an area of ground is somehow exposed so as to induce melting, it will not refreeze and may fill with meltwater. The depression is increased through subsequent melting at the frost-water interface. Examples of these are found in Alaska and Siberia. Another form of cryogenic lake, found on existing glaciers, may be formed through differential melting when dust or debris absorbs solar radiation and melts out a pocket. These lakes are even found on the sea ice of the Antarctic Ice Shelf.

Lakes with Other Origins

Solution lakes are those formed by the dissolution of soluble rock by dilute acids in water percolating through it. They result from collapsed caves and are usually small and steep-sided. Limestone is particularly susceptible to such action. The best examples are found in Florida and the Karst region along the Dalmation coast of the Adriatic Sea. Others are found in the European Alps, the Balkan Peninsula, and the Yucatan Peninsula of eastern Mexico.

Several different types of small lakes are formed in the flood plains of rivers. One of the most familiar is the *oxbow lake,* formed when the loop of a meandering river is cut off by silt deposition. Examples can be found in the flood plains of almost any river worldwide. Where a former river channel has moved as a result of sediment deposition at a bend, *scroll lakes* may form. Examples of these can be seen along the Mississippi and Minnesota rivers and the flood plain of the Parana River, Argentina (Fig. 2-4b). Flood plain lakes are connected to the river during high floods and provide a protected habitat for eggs and young of many river fish (Chap. 17, Plate 8*b*). Some South American fish migrate hundreds of kilometers from the swamps at the head of the river to breed in the flood plain lakes. Some river species in Africa migrate laterally from the river during high water to feed and breed in adjacent flood plains (Chaps. 14 and 17).

Beavers and humans are two important lake builders. The results of beavers' activities are seen throughout North America and on a few European rivers. Reservoirs have been built on small rivers for several thousand years in Sri Lanka and Egypt, although all of the large dams are recent construction. Lakes may also form accidentally when mines, gravel diggings, and quarries are abandoned. Kimberly Lake in South Africa, formed in the old DeBeers diamond mine, is probably the deepest artificial lake in the world.

In the last century huge lakes have been created throughout the world for power generation, irrigation, flood control, and drinking water supply (Fig. 20-6). Most of the world's major rivers are now dammed (Chap. 17, Plate 8*b*), and those remaining are constantly threatened. Reservoir limnology is of major interest for modern limnologists. The problems associated with impounded waters on river fisheries are considered in Chap. 14.

ORIGINS OF WETLANDS

Although fragile in some senses, wetlands plants form very stable communities that can persist for thousands of years, so long as the hydroperiod is maintained. In general the same processes of glaciation, tectonic effects, and volcanism that create lakes also created wetlands, the main difference being that the resulting basins are shallow. Typically there is less than 1 m of water present, and the area may dry out each summer. Some marshes, swamps, and bogs are formed from filled-in lakes. In many cases, the water-

FIGURE 20-6 Humans are now the main agents creating lakes, usually for power, irrigation, flood control, or as a source of drinking water. This picture shows the dam of one of the largest reservoirs, Lake Kariba, on the River Zambesi between Zambia and Zimbabwe. The lake created has an area of over 2300 km^2. Reservoirs of this size rival the largest natural lakes.

logged areas left by retreating glaciers, small land subsidences, or blockage of stream drainage create wetlands. As soon as a river forms a stable and shallow delta it will be colonized by wetlands vegetation. Along the edges of lakes and streams riparian vegetation soon becomes established, even in desert conditions (Plates 4*a*, 5*a*, 6*b*).

Change in the local microclimate or rates of plant evapotranspiration can create or destroy wetlands, especially acid peat bogs. For example, the clear-cutting of the oak-birch woodlands in several English mountain regions in 1500 to 1800 so decreased the water loss via tree leaves that they became permanently waterlogged and formed the current extensive peat bogs.

ORIGINS OF ESTUARIES

Geological events that turn rivers into lakes will create estuaries near the ocean. Most estuaries originate from the processes of glacial melt, which produces *drowned river valleys,* and *glacial scour,* which creates fijords, but some are produced by *tectonic processes* (Prichard, 1967).

Another process that creates estuaries is the production of large tidal delta regions by sedimentation where large rivers meet the sea.

Glaciation and the associated ice ages created the largest number of lakes as well as fjords and drowned river valleys. Sea level has risen as much as 400 m since the climax of the last ice age, and the meltwater has flooded many of the large river valleys created during the ice age. Most estuaries in coastal plains are of this type. Perhaps the best-studied one in the United States is the huge Chesapeake Bay on the Atlantic, but similar estuaries occur on many major rivers throughout the world. The River Thames in Britain (Chap. 22) is also a well-studied drowned valley estuary.

Where offshore barriers such as sandspits or small islands have been created in the mouth of a drowned river valley, the system is described as a *bar-built estuary*. The major difference is the restriction of water circulation with the sea, since the estuary is then almost completely surrounded by land. Some of these small estuaries may become fresh except for a lower lens of saline water and contain a very restricted fauna. Many of the complex estuaries in the Gulf of Mexico are of this type, but small, often temporary examples are found among other estuaries throughout the world.

Where large earth movements have caused a depression in the earth's crust, tectonically formed estuaries may result. San Francisco Bay was created about 10,000 years ago when the sea broke through a low point in the Coast Range at the Golden Gate to flood a tectonically depressed, marshy freshwater area. This bay continues to sink at a measurable rate. Similar examples can be found in volcanically active coastlines throughout the world.

Rivers carrying large quantities of silt, such as the Mississippi and the Nile, build out their estuaries into the sea. The very shallow, frequently changing deltas of these large rivers are often highly productive areas and serve as nurseries supporting the estuary and adjacent marine food chains (Chap. 17). These estuaries can be easily lost if the upstream load of sediment is reduced. For example, the Nile Delta in Egypt has shrunk over the last 20 years since the closing of the Aswan Dam upstream. The delta of the Mississippi, near New Orleans, has also shifted considerably due to the construction of several large flood-control dams.

EUTROPHICATION AND LAKE SUCCESSION

Historical Background

Pioneering limnologists noticed the obvious differences between mountain lakes and those in the cultivated lowlands. Swedish and German limnologists introduced the concept of the trophic state, which was originally based on two related factors: the amount of production in the surface waters (Naumann, 1919; 1921) and the conditions in the hypolimnion of stratified waters (Thienemann, 1915). Naumann tried to quantify environmental factors such as temperature, light, nutrients, and soluble gases in relation to the amount of lake phytoplankton. He introduced the word *trophic* (''nutrition'') and defined a eutrophic lake as one with high productivity. He came to believe the amount of algal biomass was correlated with the concentration of nitrogen and phosphorus. This approach is very similar to our modern definition of trophic state. (Remember that it was almost impossible at that time to obtain accurate measurements of most nutrients in lake waters.) Naumann also found that certain types of algae were characteristic of oligotrophic or eutrophic waters, an idea still in use today. Utilizing higher trophic levels, Thienemann independently classified lakes based on the presence or absence of certain benthic-dwelling midge larvae (Thienemann, 1915). *Tanytarsus* larvae characterized unproductive *sub-alpine lakes,* with little oxygen depletion in the deeper waters. *Chironomus* larvae were typical of more productive waters with low oxygen levels, which

TABLE 20-1

OLIGOTROPHIC AND EUTROPHIC LAKES

Eutrophic lakes must have *both* ample supplies of nutrients *and* high rates of primary productivity (net photosynthesis). Oligotrophic lakes lack these features. The concentration of nutrients and chlorophyll *a* as well as transparency provide an approximate way to distinguish between trophic states. The most eutrophic lakes are shallow and unstratifed and the most oligotrophic lakes are very deep. WL = ratio of watershed area to lake area. Note that there are a number of other trophic states where the effect of nutrients does not necessarily lead to high primary production. Naturally *acidotrophic* lakes (pH 2–5) are unproductive regardless of nutrient levels. *Dystrophic* lakes with high levels of brown humic acids are often unproductive, since the brown color reduces light penetration. In muddy lakes there is insufficient light for high photosynthetic rates.

Factor	Oligotrophic (unproductive)	Eutrophic (productive)
Nutrients	Low levels and low supply rates of at least one major nutrient (e.g., nitrogen, phosphorus, silica)	High winter levels and high supply rates of all major and minor nutrients
O_2	Does not vary much from saturation in epilimnion or hypolimnion ($10 \pm 10\%$)	Great variation from saturation. Depression in hypolimnion (0–100%) and supersaturation in epilimnion (100–250%)
Biota	Low primary productivity. Low densities and yields of phytoplankton and zooplankton, zoobenthos and fish	High primary productivity. High densities and yields of phytoplankton and zooplankton, zoobenthos and fish
Light	Transparent water, light penetration, often below the thermocline. Secchi depth 8–40 m	Water cloudy, light penetration relatively low, often not reaching thermocline or lake bed. Secchi depth 0.1–2 m
Basin shape and watershed	Deep lakes with steep sides. Infertile soils and undisturbed, rocky watershed. WL ratio low (e.g., 1:1).	Shallow lakes with gently sloping sides. Often unstratified. Cultivated, disturbed, or naturally fertile watershed. WL ratio high (e.g., 100:1).

he called *baltic-type lakes*. Thienemann soon adopted Naumann's terms *oligotrophic* and *eutrophic* to replace his terminology (Parma, 1980). Both viewpoints are incorporated into current definitions of trophic state.

Eutrophic, Oligotrophic, and Dystrophic Lakes

The general characteristics of oligotrophic and eutrophic lakes are summarized in Table 20-1. Lakes are "individuals" and as such are difficult to classify. There is still some discussion as to what exactly distinguishes each trophic state. Some authors have devised numerical standards based on important lake parameters. One frequently used index is the *Carlson index,* which is based on chlorophyll, secchi depth, and total

phosphorus (Carlson, 1977). Thienemann had difficulty applying his definitions to tropical lakes, and modern limnologists also find that some lakes do not fit easily into any classification system. For example, the Carlson index will not work if the phytoplankton are limited by a nutrient other than phosphorus or where secchi depth is influenced by humic acids, sediments, or other non-algae-related factors.

Eutrophic lakes are often shallow, usually less than 10 m deep, with gradually sloping edges and a large drainage area-to-lake surface ratio (Table 20-1). The most characteristic features of eutrophic lakes are high nutrients and the abundance of planktonic or attached algae. The most typical visible evidence of a eutrophic situation is the presence of surface blooms of blue-green algae. The chlorophyll pigment in the dense phytoplankton blooms absorbs light at the red and blue ends of the spectrum (Fig. 3-5a). This results in a reflectance of the yellow-green color so typical of eutrophic waters. A eutrophic state is indicated by several factors, such as variable oxygen concentrations, high nutrient levels, high chlorophyll concentrations, presence of blue-green algae, limited benthic species diversity, or type kind of benthic community. However, low water clarity is the simplest indicator of a eutrophic lake. Water transparency as measured by the secchi disk is typically less than 2 m and in extremely eutrophic situations is only a few centimeters (Table 20-1).

In temperate eutrophic lakes, hypolimnetic oxygen becomes depleted both during summer stratification and under winter ice. Tropical eutrophic lakes often have year-round depressed oxygen levels near the bottom. Most alpine and polar lakes are not naturally eutrophic. In all kinds of eutrophic lakes, water in the photic zone becomes supersaturated with oxygen during the day, due to the high rate of photosynthesis. Nocturnal dissolved oxygen values in the mixed layer may then fall below saturation, due to respiration.

The sediments of eutrophic lakes become enriched with nutrients as organic matter from the photic zone accumulates. At first this tends to increase the biomass of rooted macrophytes. Eventually, however, phytoplankton growth becomes so dense that it shades out submerged plants. Dense growths of emergent macrophytes such as cattails are less affected and are often found around the margins of eutrophic lakes and ponds. The increased supply of nutrients also stimulates periphyton. Sometimes submerged plants become so overgrown with attached algae that they die out. An excellent example of this phenomenon was described by Moss (1979) for Strumpshaw Broad, a shallow lake in eastern England (Fig. 20-7). Two hundred years ago this lake contained clear water with large areas of submerged, bottom-growing macrophytes, such as the stonewort *Chara*. Drainage from the city of Norwich through the nineteenth century

slowly increased both nitrate and phosphate loading. Periphyton increased and blanketed the *Chara*, which eventually disappeared, while phytoplankton increased and made the water turbid. Taller macrophytes that grew leaves at or near the water surface invaded the lake and reduced sediment flushing, causing the lake to fill partially with organic matter. After World War II, the liberal use of fertilizers in agriculture combined with increased waste discharges from Norwich caused very dense phytoplankton blooms. These blooms shaded out macrophytes of any kind. Strumpshaw Broad, which is a tidal but freshwater area, is now a bare mud flat at low tide.

An important feature of eutrophic lakes is the high standing crop at all levels of the food chain, including fish. Eutrophic lakes typically have large standing crops of crapie, bluegill, carp, catfish, and many other species. Because dissolved oxygen is often low and eutrophic lakes are often situated in the warm lowlands, trout are not common. In developed and developing countries alike, commercial and sport fishing in eutrophic lakes may be dependent on this high productivity. Summer and winter fish kills (Chap. 14) are typical in eutrophic waters.

Oligotrophic lakes are the opposite of eutrophic lakes. They are generally deep with steep sides and relatively small drainage areas. This is a broad generalization, because some oligotrophic lakes are no more than shallow granite pans. These are common in the Canadian Precambrian Shield and in many high mountains. Oligotrophic lakes are characterized by low nutrient levels, clear blue water (Fig. 3-6b, Plates 1a and b, 2a and b), and secchi disk transparencies of over 8 m. The clear water is due to the low number of planktonic or attached algae that can be supported by the low nutrients levels. Hypolimnetic and benthic oxygen levels throughout the year do not vary much from saturation (Fig. 7-7b). Because primary production is low, the biomass at all higher trophic levels is also small. Thus the backpacker's single panful of trout taken from a small, clear mountain lake

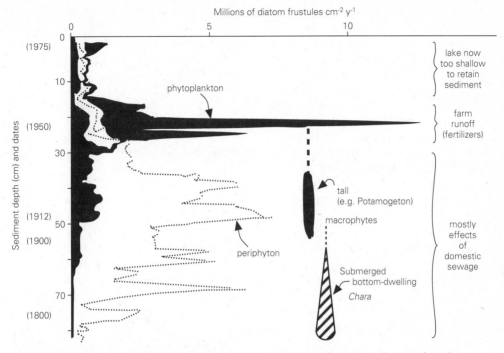

FIGURE 20-7 Cultural eutrophication: the paleolimnological record from the sediments of a culturally eutrophic lake. Nutrients from domestic sewage have been added to this shallow lake, Strumpshaw Broad, since about 1800. Prior to this time, dense growths of bottom-dwelling *Chara* grew in clear water with few periphyton or phytoplankton. As domestic sewage inputs increased between 1800 and 1900, *Chara* stands on the lake bed declined to extinction because they were shaded by coatings of periphyton diatoms as well as by phytoplankton. Macrophytes such as *Potamogeton* and *Myriophyllum,* whose leaves reach the lake surface, took the place of *Chara* and provided more substrata for different species of periphyton. All macrophytes were shaded and died out when nutrient-rich farm runoff due to increased fertilizer applications in the 1950s caused a huge bloom of phytoplankton in that decade. Organic sediments produced by the increased productivity decreased the lake volume so that it is well flushed and sediments are no longer deposited. Nutrient loading remains high but now leaves little sedimentary record. Extensively modified from Moss (1979).

may represent almost all of the year's trout production. In contrast, a similarly small but eutrophic lake or pond in the lowlands can supply many meals of catfish, bluegill, or bass before the fish stocks become seriously depleted.

Mesotrophic lakes, as the name suggests, are intermediate between oligotrophic and eutrophic lakes. They are very common water bodies and can be defined at having a secchi disk depth of 2 to 8 m.

Dystrophic lakes contain humic acids leached from decaying aquatic vegetation in the watershed. These brown acids stain the waters to a characteristic yellow-brown color (Plate 4*b*). Because they are usually acidic, dystrophic lakes are usually shallow and unproductive. Some, however, such as Tjeukemeer in the Netherlands, are very productive and contain large amounts of the floating blue-green alga *Aphanizomenon flos-aquae.* Some diatoms and desmids are characteristic of dystrophic lakes and are grown on sediments where enough light penetrates through the shallow water. Small dystrophic lakes are common in mountain regions where leachate from pine forest and bogs provides a continuous supply of humic acids.

In most lake districts a gradient of oligotrophic to eutrophic lakes can be observed. For example, in the Great Lakes of North America (Chap. 21), Lake Superior is considered oligotrophic and Lake Erie eutrophic. By the standards of many European lakes, Lake Erie might be considered only mesotrophic, since many of the world's lakes have much higher phytoplankton growth. If compared with the lakes in western North America, the Great Lakes would fall within a larger trophic range. For example, lakes Tahoe, Crater, and Waldo are more oligotrophic than Lake Superior, and Clear Lake, California is much more eutrophic than Lake Erie. There are a variety of reasons for these differences but no completely satisfactory generalities. Examples of relative trophic status and associated physical, chemical, and biological variables are given in Chap. 21 for several lake districts (Tables 21-1 to 21-4)

Eutrophication and Lake Succession

Eutrophication may be defined as the process of enrichment of a water body due to an increase in nutrient loading. The most important nutrients that cause eutrophication are phosphates, nitrates, and ammonia. Eutrophication caused by increases in carbon dioxide, silica, iron, or trace metals is less common. Eutrophication concerns inorganic nutrients; organic enrichment is usually considered a separate process and was defined by Naumann as producing *heterotrophic lakes*. In these systems bacteria play the major role, since most algae cannot use organic matter directly.

Ecologists in the early part of the twentieth century were fascinated with questions of biological succession. They were concerned with changes in animal and plant communities that occur with time, and it is not surprising that there has been considerable effort to apply the succession concept to lakes and streams. No matter whether a lake basin originated as an abandoned rock quarry or as a depression scraped out of the landscape by a glacier, a lake will change over time. Rapid initial sediment accumulation slows down as the watershed soils become vegetated and stabilized. Succession includes the initial colonization by plants and animals and a slow but progressive change in water chemistry. In new reservoirs change during the first few years is very rapid (Fig. 14-19), whatever the initial trophic state, and this probably applies to lakes created naturally as well.

One concept of lake succession considers that lakes pass through different trophic states, beginning with lower fertility or oligotrophy and gradually moving to a moderately productive or mesotrophic state. A later stage is eutrophy, and finally the lake becomes a marsh or even dry land to be invaded by trees and grasses. Too much should not be made of this general concept which is often called *lake aging*. In fact, two overriding factors control lake eutrophication: (1) mean depth of the lake and (2) size and fertility of its drainage basin. For example, the oldest lake in the world, Lake Baikal in Siberia, is very deep and still mostly oligotrophic. In contrast, shallow Lake George in Uganda is very eutrophic and was formed only 2000 years ago. The speed with which lakes change with time also depends on fluctuations in local climate, especially temperature and rainfall. Paleolimnological evidence from the study of deep lakes undisturbed by humans suggests that a lake may change from an oligotrophic to a eutrophic state but then reverse and become oligotrophic again (Fig. 20-10). This cycle may occur several times during the lake's existence and is related to regional climatic changes.

Particularly in lakes formed by glacial action, eroded sediment may reduce the depth of the lake. When combined with rising fertility from the increased drainage area-to-lake volume ratio, this results in a highly productive or eutrophic state. A simple calculation, however, shows that this may be a long process. Many lakes are situated in well-vegetated landscapes with little erosion. Sediment accumulation under these circumstances is mostly organic and due to deposition of phytoplankton and some detritus from the watershed. This sediment is partially decomposed and becomes compressed as new material piles on top. A typical sedimentation value is about 1 mm y^{-1}. Thus a lake formed after glaciation and 30 m deep would take 30,000 years to fill in. A large deep lake such a Lake Superior would take over 300,000 years to fill with sediment. Even in Lake Washington, Seattle, with an unusually high annual sedimentation rate of 3 to 5 mm per year over the past few decades, would take about 20,000 years to fill. Considering that the ice ages that created all the current glacial lakes have a periodicity of about 100,000 years, deeper lakes would be covered once again by glaciation before they had time to fill in with autochthonous sediment.

Theories about lake succession were initially based on the very obvious successions seen in small mountain lakes. The observed changes seemed to follow well-understood successions of terrestrial plants, which are thought to reach a *climax,* a stable state at which no further change takes place unless the climate changes or a large fire occurs. The succession of a European oak forest from grassland to birch and willow trees and finally to a climax mature oak woodland is an example. As mentioned earlier (Chap. 12), the main vegetation in lakes, the phytoplankton, is not necessarily specialized for a particular lake type. Most species are quite generalized and are found in lakes with a variety of trophic conditions, although their relative abundance often reflects their trophic status (Tables 19-2, 19-4).

Succession and climax in lakes is not as well based theoretically as is terrestrial succession, which is also being reevaluated. In fact, consideration of lakes throughout the world leads to the conclusion that the idea of oligotrophic to mesotrophic to eutrophic to extinction is only one of several possible routes of lake evolution. Lakes are created and may be destroyed by geologic or climatic events. The climax for many

lakes may be wetland while that of others will be determined by catastrophic events, not gradual sedimentation or inflow of nutrients. Certainly most large deep lakes, including the Great Lakes, Lake Baikal, and Crater Lake, Oregon, are more likely that they will remain oligotrophic until they are destroyed by some catastrophic process such as the one that created them. At the other end of the time scale, oxbows and scroll lakes, which are associated with rivers, may be created or disappear on an annual basis, depending on the height of the spring flood.

EUTROPHICATION IN FLOWING WATERS

Most estuaries are more productive than lakes, due to the energy subsidy provided by tidal action. Tidal mixing stirs up and recycles nutrients in shallow mud flats and flushes nutrient-laden water through salt marshes. Nutrient accumulation from extensive drainages coupled with tidal mixing cause estuaries to be among the most productive environments on earth. They are of great value as a food resource if their fertility is properly managed.

Chesapeake Bay, in the northeast United States, and the estuary of the Purari River in New Guinea are examples of eutrophic estuaries with valuable fisheries. Undesirable overproduction of algae has occurred in Chesapeake Bay and the estuarine Baltic Sea due to sewage and agricultural runoff. This has decreased the stocks of valuable bottom fish while increasing small planktonic fish. High-latitude and fjord-type estuaries are the least productive estuaries. Estuaries, like lakes, can be classified as eutrophic or oligotrophic on a relative basis.

Eutrophication in rivers and streams is in many ways similar to that found in estuaries. Once again, an energy subsidy imparted by the water flow can result in higher production for a given nutrient concentration than is usually encountered in lakes. One can find extensive attached algal growth even in the most pristine alpine streams, where nutrient levels are always low. Usually this occurs in early spring and is not often observed, since the algae are soon eaten by the stream insects. Additions of nutrients will increase the growth of aufwuchs and eventually cause a summer-long problem that cannot be grazed down by the insect larvae. The choking of some rivers with long strands of the green alga *Cladophora* can be a major eutrophication problem in temperate rivers (Lund, 1972).

CULTURAL EUTROPHICATION

Unthinking discharge of sewage and excess fertilizer into lakes and rivers has increased the algae growth in many inland and coastal waters of the world. This change is called *cultural eutrophication.* The term has become widely used and the cultural eutrophication of the Great Lakes has been a matter of discussion in newspapers and scientific journals since the 1970s.

Cultural eutrophication is not entirely a recent phenomenon. For example, a small lake along a highway, the Via Cassia north of Rome, became eutrophic after the deforestation of its watershed during the height of the Roman Empire about 2000 years ago. Examination of the sediment profile down to about 25,000 years indicated a consistent, low productivity until the building of the road (Fig. 20-8). Linsey Pond, Connecticut was originally an oligotrophic kettle lake but later had a long period of trophic equilibrium in a eutrophic state. A return to a less eutrophic state occurred following a period of soil erosion prior to the arrival of European settlers. The changes in phosphorus in the sediments of culturally eutrophic and then restored Lake Washington tracks its history of cultural eutrophication (Fig. 20-9). The 1958 sediment core contains large amounts of phosphorus in the upper few centimeters but much less prior to waste discharge. The lower concentrations now being deposited are clearly illustrated in the 1972 core, a few years after waste diversion (Fig. 20-9). Other examples are discussed in this chapter in the section on paleolimnology (Figs. 20-10, 20-11).

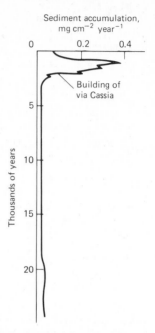

FIGURE 20-8 Accumulation of sediment in the Lago di Monterosi, Italy, over time measured by ^{14}C dating. Note the large increase when the Via Cassia was constructed by the Romans and subsequent recovery as the soil erosion decreased afterward, when the vegetation grew back and soils stabilized. Units corrected from Cowgill and Hutchinson (1970).

Eutrophic water bodies are also more productive at higher trophic levels than oligotrophic ones. Since eutrophication is so frequently linked with pollution or excessive fertilization, the point may be missed that eutrophic environments are not always undesirable. There are many naturally eutrophic lakes where large quantities of fish are harvested for food or sport. Ecosystems such as fish ponds are usually managed to maximize productivity (Fig. 15-3). If carp, bass, or *Tilapia* are the end product, highly eutrophic conditions are actually required.

Municipal sewage is one of the oldest causes of cultural eutrophication. Domestic wastewater is rich in nutrients and serves as an immediate stimulant for the growth of algae and higher aquatic plants. The use of detergents high in phosphate has stimulated cultural eutrophication

FIGURE 20-9 Changes in sediment content in Lake Washington, Seattle, before and after its restoration from a eutrophic state (see also Chap. 22). The core has been adjusted vertically to coincide with a known marker event in the lake in 1916. (*a*) The rise and fall in oscillaxanthin content, which derives from changes in the abundance of the blue-green alga *Oscillatoria agardhii*, a major component of the plankton when the lake was eutrophic. (*b*) The lower phosphorus content before waste discharge in 1941 and its rise until waste diversion in 1968. The rise and fall of oscillaxanthin coincides with the changes in phosphorus. Redrawn from Edmondson (1974b) and Griffiths and Edmondson (1975).

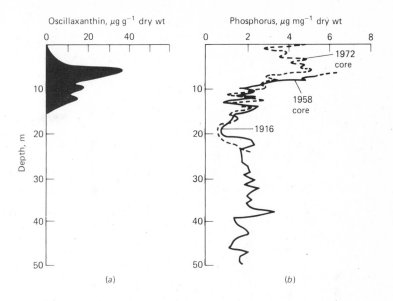

in many previously phosphorus-deficient lakes, since about half the phosphorus in raw sewage is derived from detergents. Only in the last 20 years have treatment plants been constructed that remove nutrients. Most wastewater treatment plants are designed to remove or convert organic particulates to soluble inorganics. This reduces the oxygen demand but increases the immediate eutrophication potential. Where eutrophication has become a problem, phosphates can be removed by precipitation, and more elaborate treatment plants remove nitrogen by denitrification or ion exchange. Naturally, the more advanced the treatment the more expensive and energy-demanding it becomes. In addition, sludges containing phosphate must be disposed of somewhere. Both constructed wetlands and large ponds can be designed to remove all types of nutrients but require much more space than conventional sewage treatment plants.

Urban storm runoff is an additional source of nutrients to lakes. Values of 1 to 5 mg liter^{-1} NO_3—N and 0.5 to 1.5 mg liter^{-1} PO_4—P exceed the values from undisturbed land by about one order of magnitude. Particularly high values of over 25 mg liter^{-1} NO_3—N have been found near plant nurseries that are the source of garden supplies for town dwellers. Overfertilizing of lawns and golf courses, dog excreta, feeding of "wild" birds and animals, and additional impervious land surfaces increase nutrient loads and ensure their rapid transport to the local lake. Cures are especially difficult because the volume of storm water is large. Specially designed wetlands may provide some nutrient removal for some urban runoff, but space is obviously a problem in cities.

Intensive agriculture is another source of nutrients for aquatic systems. An idea of the magnitude of this problem can be gained by considering the nutrients present in agricultural drain water. Values as high as 100 mg liter^{-1} NO_3—N and 20 mg liter^{-1} PO_4—P were recorded in California's rich Central Valley drains, and similar results are found in runoff from Iowa corn fields and cattle feed lots. These concentrations are about four times those found in undiluted treated sewage effluent. Invariably, some of the fertilizers applied are washed off by rain or during irrigation. This washout is particularly evident when nitrogenous fertilizer is applied to frozen soils in spring. During the thaw, most is washed off directly to the lake or river (Fig. 16-11).

Eutrophication can be reversed, although the

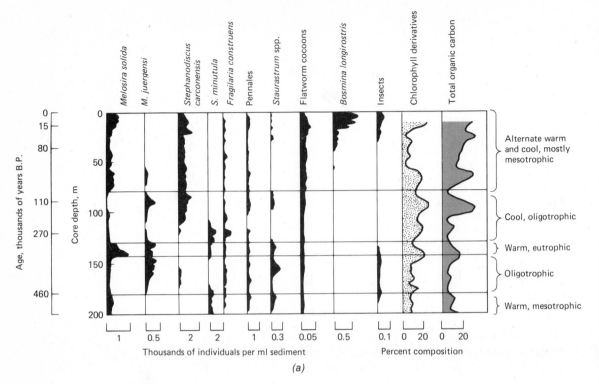

(a)

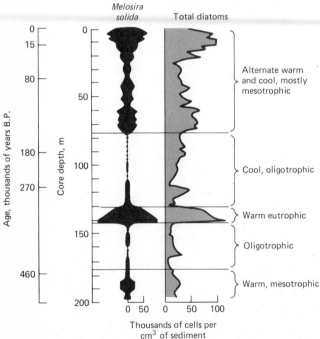

(b)

FIGURE 20-10 The paleolimnological record of the graben Lake Biwa, Japan, over the past half-million years. Two hundred meters of sediment have accumulated over this period. The lake has changed shape considerably over time. This core was taken beneath the present lake. (a) The changes in phytoplankton, zooplankton, and benthos with time and change in climate and trophic state as ice ages came and went. (b) The oscillations in the lake's trophic state from oligotrophic to eutrophic and back as indicated by changes in the most common diatoms. Redrawn from Kawanabe (1978); Fuji (1978); Mori (1974); and Horie (1981).

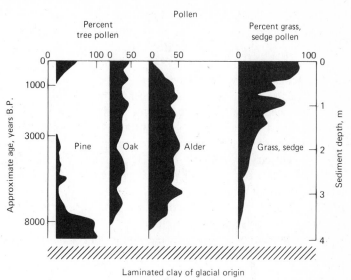

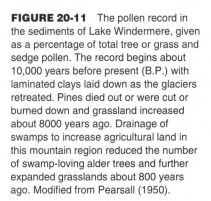

FIGURE 20-11 The pollen record in the sediments of Lake Windermere, given as a percentage of total tree or grass and sedge pollen. The record begins about 10,000 years before present (B.P.) with laminated clays laid down as the glaciers retreated. Pines died out or were cut or burned down and grassland increased about 8000 years ago. Drainage of swamps to increase agricultural land in this mountain region reduced the number of swamp-loving alder trees and further expanded grasslands about 800 years ago. Modified from Pearsall (1950).

process may be expensive and slow. The massive task of reducing the eutrophication of the Great Lakes began in the 1970s and the first signs of improvement are now apparent (Fig. 9-7). In Chap. 22, we discuss the cultural eutrophication of lakes Washington, Shagawa, and Tahoe and the subsequent restoration programs.

PALEOLIMNOLOGY

The natural process of eutrophication or its reversal may span millions of years or may be so accelerated that large changes occur in a few years. A special area of limnological investigation, called *paleolimnology,* focuses on the dimension of time.

Botanists, in their search for evolutionary evidence, long ago discovered that besides the remains of large plants in the geological records they could also identify specific vegetation by its characteristic pollen (Wright et al., 1963). Pollen grains are highly resistant to decay and exist indefinitely in marsh and lake sediments. The paleolimnologist uses pollen to reconstruct the ancient plant communities that were present in the watershed of a particular lake and thus de-

termine what climatic conditions existed. Pollen is prepared for identification by treating the sediments in a very strong base, such as sodium hydroxide. This dissolves any accumulation of diatoms. Because of their siliceous frustule (Fig. 10-2), diatoms are among the best-preserved fossils in the lake sediment. In contrast to the pollen, they are extraordinarily heat- and acid-resistant and can be cleaned of their organic matter and associated detritus by boiling in acid or burning at red heat. Their intricate structure makes them ideal for taxonomic identification, and a knowledge of their environmental requirements makes it possible to estimate temperature, light, pH, and nutrient conditions during the previous life of the lake. Other organic material, such as wood fragments, charcoal, the hard chitinous remains of zooplankton and chironomids, scales, vertebrae or spines of fish, and freshwater sponge spicules, are often identified from lake sediments.

At the chemical level, particularly in the realm of organics, the options for investigating the past history of lakes are almost unlimited. Pigments or their degradation products may be measured, as can organic carbon, nitrogen, phosphorus, and the complete range of other chemical constituents. Chlorophylls dating back as far as 30,000 years were described by Vallentyne (1960), and these, together with estimates of the organic content of the sediments, indicate the presence of different algal groups during the lake's history.

One of the most difficult and expensive aspects of paleolimnology is dating the various strata. In young glacial lakes, such as those created about 10,000 years ago in North America, the sediment consists entirely of the accumulation since glaciation. In older glacial lakes and lakes of different origins estimation of total age is more difficult. *Varves* are alternate light and dark bands in the sediment. The light portion is from inorganic accumulation during winter and early spring runoff, and the dark band represents organic deposition during the main period of plant growth. The year-by-year sedimentation rate can be estimated by counting alternate dark and light bands.

Among the most certain methods for aging particular strata in lakes is the presence of volcanic ash from known eruptions. The Katmai eruption of 1913 left an indelible layer of ash in many Alaskan lakes, and the recent Mount St. Helens eruption in Washington will provide a similar mark in lakes along the path of the ash plume. The type of glass in the volcanic ash tends to be specific for particular eruptions and can be used to date sediments over the entire area of ash fallout. As in the ocean, the magnetic orientation of iron-containing sediments may be used, since there is a growing knowledge of the magnetic changes that have occurred with time. X-ray examination of sediment cores for lead has been accomplished with interesting results, for example, pinpointing the year 1916 in Fig. 20-9 (Edmondson and Allison, 1970). Because it is so recent, the radioactive cesium layer laid down in 1963–5 following the surface testing of nuclear bombs is a particularly useful marker in paleoeutrophication studies.

Some of the most extensive paleolimnological studies have been carried out on Lake Biwa, Japan, where 1000 m of sediments accumulated over several million years, have been examined (Horie, 1981). Microfossils of zooplankton and zoobenthos over the last 500,000 years in 200 m of sediment have been quantified (Fig. 20-10a). In this sediment, the remains of several species of Cladocera and flatworm cocoons could be distinguished. Most noticeable were the intermittent presence of insects and the presence of *Bosmina* only in the last 100,000 years. In contrast, turbellarian flatworms showed little change over half a million years (Fig. 20-10a). Among the most sensitive indicators of changes in lake chemistry are the phytoplankton (Tables 21-2, 21-4). In Lake Biwa large centric diatoms such as *Melosira* or the green alga *Staurastrum* fluctuated considerably, while pennate diatoms, including *Fragilaria,* remained fairly constant (Fig. 21-10a). The changes in biota can be correlated to the changes in climate and trophic level over at least half a million years. Some diatoms, for example *Melosira solida,* were abundant only during eutrophic phases and were scarce when the climate was cool and the lake more oligotrophic. The total numbers of diatom frustules also demonstrate these changes (Fig. 20-10b). We can conclude from this long record that eutrophication is not always a one-way process but one that may reverse as climate or watershed change.

Not all sediment records are so variable as that of Lake Biwa. In eutrophic Clear Lake, sediments over 400 m deep and at least 250,000 years old have been surveyed. The large, round main basin has an extremely uniform particle composition in the upper 166 m of sediment. From this one can infer that the depth of the lake and erosion in the watershed has been rather constant. This is in marked contrast with higher latitude lakes, where glaciation has had a large effect on sedimentation rates. Clear Lake is too far south to have experienced glaciation. Nevertheless, cores from the two smaller basins, when examined for fish remains and pollen grains, show that these sections of the lake varied between shallow swamps with extensive lily beds and their present, much deeper state. The major paleolimnological events in Clear Lake concern volcanic and tectonic activity, which alternately isolated the small basins of the lake from the main lake basin. The shallow main basin has apparently sunk continually since its formation. This has produced a paradoxical paleolimnological record, which indicates that this oldest of North American lakes has always been roughly the same depth!

From the early days, humans have been attracted to the shores of lakes, which provided protection, food, and easy transport. These lake dwellers left an archeological record in the sediments beneath their wood and reed houses, which often extended out into the lake on lightweight pilings. The history of the English Lake District from the time of the Stone Age "beaker people" to modern times is preserved in the lake sediments. Similar evidence of early lake dwellers are found in some of the Swiss lakes. The early residents traveled along high ground and burned or cut the forests, reducing tree pollen in the sediments. The pollen record shows the pine's replacement by grassland, acidic sedge, and heather moors. Later, an agrarian society drained the lowland birch and alder swamps and replaced them with grasses for grazing sheep. All of this is clearly recognizable in the pollen and charcoal content of the Lake Windermere sediments (Fig. 20-11). The pollen of grasses, and especially the invasive ragweed, as well as that of cultivated cereals are used to reconstruct ancient agricultural activities.

FURTHER READING

Cushing, E. J., and H. E. Wright, Jr. (eds.). 1967. *Quaternary Paleoecology.* Yale University Press, New Haven, CN. 433 pp.

Gorham, E., J. W. G. Lund, J. E. Sanger, and W. E. Dean, Jr. 1974. "Some Relationships between Algal Standing Crop, Water Chemistry, and Sediment Chemistry in the English Lakes." *Limnol. Oceanogr.,* **19:**601–617.

Horie, S. (ed.). 1974. *Paleolimnology of Lake Biwa and the Japanese Pleistocene.* Otsu Hydrobiology Station, Kyoto University, Japan. 288 pp.

Hutchinson, G. E. 1957. *A Treatise on Limnology,* vol. 1. *Geography, Physics and Chemistry,* "Origin of Lake Basins," chap. 1, pp. 1–163. Wiley, New York.

———, and U. M. Cowgill. 1973. "The Waters of Merom: A Study of Lake Huleh. III. The Major Chemical Constituents of a 54 m Core." *Arch. Hydrobiol.,* **72:**145–185.

Lund, J. W. G. 1972. "Eutrophication." *Proc. R. Soc. London,* **180:**371–382.

Manny, B. A., R. G. Wetzel, and R. E. Bailey. 1978. "Paleolimnological Sedimentation of Organic Carbon, Nitrogen, Phosphorus, Fossil Pigments, Pollen and Diatoms in a Hypereutrophic, Hardwater Lake: A Case History of Eutrophication." *Pol. Arch. Hydrobiol.,* **25:**243–267.

National Academy of Sciences. 1969. *Eutrophication: Causes, Consequences, Correctives.* Washington. 611 pp. Includes lakes, rivers, and estuaries.

Parma, S. 1980. "The History of the Eutrophication Concept and the Eutrophication in the Netherlands." *Hydrobiol. Bull.,* **14:**5–11.

Vollenweider, R. W. 1968. *Scientific Fundamentals of the Eutrophication of Lakes and Flowing Waters, with Particular Reference to Nitrogen and Phosphorus as Factors in Eutrophication.* Technical Report no. DAS/CSJ/68.27. Organization for Economic Cooperation and Development, Paris. 159 pp.

CHAPTER 21

Comparative and Regional Limnology

OVERVIEW

Most of the basic principles of limnology can best be demonstrated by comparisons between lakes. Such comparisons are most easily made within one geographical area or *lake district*. Comparisons between lake districts then enables generalities to be drawn about eutrophication, seasonal succession in the plankton, the effects of different fish stocks, and watershed type or management. In this chapter we consider the comparative limnology of two lake districts, the English Lake District and the Laurentian Great Lakes of North America. Finally, comparison between very different types of lakes or lake districts—temperate versus semiarid, polar versus tropical, or saline versus freshwater—brings to light principles that might otherwise be missed.

Warm-water tropical lakes can be compared with cold-water alpine or polar lakes. The seasonal constancy of the flora and fauna of many tropical lakes contrasts with the very pronounced seasonal effects in polar and alpine lakes. High temperatures provide stable density stratification in tropical lakes, sometimes on a daily basis, but

unfrozen cold lakes (less than 10°C) remain unstratified, even in high summer. The effects of water temperature and degree of mixing combine to produce phytoplankton populations dominated by large diatoms in well-mixed cold water and large and buoyant colonies of blue-green algae in stable, warm-water systems. The role of light as an inhibitor of photosynthesis is pronounced in both polar and alpine lakes. Total light intensity and the ultraviolet end of the spectrum are important in the extensive benthic algal mats that develop in the shallow waters of polar regions. Similarly, submerged macrophytes coated with attached algae often dominate alpine lakes, instead of the usual phytoplankton population of lower elevation lakes.

Biological diversity of plants and animals decreases rapidly as one moves from fresh to saline lakes, and fish and macrophytes are entirely absent in the saltiest lakes. Low species diversity in saline lakes is indicative of the physiological stress produced by variable osmotic conditions. As a result of adaptation to high salinity, there is more similarity between the biota of saline lakes throughout the world than is found among freshwater lakes.

In contrast to lakes, streams have a characteristic biota the world over. Only a few streams share such special environmental conditions that they prevent the development of the typical array of organisms. Examples include polar or alpine streams and hot springs. In cold climates ice formation on the streambed and *frazil ice* in the water can be a major problem for living organisms. Springs provide a stream with the constant temperature of the ground water, where an oasis of luxuriant plant growth is likely to persist throughout the year.

In this chapter we discuss multi-lake measurements, lakes in the temperate zone, tropical lakes in tropical or arid regions, polar and alpine lakes, saline lakes, and special stream environments.

INTRODUCTION

The most efficient method to advance knowledge in limnology is through comparative studies of different types of lakes within the same geographical area. Limnology in *lake districts* (Chaps. 1, 20) considers lakes with generally similar climate, soil, and vegetation. Individual lakes within a lake district share these common denominators but are often very different in other respects. For example, they may be shallow or deep, large or small, or of very different fertility. The effects of particular environmental factors such as wind, the introduction of a particular fish, or change in nutrient levels are best studied in any one district. Famous limnologists have often been associated with lake districts, for example, Lund and Macan with the English lakes, Ohle and Ruttner with German and Austrian lakes, Birge and Juday with the Wisconsin lakes, Beadle and Talling with East African lakes, Rawson with Canadian lakes, and Welch and Eggleton with Michigan lakes. The major drawbacks of comparative limnology are the long time and comparatively high cost required before conclusions are reached.

MEASUREMENT

Gathering sufficient samples from several lakes involves considerable physical effort and a good study design. Identical methods should be used in each lake but, to avoid cross-contamination, separate plankton nets should be used for each lake, and other collection devices should be washed after use.

Relatively simple experimental designs are essential. In comparative limnology it is certain that data gaps will occur if complex apparatus is required or if sampling time is insufficient for the inevitable delays from bad weather and equipment failure. The lack of certain difficult-to-obtain information in comparative limnology is in part compensated for by the long data runs assembled using other data. Rapid synoptic sampling covering many stations in a short time can be accomplished with boats, but helicopters have been used in larger areas such as the Great Lakes, San Francisco Bay, and the River Elbe estuary in Germany and in the United States Environmental Protection Agency's survey of over 600 lakes. Remote sensing from satellites or aircraft is very useful and video images from planes can be converted quickly to a coded map of different plant communities, temperature, or chlorophyll. The classic method still employed in multilake studies is a coordinated effort by many scientists working in a particular lake district. The creation of the Experimental Lakes Area in Canada, where up to 1000 lakes could be sampled, is a good example (*J. Fish Res. Bd. Canada* **28:**123–301, Special Issue).

LAKES IN THE TEMPERATE ZONES

The temperate zones contain most of the world's extensively studied lakes. These lake districts were formed or modified by glacial action (Chap. 20) and are often situated in partially forested areas, with moderate rainfall most of the year. They often have phosphorus, nitrogen, and sili-

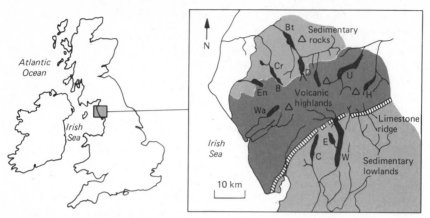

FIGURE 21-1 Fifteen of the lakes of the English Lake District (black areas) arrayed like spokes in a wheel around the central mountains. All of the lakes were formed as the most recent glacial period ended, over 10,000 years ago. W = Windermere, E = Esthwaite Water, Wa = Wastwater, En = Ennerdale Water, C = Coniston Lake, B = Buttermere, H = Haweswater, U = Ullswater, Cr = Crummock Water, D = Derwent Water, Bt = Bassenthwaite Water. The volcanic origin of the central massif (dark grey) contrasts with the sedimentary deposits of slate and sandstone (light grey) in which most of the lakes (black) actually lie. The central rocks are quite barren and produce inflows low in nutrients, while the lower terrain contains softer rocks, more vegetation, and inflows with higher nutrients (see also Chap. 16). Modified from Mitchell (1956).

con limitation. Of the many possible examples, we discuss in detail only the English Lake District and the Laurentian Great Lakes.

The English Lake District

In northwestern England about 18 lakes radiate out from a low mountain range (Fig. 21-1). Most seldom freeze and are monomictic, a few are dimictic, and some are polymictic. They have a wide variety of physical, chemical, and biological characteristics; their most important features are summarized in Tables 21-1 and 21-2. The proximity of these lakes to each other and their small size have made them an ideal subject for intensive study over many years.

Two obvious features of the biota in the English Lake District are the patterns of species abundance and the timing of the spring diatom blooms. Some species of plankton are restricted to only a few lakes, despite apparently favorable conditions in other lakes (Table 21-2). For example, the zooplankton copepods *Cyclops* and *Mesocyclops* are found together in only 3 of the 18 lakes (Chap. 13). The thermal stratification responsible for the onset of spring blooms of the diatom *Asterionella* occurs earlier in the shallow lakes because shallow lakes stratify more rapidly than deep ones (Table 21-1). The stratification prevents the algae in the epilimnion from being mixed into the dark, deeper waters, which would reduce their growth rate (Chaps. 5, 12).

One of the oldest and best-known studies in the English Lakes concerns classification of the waters by trophic level. In the 1920s, the aquatic botanist Pearsall ranked the lakes by type and abundance of algae. He also indicated the amount of agriculture in the watershed and the percentage of shallow, rocky, and thus unproductive littoral zone. His list is given in Table 21-2, which has been revised to include more modern classification. Pearsall worked when limnology was a little-known discipline, and the terms *eutrophic* and *oligotrophic* were not used as they are today. However, his rankings do not

TABLE 21-1

CHARACTERISTICS OF SELECTED LAKES IN THE ENGLISH LAKE DISTRICT

All are monomictic except for Blelham Tarn and Esthwaite Water, which are occasionally dimictic, and Bassenthwaite Water, which is polymictic (P).

Lake L, km B, km A, km²	Depth z_{max} $(\bar{z})$, m	Drainage basin area, km²	Thermocline depth, m	Typical max (min) surface temp., °C	Approximate period of thermal stratification	Winter (summer) nutrients, µg liter⁻¹		
						NO_3-N	PO_4-P	SiO_2
Windermere 17 1.5 15	67 (24)	231	5–20(N) 5–20(S)	17 (3–5)	May–end Nov.	300 (100)	3.0 (0.5)	600 (200)
Wastwater 4.8 0.8 2.9	79 (41)	49	15–20	15 (<4)	June–Dec.	>140 (~100)		
Ennerdale 3.8 0.9 2.9	45 (19)	44	15–25	19 (<4)	May–Oct.	>140 (50)		
Esthwaite 2.5 0.6 1.0	16 (6.4)	14	9–12	20 (2)	Apr.–mid-Sept.	400 (100)	2–4 (0.5)	1000 (100)
Blelham 0.8 0.3 0.11	15 (6.6)	2.3	8–10	20 (3.5)	Apr.–end Sept.	600 (200)	4 (0.5)	1000 (200)
Bassenthwaite 6.2 1.2 5.4	21 (5.5)	238	P	21 (<4)	Irregular	~250		

From Macan (1970) and Heron (1961).

TABLE 21-2

THE LAKES OF THE ENGLISH LAKE DISTRICT AS RANKED BY THEIR BIOLOGICAL DIFFERENCES

Windermere in many ways behaves like two lakes, an oligotrophic North Basin and a mesotrophic South Basin. In this table, average values for both basins are listed. For convenience, lakes Thirlmere and Haweswater have been omitted since they were much enlarged in size by dam construction just before and during the last 80 years, so some data are not comparable. Note how the 1920s trophic classification based on percent rocky bottom, calcium, or bicarbonate is supported by the distribution of phytoplankton, zooplankton, and zoobenthos.

Lake	Modern relative trophic status	1960 basin population	Secchi disk, m	Physical, % rocky and shallow bottom	Chemical, mg liter^{-1}		Phytoplankton		Zooplankton	Zoobenthos
					Ca	HCO$_3$$^-$	Asterionella*	Staurastrum*	Cyclops leuckarti*	Lymnaea palustris*
Wastwater	O	50	9.0	73	2.4	3.2	·	d	–	–
Ennerdale	O	32	8.3	66	2.2	3.5	·	d	–	–
Buttermere	O	32	8.0	50	2.1	2.6	·	·	–	–
Crummock	O	200	8.0	47	2.1	2.9	·	·	–	–
Derwentwater	M	720	5.5	33	4.5	5.4	d	·	+	–
Bassenthwaite	E	5,900	2.2	29	5.3	10.0	d	·	+	+
Coniston	M	1,400	5.4	27	6.1	10.8	d	–	+	+
Windermere	M	13,300	5.5	28	6.0	10.3	d	n	+	+
Ullswater	M	782	5.4	28	5.7	12.7	d	–	–	+
Esthwaite	E	1,200	3.1	12	8.3	18.3	d	·	+	+

From original texts by Pearsall and from Macan (1970).

* Asterionella is a common diatom in the spring bloom, Staurastrum is a desmid (green alga), C. leuckarti is a copepod zooplankter, and L. palustris is the "marsh" snail, which inhabits the littoral zone.

Key: · = present but not dominant; – = absent; + = present; n = no data.

differ greatly from those using modern information. Esthwaite Water is considered a eutrophic lake in the English Lake District (Table 21-2). It has anoxic sediments in summer, and some parts of the lake surface are occasionally covered by a thin film of the blue-green alga *Aphanizomenon flos-aquae*. These conditions are similar to those found in Clear Lake, California, which lies at the eutrophic end of the spectrum of California lakes, but there the similarity ends. Chlorophyll levels reach 300 μg liter^{-1} in Clear Lake but only about 10 μg liter^{-1} in Esthwaite. The English lake supports a moderate trout fishery, while the turbid California lake contains an excellent warm-water bass and crappie fishery.

Using biological records gathered over many years, some species of animals and plants appear to confirm Pearsall's original rankings. *Asterionella formosa* is dominant in the mesotrophic

and eutrophic lakes, while species of *Staurastrum* dominate only in the most oligotrophic ones. The zooplankter *Cyclops* and the snail *Lymnaea* are for the most part confined to the eutrophic and mesotrophic lakes (Table 21-2). The validity of rankings of this sort should be confirmed over a wide range of physical, chemical, and biological variables to be of real value in interpreting cultural eutrophication (Chap. 20). When a lake changes its rank or does not appear to be properly ranked, there may be good grounds for suspecting pollution.

The Laurentian Great Lakes

Lakes Superior, Huron, Michigan, Erie, and Ontario constitute the greatest unfrozen mass of fresh water in the world (Fig. 21-2). As with all large water bodies, the Great Lakes present se-

FIGURE 21-2 The Laurentian Great Lakes of North America formed 10,000 to 15,000 years ago. This lake district contains more fresh water than any other and consists of five major lakes. Note the small size of the drainage basins (indicated by dotted lines) relative to the size of the lakes. This tends to reduce nutrient inflow but gives most of the lakes (shown in black) a long residence time (Table 21-3). The underlying rock strata is of two types (--- marks the boundary). The northerly Precambrian rock (light grey) is not easily weathered, is overlain by extensive coniferous forests, and releases few nutrients to its drainage system. The southern rock (dark grey) is composed of more fertile sedimentary material and was overlain with deciduous forest before the recent introduction of extensive agriculture to the area. This zone releases more nutrients to the drainage system.

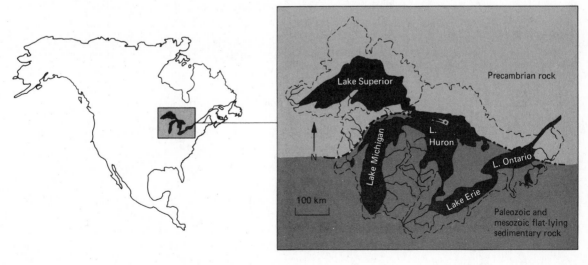

vere sampling problems. They are often stormy in summer and long cruises in large oceanographic vessels are necessary to sample them. Research vessels are not always needed. The noted physical and chemical limnologist Clifford Mortimer studied internal waves by making ingenious use of the ferries that regularly cross Lake Michigan. These lakes are particularly difficult to sample during the very cold windy winters. Most are so large and deep that they are monomictic and do not become completely ice-covered even though the winters are very cold. Lake Erie may freeze over completely during the coldest years.

Despite their size, the Great Lakes are only about 10,000 years old, like most of the English Lake District lakes, which also became free of glacial ice at the end of the Pleistocene Era. Because of their youth, the Great Lakes do not possess a large list of endemic species, such as is found in 25-million-year-old Lake Baikal, Siberia.

A summary of information on the Great Lakes is given in Tables 21-3 and 21-4. The large size of the lakes is obvious, but also important is the ratio of lake area to drainage basin area. The Great Lakes have a surface area to drainage basin ratio of about 1:2, much smaller than most lakes. Partially for this reason, the water inflow relative to lake volume is small and the lakes are low in dissolved materials. As Table 20-1 indicates, they would be oligotrophic in their natural state. The hydrologic residence time for the larger, upstream lakes, Superior and Michigan, is centuries rather than years (Table 21-3).

As with many temperate lakes, phytoplankton production throughout the summer appears most limited by supplies of phosphorus and silicon. Nitrogen limitation is less important in the Great Lakes but occurs in eutrophic inshore waters and bays such as the polluted Green Bay of Lake Michigan and the western basin of Lake Erie. The phytoplankton of the Great Lakes is dominated by diatoms, particularly the colonial pennate forms *Fragilaria, Tabellaria, Asterionella,*

the solitary pennate *Synedra,* and the chain-forming centric genus *Melosira.* Blue-green algae as single filaments or small colonies of *Lyngbia* and *Oscillatoria,* which are typical of unproductive lakes, are also widespread. In the most productive areas, such as western Lake Erie, Saginaw Bay, and Green Bay, the large colonial blue-green algae *Aphanizomenon, Anabaena,* and *Microcystis,* all characteristic of eutrophic conditions, are abundant (Table 21-4). The zooplankton in the deep, colder lakes are mostly calanoid copepods, for example, species of *Diaptomus.* Cyclopoid copepods, such as *Cyclops,* and the cladoceran zooplankters *Daphnia* or *Bosmina,* increase in importance in the more productive, warmer lakes. Rotifers and cladocerans tend to dominate the most productive, eutrophic lake basins, such as western Lake Erie. An unusually high number of limnetic zooplankton coexist in the Great Lakes. The large numbers of crustaceans are not entirely due to the lakes' large size, since this diversity is not found in large tectonic lakes. High species diversity in the Great Lakes may be due to the greater turbulence in their cold waters.

The benthos of lakes Superior and Michigan contains small populations of "relic" forms left over from the previous ice age. The shrimp *Mysis* and the amphipod *Pontoporeia,* together with some species of cold-water midge larvae, have survived in cold deep waters where oxygen is abundant and their major predators are scarce. In the benthos of the more productive parts of the lakes, where oxygen is lower, *Pontoporeia* has been replaced by chironomid larvae. A similar gradual replacement of the "relic" copepod *Limnocalanus* by *Bosmina* or *Daphnia* has occurred in the more productive sections and bays. The fish of the Great Lakes, which have been considerably modified by human activities, are discussed in Chap. 14.

Climatic variations or nutrient pollution take a long time to change large lakes with long residence times. The smaller, more frequently flushed lakes, such as Erie and Ontario, respond

TABLE 21-3

PHYSICAL AND CHEMICAL CHARACTERISTICS OF PELAGIC WATERS OF THE LAURENTIAN GREAT LAKES

Note that, as in the English Lake District, the trophic classification based on transparency (Secchi disk) or chlorophyll a is also supported by the distribution of phytoplankton, zooplankton, and zoobenthos.

Lake	L, km B, km A, km²	z_{max} ($\bar{z}$), m	Drainage basin area, km² × 10³	Thermocline depth, m	Max/min summer (winter) temp, °C	Hydraulic residence time, years	Approximate period of thermal stratification	Winter (summer) surface nutrients, µg liter⁻¹		
								NO_3-N NH_4^+-N	PO_4-P	SiO_2
Superior	560 256 82,000	406 (149)	125	10–30	14 (0.5)	184	Aug.–Dec.	280 (220)	0.5 (0.5)	2200 (2000)
Michigan	490 188 58,000	281 (85)	118	10–15	18–20 (<4)	104	July–Dec.	300 (130)	6 (5)	1300 (700)
Huron	330 292 60,000	228 (59)	128	15–30	18.5 (<4)	21	End June— Oct. or Nov.	260 (180)	0.5 (0.5)	1400 (800)
Erie*	385 91 26,000	w: 13(7.3) c: 24(18) e: 70(24)	59	w: p c: 14–20 e: 30	24 (<4)	w: 0.13 c: 1.7 e: 0.85 all: 3	mid-June— Nov.	w: 640 (80) c: 140 (20) e: 180 (20)	23 (2) 7 (1) 7 (1)	1300 (60) 350 (30) 300 (30)
Ontario	309 85 20,000	244 (86)	70	15–20	20.5 (<4)	8	End June— Nov.	280 (40)	14 (1)	400 (100)

From Schelske and Roth (1973), Dobson et al. (1974), Ragotzkie (1974), and Bennett (1978).
* For Lake Erie, w = western; c = central, e = eastern, p = polymictic.

TABLE 21-4

THE LAURENTIAN GREAT LAKES RANKED BY THEIR BIOLOGICAL AND CHEMICAL DIFFERENCES

Lake	Local trophic classification	1970 basin population, millions	Secchi disk, m	Summer surface chlorophyll, µg liter^{-1}	Chemical mg liter^{-1} Ca^{2+}	Chemical mg liter^{-1} HCO$_3{}^{-}$	Phytoplankton Tabellaria + Asterionella	Phytoplankton Aphanizomenon + Microcystis	Zooplankton Diaptomus silicis	Zooplankton Cyclops vernalis	Zoobenthos Pontoporeia
Superior	O	0.9	11.3	0.9	14	51	d	r	d	p	c
Michigan	O	7.5	4.8	1.3	37	130	d	r	c	c	d
Huron	O-M	2.0	5–9	1.8	26	200	c	p	c	c	d
Ontario	M	6.1	—	5	42	—	—	—	p	—	d
Erie, all	—	12	—	—	—	—	—	—	—	—	—
East	M	—	4.3	4.3	—	—	—	—	—	—	—
Central	E	—	4.4	5.5	38	—	p	p	p	r	r
West	E	—	2.0	11	32	—	p	d	p	r	r

From Beeton and Chandler (1963), Patalas (1971), Scheiske and Roth (1973).
Key: d = dominant; c = common; p = present in smaller amounts; r = rare or absent; – = no data; O = oligotrophic; M = mesotrophic; E = eutrophic.

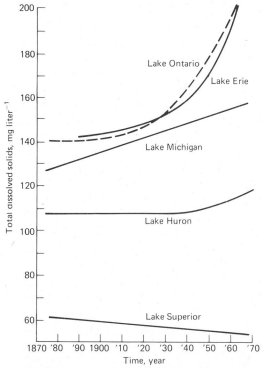

FIGURE 21-3 Changes in total dissolved solids (TDS), which are mostly calcium and magnesium sulfates, in the Laurentian Great Lakes. Note the large change in the "initial" TDS in 1870 and the rapid increases in the smaller lakes Ontario and Erie relative to Michigan. The downward trend in Superior and upward trend in Huron may not be significant. Redrawn from Beeton (1969).

more rapidly. A good example of chemical accumulation is shown in Fig. 21-3. Most waste from residential, industrial, and agricultural pollution goes into lakes Erie, Michigan, and Ontario. Superior and Huron have few large cities on their shores, and their drainage basins are too cool and rocky for intensive agriculture.

LAKES IN TROPICAL OR ARID CLIMATES

The major characteristic of lakes in tropical or arid climates is their continually high temperature. For most of the year temperatures are above 25°C, and the lowest values are approximately the highest found in temperate lakes. Lakes in the tropics range from shallow, very eutrophic waters to the deep, less productive ones.

Limnological methods in tropical lakes are similar to those generally employed at other latitudes, but some aspects deserve particular attention. Tropical lakes and their drainage basins have a variety of serious vector-borne diseases, such as malaria, bilharzia (schistosomiasis), and river blindness. Limnologists should get a full set of vaccinations and take antimalarial pills. Simple wiping off of water splashes near any snail habitat will help prevent bilharzia. More than one limnologist has been attacked by crocodiles, tossed by buffalos, threatened by elephants, or attacked by the surprisingly aggressive hippopotami. Finally, hospitals are often few and far between and travel to them is likely to be slow.

Lake George, Uganda

There are many kinds of tropical lakes, ranging from deep, meromictic Lake Tanganyika to huge shallow Lake Chad, to shallow alkaline pools that fill only in the rainy seasons. Lake George is by no means typical of all tropical lakes but has attributes that have relevance for eutrophication and seasonality beyond tropical lakes. Because of the constant water inflow and its location at the equator, there is probably less seasonality in this lake than anywhere else in the world. The constancy of the environment allows observation of a lake that has probably been at near steady-state conditions for at least 1000 years. In some ways Lake George is a huge long-term natural experiment where normal lake seasonality does not exist and the autumn blue-green algal bloom is everlasting.

Lake George is a large, shallow, polymictic, remote lake situated astride the equator, 915 m above sea level ($A = 250$ km^2, $\bar{z} = 2.4$ m, residence time = 0.36 year) in a large open plain near the Ruwenzori Mountains in the Western Great Rift Valley of Africa. Gross productivity is high, with very dense algal crops and large populations of zooplankton, zoobenthos, and fish. Papyrus swamps, common on the tributaries of African lakes, cover 60 km² adjacent to Lake George. It was studied for several years by a team of international and Ugandan limnologists, largely sponsored by the Royal Society of Britain as part of the International Biological Program (*Proc. R. Soc. London, Ser. B,* 1973, **184:**229–298). A year-round water supply comes from the Ruwenzori Mountains as well as from local runoff during the two wet seasons characteristic of this area. Incident solar energy varies annually by only 16 percent from the mean of 1700 J cm^{-2} day^{-1}. There is no significant cultural eutrophication of the basin by the sparse population of commercial *Tilapia* fishers and subsistence farmers (Fig. 21-4).

The remarkable year-round constancy of the lake is shown in Fig. 21-5a. The concentration of nutrients and the biomass of phytoplankton, chlorophyll *a,* and zooplankton are virtually unchanged over time. Detailed studies of the individual species present show that with few exceptions this seasonal constancy is typical of each component of the plankton and is not due to species replacement maintaining constant density (Burgis, 1971; Ganf, 1974). Lake George may be contrasted to temperate Loch Leven in Scotland, which is also a productive polymictic lake (Fig. 21-5b). The annual change in zooplankton in Loch Leven is enormous when compared to the slight fluctuations found in the tropical lake. In contrast to seasonal patterns, daily patterns in Lake George show very large changes (Ganf and Horne, 1975). One of the most dramatic is the daily change in dissolved oxygen from less than 100 to more than 230 percent saturation. Similar changes occur in temperature, chlorophyll, and carbon and nitrogen fixation (Fig. 21-6).

Some important conclusions can be drawn from the seasonal constancy and diurnal variability in Lake George. The plankton in temperate lakes is dominated by seasonal changes. In tropical lakes daily changes play a more important role. The closer a lake is to the equator, the more daily cycles dominate its ecology. Phytoplankton in lakes normally have a maximum growth rate of two or three divisions per week, and zooplankton grow even slower. In temperate climates the major environmental changes, such as stratification, occur only once a year and thus occur much more slowly than planktonic division rates. Thus, the plankton respond most to seasonal changes. In tropical lakes plankton experience the largest environmental changes every 24 hours and must adapt to those rather than the smaller seasonal changes. Any group of species sufficiently adaptable to grow well during a 24-hour period will tend to dominate the lake (Round, 1971; Ganf, 1974).

An outstanding physical feature of Lake George common to all tropical lakes is its high temperature, 25 to 36°C (Fig. 21-6). This has a direct effect on species composition and biological production. High temperatures produce strong temporary stratification. Blue-green algae thrive in well-stratified waters at temperatures above 20°C, but many other algae do not. In Lake George, the colonial blue-green alga *Microcystis aeruginosa* is the most abundant lake plankton

FIGURE 21-4 Subsistence-level farming and fishing typical of the drainage basin of Lake George, Uganda. The fisheries on tropical lakes are often quite productive and large number of *Talapia* are harvested, frozen, and shipped to the distant city of Narobi, Kenya. Wooden dugout canoes are now often powered by outboard motors. Note the dense papyrus stand on the unmodified lake edge.

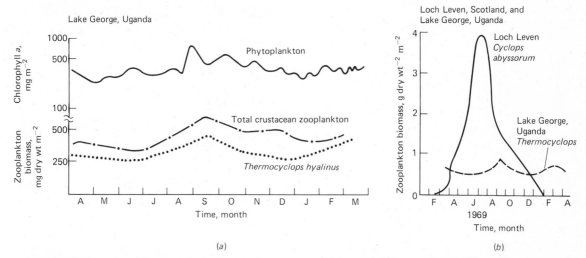

FIGURE 21-5 Seasonal changes in phytoplankton (log scale) and zooplankton (linear scale) in (a) tropical Lake George Uganda and (b) a comparable temperate lake. Note the absence of seasonal cycles in the tropical lake and the very large seasonal cycles in the temperate one. Cyclops comprise 99 percent of the zooplankton in the temperate lake. From Burgis (1974), Ganf and Viner (1973), and Bindloss et al. (1972).

at all times of year. In turn, the copepod *Thermocyclops hyalinus,* which feeds on *Microcystis,* dominates the zooplankton population in the lake at all times (Burgis, 1971). Phytoplankton comprise 99 percent of the total plant and animal plankton biomass even when the planktonic stages of the abundant midge *Chaoborus* are included (Fig. 21-5). Although Lake George is very eutrophic, with a photic zone of only about 1 m, the absolute quantity of algae is equaled by algal blooms in many eutrophic temperate lakes.

A population of about 3000 hippopotami lived in the lake in the 1970s. They graze on surrounding vegetation at night, which they digest and excrete in the lake during the day. One hippopotamus weighs as much as 60 humans, but excretion rate does not rise at a 1:1 ratio with body weight. Nevertheless, the waste from the hippo population is equivalent to that from a city of about 20,000 people. Although this would appear to be a large enrichment for a lake of this size, analysis of nitrogen shows that hippopotami wastes contribute only a few percent to the lake's

annual nitrogen inflows (Table 21-5). In these warm, shallow lakes, the natural fertility of the watershed and efficient nutrient recycling is the dominant factor.

Tropical ecosystems are usually deficient in nitrogen (Odum and Pigeon, 1970), and this is certainly the case for Lake George. About one-third of the nitrogen used for algal growth is fixed from the atmosphere by blue-green algae (Table 21-5; Horne and Viner, 1971; Burgis et al., 1973).

The zooplankton in Lake George is dominated by the raptorial cyclopoid adults and copepodites, which feed on colonies of *Microcystis.* Filter-feeding cladocerans such as *Daphnia* are uncommon because the small algae on which they feed are scarce. This situation is not necessarily common to all tropical lakes; many deeper ones, such as Lake Tanganyika, apparently have low populations of all types of algae.

The major fish species in Lake George are two herbivorous cyclids, *Haplochromis nigripinnis* and *Tilapia nilotica.* These and the dominant

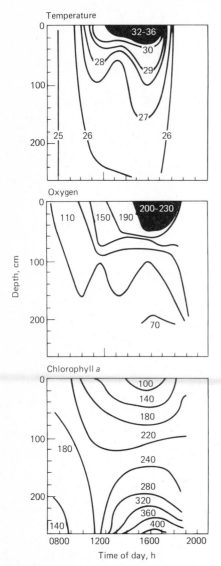

FIGURE 21-6 Diurnal changes in temperature, percentage oxygen saturation, and chlorophyll *a* with depth in shallow, eutrophic, tropical Lake George, Uganda. Oxygen isopleths are every 40 percent oxygen saturation, chlorophyll *a* every 40 µg liter^{-1}, temperature every 1°C. Note the very large diel changes in all variables, oxygen supersaturation in the upper water in the afternoon, and how the blue-green algae (chlorophyll) sank to the bottom on this calm day. Redrawn from Ganf and Horne (1975).

TABLE 21-5

NITROGEN BALANCE SHEET FOR LAKE GEORGE, UGANDA

Stream flow is a minimum value and does not include some storm runoff, which could not be measured adequately. Note the large role played by nitrogen fixation in this very productive lake.

Annual gain, metric tons		Annual loss, metric tons	
Nitrogen fixation	1280	Denitrification	?
Stream inflow	322	Stream plankton outflow	3180
Rainfall	277	Sedimentation	655
Hippopotami excretion	76–99	Commercial fish export	50–75

Modified from Horne and Viner (1971).

zooplankton *Thermocyclops hyalinus* are all dependent on *Microcystis* and other large planktonic blue-green algae. This contrasts with temperate lakes, where diatoms and green flagellates are more important for herbivores. Other tropical lakes where blue-green algae are abundant may have a food chain similar to that of Lake George. The mechanism employed by *Tilapia nilotica* to digest blue-green algae is described in Chap. 14.

Extensive free-floating growths of large aquatic plants are a feature of Lake George common to many tropical lakes but unfamiliar to most temperate limnologists. In Lake George, as in many tropical reservoirs, *Pistia,* the water lettuce, covers parts of the lake so thickly that it is impossible to drive a boat through. One-third of the water surface of the huge subtropical reservoir Lake Kariba was covered by *Salivinia,* the water fern, during the early years after its construction. They block the oxygen transfer across the lake surface and often induce anoxia in the water below. The plants eventually pile up on the downwind shores in huge rotting masses (Mitchell, 1969). Where lake levels in the tropics do not fluctuate very much, floating macrophytes are common. A major design criteria for tropical reservoirs may be to ensure sufficient water level fluctuations to strand the young plants before

(a)

(b)

FIGURE 21-7 Papyrus wetlands in tropical lakes. (*a*) Aerial view of an arm of Lake Victoria, Uganda. Note that entire bays (midcenter between darker tree-covered land and in distance) are completely filled with this tall emergent macrophyte. Papyrus swamps block small inflowing rivers to create large swamps. (*b*) The Mpanga River as it flows into Lake George, Uganda. The papyrus stands about 3 m high. In a small boat and armed with a machete, one of us made only a few yards progress in an entire afternoon through the dense root system.

they become a serious nuisance for boating, fishing, and power generation.

No discussion of tropical lakes is complete without mention of papyrus swamps, *Cyperus papyrus,* which form in the river deltas (Fig. 21-7). These wetlands slow down the seasonal heavy rains and filter out particulates. Tropical streams are usually brown with silt during rains, but after passage through a papyrus swamp the water is often so transparent that emergent plants such as lilies can grow up from the bottom.

POLAR AND HIGH ALPINE LAKES

Polar and high alpine lakes are distinguished by constant low water temperatures for all or most of the year. Large annual changes in biota are caused by the huge seasonal variations in daily total incident light. The maximum daily radiation on mountains or near the poles is greater in midsummer than that experienced by tropical lakes.

Polar and high alpine lakes are usually transparent and unproductive, with low standing crops of plankton (Plate 1*b*). Much of the plant biomass is often found in the large benthic green alga *Chara* or in a dense benthic felt of bluegreen algae, which harbors many small invertebrates. Higher plants with a covering of aufwuchs may also be more important than the plankton, especially in some alpine lakes. The small, unmodified rock and clay drainage basins of these lakes reduce annual nutrient loadings, so that it may take years to achieve even a moderately thick algal felt.

In this section we discuss two types of unpolluted lakes: coastal lakes in Antarctica, where the temperature rarely exceeds 10°C, and a lake high in the European Alps.

Limnological methods used to study these lakes are similar to those employed in other areas, but the extreme cold and remote situations of polar and alpine lakes require special attention. Hypothermia is always a danger and immersion in polar waters will kill humans in a few minutes. Whiteouts of blowing snow often reduce visibility to zero in these areas. As in tropical climates, hospitals may be far away, especially in the Antarctic.

The edges of the antarctic continent and adjacent islands contain many small lakes that are influenced by the surrounding ocean, often called *maritime lakes* (Goldman, Mason, and Wood,

1972; Heywood, 1972; Horne, 1972). Other large lakes in the interior antarctic desert, such as amictic Lake Vanda and Lake Bonney, were mentioned previously (Fig. 4-3). Antarctic maritime lakes are usually quite small and shallow ($A < 10$ ha, $z_{max} < 6$ m) and are often less than 1 m deep. These small lakes do not dry up because of their low temperature and the high humidity of the coastal zone. In common with arctic and alpine lakes, maritime antarctic lakes are usually oligotrophic in the strict sense that inflowing nutrient supplies are low. Eutrophication can occur when they receive nutrients from sea birds, seals, or people.

Maritime antarctic lakes usually have small plankton populations. The algae are often not truly planktonic but appear in the open water after being washed in from the snow or dislodged from the bottom. Antarctic phytoplankton cannot photosynthesize at high rates to compensate for their small numbers. Goldman, Mason, and Wood (1963) provided an explanation for this phenomenon that is now generally accepted for all lake and ocean surface waters. They discovered that even at sea level there was a severe *light inhibition of photosynthesis* for most of the day during the antarctic summer. The effect is due to two factors: the total amount of solar radiation and the ultraviolet part of the spectrum (Chap. 3). In the antarctic lakes, light inhibition is always more pronounced at noon, so photosynthesis is inverse to incident light energy (Fig. 21-9).

Figures 21-8 and 21-9 show the effect of vary-

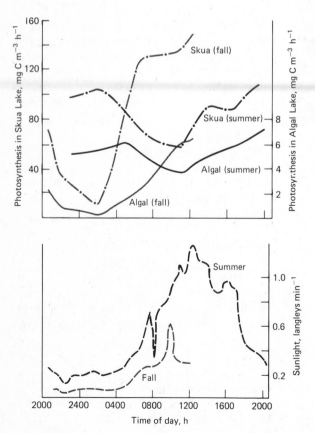

FIGURE 21-8 Diel changes in photosynthesis in typical transparent Algal Lake and in bird-fertilized Skua Lake, in Antarctic midsummer and fall (January 9–10 and February 17–18). Note that maximum production occurs at midnight and minimum at noon in the antarctic summer, but normal patterns occur with a maximum at noon in the antarctic autumn. The light reaches saturation at about 0.3 langley, which is about 20 percent of the incident light at that season. Above that level, light actually inhibits photosynthesis. Redrawn from Goldman et al. (1963; 1972).

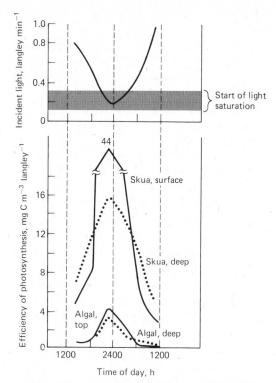

FIGURE 21-9 Inhibition of photosynthesis in antarctic midsummer (January 15, 1962) for transparent Algal Lake and turbid bird-fertilized Skua Lake. Note maximum efficiency at lowest light due to photosynthetic inhibition by high sunlight during the daytime. These lakes are very shallow, but the inhibition is reduced even in the "deep" samples, about 50 cm below the surface. ly = langleys, a unit of light-calories per square centimeter. A skua is a predatory sea bird, *Stercorarius* spp. Modified from Goldman, Mason, and Wood (1963).

ing levels of natural sunlight on phytoplanktonic carbon fixation in two contrasting antarctic lakes. In transparent Algal Lake, summer photosynthesis by the sparse phytoplankton population is low at noon, when light is highest, and maximal during the low-light period around midnight. In Skua Lake, enriched by bird droppings, overall photosynthesis is higher but shows approximately the same pattern. In the antarctic fall, a more normal pattern of maximum productivity near noon occurs in both lakes (Fig. 21-8). The

reason for this change in daily maximum is light inhibition of photosynthesis. The lower section of Fig. 21-8 shows the very high sunlight levels present for much of the day during the short antarctic summer. In contrast, levels are much lower in the fall, which is only a month later. This effect is shown most clearly in photosynthetic efficiency (Fig. 21-9).

Light inhibition of photosynthesis occurs in the upper waters of almost all lakes and seas, but overall production per unit area of lake surface may not be reduced since the production maxima can move deeper in the water column during high light. This is impossible in the very shallow antarctic, arctic, and alpine lakes. However, the lost production is compensated for by extensive growths of benthic algae and mosses, which form thick felts on the lake beds (Fogg and Horne, 1970).

The algal felts are mostly filamentous blue-green algae and dominate lake beds for several reasons. Blue-green algae are usually the first to colonize exposed surfaces, such as those left by ice scour. The upper filaments produce protective carotenoid pigments that act as a screen against inhibiting levels of sunlight. Digging through an antarctic lake's benthic felt may reveal a yellow-orange layer with a blue-green layer below. Some species of blue-green algae appear more tolerant of high light and consequently are more dominant near the surface.

The benthic felts of algae and moss provide a major habitat for antarctic lake animals. Large populations with relatively few species are typical due to the isolation of this continent from the rest of the world's land masses. In alpine and arctic lakes the felts are more diverse. Protozoans, rotifers, and crustacean copepods and cladocerans spend parts of their lives among the felt, where temperatures are often several degrees higher than in the water above. The increase in temperature is due to absorption of light energy by the felt in these transparent, shallow lakes.

Fish and all but one flying insect are absent

in the Antarctic due to the difficulty of coloniz-
ing this remote region. Fish are present or have
been introduced to most of the larger alpine and
some arctic lakes.

Alpine Lakes

Alpine lakes are found in most high mountains.
They are cold, often deep, and ice-free for much
of the summer. A most important difference from
other lakes is the increased amount of solar radiation at high altitudes. Any increased ultraviolet light due to the ozone hole in the atmosphere
(Chap. 3) would be felt strongly in alpine lakes.

Verderer Finstertaler See, in the European
Alps, is situated at 2237 m. The lake receives
very intense sunlight in summer, although day
length is shorter than in polar summers. The lake
water remains below 10°C in summer. As for
most polar or alpine systems, the structure of the
lake ecosystem is simple. Dinoflagellates are the

only common phytoplankton group, and the zooplankton community contains two rotifers and
one copepod. Two species of salmonid fish comprise the nekton in this lake (Pechlaner et al.,
1972). Mosses, blue-green algae, and epiphytic
diatoms occur on the lake bed where sufficient
light penetrates. These plants form a felt inhabited by nematodes, oligochaetes, ostracods, and
chironomid larvae.

Light inhibition of photosynthesis occurs in
the surface waters but, unlike the shallow polar
ponds, the lake is sufficiently deep for motile
algae to avoid damaging light intensities. Maximum photosynthesis in winter occurs at low light
levels just under the ice (Fig. 21-10a). In spring,
as the snow melts and the ice becomes more
transparent, the photosynthetic maximum moves
down to 5 to 15 m. Under ice-free conditions the
maximum is still deeper (Fig. 21-10a). The dominant dinoflagellates *Gymnodinium* and *Gleno-*

FIGURE 21-10 Changes in photosynthesis with depth and season in an alpine lake, Verderer
Finstertaler See. (*a*) Maximum photosynthesis occurs near the surface under ice but occurs much
deeper in summer due to light adaptation and active avoidance of high light by the dominant phytoplankter, the dinoflagellate *Gymnodinium* (see text). Values for isopleths are milligrams of carbon
fixed per cubic meter per day. (*b*) Changes in photosynthesis per algal cell with season. In winter and
spring, light levels limit production; in summer and fall, when the water surface is free of ice, nutrients
limit production (see text). (■, ●, ▲ = dark-adapted cells in late winter, spring, early summer; Δ, □ =
light-adapted cells in summer and winter. Modified from Pechlaner et al. (1972).

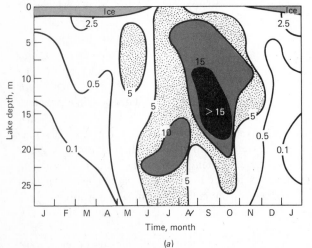

(*a*)

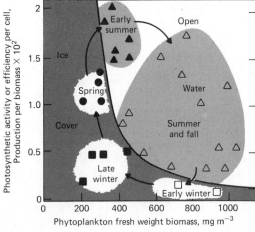

(*b*)

dinium are highly motile and phototactic and are responsible for the downward movement of maximum photosynthesis (Fig. 21-10). The adaptation of the phytoplankton to light under ice and in the open water of Verderer Finstertaler See is illustrated in Fig. 21-10*b*. In early winter phytoplankton are abundant but photosynthesize little, since they are adapted to the summer conditions of high light intensities and long days. Clumping under winter ice the motile dinoflagellates grow slowly and gradually become adapted to the dim light. Their photosynthetic efficiency rises as adaptation occurs, but their winter biomass remains small (Fig. 21-10*a*). The low biomass could also be due to winter grazing by the rotifers *Keratella hiemalis* and *Polyarthra dolichoptera,* but under-ice temperatures are always low, so grazing rates are low. The ice and snow cover take most of the spring to melt due to the high latent heat of water (Chap. 4). The eventual melt in late spring exposes the dark-adapted algae to full summer sun. Phototactic avoidance of inhibiting light intensities (Fig. 21-10) by the phytoplankton produces maximum photosynthetic efficiency at this time (Fig. 21-10*b*). This response indicates that only light was limiting growth in the dark-adapted algae. Lakes all over the world have this kind of response in spring, which has been clearly demonstrated in the English Lake District (Lund, 1949; 1950).

As summer progresses the phytoplankton efficiency decreases as biomass increases, probably due to nutrient deficiency. Some experiments indicate that Verderer Finstertaler See is phosphorus-limited in summer and fall. Different nutrients may limit algal growth in other alpine and polar lakes, since nitrogen, phosphorus, and trace metals can all stimulate growth (Goldman, 1960; Kalff, 1967; 1971).

SALINE OR ATHALASSOHALINE LAKES

There are many salt lakes throughout the world, despite their desert locations. There is almost as much saline lake water (104×10^3 km^3) as fresh

lake water (125×10^3 km^3; Table 3-1). The term *athalassohaline* is derived from Greek (*a* meaning "not"; *thalassic* meaning " sea"; *haline* meaning " salty"). Salt lakes are not connected with the ocean. There are thus two types of athalassohaline lakes: those derived from the evaporation of fresh water and the very large inland seas of marine origin, such as the Caspian Sea (Fig. 3-1).

When climates become drier or geological events change drainage basins, the lake may cease to have a significant outflow and become a *terminal* or *sink lake.* The salts in the lake are concentrated by evaporation and are no longer flushed out. The lake may dry up completely, but first it will become more saline. In the Pleistocene Era two vast lakes, Bonneville and Lahontan, covered much of the southwestern United States. The rise of the Sierra Nevada cut off most of the rain-bearing clouds from the Pacific, and now only Great Salt Lake, Utah, and lakes Walker and Pyramid, Nevada, remain as saline relics of wetter times. Other good examples of salt lakes are found in areas of drier climate, such as Australia, southwestern and northwestern United States and central Canada, South America, eastern Africa, Antarctica, Russia, and the dry northern side of the Himalayas.

Salt lakes vary from those with almost fresh waters in dry temperate climates to viscous organic soups covered with seasonal crusts of salt, such as those in tropical east Africa. Lakes are considered to be salt lakes when they contain more than 3 ppt salinity (Williams, 1978), but they can reach 350 ppt, the approximate level of saturation. Several good examples of saturating salinity can be seen in the Death Valley National Park. Salt lakes have been classified as *hyposaline* (3 to 20 ppt), *mesosaline* (20 to 50 ppt), and *hypersaline* (> 50 ppt). Seasonal rains vary the salinity and cause severe osmotic stresses. One of the most tolerant of salinity change is the brine shrimp, *Artemia salina.*

The ionic composition of salt lakes derived from the evaporation of fresh water is very different from that of the ocean. Sea water is dominated by sodium chloride and fresh water by calcium, magnesium, sulfates, and carbonates. Salt lakes can be classified by the relative dominance of the anions chloride, sulfate, or bicarbonate-carbonate (Hutchinson, 1957). High salinity alters several important physical processes. Salt lakes stratify easily and require more wind energy to destroy thermal stratification than fresh water at the same temperatures. For example, Cole (1968) measured a spectacular temperature gradient of 0.4°C cm^{-1} in a shallow Algerian salt pond. This is about 100 times greater than that found in typical freshwater lakes and results from the fact that saline water is more viscous and its temperature-density curve has a very steep slope (Fig. 21-11).

Another important physical feature of salt water is the depression of the freezing point. At high salinity, this may amount to several degrees Celsius and is sufficient to prevent some salt lakes from freezing. Mono Lake, California (elevation 1979 m), remains monomictic, although nearby lakes freeze over in winter (Fig. 21-12).

Ecologists have been attracted to salt lakes for the same reasons they are attracted to polar and alpine lakes. Under extreme conditions, simplifications in the food web reduce the factors that obscure limnological processes such as predator-prey relations. Saline lakes typically share a low diversity of organisms, which simplifies food-chain analysis. As salinity increases, diversity decreases (Table 21-6). Even on a worldwide basis the diversity of the nonmarine saline biota is much less than in fresh water. Ciliates, foraminiferans, spirochaetes, gastropod snails, oligochaete worms, crustaceans such as anostracans, copepods, cladocerans, amphipods, and

FIGURE 21-11 Change in density of saline Mono Lake, California (salinity = 70 ppt) with temperature. The curve is steeper than for pure water, and there is no density inflection at 4°C, the maximum density for pure fresh water. Redrawn from Mason (1967).

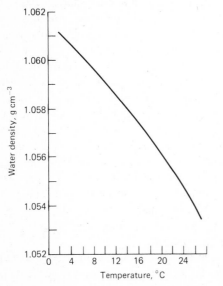

FIGURE 21-12 Conductivity (salinity), photosynthesis, and temperature profiles in amictic, desert Lake Vanda, Antarctica. Note how the salinity stabilizes the warm deeper water, which otherwise would be more buoyant and float to the surface. Modified from Goldman, Mason, and Hobble (1967).

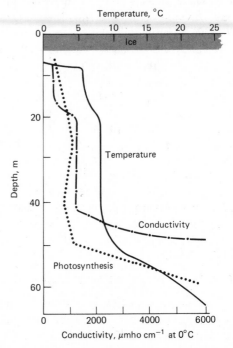

TABLE 21-6

NUMBERS OF ANIMAL SPECIES RECORDED WITHIN VARIOUS SALINITY RANGES FOR THE SALINE LAKES IN VICTORIA, AUSTRALIA

Note the rapid decline in species diversity as salinity rises above brackish water levels. A similar effect is shown in estuaries (Figs. 19-1, 19-2).

Salinity, ppt	No. of species
1–10	71
10–100	36
100–200	8
200–300	1
>300	0

From Williams (1978).

isopods, chironomids, ephydrid flies, and some mosquitoes are found (Williams, 1981; Chap. 11). At the lowest trophic level, macrophytes such as *Ruppia,* the widgeon grass, the *Halobacteria* group, and several phytoplankton, including *Dunaliella* and the blue-green algae *Spirulina,* are often dominant.

The productivity of saline lakes is often high based on a few very abundant species. Few carnivorous zooplankton occur and, because of the osmotic stress, fish are often totally absent. An exception is the tiny desert pupfish (*Cyprinodon* spp.), which is very salt-tolerant. One species has been found in salinities as high as 140 ppt (Simpson and Gunther, 1956). Some other fish can be acclimated to quite high salt levels, but usually there is a requirement of lower salinity for successful breeding. A sport fishery for corvina, which may grow to a length of 75 cm, has been maintained for several years in the increasingly saline Salton Sea. This large lake was formed accidentally by the diversion of the Colorado River in 1905 and has salinities of up to 60 ppt.

The lower trophic levels in salt lakes have very limited diversity. For example, in Mono Lake, California (salinity = 70 ppt, A = 200 km^2, $\bar{z}$ = 19 m), there are only six phytoplankton species, several protozoans, two rotifers, and one brine shrimp (Mason, 1967). Many saline lakes

are small and shallow and periodically dry up completely. This is certain to reduce diversity by providing fewer niches! Evidence of the importance of large size and depth as well as low salinity in promoting higher diversity is found in Pyramid Lake, Nevada. It has an area of 446 km^2, Z_{max} of 100 m, and a salinity of 3 to 5 ppt. This lake contains 31 phytoplankton genera, 7 zooplankton, and 3 rotifers (Galat et al., 1981).

Comparative limnological studies on animals in the Australian salt lakes (Williams, 1972) have revealed three faunal assemblages: a halobiont group (approx. 50 to 100 ppt salinity), a halophylic (salt-loving) group (approx. 10 to 60 ppt), and a salt-tolerant freshwater group (< 1 to 20 ppt).

During the drying phases of lakes, many common species die out or become rare as salinity increases. The drying up of the large Lake Chilwa, Malawi, Africa, is apparently a cyclic process and has occurred several times in the last few hundred years.

Blue-green algae, especially attached forms such as *Schizothrix* and planktonic forms such as *Anabaena* and *Nodularia,* are abundant in many salt lakes. One of the most spectacular events in many lakes of intermediate salinity is the bloom of the filamentous blue-green alga *Nodularia* (Fig. 21-13). This genus is characteristically the most visible species in summer and may cover most of Pyramid and Walker lakes in Nevada as well as much of the brackish Baltic Sea in Europe. Also abundant and characteristic of saline lakes are the brine flies and midges, some of which bite. These insects are often neglected by limnologists because they occupy the interface between open water and the dry shore, but they are a major food supply for some of the shore birds that frequent saline lakes. They were even used as food by Native Americans, who collected adult and larvae of the brine fly, *Hydropyrus,* along the foam-covered edge of Mono Lake, California.

Although fish may be absent or play a subordinate role in saline lakes, birds and reptiles

FIGURE 21-13 *Nodularia* blooms in saline, desert Pyramid Lake, Nevada. Note the very patchy distribution of this N_2-fixing blue-green alga, which is restricted to brackish water (salinity = 3 to 20 ppt) in saline lakes and estuaries. Between and underneath the patches of algae, the water is quite clear.

do not. Most of the world populations of roseate flamingos depend on saline lakes in east Africa for food and breeding sites. These birds build moundlike mud nests to prevent waterlogging during temporary flooding. The hot climate and treacherous thin salt crust prevent animal predators from crossing the drying lakes to reach these nests. The upside-down position of the head during flamingo feeding facilitates filtering out the large filaments of blue-green algae and zooplankton (Fig. 11-16).

SPECIAL STREAM ENVIRONMENTS

Unlike lakes, streams and rivers are permanent features of the landscape, although their courses and flows constantly change. Very similar-looking but taxonomically distinct organisms have evolved in rivers and their headwaters (Chap. 16). Streams have great similarity no matter where they occur, but those at high latitudes and altitudes as well as hot and cold springs share special environmental features that prevent the

usual array of organisms from developing. The specialized fauna and flora last only a short distance before representatives of the more typical stream community appear.

Some cold-water streams rarely exceed 1°C even in summer and in winter may freeze solid. However, low temperatures alone do not reduce the diversity or activity of stream biota, since stream invertebrates may be cold-adapted. Stonefly larvae, for example, often show their maximum growth during winter. A few insects survive very cold periods as eggs or in a dispause phase. Even in frozen streams the temperatures in the deeper gravels are usually above freezing, and this zone acts as a refuge. The main restriction for most insects is that warmer conditions are required for the aerial mating of adults. Suitable weather may occur for only a few days in the short arctic and alpine summers.

The main problem for stream organisms in winter is ice formation: as air cools, hoarfrost forms by condensation on vegetation along the stream edges. Ice crystals drop into the water and form nuclei for *frazil ice,* producing the effect of a snowstorm in the water. Frazil ice accumulates in large spiky masses on any solid object and forms ice caverns that disguise the familiar rocks and pools. Over time the ice becomes firmly attached as *anchor ice,* which dams and diverts water out of the streambed. Fish and insects become disoriented by the lack of recognizable objects or flow patterns in the ice caves and wander into the diverted channels. The next morning, when the ice dam melts and the water returns to its normal channel, fish and insects may become stranded and die. In some high Sierra Nevada streams the effects of ice dams are thought to be the major cause of mortality in young trout and overwintering insects (Needham and Jones, 1959).

Even without the dangers of anchor ice, the large changes in daily radiant energy in summer make cold streams an extremely variable habitat. The diel changes in flow for various types of streams fed by snow melt are shown in Fig. 21-

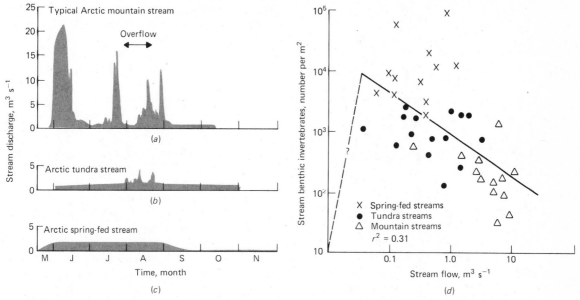

FIGURE 21-14 Stream flow and its relationship to stream animals in various types of cold-water streams in the Arctic. (*a*) The mountain stream has a highly variable discharge in summer, (*b*) the tundra stream is less variable, and (*c*) the spring-fed stream has a constant-discharge. Mountain and tundra streams usually freeze solid in winter, but spring-fed streams maintain their flow at low levels. Summer temperatures reach about 8°C for all types of streams. (*d*) Note the low benthic invertebrate populations in the continually fluctuating mountain streams relative to large numbers in the constant "Arctic oasis" of the spring-fed stream. Also note that flow characteristics only explain about one-third ($r^2 = 0.31$) of the differences in animals between streams. Much of the rest of the variation is probably due to the moderating effects of constant temperature and lack of winter freezing in the spring-fed stream. Redrawn from Craig and McCart (1975).

14. The effect in small streams is a change in flow of 10 to 20 percent per day, equivalent to a daily flood.

Large diel temperature changes occur in small streams above the tree line, and some Arctic streams may rise from 4 to 15°C between dawn and midafternoon. This increase rules out the presence of obligate cryophylic forms, which grow only at low temperatures. Most cold-stream species are not specially adapted to low temperatures (Fig. 21-15). Despite the very different temperatures, from 1 to 12°C, at which three algae grow in Montana and Wyoming, their optimal temperatures for growth in the laboratory are between about 20 and 30°C. The same general temperature relationships are found for bacteria, fungi, lichens, insects, and fish. The chironomid *Diamesa* and the colonial alga *Palmella* are among the only species that seem to be strictly confined to very cold waters and are found within a few meters of glacier ice.

A similar effect is found for cold but constant-temperature, spring-fed streams in high mountains and in the Arctic. The bright green color of the year-round moss-dominated flora near the spring outlet contrasts sharply with the winter snow. These small open areas have been called the "oases of the Arctic." As with snowmelt streams, there are no relic or endemic species present, and the only difference from more typical temperate streams is the small number of species found.

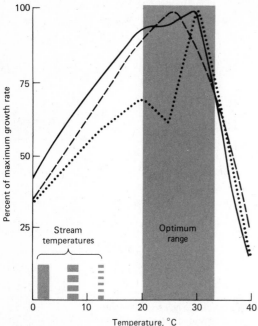

FIGURE 21-15 Growth of various types of stream algae at their normal and elevated temperatures. Solid line is the very common thallate (platelike) green alga, *Protococcus*. Dashed line is for two filamentous blue-green algae, *Oscillatoria* and *Phormidium*. Dotted line is the filamentous green alga *Zygnema*. Note that the optimal temperatures for all three groups are 20–30°C but their actual growing temperatures in the streams are 1°C (solid black, *Protococcus*), 7°C (thick dashes, blue-green algae), 12°C (thin dashes. *Zygnema*). Modified from Mosser and Brock (1976).

FURTHER READING

Bloomfield, J. A. 1978. *Lakes of New York State,* vol. 1. *Ecology of the Finger Lakes.* 499 pp. vol. 2. *Ecology of the Lakes of Western New York State.* 512 pp. Academic, New York.

Brock, T. D. 1967. "Life at High Temperatures." *Science,* **158:**1012–1019.

Brock, T. D. 1985. *A Eutrophic Lake: Lake Mendota, Wisconsin.* Springer-Verlag, New York. 308 p.

Burns, N. M. 1985. *Erie: The Lake that Survived.* Rowman & Allanheld, Littlefield, NJ. 320 p.

Cobb, C. E. 1987. "The Great Lakes' Troubled Waters." *National Geographic,* July 1987: 2–31.

Carpelan, L. H. 1958. "The Salton Sea: Physical and Chemical Characteristics." *Limnol.,* **3:**373–397.

Castenholz, R. W., and C. E. Wickstrom. 1975. "Thermal Streams." pp. 264–285. In B. A. Whitton (ed.). *River Ecology.* University of California Press, Berkeley.

Cole, G. A. 1968. "Desert Limnology." In G. W. Brown, Jr. (ed.). *Desert Biology.* Academic, New York.

Goldman, C. R. 1960. "Primary Productivity and Limiting Factors in Three Lakes of the Alaskan Peninsula." *Ecol. Monogr.,* **30:**207–270.

Heywood, R. B. 1972. "Antarctic Limnology: A Review." *Br. Antarctic Surv. Bull.,* **29:**35–65.

Macan, T. T. 1970. *Biological Studies of the English Lakes.* Elsevier, New York. 260 pp.

Mackay, N., and D. Eastburn (eds.). 1990. *The Murray (River).* Murray-Darling Basin Commission, Canberra, Australia. 363 pp.

Mitchell, P., and E. Prepas (eds.). 1990. *An Atlas of Alberta Lakes.* University of Alberta Press, Alberta. 675 p.

Schelske. C. L., and J. C. Roth. 1973. *Limnological Survey of Lakes Michigan, Superior, Huron, and Erie.* Great Lakes Research Division of the University of Michigan, Publication no. 17. 108 pp.

Wetzel, R. G. 1964. "A Comparative Study of the Primary Productivity of Higher Aquatic Plants, Periphyton and Phytoplankton in a Large, Shallow Lake." *Int. Rev. Ges. Hydrobiol. Hydrogr.,* **49:**1–61.

Williams, W. D. 1972. "The Uniqueness of Salt Lake Ecosystems." pp. 349–361. In Z. Kajak and Hillbricht-Ilkowska (eds.). *Productivity Problems of Fresh Waters.* PWN, Warsaw-Krakow.

———. 1981. "Inland Salt Lakes: An Introduction." In W. D. Williams (ed.). *Salt Lakes: Proceedings of an International Symposium on Athalassic (Inland) Salt Lakes.* Junk, The Hague.

Various authors. 1973. "Physical, Chemical, Phytoplankton, Zooplankton, Zoobenthos and Fisheries in Lake George, Uganda." *Proc. R. Soc. London,* **184:**235–346.

Various authors. 1974. *J. Fish. Res. Board Can.,* **31:**689–854. On Laurentian Great Lakes physics, chemistry, biology.

Viner, A. B. (ed.). 1987. *Inland Lakes of New Zealand.* Department of Science and Industry Research, Wellington, New Zealand. 494 pp.

CHAPTER 22

Applied Limnology

OVERVIEW

The importance of managing freshwater ecosystems is becoming more evident every year. Management should be both environmentally sound and ecologically reversible to allow for unforeseen negative effects. Here we focus on several well-documented examples of lake and river pollution and restoration that have wide application. The best understood systems are inevitably those dealing with the simplest levels of organization—nutrients, plankton, and higher aquatic plants. The best examples are found in the manipulation of medium-sized lakes—small enough for adequate sampling but large enough to minimize edge effects. In this chapter we evaluate examples of the restoration of polluted, eutrophic lakes, such as the straightforward diversion of waste from Lake Washington and phosphorus removal from wastewater entering Shagawa Lake, to more involved schemes, including diversion and dredging in Lake Trummen, Sweden. Once polluted by domestic effluent, deep oligotrophic Lake Tahoe is threatened by inflowing sediments. Methods with limited application for pollution control, such as flushing, aeration or mixing, algal or macrophyte

harvesting, and algae control by biomanipulation of the food chain, are also discussed. Older remedial measures, such as copper sulfate for algal control, are considered in light of resistance buildup and copper toxicity. Finally, we describe the successful restoration of the Central River Thames, which was so polluted by industrial and domestic wastes that in the 1950s no higher organisms could live in it.

We discuss measurements; case studies of direct waste diversion, phosphorus removal from wastewater, advanced wastewater treatment and waste diversion, and waste diversion and dredging; aeration and mixing; plant harvesting and herbicides; flushing; management of streams, rivers, and estuaries; and waste diversion, treatment, and in situ oxygenation in the River Thames.

INTRODUCTION

Managers of lakes, streams, rivers, reservoirs, wetlands, and estuaries use limnology to protect or restore water quality and the biota in lakes, rivers, and their watersheds. Limnologists work for regulatory agencies such as the U.S. Envi-

499

ronmental Protection Agency, consulting engineering firms, state or local watershed planning departments, river authorities, water departments, fish and game departments, and recreational lake communities.

Applied work differs from basic research in that it often requires a fast response to difficult questions that are not of the investigator's choosing. Entire new fields, such as biomanipulation, the use of wetlands for nutrient removal, and blue-green algae toxicity, have evolved from this approach.

Lake management requires a consensus of public opinion concerning the current versus desired status of the lake in question. Without popular and political support for the project, database-based conclusions may be ignored. Although this seems obvious at first glance, the parties involved usually have very different views on the ultimate goals. For example, real estate developers tend to have different ideas about tolerable water quality than people already living in the watershed or on the lakeshore. Establishing consensus on preserving water clarity in the Lake Tahoe basin, for example, required a decade of meetings and negotiations. Typically compromises have to be made between interests as different as builders of shopping malls, power boating lobbies, anglers, and wilderness society members.

Once the goals are defined politically, baseline limnological monitoring is required to define the problem scientifically. Such monitoring may take several months or even years. Unfortunately, political decision makers almost always require quick solutions. This invariably necessitates both compromises and shortcuts. The challenge to the limnologist is to be both fast and correct. Fortunately, an increasing number of younger limnologists have successfully accepted this challenge.

The solution to many applied problems requires the expenditure of large sums of public or private funds. The limnologist may be called upon to justify these costs in public meetings. Proposals should include realistic evaluations of the initial capital cost, long-term maintenance costs, and any secondary impacts of the management scheme.

In developed countries, increases in both population and leisure time have created public pressure to manage a variety of lakes and streams for recreation. Despite an inherent degree of incompatibility of use, these water bodies are required to meet multipurpose recreation needs, from appreciation of their beauty to fishing, duck hunting, swimming, boating, and to supply drinking water. In contrast, in most developing countries aquatic resource management is primarily concerned with water supply and food production.

Although it would be desirable to leave many beautiful lakes completely alone, it is unrealistic to assume that any lakes are now completely isolated from pollution, if only from the atmosphere. Even the most remote rock-bound lakes and streams receive traces of major and minor nutrients from aerosols and other volatile fallout from industry and agriculture. As lakes increase in recreational value with population growth, their careful management becomes essential. Virtually every lake and reservoir has more users than it had 10 years ago, and even Lake Baikal is now a tourist stop. In Southern California, 30,000 daily visitors in lines 5 miles long occasionally block major freeways as they await their turn to enter the large drinking water supply reservoirs that also serve for boating and fishing.

About half of the drinking water in the United States is derived from surface waters such as lakes, reservoirs, streams, and rivers. As these waters become more eutrophic, the higher cost of water treatment has encouraged watershed management in North America, Taiwan, South Africa, and elsewhere. Aquatic ecosystems are, and will continue to be, the ultimate sink for soluble waste. It follows that the quantitative assessment of the effects of waste discharges on the biota of receiving waters is an important field. Increasingly the question is asked, "How much treatment is enough?" Because there is not enough money to ensure that no waste is ever discharged into the waters, we must fit the treatment better to anticipated effects on the biota. If we do not accomplish this we risk a loss of beneficial use of many lakes, estuaries, and rivers.

Aquatic systems management is a vast subject, and this chapter can only cover a few examples and principles. Other assistance is to be found in the *Journal of Lake and Reservoir Management* and several texts listed in the Further Reading list at the end of the chapter.

MEASUREMENTS

Once the duration of the study and the management goals are set, what should be measured? The relative importance and economy of time and money are the deciding factors but fortunately, the most important variables do not require particularly complicated equipment or analysis. Observations necessary for management may not be strictly quantitative; for example, ''good fishing'' reflects not only a high catch rate but also species composition and fishing conditions.

Measurements used to evaluate the progress of lake restoration include secchi depth, levels of chlorophyll, attached algae, primary productivity, and oxygen, and changes in fish, zoobenthos, and zooplankton populations. All of these variables are important, but here we discuss only the example of the Secchi disk, described in Chap. 3. The Secchi disk is a useful, inexpensive method to assess water quality, particularly algae and suspended sediments (Fig. 20-1). However, the seasonal variations in water transparency prior to the pollution of lakes are usually unknown, and a level of transparency must be arbitrarily established as a goal for lake restoration. For example, a secchi depth of 50 cm indicates a severe nuisance condition for most lakes, but a fourfold increase to 2 m would provide satisfactory transparency for most observers. A fourfold change in secchi depth from, say, 2 to 8 m may not be necessary or even easily apparent to

the casual observer. Plotting transparency and algal abundance measured as chlorophyll *a* produces a hyperbolic tangent similar to that found for algal growth and nutrients (Fig. 15-7). Only over a limited range do small changes in algal concentration produce large changes in transparency (Fig. 20-1).

In some eutrophic lakes most chlorophyll is contained in large clumps of blue-green algae. Other phytoplankters are dispersed as individuals or short filaments. Clumps produce higher-than-expected transparency for any given chlorophyll level. Under such conditions, the secchi disk underestimates other nuisance conditions, such as the demand of the decaying algae on the hypolimnion oxygen supply.

Dunst et al. (1974) listed 17 types of potential methods for lake restoration, which involve lake and watershed management strategies. The best-known examples of watershed management concern sewage and other wastewater treatment or diversion. Diversion usually sends the problem elsewhere, yet has been widely used to curb wastewater inputs. Studies of wastewater diversion from lakes, such as in Lake Mendota, Lake Washington, Lake Tahoe, and Lake Zurich, are important because they illustrate the causes and effects of nutrient loading. Diversion proves that human pollution was responsible for much of the nuisance and that the gross features of eutrophication are reversible in many lakes. However, recycling from the sediments may negate the beneficial effects of major sewage diversion, especially in shallow lakes.

CASE STUDIES

Lake Washington: Direct Waste Diversion

Lake Washington is a large monomictic coastal fjord lake in Washington State ($A = 88$ km^2, $\bar{z} = 33$ m, $z_{max} = 62$ m).

Early in the twentieth century, Lake Washington was a mesotrophic to oligotrophic lake with a diatom-dominated phytoplankton and a minimum secchi depth of over 3 m. As nearby Seattle grew, the human population and pollution of Lake Washington's watershed increased. By the mid-1950s, the phytoplankton was dominated by the filamentous blue-green alga *Oscillatoria* and the secchi depth fell to about 1 m. The loss of water clarity within memory of lakeshore residents and unsightly floating mats of blue-green algae produced the necessary public demand for a lake cleanup (Edmondson, 1972*a*; 1972*b*).

The first questions asked were "What caused the deterioration?" and "What can be done to restore the lake?" The likely causes were either sewage or land drainage. Sewage inflow from nearby towns was treated and then disposed of in the lake; land drainage, chiefly discharge from agricultural, logging, and other activities, also entered the lake. Three solutions were suggested: (1) divert treated sewage out of the drainage basin; (2) change agricultural, logging, and residential development practices in the drainage basin; and (3) ignore the problem as unimportant except to property owners near the lake. A fourth solution, not technically possible in 1960, would be drastically to reduce either phosphate or nitrogen inflows by advanced wastewater treatment. Sewage phosphorus can now be removed simultaneously and a prohibition of phosphate-containing detergents enforced (see Shagawa Lake).

Lake restoration procedures were carried out, largely due to the presence at Lake Washington of an eminent limnologist, Professor W. T. Edmondson of the University of Washington. He thought it was important to differentiate between the point source inflows of sewage and the diffuse inflows, which included natural runoff and pollutants from logging. At this time the lake was receiving some 24,000 m^3 day^{-1} of secondarily treated effluent from about 70,000 people spread around the lakeshore and the immediate watershed. Sewage, therefore, seemed potentially responsible for the deterioration of the lake. Secondarily treated effluent contains 20 to 30 mg $liter^{-1}$ NH_4—N and 5 to 10 mg $liter^{-1}$ PO_4—P.

A lake nutrient budget in 1960 showed that roughly half the phosphorus input, but only 15 percent of the annual nitrogen income to the lake, was derived from sewage. Thus sewage diversion was the only alternative that would have any chance of substantially reducing the nutrient loading of the system. By 1964 point sources comprised almost 75 percent of the annual phosphorus income. Good correlation existed between the early spring concentration of phosphorus in the surface water and the crop of algae produced 3 months later (Fig. 9-5).

There was much controversy over which was the limiting nutrient for algal growth in Lake Washington. In most lakes polluted by sewage, it is unimportant which nutrient eventually becomes limiting because too much has been added of all the essential elements (Fig. 9-8). After many years of waste inflows, nitrogen usually limits growth in summer because so much more phosphorus than nitrogen has been added. Secondarily treated domestic sewage has a ratio of N:P of 3:1 by weight, while plants use N:P in a ratio of 10:1. This was not the case in Lake Washington. A good correlation between spring phosphorus and summer phytoplankton crops and a lack of a similar correlation with nitrogen told Edmondson that diversion of inflowing phosphorus alone would eliminate algal nuisance problems.

Lake Washington and Lake Zurich in Switzerland are among the first restorations in which a general theory of lake management was tested. The dramatic effects of the Lake Washington waste diversion are shown in Fig. 22-2, which demonstrates the marked increase in water transparency after the total diversion of sewage. Figure 22-2 illustrates another feature that is at first puzzling: when only 30 to 40 percent of the waste had been diverted, no change in secchi depth was noted. This was because mean epilimnial chlorophyll *a* only fell from 40 to approximately 20 μg $liter^{-1}$. Figure 22-1 shows that even large changes in concentration of chlorophyll *a* (> 20 μg $liter^{-1}$) have little effect on

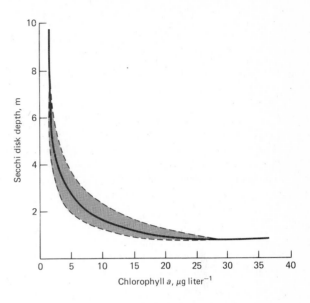

FIGURE 22-1 Generalized relationship between phytoplankton chlorophyll *a* and secchi depth in lakes. The shaded area shows the expected variability for different lakes at different seasons. This relationship will be poor if algae are present in large clumps (Fig. 12-1). Water color or turbidity from suspended sediments may also distort this relationship. Note that the transparency does not change over much of the ranges of chlorophyll in eutrophic lakes (15 to 40 μg liter^{-1}) but transparency changes greatly with only small changes in chlorophyll in mesotrophic and oligotrophic lakes (secchi depth 2 to 40 m). This has an important impact on cultural eutrophication and the restoration of lakes.

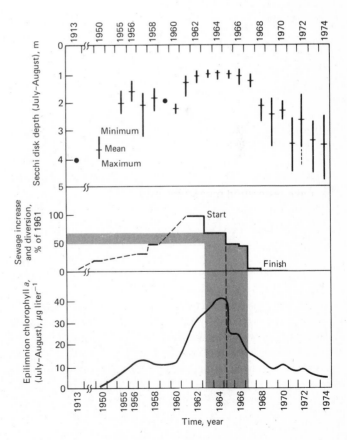

FIGURE 22-2 Cultural eutrophication in Lake Washington. The effects of sewage inflow and its diversion outside the basin as measured by water transparency (secchi disk) and epilimnetic chlorophyll *a*. Note the rapid drop in chlorophyll and subsequent increase in secchi depth after diversion of about 50 percent of the wastewater. Diversion of about 35 percent halted the deterioration of only some aspects of water quality (i.e., secchi depth but not chlorophyll *a*). Dots indicate single readings. Replotted from Edmondson (1972a; 1972b) with additional information courtesy of W. T. Edmondson.

secchi depth. Whether the lake would have shown any noticeable improvement for recreation if only half the sewage phosphorus had been diverted is uncertain (Fig. 20-2). It is likely that any increase in transparency would have taken much longer.

The effects of diversion of PO_4—P, the most important limiting nutrient for Lake Washington, are given in Fig. 22-3 where nitrate is also shown. Diversion decreased phosphorus but not nitrogen. This well-documented and successful whole-lake experiment has enabled lake man-

agers to predict with greater confidence the effects of wastewater diversion for other lakes.

Shagawa Lake: Phosphorus Removal from Wastewater

If phosphorus were the only element that controlled algal growth in Lake Washington, total sewage diversion was not essential—the same results could have been achieved with only phosphorus removal from sewage. Diversion was employed because of the close proximity of Puget Sound to Lake Washington. For inland areas like northern Minnesota, where Shagawa Lake is situated, diversion is often impractical.

The phosphorus present in treated domestic wastewater was implicated as the prime factor responsible for algal blooms in culturally eutrophic Shagawa Lake. In this case, an experimental sewage treatment plant was designed and built to remove over 99 percent of wastewater phosphorus, using chemical precipitation. Shagawa Lake ($A = 1000$ ha, $\bar{z} = 6$ m, $Z_{max} = 14$ m) is smaller, shallower, and has a shorter hydrologic residence time (8 months) than Lake Washington (3 years). Shagawa Lake is typical of many dimictic lakes that have developed nuisance algal blooms over the twentieth century. There were large spring peaks of diatoms (*Asterionella* and *Synedra*) and green algae followed by blue-green algal blooms in late summer (*Aphanizomenon* and *Anabaena*). These blooms were in marked contrast to nearby oligotrophic lakes, which presumably represented Shagawa Lake's original state. Almost all pollution appeared to come from one source—sewage from the town of Ely. This was a simple problem, at least in concept. The main inflow to the lake, apart from wastewater, was a river draining the adjacent oligotrophic Burntside Lake. In many lakes, the multiplicity of lesser nutrient inflows complicates the before-and-after picture. An annual nutrient budget established that about 80 percent of the inflowing phosphorus but only 25 percent of the nitrogen came from the domestic wastewater (Malueg et al., 1973). Bioassay ex-

FIGURE 22-3 Cultural eutrophication in Lake Washington. Changes in phosphate and nitrate from 1933 (little waste discharge) to 1963 (maximum waste discharge) to 1969 (all waste diverted). Ammonia was not measured but could be expected to be approximately 100 µg liter^{-1} (1963) and 10 to 20 µg liter^{-1} (1933 and 1969). In addition, N_2 fixation, which was not measured, probably contributed between 0.5 and 10 percent of annual inflowing nitrogen (Horne, 1977). Modified from Edmondson (1972b).

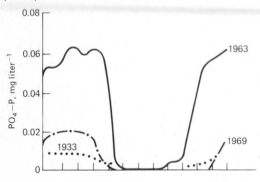

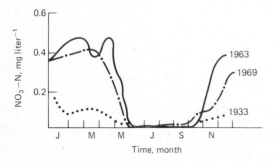

periments indicated that addition of PO_4—P to the lake water produced the greatest increase in algal growth, and a similar effect was produced by secondarily treated effluent (Powers et al., 1972). A special treatment plant was built and an extensive limnological study carried out by the U.S. Environmental Protection Agency.

The waste-treatment plant began operation during January–April 1973. The results are shown in Fig. 22-4. Virtually all phosphorus was removed from the wastewater. This reduced the annual inflow by approximately 80 percent, close to the 75 percent removed from Lake Washington. The algal levels and transparency recorded for the first year were just below the normal year-to-year variation for the pretreatment period. However, 2 years later large decreases occurred in annual mean PO_4—P and chlorophyll a. Transparency increased, but there was little change in nitrate. Because Shagawa Lake has both a short hydrologic and a short phosphorus residence time, more rapid improvement might have been expected. If phosphorus removal is to work for lakes with longer residence times, such

as the Great Lakes, the reasons for this slower response are important. In the simplest theories, nutrients are thought to spend the same residence time in the lake as the water does. In reality, summer releases of accumulated phosphate from the anoxic sediments constitute a diffuse source not considered in calculating the residence time. In the case of relatively shallow Shagawa Lake in summer, *internal loading,* that is, the rate of PO_4—P recharge from the sediments, may be as important a source of phosphorus as is the gross annual inflow.

The annual epilimnetic variations in chlorophyll a and phosphate before and after waste treatment are shown in Fig. 22-5. There was a dramatic decrease in phosphate but little change in green algae or diatom crops in spring. Presumably, the winter accumulation of phosphate is adequate to develop the spring bloom, despite the lowered waste input. The point at which the pre- and post-treatment phosphate levels are closest is in August (Fig. 22-5), due to sediment releases. Unfortunately, blue-green algal nuisance blooms and peak recreation coincide in

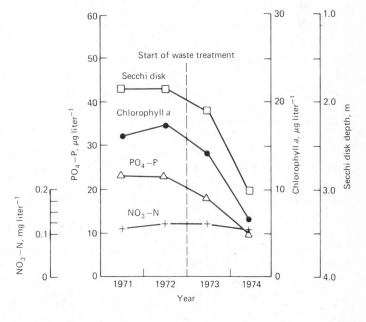

FIGURE 22-4 Cultural eutrophication in Shagawa Lake, Minnesota. Effect of removal of sewage phosphorus on lake nutrients and algal growth. The rest of the wastewater containing nitrate and ammonia was still discharged to the lake. Values are annual means for the epilimnion (0 to 5 m). Note declines in chlorophyll and phosphorus, increase in water clarity, but no change in nitrate. Redrawn from Malueg et al. (1973), with additions from Malueg (personal communication).

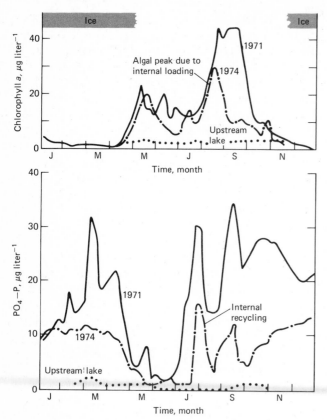

FIGURE 22-5 Cultural eutrophication in Shagawa Lake. Effect of phosphate removal on seasonal changes in phytoplankton and epilimnetic PO_4—P. Treatment started January 1973. Due to releases from anoxic sediments in August–September 1974, an unexpected autumn blue-green algal bloom was produced even after 2 years of treatment. The type of sediment release shown here—internal loading (Larson et al., 1981)—is the main reason for the lack of total success of lake restoration projects in relatively shallow stratified or unstratified lakes such as Shagawa Lake ($z = 6$ m) and failure of diversion in Lake Trummen. In contrast, deep fjord-like Lake Washington ($z = 33$ m) recovered rapidly (Fig. 22-2). Redrawn from Malueg et al. (1973).

midsummer. Since the major blue-green algae present can fix N_2 to supply much of their needs, the release of phosphate from the sediments provides all that is needed to grow a sizable algal bloom. As already noted, average chlorophyll a levels must be lowered below 20 μg liter^{-1} for differences in transparency to be obvious to the recreationist (Fig. 22-1).

Shagawa Lake's restoration program demonstrates a number of important points. After treatment, the lake's annual average limiting nutrient concentrations reached predicted levels. However, in shallow dimictic lakes annual average concentrations are of limited value for predicting the rate of supply of nutrients during midsummer. Internal loading of major nutrients from the sediments must therefore be considered. Although the percentage of phosphorus removed

from lakes Shagawa and Washington was similar, the percentage of water in contact with the bottom mud was much greater in shallow Shagawa Lake, which slowed restoration. Eventually, internal loading should diminish as nutrients are buried by fresh low-phosphorus sediments or locked into refractory compounds. The time required for shallow lakes with a thick layer of polluted sediments is at least a decade and may be even hundreds of years.

Lake Tahoe: Advanced Wastewater Treatment and Diversion

Beautiful oligotrophic Lake Tahoe sits in a graben near the crest of the Sierra Nevada Mountains on the California-Nevada border. Its water is remarkably clear; the secchi depth can approach 40 m. It is quite large ($A = 500$ km^2)

and is the tenth deepest lake in the world ($\bar{z} = 248$ m, $z_{max} = 501$ m). An improved interstate highway built in the 1960s allowed more access and attracted a large, year-round population with a recreation-based economy of gambling, skiing, boating, and fishing.

Even though the lake is so large and oligotrophic, sensitive radiocarbon assays soon revealed evidence of cultural eutrophication (Fig. 22-6). Unlike lakes Washington and Shagawa, increases in the nutrient loading rates were due to a mixture of causes: sewage disposal within

the basin, atmospheric deposition, and land erosion associated with development of houses and ski slopes. The increases would be trivial in most lakes, but the very pure water of oligotrophic lakes is very sensitive to even small increases in loading. Because of the extreme dilution in the 156 km³ of lake water (Table 2-1) and active plant uptake, it took a long time for a measurable increase in nutrient concentration to occur (Goldman, 1981). Phytoplankton primary production, stimulated by the slight nutrient increases, rose at virtually the same rate as the increase in population (Fig. 22-6).

Blue-green algae scums and cloudy water are not in evidence in the still very oligotrophic waters of Lake Tahoe. Nonetheless, two obvious signs of eutrophication are apparent. Water clarity has been decreasing. Twenty-four years of frequent secchi disk measurements have provided a sensitive measure of this slow decline (Fig. 22-7). Attached algae growing on rocks around the lake's margins provide further visual evidence of cultural eutrophication.

There was, as at Lake Washington, a fortunate coincidence of basic limnological studies carried out by Professor Goldman at the time that decisions on sewage treatment were made. The various options were (1) sewer the watershed, treat wastes to the most advanced level possible, and then dispose of the effluent in the lake; (2) pipe wastewater to the lake bottom, because such a deep lake was thought to be meromictic; (3) reuse the wastewater by spraying it on the land and forests of the lake basin; or (4) sewer the watershed and diversion waste outside the basin, as was done for Lake Washington. Waste treatment would then be combined with a land use plan to prevent uncontrolled development from further increasing erosion of the basin.

These proposals were tested in various ways.

1. A nutrient-addition bioassay devised using $^{14}CO_2$ uptake as a measure of phytoplankton responses to highly treated wastewater showed that even very small nutrient additions would have a biostimulatory effect.

FIGURE 22-6 Cultural eutrophication in ultraoligotrophic Lake Tahoe. Changes in the annual primary production in the pelagic waters in relation to the increase in permanent residents and summer visitors in the watershed. Soil and nutrients eroded during home and ski-slope construction, leachate from old septic tanks, and increased nitrogen from atmospheric pollution all reached the lake and caused primary production to increase almost fourfold. Modified from Goldman (1993).

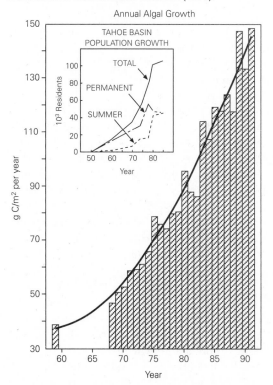

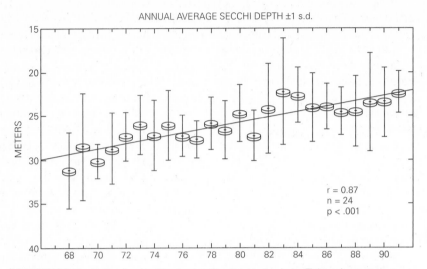

ANNUAL AVERAGE SECCHI DEPTH ±1 s.d.

FIGURE 22-7 Cultural eutrophication in ultraoligotrophic Lake Tahoe. Long-term change in water transparency in Lake Tahoe. The secchi depth has decreased at an average rate of about 0.5 m annually. Three-quarters of the variation (regression coefficient r^2 = 0.75) in secchi depth over this time is explained by the change in time. As is shown in Fig. 22-6, algal growth in the lake has increased steadily over this time. Modified from Goldman (1993).

2. This deep lake was found to be monomictic and not meromictic during most years. Thus any nutrients added to lake bottom waters would soon be circulated to the photic zone. The distribution of temperature and dissolved oxygen with depth, normally used to assess the mixing status of lakes and oceans, was not sufficiently sensitive and the mixing status was determined from measurements of nitrate with depth. A *nitrocline,* which is analogous to a thermocline was found between the low nitrate concentrations in the photic zone and the slightly higher nitrate levels of the aphotic zone (Paerl et al., 1975). In years when holomixis occurred, the nitrocline vanished. However, in other years, when winter storms were not severe, the nitrocline persisted overwinter, indicating meromixis.

3. In-basin disposal of wastewater was considered. There is sound hydrologic and economic sense in reusing wastewater within a lake basin, especially in arid regions. Usually treated wastewater, rich in nitrogen and phosphorus, is reused by spraying it over agricultural land or golf courses. After use, the excess water rejoins the natural drainage, retaining the original water balance of the basin. Because of its subalpine climate, the Tahoe basin is not suited for agriculture. Effluent was used to irrigate stands of Jeffrey pine, *Pinus jeffreyi*. Many trees were killed by waterlogging the roots. Six years after spraying ceased, Heavenly Valley Creek, which drains the sprayed area, still had average concentrations of 1 mg liter^{-1} NO_3—N, whereas similar control streams showed less than 10 percent of this level (Perkins et al., 1975).

4. Diversion out of the watershed was finally selected although, in contrast to the Lake Washington case, there was no convenient disposal area. All of the wastewater is now piped out of the Lake Tahoe basin and treated to various levels, depending on its ultimate use. The results of waste export are shown in Fig. 22-7. The increase in phytoplankton productivity since 1959 has at best only been slowed, but certainly not reversed. Human activities continue to load nutrients to the lake. Atmospheric deposition of nitrate, mostly from automobile exhausts in the cities to the west and wood-burning stoves in the local area, have increased the nitrogen load to the lake. Dry and wet fallout contain more nitrogen than phosphorus, and at Lake Tahoe the increase has been sufficient to change the limiting nutrient from nitrogen to phosphorus in the period 1980–1990.

Some attempt at restricting land disturbance from construction activity was also attempted. An \$485 million bond was passed to buy private land that was subject to erosion. Taking this erodible building land out of production has been successful in reducing sediment load to the lake. Unlike installing sewage systems, which most people think well of, land use planning with restrictions on land development is unpopular. The public controversy still continues among the various agencies of two states, five counties, and the numerous federal agencies involved.

Lake Trummen: Wastewater Diversion and Dredging

Lake Trummen, Sweden, is a small, shallow, temperate lake that was formerly oligotrophic (A = 1.0 km^2, $\bar{z}$ = about 1.5 m, z_{max} = 2.2 m). Municipal waste inflow for many years caused its eutrophication, and by the mid-1950s large blooms of blue-green algae were common. Waste discharges to the lake were diverted with the expectation that eutrophication would be reversed. Unfortunately, after 10 years no improvement was apparent.

We saw in Lake Shagawa that shallow dimictic lakes recycle phosphates from the sediments sufficiently to slow their flushing from the lake. Similar recycling of ammonia also occurs. Lake Trummen is so shallow that thermal stratification does not occur, so it is not surprising that internal loading maintained a eutrophic state. The final solution for Lake Trummen was to dredge out 0.5 m of the bottom mud to remove the nutrients that had accumulated over the years

(Bengtsson et al., 1975). Only the upper sediments contained the legacy of the previous pollution, yet this 0.5-m layer amounted to 6 million m^3 of sediment. The cost was greatly reduced by using the dredge spoils to build a park beside the lake. The interstitial waters, which are always high in nutrients (Fig. 10-5), were cleared of phosphate by precipitation with alum in a treatment lagoon before return to the lake. The cost of dredging was \$2 million (1993 U.S.), and the research program costs were similar. The success of the project can be judged in that nuisance blue-green algal blooms no longer occur (Cronberg et al., 1975). Major changes also occurred at higher trophic levels: zooplankton, especially cladocerans, were much reduced (Andersson et al., 1975). A decline was observed in the common cyprinid fish, many of which are zooplankton feeders. Benthic invertebrate populations of chironomid midge larvae, often found in eutrophic lakes, were little affected by the restoration.

In most polluted lakes, the cost of dredging and spoil disposal is prohibitive, but diversion of waste or nutrient removal should not be proposed without considering the interaction of the sediments and the overlying water.

WHEN NUTRIENT DIVERSION IS IMPOSSIBLE

Two prominent features of eutrophication are excess nutrient levels and low oxygen content of the lake bottom waters. These can be altered by physical or chemical methods. In many lakes it is not economically feasible to divert or adequately treat inflowing nutrients. For example, in Clear Lake, California, Upper Klamath Lake, Oregon, and Lake George, Uganda, natural inflows account for almost all of the nutrient input, yet these lakes are very eutrophic. In other cases, diffuse sources of nutrient inflow, such as agricultural drainage and atmospheric pollution, make water treatment impossible. Many lakes

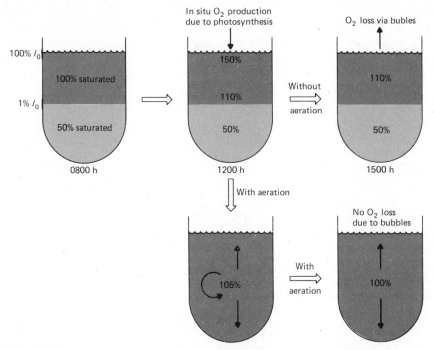

FIGURE 22-8 Artificial destratification employs compressed air pumps or giant paddles to mix oxygen-rich surface waters with the low-oxygen waters of the hypolimnion. The source of oxygen is primarily from photosynthesis in eutrophic lakes. Oxygen is normally lost to the atmosphere in the afternoon in productive lakes. Destratification moves this oxygen to the deeper waters, where it satisfies the oxygen debt built up by algal decay in the sediments.

are easily made eutrophic by small changes in the drainage basin. For small systems an approach of physical manipulation is probably the best procedure. Of the many methods available we will discuss aeration, plant harvesting, chemical control, flushing, and hypolimnetic discharge.

Aeration and Mixing

Low dissolved oxygen results in poor fish habitat, high sediment nutrient releases, and increased treatment for drinking water supplies. Oxygen can be added directly to ameliorate this situation. The simplest solution mimics nature and involves mixing the photic zone with the aphotic zone (Fig. 22-8). The resulting destrati-

fication redistributes photosynthetically produced oxygen. Destratification with compressed air is the most common method, but more efficient giant paddles or water pumps are used occasionally. The main effect of destratification is to redistribute dissolved oxygen, rather than increase its concentration. Water quality is enhanced by destratification because the oxygen precipitates soluble iron and manganese, which may impart an unpleasant taste to drinking water and produce brown stains on porcelain fixtures. Nutrient releases from the sediments are reduced by the restoration of the oxidized microzone (Fig. 10-5; Chap. 7), and toxic ammonia may be converted back to relatively harmless nitrate. Unpleasant taste and odor and hydrogen sulfide, which is associated with putrefaction, are eliminated (Barnett, 1975). In addition, oxygenated sediments allow substantial increases in benthic invertebrates, which serve as food for fish, and greatly extend the habitat for all kinds of fish.

It is also possible to aerate a lake without destratification, using a technique called *hypolimnetic aeration* (Fig. 22-9; Bernhardt, 1967; Pastorok et al., 1981). The advantage is that oxygen is added to the oxygen-depleted hypolimnion without mixing nutrients into the epilimnion. As with destratification, hypolimnetic aeration also reduces iron, manganese, hydrogen sulfide, and sediment nutrient releases. In temperate regions, hypolimnetic aeration allows trout to live in the hypolimnia of eutrophic lakes, which normally would contain insufficient oxygen to support them. Destratification would not work because the mixing of warm upper water with the hypolimnion would produce a temperature too warm for trout. A warm-water fishery in the epilimnion can be maintained simultaneously with a cold-water fishery in the hypolimnion. In eutrophic dimictic lakes, fish kills can occur in winter from oxygen depletion. Aeration in winter can reduce or eliminate fish kills that would require expensive restocking.

It is theoretically much more efficient to add oxygen alone rather than air, which is 80 percent nitrogen. The increased partial pressure of oxygen can raise the amount of oxygen at saturation from about 10 to over 30 mg liter^{-1}. Oxygen is usually supplied from large liquid oxygen tanks but can be generated on site if power is available. The simplest system, called *sidestream oxygenation,* involves the addition of oxygen to small quantities of hypolimnion water pumped into a mixing chamber. A solution supersaturated with oxygen flows back to the hypolimnion and can maintain the desired oxygen level in an otherwise anoxic region. The capital costs are small compared to hypolimnetic aeration, and it is easily adapted to changes in the oxygen demand of the sediment (Fast et al., 1975).

In eutrophic lakes and estuaries it is also possible to oxidize the superficial sediments by mixing them with an oxidizing material such as nitrate. This technique, known as *nitrate ploughing,* oxidizes, precipitates, and thus immobilizes phosphate, iron, or hydrogen sulfide. The byproduct is nitrogen gas, which causes no known environmental problems. Nitrate injection has been employed successfully in Sweden and in at least one estuary (Ripi, 1976; Horne and Roth,

FIGURE 22-9 Hypolimnetic aeration. An airlift pump on the lake bed lifts anoxic water to the surface in an inner tube and simultaneously adds oxygen. Excess gas is vented to the atmosphere and the still cold but now oxygenated water is returned to the hypolimnion via an outer tube. Stratification is preserved with this technique, so cold water salmonid fisheries can be maintained.

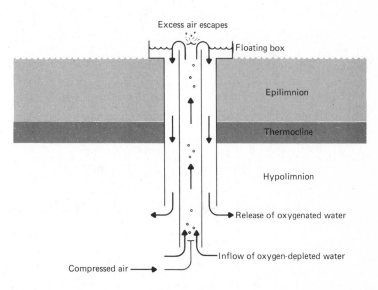

1979). In other cases the method has not always reduced eutrophication but has been proposed as an alternative to costly dredging, such as in eutrophic Lake Apopoka, Florida.

Plant Harvesting

In many lakes, nutrient inflows are so diffuse and numerous that even several nutrient treatments or diversion projects are unlikely to reverse eutrophication to the desired level. Examples are small mountain lakes where the sewage from a few scattered cabins is sufficient to produce eutrophication; small, shallow recreation lakes and stormwater detention ponds in parks or highly urbanized surroundings where street runoff is important; and larger lakes where natural inflows of nitrogen and phosphorus combine with intensive recycling to produce eutrophic conditions. In many of these cases, dredging, aeration, or both, even if effective, are uneconomical.

A major problem with these lakes is the invasion of the shallow waters by rooted aquatic macrophytes. One solution is *macrophyte harvesting* by an underwater mowing device that cuts off the plants at the stem, combined with a rake (Fig. 22-10) for transferring the cut plants to a disposal barge (Livermore and Wunderlich, 1969). Some more stubborn weeds, such as cattails, may require chopping prior to harvest to break up the tough underground mats. Many lakes are successfully ''cleaned up'' with harvesters, which, although expensive, may be rented (Nichols and Cottam, 1972). Harvested

FIGURE 22-10 Weed harvesting. Large aquatic macrophyte harvesters are available in many sizes and include models with underwater cutting blades as well as rotors for breaking up roots in the sediments. Redrawn from information provided by Aquamarine Co., Waukesha, Wisconsin.

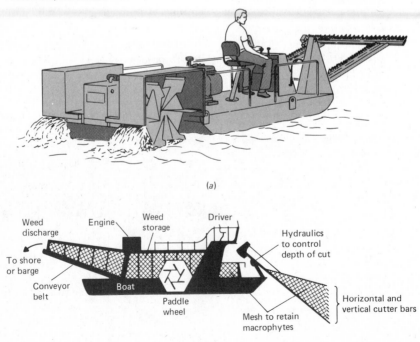

(a)

(b)

vegetation can be used for soil amendment or methane generation. Higher plant control can lead to the paradoxical situation in which the clearance of macrophyte-choked lake waters gives rise to algal blooms that cloud previously clear water.

In very large lakes, particularly those in equatorial zones, floating macrophytes can be a great nuisance by clogging outlets, harboring insect and snail hosts, and increasing water loss through transpiration. These plants are usually quite large and have descriptive common names such as water lettuce (*Pistia stratiotes*), water fern (*Salvinia molesta*), and water hyacinth (*Eichhornia crassipes*). In general, these macrophytes have a very high water content and are virtually useless as cattle feed without drying. One-third of the enormous Lake Kariba, a reservoir in central South Africa ($A = 4400$ km^2), was covered with *Salvinia* only a few years after its formation (Mitchell, 1969). Although the area covered has diminished, it continues to impede fishing and navigation. Its decay is responsible for toxic hydrogen sulfide concentrations below the thermocline in portions of the lake. At Kainji Reservoir on the Niger River in Nigeria, Africa, water level reductions during operation of the hydroelectric plant strand the plants on the shoreline. Water level control may also be used to reduce spawning success of fish likely to overpopulate the lake (Chap. 14). Lake drawdown is currently the practice in many temperate lakes for control of both floating and attached macrophytes, but this is incompatible with most recreational use. The sight of several meters of exposed mud covered with rotting weeds does not encourage tourism!

Animals such as crayfish, grass carp, talapia, nutria, capybara, and manatee may provide a degree of macrophyte control. Control has also been achieved by introducing insects that may effectively attack and destroy specific emergent or floating plants. Introductions of this sort must, of course, be undertaken with caution so as not to create new problems.

Algal harvesting, the analog of macrophyte harvesting, is much less common since it is almost impossible to pick up such small organisms with rakes typically used for macrophytes. Dense strands of the algae *Cladophora,* the blanket weed, are an exception. Experimental algae harvest rigs have been designed for the collection of concentrated surface blue-green blooms. A major difficulty with this method is the design of a harvesting screen that will collect the algae before the motion of the collecting barge dissipates the floating algae. Pilot algal harvesting devices (Fig. 22-11) have successfully been tested on the very dense algal blooms in Clear Lake, California (Oswald, 1976).

Chemical Control

The most widely used method of controlling algae in lakes is the application of *copper sulfate.* The cupric ion is toxic and acts to prevent photosynthesis or growth by affecting the cell membranes. The usual result of copper treatment is to kill the algae and disrupt the cells. The algae sink to the sediments and soluble cell contents,

FIGURE 22-11 Weed harvesting. An experimental algal harvester at work on surface films of *Aphanizomenon* (left) in Clear Lake, California. The floating blue-green algae are collected by driving the submerged blade of the leading collector under them. The resulting material is dewatered by a backwashing rotating microstrainer screen in the rear craft.

such as taste and odor compounds or toxins, remain in the water column. They are not easily biodegraded and continue to be a nuisance for lakes used for human or stock drinking water supplies. Thus copper is best used early in the bloom and not when it is dense. Copper is not a catalytic poison and is consumed in the toxic action. If the copper concentration is too low, those membrane sites not blocked by the copper ion will continue to operate and the cells will recover (Steemann Nielsen et al., 1969). Repeated applications lead to algal populations with increased copper tolerance; in some cases, resistance has built up to the point where it is uneconomical to continue (Ahlgren, 1970).

In many lakes where algae are not very abundant but float and are concentrated by wind to nuisance levels, copper treatment has been the cheapest control technique. Copper sulfate is added to surface waters to produce a concentration of about 500 μg liter^{-1}. Although this rapidly kills algae, the toxic effect lasts only a day or so and fish and zooplankton are not visibly disturbed. Presumably they migrate to avoid the high copper levels. Laboratory tests have shown that some zooplankton and fish larvae may be sensitive to ionic copper levels as low as 10 μg liter^{-1}. Nuisance blue-green algae, the prime targets of copper treatment, are affected at 5 μg liter^{-1} (Horne and Goldman, 1974; Fig. 10-10).

Flushing and Hypolimnetic Discharge

Obviously, if a nutrient-rich lake is flushed with sufficient nutrient-poor water, its water quality will improve (Welch et al., 1972). Green Lake, near Seattle, Washington ($A = 104$ ha, $\bar{z} = 3.8$ m, $z_{max} = 8.8$ m), is a small eutrophic lake that had nuisance blooms of the blue-green alga *Aphanizomenon*. When flushed with a large volume of low-nutrient water, the hydrologic residence time was reduced from 14 to 3 months. A decrease in nitrate occurred and phosphate levels were little changed. Nuisance algal levels were reduced and water clarity increased (Fig. 22-12). This form of lake management is expensive,

since only a few cities have sufficient surplus clean water available for flushing. If the lake volume is small relative to the available flushing water, it is not necessary that the flushing water be nutrient-poor, only that it be free of algae. If the flushing rate approaches the rate of cell division of the problem algae, a simple washout can be achieved. This would require replacing the lake water about every week. Even with rapid flushing, buoyant blue-green algae may resist washout if prevailing wind direction blows them away from the lake outlet.

Another method of flushing out nutrients is *hypolimnetic discharge.* In stratified eutrophic lakes, high concentrations of nutrients accumulate in the hypolimnion (Fig. 8-4a). Most reservoirs discharge at least part of their flows from the hypolimnion. This is part of the reason for the loss of productivity in the vast Lake Mead reservoir over the last decade. In small lakes it is possible to siphon some of these nutrients out of the hypolimnion in summer and thus decrease the total nutrient content at overturn. This method has been used successfully in Lake Orhid in former Yugoslavia. However, hypolimnetic discharges of anoxic, nutrient-rich water, often containing toxic levels of hydrogen sulfide, are not welcomed by fish or downstream water users. For this reason siphons are not widely used in developed areas and reservoir tailwaters are often oxygenated prior to release downstream.

STREAMS, RIVERS, AND ESTUARIES

Too many beautiful and once-productive small streams that could be restored have been regarded as hopelessly damaged. Similarly, the political difficulties of restoring larger rivers are sometimes overwhelming, since parts of the river may be in different states or even countries with no common antipollution code. This is unfortunate, because rivers and streams are usually easier to restore than lakes due to the continual supply of purer water from upstream. A united Europe, for example, may be able to mount a

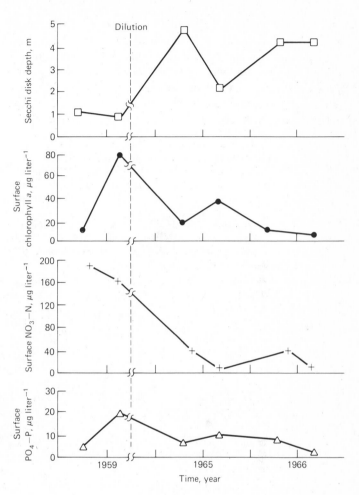

FIGURE 22-12 Flushing out nutrients. Changes in water chemistry and phytoplankton due to dilution of small, eutrophic Green Lake (Seattle, Washington) with low-nutrient water. Values are for mid-May and early August for each year. Note the rise in water clarity and decline in major nutrients after dilution. N_2-fixing blue-green algae increased in the phytoplankton in responded to the decrease in nitrate but lesser decline in phosphate. Redrawn from Oglesby (1968) and Sylvester and Anderson (1964).

more effective attack on the age-old pollution problems of the Rhine and Danube.

Frequent causes of lotic pollution are excess organic nutrient or toxicant loading. Physical damage is caused by dams, dredging, artificial canalization, accelerated watershed drainage, and removal of riparian vegetation. In extreme cases the river may be reduced to a concrete flood control channel or even be completely buried underground in a conduit.

Although desirable, it is usually uneconomical to restore portions of a river or stream. Practical considerations such as flood control, roads, bridges, docks, and housing developments that

originally changed the watercourse often still apply. During the twentieth century, extensive building in flood plains has placed artificial structures squarely in the course of flood destruction. In a few cases, for example the Kisimee River in Florida, canalization is being removed in some stretches to allow flooding once again and the regrowth of wetlands and riparian vegetation.

Restoration of the River Thames, England

A major success for river restoration at a reasonable cost has been achieved in the River Thames. This river is 380 km long, drains fertilized farmland, and eventually flows through the center of London, with a population of about 10 million. The estuarine tidal portion is about 100 km long. Although not blessed with large spawning areas upstream, the Thames had small salmon runs as well as a productive estuarine fishery.

The Thames has received the wastes of Lon-

don for almost 2000 years; King Edward III decreed some basic environmental protection regulations in 1357 in a vain attempt to reduce its smell. However, the introduction of the water closet in 1800 and the rapid increase in population to over 2 million by 1850 destroyed the fishery that had until then survived the pollution.

FIGURE 22-13 Restoration of a highly polluted river. Dissolved oxygen (DO) in the tidal River Thames over the last century. Minimum DO levels always occur during warm weather and low river discharges in late summer. Note that the minimum DO between 30 and 60 km was 20 to 30 percent saturation in 1893–1904, fell to 5 to 10 percent by 1920, and was zero in 1950–1959. The 1974 levels were similar to those of 1920. Typically, 60 to 70 percent DO saturation is now found. The major waste discharges up to 1864 and after 1880 are shown by lines and shaded area. Redrawn from DSIR (1964), Gameson and Wheeler (1977), and the Thames Region of the UK National Rivers Authority.

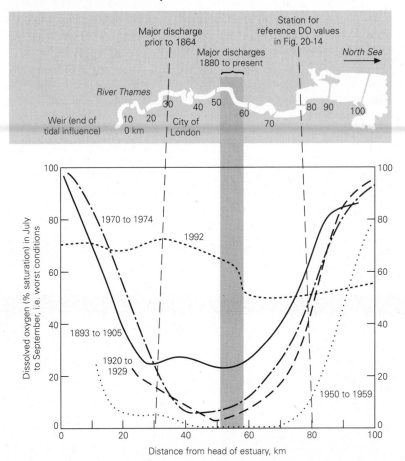

By 1850 there was an extensive stretch of low dissolved oxygen (DO) in the river, centered around the major sewage discharge in the heart of the city (km 30; Fig. 22-13). Foul smells, probably hydrogen sulfide, were common and the fishery ceased. The situation was so bad that the British Parliament, which is situated on the river bank, swiftly enacted the world's first major sewage diversion scheme. The waste was piped farther downstream and discharged during the ebb tide. The extra dilution provided by this diversion together with a precipitation treatment produced a much healthier river between 1891 and 1910 (Fig. 22-13a, b). Migratory marine fish such as smelt and flounder were once again caught in much of the river, and the DO at km 79 was adequate, even during the most critical summer periods (Fig. 22-14b, c). The traditional station used for measurements in the Thames is km 79, because its oxygen content is unaffected by variations in river discharge. The DO content of upstream stations is heavily influenced by river discharge. Fish upstream are able to survive pollution at high river discharge and, conversely, tend to suffer most during droughts. As with all urban rivers, the Thames is used as a drinking water source and the discharge is less than in historic times. This leads to a rather long hydraulic residence time of about 3 months in the summer–fall period, and no fresh water at all flows in droughts.

As the population rose and industry added more toxic material to the river, the fishery once again declined, until by 1950 there were only a few eels in a 30-km-long zone of low oxygen (Fig. 22-14). The average DO content at km 79 in autumn had fallen from 60 to 75 percent saturation in 1980–1910 to less than 10 percent (Figs. 22-13, 22-14). Depletion of oxygen was not the only factor involved in changes in the fisheries in the 1800–1920 period. During the summer and fall the anoxic mud produced hydrogen sulfide (Fig. 10-5). This toxic gas, a health hazard for all animals, became so prevalent in the 1950s that it blackened the lead-based paints on buildings near the river. A 15-year study by the government's Department of Scientific and Industrial Research (DSIR, 1964) concluded that river flow, rather than tidal mixing, was the major source of oxygen. Sewage and industrial waste rather than storm runoff were the main causes of the oxygen depletion. From this information the DSIR predicted that the oxygen deficit could be eliminated and biota restored by improved waste treatment.

It was determined that upgrading sewage treatment from the *primary* to *secondary* level would sufficiently reduce the oxygen deficit to the river and thus raise the DO content of the water. In addition it was calculated that some of the new sewage treatment plants would have to be expanded to include a final nitrification step. In this process ammonia is converted to nitrate by supplying oxygen in the treatment plant instead of in the river. The final outflow is low in biological oxygen demand but also in ammonia, which is toxic at high concentrations (Table 8-3).

The results of this restoration project are shown in Figs. 22-13 and 22-14, which demonstrate the depletion and gradual increase in DO at km 79. The relationship between oxygen in the river and upgrading of sewage treatment is shown in Figs. 22-14a and c. The low oxygen levels have been eliminated, although the level is not as high as it once was. Fish have increased from one species in 1950 to over 100 by 1992, and smelt and flounder are once again present. At km 79, DO concentration has increased from 10 to almost 60 percent during the most critical fall period (Fig. 22-14b). Anoxia has been eliminated, and much of estuary enjoys DO levels above 70 percent. The highest DO levels, found during 1893–1905, have not been reached during the autumn (Fig. 22-13) because of the oxygen demand of combined sewer overflows. In older cities such as London, Chicago, and San Francisco, sewage wastes and storm waters are carried in the same large drains. Thus after heavy rain, the wastewater treatment plants reach vol-

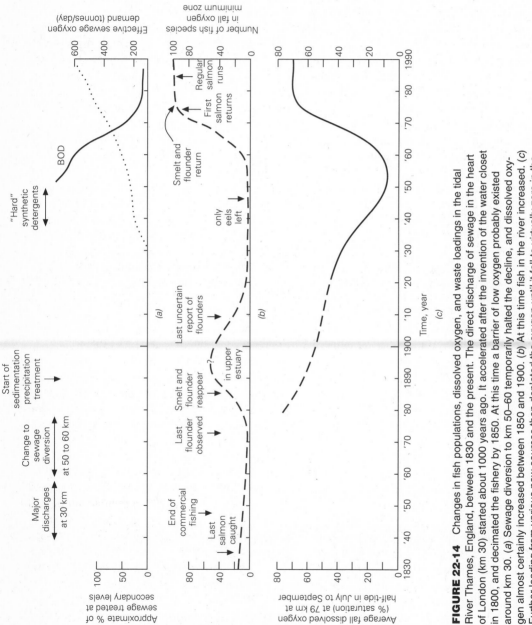

FIGURE 22-14 Changes in fish populations, dissolved oxygen, and waste loadings in the tidal River Thames, England, between 1830 and the present. The direct discharge of sewage in the heart of London (km 30) started about 1000 years ago. It accelerated after the invention of the water closet in 1800, and decimated the fishery by 1850. At this time a barrier of low oxygen probably existed around km 30. (*a*) Sewage diversion to km 50–60 temporarily halted the decline, and dissolved oxygen almost certainly increased between 1850 and 1900. (*b*) At this time fish in the river increased. (*c*) Further loading from various new sources then depleted the oxygen until it fell to virtually zero in the 1950s. At this time there were very few living macroscopic creatures in the river. As secondary treatment removed some of the biological oxygen demand of the wastewater in 1965–1970 [part (*a*)], the oxygen block diminished [part (*c*)] and smelt, flounder, and eventually salmon reappeared [part (*b*)]. Drawn from various sources including DSIR, 1964; Gameson and Wheeler 1977; personal observation of A.J. Horne and UK Thames River Authority.

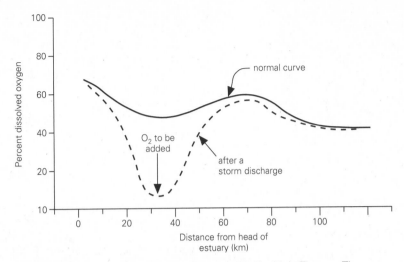

FIGURE 22-15 Mobile oxygen injection system in the River Thames. The "Thames Bubbler," is a 167 foot long barge, adds up to 30 tonnes of oxygen per day to localized areas where dissolved oxygen has become depleted by overflows from combined sewer systems following heavy rains. Using remote sensors in the river the barge can be on site within hours of a fall in DO to critical levels. The success of the bubbler and the overall pollution control system is shown by the restoration of the Thames salmon run which had been lost for over 100 years. Modified from the UK Thames River Authority.

umetric capacity and bypass the mixture of raw sewage and storm water to the rivers. When this occurs the oxygen demand in the river increases and DO in the Thames may fall below 30 percent saturation (about 2.7 mg liter^{-1}). About three times a year DO near the combined overflows falls to about 10 percent (Fig. 22-15). This relatively small area moves up and down with the tide, but if left alone it would remain for some time, given the long hydraulic residence time.

Because few fish can live at 10 percent DO, about 1 mg liter^{-1}, this area of low DO would kill fish and block the upstream and downstream migrations so vital to river and estuarine ecology. One solution would be to construct separate storm and sanitary sewers, as is done in most new cities. However, it was estimated that this would cost about $800 million (1992 U.S. dollars) and involve an enormous disruption in this densely populated city. The solution devised was

to provide local oxygenation at the overflow. A specially equipped barge is sent to the site of the low DO. It has a large molecular sieve system to separate atmospheric nitrogen from oxygen. The resultant almost pure oxygen is then added to the river to bring DO up to the minimum of 30 percent (Fig. 22-15).

In 1966 a single salmon was caught in the Thames, and the upper waters were restocked with salmon fry. By 1992, a regular run of 150 to 200 Atlantic salmon per year was established. These fish cannot pass the first locks and are spawned at a hatchery. The migrations of these pollution-intolerant fish is the final proof of success of the Thames restoration.

FURTHER READING

Bates, J. M., and C. I. Weber (eds.). 1981. *Ecological Assessments of Effluent Inputs on Communities of*

Indigenous Aquatic Organisms. ASTM Speak. Technical Publication no. 730. 370 pp.

Chapra, S. C., and K. H. Reckhow. 1983. *Engineering Approaches for Lake Management,* vol. 2. *Mechanistic Modeling.* Butterworth, Boston. 340 pp.

Cook, G. D., E. B. Welch, S. P. Peterson, and P. R. Newroth. 1993. *Lake and Reservoir Restoration.* Butterworth, Boston. 684 pp.

Esch, G. W., and R. W. McFariane (eds.). 1976. *Thermal Ecology,* vol. 2. U.S. TIS. Conf.-750425, Springfield, VA. 404 pp.

Gore, J. A. 1985. *The Restoration of Rivers and Streams: Theories and Experiences.* Butterworth, Boston. 280 pp.

Hart, C. W., and S. L. H. Fuller (eds.). 1974. *Pollution Ecology of Freshwater Invertebrates.* Academic, New York. 389 pp.

———. (eds.). 1979. *Pollution Ecology of Estuarine Invertebrates.* Academic, New York. 406 pp.

Henderson-Sellers, B., and H. R. Markland. 1987. *Decaying Lakes: The Origins and Control of Cultural Eutrophication.* Wiley, New York. 254 pp.

Hynes, H. B. N. 1966. *The Biology of Polluted Waters.* Liverpool University Press, Liverpool, England. 202 pp.

Jolley, R. L., H. Gorchev, and D. H. Hamilton (eds.). 1978. *Water Chlorination: Environmental Impact and Health Effects,* vol. 2. Ann Arbor Science, Ann Arbor, MI. 909 pp.

Mason, C. F. 1991. *Biology of Freshwater Pollution.* Wiley, New York. 351 pp.

Mintsch, W. J., and S. E. Jorgensen. 1989. *Ecological Engineering: An Introduction to Ecotechnology.* Wiley, New York. 472 pp.

Mitchell, R. (ed.). 1972, 1978. *Water Pollution Microbiology,* vols. 1, 2. Wiley, New York. 416 and 442 pp.

Reckhow, K. H., and S. C. Chapra. 1983. *Engineering Approaches for Lake Management,* vol. 1. *Data Analysis and Empirical Modeling.* Butterworth, Boston. 340 pp.

Tchobanoglous, G., and E. D. Schroeder. 1985. *Water Quality: Characteristics, Modeling, Modification.* Addison-Wesley, Reading, MA. 768 pp.

Thornton, K. W., B. C. Kimmel, and F. E. Payne. 1990. *Reservoir Limnology: Ecological Perspectives.* Wiley-Interscience, New York. 246 pp.

US EPA. 1988. *The Lake and Reservoir Restoration Guidance Manual.* Prepared by the North American Lake Management Society, L. Moore and K. Thornton (eds.). U.S. Environmental Protection Agency, Washington. 197 pp plus appendices.

Warren, C. E. 1971. *Biology, and Water Pollution Control.* W. B. Saunders, Philadelphia. 434 pp.

Weitzel, R. L. (ed.). 1979. *Methods and Measurement of Periphyton Communities: A Review.* American Society of Testing and Materials. Philadelphia. 183 pp. Periphyton means attached algae and/or aufwuchs in this review.

Welch, E. B., and T. Lindell 1980. *Ecological Effects of Waste Water.* Cambridge, New York. 337 pp.

References

Adis, J., K. Fursh, and U. Irmler. 1979. Litter production of a central Amazonian black water inundation forest. *Trop. Ecol.,* **20**:236–245.

Agassiz, L. 1850. *Lake Superior: Its Physical Character, Vegetation, and Animals.* Gould, Kendal, and Lincon, Boston. 428 pp.

Ahlgren, I. 1970. "Limnological Studies of Lake Norrviken, a Eutrophicated Swedish Lake. II. Phytoplankton and its Production," *Schweiz. Z. Hydrol.,* **32**:353–396.

Alexander, W. B., B. A. Southgate, and R. Bassindale. 1935 (reprinted 1961). "Survey of the River Tees. Part II: The Estuary—Chemical and Biological." *Dep. Sci. Ind. Res. Water Pollut. Res., Tech. Paper no. 5.* 171 pp.

Allen, K. R. 1951. "The Horokiwi Stream. A Study of a Trout Population." *Bull. Mar. New Zealand. Fish.,* **10**:1–238.

American Fisheries Society. 1966. *A Symposium on Estuarine Fisheries.* R. F. Smith (Chairman). Special Publ. No. 3. 154 pp.

Anderson, G. C., and R. P. Zeutschel. 1970. "Release of Dissolved Organic Matter by Marine Phytoplankton in Coastal and Offshore Areas of the Northeast Pacific Ocean." *Limnol. Oceanogr.,* **15**:402–407.

Anderson, H. M., and A. J. Horne. 1975. "Remote Sensing of Water Quality in Reservoirs and Lakes in Semi-Arid Climates." University of California, Berkeley, UCB-SERL Report No. 75–1. 132 pp.

Andersson, G., H. Berggren, and S. Hamrin. 1975. "Lake Trummen Restoration Project. III. Zooplankton, Macrobenthos, and Fish." *Verh. Int. Ver. Limnol.,* **19**:1097–1106.

APHA. 1992. Standard Methods for the Examination of Water and Wastewater. American Public Health Association. Washington D.C. Approx. 1500 pp.

Armstrong, F. A. J., and D. W. Schindler. 1971. "Preliminary Chemical Characterization of Waters in the Experimental Lakes Area, Northwestern Ontario." *J. Fish. Res. Board Can.,* **28**:171–187.

Arnold, D. E. 1971. "Ingestion, Assimilation, Survival, and Reproduction by *Daphnia putex* Fed Seven Species of Blue-Green Algae." *Limnol. Oceanogr.,* **16**:906–920.

Axler, R. P., G. W. Redfield, and C. R. Goldman. 1981. "The Importance of Regenerated Nitrogen to Phytoplankton Productivity in a Subalpine Lake." *Ecology,* **62**:345–354.

———, L. Paulson, P. Vaux, P. Sollberger, and D. H. Baepler. 1988. Fish Aid—The Lake Mead Fertilization Project. *Lake and Reservoir Management,* **4**:125–135.

Bachmann, R. W., and C. R. Goldman. 1965. "Hypolimnetic Heating in Castle Lake, California." *Limnol. Oceanogr.,* **10**:233–239.

Baker, A. L., and A. J. Brook. 1971. "Optical Density Profiles as an Aid to the Study of Microstratified Phytoplankton Populations in Lakes." *Arch. Hydrobiol.*, **69**:214–233.

———, ———, and A. R. Klemer. 1969. "Some Photosynthetic Characteristics of a Naturally Occurring Population of *Oscillatoria agardhii* (Gomont). *Limnol. Oceanogr.*, **14**:327–333.

Baldwin, N. S. 1964. "Sea Lamprey in the Great Lakes." *Canadian Audubon Magazine*, November-December. 7 pp.

Balon, E. K., and A. G. Coche (eds.). 1974. Lake Kariba: A Man-made Tropical Ecosystem in Central Africa." *Monogr. Biol.*, vol. 24. Junk Publishers, The Hague. 767 pp.

Barbour, C. D., and J. H. Brown. 1974. "Fish Species Diversity in Lakes." *Am. Nat.,* **108**:473–489.

Barnes, R. S. K. 1974. *Estuarine Biology.* E. Arnold, London, and Crane, Russak and Co., New York. Studies in Biology no. 49. 76 pp.

Barnes, J. R. and G. W. Minshall (eds.) 1983. *Stream Ecology: Application and Testing of General Ecological Theory.* Plenum, New York.

Barnett, R. H. 1975. "Case Study of Casitas Reservoir." ASCE Hydraulics Division: Symposium on Reaeration Research. Gatlinburg, Tenn., October.

Barret, E., and G. Brodin. 1955. "The Acidity of Scandinavian Precipitation." *Tellus*, **7**:251–257.

Bartlett, R. A. 1984. *Rolling Rivers.* McGraw-Hill, New York.

Barton, D. R. 1986. Invertebrates of the Mackenzie River system. pp. 473–492 in Davies, B. R. & K. F. Walker (eds.). 1986. *The Ecology of River Systems.* Junk Publishers, The Hague. 793 pp.

Bates, J. M., and C. I. Weber (eds.). 1981. *Ecological Assessments of Effluent Inputs on Communities of Indigenous Aquatic Organisms.* ASTM Spec. Tech. Publ. No. 730. 370 pp.

Bauer, H., M. M. Caldwell, M. Trevini, R. C. Worrest. 1982. Biological effects of UV-B radiation. *Proc. Workshop.* Munic, Min. Res. Tech. (Munich) and US EPA (Corvallis), BTP-Berict 5/82. 231 pp.

Beaumont, P. 1975. "Hydrology." pp. 1–38. In B. A. Whitton (ed.), *River Ecology.* University of California Press, Berkeley.

Beckel, A. L. 1987. Breaking New Waters. *Trans. Acad. Wisconsin Soc. Arts. Lets.* Special issue. 122 pp.

Beckett, D. C., and C. H. Pennington. 1986. Water Quality, Macroinvertebrates, Larval Fishes, and Fishes of the Lower Mississippi River—a Synthesis. Tech. Repp. E-86-12, U.S. Dept. Army Corps Engineers, Washington D.C. 123 pp. plus appendices.

———, T. P. Aartila, and A. C. Miller. 1992. "Invertebrate abundance on *Potamogeton nodusus*: Effects of Plant Surface Area and Condition." *Can. J. Zool.,* **70**:300–306.

Beeton, A. M. 1969. "Changes in the Environment and Biota of the Great Lakes." pp. 150-187. In *Entrophication: Causes, Consequences and Correctives.* National Academy of Sciences, Washington, D.C.

———, and D. C. Chandler, 1963. "The St. Lawrence Great Lakes." pp. 534-558. In D. G. Frey (ed.), *Limnology in North America.* The University of Wisconsin Press, Madison.

Begon, M., J. L. Harper, and C. R. Townsend. 1986. *Ecology.* Sinauer Assoc., Sunderland, Mass. 876 pp.

Benndorf, J. 1988. "Objectives and Unsolved Problems in Ecotechnology and Biomanipulation: A Preface." *Limnologica*, **19**:5–8.

———, and ten coauthors. 1988. "Food-web Manipulation by Enhancement of Piscivorous Fish Stocks: Long-Term Effects in the Hypertrophic Bautzen Reservoir." *Limnologica*, **19**:97–110.

Bengtsson, L., S. Fleischer, G. Lindmark, and W. Ripl. 1975. "Lake Trummen Restoration Project. 1. Water and Sediment Chemistry." *Verh. Int. Ver. Limnol.,* **19**:1080–1087.

Benke, A. C., R. L. Henry, D. M. Gillespie, and R. J. Hunter. 1985. "Importance of Snag Habitat for Animal Production in Southeastern Streams." *Fisheries*, **10**:8–13.

Bennett, E. B. 1978. "Characteristics of the Thermal Regime of Lake Superior." *J. Great Lake Res.,* **4**:310–319.

Benson, B. B., and D. M. Parker. 1961. "Relations among the Solubilities of Nitrogen, Argon, and Oxygen in Distilled Water and Sea Water." *J. Phys. Chem.,* **65**:1489–1496.

Berman, T. 1983. "Phosphorus Uptake by Micro-Plankton in Estuaries and Coastal Shelf Waters near Sapelo Island, Georgia, U.S.A." *Estuaries*, **6**:160–166.

———. 1970. "Alkaline Phosphatases and Phosphorus Availability in Lake Kinnert." *Limnol. Oceanogr.,* **15**:663–674.

———. (ed.) 1988. "The Role of Microorganisms in Aquatic Ecosystems." *Hydrobiologia, 159,* special issue. 313 pp.

——— 1990. Microbial Food Webs and Nutrient Cycling in Lakes: Changing Perspectives. pp. 511–526 in M. Tilzer and C. Serruya (eds.), *Dynamic Processes in Large Lakes.* Springer-Verlag, Berlin.

———, and W. Rhode. 1971. "Distribution and Migration of *Peridinium* in Lake Kinneret. *Mitt. Int. Ver. Theor. Agnew. Limnol.,* **19**:266–275.

Bernhardt, H. 1967. "Aeration of Wahnbach Reservoir without Changing the Temperature Profile." *J. Am. Water Works Assoc.,* **59**:943–964.

Berra, T. M. 1981. *An Atlas of Distribution of the Freshwater Fish Families of the World.* University of Nebraska Press. 197 pp.

Billaud, V. A. 1968. "Nitrogen Fixation and the Utilization of Other Inorganic Nitrogen Sources in a Sub-Arctic Lake." *J. Fish. Res. Board Canada,* **25**:2101–2110.

Bindloss, M. E., A. V. Holden, A. E. Bailey-Watts, and I. R. Smith. 1972. "Phytoplankton Production, Chemical and Physical Conditions in Loch Leven." pp. 639–659. In Z. Kajak and A. Hillbricht-Ilkowska (eds.), *Productivity Problems in Fresh Waters.* PWN (Polish Scientific Publishers), Warsaw-Krakow.

Birge, E. A. 1915. "The Heat Budgets of American and European Lakes." *Trans. Wis. Acad. Sci. Arts Lett.,* **18**:166–213.

———, and C. Juday. 1911. "The Inland Lakes of Wisconsin: The Dissolved Gases and Their Biological Significance." *Bull. Wisc. Geol. Nat. Hist. Surv.,* **22**. 259 pp.

Blake, B. F. 1977. "The Effect of the Impoundment of Lake Kainji, Nigeria, on the Indigenous Species of Mormyrid Fishes." *Freshwater Biol.,* **7**:37–42.

Blanton, J. O. 1973. "Vertical Entrainment into the Epilimnia of Stratified Lakes." *Limnol. Oceanogr.,* **18**:697–704.

Bloech, J. (ed.). 1989. Mesocosm Studies. *Hydrobiologia,* **221**.

Bloomfield, J. A. (ed.). 1978. *Lakes of New York State, Vol. I. Ecology of the Finger Lakes.* Academic, New York. 499 pp.

Blum, J. L. 1956. "The Ecology of River Algae." *Bot. Rev.,* **22**:291–341.

Bone, D. H. 1971. "Relationship between Phosphates and Alkaline Phosphatase of *Anabaena flos-aquae* in Continuous Culture." *Arch. Mikrobiol.,* **80**:147–153.

Bonetto, A. A. 1986. "Environmental Feature of the Mackenzie System." pp. 435–472. In B. R. Davies, and K. F. Walker (eds.), *The Ecology of River Systems.* Junk, The Netherlands.

Boney, A. D. 1975. *Phytoplankton.* Institute of Biology Study 52. Crane, Russak Co., New York. 116 pp.

Boyce, F. M. 1974. "Some Aspects of Great Lakes Physics of Importance to Biological and Chemical Processes." *J. Fish. Res. Board Can.,* **31**:689–730.

Boyd, C. E., and C. P. Goodyear. 1971. "Nutritive Quality of Food in Ecological Systems." *Arch Hydrobiol.,* **69**:256–270.

Boyer, L. F., R. A. Cooper, D. T. Long, and T. M. Askew. 1989. Burbot (*Lota lota*) biogenic sedimentary structures in Lake Superior. *J. Great Lakes Res.,* **15**:174–185.

Bradford, M. E. and R. H. Peters. 1987. "The Relationship between Chemically Analyzed Phosphorus Fractions and Bioavailable Phosphorus. *Limnol. Oceanogr.,* **32**:1124–1137.

Brezonik, P. L. 1973. *Nitrogen Sources and Cycling in Natural Waters.* Ecological Research Series. EPA-660/3-73-002. 167 pp.

———, and G. F. Lee. 1968. "Denitrification as a Nitrogen Sink in Lake Mendota, Wisconsin." *Environ. Sci. Technol.,* **2**:120–125.

Bricker, O. P., and R. M. Garrels. 1967. Minerologic Factors in Natural Water Equilibria." In S. O. Faust and J. V. Hunter (eds.), *Principles and Applications of Water Chemistry.* Wiley, New York.

Brinkhurst, R. O., and D. G. Cook (eds.). 1980. *Aquatic Oligochaetes.* Plenum, New York. 529 pp.

———. 1974. *The Benthos of Lakes.* Macmillan, New York.

Britt, N. W. 1955. "Stratification in Western Lake Erie in the Summer of 1953: Effects on the *Hexagenia* (Ephemeroptera) Population." *Ecology,* **36**:239–244.

Brock, T. D. 1967. "Life at High Temperatures." *Science,* **158**:1012–1019.

———. 1985. *A Eutrophic Lake: Lake Mendota, Wisconsin.* Springer-Verlag, New York. 308 pp.

Bronte, C. R., J. H. Selgby, and G. L. Curtis. 1991. "Distribution, Abundance, and Biology of the Alewife in US Waters of Lake Superior.'' *J. Great Lake Res.,* **17**:304–313.

Brooks, J. L., and S. I. Dodson. 1965. ''Predation, Body Size, and Composition of Plankton.'' *Science,* **150**:28–35.

Brooks, J. L. 1946. ''Cyclomorphosis in *Daphnia.* 1. An analysis of *Daphnia retrocurva* and *Daphnia galeata.*'' *Ecol. Monogr.,* **16**:409–447.

Brown, B. E. and J. C. Ogden. 1993. Coral Bleaching *Scientific American* January, pp. 64–70.

Brown, E. J., and D. K. Button. 1979. ''Phosphate Limited Growth Kinetics of *Selenastrum capricornutum* (Chlorophyceae).'' *J. Phycol.,* **15**:305–311.

Brown, G. W. 1970. ''Predicting the Effect of Clearcutting on Stream Temperature.'' *J. Soil Water Conserv.,* **25**:11–13.

Brown, S. L. 1981. ''A Comparison of the Structure, Primary Production, and Transpiration of Cypress Exosystems in Florida.'' *Ecol. Monogr.,* **51**:403–427.

Brunskill, G. J. 1986. ''The Parana River System.'' pp. 541–555. In B. R. Davies, and K. F. Walker (eds.), *The Ecology of River Systems.* Junk, The Netherlands.

Bryan, G. W., and L. G. Hummerstone. 1971. ''Adaptation of the polychaete *Neries diversicolor* to Estuarine Sediments Containing High Concentrations of Heavy Metals. 1. General Observations and Adaptations to Copper.'' *J. Mar. Biol. Assoc. U.K.,* **51**:845–863.

Buchanan, R. E., and N. E. Gibbons (eds.). 1974. *Bergey's Manual of Determinative Bacteriology.* 8th ed. Williams & Wilkins, Baltimore.

Burgis, M. J. 1971. ''The Ecology and Production of Copepods, Particularly *Thermocyclops hyalinus,* in the Tropical Lake George, Uganda.'' *Freshwat. Biol.,* **1**:169–192.

———. 1974. ''Revised Estimates for the Biomass and Production of Zooplankton in Lake George, Uganda.'' *Freshwater Biol.,* **4**:535–541.

———. J. P. E. C. Darlington, I. G. Dunn, G. G. Ganf, J. J. Gwahaba, and L. M. McGowan. 1973. ''The Biomass and Distribution of Organisms in Lake George, Uganda.'' *Proc. Roy. Soc. London, Ser. B,* **184**:271–298.

Burns, C. W. 1969. ''Relation between Filtering Rate, Temperature, and Body Size in Four Species of *Daphnia.*'' *Limnol. Oceanogr.,* **14**:693–700.

———. 1987. ''Insights into Zooplankton-Cyanobacteria Interactions Derived from Enclosure Studies.'' *N.Z. J. Marine Freshwat. Res.,* **21**:477–482.

———, D. J. Forsyth, J. E. Haney, M. R. James, W. Lampert, and R. D. Pridmore. 1989. ''Coexistence and Exclusion of Zooplankton by *Anabaena minutissima* var. *attenuata* in Lake Rotengaio, New Zealand.'' *N.Z. J. Marine Freshwat. Res.,* **32**:63–82.

Burns, N. W., and C. Ross. 1972. ''Project Hypo—An Intensive Study of the Lake Erie Central Basin Hypolimnion and Related Surface Water Phenomena.'' Canadian Centre for Inland Waters, Paper 6. 182 pp.

———. 1985. *Lake Erie: The Lake that Survived.* Rowman and Allanheld, New Jersey. 320 pp.

Burton, T. M., and G. E. Likens. 1973. ''The Effect of Strip-Cutting on Stream Temperatures in the Hubbard Brook Experimental Forest, New Hampshire.'' *Bioscience,* **23**:433–435.

Butler, E. I., E. D. S. Comer, and S. M. Marshall. 1969. ''On the Nutrition and Metabolism of Zoopiankton. VI. Feeding Efficiency of *Calanus* in Terms of Nitrogen and Phosphorus.'' *J. Mar. Biol. Assoc. U.K.,* **49**:977–1001.

Byron, E. R., R. P. Axler, and C. R. Goldman. 1991. ''Increased Precipitation Acidity in the Central Sierra Nevada.'' *Atmospheric Environment* **25A**:271–275.

Canadian Embassy. 1989. *Acid Rain.* Ottawa. 5 pp.

Capblancq, J. and H. Laville. 1972. ''Etude de la productivité du lac de Port-Bielh, Pyrénées centrales.'' pp. 73–88. In Z. Kajak and A. Hillbricht-Ilkowska (eds.), *Productivity Problems of Freshwaters.* PWN (Polish Scientific Publishers), Warsaw-Krakow.

Carignan, R., and J. Kalff. 1980. ''Phosphorus Sources for Aquatic Weeds: Water or Sediments?'' *Science,* **207**:987–989.

Carlson, R. E. 1977. ''A Trophic State Index for Lakes.'' *Limnol. Oceanogr.,* **22**:363–369.

Carmack, E. C., R. W. Wiegaan, R. J. Daley, C. B. J. Grey, S. Jasper, and C. H. Pharo. 1986. ''Mechanisms Influencing the Circulation and Distribution of Water Mass in a Medium-Residence Time Lake.'' *Limnol. Oceanogr.,* **31**:249–265.

Carpelan, L. H. 1958. ''The Salton Sea. Physical and Chemical Characteristics.'' *Limnol. Oceanogr.,* **3**:373–397.

Carpenter, E. J., and R. R. L. Guillard. 1971. "Intra-specific Differences in Nitrate Half-Saturation Constants for Three Species of Marine Phytoplankton." *Ecology,* **52**:183–185.

———, C. C. Remsen, and S. W. Watson. 1972. "Utilization of Urea by Some Marine Phytoplankters." *Limnol. Oceanogr.,* **17**:265–269.

Carpenter, S. R. 1980. "Enrichment of Lake Wingra by Submerged Macrophyte Decay. *Ecology,* **104**:1145–1155.

———. (ed.). 1988. *Complex Interactions in Lake Communities.* Springer, New York.

———, and J. F. Kitchell. 1988. "Consumer Control of Lake Productivity." *BioScience,* **38**:764–769.

———, J. P. Kitchell, and J. R. Hodgson. 1985 "Cascading Trophic Interactions and Lake Productivity." *BioScience,* **35**:634–639.

———, and others. 1987. "Regulation of Lake Primary Production by Food Web Structure." *Ecology,* **68**:1863–1876.

Carr, J. F., and J. K. Hiltunen. 1965. "Changes in the Bottom Fauna of Westem Lake Erie from 1930 to 1961." *Limnol. Oceanogr.,* **10**:551–569.

Carr, N. G. and B. A. Whitton (eds.). 1973. *The Biology of Blue-Green Algae.* University of California Press, Berkeley. 676 pp.

Carson, R. 1962. *Silent Spring.* Houghton Mifflin, Boston. 368 pp.

Casey, H. 1977. "Origin and Variation of Nitrate Nitrogen in the Chalk Springs, Streams and Rivers in Dorset and Its Utilization by Higher Plants." *Prog. Water Technol.,* **8**. 14 pp.

Castenholtz, R. W. 1973. "Ecology of Blue-Green Algae in Hot Springs." In N. G. Carr, and B. A. Whitton (eds.), "The Biology of Blue-Green Algae." *Bot. Monogr. No. 9*, pp. 379–414.

———, and C. E. Wickstrom. 1975. "Thermal Streams." pp. 264–285. In B. A. Whitton (ed.), *River Ecology.* University of California Press, Berkeley.

Chambrey, J. A., B. R. Davies, and P. J. Ashton. 1986. "The Orange-Vaal System." pp. 98–122. In B. R. Davies, and K. F. Walker (eds.), *The Ecology of River Systems.* Junk, The Netherlands.

Chamie, J. P. and C. J. Richardson. 1978. Decomposition in Northern Wetlands. In R.E. Good, D.F. Wigham, and R.L. Simpson (eds.), *Freshwater Wetlands—Ecological Processes and Management Potential.* Academic, New York.

Champ, M. A., D. A. Wolfe, D. A. Flemmer, and A. J. Mearns. 1987. "Long-Term Biological Records." Special Issue, *Estuaries,* **10**:181–275.

Chapman, V. J. (ed.). 1977. *Ecosystems of the World, Vol. 1: Wet Coastal Ecosystems.* Elsevier Press, New York. 428 pp.

Chapra, S. C. 1977. "Total Phosphorus Model for the Great Lakes." *J. Envir. Div. Amer. Soc. Civil Eng.,* **103**:147–161.

———, and W. C. Sonzogni. 1979. "Great Lakes Total Phosphate Budget for the Mid 1970's." *J. Wat. Poll. Cont. Fed.,* **51**:2524–2533.

———, and K. H. Reckhow. 1983. *Engineering Approaches for Lake Management. Vol. 2. Mechanistic Modeling.* Butterworth/Ann Arbor Science, Boston. 492 pp.

Charles, D. F. 1991. *Acidic Deposition and Aquatic Ecosystems.* Springer-Verlag, New York. 747 pp.

Charlton, M. N. 1987. "Lake Erie Oxygen Revisited." *J. Great Lakes Res.,* **13**:697–708.

Christie, W. J. 1974. "Changes in the Fish Species Composition of the Great Lakes." *J. Fish. Res. Board Can.,* **31**:827–854.

Clark, C. W. and D. A. Levy. 1988. "Diel Variations by Juvenile Sockeye Salmon in Lake Washington and Predator Avoidance." *Amer. Naturalist,* **13**:1271–1300.

Cloern, J. E. 1979. "Phytoplankton Ecology of the San Francisco Bay System: The Status of Our Current Understanding." pp. 247–264. In T. J. Conomos (ed.), *San Francisco Bay.* American Association for the Advancement of Science, San Francisco.

Cloern, J. E., B. E. Cole, R. J. Wong, and A. E. Alpine. 1985. Temporal dynamics of estuarine phytoplankton: a case study of San Francisco Bay. *Hydrobiologia,* **129**:153–176.

Clymo, R. S. 1965. "Experiments on Breakdown of *Sphagnum* in Two Bogs." *J. Ecol.* **53**:13–49.

Cobb, C. E. 1987. "The Great Lakes Troubled Waters." *National Geographic,* July 1987, pp. 2–31.

Cogbill, C. V. 1976. The History and Character of Acid Rain Precipitation in Eastern North America. U.S. Forest Surv. General Tech. Rpt. NE-23:363–370.

———, and Likens, G. E. 1974. "Acid Precipitation in the North East United States. *Water Resources Res.,* **10**:1133–1177.

Cole, G. A. 1968. "Desert Limnology." pp. 423–486. In G. W. Brown, Jr. (ed.), *Desert Biology*. Academic, New York.

———. 1975. *Textbook of Limnology*. Mosby, St. Louis. 426 pp.

Cole, J. J., N. F. Caraco, and G. E. Likens. 1990. "Short-Range Atmospheric Transport: A Significant Source of Phosphorus to an Oligotrophic Lake." *Limnol. Oceanogr., 35*:1230–1237.

Combs, G. F. and S. B. Combs. 1985. *The Role of Selenium in Nutrition*. Academic, New York. 523 pp.

Confer, J. L. 1972. "Interrelations among Plankton, Attached Algae, and the Phosphorus Cycle in Artificial Open Systems." *Ecol. Monogr., 42*:1–23.

Connor, W. H. and J. W. Day. 1982. The ecology of forested wetlands in the southeastern United States. pp. 69–87 in B. Gopal, R.E. Turner, R.G. Wetzel, and D.F. Whigham (eds.) *Wetlands: ecology and management*. Nat. Inst. Ecol. and Int. Sci. Publ. Jaipur, India.

Conservation 2001. 1986. Fairfield Osborn Symposium. Rockefeller University, New York.

Cook, D. G., and M. G. Johnson. 1974. "Benthic Macroinvertebrates of the St. Lawrence Great Lakes." *J. Fish. Res. Board Can., 31*:763–782.

Cook, G. D., E. B. Welsh, S. P. Peterson, and P. R. Newroth. 1993. *Lake and Reservoir Restoration*. Butterworth, Boston.

Cordone, A., S. Nichola, P. Baker, and T. Frantz. 1971. "The Kokanee Salmon in Lake Tahoe." *Calif. Fish Game, 57*:28–43.

Corner, E. D. S., and A. G. Davies. 1971. "Plankton as a Factor in the Nitrogen and Phosphorus Cycles in the Sea." *Adv. Mar. Biol., 9*:101–204.

Coull, B. C. (ed.). 1977. *Ecology of Marine Benthos*. The University of South Carolina Press, Columbia. 467 pp.

Cowgill, U. M., and G. E. Hutchinson. 1970. "Chemistry and Mineralogy of the Sediments and Their Source Materials." In "Lanula: An Account of the History and Development of the Lago di Monterosi, Latium, Italy." *Trans. Am. Philos. Soc., 60*:37–101.

Craig, P. C., and P. J. McCart. 1975. "Classification of Stream Types in Beaufort Sea Drainages between Prudhoe Bay, Alaska and the Mackenzie Delta, N. W. T. Canada." *Arctic Alpine Res., 7*:183–198.

Craik, A. D. D., and S. Leibovich. 1976. "A Rational Model for Langmuir Circulations." *J. Fluid Mech., 73*:401–426.

Cronberg, G., C. Gelin, and K. Larsson. 1975. "Lake Trummen Restoration Project. II. Bacteria, Phytoplankton and Phytoplankton Productivity." *Verh. Int. Ver. Limnol., 19*:1088–1096.

Csanady, G. T. 1969. "Dispersal of Effluents in the Great Lakes." *Water Res., 3*:835–972.

———. 1975. "Hydrodynamics of Large Lakes." *Ann. Rev. Fluid Mech., 7*:357–385.

Cummins, K. W. 1973. "Trophic Relations of Aquatic Insects." *Ann. Rev. Entomol., 18*:183–206.

———. 1974. "Structure and Function of Stream Ecosystems." *Bioscience, 24*:631–641.

———, R. C. Petersen, F. O. Howard, J. C. Wuycheck, and V. I. Holt. 1973. "The Utilization of Leaf Litter by Stream Detritivores." *Ecology, 54*:336–345.

———, G. W. Minshall, J. R. Sidell, C. E. Cushing, and R. C. Petersen. 1984. "Stream Ecosystem Theory." *Ver. Int. Verh. Limnol., 22*:1818–1927.

Currie, D. J. 1990. "Large-Scale Variability and Interactions among Phytoplankton, Bacterioplankton, and Phosphorus." *Limnol. Oceanogr., 35*:1437–1455.

———, and J. Kalff. 1984. "Can Bacteria Outcompete Phytoplankton for Phosphorus? A Chemostat Test." *Microb. Ecol., 10*:205–216.

Cushing, E. J., and H. E. Wright, Jr. (eds.). 1967. *Quaternary Paleoecology*. Yale University Press, New Haven, Conn. 433 pp.

Daget, J. 1957. Données récentes sur la poissons dans le delta central du Niger. *Hydrobiologia, 9*321–9347.

Darley, W. M. 1974. "Silicification and Calcification." pp. 655–675. In W. D. P. Stewart (ed.), "Algal Physiology and Biochemistry." *Bot. Monogr. No. 10*.

Davis, B. R. and K. F. Walker. 1986. *The Ecology of River Systems*. Junk, The Hague. 793 pp.

Day, J. A. and B. R. Davies. 1986. "The Amazon River System." pp. 289–318. In B. R. Davies, and K. F. Walker (eds.), *The Ecology of River Systems*. Junk, The Netherlands.

Day, J. W., C. A. S. Hall, W. M. Kemp, and A. Yanez-Arancibia. 1989. *Estuarine Ecology*. John Wiley, New York. 558 pp.

———, and A. Yanez-Arancibia. 1990. "Lagoon-

Estuary Ecosystems in Latin America." Special issue. *Estuaries*, **13**:118–172.

Dyer, K. and R. J. Uncles. 1990. "Physical Processes." Special issue. *Estuaries*, **13**:174–230.

de Amezaga, E., C. R. Goldman, and E. A. Stull. 1973. "Primary Productivity and the Rate of Change of Biomass of Various Species of Phytoplankton in Castle Lake California," *Verh. Int. Ver. Limnol.*, **18**:1768–1775.

de Bernardi, R., G. Giussani, and E. L. Pedretti. 1981. "The Significance of Blue-Green Algae as Food for Filterfeeding Zooplankton: Experimental Studies on *Daphnia spp.* Fed by *Microcystis aeruginosa.*" *Verh. Int. Ver. Limnol.*, **21**:477–483.

DeMort, W. R. 1986. "The Role of Taste in Food Selection by Freshwater Zooplankton." *Oecologia*, **69**:334–340.

Denison, P. J., and F. C. Elder. 1970. "Thermal Inputs to the Great Lakes 1968–2000." *Proc. 13th Conf. Great Lakes Res.*, pp. 811–828.

Dennis, W. M., and B. G. Isom. (eds.). 1984. Ecological Assessment of Macrophyton: Collection, Use, and Meaning of Data. *Amer. Soc. Test. Materials. Sp. Tech. Publ. 843.* 122 pp.

Dillon, P. J. and F. H. Rigler. 1974. "The Phosphorus-Chlorophyll Relationship in Lakes." *Limnol. Oceanogr.*, **19**:767–773.

Dillon, T. M., and T. M. Powell. 1979. "Observations of a Surface Mixed Layer." *Deep-Sea Res.*, **26A**:915–932.

———, and L. O. Myrup. 1975. "Low Frequency Turbulence and Vertical Temperature Microstructure in Lake Tahoe, California-Nevada." *Verh. Int. Ver. Limnol.*, **19**:110–115.

Dini, M. L. & S. R. Carpenter. 1991. "The Effect of Whole-Lake Fish Community Manipulations on *Daphnia* Migratory Behaviour." *Limnol. Oceanogr.*, **36**:370–377.

Dobson, H. F. H., M. Gilbertson, and P. G. Sly. 1974. "A Summary and Comparison of Nutrients and Related Water Quality in Lakes Erie, Ontario, Huron, and Superior." *J. Fish. Res. Board Can.*, **31**:731–738.

Dodge, P. D. (ed.) 1989. Proceeding of the International Large River Symposium. *Can. Spec. Publ. Fish. Aquat. Sci.*, Vol. 106.

Dodson, S. I. 1974. "Adaptive Change in Plankton Morphology in Response to Size-Selective Preda-

tion: A New Hypothesis of Cyclomorphosis." *Limnol. Oceanogr.*, **19**:721–729.

Dowd, J. E., and D. S. Riggs. 1965. "A Comparison of Estimates of Michaelis-Menten Kinetic Constants from Various Linear Transformations." *J. Biol. Chem.*, **240**:863–869.

Dring, M. 1981. Chromatic adaptation of photosynthesis in benthic marine algae: an examination of its ecological significance using a theoretical model. *Limnol. Oceanogr.* **26**:271–284

Droop, M. 1957. "Auxotrophy and Organic Compounds in Nutrition of Marine Phytoplankton." *J. Gen. Microbiol.*, **16**:286–293.

———. 1974. "The Nutrient Status of Algal Cells in Continuous Culture." *J. Mar. Biol. Assoc. U.K.*, **54**:825–855.

DSIR. 1964. "Effects of Polluting Discharges on the Thames Estuary." *Dept. Sci. Ind. Res. Water Pollut. Res. Tech. Paper No. 11*. London. 201 pp.

Dumont, H. J. 1972. "A Competition-Based Approach of the Reverse Vertical Migration in Zooplankton and Its Implications, Chiefly Based on a Study of the Interactions of the Rotifer *Asplanchna priodonta* (Gosse) with Several Crustacea Entomostraca." *Int. Rev. ges. Hydrobiol.*, **51**:1–38.

Dunst, R. C., S. M. Born, P. D. U. Hormark, S. A. Smith, S. A. Nichols, J. O. Peterson, D. R. Knauer, S. L. Sens, D. R. Winter, and T. L. Wirth. 1974. "Survey of Lake Rehabilitation Techniques and Experiences." *Wis. Dep. Nat. Resour. Tech. Bull. No. 75.* 177 pp.

Dussart, B. 1966. *Limnologie. L'étude des eux continentales.* Gauthier-Villars, Paris. 677 pp.

Edgar, L. A. 1979. "Diatom Locomotion: Computer Assisted Analysis of Cine Film." *Br. Phycol. J.*, **14**:83–101.

———. 1982. "Diatom Locomotion: A Consideration of Movement in a Highly Viscous Situation." *Br. Phycol. J.*, **17**:243–251.

———. 1984. "Diatom Locomotion." *Prog. Physiol. Res.*, **3**:47–88.

Elser, J. J., E. R. Marzolf, and C. R. Goldman. 1990. "Phosphorus and Nitrogen Limitation in the Freshwaters of North America: A Review and Critique of Experimental Enrichments." *Can. J. Fish. Aquat. Sci.*, **47**:1468–1477.

Edmondson, W. T. 1955. "Seasonal Life History of *Daphnia* in an Arctic Lake." *Ecology*, **36**:439–455.

———. 1965. "Reproductive Rate of Planktonic Rotifers as Related to Food and Temperature in Nature." *Ecol. Monogr.,* **35**:61–111.

———. 1972a. "The Present Condition of Lake Washington." *Verh. Int. Ver. Limnol.,* **18**:284–291.

———. 1972b. "Nutrients and Phytoplankton in Lake Washington." *Limnol. Oceanogr. Special Symp. Vol. 1,* pp. 172–193.

———. 1974a. "Secondary Production." *Mitt. Int. Ver. Theor. Angew Limnol.,* **20**:229–272.

———. 1974b. "The Sedimentary Record of the Euthrophication of Lake Washington." *Proc. Nat. Acad. Sci. U.S.A.,* **71**:5093–5095.

———. 1977. "Population Dynamics and Secondary Production." *Ergeb. Limnol.,* **8**:56–64.

———, and D. E. Allison. 1970. "Recording Densitometry of X-Radiographs for the Study of Cryptic Laminations in the Sediment of Lake Washington." *Limnol. Oceanogr.,* **15**:138–144.

———, and A. Litt. 1982. "*Daphnia* in Lake Washington." *Limnol. Oceanogr.,* **27**:272–293.

Egeratt, A. W. S. M., and J. L. M. Huntjens (eds.). 1975. "The Sulphur Cycle." *Plant Soil,* **48**:228 pp.

Eggers, D. M. 1978. "Limnetic Feeding Behavior of Juvenile Sockeye Salmon in Lake Washington and Predator Avoidance." *Limnol. Oceanogr.,* **23**:1114–1125.

Eisma, D., and A. J. van Bennekom. 1978. "The Zaire River and Estuary and the Zaire Outflow in the Atlantic Ocean." *Neth. J. Sea Res.,* **12**:255–272.

Elder, J. F. 1985. "Nitrogen and Phosphorus Speculation and Flux in a Large Florida River-Wetland System." *Water Resour. Res.,* **21**:724–732.

———, and A. J. Horne. 1977. "Biostimulatory Capacity of Dissolved Iron for Cyanophycean Blooms in a Nitrogen-Rich Reservoir." *Chemosphere No. 9,* pp. 525–530.

———, and ———. 1978. "Copper Cycles and $CUSO_4$ Algicidal Capacity in Two California Lakes." *Environ. Management,* **2**:17–30.

———, R. H. Fuller, and A. J. Horne. 1979. "Physiochemical Factors and their Effects on Algal Growth in a New Southern Californian Reservoir." *Water Resour. Bull.,* **15**:1608–1617.

Ellenbroek, G. A. 1987. *Ecology and Productivity of an African Wetland System: The Kafue Flats, Zambia.* Junk, The Hague. 267 pp.

Elliott, J. M. 1971. Some methods for the statistical analysis of samples of benthic invertebrates. Freshwater Biological Assoc. England. Publ. No. 25. Windermere, 144 p.

———, and P. A. Tuilett. 1977. "The Downstream Drifting of Larvae of *Dixa* (Diptera:Dixidae) in Two Stony Streams." *Freshwater Biol.,* **7**:403–407.

Elster, H-J. 1974. "History of Limnology." *Mitt. Int. Ver. Theor. Angew. Limnol.,* **20**:7–30.

Elwood, J. W., J. D. Newbold, R. V. O'Neill, R. W. Stark, and P. T. Singley. 1981. "The Role of Microbes Associated with Organic and Inorganic Substrates in Phosphorus Spiralling in a Woodland Stream." *Verh. Int. Ver. Limnol.,* **21**:850–856.

El-Zarka, S. E. D. 1973. "Kainji Lake, Nigeria." pp. 197–219. In W. C. Akerman, G. F. White, and E. B. Worthington (eds.), *Man-Made Lakes: Their Problems and Environmental Effects.* American Geophysical Union, Washington, D.C.

Emery, K. O., and G. T. Csanady. 1973. "Surface Circulation of Lakes and Nearby Land-Locked Seas." *Proc. Nat. Acad. Sci. U.S.A.,* **70**:93–97.

Eppley, R. W., J. N. Rogers, and J. J. McCarthy. 1969. "Half-Saturation Constants for Uptake of Nitrate and Ammonium by Marine Phytoplankton." *Limnol. Oceanogr.,* **14**:912–920.

———, and W. H. Thomas. 1969. "Comparison of Half-Saturation Constants for Growth and Nitrate Uptake of Marine Phytoplankton." *J. Phycol.,* **5**:375–379.

Erman, D. C., and N. A. Erman. 1975. "Macroinvertebrate Composition and Production in Some Sierra Nevada Minerotrophic Peatlands." *Ecology,* **56**:591–603.

———, J. D. Newbold, and K. B. Roby. 1977. "Evaluation of Streamside Bufferstrips for Protecting Aquatic Organisms." University of California, Davis. Water Resources Center, Publ. No. 165. 47 pp.

Esch, G. W., and R. W. McFariane (eds.). 1976. *Thermal Ecology II.* U.S. TIS. Conf.-750425. Springfield, Va. 404 pp.

Falter, C. M. 1977. "Early Limnology of Dworshak Reservoir, N. Idaho," pp. 285–294. In R. D. Andrews, et al. (eds.), *Proceedings of the Symposium on Terrestrial and Aquatic Studies in the Northwest,* EWSC Press, Washington, D.C.

———, W. J. Overholtz, and R. A. Tubb. 1975. "Hypolimnetic Oxygenation Using Liquid Oxygen.'' *Water Resour. Res.,* **11**:294–299.

Farquhar, B. W. and S. Gutreuter. 1989. ''Distribution and Migration of Adult Striped Bass in Lake Whitney, Texas.'' *Trans. Amer. Fish. Soc.,* **119**:523–532.

Fast, A. W., W. J. Overholtz, and R. A. Tubb. 1975. ''Hypolimnetic Oxygenation Using Liquid Oxygen.'' *Wat. Resour. Res.,* **11**:294–299.

Fee, E. J. 1976. ''The Vertical and Seasonal Distribution of Chlorophyll in Lakes of the Experimental Lakes Area, Northwestern Ontario: Implications for Primary Production Estimates.'' *Limnol. Oceanogr.,* **21**:767–783.

———. 1980. ''Reply to Comments by Patalas and Schindler.'' *Limnol. Oceanogr.,* **25**:1152–1153.

Fee, E. J. 1979. ''A Relation between Lake Morphometry and Primary Productivity and Its Use in Interpreting Whole-Lake Eutrophication Experiments. *Limnol. Oceanogr.,* **24**:401–418.

Fenchel T. 1988. ''Marine Planktonic Food Chains.'' *Ann. Rev. Ecol. Syst.,* **19**:19–38.

Fisher, J. B. 1982 Effects of macrobenthos on the chemical diagnosis of freshwater sediments. pp. 177–212. In P.L. McClall and M.J.S. Tevesz, *Animal-Sediment Relations: The Biogenic Alternation of Sediments.* Plenum Press, New York.

Fischer, H. B., E. J. List, R. C. Y. Koh, J. Imberger, and N. H. Brooks. 1979. *Mixing in Inland and Coastal Waters.* Academic, New York. 483 pp.

Fittkau, E. J. 1964. Remarks on Limnology of Central-Amazon Rainforest Streams.'' *Verh. Int. Ver. Limnol.,* **15**:1092–1096.

Fitzgerald, G. P. 1969. ''Field and Laboratory Evaluations of Bioassays for Nitrogen and Phosphorus with Algae and Aquatic Weeds.'' *Limnol. Oceanogr.,* **14**:206–212.

———, and T. C. Nelson. 1966. ''Extractive and Enzymatic Analyses for Limiting or Surplus Phosphorus in Algae.'' *J. Phycol.,* **2**:32–37.

Flett, R. J., D. W. Schindler, R. D. Hamilton, and N. E. R. Cambell. 1980. ''Nitrogen Fixation in Canadian Precambrian Shield Lakes.'' *Can. J. Fish. Aquat. Sci.,* **37**:494–505.

Fogg, G. E. 1969. ''The Leewenhoek Lecture, 1968. The Physiology of an Algal Nuisance.'' *Proc. Roy. Soc. London, Ser. B,* **173**:175–189.

———. 1971. ''Extracellular Products of Algae in Freshwater.'' *Arch. Hydrobiol. Beth.,* **5**:125.

———, and B. Thake. 1987. *Algal Cultures and Phytoplankton Ecology.* 3rd ed. University of Wisconsin Press, Madison. 269 pp.

———, and A. J. Horne. 1967. ''The Determination of Nitrogen Fixation in Aquatic Environments.'' pp. 115–120. In H. L. Goiterman and R. C. Clymo (eds.), *Chemical Environment in the Aquatic Habitat.* Noord-Hollandsche Uitgevers-mij., Amsterdam.

———, and ———. 1970. ''The Physiology of Antarctic Freshwater Algae.'' pp. 632–638. In M. W. Hoidgate (ed.), *Antarctic Ecology,* Academic, New York.

———, W. D. P. Stewart, P. Fay, and A. E. Walsby. 1973. *The Blue-Green Algae.* Academic, New York. 459 pp.

Folt, C., and C. R. Goldman. 1981. ''Allelopathy between Zooplankton: A Mechanism for Interference Competition.'' *Science,* **213**:1133–1135.

Forbes, S. A. 1887. ''The Lake as a Microcosm.'' *Bull. Peoria (Illinois) Sci. Assoc.* Reprinted 1925 in *Bull. Ill. Nat. Hist. Surv,* **15**:537–550.

Foree, E. J., W. J. Jewell, and P. L. McCarthy. 1971. ''The Extent of Nitrogen and Phosphorus Regeneration from Decomposing Algae.'' *Fifth International Water Pollution Research Conference.* Pergamon, London.

Forel, F. A. 1869. ''Introduction à l'étude de la faune profonde du Lac Léman.'' *Bull. Soc. Vaud. Sci. Nat. (Lausanne),* **10**:217.

———. 1892, 1895, 1904. *Le Léman: monographie limneolgique, tome (1892): Geographie, hydrographie, géologie, climatologie, hydrologie.* 543 pp.; *tome II (1895): Mecanique hydraulique, chimie, thermique, optique, acoustique.* 651 pp.; *tome III (1904): Biologie, historie, navigation, pêche,* 715 pp. Lausanne. F. Rouge, reprinted Genève, Slatkine Reprints. 1969.

———. 1901. *Handbuch der Seenkunde: allgemeine Limnologie.* Bibiiothek geographische Handbbücher, Stuttgart.

Forsberg, B. R., A. H. Devol, J. E. Richie, L. A. Martinelli, and H. dos Santos. 1988. ''Factors controlling nutrient concentrations in Amazon floodplain lakes.'' *Limnol. Oceanogr.,* **33**:41–56.

Frank, P. W., C. D. Boil, and R. W. Kelley, 1957. ''Vital Statistics of Laboratory Cultures of *Daphnia pulex* deGreer as Related to Density.'' *Physiol. Zool.,* **30**:276–305.

Fremling, C. R., J. L. Rasmussen, R. E. Sparks, S. P.

Cobb, C. F. Bryan, and T. O. Claflin. 1989. Mississippi River Fisheries: A Case History. In D. P. Dodge (ed.), *Proc. Int. Large River Symp. Can. Sp. Publ. Fish Aquat. Sci.* 106 pp.

Frey, D. G. 1963. *Limnology in North America.* University of Wisconsin Press, Madison. 734 pp.

———. 1964. "Remains of Animals in Quaternary Lake and Bog Sediments and Their Interpretation." *Ergeb. Limnol.,* **2**:1–116.

Froelich, P. N. 1988. "Kinetic Control of Dissolved Phosphate in Natural Rivers and Estuaries: A Primer on the Phosphate Buffer Mechanism." *Limnol. Oceanogr.,* **33**:649–668.

Fryer, G., and T. D. Iles. 1972. *The Cichlid Fisheses of the Great Lakes of Africa: Their Biology and Evolution.* Oliver & Boyd, Edinburgh. 641 pp.

Fuji, N. 1978. "Pollen Analysis of a 200-m Core Sample from Lake Biwa." *Verb. Int. Ver. Limnol.,* **20**:2663–2665.

Fulton, R. S. and H. W. Paerl. 1987. "Toxic and Inhibitory Effects of the Blue-Green Alga *Microcystic aeruginosa* on Herbivorous Zooplankton." *J. Plankton Res.,* **9**:837–855.

Galat, D. L., E. L. Lider, S. Vigg, and S. R. Robertson. 1981. "Limnology of a Large, Deep, North American Terminal Lake, Pyramid Lake, Nevada, U.S.A." *Hydrobiologia,* **82**:281–317.

Gameson, A. L. H., and A. Wheeler. 1977. "Restoration and Recovery of the Thames Estuary." pp. 72–101. *Recovery and Restoration of Damaged Ecosystems.* University Press of Virginia, Charlottesville.

Gammon, J. R., A. Spacie, G. Hamelink, and R. L. Kaessler. 1981. "Role of Electrofishing in Assessing Environmental Quality of the Wabash River." pp. 307–324. In J. M. Bates and C. I. Weber (eds.), *Ecological Assessment of Effluent Impacts on Communities of Aquatic Organisms.* ASTM Spec. Tech. Publ. 730.

Ganf, G. G. 1974. "Phytoplankton Biomass and Distribution in a Shallow, Entrophic Lake (Lake George, Uganda)." *Oecologia,* **16**:9–29.

———, and P. Blazka. 1974. "Oxygen Uptake, Ammonia and Phosphate Excretion by Zooplankton of a Shallow Equatorial Lake (Lake George, Uganda)." *Limnol. Oceanogr.,* **19**:313–325.

———, and A. J. Horne. 1975. "Diurnal Stratification, Photosynthesis and Nitrogen-Fixation in a Shallow, Equatorial Lake (Lake George, Uganda)." *Freshwater Biol.,* **5**:13–39.

———, and A. B. Viner. 1973. "Ecological Stability in a Shallow, Equatorial Lake (Lake George, Uganda)." *Proc. Roy. Soc. London, Ser. B,* **184**:321–346.

Garstang, E. O. 1986. *Freshwater Vegetation Management.* Thomas Publ. Fresno, California. 377 p.

Geller, W. 1986. "Diurnal Vertical Migration of Zooplankton in a Temperate Great Lake (L. Constance): A Starvation Avoidance Mechanism?" *Arch. Hydrobiol/Suppl,* **74**:1–60.

———. 1991. Die Planktongemeinschaft als dynamisches System. pp. 31–47 in *Okologie der oberbayerischen Seen,* F. Pfeil, Munich, Germany.

———, R. Berberovic, U. Gaedke, H. Muller, H-R. Pauli, M. M. Tilzer, and T. Weisse. 1991. "Relations among the Components of Autotrophic and Heterotrophic Plankton during the Seasonal Cycle 1987 in Lake Constance." *Ver. Int. Ver. Limnol.,* **24**:831–836.

Gerloff, G. C., and F. Skoog. 1954. "Cell Contents of Nitrogen and Phosphorus as a Measure of Their Availability for Growth of *Microcystis aeruginosa.*" *Ecology,* **35**:348–353.

———, and ———. 1957. "Availability of Iron and Manganese in Southern Wisconsin Lakes for the Growth of *Microcystis aeruginosa.*" *Ecology,* **38**:551–556.

Gersberg, R., K. Krohn, N. Peek, and C. R. Goldman. 1976. "Denitrification Studies with ^{13}N labelled Nitrate." *Science,* **192**:1229–1231.

Gessner, F. 1955. *Hydrobotanik, vol. I: Energiehaushalt.* VEB Deutsche Verlag Wissenschaft, Berlin. 517 pp.

———. 1959. *Hydrobotanik, vol. II: Stoffhaushalt.* VEB Deutsche Verlag Wissenschaft, Berlin. 701 pp.

Giesy, J. P. 1980. "Microcosms in Ecological Research." Technical Information Center. U.S. Department of Energy. Springfield, Va. DOE Symposium Series 52. Conf.-781101. 1101 pp.

Gilbert, J. J., and G. A. Thompson. 1968. "Alpha Tocopherol Control of Sexuality and Polymorphism in the Rotifer Asplanchna." *Science,* **159**:734–738.

———. 1966. "Rotifer Ecology and Embryological Induction." *Science,* **151**:1234–1237.

Gilinsky, E. 1984. "The Role of Fish Predation and

Spacial Heterogeneity in Determining Benthic Community Structure.'' *Ecology*, **65**:544–468.

Gold, K. 1964. ''Aspects of Marine Dinoflagellate Nutrition Measured by ¹⁴C Assimilation.'' *J. Protozool.*, **11**:85–89.

Goldman, C. R. 1960. ''Primary Productivity and Limiting Factors in Three Lakes of the Alaskan Peninsula.'' *Ecol., Monogr.*, **30**:207–270.

———. 1961. ''The Contribution of Alder Trees (*Ainus tenitifolia*) to the Primary Productivity of Castle Lake, California.'' *Ecol. Monogr.*, **42**:282–288.

———. 1965. ''Micronutrient Limiting Factors and Their Detection in Natural Phytoplankton Populations.'' pp. 121–135. In C. R. Goldman (ed.), ''Primary Productivity in Aquatic Environments.'' *Mem. 1st. Ital. Idrobiol.*, 18(suppl.).

———. 1968a. ''The Use of Absolute Activity for Eliminating Serious Errors in the Measurement of Primary Productivity with 14C.'' *J. Cons. Perm. Int. Explor. Mer.*, **32**:172–179.

———. 1968b. ''Aquatic Primary Production.'' *Am. Zool.*, **8**:31–42.

———. 1969. ''Photosynthetic Efficiency and Diversity of a Natural Phytoplankton Population in Castle Lake, California.'' Proceedings IBP/PP Technical Meeting, *Prediction and Measurement of Photosynthetic Productivity*. pp. 507–517.

———. 1972. ''The Role of Minor Nutrients in Limiting the Productivity of Aquatic Ecosystems.'' *Symposium on Nutrients and Eutrophication*, vol. 1, pp. 21–33. American Society of Limnology and Oceanography.

———. 1981. ''Lake Tahoe: Two Decades of Change in a Nitrogen Deficient Oligotrophic Lake.'' *Verh. Int. Ver. Limnol.*, **21**:45–70.

———. 1988. ''Primary Productivity, Nutrients, and Transparency during the Early Onset of Eutrophication in Ultra-Oligotrophic Lake Tahoe, California-Nevada.'' *Limnol Oceanogr.*, **33**:1321–1333.

Goldman, C. R. 1993. The conservation of two large lakes: Tahoe and Baikal. *Verh. Int. Ver. Limnol.*, **25**:388–391.

———, and R. C. Carter. 1965. ''An Investigation by Rapid Carbon-14 Bioassay of Factors Affecting the Cultural Eutrophication of Lake Tahoe, California-Nevada.'' *J. Water Pollut. Control Fed.*, **37**:1044–1059.

———, E. A. Stull, and E. de Amezaga. 1973. Vertical patterns of primary productivity in Castle Lake, California. *Ver. Int. Ver. Limnol.* **18**:1760–1767.

———, and R. W. Hoffman. 1977. ''Environmental Aspects of the Purari River Scheme.'' pp. 325–341. In J. H. Winslow (ed.), *The Melanesian Environment*. Australian National University Press, Canberra.

———, and D. T. Mason. 1962. ''Inorganic Precipitation of Carbon in Productivity Experiments Utilizing Carbon-14.'' *Science,* **136**:1049–1050.

———, M. D. Morgan, S. T. Threlkeld, and N. Angeli. 1979. A population dynamics analysis of the cladoceran disappearance from Lake Tahoe, California-Nevada. *Limnol. Oceanogr.* **24**:289–297.

———, ———, and J. E. Hobble. 1967. ''Two Antarctic Desert Lakes.'' *Limnol. Oceanogr.*, **12**:295–310.

———, ———, and B. J. B. Wood. 1963. ''Light Injury and Inhibition in Antarctic Freshwater Phytoplankton.'' *Limnol. Oceanogr.*, **8**:313–322.

———, and ———. 1972. ''Comparative Study of the Limnology of Two Small Lakes on Ross Island, Antarctica.'' *Antarct. Res. Ser.*, **20**:1–50.

———, M. D. Morgan, S. T. Threlkeld, and N. Angeli. 1979. ''A Population Dynamics Analysis of the Cladoceran Disappearance from Lake Tahoe, California-Nevada.'' *Limnol. Oceanogr.*, **24**:289–297.

———, and R. G. Wetzel. 1963. ''A Study of the Primary Productivity of Clear Lake, Lake County, California.'' *Ecology*, **44**:283–294.

———, N. Williams, and A. J. Horne. 1975. ''Prospects for Micronutrient Control of Algal Populations.'' pp. 97–105. In P. L. Brezonik and J. L. Fox (eds.), *Water Quality Management through Biological Control*. University of Florida, Gainesville, Engineering Science Report ENV-07-75-1.

———, A. D. Jassby, and E. De Amezaga. 1990. ''Forest Fires, Atmospheric Deposition, and Primary Productivity at Lake Tahoe, California-Nevada. *Ver. Int. Ver. Limnol.*, **24**:499–503.

Golterman, H. L. 1975a. *Physiological Limnology*. Elsevier Scientific Publishing Co., New York. 489 pp.

———. 1975b. ''Chemistry of Running Waters.'' pp. 39–80. In B. A. Whitton (ed.), *River Ecology*. Blackwell, Oxford.

————, and R. S. Clymo (eds.). 1967. *Chemical Environment in the Aquatic Habitat.* Noord-Hollandsche Uitgevers-Mij., Amsterdam. 322 pp.

———— and M. A. M. Ohnstad. 1978. *Methods for Physical and Chemical Analysis of Fresh Waters.* 2d ed. Blackwell Scientific Publishers, Oxford. IBP Handbook, No. 8. 213 pp.

Good, R. E., D. F. Wigham, and R. L. Simpson (eds.) 1978. *Freshwater Wetlands: Ecological Processes and Management Potential.* Academic, New York.

Gore, J. A. 1985. *The Restoration of Rivers and Streams: Theories and Experiences.* Butterworth, Stoneham, Mass.

Gorham. E. 1955. "On the Acidity and Salinity of Rain." *Geochim. Cosmochim. Acta,* **7**:231–239.

————. 1964. "Morphometric Control of Annual Heat Budgets in Temperate Lakes." *Limnol. Oceangr.,* **9**:525–529.

————, J. W. G. Lund, J. E. Sanger, and W. E. Dean, Jr. 1974. "Some Relationships between Algal Standing Crop, Water Chemistry, and Sediment Chemistry in the English Lakes." *Limnol. Oceanogr.,* **19**:601–617.

Granhall, U., and A. Lundgren. 1971. "Nitrogen Fixation in Lake Erken." *Limnol. Oceanogr.,* **16**:711–719.

Grant, J. W. G., and I. A. E. Bayly. 1981. "Predator Induction of Crests in Morphs of the *Daphnia carinata* King Complex." *Limnol. Oceanogr.,* **26**:201–218.

Griffith, E. J., A. Beeton, J. M. Sponser, and D. T. Mitchell (eds.). 1973. *Handbook of Environment Phosphorus.* Wiley, New York. (See especially chapters by H. L. Goiterman, "Vertical Movement of Phosphate in Freshwater," and F. H. Rigier, "A Dynamic View of the Phosphorus Cycle in Lakes.")

Griffiths, B. M. 1939. "Early References to Waterblooms in British Lakes." *Proc. Limn. Soc. London,* **151**:12–19.

Griffiths, M., and W. T. Edmondson. 1975. "Burial of Oscillaxanthin in the Sediment of Lake Washington." *Limnol. Oceanogr.,* **20**:945–952.

Gross, M. G. 1977. *Oceanography.* 2d ed. Prentice Hall, Englewood Cliffs, N.J. 497 pp.

Groth, P. 1971. "Untersuchungen über einige Spurenelemente in Seen" ("Investigations of Some Trace Elements in Lakes"). *Arch. Hydrobiol.,* **68**:305–375 (summary in English).

Gudmundsson, F. 1979. "The Past Status and Exploitation of the Mývatn Waterfowl Populations." In P. M. Jonasson (ed.), "Lake Myvatn." *Oikos,* **32**:232–249.

Guillard, R. R. L., and P. Kilham. 1977. "The Ecology of Marine Planktonic Diatoms." pp. 372–469. In D. Werner (ed.), *The Biology of Diatoms.* University of California Press, Berkeley.

Gunter, G. 1967. "Some Relationships of Estuaries to the Fisheries of the Gulf of Mexico." pp. 621–638. In G. H. Lauff (ed.), *Estuaries.* American Association for the Advancement of Science, publ. no. 83, Washington, D.C.

Guseva, K. A. 1939. "Bloom on the Ucha Reservoir." *Biul Moskov. Obshch. Ispytat. Prirody, Otdel. Biol.,* **48**:30. Reprinted in *Nat. Res. Council Can.,* technical translation 879 by G. Bekov, 1960.

Haines, T. A. 1981. "Acidic Precipitation and Its Consequences for Aquatic Ecosystems: A Review. *Trans. Amer. Fish. Soc.,* **110**:669–707.

Hakanson, L. 1981. *A Manual of Lake Morphometry.* Springer-Verlag, New York. 78 pp.

Hall, C. A. S. 1977. "Models and the Decision-making Process: The Hudson River Power Plant Case." In C. A. S. Hall and J. W. Day (eds.), *Ecosystem Modeling in Theory and Practice.* Wiley, New York. 684 pp.

Hall, D. J., W. E. Cooper, and E. E. Werner. 1970. "An Experimental Approach to the Production Dynamics and Structure of Freshwater Animal Communities." *Limnol. Oceanogr.,* **15**:839–928.

————, S. T. Threlkeld, C. W. Burns, and P. H. Crowley. 1976. "The Size Efficiency Hypothesis and the Size Structure of Zooplankton Communities." *Ann. Rev. Ecol. Syst.,* **7**:177–208.

Hammer, D. A. (ed.) 1989. *Constructed Wetlands for Wastewater Treatment: Municipal, Industrial, and Agricultural.* Lewis Publ. Chelsea, Michigan. 831 p.

Hamilton-Taylor, J., and M. Wills. 1991. "A Quantitative Assessment of the Sources and General Dynamics of Trace Metals in a Soft-Water Lake." *Limnol. Oceanogr.,* **5**:840–851.

Haney, J. F. 1973. "An in situ Examination of the Grazing Activities of Natural Zooplankton Communities." *Arch. Hydrobiol.,* **72**:87–132.

————. 1987. "Field Studies on Zooplankton-Cyanobacteria Interactions." *N.Z. J. Mar. Freshwat. Res.,* **21**:467–475.

Harmon, M. E., J. R. Franklin, F. J. Swanson, J. D. Lattin, S. V. Gregory, N. H. Anderson, S. P. Cline, N. G. Aumen, J. R. Sidell, G. W. Lienkaemper, K. Cromack, and K. W. Commins. 1986. Ecology of coarse woody debris in temperate ecosystems. *Adv. Ecol. Res.* **15**:133–302.

Hart, C. W. and S. L. Fuller (eds.). 1974. *Pollution Ecology of Freshwater Invertebrates.* Academic, New York, 398 pp.

———, and ——— (eds.). 1979. *Pollution Ecology of Estuarine Invertebrates.* Academic, New York. 406 pp.

Harbeck, G. E. 1955. "The Effect of Salinity on Evaporation." *U.S. Geol. Surv. Prof. Pap.*, 272A. 6 pp.

Harding, D. 1966. "Lake Kariba. The Hydrology and Development of Fisheries in Man-Made Lakes." *Symp. Inst. Biol.*, **15**:7–20.

Hargrave, B. T., and G. H. Geen. 1968. "Phosphorus Excretion by Zooplankton." *Limnol. Oceanogr.*, **13**:332–342.

Harkness, W. J. K., and J. R. Dymond. 1961. "The Lake Sturgeon. The History of Its Fishery and Problems of Conservation." *Ont. Dep. Lands For., Fish Wildl. Br.* 121 pp.

Harmon, M. E., J. R. Franklin, F. J. Swanson, J. D. Lattin, S. V. Gregory, N. H. Anderson, S. P. Cline, N. G. Aumen, J. D. Sidell. G. W. Lienkaemper, K. Cromak, and K. W. Cummins. 1986. "Ecology of Coarse Woody Debris in Temperate Ecosystems." *Adv. Ecol. Res.*, **15**:133–302.

Harper, M. A. 1977. Movements. pp. 224–249 In D. Werner (ed.) *The Biology of Diatoms.* University of California Press Berkeley.

Harris, G. P. 1986. *Phytoplankton Ecology: Structure, Function, and Fluctuations.* Chapman and Hall, London. 384 pp.

Harrison, M. J., R. E. Pacha, and R. Y. Morita. 1972. "Solubilization of Inorganic Phosphates by Bacteria Isolated from Upper Klamath Lake Sediment." *Limnol. Oceanogr.*, **17**:50–57.

Hart, C. W., and S. L. H. Fuller (eds.). 1974. *Pollution Ecology of Freshwater Invertebrates.* Academic, New York. 389 pp.

———, and ——— (eds.). 1979. *Pollution Ecology of Estuarine Invertebrates.* Academic, New York. 406 pp.

Harvey, H. W. 1937. *The Chemistry and Fertility of Sea Waters.* Cambridge University Press, England. 240 pp.

Hasler, A. D. 1966. *Underwater Guideposts: Homing of Salmon.* The University of Wisconsin Press, Madison.

Havel, J. 1986. Predator-Induced Defences: A review. pp. 267–279. In W. C. Kerfoot and A. Sih (eds.), *Predation: Direct and Indirect Impacts on Aquatic Communities.* University of New England Press.

Hawkins, C. P., and J. R. Sidell. 1981. "Longitudinal and Seasonal Changes in Functional Organization of Macroinvertebrate Communities in Four Oregon Streams." *Ecology*, **62**:387–397.

Healy, F. P. 1977. "Ammonia Uptake by Some Freshwater Algae." *Can. J. Bot.*, **55**:61–69.

Hebert, P. D. N., and P. M. Grewe. 1985. *"Chaeoboris* Introduced Shifts and the Morphology of *Daphnia ambigua." Limnol. Oceanogr.*, **30**:1291–1296.

Hecky, R. E., E. J. Fee, H. Kling, and J. W. M. Rudd. 1978. "Studies on the Planktonic Ecology of Lake Tanganyika." Canadian Fisheries and Marine Services. Technical Report 816, Winnipeg. 51 pp.

Hedges, J. I., W. A. Clark, P. D. Quay, J. E. Richy, A. D. Devol, and U. de M. Santos. 1986. "Composition and Fluxes of Particulate Material in the Amazon River." *Limnol. Oceanogr.*, **31**:717–738.

Hendersen-Sellers, B. and H. R. Markland. 1987. *Decaying Lakes: The Origins and Control of Cultural Eutrophication.* Wiley, New York. 254 pp.

Hensen, V. 1887. "Über die Bestimmung des Planktons oder des in Meere treibenden Materials on Pflanzen und Thieren." *Ber. Kommn Wiss. Unters. dt. Meere.*, **5**:1–109.

Heron, J. 1961. "The Seasonal Variation of Phosphate, Silicate, and Nitrate in the Waters of the English Lake District." *Limnol. Oceanogr.*, **6**:338–346.

Herdendorf, C. E. 1990. Distribution of the World's Large Lakes. pp. 3–38. In M. M. Tilzer and C. Serruya (eds.), *Large Lakes: Ecological Structure and Function.* Springer-Verlag, Berlin.

Hewett, S. W. amd B. S. Johnson. 1987. "A Generalized Bioenergetics Model of Fish Growth for Microcomputers." Univ. Wisconsin Sea Grant Tech. Rpt. WIS-SG87-145.

Heywood, R. B. 1972. "Antarctic Limnology: A Review." *Br. Antarct. Surv. Bull.*, No. 29, pp. 35–65.

Hoagland, K. D., S. E. Roemer, and J. R. Rosowski.

1982. "Colonization and Community Structure of Two Periphyton Assemblages, with Emphasis on the Diatoms (Bacillariophyceae)." *Am. J. Bot.*, **69**:188–213.

Holm, L. G., L. W. Weldon, and R. D. Blackburn. 1969. "Aquatic Weeds." *Science*, **166**:699–709.

Holm, N. P., and D. E. Armstrong. 1981. "Role of Nutrient Limitation and Competition in Controlling the Populations of *Asterionella formosa* and *Microcystis aeruginoas* in Semicontinuous Culture." *Limnol. Oceanogr.*, **26**:622–634.

Hook, D. D., and others 1988. *The Ecology and Management of Wetlands. Vol. 1. Ecology of Wetlands.* 592 pp. *Vol 2. Management, Use, and Value of Wetlands.* 394 pp. Timber Press, Portland, Ore.

Horie, S. (ed.). 1974. *Paleolimnology of Lake Biwa and the Japanese Pleistocene.* Otsu Hydrobiology Station, Kyoto University, Japan. 288 pp.

———. 1981. "On the Significance of Paleolimnological Study of Ancient Lakes—Lake Biwa and Other Relic Lakes." *Verh. Int. Ver. Limnol.*, **21**:13–44.

Horne, A. J. 1972. "The Ecology of Nitrogen Fixation on Signy Island, South Orkney Islands." *Br. Antarct. Surv. Bull.*, **27**:1–18.

———. 1975. "The Ecology of Clear Lake Phytoplankton." Special report of the Clear Lake Algal Research Unit, Lakeport, Calif. 116 pp.

———. 1977. "Nitrogen Fixation—A Review of This Phenomenon as a Polluting Process." *Prog. Water Technol.*, **8**:357–372.

———. 1978. "Nitrogen Fixation in Entrophic Lakes." pp. 1–30. In R. Mitchell (ed.), *Water Pollution Microbiology,* vol. 2. Wiley, New York.

———. 1979a. "Management of Lakes Containing N_2-fixing Blue-Green Algae. "*Arch. Hydrobiol. Beth.*, **13**:133–144.

———. 1979b. "Nitrogen Fixation in Clear Lake, California. IV. Diel Studies on *Aphanizomenon* and *Anabaena* Blooms." *Limnol. Oceanogr.*, **24**:329–341.

———, and C. J. W. Carmigelt. 1975. "Algal Nitrogen Fixation in California Streams: Seasonal Cycles." *Freshwat. Biol.*, **5**:461–470.

———, and G. E. Fogg. 1970. "Nitrogen Fixation in Some English Lakes." *Proc. Roy. Soc. London,* Ser. B. **175**:351–366.

———, ———, and D. J. Eagle. 1969. "Studies in situ of the Primary Production of an Area of Inshore Antarctic Sea." *J. Mar. Biol. Assoc. U.K.*, **49**:393–405.

———, and C. R. Goldman. 1972. "Nitrogen Fixation in Clear Lake, California. 1. Seasonal Variation and the Role of Heterocysts." *Limnol. Oceanogr.*, **17**:678–692.

———, and ———. 1974. "Supression of Nitrogen Fixation by Blue-Green Algae in an Entrophic Lake with Trace Additions of Copper." *Science*, **83**:409–411.

———, P. Javornicky, and C. R. Goldman. 1971. "A Freshwater 'Red Tide' on Clear Lake, California." *Limnol. Oceanogr.*, **16**:684–689.

———, and W. J. Kaufman. 1974. "Biological Effects of Ammonia Salts and Dilute, Treated Petroleum Refinery Effluent on Estuarine Aufwuchs, Phytoplankton and Fish Communities." Sanitary Engineering Research Laboratory, University of California, Berkeley. UCB-SERL Rep. No. 74-5. 112 pp.

———, and J. C. Roth. 1979. "Nitrate Ploughing to Eliminate Hydrogen Sulfide Production in the Tillo Mudflat." Report to City of South San Francisco, Public Works Department, February. 23 pp.

———, ———, D. Kelley, and F. McLaren. 1979. "A Biological Survey of Martis Creek, California." McLaren Environmental Engineering, Sacramento, Calif.

———, and A. B. Viner. 1971. "Nitrogen Fixation and Its Significance in Tropical Lake George, Uganda." *Nature*, **232**:417–418.

———, and R. C. Wrigley. 1975. "The Use of Remote Sensing to Detect How Wind Influences Planktonic Blue-Green Algal Distribution." *Verh. Int. Ver. Limnol.*, **19**:784–791.

———, and D. L. Galat. 1985. "Nitrogen Fixation in an Oligotrophic, Saline Desert Lake: Pyramid Lake, Nevada. *Limnol. Oceanogr.*, **30**:1229–1239.

———, and M. L. Commins. 1987. "Macronutrient Controls on Nitrogen Fixation in Planktonic Cyanobacterial Populations." *N.Z. J. Freshwat. Marine Biol.* **21**:413–423.

———, and J. C. Roth. 1989. Selenium detoxification studies at Kesterson Reservoir wetlands: Depuration and biological population dynamics measured using an experimental mesocosm and pond 5 under permanently flooded conditions. University of California, Berkeley. Environmental Engineering and Health Sciences Laboratory Rept. No. 89-4. 107 pp. plus appendix (89 pp.).

Houston, K. A. and J. R. M. Kelso. 1991 "Relation of Sea Lamprey Size and Sex Ratio to Salmonid Availability in the Great Lakes." *J. Great Lakes Res.,* **17**:270–280.

Howarth, R. W., R. Marino, J. Lane, and J. J. Cole. 1988. "Nitrogen Fixation in Freshwater, Estuarine, and Marine Ecosystems. 1. Rates and Importance." *Limnol. Oceanogr.,* **33**:669–687.

———, ———, and ———. 1988. "Nitrogen Fixation in Freshwater, Estuarine, and Marine Ecosystems. 2. Biogeochemical Controls." *Limnol. Oceanogr.,* **33**:688–701.

Hrbáček, J. 1962. "Species Composition and the Amount of Zooplankton in Relation to the Fish Stock." *Rozpr. Cesk. Akad. Ved. Rada Mat. Prir. Ved.,* **72**:1–116.

Huber, A. L. 1986. "Nitrogen Fixation by *Nodularia spumigena* Mertens (*Cyanobacteriaceae*). I Field Studies and the Contribution of Blooms to the Nitrogen Budget of the Peel-Harvey Estuary, Western Australia." *Hydrobiologia,* **131**:193–203.

Hunt, E. G., and A. I. Bischoff. 1960. "Inimical Effects on Wildlife of Periodic DDT Applications to Clear Lake." *Cal. Fish Game,* **46**:91–106.

Hutchins, D. A., J. G. Reuter, and W. Fish. 1991. "Siderophore Production and Nitrogen Fixation Are Mutually Exclusive Strategies." *Limnol. Oceanogr.,* **36:**1–12.

Hutchinson, G. E. 1957, 1967, 1975. *A Treatise on Limnology.* Vol. I (1957): *Geography, Physics and Chemistry,* 1015 pp.; Vol. II (1967): *Introduction to Lake Biology and the Limnoplankton,* 1115 pp.; Vol. III (1975): *Limnological Botany,* 660 pp. Wiley, New York. Vol. IV. (1993): *The Zoobenthos,* 944 pp.

———, and U. M. Cowgill. 1973. "The Waters of Merom: A Study of Lake Huleh. III. The Major Chemical Constituents of a 54 m Core." *Arch. Hydrobiol.,* **72**:145–185.

Hutchinson, G. L., and F. G. Viets. 1969. "Nitrogen Enrichment of Surface Water by Absorption of Ammonia Volatilized from Cattle Feed-Lots." *Science,* **166**:514–515.

Hyatt, K. D. and J. D. Stockner. 1985. "Responses of Sockeye Salmon (*Oncorhynchus nerka*) to Fertili-

zation of British Colombia Coastal Lakes." *Can. J. Fish. Aquat. Sci.,* **42:**320–331.

Hynes, H. B. N. 1966. *The Biology of Polluted Waters.* University of Liverpool Press, England. 202 pp.

———. 1972. *The Ecology of Running Waters.* University of Toronto Press, Toronto. 555 pp.

———. 1975. "The Stream and Its Valley." *Verh. Int. Ver. Limnol.,* **19**:1–15.

Imberger, J. 1985. "The Diurnal Mixed Layer." *Limnol. Oceanogr.,* **30**:737–770.

———, and J. C. Patterson. 1990 "Physical Limnology." *Adv. Appl. Mechanics,* **27**:303–471.

International Association of Theoretical and Applied Limnology. 1971. "Factors That Regulate the Wax and Wane of Algal Populations." Symposium No. 19. *Mitt. Int. Ver. Theor. Angew. Limnol.* 318 pp.

Isom, B. G., S. D. Dennis, and J. M. Bates (eds.). 1986. *Impact of Acid Rain and Deposition on Aquatic Biological Systems.* ASTM Publication 04-928000-16 Philadelphia. 114 pp.

Itasaka, O., and M. Koyama. 1980. "Elementary Components in Water." p. 28. In S. Mori (ed.), *An Introduction to the Limnology of Lake Biwa.* Shizouka Women's University, Japan.

Ivlev, V. S. 1939. "Transformation of Eneregy by Aquatic Animals. Coefficient of Energy Consumption by *Tubifex tubifex* (*Oligochaeta*)." *Int. Rev. Ges. Hydrobiol. Hydrograph.,* **38**:449–458.

———. 1963. "On the Utilization of Food by Plankton-Eating Fishes." *Fish. Res. Board Can.* (Translation Series No. 447, 17 pp.)

Jackson, P. B. M. 1962. "Why Do Nile Crocodiles Attack Boats?" *Copeia,* **1**:204–206.

James, H. R., and E. A. Birge. 1938. "A Laboratory Study of the Absorbtion of Light by Lake Waters." *Trans. Wis. Acad. Sci. Arts Lett.,* **31**:1–154.

Jansson, B-O., and F. Wulff. 1977. "Baltic Ecosystem Modeling." pp. 323–343. In C. A. S. Hall and J. W. Day (eds.), *Ecosystem Modeling in Theory and Practice.* Wiley, New York. 684 pp.

Jansson, M., H. Olsson, and K. Pettersson. 1988. "Phosphatases: Origin, Characteristics and Function in Lakes." *Hydrobiologia,* **170**:157–175.

Jassby, A. D., and C. R. Goldman. 1974. "Loss Rates from a Lake Phytoplankton Community." *Limnol. Oceanogr.,* **19**:618–627.

Jefferies, R. L., and A. J. Davy (eds.). 1979. *Ecolog-*

ical Processes in Coastal Environments. Blackwell Press, Oxford. 684 pp.

Jenkin, P. M. 1936. "Reports on the Percy Staden Flamingos." *Phil. Trans. Roy. Soc. Lond. B,* **240**:401–493.

———. 1942. "Seasonal Changes in the Temperature of Windermere (English Lake District)." *J. Animal. Ecol.,* **11**:248–269.

Jenkins, D. 1975. "The Analysis of Nitrogen Forms in Waters and Wastewaters." *Proc. Conf on Nitrogen as a Water Pollutant.* IAWPR. vol. 1. 30 pp.

Jerlov, N. G. 1968. *Optical Oceanography.* Elsevier Press, London. 194 pp.

Jobling, M. 1981. "Temperature Tolerance and the Final Preferendum: Rapid Methods for the Assessment of Optimum Growth Temperatures." *J. Fish. Biol.,* **19**:439–455.

Johannes, R. E. 1968. "Nutrient Regeneration in Lakes and Oceans." *Adv. Miirobiol. Sea,* **1**:203–213.

Jolley, R. L., H. Gorchev, D. H. Hamilton (eds.). 1978. *Water Chlorination: Environmental Impact and Health Effects,* vol. 2. Ann Arbor Science, Ann Arbor, Mich. 909 pp.

Johnson, R. K., B. Bostrom, and W. van der Bund. 1989. Interactions between *Chironomus plumosa* (L.) and the microbial community in surficial sediments of a shallow, eutrophic lake. *Limnol. Oceanogr.,* **34**:992–1003.

Jónasson, P. M. 1978. "Zoobenthos of Lakes." *Verh. Int. Ver. Limnol.,* **20**:13–37.

———. 1990. "Energy Budget of Lake Esrom, Denmark." *Verh. Int. Ver. Limnol.,* **24**:632–640.

———, E. Lastein, and A. Rebsdorf. 1974. "Production, Insulation and Nutrient Budget of Lake Esrom." *Oikos,* **25**:255–277.

Jones, J. G. 1971. "Studies on Freshwater Bacteria: Factors Which Influence the Population and Its Activity." *J. Ecol.,* **59**:593–613.

———. 1972. "Studies on Freshwater Microorganisms. Phosphatase Activity in Lakes of Differing Degrees of Eutrophication." *J. Ecol.,* **60**:777–791.

———. 1977. "Variation in Bacterial Populations in Time and Space." *Freshwat. Biol. Assoc. Ann. Rep.* No. 5, pp. 55–61.

Jones, K., and W. D. P. Stewart. 1969. "Nitrogen Turnover in Marine and Brackish Habitats. III. The Production of Extracellular Nitrogen by *Calothrix*

scopulorum. J. Mar. Biol. Assoc. U.K., **49**:475–488.

Jørgensen, C. B. 1966. *Biology of Suspension Feeding.* Pergamon, New York. 357 pp.

Junk, W. J. 1970. "Investigations on the Ecology and Production Biology of the 'Floating Meadows' (*Paspalo-Echinocloetum*) in The Middle Amazon. 1. The Floating Vegetation and Its Ecology." *Amazoniana,* **2**:449–495.

———. 1986. Aquatic Plants of the Amazon system. pp. 319–337. In B. R. Davis and K. F. Walker, *The Ecology of River Systems.* Junk, The Hague.

———, and C. Howard-Williams. 1984. Ecology of Aquatic Macrophytes in Amazonia. pp. 269–293. In H. Siroli (ed.), *Limnology and Landscape Ecology of a Mighty Tropical River and Its Basin.* W. Junk, Dordrecht.

———, P. B. Bailey, and R. E. Sparks. 1989. "The Flood Pulse Concept in River-Flood Plain Systems. pp. 110–127. In D. P. Dodge (ed.), *Proc. Int. Large River Symp. Can. Sp. Publ. Fish. Aquat. Sci.* 106.

Kajak, Z. 1988. "Considerations on Benthos Abundance in Freshwater, Its Factors and Mechanisms. *Int. Rev. Ges. Hydrobiol.,* **73**:5–19.

Kalff, J. 1967. "Phytoplankton Dynamics in an Arctic Lake." *J. Fish. Res. Board Can.,* **24**:1861–1871.

———. 1971. "Nutrient Limiting Factors in an Arctic Tundra Pond." *Ecology,* **52**:655–659.

Karanas, J. K., H. Van Dyke, and R. C. Worrest. 1981. "Impact of UV-B Radiation on the Fucundity of the Copepod *Acartia clausii. Mar. Biol.,* **65**:125–133.

Kaushik, N. K., and H. B. N. Hynes. 1971. "The Fate of the Dead Leaves That Fall into Streams." *Arch. Hydrobiol.,* **68**:465–515.

Kawanabe, H. 1978. "Some Biological Problems." *Verh. Int. Ver. Limnol.,* **20**:2674–2677.

Keeney, D. R. 1972. "The Fate of Nitrogen in Aquatic Ecosystems." *Univ. Wis. Water Resour. Cent. Lit. Revs.,* 3. 59 pp.

———, R. L. Chen, and D. A. Graetz. 1971. "Importance of Denitrification and Nitrate Reduction in Sediments to the Nitrogen Budget of Lakes." *Nature,* **233**:66–67.

Keirn, M. A., and P. L. Brezonik, 1971. "Nitrogen Fixation by Bacteria in Lake Mize, Florida, and in Some Lacustrine Sediments." *Limnol. Oceanogr.,* **16**:720–731.

Kellogg, W. W., R. D. Cadle, E. R. Allen, A. L. Lazrus, and E. A. Martell. 1972. "The Sulfur Cycle." *Science*, **175**:587–596.

Kelts, K., and K. J. Hsu. 1978. "Freshwater Carbonate Sedimentation." pp. 295–323. In A. Lerman (ed.), *Lakes: Chemistry, Geology, Physics*. Springer-Verlag, New York.

Kennedy, V. S. (ed.). 1980. *Estuarine Perspectives*. Academic Press, New York. 533 pp.

Kenoyer, G. J., and M. P. Anderson. 1989. "Groundwater's Dynamic Role in Regulating Acidity and Chemistry in a Precipitation-Dominated Lake." *J. Hydrol.*, **109**:287–306.

Kerfoot, W. C. (ed.). 1980. *Evolution and Ecology of Zooplankton Communities*. Special Symposium Vol. 3, American Soceity of Limnology and Oceanography. University of New England Press, New Hampshire. 793 pp.

———, and A. Sih (eds.). 1987. *Predation: Direct and Indirect Impacts on Aquatic Communities*. University of New England Press, New Hampshire. 386 pp.

Kilham, P., and D. Tilman. 1979. "The Importance of Resource Competition and Nutrient Gradients for Phytoplankton Ecology." *Arch. Hydrobiol. Beth.*, **13**:110–119.

King, C. E. 1967. "Food, Age and the Dynamics of a Laboratory Population of Rotifers." *Ecology*, **48**:111–128.

——— (ed.). 1977. *Proceedings of the First International Rotifer Symposium*. Springer-Verlag, New York.

Kipling, C. 1976. "Year Class Strengths of Perch and Pike in Windermere." *Freshwat. Biol. Assoc. Ann. Rep.* No. 44, pp. 68–75.

———, and W. E. Frost, 1970. "A Study of the Mortality, Population Numbers, Year Class Strengths, Production and Food Consumption of Pike, *Esox lucius*, in Windermere from 1944 to 1962." *J. Anim. Ecol.*, **39**:115–157.

Kirchner, W. B. 1975. "An Examination of the Relationship between Drainage Basin Morphology and the Export of Phosphorus." *Limnol. Oceanogr.*, **20**:267–270.

Kitchell, J. F. and L. B. Crowder. 1986. "Predator-Prey Interactions in Lake Michigan: Model Predictions and Recent Dynamics." *Env. Bio. Fish.*, **16**:205–211.

Kittel, T., and P. J. Richerson. 1978. "The Heat Budget of a Large Tropical Lake, Lake Titicaca (Peru-Bolivia)." *Verh. Int. Ver. Limnol.*, **20**:1203–1209.

Kitting, C. L. 1984. "Selectivity by Dense Populations of Small Invertebrates Foraging among Seagrass Blade Surfaces." *Estuaries*, **7**:276–288.

Knighton, A. D. 1976. "Stream Adjustment in a Small Rocky Mountain Basin." *Arctic Alpine Res.*, **8**:197–212.

Koehl, M. A. R., and J. R. Strickler. 1981. "Copepod Feeding Currents: Food Capture at Low Reynolds Number." *Limnol. Oceanogr.*, **26**:1062–1073.

Kozhov, M. 1963. *Lake Baikal and Its Life*. Junk Publishers, The Hague. 344 pp.

Krueger, D. A., and S. I. Dodson. 1981. "Embryological Induction and Predation Ecology in *Daphnia Pulex*." *Limnol. Oceanogr.*, **26**:219–223.

Kusnezow, S. I. 1959. *Die Rolle der Mikroorganismen im Stoflkreislauf der Seen*. Deutsches Verlag der Wissenschaften, Berlin.

Lagler, K. F., J. E. Bardach, R. R. Miller, and D. R. M. Passino. 1977. *Icththyology*. 2d ed. Wiley, New York. 506 pp.

Lallatin, R. D. 1972. "Alternative Eel River Projects and Conveyance Routes. Appendix C. Clear Lake Water Quality." California Department of Water Resources, Red Bluff. 145 pp.

Lampert, W. 1978. "Climatic Conditions and Planktonic Interactions as Factors Controlling the Regular Succession of Spring Algal Bloom and Extremely Clear Water in Lake Constance." Ver. Int. Ver. Limnol. **20**:969–974.

Lampert, W. (ed.). 1985. "Food Limitation and the Structure of Zooplankton Communities." *Arch. Hydrobiol.*, vol 21, 497 pp.

———. 1989. "The Adaptive Significance of Diel Vertical Migration of Zooplankton. *Functional Ecology*, **3**:21–27.

———. 1987. "Laboratory Studies on Zooplankton-Cyanobacteria Interactions." *N. Z. J. Mar. Freshwat. Res.*, **21**:483–490.

———, W. Fleckner, H. Rai, and B. E. Taylor. 1986. "Phytoplankton Control by Grazing Zooplankton: A Study on the Spring Clear-Water Phase. *Limnol. Oceanogr.*, **31**:478–490.

Lander, G. W., and K. F. Liem. 1981. "Prey Capture by *Luciocephalus pulcher*. Implications for Models of Jaw Protrusion in Teleost Fishes.'' *Environmental Biology of Fishes,* **6**:257–268.

Lang, W. 1971. ''Limiting Nutrient Elements in Filtered Lake Erie Water.'' *Water Res.,* **5**:1031–1048.

Larimore, R. W., L. Durham, and G. W. Bennett. 1950. ''A Modification of the Electric Fish Shocker for Lake Work.'' *J. Wildl. Manag.,* **14**:320–323.

Larsen, D. P., D. W. Schults, and K. W. Malueg. 1981. ''Summer Internal Phosphorus Supplies in Shagawa Lake, Minnesota.'' *Limnol. Oceanogr.,* **26**:740–753.

Larsson, U., R. Elmgren, and F. Wulff. 1985. ''Eutrophication and the Baltic Sea: Causes and Consequences.'' *Ambio.,* **14**:9–14.

Laskin, A. I., and H. A. Lechavalier (eds.). 1977. *CRC Handbook of Microbiology* (2nd ed.) *Vol. I. Bacteria.* 757 pp. *Vol. II. Fungi, Algae, Protozoa, and Visuses.* CRC Press, West Palm Beach, Florida. 874 pp.

Lathrop, R. G., J. R. Vande Castle, and T. M. Lillesand. 1990. ''Monitoring River Plume Transport and Mesoscale Circulation in Green Bay, Wisconsin Through Satillite Remote Sensing.'' *J. Great Lakes Res.,* **16**:471–484.

Lauff, G. (ed.). 1967. *Estuaries.* American Association for the Advancement of Science, Washington. Publication 83. 757 pp.

Lebo, M. E. 1990. ''Phosphate Uptake along a Coastal Plain Estuary.'' *Limnol. Oceanogr.,* **35**:1279–1289.

LeCren, E. D. 1958. ''Observations on the Growth of Perch (*Perca fluviatilis*) over Twenty-Two Years with Special Reference to the Effects of Temperature and Changes in Population Density.'' *J. Anim. Ecol.,* **27**:287–334.

Lee, D. H. K. 1970. ''Nitrates, Nitrites, and Methemoglobinemia.'' *Environ. Res.,* **3**:484–511.

Lefevre, M., H. Jakob, and M. Nisbet. 1952. ''Auto et hetero-antagonisme chez les algues d'eau douce.'' *Ann. Stat. Cent. Hydrobiol. Appl.,* **4**:5–197.

Lehman, J. T. 1980. ''Release Cycling of Nutrients between Planktonic Algae and Herbivores.'' *Limnol. Oceanogr.,* **25**:620–632.

———, and D. Scavia. 1982. ''Microscale Nutrient Patches Produced by Zooplankton.'' *Science,* **216**:729–730.

———, and T. Naumoski. 1986. ''Net Community Production and Hypolimnetic Nutrient Regeneration in a Michigan Lake.'' *Limnol. Oceanogr.,* **31**:788–797.

Lemmin, U., J. T. Scott, and U. H. Czapski. 1974. ''The Development from Two-Dimensional to Three-Dimensional Turbulence Generated by Breaking Waves.'' *J. Geophys. Res.,* **79**:3442–3448.

Lemoalle, J. 1975. L'activite photosynthetique du phytoplancton en relation avee le niveau des eux de lac Tchad (Afrique). *Verh. Int. Ver. Limnol.,* **19**:1399–1403.

Leonard, R. L., L. A. Kaplan, J. F. Elder, R. N. Coats, and C. R. Goldman. 1979. ''Nutrient Transport in Surface Runoff from a Subalpine Watershed, Lake Tahoe Basin, California.'' *Ecol. Monogr.,* **49**:281–310.

Leopold, L. B., M. G. Wolman, and J. P. Miller. 1964. *Fluvial Processes in Geomorphology.* Freeman, San Francisco. 522 pp.

Lerman, A. (ed.). 1978. *Lakes—Chemistry, Geology, Physics.* Springer-Verlag, New York. 363 pp.

Lesht, B. M., T. D., Fontiane, and D. M. Dolan. 1991. ''Great Lakes Total Phosphorus Model. Post Audit and Regionalized Sensitivity Analysis. *J. Great Lakes Res.,* **17**:3–17.

Leslie, J. 1838. ''Treatise on Various Subjects of Natural and Chemical Philosophy.'' Cited in Murray and Pullar (1910), pp. 91–92.

Levine, S. N., and W. M. Lewis. 1987. ''A Numerical Model of Nitrogen Fixation and Its Application to Lake Valencia, Venezuela.'' *Freshwat. Biol.,* **17**:265–274.

Lewin, J. C. 1962. ''Silicification.'' pp. 445–455. In R. A. Lewin (ed.), *Physiology and Biochemistry of Algae.* Academic, London.

Lewis, W. M. 1973. ''The Thermal Regime of Lake Lanao (Philippines) and Its Theoretical Implications for Tropical Lakes.'' *Limnol. Oceanogr.,* **18**:200–217.

———, 1979. *Zooplankton Community Analysis-Studies on a Tropical System.* Springer Verlag, New York. 163 pp.

Likens, G. E., F. H. Borman, N. M. Johnson, D. W. Fisher, and R. S. Pierce. 1970. ''Effects of Forest Cutting and Herbicide Treatment on Nutrient Budgets in the Hubbard Brook Watershed Ecosystem.'' *Ecol. Monogr.,* **40**:23–47.

————, R. S. Pierce, J. S. Eaton, and N. M. Johnson. 1977. *Biogeochemistry of a Forested Ecosystem.* Springer-Verlag, New York. 146 pp.

————, and N. M. Johnson. 1969. "Measurement and Analysis of the Annual Heat Budget for the Sediments in Two Wisconsin Lakes." *Limnol. Oceanogr.,* **14**:115–135.

Lindegaard, C., and P. M. Jónasson. 1979. "Abundance, Population Dynamics and Production of Zoobenthos in Lake Mývatn, Iceland." In P. M. Jónasson (ed.), "Lake Mývatn." *Oikos,* **32**:202–227.

Lindeman, R. L. 1942. "The Trophic-Dynamic Aspect of Ecology." *Ecology,* **23**:399–418.

Lindstrom, K. and W. Rodhe. 1977. "Selenium as a Micronutrient for the Dinoflagellate *Peridinium cinctum fa. westii.*" *Verh. Int. Ver. Limnol.,* **21**:168–173.

Livermore, D. F., and W. E. Wunderlich. 1969. "Mechanical Removal of Organic Production from Waterways." pp. 494–519. In *Eutrophication: Causes, Consequences, Correctives.* National Academy of Sciences, Washington, D.C.

Livingstone, D. A. 1963. "Mean Composition of World River Water. Chemical Composition of Rivers and Lakes. Data of Goechemistry 6th ed. Chap. G." *U.S. Geol. Surv. Prof. Pap.* 400-G. pp. 1–64.

Livingstone, R. J. (ed.). 1979. *Ecological Processes in Coastal and Marine Systems. Marine Science,* vol. 10. Plenum, New York. 548 pp.

————. 1984. The Ecology of the Apalchicola Bay System: An Estuarine Profile. U.S. Fish and Wildlife Service. FWS/OBS 82/05. 148 pp.

Lock, M. A., and D. D. Williams (eds.). 1981. *Perspectives in Running Water Ecology.* Plenum Press, New York.

Lorenz, J. R. 1863. "Brackwasserstudien an der Elbemündung." *Sitzungsber. math-naturwiss. Kl. Kaiser Akad. Wiss. Wein.,* **48**(2):602–613.

Losee, R. F., and R. G. Wetzel. 1988. "Water Movement within Submersed Littoral Vegetation." *Int. Ver. Agnew. Limnol. Verh.,* **23**:62–66.

Lowe-McConnell, R. H. 1986. Fish of the Amazon System. pp. 339–351. In B. R. Davis and K. F. Walker (eds.), *The Ecology of River Systems.* Junk, The Hague.

Luecke, C., M. J. Vanni, J. J. Magnuson, J. F. Kitchell, and P. T. Jacobson. 1990. "Seasonal Regulation of

Daphnia Populations by Planktiverous Fish: Implications for the Spring Clear-Water Phase." *Limnol. Oceanogr.,* **35**:1718–1733.

————. 1990. "Changes in Abundance and Distribution of Benthic Macroinvertebrates after Introduction of Cutthroat Trout into a Previously Fishless Lake." *Transactions of the American Fisheries Society,* **119**:1010–1021.

Lund, J. W. G. 1949, 1950. "Studies on *Asterionella.* 1. The Origin and Nature of the Cells Producing the Spring Maximum." *J. Ecol.,* **37**:389–419 (1949); and II. "Nutrient Depletion and the Spring Maximum." *J. Ecol.,* **38**:1–35 (1950).

————. 1954. "The Seasonal Cycle of the Plankton Diatom, *Melosira italica* (Ehr.) Kutz. subsp. *subarctica O.* Mull." *J. Ecol.,* **42**:151–179.

————. 1964. "Primary Production and Periodicity of Phytoplankton." *Verh. Int. Ver. Limnol.,* **15**:37–56.

————. 1965. "The Ecology of Freshwater Phytoplankton." *Biol. Revs,* **40**:231–293.

————. 1971. "An Artificial Alternation of the Seasonal Cycle of the Plankton Diatom *Melosira italica* subsp. *subarctica* in an English Lake." *J. Ecol.,* **59**:521–533.

————. 1972. "Eutrophication." *Proc. Roy. Soc. Lond. Ser. B.,* **180**:371–382.

————, C. Kipling, and E. D. Le Cren. 1958. "The Inverted Microscope Method of Estimating Algal Numbers and the Statistical Basis of Estimations by Counting." *Hydrobiologia,* **11**:143–170.

Mackay, N. and D. Eastburn (eds.). 1990. *The Murray* (River). Murray-Darling Basin Commission, Canberra, Australia. 363 pp.

Macan, T. T. 1970. *Biological Studies of the English Lakes.* American Elsevier, New York. 260 pp.

————. 1974. "Running Water." *Mitt. Int. Ver. Theor. Angnew. Limnol.,* **20**:301–321.

McCarthy, J. J. 1972. "The Uptake of Urea by Marine Phytoplankton." *J. Phycol.,* **8**:216–222.

McHarg, L. L., and M. G. Clarke. 1973. "Skippack Watershed and the Evansburg Project: A Case Study for Water Resources Planning." pp. 299–330. In C. R. Goldman, J. McEvoy, and P. J. Richerson (eds.), *Environmental Quality and Water Development.* Freeman, San Francisco.

MacIsaac, J. J., and R. C. Dugdale. 1969. "The Kinetics of Nitrate and Ammonia Uptake by Natural

Populations of Marine Phytoplankton." *Deep-Sea Res.*, **16**:45–57.

MacKenthun, K. M., et al., 1964. "Limnological Aspects of Recreational Lakes." *U.S. Public Health. Serv. Publ.* 1167. 176 pp.

McLaren, F. R. 1977. "Water Quality Studies of the Truckee River." McLaren Environmental Engineering, Sacramento, Calif.

———, A. J. Horne, D. Kelley, and J. C. Roth. 1979. "Studies of Martis Creek, 1979." McLaren Environmental Engineering, Sacramento, Calif.

McMahon, J. W. 1969. "The Annual and Diurnal Variation in the Vertical Distribution of Acid Soluble Ferrous and Total Iron in a Small Dimictic Lake." *Limnol. Oceanogr.*, **14**:357–367.

McQueen, D. J., J. R. Post, and E. L. Mills. 1986. "Trophic Relationships in Freshwater Pelagic Ecosystems." *Can. J. Fish. Aquat. Sci.*, **43**:1571–1581.

Macnae, W. 1967. "Zonation within Mangroves Associated with Estuaries in Queensland." pp. 432–441. In G. H. Lauff (ed.), *Estuaries*. American Association for the Advancement of Science, publ. no. 83, Washington, D.C.

McRoy, C. P., and R. J. Barsdate. 1970. "Phosphate Absorption in Eelgrass." *Limnol. Oceanogr.*, **15**:6–13.

———, and N. Nebert. 1972. "Phosphorus Cycling in an Eelgrass (*Zostera marina* L.) Ecosystem." *Limnol. Oceanogr.*, **17**:58–67.

Magee, P. N. 1977. "Nitrogen as a health hazard." *Ambio.*, **6**:123–125.

Magnuson, J. J. 1962. "An Analysis of Aggressive Behavior, Growth and Competition for Food and Space in Medaka, *Oryzias latipes Pisces (Cyprinodontidae)*." *Can. J. Zool.*, **40**:313–363.

———, L. B. Crowder, and P. A. Medvick. 1979. "Temperature as an Ecological Resource." *American Zoologist*, **19**:331–343.

Maitiand, P. S. 1974. "The Conservation of Freshwater Fishes in the British Isles." *Biol. Conserve*, **6**:7–14.

Malueg, K. W., R. M. Brice, D. W. Schults, and D. P. Larson. 1973. "The Shagawa Lake Project." U.S. Environmental Protection Agency, EPA R3-73-026. 49 pp.

Mangelsdorf, P. C. 1967. "Salinity Measurements in Estuaries." pp. 71–79. In G. H. Lauff (ed.), *Estu-aries*. American Association for the Advancement of Science, publ. no. 83, Washington, D.C.

Mann, K. H. 1988. "Production and Use of Detritus in Various Freshwater, Estuarine, and Coastal Marine Ecosystems." *Limnol. Oceanogr.* **22**:910–930.

———, R. H. Britton, A. Kowalczewski, T. J. Lack, C. P. Mathews, and I. McDonald. 1972. "Productivity and Energy Flow at All Trophic Levels in the River Thames, England." pp. 579–596. In Z. Kajak and A. Hilibricht-Ilkowska (eds.), *Productivity Problems of Freshwater*. PWN (Polish Scientific Publishers), Warsaw Krakow.

Manny, B. A. 1972. "Seasonal Changes in Dissolved Organic Nitrogen in Six Michigan Lakes." *Verh. Int. Ver. Limnol.*, **18**:147–156.

———, R. G. Wetzel, and R. E. Bailey. 1978. "Paleolimnological Sedimentation of Organic Carbon, Nitrogen, Phosphorus, Fossil Pigments, Pollen and Diatoms in a Hypereutrophic, Hardwater Lake: A Case History of Eutrophication." *Pol. Arch. Hydrobiol.*, **25**:243–267.

Margalef, R. 1965. "Ecological Correlations and the Relationship between Primary Produtivity and Community Structure." pp. 355–364. In C. R. Goldman (ed.), "Primary Productivity in Aquatic Environments." *Mem. Ist. Ital. Idrobiol.*, **18** (suppl.).

Marker, A. F. H. 1976a. "The Benthic Algae of Some Streams in Southern England 1. Biomass of the Epilithon in Some Small Streams." *J. Ecol.*, **64**:343–358.

———. 1976b. "The Benthic Algae of Some Streams in Southern England. II. The Primary Production of the Epilithon in a Small Chalkstream." *J. Ecol.*, **64**:359–373.

Marshall, N. B. 1966. *The Life of Fishes.* Universe Books, New York, 402 pp.

Mason, C. F. 1991. *Biology of Freshwater Pollution.* Wiley, New York. 351 pp.

Mason, D. T. 1967. "Limnology of Mono Lake, California." *University of California Berkeley Publ. Zool.*, **82**. 110 pp.

Mathews, C. P., and A. Kowalcezwki. 1969. "The Disappearence of Leaf Litter and Its Contribution to Production in the River Thames." *J. Ecol.*, **57**:543–552.

Mathews, W. J., L. G. Hill, D. R. Edds, and F. P. Gelwink. 1989. "Influence of Water Quality and

Season on Habitat Use by Striped Bass in a Large Southwestern Reservoir.'' *Trans. Am. Fish. Soc.,* **118**:243–250.

Mayer, J. R., W. M. Bernard, W. J. Metzger, T. A. Storch, T. A. Earlandson, J. R. Luensman, S. A. Nicholson, and R. T. Smith. 1978. Chautauqa Lake—Watershed and Lake Basins. pp. 2–103. In J. A. Bloomfield (ed.), *Lakes of New York State,* Vol. II. Academic Press, New York.

Megusar, F., and M. Gantar (eds.). 1986. *Perspectives in Microbial Ecology.* Slovene Soc. Microbiol., Ljubjana, 684 pp.

Melack, J. M. 1976. ''Primary Productivity and Fish Yields in Tropical Lakes.'' *Trans. Am. Fish. Soc.,* **105**:575–580.

Merrit, R. W. and K. W. Commins (eds.). 1984. *An introduction to the Aquatic Insects of North America.* Second edition. Kendall-Hunt, Dubuque, Iowa.

Messer, J. and P. L. Brezonik, 1983. ''Comparison of Denitrification Rate Estimation Techniques in a Large, Shallow Lake.'' *Water Res.,* **17**:631–640.

Meyer, H., and K. Mobius. 1865, 1872. *Fauna der Kieler,* bucht 1 (1865), pp. 1–88; bucht 2 (1872), pp. 1–139.

Micklin, P. P. 1988. Dessication of the Aral Sea: A water management disaster in the Soviet Union. *Science* **241**:1170–1176.

Mill, H. R. 1895. ''Bathymetric Survey of the English Lakes.'' *Geogr. J.,* **6**:46–73.

Miller, R. G. 1951. ''The Natural History of Lake Tahoe Fishes.'' Ph.D. thesis, Stanford University, Stanford, Calif. 160 pp.

Miller, T. J., L. B. Crowder, J. A. Rice, and E. A. Marschall. 1988. ''Larval Size and Recruitment Mechanisms in Fishes: Toward a Conceptual Framework.'' *Can. J. Fish. Aquatic Sci.,* **45**:1657–1670.

Miller, W. E., T. E. Mahoney, and J. C. Greene. 1974. ''Algal Productivity in 49 Lake Waters as Determined by Algal Assays. *Water Res.,* **8**:667–679.

Milliman, J. D., and E. Boyle. 1975. ''Biological Uptake of Dissolved Silica in the Amazon River Estuary.'' *Science,* **189**:995–997.

Minshall, G. W. 1978. ''Autotrophy in Stream Ecosystems.'' *Bioscience,* **28**:767–771.

———, R. C. Petersen, K. W. Cummins, T. L. Bott, J. R. Sidell, C. E. Cushing, and R. L. Vannote.

1983. ''Interbiome Comparison of Stream Ecosystem Dynamics.'' *Ecol. Monogr.,* **53**:1–25.

Mitchell, D. S. 1969. ''The Ecology of Vascular Hydrophytes on Lake Kariba.'' *Hydrobiologia,* **34**:448–464.

Mitchell, G. H. 1956. ''The Geological History of the Lake District.'' *Proc. Yorks. Geol. Soc.,* **30**.

Mitchell, P., and E. Prepas. 1990. *Atlas of Alberta Lakes,* University of Alberta Press, Edmonton. 675 pp.

Mitchell, R. (ed.). 1972, 1978. *Water Pollution Microbiology,* vols. I and II. Wiley, New York. 416 and 442 pp.

Mitsch, W. J. and K. C. Ewel. 1979. ''Comparative Biomass and Growth of Cypress in Florida Wetlands.'' *Am. Midland Naturalist,* **101**:417–426.

Mitsch, W. J. and J. G. Gosslink. 1993. *Wetlands.* Van Nostrand Reinhold, New York. 722 pp.

———, and S. E. Jorgensen. 1989. *Ecological Engineering: An Introduction to Ecotechnology.* Wiley, New York. 472 pp.

Mittelbach, G. G. 1988. ''Competition among Refuging Sunfishes and Effects of Fish Density on Littoral Zone Invertebrates. *Ecology,* **69**:614–623.

Monteleone, D. M. 1992. ''Seasonality and Abundance of Icthyoplankton in Great South Bay, New York.'' *Estuaries,* **15**:230–238.

Moore, J. M. and S. Ramamoorthy. 1984. *Heavy Metals in Natural Waters.* Springer-Verlag, New York. 288 pp.

Moore, J. W. 1976. ''Seasonal Succession of Algae in Rivers. 1. Examples from the Avon, a Large Slowflowing River.'' *J. Phycol.,* **12**:342–349.

Mordukai-Boltovskoi, P. D. (ed.). 1979. ''The River Volga and Its Life.'' *Monogr. Biol.,* vol. 33. 473 pp.

Morgan, M. D. 1980. ''Life History Characteristics of Two Introduced Populations of *Mysis relictis.*'' *Ecology,* **61**:551–561.

Mori, S. 1974. ''Diatom Succession in a Core from Lake Biwa.'' pp. 247–254. In S. Hori (ed.), ''Paleolimnology of Lake Biwa and the Japanese Pleistocene.'' *Contrib. Paleolimnol. L. Biwa,* No. 43. Otsu, Japan.

———, and T. Miura. 1980. ''List of Plant and Animal Species Living in Lake Biwa.'' *Memoirs Fac. Sci. Kyoto Univ. Ser. Biol.,* **8**:1–33.

Moriarty, D. J. W. 1973. ''The Physiology of Digestion of Blue-Green Algae in the Cichlid Fish, *Talapia nilotica.*" *J. Zool. London,* **171**:25–39.

——, J. P. E. C. Darlington, I. G. Dunn, C. M. Moriarty, and M. P. Tevlin. 1973. "Feeding and Grazing in Lake George, Uganda." *Proc. Roy. Soc. Lond. Ser. B,* **184**:299–319.

Morisawa, M. 1968. *Streams, Their Dynamics and Morphology.* McGraw-Hill, New York. 175 pp.

Morris, I. 1974. "Nitrogen Assimilation and Protein Synthesis." pp. 583–609. In W. D. P. Stewart (ed.), "Algal Physiology and Biochemistry." *Bot. Monograph.,* **10**.

—— (ed.). 1980. *The Physiological Ecology of Phytoplankton.* University of California Press, Berkeley. 625 pp.

Morris, R. H., D. P. Abbott, and E. C. Haderlie. 1980. *Intertidal Invertebrates of California.* Stanford University Press Stanford California. 690 pp.

Mortimer, C. H. 1941, 1942. "The Exchange of Dissolved Substances between Mud and Water in Lakes." *J. Ecol.,* **29**:280–329, (1941); **30**:147–201 (1942).

——. 1971. "Chemical Exchanges between Sediments and Water in the Great Lakes—Speculations on Probable Regulatory Mechanisms." *Limnol. Oceanogr.,* **16**:387–404.

——. 1974. "Lake Hydrodynamics." *Mitt. Int. Ver. Theor. Angew. Limnol.,* **20**:124–197.

——. 1981. "The Oxygen Content of Air-Saturated Freshwaters over Ranges of Temperature and Atmospheric Pressure of Limnological Interest." *Mitt. Int. Ver. Theor. Angew. Limnol.,* No. 22. 22 pp.

——. 1988. "Discoveries and Testable Hypotheses Arising from Coastal Zone Scanner Imagery of Southern Lake Michigan." *Limnol. Oceanogr.,* **33**:203–226.

——, and E. B. Worthington. 1942. "Morphometric Data for Windermere." *J. Anim. Ecol.,* **11**:245–247.

Moss, B. 1972. "The Influence of Environmental Factors on the Distrbution of Freshwater Algae: An Experimental Study. 1. Introduction and the Influence of Calcium Concentration." *J. Ecol.,* **60**:917–932.

——. 1979. "Algal and Other Evidence for Major Changes in Strumpshaw Broad, Norfolk, England in the Last Two Centuries." *Br. Phycol. J.,* **14**:263–283.

——. 1980. *Ecology of Fresh Waters.* Blackwell, Oxford. 332 pp.

——. 1981. "The Composition and Ecology of Periphyton Communities in Freshwaters. II. Inter-Relationships between Water Chemistry, Phytoplankton Populations and Periphyton Populations in a Shallow Lake and Associated Experimental Reservoirs ("Lund tubes"). *Br. Phycol. J.,* **16**:59–76.

Mosser, J. L., and T. D. Brock. 1976. "Temperature Optima for Algae Inhabiting Cold Mountain Streams." *Arctic Alpine Res.,* **8**:111–114.

Moyle, P. B. 1976. *Inland Fishes of California.* University of California Press, Berkeley. 405 pp.

——, and J. J. Cech. 1988. *Fishes: An Introduction to Ichthyology.* 2nd edition. Prentice Hall, Englewood Cliffs, New Jersey.

Mullin, M. M., and P. M. Evans. 1974. "The Use of a Deep Tank in Plankton Ecology. II. Efficiency of a Planktonic Food Chain." *Limnol. Oceanogr.,* **19**:902–911.

Murphy, C. B. 1978. Onondaga Lake. Pp. 224–365. In J. A. Bloomfield (ed.), *Lakes of New York State,* Vol II. Academic New York.

Murphy, C. R. 1972. "An Investigation of Diffusion Characteristics of the Hypolimnion of Lake Erie." pp. 39–44. In N. M. Burns and C. Ross (eds.), "Project Hypo—An Intensive Study of the Lake Erie Central Basin Hypolimnion and Related Surface Water Phenomena." Canadian Centre for Inland Waters, Paper 6.; U.S. EPA Tech. Rep. TS-05-71-208-24.

Murray, J., and L. Pullar. 1910. *Bathymetric Survey of the Scottish Lochs.* Vol. 1. Challenger Office, Edinburgh. 785 pp.

Myrup, L. O., T. M. Powell, D. A. Godden, and C. R. Goldman. 1979. "Climatological Estimate of the Average Monthly Energy and Water Budgets of Lake Tahoe, California-Nevada." *Water Resour. Res.,* **15**:1499–1508.

National Academy of Sciences. 1969. *Eutrophication: Causes, Consequences, Correctives.* Washington, D.C. 611 pp. Includes lakes, rivers, and estuaries.

——. *Nitrates: An Environmental Assessment.* Environmental Studies Board. National Research Council. Washington, D.C. 750 pp.

——. 1978. Nitrates: an environmental assessment. Environmental Studies Board. National Research

Council, National Academy of Sciences, Washington, DC. 78-62316. 723 pp.

National Research Council, 1992. Wetlands. pp. 262–340. In *Restoration of Aquatic Ecosystems*. National Research Council, Washington, D.C.

Naumann, E. 1919. Nagra synpunker angaende planktons okologi. Med sarskild hansyn till fytoplankton. *Svensk bot. Tidskr.*, **13**:129–158.

———. 1921. Einige Grundlinien der regionalen Limnologie. *Lunds Universitets Årsskrift N.F. II*, **17**:1—22.

Nauwerck, A. 1963. "Die Beziehungen Zwischen Zooplankton und Phytoplankton im See Erken." *Symb. Bot. Ups.*, **17**:1–163.

Needham, P. R., and A. C. Jones. 1959. "Flow, Temperature, Solar Radiation and Ice in Relation to Activities of Fishes in Sagehen Creek, California." *Ecology*, **40**:465–474.

Neess, J. C., R. C. Dugdale, V. A. Dugdale, and J. J. Goering. 1962. "Nitrogen Metabolism in Lakes. 1. Measurement of Nitrogen Fixation with ^{15}N. *Limnol. Oceanogr.*, **7**:163–169.

Neilands, J. B. 1981. "Microbial Iron Compounds." *Ann. Rev. Biochem.*, **50**:715–731.

Nelson, D. M., J. J. Goering, S. S. Kilham, and R. R. L. Guillard. 1976. "Kinetics of Silicic Acid Uptake and Rates of Silica Dissolution in the Marine Diatom *Thalassiosira pseudonana.*" *J. Phycol.*, **12**:246–252.

Newell, R. C. 1970. *Biology of Intertidal Animals*. American Elsevier, New York. 555 pp.

Nichols, F. H. 1979. "Natural and Anthropogenic Influences on Benthic Community Structure in San Francisco Bay." pp. 409–426. In T. J. Conomos (ed.), *San Francisco Bay*. American Association for the Advancement of Science, San Francisco.

Nichols, S. A., and G. Cottam. 1972. "Harvesting as a Control for Aquatic Plants." *Water Res. Bull.*, **8**:1205–1210.

Nisho, T., I. Koike, and A. Hatorri. 1983. "Estimates of Dentrification and Nitrification in Coastal and Estuarine Sediments." *Appl. Environ. Microbiol.*, **45**:444–450.

Nizan., S., C. Dimentman, and M. Shilo. 1986. "Acute Toxic Effects of the Cyanobacterium *Microcytis aeruginosa* on *Daphnia magna. Limnol. Oceanogr.*, **31**:497–502.

Northcoate, T. G. 1988. "Fish in the Structure and Function of Freshwater Ecosystems: A "Top-Down" View." *Can J. Fish. Aquat. Sci.*, **45**:361–379.

O'Brien, W. J., B. T. Evans, and G. L. Howick. 1986. A new view of the predation cycle of a planktivorous fish, white crappie (*Pommoxis annularis*). *Can. J. Fish. Aquat. Sci.*, **43**:1894–1889.

O'Gorman, R. and Schneider, C. P. 1986. "Dynamics of Alewifes in Lake Ontario Following a Mass Mortality." *Trans. Am. Fish. Soc.*, **115**:1–14.

Odum, E. P. 1971. *Fundamentals of Ecology*. 3d ed. W. B. Saunders, Philadelphia. 574 pp.

———, and A. de la Cruz. 1967. "Particulate Organic Detritus in a Georgia Salt Marsh-Estuarine Ecosystem." pp. 383–388. In G. H. Lauff (ed.), *Estuaries*. American Association for the Advancement of Science, publ. no. 83. Washington, D.C.

Odum, H. T. and R. F. Pigeon (eds.). 1970. "A Tropical Rain Forest. A Study of Irradiation and Ecology." Office of Information Services, U.S. Atomic Energy Commission, Washington, D.C. 1684 pp.

Officer, C. B. 1976. *Physical Geography of Estuaries*. Wiley-Interscience, New York. 465 pp.

Oglesby, R. T. 1968. "Effects of Controlled Nutrient Dilution of a Entrophic Lake." *Water Res.*, **2**:106–108.

———. 1978. "The Limnology of Cayuga Lake." pp. 1–20. In J. A. Bloomfield (ed.), *Lakes of New York State*, Vol. 1. *Ecology of the Finger Lakes*. Academic, New York.

Ohle, W. 1952. "Die Hypolimnishe Kohlendioxydakkumulation als produktionsbiologischer Indikator." *Arch Hydrobiol.*, **46**:153–285.

Ólafsson, J. 1979. "The Chemistry of Lake Mývatn." *Oikos*, **32**:82–112.

Olausson, E., and I. Cato. 1980. *Chemistry and Biogeochemistry of Estuaries*. Wiley-Interscience, New York. 452 pp.

Omernik, J. M. 1976. The Influence of Land Use on Stream Nutrient Levels." U. S. EPA-600/3-76-014. Corvallis, Ore. 68 pp. plus appendix.

Orth, R. J., K. L. Heck, and M. P. Weinstein (eds.). 1984. "Faunal Relationships in Seagrass and March Ecosystems." Special Issue, *Estuaries*, **7**:276–470.

Oswald, W. J. 1976. "Removal of Algae in Natural Bodies of Water." University of California, Berkeley. Sanitary Eng. Res. Lab. Rep. UCB-SERL No. 76-1. 140 pp.

Overbeck, J., and H. D. Babenzien. 1964. "Bakterien

und Phytoplankton eines Kleingewässers im Jahreszyklus.'' *Z. Allg. Mikrobiol.*, **4**:59–76.

Paasche, E. 1973. ''Silicon and the Ecology of Marine Planktonic Diatoms. II. Silicate-Uptake Kinetics in Five Diatom Species.'' *Mar. Biol.*, **19**:262–269.

Paerl, H. 1973. ''Detritus in Lake Tahoe: Structural Modification by Attached Microflora.'' *Science*, **180**:496–498.

———, R. C. Richards, R. L. Leonard, and C. R. Goldman. 1975. ''Seasonal Nitrate Cycling as Evidence for Complete Vertical Mixing in Lake Tahoe, California-Nevada.'' *Limnol. Oceanogr.*, **20**:1–8.

———, , K. L. Webb, J. Baker, and W. J. Wiebe. 1981. Nitrogen Fixation in Waters. pp. 193–240. In W. J. Broughton (ed.), *Nitrogen Fixation. Vol. 1. Ecology.* Clarendon Press, Oxford.

Paller, M. H. 1987. ''Distribution of Larval Fish between Macrophyte Beds and Open Channels in a Southeastern Floodplain Swamp.'' *J. Freshwat. Ecol.*, **4**:191–200.

Pamatmat, M. M., and K. Banse. 1969. ''Oxygen Measurements by the Seabed. II. In Situ Measurements to a Depth of 180 m.'' *Limnol. Oceanogr.*, **14**:250–259.

Park, C. C. 1987. *Acid Rain: Rhetoric and Reality.* Methuen, London. 272 pp.

Parma, S. 1980. ''The History of the Eutrophication Concept and the Eutrophication in the Netherlands.'' *Hydrobiol. Bull.* (Amsterdam), **14**:5–11.

Parsons, T. R., Y. Maita, and C. M. Lalli. 1984. *A Manual of Sea Water Analysis.* Pergammon, Oxford. 173 pp.

Parsons, T. R., Yoshiaki, M., and C. M. Lalli. 1984. *A Manual of Biological Methods for Seawater Analysis.* Pergammon, Oxford. 172 pp.

Pasciak, W. J., and J. Gavis. 1974. ''Transport Limitation of Nutrient Uptake in Phytoplankton.'' *Limnol. Oceanogr.*, **19**:881–888.

Pastorok, R. A., M. W. Lorenzen, and T. C. Ginn. 1981. ''Artificial Aeration and Oxygenation of Reservoirs: A Review of Theory, Techniques, and Experiences.'' Tetra-Tech. Co. Final Rep. TC-3400. Waterways Experimental Station U.S. Army Corps of Engineers. 192 pp. plus appendix.

Patalas, K. 1969. ''Composition and Horizontal Distribution of Crustacean Zooplankton in Lake Ontario.'' *J. Fish. Res. Board Can.*, **26**:2135–2164.

———. 1971. ''Crustacean Plankton and the Eutro-phication of St. Lawrence Great Lakes. *J. Fish. Res. Board Can.*, **29**:1451–1462.

———. 1984. ''Mid-Summer Mixing Depths in Lakes of Different Latitudes. *Verh. Int. Ver. Limnol.*, **22**:97–102.

Patrick, R., B. Crum, and J. Coles. 1969. ''Temperature and Manganese as Determining Factors in the Presence of Diatom or Blue-Green Algal Floras in Streams.'' *Proc. Nat. Acad. Sci. U.S.A.*, **64**:472–478.

Patterson, C. C., and J. D. Salvia. 1968. ''Lead in the Modern Environment, How Much Is Natural?'' *Scientist and Citizen*, **10**:66–79.

Paulson, L. J. 1980. ''Models of Ammonia Excretion for Brook Trout (*Salvelinus fontinalis*) and Rainbow Trout (*Salmo gairdneri*).'' *Can. J. Fish. Aquatic Sci.*, **37**:1421–1425.

Payne, A. I. 1986. *The Ecology of Tropical Lakes and Rivers.* John Wiley. New York. 301 pp.

Pearsall, W. H. 1932. ''Phytoplankton in English Lakes. II. The Composition of the Phytoplankton in Relation to Dissolved Substances.'' *J. Ecol.*, **20**:24–262.

———. 1950. *Mountains and Moorlands.* Collins, London. 312 pp.

———, and W. Pennington. 1973. *The Lake District.* Collins, London. 320 pp.

Pearson, W. D., and R. H. Kramer. 1972. ''Drift and Production of Two Aquatic Insects in a Mountain Stream.'' *Ecol. Monogr.*, **24**:365–385.

Pechlaner, R., G. Bretschko, P. Gollmann, H. Pfeifer, M. Tilzer, and H. P. Weissenbach. 1972. ''The Production Processes in Two High Mountain Lakes (Vorder and Hinterer Finstertaler See), Kuhtai, Austria.'' pp. 239–269. In Z. Kajak and A. Hillbricht-Ilkowska (eds.), *Productivity Problems of Freshwaters*, PWN (Polish Scientific Publishers), Warsaw-Krakow.

Pennak, R. W. 1971. ''Towards a Classification of Lotic Habitats.'' *Hydrobiologia*, **38**:321–334.

———. 1978. *Freshwater Intertebrates of the United States.* 2d ed. Wiley, New York. 803 pp.

Perkins, E. J. 1974. *Biology of Estuaries and Coastal Waters.* Academic, New York. 678 pp.

Perkins, M. A., C. R. Goldman, and R. L. Leonard. 1975. ''Residual Nutrient Discharge in Streamwaters Influenced by Sewage Effluent Spraying.'' *Ecology*, **56**:453–460.

Peskova, H. 1990. ''Original Secchi Disc Experiments

Held on Papal Fleet in Mediterranean Sea. *Lake Watch*, **5**:4. (Newsletter of the Minnesota Pollution Control Agency: Citizens Lake-Monitoring Program.)

Peterman, R. M., and M. J. Bradford, 1987. "Wind Speed and Mortality Rate of a Marine Fish, the northern anchovy (*Engraulis mordax*). *Science* **235**:354–356.

Petr. T. 1986. "The Volta River System." pp. 163–184. In B. R. Davies, and K. F. Walker (eds.), *The Ecology of River Systems.* Junk, The Netherlands.

Pettersson, K. 1980. "Alkaline Phosphatase Activity and Algal Surplus Phosphorus as Phosphorus-Deficiency Indicators in Lake Erken." *Arch. Hydrobiol.,* **89**:54–87.

Pfeifer, R. F., and W. F. McDiffett. 1975. "Some Factors Affecting Primary Productivity of Stream Riffle Communities." *Arch. Hydrobiol.,* **75**:306–317.

Pierson, W. R., W. W. Brachaczek, S. M. Japar, G. R. Cass, and P. A. Solomon. 1988. "Dry Deposition and Dew Chemistry in Claremont, California, during the 1985 Nitrogen Species Methods Comparison Study." *Atmospheric Environment*, **22**:1657–1663.

Poe, T. P., C. O. Hatcher, C. L. Brown, and D. W. Schloesser. 1986. "Comparison of Species Composition and Richness of Fish Assemblages in Altered and Unaltered Littoral Habitats." *J. Freshwat. Ecol.,* **3**:525–536.

Polmiluyko, V. P., and M. V. Ochkivskaya. 1970. "Comparison of Nitrate Reductase Activity in *Microcystis aeruginosa* and *Chlorella vulgaris* in Culture." *Hydrobiol. J. (USSR)*, **6**:77–80.

Pomeroy, L. R., H. M. Matthews, and H. S. Min. 1963. Excretion of Soluble Organic Compounds by Zooplankton." *Limnol. Oceanogr.,* **8**:50–55.

Pond, S. and G. L. Pickard. 1978. *Introductory Dynamic Oceanography*. Pergamon, New York. 241 pp.

Porter, K. G. 1976. "Enhancement of Algal Growth and Productivity by Grazing Zooplankton." *Science*, **192**:1332–1334.

———. 1977. "The Plant-Animal Interface in Freshwater Ecosystems." *Am. Sci.,* **65**:159–170.

———, and R. McDonough. 1984. "The Energetic Cost of Response to Blue-Green Algal Filaments by Cladocerans. *Limnol. Oceanogr.,* **29**:365–369.

———, E. B. Sheer, B. F. Sheer, M. L. Pace, and R.

W. Sanders. 1985. "Protozoa in Planktonic Food Webs." *J. Protozoology*, **32**:409–415.

———. 1988. "Phagotrophic Phytoflagellates on Microbial Food Webs." *Hydrobiologia,* **159**:89–98.

Post, J. R. and D. Cucin 1984. Changes in the Benthic Community of a Small Precambrian Lake following the Introduction of the Yellow Perch, *Eylga flavescens Can. J. Fish. Aquat. Sci.* **41**:1496–1501.

Powell, T., and A. Jassby. 1974. "The Estimation of Vertical Eddy Diffusivities below the Thermocline in Lakes." *Water Resour. Res.,* **10**:191–198.

Powers, C. F., D. W. Schults, K. W. Malueg, R. M. Brice, and M. D. Schuldt. 1972. "Algal Responses to Nutrient Additions in Natural Waters. II. Field Experiments." *Limnol. Oceanogr. Special Symp.* vol. I., pp. 141–154.

Prepas, E., and F. H. Rigler. 1978. "The Enigma of *Daphnia* Death Rates." *Limnol. Oceanogr.,* **23**:970–988.

———, and D. O. Trew. 1983. "Evaluation of the Phosphorus-Chlorophyll Relationship for Lakes off the Precambrian Shield in Western Canada." *Can. J. Fish. Aquat. Sci.,* **40**:27–35.

Preston, T., W. D. P. Stewart, and C. S. Reynolds. 1980. "Bloom-forming Cyanobacterium *Microcystis aeruginosa* overwinters on Sediment Surface." *Nature*, **288**:365–367.

Prichard, D. W. 1967. "What Is an Estuary? Physical Viewpoint." pp. 3–5. In G. H. Lauff (ed.), *Estuaries*. American Association for the Advancement of Science, Washington, D.C.

Priscu, J. C. 1982. "Physiological Ecology of Castle Lake Phytoplankton: A Comparison of Shallow and Deep-Water Communities." Ph.D. Thesis. University of California, Davis.

———. 1983. "Suspensoid Characteristics in Subalpine Castle Lake, California. II. Optical Properties." *Arch. Hydrobiol.,* **97**:425–433.

Prophet, C. W., Bungardt, T. B., and N. K. Prophet. 1989. "Diel Movement and Seasonal Distribution of Walleye, *Stizostedion vitreum*, in Marion Reservoir, Based on Ultrasonic Telemetry." *J. Freshwat. Ecol.,* **5**:177–185.

———. 1991. "Diel Activity and Seasonal Movements of Striped Bass x White Bass Hybrids in Marion Reservoir, Kansas. *J. Freshwat. Ecol.,* **6**:305–313.

Provasoli, L. 1963. "Organic Regulation of Phytoplankton Fertility.'' In M. N. Hill (ed.), *The Sea*, **2**:165–219.

Ragotzkie, R. A. 1974. ''The Great Lakes Rediscovered.'' *Am. Sci.*, **62**:454–464.

———. 1978. ''Heat Bugets of Lakes.'' pp. 1–19. In A. Lerman (ed.), *Lakes—Chemistry, Geology, Physics*. Springer-Verlag, New York.

Ranwell, D. S. 1972. *Ecology of Salt Marshes and Dunes*. Chapman & Hall, London. 258 pp.

Rasmussen, R. A., J. Krasnec, and D. Pierotti. 1976. ''N$_2$O Analysis in the Atmosphere via Electron Capture-Gas Chromatography.'' *Geophys. Res. Letts.*, **3**:615–618.

Raven, J. A. 1983. The transport and function of silicon in plants. *Biol. Revs.* **58**:179–207.

———, 1984. *Energetics and Transport in Aquatic Plants* Marine Biological Laboratory Lectures in Biology Vol 4, 587 pp.

Ravera, O. 1953. ''Gli Stadi di Sviluppo dei Copepodi Pelagici del Lago Maggiore.'' *Mem. Ist. Ital. Idrobiol.*, **7**:129–151.

Ravesi. E. M. 1976. ''Nitrite additives—harmful or necessary?'' *Mar. Fish. Rev.*, **38**:24–30.

Rawson, D. S. 1952. ''Mean Depth and the Fish Production of Large Lakes.'' *Ecology*, **33**:513–521.

———. 1955. ''Morphometry as a Dominant Factor in the Productivity of Large Lakes.'' *Verh. Int. Ver. Limnol.*, **12**:164–175.

Reckhow, K. H. and S. C. Chapra. 1983. *Engineering Approaches for Lake Management. Vol. 1. Data Analysis and Empirical Modeling*. Butterworth, Boston. 340 pp.

Reddy, K. R., W. H. Patrick, and C. W. Lindau. 1989. Nitrification-denitrification at the plant root-sediment interface in wetlands. *Limnol. Oceanogr.* **34**:1004–1013.

Regier, H. A., and K. H. Lotus. 1972. ''Effects of Fisheries Exploitation on Salmonid Communities in Oligotrophic Lakes.'' *J. Fish. Res. Board Can.*, **29**:959–968.

Reid, G. K., and R. D. Wood. 1976. *Ecology of Inland Waters and Estuaries*. 2d ed. Van Nostrand, New York. 485 pp.

Reid, P. C. 1975. ''Large Scale Changes in North Sea Phytoplankton.'' *Nature*, **257**:217–219.

Remane, A., and C. Schlieper. 1971. *Biology of Brackish Water*. 2d ed. Schweizerbart' sche, Stuttgart.

Resh, V. H. 1979. ''Sampling Variability and Life History Features: Basic Considerations in the Design of Aquatic Insect Studies.'' *J. Fish Res. Board Can.*, **36**:290–311.

———, and D. M. Rosenberg (eds.). 1984. *The Ecology of Aquatic Insects*. Praeger Scientific, New York. 625 pp.

Reuter, J. E. 1982. ''Nitrogen Assimilation of the Epilithic Periphyton Community in Lake Tahoe, California-Nevada.'' Ph.D. thesis. University of California, Davis.

Reynolds, C. S. 1971. ''The Ecology of the Planktonic Blue-Green Algae in the North Shropshire Meres.'' *Field Stud.*, **3**:409–432.

———. 1973. ''Growth and Buoyancy of *Microcystis aeruginosa*, Katz amend. Elenkin, in a Shallow Entrophic Lake.'' *Proc. Roy. Soc. Lond. Ser. B*, **184**:29–50.

———, R. L. Oliver, and A. E. Walsby. 1987. ''Cyanobacteria Dominance: The Role of Buoyancy Regulation in Dynamic Lake Environments.'' *N.Z. J. Mar. Freshwat. Res.*, **21**:379–390.

Richardson, C. J., and P. E. Marshall. 1986. ''Processes Controlling Movement, Storage, and Export of Phosphorus in a Fen Peatland.'' *Ecol. Monogr.*, **56**:279–302.

Richardson, J., and D. Livingstone. 1962. ''An Attack by a Nile Crocodile on a Small Boat.'' *Copeia*, **1**:203–204.

Richerson, P. J., C. Widmer, and T. Kittel. 1977. ''The Limnology of Lake Titicaca (Peru-Bolivia), a Large, High-Altitude Tropical Lake.'' Institute of Ecology, publ. no. 14, University of California, Davis. 78 pp.

Richter, D. D., C. W. Ralston, and W. R. Harms. 1982. ''Prescribed Fire: Effects on Water Quality and Forest Nutrient Cycling.'' *Science*, **215**:661–663.

Ricker, W. E. 1975. *Computation and Interpretation of Biological Statistics of Fish Populations*. Department of Environment Fisheries and Marine Service, Ottawa, Canada. 382 pp.

Riemann, B., and M. Sondergaard. 1986. *Carbon Dynamics in Eutrophic, Temperate Lakes*. Elsevier, Amsterdam. 284 pp.

Rigler, F. H. 1973. ''A Dynamic View of the Phosphorus Cycle in Lakes.'' pp. 539–572. In E. J. Griffisth, A. Beeton, J. M. Spenser, and D. T. Mitchell (eds.), *Environmental Phosphorus Handbook*. Wiley, New York.

Ringler, N. H., and J. D. Hall. 1975. "Effects on Logging on Water Temperature and Dissolved Oxygen in Spawning Beds." *Trans. Am. Fish. Soc.*, **104**:111–121.

Ripl, W. 1976. "Biochemical Oxidation of Polluted Lake Sediment with Nitrate—A New Lake Restoration Method." *Ambio*, **5**:132–135.

Risotto, S. P. and R. E. Turner. 1985. Annual fluctuations in abundance of the commercial fisheries of the Mississippi River and Tributaries. *N. Am. J. Fish Manage.* 557–574.

Roberts, L. 1989. "Does the Ozone Hole Threaten Antarctic Life?" *Science*, **244**:288–299.

Rodhe, W. 1948. "Environmental Requirements of Freshwater Plankton Algae. VII. Iron as a Limiting Factor for Growth." *Symb. Bot. Ups.*, **10**:104–117.

———. 1965. "Standard Correlations between Pelagic Photosynthesis and Light." pp. 365–382. In C. R. Goldman (ed.), "Primary Productivity in Aquatic Environments." *Mem. Ist. Ital. Idrobiol,* **18** (suppi).

———. 1979. "The Life of Lakes." *Arch. Hydrobiol. Beth.,* **3**:5–9.

Ronner, U. 1985. "Nitrogen Transformations in the Baltic Proper: Denitrification Counteracts Eutrophication." *Ambio*, **14**:134–138.

Rosa, F. and N. M. Burns. 1987. "Lake Erie Central Basin Oxygen Depletion Changes." *J. Great Lakes Res.,* **13**:684–696.

Roth, J. C. 1968. "Benthic and Limnetic Distribution of Three *Chaoborus* Species in a Southern Michigan Lake (Diptera, *Chaoboridae*)." *Limnol. Oceanogr.,* **13**:242–249.

———, and A. J. Horne. 1981. "Algal Nitrogen Fixation and Microcrustacean Abundance: An Unregarded Interrelationship between Zoo- and Phytoplankton." *Verh. Int. Ver. Limnol.,* **21**:333–338.

———, and S. E. Neff. 1964. "Studies of Physical Limnology and Profundal Bottom Fauna, Mountain Lake, Virginia." *Va. Agric. Exp. Stn. Tech. Bull.,* **169**. 44 pp.

Round, F. E. 1971. "The Growth and Succession of Algal Populations in Freshwaters." *Mitt. Int. Ver. Theor. Agnew. Limnol.,* **19**:70–99.

———. 1973. *The Biology of the Algae.* Edward Arnold, London. 278 pp.

——— (ed.). 1988. *Algae and the Aquatic Environment.* Biopress, Bristol, England. 460 pp.

Roy, D. 1989. Physical and Biological Factors Controlling the Distribution and Abundance of Fish in the Hudson/James Bay Rivers. In Dodge, P. D. (ed.), Proceeding of the International Large River Symposium. *Can. Sp. Publ. Fish. Aquat. Sci.*, Vol. 106.

Rudd, R. L. 1964. *Pesticides in the Living Landscape.* University of Wisconsin Press, Madison. 320 pp.

Russell, F. S., A. J. Southward, G. T. Boalch, and E. I. Butler. 1971. "Changes in Biological Conditions in the English Channel off Plymouth during the Last Half-Century." *Nature*, **234**:468–470.

Russell-Hunter, W. D. 1968. *A Biology of Lower Invertebrates.* Macmillan, New York. 181 pp.

———. 1969. *A Biology of Higher Invertebrates.* Macmillan, New York. 224 pp.

Ruttner, F. 1963. *Fundamentals of Limnology.* English translation by D. G. Frey and F. E. J. Fry. Toronto University Press, Canada. 307 pp. (First German edition in 1940.)

Ruttner-Koliska, A. 1972. "Das Zooplankton der Binnengewässer. I. Tiel. Rotatoria." *Die Binnengewässer,* **26**:99–234.

Ryder G. I. and D. Scott. 1988. "The Applicability of the River Continuum Concept to New Zealand Streams." *Verh. Int. Ver. Limnol.,* **23**:1441–1445.

Ryder, R. A. 1965. "A Method for Estimating the Potential Fish Production of North-Temperate Lakes." *Trans. Amer. Fish Soc.,* **94**:214–218.

Rzoska, J. (ed.). 1976. *The Nile: Biology of an Ancient River. Junk,* The Hague. 417 pp.

Sas, H. (ed.). 1989. *Lake Restoration by Reduction of Nutrient Loading: Expectations, Experiences, Extrapolations.* Academia Verlag Richartz, St. Augustin, Germany, 497 pp.

Saunders, G. W. 1971. "Carbon Flow in the Aquatic System." In J. Cairns (ed.), *Structure and Function of Freshwater Microbial Communities.* Research Division Monograph 3, pp. 31–45. Virginia Polytechnic Institute, Blacksburg.

Savino, J. F. and R. A. Stein. 1982. "Predator-Prey Interaction between Largemouth Bass and Bluegills as Influenced by Simulated Submerged Vegetation." *Trans. Amer. Fish. Soc.* **111**:255–266.

Scavia, D., R. P. Canale, W. F. Powers, and J. L. Moody. 1981. "Variance Estimates for a dynamic Eutrophication Model of Saginaw Bay, Lake Huron." *Water Resour. Res.,* **17**:1115–1124.

———, G. H. Fahnenstiel, M. S. Evans, D. J. Jude,

and J. T. Lehman. 1986. "Influence of Salmonine Predation and Weather on the Long-Term Water Quality Trends in Lake Michigan." *Can. J. Fish. Aquat. Sci.,* **43**:435–443.

Schaffner, W. R., and R. T. Oglesby. 1978. Limnology of Eight Finger Lakes. pp. 312–470. In J. A. Bloomfield (ed.), *Lakes of New York State*, Vol I. Academic, New York.

Schelske, C. L. 1962. "Iron, Organic Matter and Other Factors Limiting Primary Productivity in a Marl Lake." *Science,* **136**:45–46.

———, and J. C. Roth. 1973. "Limnological Survey of Lakes Michigan, Superior, Huron, and Erie." *Great Lakes Res. Div., Univ. Mich.,* Publ. 17. 108 pp.

———, and E. F. Stoermer. 1972. "Phosphorus, Silica, and Eutrophication of Lake Michigan." *Limnol. Oceanogr.,* Special Symposium, vol. 1, pp. 157–170.

Schindler, D. W. 1980. "The Effect of Fertilization with Phosphorus and Nitrogen versus Phosphorus Alone on Eutrophication of Experimental Lakes." *Limnol. Oceanogr.,* **25**:1149–1152.

———. 1971. "Light, Temperature, and Oxygen Regimes of Selected Lakes in the Experimental Lakes Area, Northwestern Ontario." *J. Fish. Res. Board Can.,* **28**:157–169.

———, K. H. Mills, D. F. Malley, D. L. Findllay, J. A. Shearer, J. J. Davies, M. A. Turner, G. A. Linsey, and D. R. Cruikshank. 1985. "Long-Term Ecosystem Stress: The Effects of Years of Experimental Acidification on a Small Lake." *Science,* **228**:1395–1401.

Schindler, O. 1957. *Freshwater Fishes.* Translated and edited by P. A. Orkin. Thames and Hudson, London. 243 pp.

Schmidt, G. W. 1969. "Vertical Distribution of Bacteria and Algae in a Tropical Lake." *Int. Res. Ges. Hydrobiol.,* **54**:791–797.

———. 1973a. "Primary Productivity of Phytoplankton in Three Types of Amazon Water, 2. The Limnology of a Tropical Flood-Plain Lake in Central Amazonia (Lago de Castanho)." *Amazoniana,* **4**:139–203.

———. 1973b. "Primary Productivity of Phytoplankton in Three Types of Amazon Water, 3. Primary Productivity of Phytoplankton in a Tropical Flood-Plain Lake of Central Amazonia." *Amazoniana,* **4**:379–404.

Sculthorpe, C. D. 1967. *The Biology of Vascular Plants.* Edward Arnold, London 610 pp.

Seitzinger, S. P. 1988. "Denitrification in Freshwater and Coastal Marine Ecosystems: Ecological and Geochemical Significance." *Limnol. Oceanogr.,* **33**:702–724.

Seliger, H. H., J. H. Carpenter, M. Lotus, and W. D. McElroy. 1970. "Mechanisms for the Accumulation of High Concentrations of Dinoflagellates in a Bioluminescent Bay." *Limnol. Oceanogr.,* **15**:234–245.

Sellers, C. M., A. G. Heath, and M. L. Bass. 1975. "The Effect of Sublethal Concentrations of Copper and Zinc on Ventilatory Activity, Blood Oxygen, and pH in Rainbow Trout (*Salmo gardneri*). *Water Res.,* **9**:401–408.

Sellery, G. C. 1956. *E. A. Birge, a Memoir.* The University of Wisconsin Press, Madison. 221 pp. [With an appraisal of Birge, the limnologist, "An Explorer of Lakes," by C. H. Mortimer, pp. 165–211.]

Serruya, C., and U. Pollingher. 1971. "An Attempt at Forecasting the *Peridinium* Bloom in Lake Kinneret (Lake Tiberias)." *Mitt. Int. Ver. Theor. Angew. Limnol.,* **19**:277–291.

Shaffer, J. M. and U. Ronner. 1984. "Denitrification in the Baltic Proper Deep Water." *Deep Sea Res.,* **31**:197–220.

Shapiro, J. 1960. "The Cause of a Metalimnetic Minimum of Dissolved Oxygen." *Limnol. Oceanogr.,* **5**:216–227.

———. 1973. "Blue-Green Algae: Why They Become Dominant." *Science,* **179**:382–384.

———. 1989. "Current Beliefs Regarding Dominance by Blue-Greens: The Case for the Importance of CO_2 pH. *Verh. Int. Ver. Limnol.,* **24**:38–54.

———, W. T. Edmondson, and D. E. Allison. 1971. "Changes in the Chemical Composition of Sediments in Lake Washington, 1958–1970." *Limnol. Oceanogr.,* **16**:437–452.

———, and D. L. Wright. 1984. "Lake Restoration by Biomanipulation: Round Lake, Minnesota, the First Two Years." Freshwat. Biol., **14**:371–383.

Shaw, R. D., J. F. H. Shaw, H. Friker, and E. E. Prepas. 1990. "An Integrated Approach to Quantify Groundwater Transport of Phosphorus to Narrow Lake, Alberta. *Limnol. Oceanogr.,* **35**:870–886.

Simpson, D. G., and G. Gunther. 1956. "Notes on Habits, Systematic Characters, and Life Histories of Texas Saltwater Cyprinodonts.'' *Tulane Stud. Zool. Bot.,* **4**:115–134.

Skabitchewsky, A. P. 1929. ''Über die biologie von *Melosira baicalensis* (K. Meyer).'' *Wisl. Russ. Gidrobiol. Zh.,* **8**:93–114.

Skreslet, S. (ed.). 1986. *The Role of Freshwater Outflow in Coastal Marine Ecosystems.* Springer-Verlag, Berlin. 453 pp.

Smayda, T. J. 1957. ''Phytoplankton Studies in Lower Narragansett Bay.'' *Limnol. Oceanogr.,* **2**:342–358.

———. 1980. Phytoplankton seasonal succession, pp. 493–570 in I. Morris (ed.), *The physiological ecology of phytoplankton.* Univ. California Press, Berkeley.

Smith, C. S., and M. S. Evans. 1986. ''Phosphorus Transfer from Sediments by *Myriophyllum spicatum.*'' *Limnol. Oceanogr.,* **31**:1312–1321.

Smith, I. R. 1975. ''Turbulence in Lakes and Rivers.'' *Freshwat. Biol. Assoc.,* U.K. Publ. 29. 79 pp.

Smith, M. S., M. K. Firestone, and J. M. Tiedje. 1978. ''The Acetylene Inhibition Method for Short Term Measurement of Soil Denitrification and Its Evaluation Using ^{13}N.'' *Soil. Sci. Soc. Amer. J.*

Smith, N. J. H. 1981. *Man, Fishes, and the Amazon.* Columbia University Press. 180 pp.

Smith, R. A. 1852. ''Relationship of Sooty Skies and Acid Precipitation in Manchester, England.'' Referred to in *National Geographic,* November 1981, p. 661.

Smith, R. C. 1968. ''The Optical Characterization of Natural Waters by Means of an 'Extinction Coefficient'.'' *Limnol. Oceanogr.,* **13**:423–429.

———, J. E. Tyler, and C. R. Goldman. 1973. ''Optical Properties and Color of Lake Tahoe and Crater Lake.'' *Limnol. Oceanogr.,* **18**:189–199.

Smith, S. H. 1968. ''Species Succession and Fishery Exploitation in the Great Lakes.'' *J. Fish. Res. Board Can.,* **25**:667–693.

Smith, V. H. 1982. ''The Nitrogen and Phosphorus Dependence of Algal Biomass in Lakes: An Empirical and Theoretical Analysis.'' *Limnol. Oceanogr.,* **27**:1101–1112.

Smith, V. A. 1983. ''Low Nitrogen to Phosphorus Ratios Favor Dominance by Blue-Green Algae in Lake Phytoplankton.'' *Science,* **221**:669–671.

Smyly, W. J. P. 1978. ''Strategies for Coexistence in Two Limnetic Cyclopoid Copepods.'' *Verh. Int. Ver. Limnol.,* **20**:2501–2504.

Solórzano, L. 1969. ''Determination of Ammonia in

Natural Waters by the Phenolhypochlorite Method.'' *Limnol. Oceanogr.,* **14**:799–801.

Sommer, U., Z. Gliwicz, W. Lampert, and A. Duncan. 1986. ''The PEG-Model of Seasonal Succession of Phytoplankton in Fresh Waters. *Arch Hydrobiol.,* **106**:433–471.

Sørensen, J. 1978. ''Capacity for Denitrification and Reduction of Nitrate to Ammonia in a Coastal Marine Sediment.'' *Appl. Environ. Microbiol.,* **35**:301–305.

Spigarelli, S. A. (ed.). 1990. ''Fish Community Health: Monitoring and Assessment in Large Lakes. *J. Great Lakes Res.,* **16**:403–469.

Stacey, M. W., S. Pond, and P. H. LeBlond. 1986. ''A Wind-Forced Ekman Spiral as a Good Statistical Fit to Low-Frequency Currents in a Coastal Strait.'' *Science,* **233**:470–472.

Stanford, J. A., and J. V. Ward. 1986. Fish of the Colorado System. pp. 385–402. In B. R. Davis and K. F. Walker (eds.), *The Ecology of River Systems.* Junk, The Hague.

———, and A. P. Covich (eds.). 1988. ''Community Structure and Function in Temperate and Tropical Streams.'' *J. North Am. Benthological Soc.,* **7**:261–529.

Steele, J. H. 1974. *The Structure of Marine Ecosystems.* Blackwell Scientific Publications, Ltd., Oxford. 128 pp.

Steeman Nielsen, E. L., L. Kamp-Nielsen, S. Wium-Anderson. 1969. ''The Effect of Deleterious Concentrations of Copper on the Photosynthesis of *Chlorella pyrenoidosa.*'' *Physiol. Plant. Pathol.,* **22**:1121–1131.

———, and S. Wium-Anderson. 1971. ''The Influence of Cu on Photosynthesis and Growth in Diatoms.'' *Physiol. Plant. Pathol.,* **24**:408–414.

Stephens, R. T. T. 1983. Native fish in the Lake. pp. 111–118. In D. J. Forsyth and C. Howard-Williams (eds.), *Lake Taupo.* Div. Sci. Indust. Res. Wellington, New Zealand.

Stewart, D. J. and M. Ibarra. 1991. ''Predation and Production by Salmonid Fishes in Lake Michigan.'' *Can. J. Fish. Aquat. Sci.,* **48**:909–922.

Stewart, K. M. 1972. ''Isotherms under Ice.'' *Verh. Int. Ver. Limnol.,* **18**:303–311.

———. 1973. ''Detailed Time Variations in Mean Temperature and Heat Content of Some Madison Lakes.'' *Limnol. Oceanogr.,* **18**:218–226.

Stewart, K. M. 1976. ''Oxygen Deficits, Clarity, and

Eutrophication in Some Madison Lakes." *Int. Rev. Ges. Hydrobiol.*, **61**:536–549.

Stewart, W. D. P. 1967. "Transfer of Biologically Fixed Nitrogen in a Sand Dune Slack Region." *Nature*, **214**:603–604.

——— (ed.). 1974. *Algal Physiology and Biochemistry*. Botanical Monographs, vol. 10. University of California Press, Berkeley.

———, and G. Alexander. 1971. "Phosphorus Availability and Nitrogenase Activity in Aquatic Blue-Green Algae." *Freshwat. Biol.*, **1**:389–404.

———, G. P. Fitzgerald, and R. H. Burris. 1967. "In situ Studies on N_2-fixation Using the Acetylene Reduction Technique." *Proc. Nat. Acad. Sci. U.S.A.*, **58**:2071–2078.

Stillinger, F. H. 1980. "Water Revisited." *Science*, **209**:451–457.

Stockner, J. G. 1987. "Lake Fertilization: The Enrichment Cycle and Lake Sockeye Salmon (*Oncorhynchus nerka*) Production." pp. 198–215. In H. O. Smith, L. Margolis, and C. C. Wood (eds.), *Sockeye Salmon Population Biology and Future Management*. Can. Sp. Publ. Fish. Aquat. Sci. **96**:486 pp.

Stockner, J. G. and K. S. Shortreed. 1989. "Algal Picoplankton Production and Contribution to Food-Webs in Oligotrophic British Columbia Lakes." *Hydrobiologia*, **173**:151–166.

Stone, R. W., W. J. Kaufman, and A. J. Horne. 1973. "Long-Term Effects of Toxicants and Biostimulants on the Waters of Central San Francisco Bay." University of California, Berkeley, Sanitary Eng. Research Lab. UCB-SERL Rep. No. 73-1. 111 pp.

Storrs, P. N., E. A. Pearson, and R. E. Selleck. 1966. "A Comprehensive Study of San Francisco Bay, A Final Report." University of California, Berkeley. UCB-EEHSL Rept. No. 67–2.

Strahler, H. N. 1957. "Quantitative Analysis of Watershed Geomorphology." *Am. Geophys. Union Trans.*, **33**:913–920.

Strickland, J. D. H., O. Holm-Hansen, R. W. Eppley, and R. J. Linn. 1969. "The Use of a Deep Tank in Plankton Ecology. 1. Studies of the Growth and Composition of Phytoplankton Crops at Low Nutrient Levels." *Limnol. Oceanogr.*, **14**:23–34.

Strahler, H. N. 1957. "Quantitative Analysis of Watershed Geomorphology." *Am. Geophys. Union Trans.*, **33**:913–920.

Strong, A. E. and B. J. Edie. 1978. Satillite observa-
tions of calcium carbonate precipitations in the Great Lakes. *Limnol. Oceanogr.* **23**:877–887.

Stumm, W. and J. O. Leckie. 1971. "Phosphate Exchange with Sediments: Its Role in the Productivity of Surface Waters." *Proceedings of Fifth International Water Pollution Conference*. Pergamon, London.

Sugawara, K. 1939. "Chemical Studies in Lake Metabolism." *Bull. Chem. Soc. Japan,* **14**:375–451.

Suttle, C. A., and P. J. Harrison. 1988. "Ammonium and Phosphate Uptake Rates, N:P Supply Ratios, and Evidence for N and P Limitation in Some Oligotrophic Lakes." *Limnol. Oceanogr.,* **33**:186–202.

Swale, E. M. F. 1969. "Phytoplankton in Two English Rivers." *J. Ecol.,* **57**:1–23.

Swift, M. C. 1970. "A Qualitative and Quantitative Study of Trout Food in Castle Lake, California." *Calif. Fish Game*, **56**:109–120.

Sylvester, R. O., and G. C. Anderson. 1964. "A Lake's Response to Its Environment." *J. Sanit. Eng. Div. Am. Soc. Civ. Eng.,* **90**.

Tabor, R. A. and W. A. Wurtsbaugh. 1991. "Predation Risk and the Importance of Cover for Juvenile Rainbow Trout in Lentic Systems." *Trans. Am. Fish. Soc.,* **120**:728–738.

Talling, J. F. 1957. The Longitudinal succession of water characteristics in the White Nile River. *Hydrobiologia* **11**:73–89.

———. 1969. "The Incidence of Vertical Mixing, and Some Biological and Chemical Consequences, in Tropical African Lakes." *Verh. Int. Ver. Limnol.,* **17**:998–1012.

———. 1970. "Generalized and Specialized Features of Phytoplankton as a Form of Photosynthetic Cover." pp. 431–446. In *Prediction and Measurement of Photosynthetic Activity*. Centre for Documentation, Wageningen, Netherlands.

———. 1971. "The Underwater Light Climate as a Controlling Factor in the Production Ecology of Freshwater Phytoplankton." *Mitt. Int. Ver. Theor. Angew. Limnol.,* **19**:214–243.

———. 1976. "The Depletion of Carbon Dioxide from Lake Water by Phytoplankton." *J. Ecol.,* **64**:79–121.

Tarapchak, S. J., and C. Rubitschun. 1981. "Comparisons of Soluble Reactive Phosphorus and Orthophosphorus Concentrations at an Offshore Station in Southern Lake Michigan." *J. Great Lakes Assoc.,* **7**:290–298.

Tchobanoglous, G., and E. D. Schroeder. 1985. *Water Quality: Characteristics, Modeling, Modification.* Addison-Welsley, Reading, Mass. 768 pp.

Teal, J. M. 1957. "Community Metabolism in a Temperate Cold Spring." *Ecol. Monogr.,* **27**:283–302.

Thienemann, A. 1915. "Physikalische und chemische Untersuchungen in den Marren der Eifel." *Ver. Naturh. Ver preuss. Rheinl.,* **71**:281–389.

———. 1922. "Die beiden Chironomus Arten Tiefenfauna der norddeutschen Seen. Ein hydrobiologisches Problem." *Arch. Hydrobiol.,* **13**:609–646.

Thompson R. O., and J. Imberger. 1980. Response of a Numerical Model of a Stratified Lake to Wind Stress. pp. 562–570. In *Stratified Flows.* Proc. 2nd Int. Symp., Trondheim.

Thornton, K. W., B. C. Kimmel, and F. E. Payne. 1990. *Reservoir Limnology: Ecological Perspectives.* Wiley, New York. 246 p.

Thorpe, S. A. 1971. "Experiments on Instability of Stratified Shear Flows: Miscible Fluids." *J. Fluid Mech.,* **46**:299–319.

———. 1977. "Turbulence and Mixing in a Scottish Loch." *Phil. Trans. Roy. Soc. Lond., Ser. A,* **286**:125–181.

Tilman, D. 1978. "The Role of Nutrient Competition in a Predictive Theory of Phytoplankton Population Dynamics." *Mitt. Int. Ver. Theor. Angew. Limnol.,* **21**:585–592.

———, and S. S. Kilham. 1976. "Phosphate and Silicate Growth and Uptake Kinetics of the Diatoms *Asterionelia formosa* and *Cyclotella meneghiniana* in Batch and Semi-Continuous Culture." *J. Phycol.,* **12**:375–383.

Tilman, D. 1982. *Resource competition and community structure.* Princeton.

Tilzer, M. M. 1983. "The Importance of Fractional Light Absorption by Photosynthetic Pigments for Phytoplankton Productivity in Lake Constance." *Limnol. Oceanogr.,* **28**:833–846.

———. 1984. "Seasonal and Diurnal Shifts of Photosynthetic Quantum Yields in the Phytoplankton of Lake Constance." *Verh. Int. Ver. Limnol.,* **22**:958–962.

———. 1990. Specific Properties of Large Lakes. pp. 39–44 in M. M. Tilzer, and C. Serruya (eds.), *Large Lakes: Ecological Structure and Function.* Springer-Verlag, Berlin.

———, and A. J. Horne. 1979. "Diel Patterns of Phytoplankton Productivity and Extracellular Release in Ultra-Oligotrophic Lake Tahoe." *Int. Rev. Ges. Hydrobiol.,* **64**:157–176.

———, C. R. Goldman, and E. de Amezaga. 1975. "The Efficiency of Photosynthetic Light Energy Utilization by Lake Phytoplankton." *Verh. Int. Ver. Limnol.,* **19**:800–807.

———, and C. Serruya (eds.). 1990. *Large Lakes: Ecological Structure and Function.* Springer-Verlag, Berlin. 691 pp.

Timm, T. 1980. "Distribution of Aquatic Oligochaetes." pp. 55–77. In R. O. Brinkhurst and D. G. Cook (eds.), *Aquatic Oligochaete Biology.* Plenum, New York.

Tjossem, S. F. 1990. "Effects of Fish Chemical Clues on Vertical Migration of *Chaoborus. Limnol. Oceanogr.,* **35**:1456–1468.

Toetz, D. W. 1971. "Diurnal Uptake of NO_3 and NH_4 by a *Ceratophylium*-Periphyton Community." *Limnol. Oceanogr.,* **16**:819–822.

Tomlinson, T. E. 1970. "Trends in Nitrate Concentration in English Rivers in Relation to Fertilizer Use." *Water Treat. Exam.,* **19**:277–293.

Torrey, M. S., and G. F. Lee. 1976. "Nitrogen Fixation in Lake Mendota, Madison, Wisconsin." *Limnol. Oceanogr.,* **21**:365–378.

Townsend, C. R., and A. G. Hildrew. 1984. "Longitudinal Patterns in Detritivore Communities of Acid Streams: A Consideration of Alternative Hypotheses." *Verh. Int. Ver. Limnol.,* **22**:1953–1958.

———, and A. G. Hildrew. 1988. "Pattern and Process in Low-Order Acid Streams." *Verh. Int. Ver. Limnol.,* **23**:1267–1271.

Trodahl, H. J., and R. G. Buckley. 1989. "Ultraviolet Light under Sea Ice during the Antarctic Spring." *Science,* **245**:194–195.

Truesdale, G. A., A. L. Downing, and G. F. Lowden. 1955. "The Solubility of Oxygen in Pure Water and Seawater." *J. Appl. Chem.,* **5**:53–62.

Trussell, R. P. 1972. "The Percent Unionized Ammonia in Aqueous Ammonia Solutions at Different pH Levels and Temperatures." *J. Fish. Res. Board Can.,* **29**:1505–1507.

Tuite, C. H. 1981. "Standing Crop Densities and Distribution of *Spirulina* and Benthic Diatoms in East African Alkaline Saline Lakes." *Freshwat. Biol.,* **11**:345–360.

Tyler, J. E. 1968. "The Secchi Disc." *Limnol. Oceanogr.,* **13**:1–6.

———, and R. W. Priesendorfer. 1962. "Transmission of Energy within the Sea.'' In M. N. Hill (ed.), *The Sea,* **1**:397–451.

Tyler, M. A., and H. H. Seliger. 1978. ''Annual Subsurface Transport of a Red Tide Dinoflagellate to Its Bloom Area: Water Circulation Patterns and Organism Distributions in the Chesapeake Bay.'' *Limnol. Oceanogr.,* **23**:227–246.

Urabe, J. 1990. ''Stable Horizontal Variation in the Zooplankton Community Structure of a Reservoir Maintained by Predation and Competition.'' *Limnol. Oceanogr.,* **35**:1703–1717.

Vallentyne, J. R. 1960. ''Fossil Pigments.'' pp. 83–105. In M. B. Allen (ed.). *Comparative Biochemistry of Photoreactive Systems.* Academic, New York.

Vanni, M. J., C. Luecke, J. F. Kitchell, and J. J. Magnuson. 1990. ''Effects of Planktivorous Fish Mass Mortality on the Plankton Community of Lake Mendota, Wisconsin: Implications for Biomanipulation.'' *Hydrobiologia,* **200/201**:329–336.

Vannote, R. L., G. M. Minshall, K. W. Cummins, J. R. Sidel, and C. E. Cushing. 1980. ''The River Continum Concept.'' *Can. J. Fish. Aquat. Sci.,* **37**:130–137.

Various authors. 1973. ''Physical, Chemical, Phytoplankton, Zooplankton, Zoobenthos and Fisheries in Lake George, Uganda.'' *Proc. Roy. Soc. London, Ser. B,* **184**:235–346.

——. 1974. *J. Fish. Res. Board Can.,* **31**:689–854. On Laurentian Great Lakes physics, chemistry, biology.)

Verry, E. S., and D. R. Timmons. 1982. ''Waterborne Nutrient Flow through an Upland Peatland Watershed in Minnesota.'' *Ecology,* **63**:1456–1467.

Vincent, W. F. (ed.). 1989. ''Dominance of Bloom-Forming Cyanobacteria (Blue-Green Algae).'' *N.Z. J. Mar. Freshwat. Res.,* **21**:361–542.

Viner, A. B. 1969. ''The Chemistry of the Water of Lake George, Uganda.'' *Verh. Int. Ver. Limnol.,* **17**:289–296.

——. 1972. ''Responses of a Mixed Phytoplankton Population to Nutrient Enrichments of Ammonia and Phosphate, and Some Associated Ecological Implications.'' *Proc. Roy. Soc. Lond., Ser. B,* **183**:351–370.

—— (ed.). 1987. *Inland Lakes of New Zealand.* Dept. Sci. Indust. Res., Wellington, New Zealand, 494 pp.

——, and I. R. Smith. 1973. ''Geographical, His-

torical and Physical Aspects of Lake George.'' *Proc. Roy. Soc. Lond., Ser. B,* **184**:235–270.

Visser, S. A., and J. P. Villeneuve. 1975. ''Similarities and Differences in the Chemical Composition of Waters from West, Central and East Africa.'' *Verh. Int. Ver. Limnol.,* **19**:1416–1425.

Vollenweider, R. A. 1965. ''Calculation Models of Photosynthesis Depth Curves and Some Implications Regarding Day Rate Estimates in Primary Production Measurements.'' pp. 425–457. In C. R. Goldman (ed.), ''Primary Productivity in Aquatic Environments.'' *Mem. Ist. Ital. Idrobiol.,* **18** (suppl.).

——. 1968. *Scientific Fundamentals of the Eutrophication of Lakes and Flowing Waters, with Particular Reference to Nitrogen and Phosphorus as Factors in Eutrophication.* Tech. Rept. No. DAS/CSJ/68.27. Organization for Economic Cooperation and Development, Paris. 159 pp.

——. 1969. *A Manual on Methods for Measuring Primary Production in Aquatic Environments.* IBP Handbook No. 12. Davis, Philadelphia. 213 pp.

——. 1976. ''Advances in Defining Critical Loading Levels of Phosphorus in Lake Eutrophication.'' *Mem. Ist. Ital. Idrobiol.,* **33**:53–83.

Waananen, A. O., D. D. Harris, and R. C. Williams. 1970. ''Floods of December 1964 and January 1965 in the Four Western States. Part 2. Stream Flow and Sediment Data.'' *U.S. Geol. Surv. Water-Suppl. Pap.* 18665. 861 pp.

Walker, W. W. 1979. ''Use of Hypolimnetic Oxygen Depletion Rates as a Trophic State Indicator for Lakes.'' *Water Resour. Res.,* **15**:1463–1470.

Walls, M., and M. Ketola. 1989. ''Effects of Predator-Induced Spines on Individual Fitness in *Daphnia pulex. Limnol. Oceanogr.,* **34**:390–396.

Walsby, A. E. 1972. ''Structure and Function of Gas Vacuoles.'' *Bacteriol Revs.,* **36**:1–32.

——. 1974. ''The Extracellular Products of *Anabaena cylindrica* Lemm. 1. Isolation of a Macromolecular Pigment-Peptide Complex and Other Components.'' *Br. Phycol. J.,* **9**:371–381.

——, and C. S. Reynolds. 1979. ''Sinking and Floating in Phytoplankton Ecology.'' In I. Morris (ed.), *The Ecology of Phytoplankton.* Blackwell Scientific Publications, Ltd., Oxford.

——, and A. Xypolyta. 1977. ''The Form Resistance of Chitin Fibres Attached to the Cells of *Thalassiosira fluvitalis* Hustedt.'' *Br. Phycol. J.,* **12**:215–223.

————, C. S. Reynolds, R. L. Oliver, and J. Kromkamp. 1989. The Role of Gas Vacuoles and Carbohydrate Content in the Buoyancy and Vertical Distribution of *Anabaena minutissima* in Lake Rotongaio, New Zealand. In W.F. Vincent (ed.), "Cyanobacterial Growth and Dominance in Two Eutrophic Lakes." *Arch. Hyydrobiol. Beih.,* **32**:1–25.

Ward, H. B., and G. C. Whipple. 1959. In W. T. Edmondson (ed.), *Freshwater Biology.* 2d ed. Wiley, New York. 1248 pp.

Ward, J. V. 1986. "Altitudinal Zonation in a Rocky Mountain Stream." *Arch. Hydrobiol. Suppl.,* **74**:133–199.

————. 1992. *Aquatic Insect Ecology.* John Wiley, New York. 438 pp.

————, and J. A. Stanford (eds.). 1979. *The Ecology of Regulated Streams.* Plenum, New York. 398 pp.

Warren, C. E. 1971. *Biology and Water Pollution Control.* W. B. Saunders, Philadelphia. 434 pp.

Warrest, R. C., U. Krystyna, J. D. Scott, D. H. Brooker, B. E. Thompson, and H. Van Dyke. "Sensitivity of Marine Phytoplankton to UV-B Radiation: Impact upon a Model Ecosystem." *Phytochem. Phytol.,* **33**:223–227.

Watt, W. D. 1966. "Release of Dissolved Organic Material from the Cells of Phytoplankton Populations." *Proc. Roy. Soc. Lond., Ser. B,* **164**:521–551.

Weatherley, A. H., and P. Dawson. 1972. "Zinc Pollution in a Freshwater System: Analysis and Proposed Solutions." *Search,* **4**:471–476.

Weitzel, R. L. (ed.). 1979. *Methods and Measurement of Periphyton Communities: A Review.* Am. Soc. Testing and Materials, Philadelphia. 183 pp.

Welch, E. B. (ed.). 1980. *Ecological Effects of Waste Water.* Cambridge, New York. 337 pp.

————, J. A. Buckley, and R. M. Bush. 1972. "Dilution as an Algal Bloom Control." *J. Water Pollut. Control Fed.,* **44**:2245–2265.

Welch, H. 1967. "Energy Flow through the Major Macroscopic Components of an Aquatic Ecosystem." Ph.D. thesis, University of Georgia, Athens.

Welch, P. S. 1935. *Limnology.* McGraw-Hill, New York. 472 pp. (2d ed., 1952, 536 pp.)

Welcomme, R. I. 1976. "Some General and Theoretical Considerations on the Fish Yield of African Rivers. *J. Fish Biol.,* **8**:351–364.

————. 1988. "Concluding Remarks I: On the Nature of Large Tropical Rivers, Floodplains, and Future Research Directions." *North Am. Benthological Assoc.,* **7**:525–526.

Weller, R. A., J. P. Dean, J. Marra, J. F. Price, E. A. Francis, and D. C. Boardman. 1985. "Three-Dimensional Flow in the Upper Ocean." *Science,* **227**:1552–1556.

Werner, D. (ed.). 1977. *Biology of Diatoms.* University of California Press, Berkeley. 498 pp.

Werner, E. E., J. F. Gilliam, D. J. Hall, and G. G. Mittelbach. 1983. "Experimental Tests of the Effects of Predation Risk on Habitat Use in Fish: The Role of Relative Habitat Profitability." *Ecology,* **64**:1540–1548.

Werner, E. (ed.). 1977. *The Biology of Diatoms.* Botanical Monographs Vol. 13, University of California Press.

Westlake, D. F., H. Casey, F. H. Dawson, M. Ladle, R. H. K. Mann, and A. F. H. Marker. 1972. "The Chalk-Stream Ecosystem." pp. 613–635. In Z. Kajak and A. Hilibricht-Ikowska (eds.), *Productivity Problems of Freshwaters.* PWN (Polish Scientific Publishers), Warsaw-Krakow.

Wetzel, R. G. 1960. "Marl Encrustation on Hydrophytes in Several Michigan Lakes." *Oikos,* **11**:223–236.

————. 1964. "A Comparative Study of the Primary Productivity of Higher Aquatic Plants, Periphyton and Phytoplankton in a Large, Shallow Lake." *Int. Rev. Ges. Hydrobiol. Hydrogr.,* **49**:1–61.

————. 1983. *Limnology.* W. B. Saunders, Philadelphia. 743 pp.

————. 1990. "Land Water Interfaces: Metabolic and Limnological Regulators. The Edgardo Baldi Memorial Lecture." *Verh. Int. Ver. Limnol.,* **24**:6–24.

————, and A. Otsuki. 1974. "Allochthonous Organic Carbon of a Marl Lake." *Arch. Hydrobiol.,* **73**:31–56.

————, and G. E. Likens. 1991. *Limnological Analysis.* W. B. Saunders, Philadelphia. 391 pp.

Whitton, B. A. 1970. "Toxicity of Heavy Metals to Freshwater Algae: A Review." *Phykos,* **9**:116–125.

———— (ed.). 1975. *Studies in Ecology, Vol. 2: River Ecology.* University of California Press, Berkeley. 725 pp.

Wiley, J. M., and S. L. Kohler. 1984. Behavioral Adaptations of Aquatic Insects. pp. 101–133. In V. H. Resh and D. M. Rosenberg (eds.), *The Ecology of Aquatic Insects.* Praeger Publishers, New York.

Williams, L. R. 1971. "A Possible Role of Heteroinhibition in the Production of *Anabaena flos-aquae*

Waterblooms.'' Ph.D. thesis, Rutgers University, New Brunswick, New Jersey. 88 pp.

Williams, W. D. 1972. "The Uniqueness of Salt Lake Ecosystems.'' pp. 349–361. In Z. Kajak and A. Hillbricht-Ilkowska (eds.), *Productivity Problems of Freshwaters*. PWN (Polish Scientific Publishers), Warsaw-Krakow.

———. 1978. "Limnology of Victorian Salt Lakes, Australia.'' *Verh. Int. Ver. Limnol., 20*:1165–1174.

———. 1981. "Inland Salt Lakes: An Introduction.'' In W. D. Williams (ed.), *Salt Lakes: Proceedings of an International Symposium on Athalassic (Inland) Salt Lakes*. Junk Publishers, The Hague.

Willoughby, L. G. 1969. "A Study of the Aquatic Actinomycetes of Bleham Tarn.'' *Acta Hydrobiol. Hydrographia Protistol., 34*:465–483.

Wilson, C. B., and W. W. Walker. 1989. "Development of Lake Assessment Methods Based upon the Aquatic Ecoregion Concept.'' *Lake Reservoir Management, 5*:11–22.

Williams, W. F., and J. W. Barko. 1991. "Estimation of Phosphorus Exchange between Littoral and Pelagic Zones during Nighttime Convective Circulation.'' *Limnol. Oceanogr., 36*:179–187.

Wiley, M. L. (ed.). 1978. *Estuarine Interactions*. Academic, New York. 603 pp.

Winberg, G. G. 1970. "Energy Flow in the Aquatic Ecological System.'' *Pol. Arch. Hydrobiol., 17*:11–19.

Wolfe, D. A. (ed.). 1986. *Estuarine Variability*. Academic, New York. 509 pp.

Wright, H. E., T. C. Winter, and H. L. Patten. 1963. "Two Pollen Diagrams from Southeastern Minnesota; Problems in the Regional Late-Glacial and Post-Glacial Vegetation History.'' *Geol. Soc. Am. Bull., 74*:1371–1396.

Wright, J. C. 1965. "The Population Dynamics and Production of *Daphnia* in Canyon Ferry Reservoir, Montana.'' *Limnol. Oceanogr., 10*:583–590.

Wright, R. T., and J. E. Hobble. 1966. "Use of Glucose and Acetate by Bacteria and Algae in Aquatic Ecosystems.'' *Ecology, 47*:447–464.

Wrigley, R. C., and A. J. Horne. 1974. "Remote Sensing and Lake Eutrophication.'' *Nature, 250*:213–214.

———, and ———. 1975. "Surface Algal Circulation Patterns in Clear Lake by Remote Sensing.'' *NASA Tech. Memo.* X-62,451. 11 pp.

Wurtsbaugh, W. A. 1988. "Iron, Molybdenum, and Phosphorus Limitation of N_2-Fixation Maintains Nitrogen Limitation in the Great Salt Lake Drainage.'' *Verh. Int. Ver. Limnol., 23*:121–130.

———, and A. J. Horne 1983. "Iron in Eutrophic Clear Lake, California: Its Importance for Algal Nitrogen Fixation and Growth.'' *Can. J. Fish. Aquat. Sci., 40*:1419–1429.

———, and H. Li. 1985. "Diel Migrations of a Zooplanktivorous Fish (*Megidis beryllina*) in Relation to the Distribution of its Prey in a Large Eutrophic Lake.'' *Limnol.* Oceanogr., 30:565–576.

———, R. W. Brocksen, and C. R. Goldman. 1975. "Food and Distribution of Underyearling Brook and Rainbow Trout in Castle Lake, California.'' *Trans. Amer. Fish. Soc., 104*:88–95.

Wyatt, P. J., and C. Jackson. 1989. "Discrimination of Phytoplankton via Light-Scattering Properties.'' *Limnol. Oceanogr., 34*:96–112.

Young, J. O. 1975. "Preliminary Field and Laboratory Studies on the Survival and Spawning of Several Species of Gastropoda in Calcium-Poor and Calcium-Rich Waters.'' *Proc. Malac. Soc. London, 41*:429–437.

Yurk, J. J., and J. J. Ney. 1989. "Phosphorus-Fish Community Biomass Relationships in Southern Appalachian Reservoirs: Can Lakes Be Too Clean for Fish?'' *Lake Reservoir Management, 5*:83–90.

Zaret, T. M., and R. T. Paine. 1973. "Species Introduction in a Tropical Lake.'' *Science, 182*:449–455.

Zehr, J. P., R. P. Axler, and C. R. Goldman. 1985. "Heterotrophic Mineralization of Amino Acid Nitrogen in Subalpine Castle Lake, California.'' *Marine Chemistry, 16*:343–350.

Zenkevitch, L. 1963. *Biology of the Seas of the U.S.S.R.* G. Allen, London. 955 pp.

Zevenboom, W., and L. R. Mur. 1978. "On Nitrate Uptake by *Oscillatoria agardhii*.'' *Verh. Int. Ver. Limnol., 20*:2302–2307.

———, G. J. DeGroot, and L. R. Mur. 1980. "Effects of Light on Nitrate-Limited *Oscillatoria agardhii* in Chemostat Culture.'' *Arch. Mikrobiol., 125*:59–65.

———, and L. R. Mur. 1981. "Ammonia-Limited Growth and Uptake by *Oscillatoria agardhii* in Chemostat Culture.'' *Arch. Mikrobiol., 129*:61–66.

Name Index

Subject Index

The abbreviations t and f stand for table and figure respectively.